Ian Worthington · Chris Britton · Andy Rees

# Economics for Business

## Blending Theory and Practice

FINANCIAL TIMES
Prentice Hall

*An imprint of* **Pearson Education**

Harlow, England · London · New York · Reading, Massachusetts · San Francisco · Toronto · Don Mills, Ontario · Sydney
Tokyo · Singapore · Hong Kong · Seoul · Taipei · Cape Town · Madrid · Mexico City · Amsterdam · Munich · Paris · Milan

**Pearson Education Limited**

Edinburgh Gate
Harlow
Essex CM20 2JE
England

and Associated Companies throughout the world

*Visit us on the World Wide Web at:*
www.pearsoneduc.com

---

**First Published 2001**

ISBN 0  273 63245 0

*British Library Cataloguing-in-Publication Data*
A catalogue record for this book is available from the British Library

*Library of Congress Cataloging in Publication Data*
Worthington, Ian.
        Economics for business : blending theory and practice/Ian Worthington, Chris Britton,
    Andy Rees.
            p. cm.
        Includes bibliographical references and index.
        ISBN 0-273-63245-0 (alk.paper)
            1. Managerial economics. I. Britton, Chris. II. Rees, Andy. III. Title.

    HD30.22.W67 2001
    338.5'024'658--dc21                                          00-065412


10   9  8  7  6  5  4  3  2  1
05 04 03 02 01

Typeset by 30 in 9$\frac{1}{2}$/12pt New Century Schoolbook
Printed at Ashford Colour Press Ltd, Gosport

For Margaret, Nick, Lindsey and all the children
and in memory of David, Jim and John

# Contents

# Preface

This book has been written primarily, though not exclusively, for students studying business economics as part of a degree, diploma or professional course in business studies. Its main aim is to illustrate how the ideas and perspectives of economists can help us to make sense of the world in which we live and especially to describe and analyse the fundamental processes of production and consumption that are central to our daily lives.

The book's title has been chosen deliberately to emphasise our belief that a blend of theory and practice provides a much fuller understanding of the business world than one which is either simply abstract and theoretical or alternatively overly descriptive. Moreover, as teachers of business studies and economics we have started from the premise that relative simplicity rather than complexity of presentation makes for a better understanding both by ourselves and our readers. This approach is not meant to be either insulting or patronising, but simply to underline our conviction – based on many years of experience in teaching and research – that communicating ideas which can at times be complex is always best served by a reader-centred approach.

In choosing the 16 chapters in this book we have attempted to cover all the mainstream topics normally examined within a business economics module/ course, while at the same time offering students and tutors a degree of flexibility by adding extra chapters on a number of areas of contemporary interest and relevance. Many of these additional chapters help to provide links with other modules on a business programme and can easily be accommodated within either a modular or linear structure according to particular needs and/or preferences.

In preparing this text we owe a debt of gratitude to many people, not least to our past and present students who have been – and continue to be – a source of inspiration, albeit sometimes unwittingly. To Janice Cox and Zoe Lewin who expertly typed a large part of the text from our scrawled hand-writing we offer sincere thanks for their hard work and patience in the face of very trying circumstances. Special thanks must also go to the staff of De Montfort University Library for all their help over the years and particularly to Sadie McClelland, Paula Parish, Laura Prime and Paula Harris at Pearson who have supported us throughout and have kept faith with the project. We also acknowledge the contributions of our colleagues Katherine Duffy amd Dean Patton and the views and observations of our anonymous reviewers who provided us with particularly helpful and supportive comments at the draft stage.

As any author will verify, preparing a book invariably imposes a substantial cost on others, particularly one's family who become increasingly obsessed with the completion date. Well here it is – it is to you, and those no longer with us, that quite rightly we dedicate this book with our thanks for your forbearance and more especially with our love.

*Ian Worthington*                                                                                            *September 2000*
*Chris Britton*
*Andy Rees*

# Acknowledgements

We are grateful to the following for permission to reproduce copyright material:

Figure 2.5 from Williamson, O.E., 'The Economics of organization: the transaction cost approach', *American Journal of Sociology*, 87 (1981), The University of Chicago Press, Chicago, IL, Tables 8.4 and 8.5 from *Driving Productivity and Growth in the UK Economy*, McKinsey Global Institute (1988), Washington, DC; Figures 8.5, 8.6 and Table 8.6 from *The Advertising Statistics Yearbook, 1999*, NCT Publications Ltd., Henley-on-Thames; Figures 8.7 from *OECD Economic Outlook*, 62 (December 1997) copyright OECD, 1997; Figure 10.9 is reproduced with permission of the Bank of England; Table 10.10 from *Measuring Globalisation: The Role of Multinationals in OECD Economies 1999 Edition*, copyright OECD, 1999; Figure 11.3 from DTI, Crown copyright is reproduced with permission of the Controller of Her Majesty's Stationery Office; Figure 13.11 from *General Household Survey (1996)*, National Statistics © Crown copyright, 2000; Figure 13.8 from Atkinson, J., 'Manpower strategies for flexible organisations', *Personnel Management*, August 1984; Figure 16.2 from Bowers, D. (1991) *Statistics for Economics and Business*, Macmillan, Basingstoke.

While every effort has been made to trace the owners of copyright material, in a few cases this has proved impossible and we take this opportunity to offer our apologies to any copyright holders whose rights we may have unwittingly infringed.

# The firm in its environment

# CHAPTER 1

# Studying business economics

Ian Worthington

**Objectives**

1 To provide a rationale for the study of business economics.

2 To outline the broad environmental influences faced by businesses.

3 To examine key concepts relevant to the study of business decision-making and economics.

4 To identify the central themes inherent in this text.

## 1.1 Introduction: why study economics?

There is an old joke in business circles about laying every economist in the world end to end and never reaching a conclusion. Underlying this witticism are at least two important and interrelated questions. Why should people in the business world listen to so-called 'experts' when they seem unable to agree amongst themselves about everyday issues and events? What can businessmen and women, dealing with day-to-day problems and concerns, really learn from people who tend to operate in a world which appears to be dominated by abstract theories and ideas? Put another way, what benefits can practitioners – and for that matter students possibly contemplating a career in business – gain from studying a subject which can appear at best impractical and at worst irrelevant?

When confronted with questions of this type there is a great temptation to seek refuge in the old adage about undertaking learning for its own sake, but to sceptics this approach usually appears unconvincing and evasive and is, in our view, too defensive. Years of studying, teaching and researching in the broad area of **economics** has convinced us that the economist's view of the world – as encapsulated in economic ideas, concepts, theories and models – helps us to understand more fully those aspects of human behaviour which are the very essence of business activity: namely, production and consumption. In the jargon, economics provides us with a framework of analysis which can be useful in interpreting and explaining some of the most important and recurring aspects of human behaviour and experience; it helps us to make more sense of the world in which we live and to explain how, why, and in some cases where and when, situations which we encounter on a regular basis are likely to occur (e.g. why house prices are more expensive in certain parts of the country, why retailers alter their prices, why the cost of borrowing may rise).

**economics** the study of those aspects of behaviour and those institutions involved in the use of scarce resources to produce and distribute goods and services to satisfy human wants

The claim is not that studying economics will invariably provide us with the 'right' answers to business problems, but that it gives us an insight into the nature of the problems themselves and their possible causes and thus helps decision-makers – at home, in firms and in government – to search for solutions which are appropriate to the circumstances with which they are confronted. The economic way of thinking is not a substitute for common sense, intuition or judgement or for other conceptual and analytical approaches to decision-making and problem-solving, it is just one part of the intellectual armoury we have at our disposal when called upon to explain or react to a situation; it should be used as and when necessary.

## 1.2    What is business economics?

**business economics** the study of the firm and of the environment in which it operates and makes its decisions

There is some dispute in academic circles as to what should be included in a course on **business economics** and to what extent, as an area of study, it differs from, say, managerial economics or industrial economics; we have no inclination to enter into this debate. To us business economics is essentially about the firm or enterprise and in particular about the factors which help to influence its decisions concerning the acquisition of productive resources and the transformation of these resources into goods and services to satisfy human needs and wants: it is about the processes of **production** and **consumption**. Apart from obvious concerns with costs, revenues and profitability, there is ample empirical evidence to indicate that in a market-based economy business decisions are shaped by a range of other influences including the firm's objectives, the competitive nature of the market(s) in which it operates and the opportunities and constraints provided by the broader environment in which it exists and carries out its activities. The economist's view of these influences on business decision-making form the subject matter of this book.

**production** the conversion by firms of inputs into outputs, usually with a view to making profits

**consumption** using up goods and services to satisfy human wants; normally achieved through the act of purchasing

In focusing on production and consumption processes, business economists traditionally seek answers to a number of key questions. These include:

- How can we explain what underlies consumer behaviour?
- What factors affect consumer demand for goods and services?
- How do consumers respond to price signals?
- To what extent is a person's demand influenced by changes in income or in the prices of competitive products?
- How do firms organise themselves to meet consumer demands?
- What factors influence a firm's behaviour?
- What is the relationship between a firm's output, its costs and its profitability?
- How do firms decide on their pricing strategy?
- To what degree does the structure of the market in which a firm operates affect its conduct and performance?
- How far can a firm influence the degree of competition in the market place?

**internal environment** those influences within the firm which affect its operations and decisions and which invariably affect its performance

These, and other questions, are the 'stuff' of business economics; they are also central concerns of decision-makers in business organisations.

In examining questions that are essentially to do with demand, supply, markets and prices, business economics looks not only at the influences within a firm's **internal environment**, but also at how firms as producers interact with their consumers and with other businesses (e.g. as suppliers, customers or competitors) and to what extent such interactions might affect and explain their behaviour. Increasingly it is also concerned to describe and analyse other aspects of the relationship between a firm and its **external environment**, including the role of government in shaping business behaviour, the impact of business activity on the natural environment and the nature of the market for resources such as labour. These are issues which we believe should also be examined as part of a business economics course, together with the question of how insights offered by economists can help to shape business strategy.

**external environment**
those influences which lie outside the firm but which affect its internal operations and decisions and may affect its performance

## 1.3    The firm in its environment: an overview

### 1.3.1  A generic model of business activity

In a modern economy most decisions about what goods and services should be produced are taken within an organisational context and even a cursory investigation of the world of business reveals the wide variety of organisations involved, ranging from the small local supplier of a single product (e.g. a local plumber) to the huge, multibillion dollar **transnational corporation** producing and trading on a global scale (e.g. Ford). While it is possible to identify significant differences between organisations in terms of their relative size, scale of operations, market reach, finance, legal status and so on, all businesses have at least one thing in common: their activities essentially involve the acquisition of productive resources (or 'inputs') and the conversion or transformation of these resources into goods or services or other forms of 'output' to satisfy the demands of their customers or clients. This **process of transformation** is illustrated in Figure 1.1.

**transnational corporation**
a firm which has the power to control and co-ordinate operations in more than one country

**transformation process**
the process of converting inputs into outputs

**firm**  the business organisation or enterprise which transforms inputs into outputs and makes the latter available for consumption

The linking mechanism in this process is, of course, the **firm** (or **business organisation/enterprise**) which is responsible for making a variety of decisions, ranging from resource acquisition through production to marketing and distribution. Implicit in the notion of the firm are those internal aspects of its operations which will have an important influence on the decision-making process, such as the firm's objectives, its structure, management and organisational culture, and some of these issues are explored in Chapters 2 and 6. For anyone wishing to study this area from an organisational and management

**Figure 1.1  The business organisation as a transformation system**

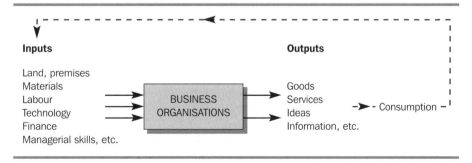

point of view we have recommended some of the more recent contributions to the debate in the further reading section at the end of this chapter.

One benefit of portraying business activity in this generic way is that it reminds us that a firm's decisions on resource acquisition and production are ultimately linked with decisions on consumption and that it is largely through the latter that most businesses are able to acquire and replenish the resources on which production depends. The model also illustrates that what is a resource or input for one organisation is frequently the output of another organisation (e.g. capital equipment, raw materials), whether produced by a firm in the domestic economy or imported from elsewhere. These, and other linkages, serve to demonstrate the complex and integrated nature of business activity in the early twenty-first century and help to underline the degree to which the fortunes of any one organisation are linked to decisions by both consumers and by other producers, a point readily understood by a business faced with falling demand for its products or supply difficulties or the all too common problem of bad debts.

### 1.3.2 The firm's external environment

Business decisions are not only shaped by internal considerations but also by influences which lie outside the organisation, in what is termed its 'external environment'. This external environment or context comprises a wide range of spatially diverse influences – economic, political, legal, social, technological, etc. – which affect business activity in a variety of ways and impinge on all aspects of the transformation process through to, and including, eventual consumption. This notion of the firm's external environment is illustrated in Figure 1.2.

In considering a firm's external environment, a useful distinction can be made between those factors which tend to have a more immediate effect on the day-to-day operations of the enterprise and those which will tend to have a more general influence on the decisions made by a firm's management. For most firms the **immediate** or **operational environment** will include suppliers, labour markets, financiers, customers and competitors and may also include trading organisations, trade unions and possibly a parent company. In contrast the **general** or **contextual environment** comprises those broader macroenvironmental variables – including the economic, political, social, cultural, demographic, legal and technological influences on business – which affect organisations in general

**operational environment**
those aspects of a firm's external environment which tend to have an influence at an operational level

**contextual environment**
the broad macroenvironmental context in which firms exist and operate

**Figure 1.2   The firm in its environment**

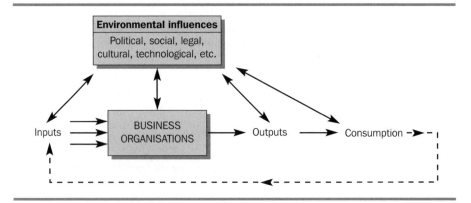

**Figure 1.3  Two levels of environment**

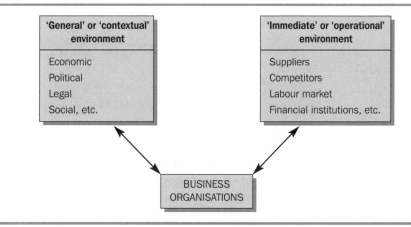

**Figure 1.4  Environmental influences on a firm's marketing system**

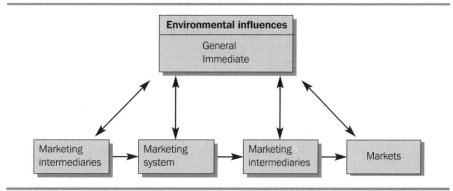

and which emanate not only from local and national sources but also from international and supranational developments. This distinction between the two levels of external environment is shown in Figure 1.3.

It is worth noting that this type of analysis can equally be extended to the different functional areas of a firm's activities, such as marketing, human resource management, production or finance, as illustrated in Figure 1.4. This can be useful in at least two ways. First it serves to emphasise how specific activities within a firm are influenced by external factors, thereby underlining the importance of the interface between an organisation's internal and external environments. Second, by drawing attention to this interface, it reminds us that while decision-makers are often able to exercise some degree of control over the internal aspects of the organisation, they often find it very difficult, if not impossible, to control the external environment against which these decisions are made.

## 1.4  Macro and microeconomic influences on the firm

A comprehensive analysis of the different external factors affecting businesses can be found in our companion book *The Business Environment* (Worthington and

Britton 2000);[1] for convenience, in this and the following section we have given a brief summary of some of the key economic influences operating at both the macro and micro levels which can impinge upon business decisions. Links between these variables and the text are indicted by the chapter references (in parentheses).

### 1.4.1 Macroeconomic

**macroeconomic environment** those economy-wide influences that are part of the context in which individual business decisions are made

The **macroeconomic environment** of the firm comprises those broad economic aggregates which are part of the background against which individual business decisions are made; these include such considerations as employment/unemployment levels, growth rates, inflation rates, external trade patterns and the overall level and pattern of economic activity. The rate of inflation, for example, can affect not only the willingness and ability of a business to borrow money to invest in producing output, but may also influence consumer spending plans and this in turn may have an impact on a firm's output and investment decisions. Levels of employment/unemployment can affect businesses not simply through the impact on the labour market (see Chapter 13), but also through their potential effect on consumption, given that rising unemployment tends to result in a fall or a slowing down in the rate of consumer spending in the economy.

**fiscal policy** that aspect of government policy concerned with raising revenue, primarily through taxation, and using that revenue to fund government (or public) expenditure

**monetary policy** that part of government policy concerned with the amount of money in circulation and with interest rates

An important influence within this macroeconomy of business is the democratically elected government which plays a key role in setting objectives for the economy as a whole and can, through the use of **fiscal** and **monetary policy** have a major impact on both the demand and supply side of business activity (see Chapter 12). Equally, through policy and/or legislation of a more direct and targeted kind, government can be influential in shaping business decisions in a wide variety of areas, ranging from where to locate the enterprise to whether a merger with other organisations is either desirable or possible (Chapter 11).

### 1.4.2 Microeconomic

**microeconomic influences** those economic influences which operate at the level of the individual business or within the market or industry to which it belongs

**Microeconomic influences** are those which operate at the level of the individual business organisation or within the market or industry in which a firm operates. Foremost amongst those would be the influence of suppliers, customers and competitors – encapsulated in Porter's model of the five forces affecting firms in competitive markets (see Chapter 7).

As far as suppliers are concerned, firms tend to be confronted with a number of important questions concerning sources of supply: for example, what is the relative cost and reliability of buying from alternative suppliers? is it better to produce a good or service 'in-house' or to buy it in from another organisation (see Chapter 2)? is the firm the source or recipient of pressures within the supply chain which have an impact at operational level (Chapter 14)? The answers to these, and other supply-side questions, will ultimately have an impact on the firm's costs of production and hence – other things being equal – on its profitability as an organisation (Chapter 5).

Customers and competitors are no less important to a firm's fortunes and their relevance to business decisions can be illustrated in a variety of ways. A business, for instance, needs ideally to understand which factors are likely to affect an individual's demand and to consider how price, or other variables, can be manipulated to influence consumer buying decisions (Chapter 3). The extent to which a firm is able to manipulate such variables tends to depend to a large degree on market conditions and in particular on the nature and level of competition it faces from other producers in the market (Chapter 7). In short, the **market structure** within which a firm operates (especially the degree of actual and potential competition) is likely to affect the decisions it takes and potentially the outcome of those decisions – a view exemplified by the Structure–Conduct–Performance model discussed in Chapters 7 and 8.

**market structure** the underlying characteristics of a market, which govern the competitive relations between suppliers

## 1.5  Key concepts

To highlight the links between business decision-making and the study of economics, it is useful to begin with a review of some of the key concepts familiar to the economist. These include:

- scarcity and choice
- opportunity cost
- resource allocation
- firm
- market
- industry.

### 1.5.1 Economic scarcity

As indicated above, economics is concerned with how society tackles the basic problem of resource allocation. At the heart of this problem lie the concepts of scarcity, choice and opportunity cost.

To the economist, **scarcity** is the idea that no society ever has sufficient resources to meet all the actual and potential demands for those resources. Scarcity, in other words, is a relative concept and is one which can be applied to the situation faced by individuals, firms, governments and society in general. At the macro level, for example, scarcity implies that the total goods and services that people would like to consume consistently exceed the economy's capacity to produce them, i.e. society's demands are infinite (unlimited), whilst its resources such as land, labour and capital are finite (limited). At the micro level the term tends to be applied to situations in which individual or collective needs and wants consistently outstrip the financial means available to satisfy them, as exemplified by the inability of governments to provide the best health care, education, defence, public transport, and so on, at a time and place and of a quality demanded by the user.

**economic scarcity** a situation in which economic resources are finite but the demand for those resources is infinite; consequently human wants exceed the economy's capacity to satisfy those wants

### 1.5.2 Choice

Scarcity and **choice** go hand in hand. Given that individuals, firms, governments and society in general are unable to meet all their demands, it follows that choices have to be made concerning how the available resources should be used. An individual, for instance, might have to choose between changing the car or going on a foreign holiday; a firm might have to decide between increasing its

**choice** the requirement to decide between alternative ways of using scarce resources whether by individuals, firms or governments

expenditure on research and development or building a new administration block. Governments, too, face similar dilemmas: more spending on health or education or welfare? The choices that are ultimately made – both individually and collectively – determine how resources are allocated within the economy.

### 1.5.3 Opportunity cost

As everyone is aware, making a choice between alternatives inevitably involves a sacrifice: what might broadly be called a 'cost'. Whereas an accountant usually measures cost in monetary terms (e.g. cost of labour, overheads), the economist also takes into consideration the opportunity that has been sacrificed of taking an alternative course of action. This sacrifice represents the **opportunity cost** or **real cost** of a decision between alternatives. Thus the real cost of an extra £1 billion spending on the NHS is £1 billion not spent on education (or public transport or roads, etc.); the firm's decision to build a new administration block means that it has sacrificed the opportunity of spending more on research and development or some other area of corporate investment (see Appendix 1.1).

**opportunity cost** the 'real' cost of a decision measured in terms of the best alternative which has been sacrificed

---

**Mini case**    **Thinking like an economist**

'Cost' is a fundamental concept and one you might assume is readily understood by all. Ask an accountant and an economist to explain the meaning of cost, however, and you will get a different answer. To the accountant cost represents what has been expended on inputs into the production process in order to produce output: the amount spent on wages, materials, energy, overheads and so on. These are the 'monetary values' associated with using resources. The economist, in contrast, is concerned with the 'real values' of resource utilisation. The measurement of cost, in other words, also contains a calculation of the opportunities that have been lost or the alternatives that have been sacrificed in deciding on a particular course of action. An accountant would tell you that the cost of buying this book is the price you paid for it when you purchased it; the economist would say that its real cost was what else you could have done with your money – the missed opportunity of spending your cash on something else. Perish the thought!

---

### 1.5.4 Resource allocation

As indicated above, from a societal point of view the significance of the existence of economic scarcity is that it gives rise to a need to allocate resources among alternative uses. This basic problem of **resource allocation** poses three major dilemmas for any society:

**resource allocation** the question of how scarce resources should be utilised

- *What* should the available resources be used for? That is, what goods and services should be produced (or not produced) with the given resources?
- *How* best should the resources be used? For example, in what combinations, using what techniques and what methods?

■ *For whom* should the goods or services be produced and distributed? Who gets what, how much and on what basis?

The ways in which a society solves these problems indicates the type of economic system it possesses (see Appendix 1.2). In a **market-based economy**, the market mechanism is the key to resource allocation with the price synchronising the actions of buyers and sellers. In contrast, in **planned** or **command economies**, the state and its agencies are largely responsible for deciding on questions of production, distribution and allocation.

In practice, of course, allocative decisions tend to be solved in a variety of ways – including barter, price signals and the market, queuing and rationing, government instruction and corruption – whatever the economic and political system in force at the time. The fact that a country has a market-based system does not mean that all decisions on resource allocation will inevitably be determined by price; apart from the key role of government in production and consumption decisions, businesses, too, sometimes make buying and selling decisions based on factors other than price (e.g. when a manager chooses to use a supplier because he/she is a friend).

**market-based economy** an economy in which the market mechanism is the major determinant of resource allocation

**command economy** an economy in which the state and its agencies decide what goods and services are produced, how they are produced and how the resultant output is distributed

### 1.5.5 Firm

The concept of **firm** (or **enterprise**) implies deliberate organisation for productive purposes; it evokes notions of ownership and control, direction and co-ordination, and processes of decision-making and risk-taking. As indicated previously, the structures to which the term can be applied range from the very simple type of business enterprise owned and run by one person to the highly complex, multinational corporation, with component elements (units) spread across the globe and operating with different degrees of autonomy at different times and/or in different locations.

Whereas traditional (neo-classical) theories of the firm generally treat the business organisation in a highly abstract way, more recent contributions recognise the complexities of **entrepreneurial** activity and provide a more realistic view of the role of firms in converting inputs into outputs. Firms are no longer simply viewed as entities with a collective mind which responds in a predictable way in pursuit of profit maximisation; they are seen as shifting arenas of decision-making in which different **stakeholder groups** – often with conflicting objectives and different degrees of power and influence – operate. Chapter 6 examines some of the major discussions on a firm's objectives; Chapter 2 looks at the notion of transaction costs and highlights the problem of identifying where the 'boundary of a firm' is drawn.

**entrepreneurial** wealth-creating and risk-taking activities by individuals

**stakeholder groups** groups who have an interest in the performance of an organisation

### 1.5.6 Industry

An **industry** is normally defined according to the technical and physical characteristics of the output it produces; it comprises all businesses producing goods within the particular category under investigation (e.g. the brewing industry; the car industry). In the UK, for instance, the Standard Industrial Classification (SIC) of economic activity is used as the official means of classifying industries. This system of classification – whilst not without its problems

**industry** all businesses producing a particular product or service

– provides data at a substantial level of disaggregation and allows acceptable comparisons to be made both over time and between countries.

### 1.5.7 Market

**market** a situation in which buyers and sellers come together to effect an exchange

A **market** is an exchange mechanism which brings together buyers and sellers; in essence it is any situation in which someone wishing to buy and someone wishing to sell come together to effect an exchange. This meeting may be face to face, but it frequently involves other forms of contact (e.g. phone, fax, mail, email, internet) where buyers and sellers do not physically meet. In short, a market is not confined to any particular geographical location; the emphasis is not on place but on the activity of buying and selling (i.e. demand and supply). As a consequence, it is sometimes difficult to decide – as in the case of the terms 'firm' and 'industry' – where to draw the boundary of a market (e.g. is the market for real ale separate from the market for other beer products or, for that matter, for alcoholic drinks generally?).

## 1.6    Key themes

A number of key themes run through the text and it is useful to draw attention to these at this point.

### 1.6.1 Blending theory and practice

Economic theory provides useful insights into the world of business and it will be clear from the analysis below that many of the preoccupations of the economist (e.g. prices, costs, supply, demand, competition, markets) are of central relevance to managers. Theory, however, should not replace practice, but should be used in conjunction with it, wherever possible, to aid our understanding of business decisions and managerial action.

### 1.6.2 Blending old and new

**perfect competition** a theoretical market structure where consumers and producers are so numerous as to have no influence over market prices

**Porter's five-forces model** a model of the competitive forces within an industry developed by Michael Porter

**neo-classical** a school of economic thought in the tradition of classical economics which forms the foundation of much of current teaching in business economics

Many economic theories and models can appear abstract and unrealistic (e.g. **perfect competition**) and this has done much to blacken the name of economics in the eyes of businessmen and women. Some of the more recent developments in the field appear to have been more favourably received by the business community (e.g. **Porter's five-forces model**) and it is tempting to concentrate on these alone. We believe that a better option is to blend some of the **neo-classical** approaches with some of the more modern insights into how business organisations operate; in our opinion a synthesis of the two provides a fuller understanding of the influences on business decisions.

### 1.6.3 Micro and macro perspectives

Business economics has traditionally had a microeconomic focus, with the emphasis on firms, industries and markets, rather than on economy-wide aspects. While this is a legitimate approach, ignoring the macroeconomic influences on firms seems to us to provide only a partial view of the factors which affect a firm's operations and decisions. Some discussion of the macroeconomic context against which business activity occurs is both desirable and valuable (see Chapter 12).

### 1.6.4 Thinking about variables

Like practitioners, economists recognise that buying and selling activity is not static; it varies according to the underlying determinants such as price, the number of substitutes available, seasonal influences and so on. Identifying the variables, the relationships between them and how they can affect the eventual outcome is one of the keys to thinking like an economist. Another is recognising that decisions need to be viewed against a time context; what might be appropriate in the short run is not necessarily advisable/possible in the longer term or vice versa.

### 1.6.5 Thinking incrementally

On the whole, choices by individuals and firms about production and consumption tend to involve small (i.e. incremental) adjustments to existing behaviour (e.g. buying or producing a little bit more (or less) of a good or service) rather than all-or-nothing decisions. Such **marginal changes** are central to the analysis in a number of the chapters below (e.g. Chapters 3 and 5).

**marginal changes** small changes in the quantity of a variable

### 1.6.6 Thinking about linkages

Business economics is not a discrete discipline; it is an area of study which draws heavily on economic concepts, theories and models but which also utilises ideas and approaches from other subject areas including marketing and human resource management. While this blending of knowledge may be anathema to the purist, we strongly believe that an eclectic approach is to be encouraged; it is, after all, central to the whole concept of a business studies degree.

## 1.7    The structure of the book

We have divided the book into five main sections, grouping chapters into what we hope appears to be a logical order. As anyone teaching in this field will recognise, it is very much a question of personal choice of how to handle the large amount of material normally covered in a course on business economics. Readers and tutors are at liberty to switch chapters around to suit their own needs or preferences.

Following a general discussion of business economics and the internal environment of the firm in this opening section, we turn our attention to what are normally the core areas of study for students of business economics. Section 2 looks at the key processes of consumption and production, focusing on the central concepts of demand and supply and how these relate to notions such as consumer behaviour, costs and profits. While profit is seen to be a major driving force influencing the behaviour of private sector businesses, Chapter 6 illustrates that this is only one of the objectives a firm may pursue and which can shape its operations and decisions.

In Section 3 we examine the idea of markets and prices, looking at important questions such as how the structure of the market in which a firm operates can influence its conduct and performance and what insights economists can offer with regard to how prices are determined under different market conditions. In keeping with the subtitle of this book we also look at different pricing strategies used by business organisations in the 'real' world and at how firms in international markets can be affected by factors such as fluctuating exchange rates.

In the fourth section we examine a number of areas of contemporary relevance, which frequently give rise to interactions between government, firms and markets. Depending on the subject matter, the approach to the material in this part of the book is at certain times theoretical and at other times empirical. Moreover the analysis is sometimes at the micro level and sometimes at the macro level. To us this is consistent with our view that a subject such as business economics needs a flexible and eclectic approach: one which attempts to blend theory and practice and which draws from different disciplines and subject areas in trying to understand the various influences on business decisions.

In the final section we look at some of the links which exist between the study of business economics and business decision-making and how decision-makers can obtain and analyse data and information to guide their actions. We see Section 5 very much as a bridge to subsequent areas of study in an undergraduate business programme and one which, we hope, will underpin the reader's understanding of the integrated and multidisciplinary nature of a degree or diploma course in business studies.

Within each chapter we have used a standardised layout for the convenience of the reader. Every chapter starts with a specification of the chapter's objectives, followed by the main text which is split into numbered sections. Key terms are highlighted in **bold letters** on the first occasion they appear, when a definition is also provided in the margin. Most of these terms are subsequently highlighted elsewhere in the text.

Each chapter contains mini cases within the text to highlight key discussion points and ends with a case study, many of which use examples from both UK and international sources. As with much of the text, some of the case study and mini case material is generic in nature and is therefore applicable to students of all nationalities. At the end of each chapter there are a number of review and discussion questions and assignments designed to encourage readers to test their understanding and application of the material from the chapter. The chapters conclude with suggested further reading and, in some cases, with appendices related to the text.

## 1.8   Choosing a route through the text

Every university and college degree or diploma course/module in business economics is to a certain extent unique to the institution. Moreover, students joining a particular business studies programme come from different educational backgrounds, with varying amounts of knowledge and understanding of the subject matter. In the planning and execution of this book we have attempted to take both of these factors into consideration.

In providing 16 chapters built around a common core found in most business economics courses (or modules), we have attempted to provide a text which is relevant yet flexible and which can suit the demands of both a linear degree and a one-term or one-semester modular programme. Where students have little or no prior knowledge of economics and only require a relatively non-technical introduction to the subject matter, we would recommend Chapters 1–3, 5–10 and Chapter 12 as a useful course structure. Where necessary this can be supplemented with other chapters, depending on the degree of complexity required (e.g. Chapters 4 and 16) and/or the wish to examine issues of contemporary interest (e.g. Chapters 13 and 14) or of relevance to later parts of the degree programme (e.g. Chapter 15).

While accepting that no book can ever hope to satisfy everyone's needs simultaneously or cover every possible topic which could be included under the title 'business economics', we would welcome your views on how we could improve on the current text. As we aim to demonstrate below, in a competitive market place the views of the customer must remain paramount if the 'product' is to have a successful and extended life cycle!

## 1.9  Conclusion

A primary aim of the firm in a capitalist economy is to be profitable by producing and/or selling a good or service for more than it costs the organisation to make or acquire. In seeking to achieve this objective, business decision-makers have to make choices about what products to produce, where to acquire the necessary resources, whether to provide a service in house or buy it in, what prices to charge customers, how to respond to competitor decisions, what markets to operate in and so on. These are key questions for any business organisation; they are equally central concerns within the field of business economics.

In asking questions about what shapes business behaviour and the broader environment in which that behaviour occurs, economists make use of an array of concepts, models, theories and analytical techniques to help us understand the day-to-day processes of production and consumption. Using the economist's 'toolkit' helps to enhance our understanding of the world in which we live and both complements and augments knowledge and insights derived from other disciplines as well as from practical experience. For students studying at degree, diploma and professional level, business economics is a key component of a business studies programme, alongside subjects such as accounting, human resource management, law, marketing and statistics.

## Notes and references

1. Worthington, I. and Britton, C. (2000), *The Business Environment*, 3rd edition, Financial Times Prentice Hall, Harlow.

| Case study | **Problems at Rover** |

In the mid-1990s BMW acquired Rover cars from British Aerospace and with it a number of famous brand names which included MG, Land Rover and the Mini. Some five years later the German car manufacturer announced its decision to break up the Rover Group, divesting itself of the Rover Car Company, getting rid of the old Mini brand and selling off Land Rover. This decision – announced in March 2000 – came at a time when the British government had indicated its willingness to subsidise expansion at the Longbridge plant and ran counter to the general trend towards motor industry takeovers and alliances which were seen as a key to company survival.

The evidence suggests that BMW's decision was driven first and foremost by commercial considerations. Having acquired Rover and invested in a number of new models, the parent company subsequently saw a decline in sales of the Rover brand and in Rover's share of the UK car market (e.g. in January 2000 market share was just over 5 per cent; by comparison it had been 40 per cent in the 1960s). Estimates suggest that prior to the announcement Rover was costing BMW around £2 million a day, with losses in 1999 said to be in the region of £800 million. Far from enhancing BMW's profitability, Rover appears to have been something of a liability to the parent company, hence the decision to sell off the profitable parts of the group and to dispose of the others as cheaply as possible.

A number of factors have been put forward to explain the underlying causes of the decline in Rover's fortunes. These centre around questions of demand, supply, cost, price and competition, concepts which are readily familiar to the business economist.

- *Supply* – there was over-capacity in the world car market, making trading conditions difficult for mass production car firms. Many Rover cars had to be stockpiled at considerable cost to the company.
- *Demand* – despite the critical acclaim afforded the new Rover 75 model, Rover cars were not generally selling in sufficient quantities in the showrooms. UK consumers appeared reluctant to buy new cars in the expectation that cars prices would fall because of excess supply and pressure on car manufacturers by the UK competition authorities.
- *Costs* – while there had been significant productivity gains in Rover plants, BMW was not able to deliver the kind of economies of scale and improvements in productivity needed to save the relatively ageing Longbridge plant.
- *Prices* – with most components sourced in the UK and a strong £/Dmark exchange rate Rover cars were more expensive in export markets.
- *Competition* – Rover models faced severe competition from larger car producers which enhanced the importance of reducing unit costs and selling at competitive prices. Sterling's strength affected BMW's investment plans.
- *Other factors* – BMW executives claimed that the UK's failure to join the 'euro' had been a contributory factor in its decision to dispose of Rover. Press reports of continuing problems with BMW's relationship with Rover seem to have been fuelled by adverse remarks by BMW executives.

Postcript: BMW eventually sold Rover in May 2000 to the Phoenix consortium for a token £10. It remains to be seen whether this will help to safeguard the Longbridge plant in the longer term as a site for mass car production. Ford's decision to cease mass car production at its Dagenham plant in the UK and concentrate production on other sites suggests that there may be difficult times ahead for the Longbridge workers and management.

## Review and discussion questions

1 If you were being interviewed for a job, how would you convince your interviewer that studying business economics was useful for a career in business?

2 How does economic scarcity differ from shortages? Are there any goods which are not scarce?

3 The Millennium Commission contributed hundreds of millions of pounds of public money to the Millennium Dome project. How would an economist calculate the 'real cost' of this enterprise?

4 With regard to Figure 1.5 explain the following: (1) why is the production possibility function a curved rather than a straight line joining x and y? (2) what can you deduce about a firm currently operating at point w, i.e. producing Ou units of A and Ot units of B? (3) under what circumstances could the firm operate at point r?

## Assignments

1 Imagine you own a small shop selling groceries, newspapers, cigarettes, etc. A number of your regular customers have asked you to provide a range of fresh sandwiches which they are likely to purchase on a daily basis. Draw up a list of the anticipated costs and benefits of providing this service (hint: think like an economist).

2 Given the over-capacity in the world car market referred to in the case study, what do you predict are likely to be the consequences for mass production car firms?

## Further reading

### Economics and business texts

Cook, M. and Farquharson, C. (1998), *Business Economics:Strategy and Applications*, Pitman Publishing, London.

Sloman, J. and Sutcliffe, M. (2001), Economics for Business, 2nd edition, Financial Times Prentice Hall, Harlow.

Worthington, I. and Britton, C. (2000), *The Business Environment*, 3rd edition, Financial Times Prentice Hall, Harlow.

### Organisation and management texts

Fincham, R. and Rhodes, P. (1999), *Principles of Organizational Behaviour*, 3rd edition, Oxford University Press, Oxford.

Hall, R. H. (1999), *Organizations: Structures, Processes and Outcomes*, 7th edition, Prentice Hall, Old Tappan, NJ.

Mullins, L. (1999), *Management and Organisational Behaviour*, 5th edition, Financial Times Prentice Hall, Harlow.

## Appendix 1.1    Illustrating opportunity cost

The idea of opportunity cost can be illustrated diagrammatically using what is called a 'production possibility curve or function'. In essence this curve illustrates the maximum output that can be achieved for two alternative goods or services, given the current level of resources available and assuming that there is maximum efficiency in production. In Figure 1.5 the firm (or country) uses its resources to produce two products, A and/or B. Using all its resources to produce just A would result in a maximum output of Ox units of A and no units of B; while using them just for producing B would yield Oy units of B and no units of A. Joining the two points x and y gives all possible combinations of output of the two goods that can be achieved by the firm (or country) given current resources (e.g. Os units of A and Ot units of B or Ou units of A and Ov units of B). As can be seen in Figure 1.5 producing more of one product involves sacrificing a certain level of output of the other: this is the opportunity cost.

You can develop your understanding of this idea by attempting question 4 in the Review and discussion questions on p. 17.

**Figure 1.5  The production possibility curve**

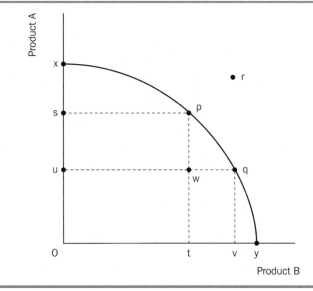

**Appendix 1.2**    ## Scarcity, choice and resource allocation

**Figure 1.6  Economic systems**

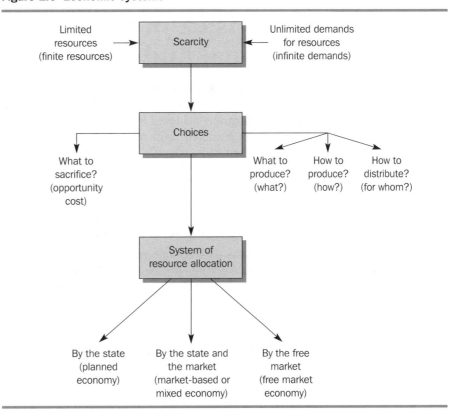

# CHAPTER 2

# Organisation for production: practical and theoretical perspectives

Chris Britton

**Objectives**

1 To give students a full understanding of the different legal structures which can be adopted by the business organisation, and their implications.

2 To look at the different internal organisational structures that exist, and their relative advantages and disadvantages.

3 To consider some of the recent developments in business economics which concentrate on theoretical issues such as the existence and the size of firms.

4 To give students an awareness of the principal-agent problem in the business setting and mechanisms which can be used to alleviate it.

## 2.1 Introduction

The production of goods and services in our economy takes place mainly within organisations, whether in the private sector or the public sector. Early business economists saw the business organisation as a 'black box' which, irrespective of its legal form or internal structure, acted as a single decision-making unit whose objective was to maximise profit. It was seen as powerless in the face of market conditions. Given these assumptions it was therefore deemed unnecessary to consider the internal organisation of the firm.

Over time this view has changed. The debate over ownership and control has questioned the objective of profit maximisation (see Chapter 6). The firm is no longer seen as powerless in the face of market forces and there is an acceptance that the firm is actually made up of a coalition of individuals, all of whom might have conflicting interests. It has become necessary, therefore, to look at the internal structure of organisations and the ways in which decisions are made. In this chapter we look at the types of business organisation which exist – their legal status and their organisational structures – in both the private and the public sectors, using the UK as our example. Similar structures exist in most other countries.

Consideration is also given to three relatively new theoretical approaches in business economics concerning the organisation for production:

■ transactions cost economics, which asks the question, why do firms exist at all?
■ other approaches to the existence of firms, e.g. the resource-based view.
■ principal–agent theory which looks at the way in which the interests of the various individuals and groups within the firm can be aligned.

The chapter ends with a consideration of two alternatives to the firm as the basic unit of production – networking and the virtual organisation.

## 2.2   Legal structures

### 2.2.1 Private sector organisations

**legal structure** the legal definition of the firm according to its characteristics (e.g. sole proprietor, partnership, limited company)

The choice of **legal structure** is a complex one and, for businesses in the private sector, the choice of legal structure has important implications. Amongst the factors which the aspiring entrepreneur has to take into account when deciding what form of business enterprise to establish are:

■ the degree of personal liability
■ the willingness to share decision-making powers and risks
■ the cost of establishing the business
■ the legal requirements concerning the provision of public information
■ the taxation position
■ commercial needs, including access to capital
■ business continuity.

Important issues like the objectives of the organisation or who its **stakeholders** are will have an impact upon legal structure. Once the legal structure has been determined this in turn will impact upon these determining factors. Profit maximisation, for example, is much more likely to be the objective of the sole trader or partnership, since any profits will accrue directly to the owners. In companies where decisions are taken by managers rather than owners there is the possibility of a conflict of goals.

#### The sole trader

**sole trader/proprietor** an unincorporated business owned and run by one individual

A **sole trader** (or sole proprietor) is a business owned by one individual who is self-employed. Normally using personal funds to start the business, the sole trader makes all of the operational and strategic decisions regarding the firm. All profits which result from the operation of the business accrue to the owner and it is common for sole traders to reinvest a considerable proportion of these in the business. In the case of losses, these too are the responsibility of the sole trader who has **unlimited personal liability** for the debts of the business.

**unlimited personal liability** where the owner of the business is personally liable for all the firm's debts

Despite this major disadvantage, sole proprietorship tend to be the most popular form of business organisation numerically (see mini case on legal structures, p. 29). In some sectors – notably personal services, retailing, building – the percentages are even higher. Why is this the case?

- Part of the reason for this is the relative ease with which an individual can establish a business of this type. Despite some minor restrictions concerning the use of a business name, firms with a turnover less than £50,000 (in 1998) do not have to register for value added tax and there is no requirement to file annual reports except for tax purposes.
- Many sole proprietors are individuals who enjoy being their own boss – they have almost complete control over the running of the business and are likely to be highly motivated. In addition to this 'pull' factor, the 'push' of unemployment is often an important factor and one which clearly accounts for some of the growth in the number of small businesses in the UK in the 1980s.

**cash flow** the flow of money to and from an organisation in a given period

There are, however, problems in being a sole trader – there is a very high mortality rate amongst businesses of this kind particularly during a recession. Reasons for this include **cash flow** problems from late payment of bills, the effects of increased competition, higher interest rates and falling demand. These problems affect all businesses but there are some which are specific to small firms, such as lack of funds for expansion, poor marketing, lack of research of the market place and insufficient management skills. Where such constraints exist, the sole trader may be tempted to look to others to share the burdens and the risks by establishing a partnership or co-operative or limited company.

### The partnership

**partnership** an unincorporated business of between two and 20 individuals

A **partnership** is the voluntary combination of between two and 20 individuals who work together in business, although some partnerships of over 20 are allowed, especially in professional services. Like the sole trader, this form of business organisation does not have its own distinct legal personality and hence the owners – the partners – have unlimited personal liability both jointly and severally. The Partnership Act (1890) lays down a minimum code which governs the relationship between partners but it is common practice for partnerships to have their own Deed of Partnership or Articles which clarify issues like the share of partners in the capital and profits or losses and provide the legal framework within which the enterprise exists and its co-owners operate.

The main advantage of partnerships over being a sole trader is that they permit the sharing of responsibilities and tasks and it is common in a partnership for individuals to specialise to some degree in particular aspects of the organisation's work. Added to this is the wider access to capital for the business. These two factors alone tend to make a partnership an attractive proposition for some would-be entrepreneurs; whilst for others the rules of their professional body – which often prohibits its members from forming a company – effectively provide for the establishment of this type of organisation.

On the downside, the sharing of decisions and responsibilities may represent a problem, particularly where partners are unable to agree over the direction the partnership should take or the amount to be reinvested in the business, unless such matters are clearly specified in a formal agreement. A more intractable problem is the existence of unlimited personal liability. To overcome this problem, many individuals, especially in manufacturing and trading, look to the limited company as the type of organisation which can combine the benefits of joint ownership and limited personal liability – a situation not necessarily always borne out in practice.

### Limited companies

**company** a corporate association having a legal identity in its own right

In law a **company** is a corporate association having a legal identity in its own right. This means that all property and other assets owned by the company belong to the company and not to its members (owners). By the same token, the personal assets of its members (the shareholders) do not normally belong to the business, such that in the event of insolvency an individual's liability is limited to the amount invested in the business.

Companies are essentially business organisations consisting of two or more individuals who have agreed to embark on a business venture and who have decided to seek corporate status rather than to form a partnership. Such status could derive from an Act of Parliament or a Royal Charter, but is almost always nowadays achieved through 'registration', the terms of which are laid down in the various Companies' Acts. Under the legislation – the most recent of which dates from 1985 and 1989 – individuals seeking to form a company are required to file numerous documents, including a Memorandum of Association and Articles of Association, with the Registrar of Companies. If satisfied, the Registrar will issue a Certificate of Incorporation, bringing the company into existence as a legal entity.

**public limited company** a limited company whose shares can be bought and sold by the public

Under British law a distinction is made between public and private companies. **Public limited companies** (plcs) – not to be confused with public corporations which are state-owned businesses – are those limited companies which satisfy the conditions for being a 'plc'. These conditions require the company to have

- a minimum of two shareholders
- at least two directors
- a minimum (at present) of £50,000 of authorised and allotted share capital
- the right to offer its shares (and debentures) for sale to the general public
- a certificate from the Registrar of Companies verifying that the share capital requirements have been met
- a memorandum which states it is to be a public company.

A company which meets these conditions must include the title 'public limited company' or 'plc' in its name and is required to make full accounts available for public inspection. Any company unable or unwilling to meet these conditions is therefore, in the eyes of the law, a **private limited company**, normally signified by the term 'Limited' or 'Ltd'.

**private limited company** a limited company whose shares cannot be offered to the general public

Like the public limited company, the private company must have a minimum of two shareholders, but its shares cannot be offered to the public at large, although it can offer them to individuals through its business contacts. This restriction on the sale of shares, and hence on its ability to raise considerable sums of money on the open market, normally ensures that most private companies are either small or medium-sized, and are often family businesses operating in a relatively restricted market, although there are some notable exceptions to this general rule (e.g. Clarks Shoes, Virgin). In contrast, public companies – many of which began life as private companies prior to **'going public'** – often have many thousands, even millions, of owners (shareholders) and normally operate on a national or international scale, producing products as diverse as computers, petrochemicals, cars and banking services. Despite being outnumbered numerically by their private counterparts, public companies

**going public** the process by which private limited companies become public limited companies

dwarf private companies in terms of their capital and other assets, and their collective influence on output, investment, employment and consumption in the economy is immense.

**company director**
a person appointed to run a company and to represent the interests of shareholders

Both public and private companies act through their **directors**. These are individuals chosen by a company's shareholders to manage its affairs and to make the major decisions concerning the strategic direction of the company. The appointment and powers of directors are outlined in the Articles of Association (the 'internal rules' of the organisation) and so long as the directors do not exceed their powers, the shareholders do not normally have the right to intervene in the day-to-day management of the company. It is usual for a board of directors to have both a chairperson and a managing director, although many companies choose to appoint one person to both roles. The

**managing director** a company director responsible for the day-to-day running of the company

**managing director**, or chief executive, fulfils a pivotal role in the organisation, by forming the link between the board and the management team of senior executives. Central to this role is the need not only to interpret board decisions but to ensure that they are put into effect by establishing an appropriate structure of delegated responsibility and effective systems of reporting and control (organisational structure is considered in Section 2.3). This close contact with the day-to-day operations of the company places the appointed individual in a position of considerable authority and they will invariably be able to make important decisions without reference to the full board. This authority is enhanced where the managing director is also the person chairing the board of directors and/or is responsible for recommending individuals to

**executive director** a director of a company who is a full-time employee and usually has responsibility for a particular activity

serve as **executive directors** (i.e. those with functional responsibilities such as production, marketing, finance).

Like the managing director, most, if not all, executive directors will be full-time executives of the company, responsible for running a division or functional area within the framework laid down at board level. In contrast,

**non-executive director** a director not involved in the day-to-day management of the organisation, but usually appointed for specialist expertise

other directors will have a **non-executive** role and are usually part-time appointees, chosen for a variety of reasons including their knowledge, skills, contacts, influence, independence or previous experience. Sometimes, a company might be required to appoint such a director at the wishes of a third party, such as a merchant bank which has agreed to fund a large capital injection and wishes to have representation on the board. In this case, the individual tends to act in an advisory capacity – particularly on matters of finance – and helps to provide the financing institution with a means of ensuring that any board decisions are in its interests.

In Britain the role of company directors and senior executives in recent years has come under a certain amount of public scrutiny and has culminated in a number of enquiries into issues of power and pay. In the Cadbury Report (1992), a committee, with Sir Adrian Cadbury as chairperson, called for a non-statutory code of practice which it wanted to be applied to all listed public companies. Under this code the committee recommended:

- a clear division of responsibilities at the head of a company to ensure that no individual had unfettered powers of decision;
- a greater role for non-executive directors;
- regular board meetings;
- restrictions on the contracts of executive directors;

- full disclosures of directors' total enrolments;
- an audit committee dominated by non-executives.

The committee's stress on the important role of non-executive directors was a theme taken up in the Greenbury Report (1995) which investigated the controversial topic of executive salaries in the wake of a number of highly publicised pay rises for senior company directors. Greenbury's recommendations included:

- full disclosure of directors' pay packages, including pensions;
- shareholder approval for any long-term bonus scheme;
- remuneration committees consisting entirely of non-executive directors;
- greater detail in the annual report on directors' pay, pensions and perks;
- an end to payments for failure.

Greenbury was followed by a further investigation into corporate governance by a committee under the chairmanship of ICI chairman Ronal Hampel. The Hampel Report (1998) called for greater shareholder responsibility by companies and increased standards of disclosure of information; it supported Cadbury's recommendation that the role of chairman and chief executive should normally be separated. As might have been anticipated, the Hampel Report advocated **self-regulation** as the best approach for UK companies. Time will tell how far public companies are prepared to go to implement the various recommendations and whether self-regulation will be sufficient to ensure compliance with the spirit as well as the letter of the law.

**self-regulation** the regulation of behaviour by companies themselves without any outside influence

### Co-operatives

#### Consumer co-operative societies

**consumer societies** self-help organisations formed originally to benefit consumers

**Consumer societies** are basically 'self-help' organisations which have their roots in the anti-capitalist sentiment which arose in mid-nineteenth-century Britain and which gave rise to a consumer co-operative movement dedicated to the provision of cheap, unadulterated food for its members and a share in its profits. Today this movement boasts a multibillion pound turnover, a membership numbered in millions and an empire which includes 3,000 food stores, numerous factories and farms, dairies, travel agencies, opticians, funeral parlours, a bank and an insurance business. Taken together, these activities ensure that the 'Co-op' remains a powerful force in British retailing.

Although the co-operative societies, like companies, are registered and incorporated bodies – in this case under the Industrial and Provident Societies Act – they are quite distinct trading organisations. These societies belong to their members (i.e. invariably customers who have purchased a share in the society) and each member has one vote at the society's annual meeting which elects a committee (or board) to take responsibility for running the organisation. This committee appoints managers and staff to run its various stores and offices and any profits from its activities are supposed to benefit the members. Originally this took the form of a cash dividend paid to members in relation to their purchases, but this has largely disappeared, having been replaced either by trading stamps or by investment in areas felt to benefit the consumer (e.g. lower prices, higher-quality products, modern shops, etc.) and/or the local community (e.g. charitable donations, sponsorship).

The societies differ in other ways from standard companies. For a start, shares are not quoted on the Stock Exchange and members are restricted in the number of shares they can purchase and in the method of disposal. Not having access to cheap sources of capital on the stock market, co-operatives rely heavily on retained surpluses and on loan finance, and the latter places a heavy burden on the societies when interest rates are high. The movement's democratic principles also impinge on its operations and this has been a bone of contention in recent years as members have complained about their increasing remoteness from decision-making centres. Some societies have responded by encouraging the development of locally elected committees, to act in an advisory or consultative capacity to the society's board of directors and it looks likely that others will be forced to consider similar means of increasing member participation, which still remains very limited.

### Workers' co-operatives

**workers' co-operatives**
a business owned by the people working in it

In Britain, **workers' co-operatives** are found in a wide range of industries including manufacturing, building and construction, engineering, catering and retailing. They are particularly prevalent in printing, clothing and in wholefoods and some have been in existence for over a century. The majority, however, are of fairly recent origin, having been part of the growth in the number of small firms which occurred in the 1980s.

As the name suggests, a workers' co-operative is a business in which the ownership and control of the assets are in the hands of the people working in it, having agreed to establish the enterprise and to share the risk for mutual benefit. Rather than form a standard partnership, the individuals involved normally register the business as a friendly society under the Industrial and Provident Societies Acts (1965–78), or seek incorporation as a private limited company under the Companies Act (1985). In the case of the former, seven members are required to form a co-operative, whilst the latter only requires two. In practice, a minimum of three or four members tends to be the norm and some co-operatives may have several hundred participants, frequently people who have been made redundant by their employers and who are keen to keep the business going.

The central principles of the movement – democracy, open membership, social responsibility, mutual co-operation and trust – help to differentiate the co-operative from other forms of business organisation and govern both the formation and operation of this type of enterprise. Every employee may be a member of the organisation and every member owns one share in the business, with every share carrying an equal voting right. Any surpluses are shared by democratic agreement and this is normally done on an equitable basis, reflecting, for example, the amount of time and effort an individual puts into the business. Other decisions, too, are taken jointly by the members and the emphasis tends to be on the quality of goods or services provided and on creating a favourable working environment, rather than on the pursuit of profits – although the latter cannot be ignored if the organisation is to survive. In short, the co-operative tends to focus on people and on the relationship between them, stressing the co-operative and communal traditions associated with its origins, rather than the more conflictual and competitive aspects inherent in other forms of industrial organisation.

Despite these apparent attractions, workers' co-operatives have never been as popular in Britain as in other parts of the world (e.g. France, Italy, Israel), although a substantial increase occurred in their number in the 1980s, largely as a result of growing unemployment, overt support across the political spectrum and the establishment of a system to encourage and promote the co-operative ideal (e.g. Co-operative Development Agencies). More recently, however, their fortunes have tended to decline, as **employee shareholding and profit schemes** (ESOPs) have grown in popularity. It seems unlikely that workers' co-operatives will ever form the basis of a strong third sector in the British economy, between the profit-orientated firms in the private sector and the nationalised and municipal undertakings in the public sector.

**employee shareholding and profit schemes**
where firms offer profit-sharing or shares in the company to employees to increase motivation and involvement

### 2.2.2 Public sector business organisations

Public sector organisations come in a variety of forms which include:

- central government departments (e.g. Department of Trade and Industry)
- local authorities (e.g. Lancashire County Council)
- regional bodies (e.g. the former regional health authorities)
- quangos (e.g. the Arts Council)
- central government trading organisations (e.g. HMSO)
- public corporations and nationalised industries (e.g. the Post Office).

Here, attention is focused on those public sector organisations which most closely approximate businesses in the private sector, namely public corporations and municipal enterprises.

**Public corporations**

Private sector business organisations are owned by private individuals and groups who have chosen to invest in some form of business enterprise, usually with a view to personal gain. In contrast, in the public sector the state owns assets in various forms, which it uses to provide a range of goods and services felt to be of benefit to its citizens, even if this provision incurs the state in a 'loss'. Many of these services are provided directly through government departments (e.g. social security benefits) or through bodies operating under delegated authority from central government (e.g. local authorities, health authorities). Others are the responsibility of state-owned industrial and commercial undertakings, specially created for a variety of reasons and often taking the form of a **'public corporation'**. These state corporations are an important part of the public sector of the economy and still contribute significantly to national output, employment and investment. Their numbers, however, have declined substantially following the wide-scale **privatisation** of state industries which occurred in the 1980s and this process looks set to continue in the foreseeable future (see Chapter 11).

**public corporation** a state-owned organisation set up to run a nationalised industry or to provide a national service

**privatisation** the transfer of ownership of public assets into private hands

Public corporations are statutory bodies, incorporated (predominantly) by special Act of Parliament and like companies have a separate legal identity from the individuals who own and run them. Under the statute setting up the corporation, reference is made to the powers, duties and responsibilities of the organisation and to its relationship with the government department which oversees its operations. In the past these operations have ranged from providing a variety of national and international postal services (the Post Office), to the provision of entertainment (the BBC), an energy source (British Coal) and a national rail network (British Rail). Where such provision involves the organisation in a considerable degree of direct contact with its customers from whom it derives most of its revenue, the corporation tends to be called a **nationalised industry**. In reality, of course, the public corporation is the legal form through which the industry is both owned and run and every corporation is to some degree unique in structure as well as in function.

**nationalised industry** an industry which has been taken into public ownership and control

As organisations largely financed as well as owned by the state, public corporations are required to be publicly accountable and hence they invariably operate under the purview of a 'sponsoring' government department, the head of which (the Secretary of State) appoints a board of management to run the organisation. This board tends to exercise a considerable degree of autonomy in day-to-day decisions and operates largely free from political interference on most matters of a routine nature. The organisation's strategic objectives, however, and important questions concerning reorganisation or investment, would have to be agreed with the sponsoring department, as would the corporation's performance targets and its external financing limits.

The link between the corporation and its supervising ministry provides the means through which Parliament can oversee the work of the organisation and permits ordinary Members of Parliament to seek information and explanation through question time, through debates and through the select committee system. Additionally, under the Competition Act (1980), nationalised industries can be subject to investigation by the Competition Commission (formerly the Monopolies and Mergers Commission), and this too presents opportunities for further parliamentary discussion and debate, as well as for government action (see Chapter 11).

**consumer/consultative councils** bodies set up to consider complaints from customers of a nationalised industry and to offer advice to the board of the public corporation

A further opportunity for public scrutiny comes from the establishment of industry-specific **consumer** or **consultative councils**, which consider complaints from customers and advise both the board and the department concerned of public attitudes to the organisation's performance and to other aspects of its operations (e.g. pricing). In a number of cases – including the former British Rail – pressure on government from consumers and from other sources has resulted in the establishment of a 'customers' charter', under which the organisation agrees to provide a predetermined level of service or to give information and/or compensation where standards are not achieved. Developments of this kind are already spreading to other parts of the public sector and in future may be used as a means by which governments decide on the allocation of funds to public bodies, as well as providing a vehicle for monitoring organisational achievement.

**regulatory bodies** groups of individuals who have the responsibility of overseeing the activities of privatised industries

It is interesting to note that mechanisms for public accountability and state regulation have been retained to some degree even where public utilities have been privatised (i.e. turned into public limited companies). Industries such as gas, electricity, water and telecommunications are watched over by newly created **regulatory bodies** which are designed to protect the interests of consumers, particularly with regard to pricing and the standard of service provided (see Chapter 11). Ofgas (which regulates British Gas), for example, monitors gas supply charges to ensure that they reasonably reflect input costs and these charges can be altered by the 'regulator' if they are seen to be excessive. Similarly, in the case of non-gas services, such as maintenance, the legislation privatising the industry only allows prices to be raised to a maximum of the current rate of inflation less 2 per cent, to ensure that the organisation is not able to take full advantage of its monopoly power.

An additional source of government influence comes from its ownership of a **'golden share'** in a privatised state industry which effectively gives the government a veto in certain vital areas of decision-making. This notional shareholding – which is written into the privatisation legislation – tends to last for a number of years and can be used to protect a newly privatised business from a hostile takeover, particularly by foreign companies or individuals. Ultimately, however, the expectation is that this veto power will be relinquished and the organisation concerned will become subject to the full effects of the market: a point exemplified by the government's decision to allow Ford to take over Jaguar in 1990, having originally blocked a number of previous takeover bids.

The existence of a 'golden share' should not be equated with the decision by government to retain (or purchase) a significant proportion of issued shares in a privatised (or already private) business organisation, whether as an investment and/or future source of revenue, or as a means of exerting influence in a particular industry or sector. Nor should it be confused with government schemes to attract private funds into existing state enterprises, by allowing them to achieve notional company status in order to overcome Treasury restrictions on borrowing

**golden share** where the government retains a significant share in a privatised company in order to influence future decisions

---

**Mini case** | **Organisational legal structures**

Data is collected by the government in the UK on the legal structure of organisations: Table 2.1 shows the percentage breakdown for 1996.

**Table 2.1  Legal structure of business organisations, UK, 1996**

|  | Number (000) | Percentage |
|---|---|---|
| Sole proprietor | 598,170 | 39 |
| Partnership | 388,130 | 25 |
| Limited company | 522,620 | 34 |
| Public and non-profit-making organisations | 28,725 | 2 |

Source: Adapted from Tables 3A, 3B, 3C, 3D PA 1003, National Statistics © Crown copyright (1996).

The most popular legal structure is the sole proprietor. It is difficult to ascertain the next most numerous, since private and public limited companies are grouped together in the figures. It is clear from the table that the partnership is also a very popular legal structure. Therefore it seems that the disadvantage of unlimited liability is overcome by the advantages of these legal structures.

This pattern is repeated in most other European countries but there are some cultural differences.[1] In Germany for example the private limited company is very important – many companies in the limited company category are family-run.

imposed on public bodies. In the latter case, which often involves a limited share issue, government still retains full control of the organisation by owning all (or the vast majority) of the shares – as in the case of Rover prior to its sale to British Aerospace. Should the government wish to attract additional funds into the organisation or ultimately to privatise it, it can do so relatively easily by selling all or a proportion of its holding to private investors.

### Municipal enterprises

Local authorities have a long history of involvement in business activity. In part this is a function of their role as major providers of public services (e.g. education, housing, roads, social services) and of their increasing involvement in supporting local economic development initiatives. But their activities have also traditionally involved the provision of a range of marketable goods and services, not required by law but provided voluntarily by a local authority and often in direct competition with the private sector (e.g. theatres, leisure services, museums). Usually such provision has taken place under the aegis of a local authority department which appoints staff who are answerable to the council and to its committees through the department's chief officer and its elected head. Increasingly, though, local authorities are turning to other organisational arrangements – including the establishment of companies and trusts – in order to separate some of these activities from the rest of their responsibilities and to create a means through which private investment in the enterprise can occur.

One example of such a development can be seen in the case of local-authority-controlled airports which are normally the responsibility of a number of local authorities who run them through a joint board, representing the interests of the participating district councils (e.g. Manchester Airport). Since the Airports Act of 1986, local authorities with airports have been required to create a limited company in which their joint assets are vested and which appoints a board of directors to run the enterprise. Like other limited companies, the organisation can, if appropriate, seek private capital and must publish annual accounts, including a profit and loss statement. It can also be privatised relatively easily if the local authorities involved decide to relinquish ownership (e.g. East Midlands Airport).

Such developments – which have parallels in other parts of the public sector – can be seen to have had at least four benefits:

- They have provided a degree of autonomy from local authority control which is seen to be beneficial in a competitive trading environment.
- They have given access to market funds by the establishment of a legal structure which is not fully subject to central government restrictions on local authority borrowing.
- They have helped local authority organisations to compete more effectively under compulsory competitive tendering (CCT), by removing or reducing charges for departmental overheads that are applied under the normal arrangements.
- They have provided a vehicle for further private investment and for the ultimate privatisation of the service.

Given these benefits and the current fashion for privatisation, there is little doubt that they will become an increasing feature of municipal enterprise in the foreseeable future.

## 2.3    Organisational structure

As we have seen, business organisations convert inputs into output. Inputs include people, finance, materials and information, provided by the environment in which the organisation exists and operates. Outputs comprise such things as goods and services, information, ideas and waste, discharged into the environment for consumption by 'end' or 'intermediate' users and in some cases representing inputs used by other organisations (see Chapter 13). Apart from the very simplest form of enterprise in which one individual carries out all tasks and responsibilities, business organisations are characterised by a **division of labour** which allows employees to specialise in particular roles and to occupy designated positions in pursuit of the organisation's objectives. The resulting pattern of relationships between individuals and roles constitutes what is known as the **organisational structure** and represents the means by which the purpose and work of the enterprise is carried out. It also provides a framework through which communications can occur and within which the processes of management can be applied.

**division of labour** the breakdown of the production process into small parts so that specialisation can take place among employees

**organisational structure** the possible ways in which a firm can organise itself, for example by function by product or service

Responsibility for establishing the formal structure of the organisation lies with management and a variety of options is available. Whatever form is chosen, the basic need is to identify a structure which will best sustain the success of the enterprise and will permit the achievement of a number of important objectives. Through its structure an organisation should be able to:

- achieve efficiency in the utilisation of resources
- provide opportunities for monitoring organisational performance
- ensure the accountability of individuals
- guarantee co-ordination between the different parts of the enterprise
- provide an efficient and effective means of organisational communication
- create job satisfaction, including opportunities for progression
- adapt to changing circumstances brought about by internal or external developments.

In short, structure is not an end in itself, but a means to an end, and should ideally reflect the needs of the organisation within its existing context and in light of its future requirements. Five main methods of grouping activities in business organisations are considered below.

### 2.3.1 Functional organisation

The functional approach to organisations is depicted in Figure 2.1. As its name indicates, in this type of structure activities are clustered together by common purpose or function. All marketing activities, for example, are grouped together as a common function, typically within a marketing department. Similarly, other areas of activity, such as production, finance, personnel and research and development have their own specialised sections or departments, responsible for all the tasks required of that function.

**Figure 2.1  A functional organisation structure**

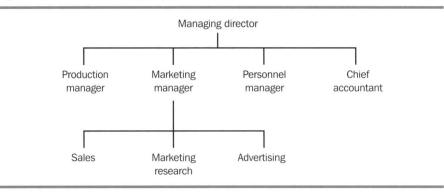

**functional organisation**
where the firm is organised
into departments according
to function, such as
marketing or finance

Apart from its obvious simplicity, the **functional organisation** structure allows individuals to be grouped together on the basis of their specialisms and technical expertise and this can facilitate the development of the function they offer, as well as providing a recognised path for promotion and career development. On the downside, functional specialisation, particularly through departments, is likely to create sectional interests which may operate to the disadvantage of the organisation as a whole, particularly where inequalities in resource allocation between functions becomes a cause for inter-function rivalry. It could also be argued that this form of structure is most suited to single-product firms and that it becomes less appropriate as organisations diversify their products and/or markets. In such circumstances, the tendency will be for businesses to look for the benefits which can arise from specialisation by product or from the divisionalisation of the enterprise.

### 2.3.2  Organisation by product or service

**product-based structure**
where the organisational
structure is based around
products

In this case the division of work and the grouping of activities is dictated by the **product** or **service** provided (a **product-based structure**, see Figure 2.2), such that each group responsible for a particular part of the output of the organisation may have its own specialist in the different functional areas (e.g. marketing, finance, personnel). One advantage of this type of structure is that it allows an organisation to offer a diversified range of products, as exemplified by the differ-

**Figure 2.2  A product-based structure**

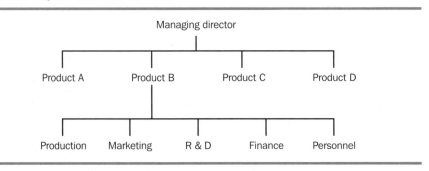

ent services available in National Health Service hospitals (e.g. maternity, orthopaedic, geriatric, etc.). Its main disadvantage is the danger that the separate units or divisions within the enterprise may attempt to become too autonomous, even at the expense of other parts of the organisation, and this can present management with problems of co-ordination and control.

### 2.3.3 The divisional structure

As firms diversify their products and/or markets – often as a result of merger or takeover – a structure is needed to co-ordinate and control the different parts of the organisation. This structure is likely to be the **divisional (or 'multi-divisional') company**.

**divisional (or multi-divisional) company** a business which is split into self-contained units (or divisions)

A divisionalised structure is formed when an organisation is split up into a number of self-contained business units, each of which operates as a **profit centre**. Such a division may occur on the basis of product or market or a combination of the two, with each unit tending to operate along functional or product lines, but with certain key functions (e.g. finance, personnel, corporate planning) provided centrally, usually at company headquarters (see Figure 2.3).

**profit centre** a division which has responsibility for its own revenue and costs and therefore its own profits

The main benefit of the multidivisional company is that it allows each part of what can be a very diverse organisation to operate semi-independently in producing and marketing its products, thus permitting each division to design its offering to suit local market conditions – a factor of prime importance where the firm operates on a multinational basis. The dual existence of divisional profit centres and a central unit responsible for establishing strategy at a global level can, however, be a source of considerable tension, particularly where the needs and aims of the centre appear to conflict with operations at the local level or to impose burdens seen to be unreasonable by divisional managers (e.g. the allocation of central overhead costs).

**holding company** a company that controls one or more other companies

Much the same kind of arguments apply to the **holding company**, though this tends to be a much looser structure for managing diverse organisations

**Figure 2.3 A divisional structure**

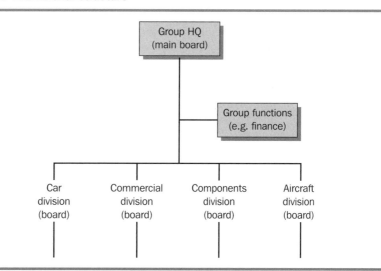

favoured by both UK and Japanese companies. Under this arrangement, the different elements of the organisation (usually companies) are co-ordinated and controlled by a parent body which may be just a financial entity established to maintain or gain control of other trading companies (e.g. Lonhro). Holding companies are associated with the growth of firms by **acquisition** which gives rise to a high degree of product or market diversification. They are also a popular means of operating a **multinational organisation**.

**acquisition** the takeover of one company by another

**multinational organisation (or enterprise)** a company which owns production or service facilities in two or more countries

**matrix organisation** combines functional specialisms with structures built around projects or programmes

### 2.3.4 Matrix structures

A **matrix** is an arrangement for combining functional specialisation (e.g. through departments) with structures built around products or projects or programmes (Figure 2.4). The resulting grid (or matrix) has a two-way flow of authority and responsibility. Within the functional elements, the flow is vertically down the line from superior to subordinate and this creates a degree of stability and certainty for the individuals located within the department or unit. Simultaneously, as a member of a project group or product team, an individual is normally answerable horizontally to the project manager whose responsibility is to oversee the successful completion of the project, which in some cases may be of very limited duration.

Matrix structures offer various advantages, most notably flexibility, opportunities for staff development, an enhanced sense of ownership of a project or programme, customer orientation and the co-ordination of information and expertise. On the negative side, difficulties can include problems of co-ordination

**Figure 2.4  A matrix structure in a business school**

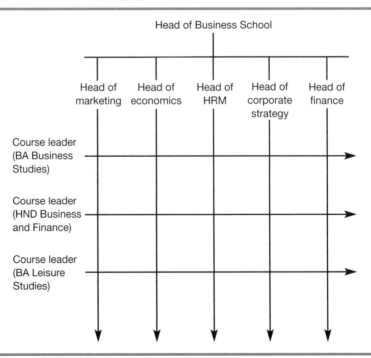

and control, conflicting loyalties for staff and uncertain lines of authority. It is not uncommon in an organisation designed on matrix lines for project or programme leaders to be unsure of their authority over the staff from the contributing departments. Nor is it unknown for functional managers to withdraw their co-operation and/or support for projects located outside their immediate sphere of influence.

### 2.3.5 Project teams

**project team** a temporary structure within an organisation put together to work on a specific project

Despite its flexibility, the matrix often has a degree of permanence; in contrast, the **project team** is essentially a temporary structure established as a means of carrying out a particular task, often in a highly unstable environment. Once the task is complete, the team is disbanded and individuals return to their usual departments or are assigned to a new project.

Fashioned around technical expertise rather than managerial rank and often operating closely with clients, project teams are increasingly common in high technology firms, construction companies and in some types of service industry, especially management consultancies and advertising. Rather than being a replacement for the existing structure, they operate alongside it and utilise in-house staff (and in some cases, outside specialists) on a project-by-project basis. Whilst this can present logistical and scheduling problems and may involve some duplication of resources, it can assist an organisation in adapting to change and uncertainty and in providing products to the customer's specifications. Project teams tend to be at their most effective when objectives and tasks are well defined, when the client is clear as to the desired outcome and when the team is chosen with care.

## 2.4    Theoretical approaches to the organisation

### 2.4.1 Transactions cost economics

**transactions cost economics** a theoretical approach which looks at the make-or-buy decision as based on the relative costs of transactions

**Transactions cost economics** (TCE) is essentially concerned with the make or buy decision. It considers the relative merits of carrying out transactions within the boundary of the firm and between different firms in the market. It therefore has something to say about:

- the existence of firms in the first place
- the size and growth of firms, and
- the internal governance structures in organisations.

Only the first two will be discussed in detail in this section; the third aspect will be considered only in passing.

**bounded rationality** the idea that although human beings might act rationally, there are limits to their ability to process information and formulate and solve problems

TCE comes from economics, organisational theory and contract law. Williamson (1981) said that whether a firm produced something itself or bought it from the market depended upon the relative costs involved.[2] The two main underlying assumptions of TCE are: firstly, that there is **bounded rationality**[3] – human beings are rational but there are limits to their abilities to process information and formulate and solve problems; and, secondly, that at least some agents are given to opportunistic behaviour because they follow their own self-interest. These two assumptions imply that contracts are needed for a transaction to take place.

The process of exchange brings problems of information and enforcement. For example, an individual having alterations done to his home has two choices: to do it himself or to employ specialists to do it for him. Employing specialists brings the benefits of specialisation but also brings some problems like:

- finding the specialists
- assessing their abilities
- forming agreements with the specialists
- monitoring the work
- enforcing and co-ordinating the contract.

These problems can be grouped under two headings – information deficiencies and problems of enforcement – and both of these will carry a cost.

### Information deficiencies

There are two types of information deficiency. Firstly, the individual does not have information on the location of possible specialists or their abilities and the individual might not know exactly what he wants and will therefore have to rely on the judgement of the specialist. In other words, there is **asymmetric information** between the buyer and the seller – the seller is better informed than the buyer. The classic example from the literature is the case of second-hand cars when the buyer has problems in determining whether or not he is buying a 'lemon'.[4] This type of information deficiency is called ex ante or **adverse selection**, since it takes place prior to a transaction being agreed. The second type of information deficiency stems from the buyer's inability to observe the actions taken by the seller. This is called ex post or **moral hazard**, as it takes place after a contract has been agreed. If the buyer cannot observe the actions of the seller it is impossible for him to know whether the seller is putting in sufficient effort on behalf of the buyer. This is also known as the principal-agent problem which is considered later.

These information deficiencies carry a cost. The individual will have to spend time finding architects, builders, plumbers and electricians and time assessing their abilities. Some information is relatively easy to find (e.g. information on price can be obtained by asking for a number of quotes), but assessing the quality of the contractors is much more difficult.

### Problems of enforcement

In order for the building alterations to go ahead, some kind of contract is required. The drawing up of a contract carries a cost. Once drawn up there is a need for the contract to be monitored and enforced; this also carries a cost. These are called **governance costs**.

Whether or not the individual chooses to do the house alterations himself will depend upon the relative costs involved in overcoming the information deficiencies and the problems of enforcement. For these two reasons there are costs involved in carrying out a transaction. These are called transaction costs.

Coase (1937) sees these costs as the reason for the existence of firms:[5]

> The main reason why it is profitable to establish a firm would seem to be that there is a cost of using the price mechanism (p. 390).

**asymmetric information** when one party to a transaction has more information than the others

**adverse selection** asymmetric information which occurs prior to the transaction being agreed

**moral hazard** asymmetric information which occurs after a transaction has been agreed

**governance costs** the costs involved in the monitoring and enforcement of a contract

Assume that the firm has two choices – to produce a component itself or to buy it from another firm (i.e. go to the market). The choice facing the firm is similar to the choice facing the individual above; which the firm chooses depends upon their relative costs.

In Figure 2.5 there are three stages in the production process within the firm, $S_1$, $S_2$ and $S_3$. Raw materials R are purchased from the market. Components (C) are added at each stage of the production process and can either be produced within the firm, $C_1$–O, $C_2$–O and $C_3$–O or bought in from outside, $C_1$–B, $C_2$–B and $C_3$–B. Distribution of the finished product can also be done in house (D–O) or through the market (D–B). The dotted lines represent potential transactions while the solid lines represent actual transactions. It can be seen that the firm has chosen to produce component 2 in house while it purchases components 1 and 3 from the market. It has also chosen to distribute the product itself. The thickened line represents the 'efficient boundary' of the firm. When components are produced in house, the form of governance of the transaction is through the existing organisational hierarchy and control is exercised through the employment contract between the employees of the firm and the firm itself. When components are bought in from outside the transaction is governed by normal contract law.

TCE can be used to determine the size and growth of firms and the degree of **vertical integration** that takes place within an industry. The way in which the firm decides which component to produce and which to buy depends upon the relative transactions cost (as does the decision of whether to distribute the finished good itself or not). These will depend upon:

**vertical integration** the undertaking by a firm of successive stages in the production process

**site specificity** assets used in the production process which are located in proximity to one another

**physical asset specificity** where there are specialised physical assets used in the production process

**human asset specificity** when specific human assets are required by a production process

1 *The presence of specific assets.* These are specialised assets used in the production process. There are three types of asset specificity: **site specificity**, where stations need to be located next to one another in order to cut down on transportation costs; **physical asset specificity** where a highly specialised piece of equipment is needed to produce a component; and **human asset specificity**, where specific human assets are required for production, i.e. where the effect of learning by doing is high. The less specific the assets the more advantages the market will enjoy over the firm in both production and governance costs. The greater the need for specific assets, the greater is

**Figure 2.5 The efficient boundary of the firm**

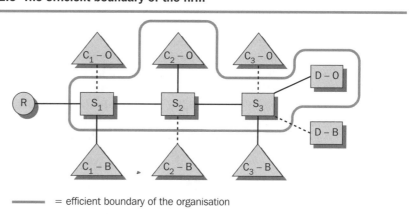

——— = efficient boundary of the organisation

*Source:* Williamson, 'The Economics of organization', *American Journal of Sociology*, 87, 1981.

the possibility that the assets will be purchased by the firm and governance will be through the internal organisation.

2 The *uncertainty* involved in the outcome. For standardised products it is more likely that components would be bought in from outside, since the problem of monitoring would be less costly.

3 The *frequency* of the transaction. If the transaction is a recurring one it is more likely that production would take place in house.

**production cost economies** economies of scale which occur in production

**economies of scale** factors which lead to falling average cost when the scale of production is increased

**governance economies** cost savings which are involved in the governance of contracts

There are two types of economies involved in the make or buy decision which favour either the firm or the market. The first are **production cost economies**, where the market is likely to have the advantage. If the needs of the firm with respect to the component are small compared to the total market, the market will have **economies of scale** since it can pool risks by aggregating demands. The second are **governance economies** – the cost of monitoring and co-ordinating a transaction and the cost of enforcing a contract. Here the firm might have the advantage since a governance hierarchy will already be in existence in the internal organisation of the firm.

One criticism of TCE is that by making the assumption that some will act opportunistically, TCE tends to concentrate on the two extreme cases of market and hierarchies. However, there are intermediate market structures, many of which have received a great deal of attention in recent years in the business economics literature (e.g. networks, joint ventures, strategic alliances and franchises), which will be considered in Section 2.5. All of these structures require trust between partners. Ring and Van de Ven (1992) recognise two intermediate structures: relational contracting and recurrent contracting.[6] **Recurrent contracts** tend to be relatively short-term contracts between legally separate entities where the assets being exchanged have a moderate degree of transaction specificity. **Relational contracts** are longer-term relationships which involve the joint specification of the terms of the exchange which cannot be completely specified beforehand. In the case of recurrent contracting the governance mechanism is predominantly market-based, while in the case of relational contracting the governance mechanism is largely bilateral.

**recurrent contracts** relatively short-term contracts between legally separate entities

**relational contracts** long-term contracts between legally separate entities

### 2.4.2 Other theoretical approaches

The resource-based view (RBV) of the firm comes out of the work by Penrose (1959) in the 1950s.[7] She argued that firms diversify because market imperfections make it difficult for the market properly to evaluate new products or technologies. Therefore the firm diversifies and uses the new technologies or produces the new products itself, and in doing so develops unique capabilities or 'resources'. The work was taken up by strategists in the 1980s and formalised into a theory by Barney in 1991.[8] In the RBV the firm is seen as a bundle of resources which includes 'all assets, capabilities, organisational processes, firm attributes, information, knowledge, etc. controlled by a firm' (Barney 1991, p. 101).

The resources of the firm are divided into three categories:

- *physical capital resources* – which include the firm's plant and equipment, geographical location and access to raw materials;
- *human capital resources* – which include training, experience, judgement relationships and insights of individual managers;

- *organisational capital resources* – which include the firm's formal reporting structure, and its formal and informal planning, controlling and co-ordinating systems.

**competitive advantage**
an advantage over
competitors gained by giving
consumers better value

Each firm is comprised of a unique bundle of these resources, and the firm's ability to access these resources and use them effectively gives rise to **competitive advantage**.

Barney's article used the RBV to suggest a strategy for the firm in developing a sustained competitive advantage over its current or potential competitors. For a resource to be the basis for competitive advantage for a firm it must have four characteristics: it must be valuable; it must be rare among the firm's competitors; it must be difficult to imitate; and there cannot be strategically equivalent substitutes. If this is the case a firm will enjoy a competitive advantage over its competitors which can be sustained over time. Prahalad and Hamel[9] call these resources the 'core competencies' of the firm and argue that these are crucial in the pursuit of competitive success.

As well as the development of strategy, the RBV has something to say about the 'make or buy' debate (see mini case study on outsourcing human resources (HR)), but the outcomes are not necessarily the same as for the TCE approach. According to the RBV the firm should retain those functions which are the source of competitive advantage and outsource the rest. It therefore provides an insight into the determination of firm size. What is more difficult to determine is which resources are those that confer competitive advantage.

**Mini case**   ## Outsourcing in the human resource function

Outsourcing within the human resources function is receiving a great deal of attention at present in both the theoretical literature and the practitioner press. The trend towards increased outsourcing which has been evident in the USA for some time is now evident in the UK. What is the motivation for outsourcing?

Scott Lever (1997) looked at the outsourcing decision in the case of six HR functions (payroll, benefits payments, training, HR information systems, compensation and recruitment) and tested three hypotheses regarding the motivation for outsourcing:[10]

- **Hypothesis 1** was that these HR functions were outsourced because it led to a cost saving (the TCE approach).
- **Hypothesis 2** was that these functions were outsourced as a means of risk reduction.
- **Hypothesis 3** was that outsourcing took place so that firms could concentrate on their core competencies (the RBV approach).

The sample included 69 US firms of varying size and the mean value of outsourcing by function and the percentage of firms which outsourced the functions are shown in Table 2.2. The mean value of outsourcing is obtained from a six point scale, where higher values indicated that a higher proportion of the activity is outsourced. Payroll was the activity which was most outsourced (3.33) while benefits was the activity outsourced by the highest number of companies (75 per cent) in the survey. Compensation was the least outsourced (1.34) and by the smallest number of companies (17 per cent).

**Table 2.2  The degree of outsourcing in HR**

| HR function | Mean level of outsourcing | Number of firms outsourcing (percentage in brackets) |
| --- | --- | --- |
| Payroll | 3.33 | 43 (62) |
| Benefits | 2.58 | 52 (75) |
| Training | 2.37 | 44 (65) |
| HR information systems | 1.55 | 21 (30) |
| Compensation | 1.34 | 12 (17) |
| Recruiting | 1.75 | 35 (50) |
| Total | | 69 |

*Source*: Adapted from Lever (1997).

Each of the three motivations for outsourcing was operationalised into a number of questions which were posed to the survey respondents. The results of the survey indicate support for all three hypotheses, depending upon the function under consideration. Table 2.3 summarises Lever's results; the last row refers to the level of organisational support for outsourcing in general, which had a positive effect on the outsourcing of all the HR activities investigated.

**Table 2.3  Results of research**

| Activity hypothesis | Payroll | Benefits | Training | HR info. systems | Recruitment |
| --- | --- | --- | --- | --- | --- |
| Cost | * | | * | | |
| Risk | | | | | * |
| Competency | | | * | | |
| Org. level | * | * | * | * | * |

*Source*: Lever (1997).

Cost reduction was an issue for two of the activities – payroll and training – but only for payroll was the outsourcing decision based purely on the basis of cost. For training, in addition to cost, the development of competency within the organisation was also found to be important in the decision. Although the research is based on a small sample and is therefore difficult to generalise, it indicates that many issues (including cost and competency) influence the outsourcing decision and therefore the size of the firm.

**team production** where output is the result of the combined activities of several team members

The business organisation was seen as an example of **team production** by Alchian and Demsetz (1972).[11] Team production occurs when output is produced by the simultaneous co-operation of several team members and where the joint use of inputs is more productive than the separate use of inputs. The use of a production line, for example, breaks the production process down into its component parts so that specialisation can take place. Thus the firm will experience economies of scale, average costs will fall and the enterprise will become more efficient. Because a business organisation can operate in this way, the firm is seen as a better co-ordinator of economic activity than the market.

**productivity** the relationship between factor inputs and outputs

Team production carries with it a fundamental problem because the rewards of each team member must be determined in some way by their **productivity**. The productivity of any one individual on the production line depends upon the actions of those that are stationed before them and the productivity of the whole production line depends on the productivity of all. The whole firm can be seen as an example of team production where the productive process is split between jobs, specialisms and functions such as marketing and finance. The productivity of the firm as a whole depends upon the actions of everyone. If this is the case it becomes very difficult to separate out the contribution of each member of the team to the final output and this introduces the possibility and the opportunity of shirking on the part of team members.

According to Alchian and Demsetz there is a need for someone to monitor the activities of team members, and this is best done within the firm. If team members are monitored, their productivity can be determined and they can be rewarded accordingly. The notion of the firm used here is the classical entrepreneurial firm which has one owner/manager who has the power to monitor employees, draw up contracts, modify contracts and ultimately to hire and fire. Through the actions of this person, the firm takes on the characteristics of an efficient market by making the most efficient use of a set of inputs.

### 2.4.3 Principal–agent theory

Principal–agent (P–A) theory provides an understanding of:

- the internal organisation of the firm
- the relationship between the firm's owners and managers
- the relationships that exist between the firm and outside parties.

**principal** the individual or organisation that hires another to carry out a task

**agent** an individual or organisation hired by another to carry out a task on their behalf

A **principal** hires an **agent** to act on her behalf. There are many examples of the principal–agent relationship – the individual hires a builder to carry out alterations on her house, the manager hires employees, shareholders hire managers, the firm hires a subcontractor. P–A theory accepts that there is incomplete information and uncertainty and that inherent in the P–A relationship is a series of problems. Firstly, there is an imbalance in power between the principal and the agent; secondly, there is likely to be a divergence of interests between the principal and the agent and the possibility of opportunism exists. Agency theory concentrates on the opportunism by the agent and the mechanisms used to alleviate the problem. If the interests of the principal and the agent differ there is no inherent incentive for the agent to expend maximum effort on behalf of the principal. P–A theory looks at ways of aligning the interests of the principal and agent. Since the agent is assumed to act rationally, it is possible to design incentive systems to reduce the risk of opportunistic behaviour by the agent.

The example of the shareholder–manager relationship can be used to illustrate the P–A problem. The manager implements policies which generate income. What happens to this income? At one extreme this income can all be paid out as profit to the shareholders or at the other extreme can all be taken in benefits (like company cars, health benefits, etc.) by the manager. Using **indifference curve analysis** (see Chapter 4) the equilibrium combination of profits and benefits can be derived. It can also be shown that if the manager is only part owner of the firm the equilibrium position will result in a lower level of profits and a higher level of benefits than if the manager were the owner of the firm. What is happening is the pursuit of sub-goals. The interests of the principal (shareholder) and the agent (manager) are not the same. The owner/shareholder of the firm wishes to maximise profits while the manager wishes to maximise benefits for himself. For the efficient operation of the firm some incentive mechanism is needed to align these interests. In the case of the sole trader or partnership, there is no such conflict, since the owners are also the decision-makers.

Incentives can be created through payment structures. Because the agency literature concentrates on reducing the opportunism by the agent, it attempts to design a payment structure which aligns the interests of the principal and the agent as much as possible and ensures the maximum effort on the part of the agent. In designing a payment structure there are two extremes: piece rates, where the agent is rewarded wholly on the basis of output produced; or fixed wages which are paid irrespective of output.

Each of these extremes has its problems. Having an incentive system based on output only will tend to encourage quantity at the expense of quality. It would only work in situations where the quality of the product can be easily monitored and where output was directly dependent on effort. It is often the case that output depends upon factors other than the effort of the individual alone, for example output may be affected by the efforts of others or chance factors beyond the control of the individual. In such situations piece rates have the effect of shifting all of the risk to the agent, and this might not be acceptable to the agent. At the other extreme, fixed payments irrespective of output will tend to encourage quality at the expense of quantity. Here payment can be based on behaviour, but this only works if behaviour is observable and this is often not the case. Eisenhardt (1989) talks about the 'programmability' of a task, where a programmable task is one where the required behaviour can be precisely defined.[12] The more programmable a task the more likely it is to be rewarded by behaviour-based compensation, whereas less programmable tasks are more likely to be rewarded by outcome-based payments. Between the two extremes are incentive structures which combine elements of both: where a fixed wage is paid irrespective of output and a commission is paid in excess of this which is related to output. This marginal payment (or **performance-related pay**) acts as an incentive, since it is dependent on results. Share options would be an example of such an incentive system in the shareholder/manager relationship.

**indifference curve analysis** a method of analysing choice between two variables subject to constraints

**performance-related pay** that part of payment which is related to the performance of the recipient

The incentive system needs to balance two conflicting objectives – reducing the possibility of opportunism (and ensuring maximum effort by the agent), while taking account of the possible risk aversion of the agent. It is unlikely, given the problems inherent in the P–A situation, that the payment system would be fixed, as this encourages opportunistic behaviour, or would be completely dependent upon outcome, as this is too risky for the agent. Instead it will be a combination of the two extremes, containing a fixed element and an element dependent on performance. There are many possible solutions to the P–A problem depending upon:

- the attitude towards risk
- what is observable
- the cost of monitoring

and this explains why there are different types of employment contracts in every organisation. It also applies to contracts the firm has with other organisations.

## 2.5    Networking and the virtual organisation

**virtual (or network-based) organisation** one where a core operating company outsources most of its processes to a network of other companies

The **virtual organisation** is a **network-based structure** built on partnerships where a small core operating company outsources most of its processes. It is a network of small companies which specialise in various aspects of production. The organisation can be very big in trading terms but very small in the numbers of permanent staff. The process is typically mediated by information technology. From the TCE approach, the virtual organisation can be seen as a response to the need to reduce transactions costs. From the RBV approach, the virtual organisation concentrates on core competencies and uses partners in networks to expand its strategic scope and adaptability.

The main benefit of the virtual structure is that it helps organisations to deal with uncertainty. When virtual organisations are managed properly they can simultaneously increase efficiency, flexibility and responsiveness to changes in market conditions. The organisation is reaping the benefits of specialisation without having to develop those specialisms itself. Therefore overhead costs are minimised, as too are training costs and support costs. Information technology assumes many of the co-ordinating and managing roles that managers and committees carry out in large organisations. Information technology enables communication and the sharing of information across geographical boundaries. It is often the case, however, that the creation of a virtual organisation is driven solely by cost considerations rather than strategic considerations, in which case the benefits might not be realised. There will be a loss of control over outsourced activities and it may actually cost more to manage such activities. The organisation can become locked into contracts and specific relationships so that flexibility is reduced. There may be a lack of commitment of key resources (i.e. contractors) to the company and the loss of a contractor will be very serious.

There is some evidence that the incidence of virtual organisations is on the increase, facilitated by developments in information technology. It is a matter of 'wait and see' if this will become the dominant organisational structure in the future.

## 2.6 Conclusion

In this chapter we have looked at the internal structure of the business unit from a variety of viewpoints – the legal structure, the organisational structure and from a theoretical view. The internal structure of the organisation is important, since like market structure and conduct (see Chapters 7 and 8) it will affect the performance of the organisation. Economics has moved away from its early position of viewing the organisation simply as a black box which maximises profit.

In terms of legal structure, the sole trader is the most common in the UK, followed closely by the limited company and then the partnership. As the mini case study (p. 29) points out, there are some differences in this pattern between countries, but the sole proprietorship remains an important legal structure for reasons discussed in the text. Five organisational structures were considered – organisation by function, organisation product or service, the divisional structure, the matrix structure and organisation by project teams – along with their relative costs and benefits.

Several theoretical approaches to the organisation were considered. The transactions cost economics approach was covered in some detail. It looks at the make-or-buy decision facing organisations and therefore says something about the existence of firms and their size. The other approaches that were discussed – although mainly based in the strategy literature – still have something to say about the size and the existence of the firm. The mini case (p. 39–40) brings these together by looking at the outsourcing of human resources from two of the theoretical approaches. The principal–agent approach also looks at the internal working of the organisation but from a rather different stance – it looks at how incentives are created. Although the discussion was largely limited to relationships within the organisation, the principles apply equally to the relationships which exist between firms in a networking arrangement, for example.

**Case study** | ## Executive recruitment consultancy as an example of the principal–agent problem

The use of executive search and selection consultancies is an example of an agency relationship, where the client company (the principal) delegates executive recruitment to a recruitment consultancy (the agent) who performs that work.

In executive search there is the possibility of opportunistic behaviour by both principal (client) and agent (consultant). The client may attempt to renegotiate terms after the start of an assignment or even pull out of the assignment. The risk of this is greater if the agent has to purchase specific assets for the job. In executive search there are no large-scale investments necessary as there are in manufacturing, but there are physical assets (databases) which are specific to recruitment and there is also a high degree of human asset specificity (personal contacts). However, the process of an assignment involves an outlay of expenditure by the consultant on behalf of the client (the cost of research) and once this expenditure has been made the balance of power changes in favour of the client. An important factor which will serve to constrain possible opportunism by the client is the considerable amount of commercially sensitive information the client will have to reveal to the consultant in the process of the assignment.

Opportunistic behaviour by the consultant may derive from insufficient effort being put into the assignment. The client is faced with a number of problems: firstly, the client cannot observe the actions of the consultant; secondly, given the intangible nature of services, it is often difficult to define or observe the output of the process, and it will certainly be difficult to assess or measure quality; the covert nature of the process of executive search only serves to exacerbate this. Thirdly, there are exogenous factors which are beyond the control of the consultant but will affect the outcome of the assignment. It is hard for the client to differentiate between the effects of these factors on outcome and the results of the genuine effort of the consultant. An assignment carried out badly might result in the appointment of the wrong individual and, given the nature of the process, this might not be evident until some time after appointment.

The standard way of reducing the possibility of opportunism is through the payment system. In executive search the most common fee structure is 33 per cent of the first year's remuneration package of the successful candidate. This is increasingly based on the *anticipated* first year's remuneration so that effectively it is fixed in advance. This has the advantage of removing one type of opportunism by the consultant – that of pushing the candidate who commands the highest salary in order to maximise fee income – but introduces the possibility of another. If the consultant is being paid a fixed fee agreed beforehand, there is no incentive for the consultant to maximise his effort. This problem is partly overcome in executive search by the way in which the fees are paid.

In executive search and selection, payment of fees in three instalments is most common: one-third at the beginning, one-third on production of a short list and one-third on completion of the assignment. The division of the fee into instalments, the last one of which is paid only on the appointment of the successful candidate, serves to minimise the possibility for opportunism from both client and consultant. The initial payment represents a form of pre-commitment and once it has been paid the client will be less likely to cancel the assignment. Making the last payment dependent upon the successful completion of the assignment acts as an incentive to the consultancy to maximise its efforts. It is becoming increasingly common for clients to seek some fee retention until after the appointee has been in post for some time, which partly overcomes the difficulty of observing quality within a specified period of time.

The possibility of opportunistic behaviour has not been completely eradicated by the payment system, and there are other factors which help the situation:

- There are several professional associations to which consultancies belong and these carry their own codes of conduct.
- The majority of consultancies operate according to their own code of conduct, even in the absence of professional body membership.

▶

- The majority of consultancies offer a variety of guarantees, like guaranteeing to find a replacement for the placed candidate if he/she leaves within an agreed time period.
- Consultancies usually draw up an assignment specification in conjunction with the client in advance of an assignment which clearly sets out the procedures of the assignment and the timetable to be followed.
- As in many other services, recommendation is a big source of new business for consultancies and there is high reliance on repeat business. This means that reputation is crucial and consultancies are unlikely to do anything that will harm their reputation.
- There has been an increase in the incidence of 'partnering' as consultancies form long-term relationships with companies and carry out other activities as well as recruitment.

All of these factors serve to engender trust and increase the amount of information available about the process and therefore reduce the possibility of opportunistic behaviour.

## Notes and references

1. Worthington, I. and Britton, C. (2000), *The Business Environment*, 3rd edition, Financial Times Prentice Hall, Harlow.
2. Williamson, O. E. (1981), 'The Economics of organization: the transaction cost approach', *American Journal of Sociology*, 87, pp. 548–577.
3. Simon, H. A. (1957), *Models of Man*, Wiley, New York.
4. Akerlof, G. A. (1970), 'The market for "lemons" : quality uncertainty and the market mechanism', *Quarterly Journal of Economics*, 89(3), pp. 345–364.
5. Coase, R. H. (1937), 'The nature of the firm', *Economica*, NS, 4, pp. 386–405.
6. Ring, P. S. and Van de Ven, A. H. (1992), Structuring co-operative relationships between organisations, *Strategic Management Journal*, 13, pp. 483–498.
7. Penrose, E. T. (1959), *The Theory of the Growth of the Firm*, Wiley, New York.
8. Barney, J. (1991), 'Firm resources and sustained competitive advantage', *Journal of Management*, 17(1), pp. 99–120.
9. Prahalad, C. K. and Hamel, G. (1990), 'The core competence of the corporation', *Harvard Business Review*, 68(3), pp. 79–91.
10. Lever, S. (1997), 'An analysis of managerial motivations behind outsourcing practices in human resources', *Human Resource Planning*, 20(2), pp. 37–47.
11. Alchian, A. and Demsetz, H. (1972), 'Production, information costs, and economic organisation', *American Economic Review*, 62(5), pp. 777–795.
12. Eisenhardt, K. M. (1989), 'Agency theory: an assessment and review', *Academy of Management Review*, 14(1), pp. 57–74.

## Review and discussion questions

1 Numerically, the sole trader is the most popular form of business organisation throughout Europe. How would you account for this?

2 What criteria can be used to determine which are the *core competencies* of the organisation?

3 According to the transactions cost economics theory why does Marks and Spencer continue to buy clothes from independent producers rather than set up its own production capacity?

4 Referring to the case study on the principal–agent problem, what mechanisms are in place to reduce the possibility of opportunistic behaviour by the agent in the case of a car mechanic and an estate agency?

## Assignments

1 A firm is considering the relationship it has with one of its suppliers of an essential component in the production process. The two possibilities under consideration are to continue to buy the component from the independent firm or to take over the firm and internalise the production of the component. What are the factors which need to be considered in such a choice?

2 You work in a local authority business advice centre. One of your clients wishes to start a business in some aspect of catering. Advise your client on the advantages and disadvantages of the various legal forms the proposed enterprise could take.

## Further reading

Mintzberg, H., Ahlstrand, B. and Lampel, J. (1998), *Strategy Safari*, Prentice Hall, Harlow.

Worthington, I. and Britton, C. (2000), *The Business Environment*, 3rd edition, Financial Times Prentice Hall, Harlow.

# Demand and supply

# CHAPTER 3

# Consumer and market demand

Andy Rees

**Objectives**

1 To outline the factors affecting the demand for goods and services.

2 To consider how demand may vary with price and other factors

3 To explain the concept of 'consumer surplus'.

4 To examine ideas of 'elasticity' and their relevance to business organisations.

5 To highlight criticisms of demand theory.

## 3.1 Introduction

**demand** the willingness to pay a sum of money for a given amount of a specific good or service

What determines the **demand** for a good or service? For basic commodities such as petrol, price is clearly a dominant factor. With other goods, although price is still important, the consumer may be more concerned with reliability, design and the desire to be in fashion.

The successful firm will seek to understand the factors determining demand for its product. Armed with such knowledge the firm might propose modifying the characteristics of the product range in response to a change in consumer tastes. Alternatively, an improvement in the general economic environment might facilitate a price increase with little effect upon sales. Such market awareness is crucial for the well-being of the enterprise. If one firm can react more quickly or more successfully than others it will increase its market share.

Rather than simply reacting to consumer tastes and market conditions, the firm may attempt to influence and manipulate demand through marketing and advertising. It might even attempt to generate demand for a good where previously none existed.

In this chapter we will study the factors influencing demand and demonstrate how an understanding of such factors is vital to the well-being of the firm.

## 3.2 The demand curve

Imagine the many factors that could affect the demand for a single good, for example an individual brand of lager. These would include:

- the price of that brand (P)
- the price of other brands, including other non-lager drink substitutes ($P_S$)
- the disposable income of lager drinkers (Y)
- the price of complementary goods, for example the admission price to student night clubs ($P_C$)
- the volume and quality of advertising on this and competing brands (A)
- the tastes of the consumer (T)
- the perceived quality of the product (Q).

The above list is clearly not exhaustive. For example, more lager is sold in hot weather and a variable could be included to reflect the average daily temperature. Or, particularly with relevance to consumer durable goods such as dishwashers, the availability and terms of credit may be of particular importance. With stocks and shares current demand may be influenced by the expectation of future price changes.

The firm's knowledge of all the above factors is unlikely to be perfect, particularly as not all factors are directly under its control. Accordingly the firm may expend time and money in generating valuable market information: for example, investigating the effect of a design change upon demand or the influence of a change in the general economic environment upon its fortunes. As noted, an understanding of these factors is of vital importance to the firm. (The principles involved in forecasting future levels of demand will be considered in Chapter 16.)

**demand function** the relationship between the quantity of a good the consumer wishes to buy and all the factors determining that demand

The factors influencing the demand for a product can be expressed as a **demand function**. For instance, with regards to our above example, the quantity demanded (d) is influenced by price, the price of other brands, income and so on. In short:

$$Q_d = f (P, P_S, Y, P_C, A, T, Q, ..., etc.).$$

The equation states that the quantity demanded of this brand of lager, the **dependent variable**, is a function of the variables outlined, referred to as **independent** or **explanatory variables**. Demand is measured over a determined time period, such as a month or a financial year.

**dependent variable** a variable whose value is determined by the value(s) of some other variable(s)

**independent variable** a variable whose value determines the value of some other (the dependent) variable

By tradition we study the influence of the independent variables in isolation from one another: for example, how a change in the price of the lager influences demand when all other factors remain constant. This is referred to as a *ceteris paribus* approach, i.e. 'other things remaining equal'. In reality, 'other things' are unlikely to do so and in consequence it may prove difficult to isolate the influence of a single independent variable, as when a price decrease is matched by competitors, or general economic conditions change and affect the disposable income of lager drinkers. Equally the government might even launch a campaign aimed to encourage more temperate drinking habits. Therefore, in reality, isolating the effect of single independent variables may prove problematic. Solutions can be sought through statistical analysis (see Chapter 16 on forecasting).

**explanatory variable** a variable whose value explains the value of some other (the dependent) variable

**ceteris paribus** Latin for 'other things being equal' – an approach used by economists to isolate the subject of study so that changes external to it need not be considered

Nevertheless, our *ceteris paribus* approach will provide invaluable insights into consumer behaviour and the operation of markets.

**demand curve** a curve relating price per unit of a particular product to the quantity the consumer wishes to buy

Traditionally economists present the demand function in diagrammatic form as illustrated in Figure 3.1. The **demand curve** indicates levels of demand for a good at a range of price levels, *ceteris paribus*. At a price of $P_1$ then $Q_1$ units are demanded. If price falls to $P_2$ demand rises to $Q_2$.

**Figure 3.1  The demand curve**

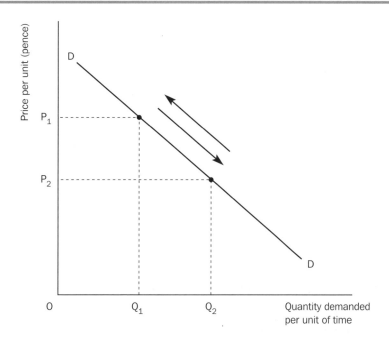

The continuous shape of the demand curve implies a knowledge of demand over a full range of prices. This may not accord with reality, in that the firm is more likely to have a knowledge of demand over a more limited price range. Indeed, knowledge of demand over a wider range may be irrelevant to the firm in that it would never consider marketing the good at very high or low prices.

The above demand curve is drawn as a straight line, i.e. it is linear. This should be seen as a convenient simplification for diagrammatic purposes and unlikely to reflect real world conditions. We will discuss the implication of the shape of the demand curve later in the chapter.

The downward slope of the demand curve indicates an inverse relationship between price and quantity demanded, 'ceteris paribus', i.e. as price falls from $P_1$ to $P_2$ in Figure 3.1, quantity demanded rises from $Q_1$ to $Q_2$, and vice versa. This inverse relationship is referred to as 'the law of demand'. While such a relationship might appear readily acceptable, it is worthy of further consideration.

### 3.2.1 The substitution and income effects

The inverse relationship can be explained by the combined influence of the substitution and income effects.

**'Substitution effect'**

As price falls the good becomes cheaper relative to other goods, i.e. its relative price falls. Other goods whose prices have not changed now become relatively more expensive. Consumers might therefore substitute expenditure towards the good whose price has fallen. The strength of this effect depends upon the substitutability and availability of alternatives. The process is reversed for a price rise. The **substitution effect** would therefore be consistent with our 'law of demand'.

### 'Income effect'

A price decrease has no effect upon **nominal income**, i.e. the monetary value of a consumer's disposable income is unaltered. However, it clearly influences **real income** as the consumer is now relatively better off. The degree to which this is the case depends upon the size of the price change and the significance of the good in overall expenditure. For example, a relatively large decrease in the price of electricity would have a significant effect upon the real income of most households. This increase in real income is equivalent to a change in nominal income, as the consumer may now take the opportunity to redistribute expenditure. This could result in more or less units being consumed of this and other goods.

Where an increase in real or nominal income encourages the consumer to buy more units the good is referred to as **normal**; most goods fit this category. An **inferior good** is one where fewer units would be purchased. For example, following an increase in real income the consumer might consume fewer 'cheap' goods and move towards more 'expensive' alternatives, such as travelling by taxi instead of bus, or eating in restaurants rather than buying 'takeaways'. For this consumer bus travel and 'takeaway food' would be classed as inferior goods. Given consumer ambitions, we all have examples of such inferior goods. Think of your own examples.

As outlined, a price change causes a combined substitution and income effect. With normal goods both work together to ensure an inverse relationship between price and quantity demanded for both price increases and decreases. However, with inferior goods the income effect works against the substitution effect. For example, a decrease in price raises real income and discourages consumption of the inferior good. The substitution effect still encourages consumption. Nevertheless, in such a circumstance it would be unusual for the income effect to outweigh the substitution effect and our 'law of demand' normally remains intact. In a total market situation this would almost certainly be the case given that the number of consumers with an income effect stronger than their substitution effect would be more than balanced out by consumers for whom this was not the case.

Goods where the income effect does outweigh the substitution effect are commonly referred to as **Giffen goods**.[1] Examples are basic bulk foods such as rice and potatoes in near-subsistence societies. Here, for example, following a price fall, consumers may take the opportunity to diminish their consumption of a basic food and redistribute income towards less basic alternatives. The result might be a meal with rice and a little meat rather than all rice. Alternatively, an increase in the price of rice might force the consumer to curtail meat consumption and maintain their food bulk through increasing rice consumption. Such behaviour has been observed in very poor societies.

---

**substitution effect** the change in quantity demanded of a good or service resulting solely from a change in its price relative to the prices of other goods

**nominal income** the face value or monetary value of income. The nominal value of income is unaffected by price inflation

**real income** the purchasing power of income. Whilst price inflation would not affect actual or money income, real income would decrease

**normal good** a good that a consumer will buy more of as either their real or nominal income rises and vice versa

**inferior good** a good the consumer buys less of as either their real or nominal income rises, and vice versa

**Giffen goods** such strongly inferior goods that if their price changes the income effect outweighs the substitution effect, resulting in a direct relationship between price and quantity demanded and an upward-sloping demand curve

### 3.2.2 **Other instances where the 'law of demand' might appear breached**

These could include:

**speculative demand**
buying a good or service
now in the expectation that
price might rise even further
in the future

### Speculative demand

An increase in house prices might create the expectation that prices will rise even further in the near future, fuelling increased demand at the current price. Similarly, in stock markets an increasing share price might lead to increased demand, on the expectation that prices will rise further. In both examples, the prediction is likely to come true. The increase in demand leads directly to higher prices, further fuelling speculative expectations.

### Conspicuous consumption

Most of us are concerned with our image and place particular emphasis upon being in or out of fashion. Many like to follow trends and be part of a crowd, others are concerned to be different. Some gain specific satisfaction from consuming expensive goods with a high **conspicuous price**.

**conspicuous price**  the
price that others believe you
paid for the good – most
relevant where the
consumer gains satisfaction
from consuming a good with
a known high price

The conspicuous price can generally be defined as the price that other people think the consumer paid for the good, or, more exactly, the price that the consumer thinks other people think they paid for the good (e.g. the satisfaction gained by the owner of a Ferrari believing that others see the car as a highly priced luxury). As noted, what is important is the price that the consumer thinks others think was paid for the good. In reality, the consumer may be mistaken. For instance, I may be happy to wear a particular article of clothing in the belief that others see it as both expensive and exclusive. In both respects I may be wrong. However, so long as I continue to believe that others think it is both expensive and exclusive I may continue to consume the good.

Conspicuous prices might cause an upward sloping-demand curve, as when a rising price increases the 'conspicuous price' this could have the net effect of increasing demand. Note, however, that although the higher price might encourage some consumers it will discourage others, and the net effect could still be a fall in overall demand. The influence of conspicuous prices upon consumption is often referred to as a **Veblen effect**.

**Veblen effect**  the
influence of conspicuous
prices upon consumption
most relevant with
ostentatious goods

This effect is illustrated in Figure 3.2. Between points S and R the demand curve is upward sloping, indicating that when price rises from S the 'conspicuous price' effect outweighs any normal price effect. Clearly, the demand curve would not be permanently upward sloping. After point R the 'conspicuous price effect' becomes outweighed by the normal price effect, and there must be a price ($P_n$) where demand is zero. Similarly, below point S the demand curve takes on a normal downward slope, as any 'conspicuous price effect' becomes relatively insignificant at low prices and is outweighed by the usual price effect. $Q_n$ denotes the level of demand if price were zero. The demand curve therefore takes on a backward S shape.

As noted, the existence of a 'conspicuous consumption effect' does not guarantee an upward sloping demand curve over any portion of the curve. So long as the price effect dominates, then our 'law of demand' remains intact.

**bandwagon effect**  the
means by which an
individual's consumption of
a given good might be
stimulated by the
consumption of other
consumers

It is interesting to note that consumers often do not consume in isolation from each other and are therefore likely to be either encouraged or discouraged by the actions and assumed thoughts of others. Where consumers are motivated to 'follow the crowd', this is referred to as a **bandwagon effect**;

**Figure 3.2 Conspicuous prices/Veblen effect**

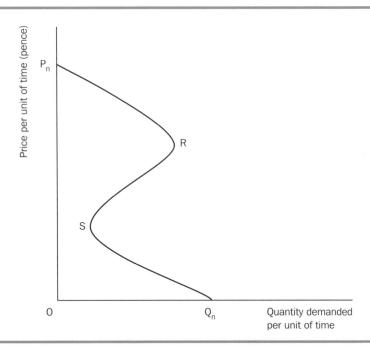

**snob effect** the desire by individual consumers for exclusiveness in their consumption of a particular good and therefore to be discouraged by the consumption of others

where consumers wish to be exclusive, as a **snob effect**; and as a Veblen effect where they are concerned with the 'conspicuous price'.[2]

## 3.3 The market demand curve

**market demand curve** the aggregation of all individual demand curves for a specific good or service showing the total demand at each price

The **market demand curve** represents the summation of total consumer demand at all prices. Figure 3.3 indicates how such a curve can be derived.

Figure 3.3 assumes a simple market situation with only two consumers. At any price above $P_1$ only consumer 2 is in the market and that section of their demand curve is also the market demand curve. At prices below $P_1$ both individuals consume and the market demand curve becomes a horizontal summation of the two curves. For example, with a price of P then $Q_4 = Q_1 + Q_3$. If further consumers joined the market their demand curves would be added horizontally in a similar fashion and the market demand curve would shift to the right.

However, as previously observed, consumers do not always consume in isolation. It is possible that a third consumer coming onto the scene might influence the consumption of the first two. For example, if consumers 1 and 2 become aware that others are now consuming a good that they believed to be relatively exclusive, they might cease or diminish their own consumption. In practice we are not always fully aware of the consumption of others. Although an individual might think themselves to be wearing a fashion widely worn by others, this may not be the case. Consumers seldom have a completely accurate picture of market conditions. That said, the principle holds that the market demand curve is a horizontal summation of the individual demand curves.

**Figure 3.3    The market demand curve**

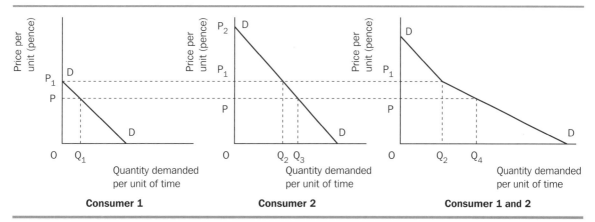

Consumer 1                    Consumer 2                    Consumer 1 and 2

## 3.4    Consumer surplus

Figure 3.3 indicates that consumer 2 generally placed a higher value on the good than consumer 1. While consumer 2 would be willing to purchase units at a price between $P_1$ and $P_2$, consumer 1 will only purchase at prices less than $P_1$.

## 3.4    Consumer surplus

Figure 3.3 indicates that consumer 2 generally placed a higher value on the good than consumer 1. While consumer 2 would be willing to purchase units at a price between $P_1$ and $P_2$, consumer 1 will only purchase at prices less than $P_1$.

With a price of P, consumer 2 is willing to buy up to $Q_3$ units. This last unit, the $Q_3$'rd, is referred to as the **marginal unit**, and previous units as **intra-marginal units**. The consumer consumes up to the margin where the value received from consuming that last unit is represented by the price they pay. Consumer 2 would not be willing to pay more than P for unit $Q_3$. However, by inference, they would have been willing to pay more for the intra-marginal units. For example, consumer 2 would have paid $P_1$ for unit $Q_2$.

**marginal unit** the last unit consumed in a given time period

**intra-marginal unit** the units consumed prior to the last or marginal unit

The consumer therefore receives a surplus on intra-marginal units in that they would have been willing to pay a higher price for those units. The difference between what the consumer actually pays for a commodity and the maximum sum they would have been willing to pay is referred to as **consumer surplus**.

**consumer surplus** the difference between the total amount of money an individual would be prepared to pay for a given quantity of a good and the amount actually paid

The principle of consumer surplus is illustrated in Figure 3.4 showing consumer 2's demand curve taken from Figure 3.3. $Q_3$ units are demanded at a price of P, and the area $OPXQ_3$ represents total expenditure on the good (i.e. the price of P multiplied by the number of units consumed). As noted, the consumer would have been willing to pay more for intra-marginal units. For example, although they only pay a price of P for unit $Q_2$, they would have been willing to pay $P_1$. $P_1$ minus P represents the consumer surplus gained on unit $Q_3$. If we were to assume a large number of units from zero to $Q_3$ and further assume that the consumer pays the price they would have been willing to pay for each unit, then total expenditure for all $Q_3$ units would be approximated by the total area $OAXQ_3$. However, given that they actually pay only P for all those units then total expenditure is only $OPXQ_3$, and consumer surplus would approximate:

$$OAXQ_3 - OPXQ_3 = PAX$$

i.e. the amount they would be willing to pay – the amount paid = consumer surplus.

**Figure 3.4  Consumer surplus**

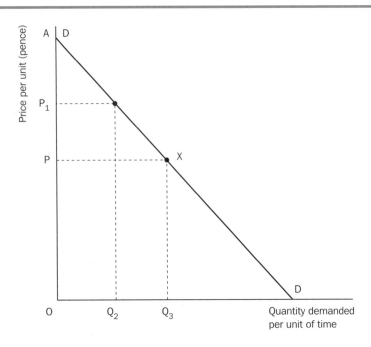

The concept of consumer surplus is clearly of interest to the firm as it represents a possible source of additional revenue. For example, rather than charge the same price for all units, the firm might sell intra-marginal units at a higher price. Or, if a firm wishes to sell additional units, it has the possibility of selling those additional units at a lower price, leaving the previous units sold at the original price. This strategy is often used by holiday firms to sell off unsold holidays prior to the start of the holiday package. Such strategies are generally referred to as **price discrimination** and will be considered in Chapter 9.

The concept of the consumer's 'willingness to pay' is also of relevance in public policy making, in that it may be used to place a monetary value on activities that do not appear to have a market price. Thus if a local council is considering sacrificing a local beauty spot to build a civic amenity, it might attempt to place a monetary value on that beauty spot by asking residents how much they might be willing to pay to preserve it (see, e.g., Chapter 14). It is easy to imagine the difficulties involved in such an exercise.[3]

**price discrimination**
where different buyers or groups of buyers are charged different prices for an identical good

## 3.5    Other determinants of demand

In Section 3.2 we noted that demand is influenced by a range of independent variables. So far we have concentrated upon the price of the good. Let us now consider the other main determinants. Again, we use a *ceteris paribus* approach.

A change in these other variables shifts the demand curve. This provides a distinction between:

1  changes in demand due to adjustments in the price of the good, causing movements up or down an existing demand curve (as seen in Figure 3.1), known as **extensions** or **contractions in demand**;

2  changes, or shifts in demand, due to a change in one of the other variables affecting demand, causing a movement to either the left or right of the original demand curve, (as illustrated in Figure 3.5), known as **increases** or **decreases in demand**.

Although we have identified many independent or explanatory variables affecting the demand for a good, we will concentrate upon the influence of:

- the price of other goods
- consumers' disposable income
- consumer tastes.

The influence of other independent variables would be analysed in a similar fashion. A measure of the influence of these independent variables upon demand is provided by the concept of 'elasticity of demand' which will be considered below (see Section 3.6).

### 3.5.1 The price of other goods

The degree to which a change in the price of another good influences demand depends upon the size of that change and the relationship between the goods. The goods can be seen to be either **complements** or **substitutes** and have a particular degree of complementarity or substitutability.

For example, an increase in the price of cinema tickets would diminish cinema attendance and might also result in the sale of less popcorn. To many cinema fans, popcorn is a complementary good to cinema attendance; they always buy popcorn to accompany the film. Popcorn and cinema attendance would therefore be classified as complementary goods.

Figure 3.5 shows three demand curves for popcorn, each associated with a different price of cinema tickets. Imagine initially that the price of cinema tickets is such that $D_1D_1$ represents the demand curve for popcorn. If the price of cinema tickets were now to rise, this demand curve would shift to $D_2D_2$, less popcorn being purchased at all prices. Conversely, if the price of cinema tickets had fallen, the demand curve shifts outwards to $D_3D_3$ and more popcorn is consumed. Would a change in the price of popcorn have a similar effect upon the demand for cinema tickets? This must be less pronounced. Few, if any, people will stop attending the cinema if the price of popcorn increases.

If cinemas introduced a promotional event on 'pick and mix' sweets, offering them at a reduced price, the demand for popcorn would be likely to fall, shifting the demand curve from $D_1D_1$ to $D_2D_2$, i.e. 'pick and mix' sweets acting as a substitute for popcorn. Alternatively, if the price of 'pick and mix' increased, the demand curve for popcorn would shift to the right.

Clearly there are many other examples of complementary and substitute goods. List some of your own examples.

---

**extension in demand**
a rise in demand and a corresponding movement down a demand curve due to a fall in price

**contraction in demand**
a fall in demand and a corresponding movement up the demand curve due to an increase in price

**increase in demand**
an increase in demand brought about by a change in a dependant variable other than price, causing the demand curve to shift to the right

**decrease in demand**
a fall in demand due to a change in a dependent variable other than price causing the demand curve to shift to the left

**complements**  goods are complements or complementary when an increase in the demand for one results in an increase in the demand for the other and vice versa

**substitutes**  goods that fulfil a similar function or serve a similar taste in the eyes of consumers. Two goods are substitutes if a rise in the price of one results in a fall in the demand for the other

**Figure 3.5  Change in the price of another good**

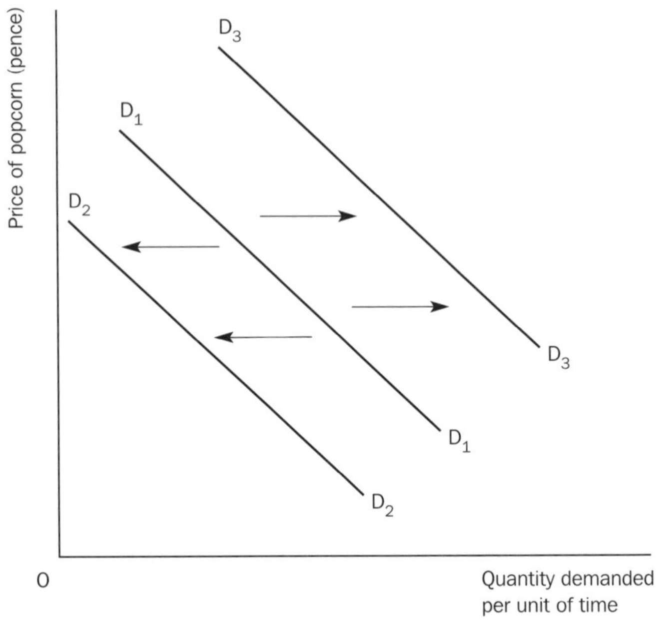

### 3.5.2 Consumers' disposable income

As noted in Section 3.2, an income change encourages consumers to redistribute their expenditure between goods. Rising incomes increase the consumption of normal goods; falling incomes have the opposite effect. In contrast the consumption of inferior goods declines following an increase in income, and vice versa. It is also possible that a change in income might not affect the consumption of a good. These various possibilities are illustrated in Figure 3.6.

The diagrams in Figure 3.6 show how demand may vary with changes in disposable income. The curve plotting income against demand is generally referred to as an Engel curve after Ernst Engel (1821–96), a German statistician who investigated the impact of income changes upon the food consumption of Belgian families in the mid-nineteenth century. His general conclusion was that as income rises the proportion of income spent on food declines. This proposition is commonly referred to as **Engel's law**. The 'law' is then often extended to imply that the proportion of expenditure on all necessities (e.g. food) declines as incomes rise. In contrast, the proportionate expenditure on luxuries (or, non-necessities) would increase.

Whilst the above is likely to be true, we must be guarded, as was Engel, in such generalisations. One person's luxury might be another's necessity, and goods that were once thought luxuries might later become necessities (e.g. many now see a colour television and video player as a necessity). Nevertheless, the implications of the general proposition are certainly echoed in business. Thus, while supermarkets are not so adversely affected in an economic recession, as consumers continue to buy foodstuffs, providers of luxury overseas holidays might experience a significant fall in demand during such a period.

**Engel's law**  the proposition that with given tastes and preferences the proportion of income spent on food falls as income rises

**Figure 3.6  Quantity demanded against income: the Engel curve**

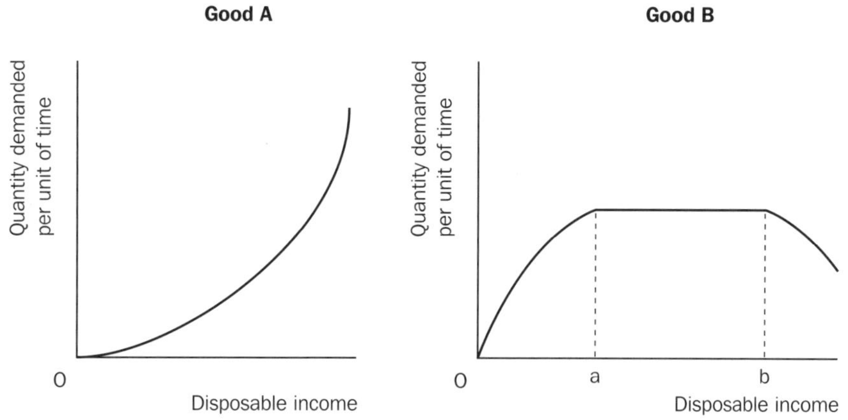

The Engel curve slopes upwards so long as the good is normal. For 'good A' in Figure 3.6, the curve slopes upwards at an increasing rate as the proportion of income spent on the good increases (i.e. rising income leads to a greater than proportionate rise in expenditure). Conversely, if income falls, the proportion of income expended also falls.

For good B in Figure 3.6 the curve increases at a decreasing rate up to a disposable income of a, showing that the proportion of income spent on the good is falling. If income fell below a the proportion of income spent on the good would rise. As income rises from a to b, consumption of good B is unchanged. The income effect is neutral. Beyond b the good is inferior and becomes increasingly so as the curve declines at an increasing rate. An example of such a good might be baked beans for a typical student. Up to a the student buys more of this most 'useful necessity', although starting to spend proportionally more on other more luxurious foods, including the possibility of eating out. Consumption is then constant between a disposable income of a to b. Beyond b consumption falls as the student discovers more eclectic tastes!

The concept of income elasticity (see Section 3.6.6) provides a measure of the responsiveness of demand to a change in income. In relation to our investigation of demand, a change in income causes the demand curve to shift. For example, referring back to Figure 3.5, if popcorn were a normal good then an increase in income would shift the curve to the right, or to the left following a fall in income. The degree of shift is greater the stronger the normality of the good and the larger the change in income. The reverse would be the case if the good were inferior.

### 3.5.3 Consumer Tastes

A shift in consumer tastes towards the good – perhaps brought about by a successful advertising campaign – would move the demand curve to the right. This can again be illustrated through our popcorn example in Figure 3.5 as a movement from $D_1D_1$ to $D_3D_3$. The same rightward shift could be brought about by the increased popularity of cinema attendance, on the assumption that the

**Mini case**    ## Young drinkers move away from lager?

The draught beer market in recent years has witnessed the strong growth of lager drinking at the expense of the traditional cask beers beloved by the Campaign for Real Ale and the keg beers introduced in the 1970s. The shift towards lager drinking was encouraged through active advertising portraying lager drinking to be fashionable, and lager to be a high-quality commodity. This allowed lager to be sold at a premium price, typically in excess of beer prices. Many adverts were specifically aimed at the youthful end of the market.

In terms of our analysis, the shift in taste towards lager had the effect of shifting the demand curve for lagers to the right, with a corresponding leftwards shift in the demand curve for beers.

Even more recently we have seen the expansion of so-called 'nitrokeg' beers, typified by the current market leader Caffreys, introduced by Bass in March 1994. These are 'smooth flow' beers of a similar type to Guinness. (The 'smoothness' of 'nitrokeg' beers is brought about by a conditioning of the beer in the keg with a mixture of nitrogen and carbon dioxide.) The view of the industry is that they particularly appeal to younger drinkers who are believed to enjoy the spectacle of watching the 'smooth flowing beer' settle slowly in the glass. The smooth taste of these new 'nitrokegs' is also appealing to many drinkers, as they can be looking for a change from lager that does not involve moving over to the 'more challenging' tastes of traditional beers.

Although 'nitrokeg, beers' only accounted for 12.5 per cent of the market in 1996 this represented a significant share considering their introduction only approximately two years previously. It is anticipated that their market share will continue to increase. Indeed, Vaux, the Sunderland-based hotel, pubs and brewing group, was quoted in the *Guardian* (13 May 1998) as believing that these 'new trendy bitters' will eventually lead to the death of lager. Vaux and other major breweries are certainly encouraging this trend through extensive advertising. For example, Vaux have agreed a £2 million renewal of their sponsorship deal with Sunderland Football Club until 2001 to advertise their 'smooth flow' brand Lambtons on the players' shirts. Other extensively advertised 'smooth flow' beers currently on the market include Kilkenny, (produced by Guinness); Whitbread's Boddington Gold; and Carlsberg-Tetley's Tetley Smooth.

Markets such as beer are clearly influenced by changing consumer tastes, often encouraged by advertising strategies. If 'nitrokeg beers' do come to dominate the draught beer market it is likely that they will eventually be toppled by a new 'drinking craze'.

goods are complementary. A leftward shift ($D_1D_1$ to $D_2D_2$) might be caused by a decrease in the popularity of cinema attendance; the successful advertising of a popcorn substitute; or a food scare allegedly linked to popcorn consumption!

## 3.6    Elasticity

In Section 3.2 we presented the demand curve as downward sloping, illustrating an inverse correlation between price and quantity demanded. Although such a correlation would be known to businesses, they are likely to be more concerned with the degree of responsiveness of demand to a change in price. By how much might demand change if price were decreased, and would the increased sales at a lower price lead to a higher or lower sales revenue? For example, a professional football team who typically have a half-empty stadium know that reducing ticket prices will sell more tickets. However, whether revenue from tickets sales increases depends upon the responsiveness of demand to the fall in price. Indeed, increasing price might result in smaller crowds, yet at same time increase overall revenue.

A measurement of the responsiveness of demand to a change in one of our independent variables is provided by the concept of **elasticity**. An elasticity measures the responsiveness of one variable to changes in another. For example, with regard to the various independent variables that affect demand for a specific good:

**elasticity** a measure of the change in one variable brought about by a change in another

$$\text{An } \textbf{elasticity of demand} = \frac{\text{Percentage (\%) change in the demand for good A}}{\text{Percentage (\%) change in an independent variable}}$$

**elasticity of demand** a measurement of the change in demand for a good brought about by a change in one of the independent variables that help determine its demand

We measure changes proportionately (i.e. as a percentage change) rather than in absolute terms. In so doing we obtain a measurement that is independent of the unit of measurement of the numerator and denominator. For example, a percentage change in price would be the same whether measured in pounds sterling or the equivalent value of US dollars.

We will concentrate upon three elasticities:

- price elasticity of demand
- cross-price elasticity of demand
- income elasticity of demand.

**price elasticity of demand** a measure of the degree of responsiveness of the quantity demanded of a good to a change in its price

### 3.6.1  Price elasticity of demand ($E_p$)

$$E_p = \frac{\% \text{ change in demand}}{\% \text{ change in price of the good}}$$

In terms of formula, the inverse relationship between price and quantity demanded (i.e. the 'law of demand') provides a negative solution. For example, with a positive denominator (an increase in price) and a negative numerator (a decrease in demand) the solution is negative. However, by convention the minus sign is omitted and **price elasticity** is presented as a positive figure.

If a percentage change in price brings about a greater percentage change in demand then price elasticity as a numerical value is greater than 1 and demand is referred to as being **relatively price elastic**. Alternatively, if demand had changed by a lower percentage than the percentage change in price then price elasticity is less than 1, and demand is **relatively price inelastic**. These concepts provide us with a useful piece of jargon. For example, we might generally state that demand for cigarettes is strongly inelastic, implying that an increase in price has little influence upon demand. Alternatively, we might

**relatively price elastic** where a percentage change in price of a good brings about a greater than proportional change in quantity demanded

**relatively price inelastic**
where a percentage change
in the price of a good brings
about a less than
proportional change in its
quantity demanded

observe that the demand for a single brand of cigarettes (*ceteris paribus*) is relatively elastic, given that smokers could switch brands and thus could be price
sensitive. We will see later how actual calculations of elasticity are made.

Table 3.1 provides a summary of the ranges of price elasticity; a descriptor;
and the predicted change in total revenue received by the firm (or, total expenditure by consumers) as a result of the price change. These elasticities are
illustrated in Figure 3.7.

As indicated in Table 3.1, price elasticity ranges from zero (perfectly inelastic)
to infinity (perfectly elastic). Perfect inelasticity (Figure 3.7a) might be illustrated by an individual who always buys a particular morning newspaper
irrespective of price. A situation of perfect elasticity (Figure 3.7e) might appear
unlikely, although we will see later how this applies to firms in highly competitive markets. An implication of such a demand curve would be that the firm can
sell more without changing price. If the firm were to attempt to increase the
price above P they would lose all custom, and the firm would not consider lowering the price below P because they can anyway sell all they wish at that price.

**rectangular hyperbola**
where a demand curve is a
rectangular hyperbola then
any proportional change in
price for that good will be
matched by an equal
proportional change in
quantity demanded

The demand curve illustrating unitary elasticity (Figure 3.7c) is called a
**rectangular hyperbola**. The property of this demand curve is such that if you
multiply price by quantity relative to any point on the curve the value of total
revenue (or total expenditure) is constant. This might depict an individual who
always spends a fixed sum of money on a good in a given time period: for
example, a fixed weekly budget of £10 to spend on beer. If the price of beer

## Table 3.1  Price elasticity: value, terminology, descriptor and total revenue

| Value of $E_p$ | Terminology | Descriptor | Change in total revenue from sales (TR) |
|---|---|---|---|
| 0 | Perfectly inelastic | A price change has no effect upon demand (see Fig. 3.7a). | Increased price leads to increased TR (and vice versa). |
| >0 <1 (i.e. greater than 0, but less than 1) | Relatively inelastic | A % change in price leads to a smaller % change in demand (see Fig. 3.7b). | Increased price leads to increased TR (and vice versa). |
| 1 | Unitary elasticity | A % change in price leads to the same % change in demand (see Fig. 3.7c). | Any price change leaves TR constant. |
| >1 <∞ (i.e. greater than 1, but less than infinity) | Relatively elastic | A % change in price leads to a greater % change in demand (see Fig. 3.7d). | Increased price leads to decreased TR (and vice versa). |
| ∞ (i.e.: infinity) | Perfectly elastic | A small % price change leads to an infinitely large % change in demand (see Fig. 3.7e). | A price rise results in zero TR. |

**Figure 3.7  Demand curves illustrating a range of price elasticities**

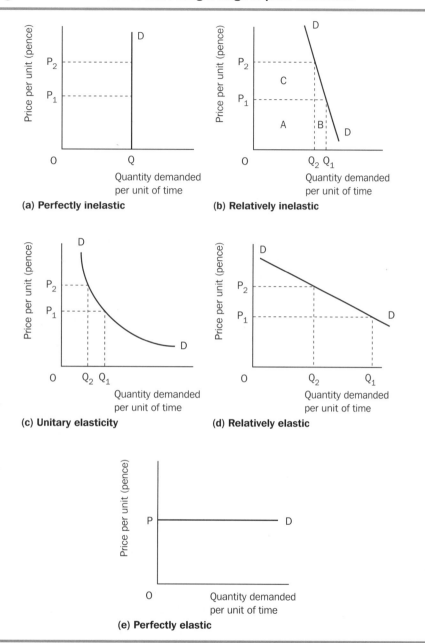

(a) **Perfectly inelastic**

(b) **Relatively inelastic**

(c) **Unitary elasticity**

(d) **Relatively elastic**

(e) **Perfectly elastic**

were to rise by 5 per cent, consumption falls by 5 per cent and the £10 budget is spent. Price elasticity therefore equals 1, neither elastic nor inelastic.

Figure 3.7b shows a relatively price inelastic demand curve. As indicated in Table 3.1, a price increase leads to an increase in total revenue, that is:

■ at $P_1$ total revenue (TR) from sales = $P_1 \times Q_1$

= areas A + B

- at $P_2$ total revenue (TR) from sales = $P_2 \times Q_2$
$$= \text{areas A} + \text{C}$$

- given that C > B then TR will rise.

Alternatively, if price were to fall from $P_2$ to $P_1$ then TR would fall.

Figure 3.7d shows a relatively price elastic demand curve. In this case a fall in price results in an increase in total revenue, and vice versa. Therefore:

1 When demand is **price inelastic**:
   - a price rise will increase total revenue; consumer expenditure on the good increases;
   - a price fall will decrease total revenue; consumer expenditure decreases.
2 When demand is **price elastic**:
   - a price rise will decrease total revenue or total expenditure;
   - a price fall will increase total revenue or total expenditure.

Such changes in revenue as prices change are, of course, relevant to businesses and can affect their pricing decisions (see Section 3.6.5).

### 3.6.2 Calculating Price Elasticity

From the information provided in Figure 3.8 imagine a price rise from 40p to 60p and a fall in demand from 25 to 20 units; thus:

$$E_p = \frac{\% \text{ change in Q}}{\% \text{ change in P}}$$

$$= \frac{\Delta Q}{Q} \times 100 \bigg/ \frac{\Delta P}{P} \times 100$$

where:

$\Delta$ = 'change in'
$\Delta Q$ = absolute change in quantity demanded
$\Delta P$ = absolute change in price
$Q$ = original quantity demanded
$P$ = original price

$$= \frac{5/25 \times 100}{20/40 \times 100} = \frac{20\%}{50\%} = 0.4.$$

This shows demand is inelastic. However, a problem of this measurement is that if you were to then measure elasticity when the price fell from 60p to 40p the answer would be different, that is:

$$Ep = \frac{\Delta Q}{Q} \times 100 \bigg/ \frac{\Delta P}{P} \times 100$$

$$= \frac{5/20 \times 100}{20/60 \times 100} = \frac{20\%}{33.3\%} = 0.75.$$

The reason for the variation is that the percentage change in each case is measured from a different base. When the price rises from 40p to 60p, this is a 50 per cent rise. When it falls from 60 to 40p it is only a 33.3 per cent fall. The value of

**Figure 3.8  Measuring price elasticity**

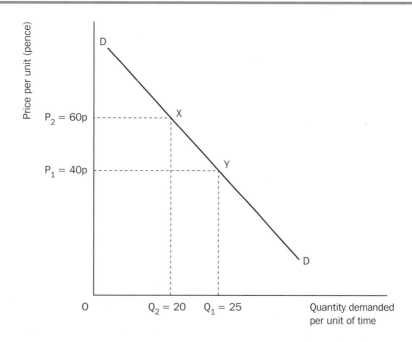

elasticity therefore varies (the value 0.4 actually represents elasticity at point Y, and 0.75 the value at point X, as we will see below when we discuss the concept of point elasticity). Note that, as points X and Y in the diagram come closer together, the difference in the calculation for a price increase or decrease diminishes.

To avoid ambiguity it is usual to measure elasticity as the percentage change from the average value of price and quantity before and after the change. The value of price elasticity will then be identical for either increases or decreases in price, that is:

$$E_p = \frac{\% \text{ change in Q}}{\% \text{ change in P}}$$

$$= \frac{\Delta Q}{0.5(Q_1 + Q_2)} \times 100 \Big/ \frac{\Delta P}{0.5(P_1 + P_2)} \times 100$$

$$= \frac{5/22.5 \times 100}{20/50 \times 100} = \frac{22.2\%}{40\%} = 0.55$$

**arc elasticity of demand**
a measurement of elasticity between two distinct points on a given demand curve

**point elasticity** the measurement of elasticity at a single point on a demand curve

The above calculation provides us with a measurement of **arc elasticity of demand.** That is, we are measuring elasticity *between* points X and Y on the curve. (We are in effect measuring it at a point equidistant between point X and Y.)

Imagine that X and Y are now so close together they are virtually a single point, i.e. there is an *extremely* small change in price, such that we are effectively looking at a single point on the demand curve. If we were now to measure elasticity we are effectively measuring that elasticity at a single point. This would be referred to as **point elasticity**. We can now use our original equation:

$$E_p = \frac{\Delta Q}{Q} \times 100 \Big/ \frac{\Delta P}{P} \times 100 \qquad \text{(eq. 1)}$$

or, cancelling the 100s, and rearranging the terms:

$$E_p = \frac{\Delta Q}{Q} \Big/ \frac{\Delta P}{P} \qquad \text{(eq. 2)}$$

$$= \frac{\Delta Q}{Q} \times \frac{P}{\Delta P} \qquad \text{(eq. 3)}$$

$$= \frac{\Delta Q}{\Delta P} \times \frac{P}{Q} \qquad \text{(eq. 4)}$$

Equation 4 tells us that price elasticity at any point on the demand curve equals the ratio of price to quantity (P/Q) multiplied by the ratio of the change in quantity to the change in price ($\Delta Q/\Delta P$), where $\Delta Q/\Delta P$ represents the slope of the demand curve.

By mathematical convention it is usual to express the slope as the ratio $\Delta P/\Delta Q$. Therefore, $\Delta Q/\Delta P$ represents the inverse of the slope. From Figure 3.9 note that this ratio would be constant on a linear demand curve, i.e. the ratio would be the same between any two points on the curve. It also represents the slope at a single point.

Price elasticity at any point on the demand curve therefore equals the ratio P/Q multiplied by a constant, K:

$$= K \times \frac{P}{Q} \qquad \text{(eq. 5)}$$

**Figure 3.9 The value of elasticity along a linear demand curve**

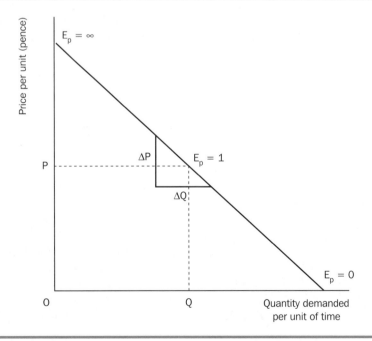

Figure 3.9 illustrates how price elasticity would vary over the length of a linear demand curve.

If Q = O then:

$$E_p = K \times P/O = \infty$$

Elasticity is infinity or perfectly inelastic.

As we move down the demand curve the ratio P/Q falls. Demand is becoming increasingly less elastic.

Halfway along the curve price elasticity is unitary. This marks the boundary between elastic and inelastic. Below this point demand becomes increasingly inelastic.

If P = O then:

$$E_p = K \times O/Q = O$$

Demand is perfectly inelastic.

We can now also see that although the curves in Figure 3.7b and Figure 3.7d were portrayed respectively as relatively inelastic and elastic the value of elasticity varies over the length of such curves. Even a 'shallow' curve such as in Figure 3.7d would have sections which are relatively inelastic.

The principle of point elasticity can be used to estimate elasticity on a non-linear demand curve. Consider Figure 3.10. At point X, elasticity equals P/Q multiplied by the inverse of the gradient of the demand curve at that point. The gradient can be found by measuring the slope of a tangent to the curve at point X, i.e. ΔQ/ΔP.

### 3.6.3 Revenue and price elasticity

Table 3.2 provides an example of a demand relationship. As price falls (column 1), demand increases (column 2). Note:

**Figure 3.10  Price elasticity on a non-linear demand curve**

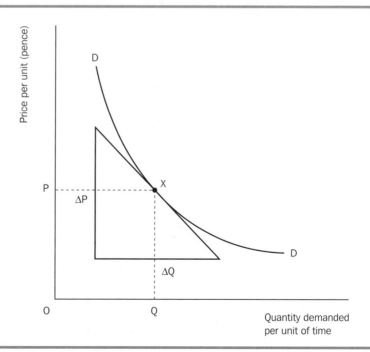

**Table 3.2  Total revenue, marginal revenue and elasticity**

| Column 1 | Column 2 | Column 3 | Column 4 | Column 5 |
|---|---|---|---|---|
| Price or AR (pence) | Quantity | Total revenue (pence) | Marginal revenue (pence) | Elasticity |
| 10 | 1 | 10 | – | – |
| 9 | 2 | 18 | 8 | 6.33 |
| 8 | 3 | 24 | 6 | 3.40 |
| 7 | 4 | 28 | 4 | 2.14 |
| 6 | 5 | 30 | 2 | 1.44 |
| 5 | 6 | 30 | 0 | 1.00 |
| 4 | 7 | 28 | –2 | 0.69 |
| 3 | 8 | 24 | –4 | 0.47 |
| 2 | 9 | 18 | –6 | 0.29 |
| 1 | 10 | 10 | –8 | 0.16 |
| 0 | 11 | 0 | –10 | 0.05 |

$E_p > 1$

$E_p = 1$

$E_p < 1$

$$\text{Total revenue (TR)} = P \times Q$$

$$\text{therefore ....} \qquad P = TR/Q$$

$$= \text{average revenue (AR) per unit sold.}$$

So long as all units are sold at the same price the demand curve is also an average revenue curve. However, in certain circumstances businesses may choose to sell certain units at a different price. For example, prior to take-off an airline might sell unsold seats at a discount. This is an example of **price discrimination** (see Chapter 9). In such a case the demand curve and the **average revenue curve** would diverge.

Column 3 indicates total sales revenue $(P \times Q)$ and column 5 price elasticity estimated on the basis of arc elasticity. As the price falls from 10p to 9p **total revenue** rises and the proportionate increase in quantity demanded is greater than the proportionate fall in price, i.e., $E_p > 1$. As the price continues to fall towards 6p, the demand remains price elastic, although its value is falling. Total revenue therefore increases at a decreasing rate. When the price falls to 5p, total revenue reaches a peak and price elasticity equals unity. When the price falls below 5p, demand is price inelastic and becoming increasingly so. Total revenue now falls at an increasing rate.

Column 4 shows **marginal revenue**. This is defined as the change in total revenue from selling either one extra, or one less, unit. For example, as the price falls from 9p to 8p to sell the third unit total revenue rises from 18p to 24p, demand being price elastic. The marginal revenue (MR) from selling the extra third unit is therefore 6p (i.e. 24p minus 18p). Note that marginal revenue for the third unit is less than the price at which it is sold, because to sell that extra unit the price of previous units, the intra-marginal units, is also decreased.

When price falls over the inelastic section of the demand curve total revenue falls and marginal revenue is negative. For example, in selling the ninth unit total revenue falls from 24p to 18p and marginal revenue is minus 6p.

The above relationship between price (average revenue), marginal revenue, total revenue and price elasticity is shown graphically in Fig. 3.11. As price

**average revenue curve** a curve relating average revenue per unit of a specific good against the number of units sold – where all units are sold at the same price the average revenue curve and corresponding demand curve coincide

**total revenue** the number of units sold multiplied by the sale price of each unit

**marginal revenue** the change in total revenue from selling one more or one less unit

**Figure 3.11 (a) Price elasticity, average revenue and marginal revenue; (b) total revenue and price elasticity**

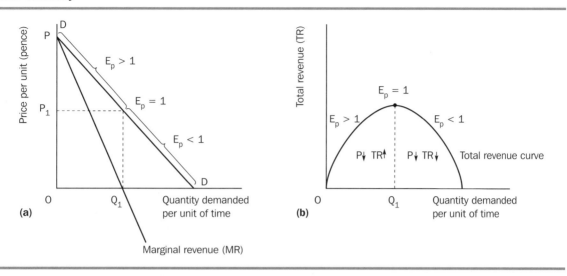

(a)

(b)

Marginal revenue (MR)

falls from P to $P_1$ then $E_p > 1$, yet falling. TR therefore increases at a decreasing rate and MR is positive, yet falling. At $P_1$, $E_p = 1$ and TR is maximised. MR = 0 at the corresponding output, $Q_1$. With price falling below $P_1$ then $E_p < 1$ and becomes increasingly inelastic. TR therefore falls at an increasing rate with MR becoming increasingly negative.

We have noted that marginal revenue is the change in total revenue brought about by a one unit change in quantity sold. This can be expressed as:

$$\text{Marginal revenue (MR)} = \frac{\text{Change in total revenue}}{\text{change in quantity}}$$

$$= \frac{\Delta TR}{\Delta Q}$$

If we move from point a to point b on the total revenue curve in Figure 3.12, marginal revenue would be represented by the slope of the line (the cord) between a and b (= $\Delta TR/\Delta Q$). As the number of units on the quantity axis increases, the distance $\Delta Q$ falls and the length of the cord diminishes. As $\Delta Q$ approaches zero a continuation of the cord could be seen as a tangent to the total revenue curve at that point (see point X on Figure 3.12).

A tangent drawn to the total revenue curve at any point therefore approximates the value of marginal revenue at that level of output, e.g. at point X, MR = $\Delta TR^*/\Delta Q^*$. As we move up the total revenue curve the slope of such tangents falls (marginal revenue is falling). At $Q_1$, a tangent to the total revenue curve is horizontal and marginal revenue is zero. Beyond $Q_1$ tangents are negatively sloped and marginal revenue is negative. Marginal revenue becomes increasingly negative as output rises from $Q_1$.

**ray** a straight line drawn from the origin of two axes to a point on a curve

The slope of a **ray** to the total revenue at any point on Figure 3.12 represents average revenue, or price. For example, at output $Q_2$, average revenue = $TR^*/Q_2$. As output increases the slope of a ray falls, i.e. price falls to increase

**Figure 3.12 Price elasticity: average revenue and marginal revenue on a total revenue curve**

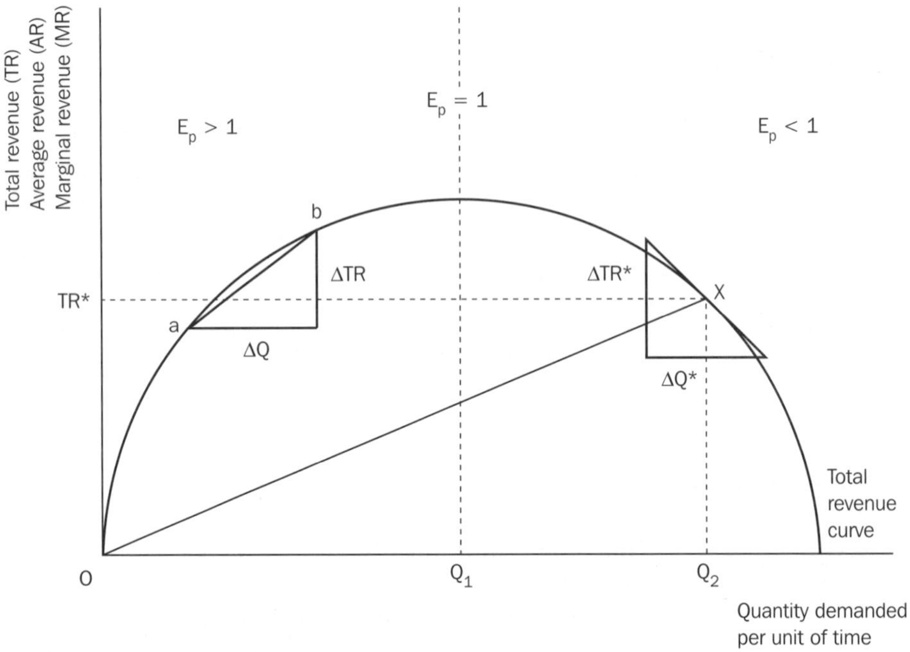

sales. At all points on the total revenue curve, with the exception of when output is zero, the slope of a ray is greater than a slope of a tangent, i.e. price exceeds marginal revenue. This is illustrated at point x on Figure 3.12

The information shown on Figure 3.11a is therefore also available on Figure 3.11b.

A clear understanding of the relationship between price, elasticity and total revenue is essential to our analysis.

### 3.6.4 The determinants of price elasticity

The main determinants are:

**The availability of substitutes**

The greater and closer the number of substitutes, the higher the elasticity. For example, the price elasticity of a single brand of chocolate is relatively elastic given the wide availability of substitutes. If the price of just one brand were to rise, this would be likely to cause a proportionally large decrease in demand for the brand. Alternatively, demand for petrol is likely to be inelastic given most drivers' unwillingness to consider alternative means of transport.

**The need satisfied by the good**

Where a good is seen as a **necessity** it will generally be price inelastic. For example, food as a general commodity is price inelastic over a wide price

**necessities** a good is a necessity when it is considered by the consumer to be an essential purchase

**luxuries** a good can be considered a luxury by the consumer where it is not an essential purchase, generally taking up a larger proportion of expenditure as income increases

range. Alternatively, non-necessities or **luxuries** are more likely to be elastic. Thus although an annual holiday might be seen as a necessity by most families, a holiday abroad might be considered a luxury and prone to cancellation by many families if its price increased.

As noted previously, caution should be taken with the above generalisations. One person's necessity might be another's luxury, and goods that were once luxuries might become necessities.

### The time period

Consumers often take time to adjust their consumption patterns to price changes. Generally, demand becomes more price elastic over time. For example, an increase in the price of domestic gas might have little immediate impact upon consumption. However, if the price differential between gas and other fuels continues, consumers might then take the opportunity to replace their gas appliances with electric ones and/or improve their house insulation. Gas appliances might only be replaced once they become obsolete or worn out. Demand then becomes more elastic over this longer time.

A time lag might also allow producers to develop and introduce substitutes, like the development of a wider range of increasingly fuel-efficient cars following the increase in motoring costs after the first OPEC oil price increases of the mid-1970s.

### The proportion of income spent on the good

It is commonly observed that the larger the proportion of income spent on a good the greater the elasticity, and vice versa. This is largely due to the impact of the price change upon real income, in that where a good takes up a relatively large portion of income a price change has a significant effect upon real income. Where the good is normal the impact upon demand will therefore be relatively strong and elasticity high. Conversely, if the good were inferior, demand might be inelastic. In fact, as we have seen in the case of a Giffen good, not only would expenditure on the good fall following a fall in price, but so would the number of units consumed. The above observation therefore needs to be treated cautiously.

Although we have isolated a number of factors likely to affect the value of price elasticity, the elasticity for a single good will be determined by a combination of such factors. For instance, the demand for salt is generally inelastic due to a lack of substitutes, its position as a necessity and the small amount of income spent on that good. Although expenditure on petrol might take up a relatively large portion of many people's income, the lack of available substitutes leads to its having an inelastic demand. Remember, however, that the demand for different brands of petrol is generally price elastic, hence the success of petrol stations at supermarkets which sell petrol at lower prices and in convenient locations.

### 3.6.5 The importance of the concept of price elasticity to the firm

An understanding of price elasticity can be important to the firm when determining pricing strategy. For example, a firm might aim to increase sales by 15 per cent over the next year. If it were to rely upon price to achieve this goal, an estimate of price elasticity would help it to determine the necessary price decrease to achieve the target sales growth.

Further, if a firm knew that the demand for its good was price inelastic, it might safely increase price and suffer a relatively small loss in market share whilst at the same time increasing its total revenue. Moreover, the decreased costs brought about by lower production must by definition result in increased profitability. Alternatively, lowering price must decrease profits as revenue falls and costs increase with higher levels of production. A consideration of revenue and cost might also make the firm wary of decreasing price if demand were known to be price elastic, for although revenue would rise, so would costs due to increased production. The firm would need to estimate whether the increasing revenue is sufficient to outweigh increasing costs. A detailed analysis of costs, revenue and profit will be undertaken in Chapter 5.

It is always in the interest of the firm to decrease the substitutability of its product against those of rival producers. In so doing its good becomes less price elastic. This could be achieved by increasing consumer loyalty through successful branding, possibly brought about and maintained through continuous advertising. Where the producer possesses a **dominant brand** this allows pricing at a premium over cost. Note, for example, the willingness of many supermarket shoppers to pay high prices for branded goods over the supermarket's own brand, although in many cases the product might be virtually identical.

**dominant brand** the market leading brand within a range of similar products

We noted previously the practice of price discrimination where producers might sell the same good at different prices. We will see in Chapter 9 that a knowledge of the price elasticities in different markets is necessary for successful price discrimination.

A knowledge of price elasticity is also of relevance to governments when determining taxation strategies. For example, although high taxes levied on such goods as tobacco and alcohol might be rationalised by governments as aimed at discouraging consumption, the low price elasticity of such goods also makes the tax lucrative as a source of government revenue.

The firm's knowledge of price elasticity is unlikely to be fully accurate due to problems in estimation and information that might be correct at one moment but might rapidly become inaccurate as market conditions change (e.g. a rival firm might restyle and relaunch its product range). Obtaining market information can also be costly and beyond the reach or capability of many firms. We should not therefore assume that firms have a full knowledge of price elasticities.

### 3.6.6 Income elasticity of demand

We have seen that a change in disposable income shifts the demand curve to the left or right depending upon whether the good is normal or inferior, and if disposable income increases or decreases. The responsiveness of demand to changes in disposable income is measured by the **income elasticity of demand**:

**income elasticity of demand** a measure of the responsiveness of demand for a good or service to a change in the consumer's income

$$\text{Income elasticity } (E_y) = \frac{\text{Percentage change in quantity demanded}}{\text{Percentage change in disposable income}}$$

Table 3.3 shows the range of income elasticities. For normal goods income elasticity is positive. Where $E_y$ is greater than 1, demand is **income elastic**: the percentage change in quantity demanded exceeds the percentage change in disposable income. This would be the case for good A in Figure 3.6 where the Engel curve was rising at an increasing rate. As noted, such goods may be termed luxuries.

**income elastic** when demand for a good increases less than the increase in disposable income

**Table 3.3  Income elasticity**

| Value of $E_y$ | Terminology | Descriptor | Type of good |
| --- | --- | --- | --- |
| $E_y > 0 < 1$ (i.e. greater than zero, but less than 1) | Income inelastic | A change in income leads to a less than proportionate change in demand | Normal good 'necessities' |
| $E_y > 1$ | Income elastic | A change in income leads to a greater than proportionate change in demand | Normal good 'luxuries' |
| $E_y = 0$ | Unitary elasticity | Demand stays constant despite a change in income | |
| $E_y < 0$ | Negative elasticity | Quantity demanded falls as income increases and vice versa | Inferior good |

**income inelastic** when demand for a good increases less than the increase in disposable income

Where $E_y$ is positive and less than 1, demand is **income inelastic**. The percentage change in demand is less than the percentage change in income. Such goods may be classified as necessities. This would correspond to good B on Figure 3.6 up to an income of a.

If $E_y$ were zero, demand is unaffected by a change in disposable income. This corresponds to good B in Figure 3.6 from a disposable income of a to b. Where demand decreases following an increase in disposable income, $E_y$ is negative and the good is inferior. This corresponds to good B on Figure 3.6 beyond an income of b. For a good to have a negative income elasticity then it must have been normal over lower levels of income.

**The importance of income elasticity to the firm**

The concept of income elasticity can help explain the changing structure of an economy. As the economy grows, and disposable income increases, those sectors producing goods and services which are income elastic expand relative to those producing goods and services of a lower or negative income elasticity.[4] This need not mean that all firms within a sector share the same experience. Some will always perform better or worse than the average. Nevertheless, over a period of time, the value of income elasticity can be an important explanatory factor of a sector's or firm's performance.

As regards future investments, if you were confident of rising incomes, it might be good advice to invest in those sectors where demand is income elastic. Firms in such sectors certainly pay particular attention to forecasts of aggregate economic activity, and knowledge of the income elasticity of demand for their goods is invaluable in determining long-term investment strategies. Firms producing goods with a low elasticity might be comforted in the knowledge that they should not be hit so severely in a recession.

### 3.6.7 Cross-elasticity of demand

We have seen how a change in the price of one good may shift the demand curve for another good to the left or right depending upon the relationship between the goods and the direction of the price change. The relationship between goods can be measured by **cross-price elasticity of demand**. For example, the influence of a change in the price of good B upon the demand for good A is measured as follows:

**cross-price elasticity of demand** a measure of the responsiveness of the quantity demanded of one good to changes in the price of another good

$$\text{Cross-elasticity of demand } (E_x) = \frac{\text{Percentage change in quantity demanded of good A}}{\text{Percentage change in price of B}}$$

Whether cross-elasticity is positive or negative depends upon the relationship between the goods (see Table 3.4).

If A and B are substitutes, an increase in the price of B increases the demand for A, and $E_x$ is positive (i.e. the numerator and denominator in the equation are both positive). If the price of B falls, the demand for A falls and $E_x$ is still positive (i.e. the numerator and denominator are both negative, and a minus divided by a minus gives a positive solution).

If A and B are complementary, a change in the price of B has an inverse effect upon the demand for A. Cross-elasticity is therefore negative as both a +/– and a –/+ give a negative solution.

The value of $E_x$ is larger the closer the goods are substitutes. Thus, the value would be greater between an Audi and a BMW car than say between an Audi and Skoda. The more similar the goods are in the eye of the consumer the greater the value of $E_x$. Where two goods are homogeneous (i.e. perfect substitutes) $E_x$ approaches infinity.

The closer the complementarity between any two goods the lower the value of $E_x$. For example, bread and butter or margarine might be closer complements than bread and marmalade on the basis that whilst nearly everyone spreads butter or margarine on their bread, far fewer also use marmalade.

If the goods are unrelated a change in the price of B has no effect on the demand for A, and $E_x$ equals zero. Note, however, that a wide range of related and unrelated goods compete for a consumer's finite income, and in this sense

**Table 3.4  Cross-elasticity**

| Value of $E_x$ | Terminology | Descriptor | Type of goods |
| --- | --- | --- | --- |
| $E_x > 0$ | Positive cross-elasticity | Increase in the price of good B leads to an increase in the demand for good A and vice versa | Substitutes |
| $E_x < 0$ | Negative cross-elasticity | Increase in the price of good B leads to an decrease in the demand for good A and vice versa | Complements |
| $E_x = 0$ (or, approaches zero) | Zero cross-elasticity | A change in the price of B has no effect upon the demand for A | Little or no relationship between the goods |

goods might appear substitutes or complements. For example, a decrease in the price of beer might lead to an increase in the demand for student text-books. Does this make beer and textbooks complementary? Although this is a possibility for some students, the more likely explanation is the price inelastic-ity of demand for beer leading to less expenditure on beer and more income being available to be spent on other goods, including academic texts!

The value of $E_x$ is unlikely to be symmetric between any two goods (i.e. the effect of a percentage change in the price of B upon the demand for A might not be the same as a change in the price of A upon the demand for B). Hence, as noted previously, although an increase in the price of cinema tickets might have a certain impact upon the demand for popcorn sales, the same propor-tionate change in the price of popcorn would have little, if any, effect upon the demand for cinema tickets.

The concept of cross-elasticity can also be used to define those products to be included in a given market. For example, the automobile industry consists of a number of markets, ranging from the luxury car market to the small car market and including the 'classic car' and 'four-wheel drive' markets, etc. Different models of car might be placed in particular markets depending on their sharing a similar cross-elasticity. Given the varying degree of substitutability between different cars, the value of $E_x$ would differ between any two models that might be placed in the same market. Boundaries between markets might appear as gaps in the chains of substitutability as measured by $E_x$.[5]

### 3.6.8 The importance of cross-elasticity to the firm

In competitive markets firms should be aware of how a change in a rival's price will affect demand for their own goods. A high value of cross-elasticity implies strong interdependence between firms and this could influence a firm's pricing strategy, as when one supplier is unwilling to embark upon a price cut in case this leads to retaliatory price cuts from its competitors. Firms also often produce a range of products, many of which compete with each other, as in the case of cigarette or detergent manufacturers. In such circumstances the firm should also be aware of the cross-elasticity between its own brands when price setting.

Knowledge of the strength of cross-elasticities is also relevant when firms are supplying complementary goods, as illustrated by the case of suppliers of computer software who have experienced significant increases in demand as a result of the increased popularity of home computers.

### 3.6.9 Other elasticities

As indicated in Section 3.6, an elasticity is a general concept measuring the responsiveness of one variable to a change in another. Other commonly used elasticities include:

**price elasticity of supply** a measure of the response of quantity supplied to a change in price

### Price elasticity of supply

$$E_s = \frac{\text{Percentage change in quantity supplied}}{\text{Percentage change in price}}$$

This is normally positive, reflecting the upward slope of the supply curve, i.e. an increase in market price encouraging producers to increase supply, and vice versa. The value of $E_s$ will be determined primarily by the number of firms supplying the good; how costs respond to output changes; and, the period of time over which supply is measured. Generally, as with all elasticities, $E_s$ is higher over a longer time period.

The supply curve, and connected concepts, will be discussed fully in Chapter 5.

**advertising elasticity** a measure of the effect of a change in advertising upon the sales of a given good

### Advertising elasticity

$$E_a = \frac{\text{Percentage change in quantity demanded of good A}}{\text{Percentage change in expenditure on advertising good A}}$$

The value should always be positive. If $E_a < 1$, i.e. inelastic, proportionally large amounts of expenditure would be needed to increase demand. In such circumstances the firm might seek alternative ways of increasing demand. The most successful advertising campaigns are those with the highest elasticity. We would also generally expect to observe eventual diminishing returns to advertising, i.e. as expenditure on a given advert increases, the percentage increase in generated demand will eventually decline.

**cross-advertising elasticity** a measure of the responsiveness of the quantity of demand of one good to a change in the expenditure upon advertising on another good

We may also have a **cross-advertising elasticity**. This measures the influence of a change in advertising expenditure on good A upon the demand for good B. The value could be positive or negative depending upon the relationship between the goods, i.e. positive for complements and negative for substitutes.

### Conjectural price flexibility

$$E_c = \frac{\text{Expected percentage change in the price charged by firm B}}{\text{Actual percentage change in price charged by firm A}}$$

This elasticity can be used to measure the conscious interdependence between firms, i.e. the degree to which firm A forecasts its rival, firm B, would change price in retaliation to its own price change. In **oligopolistic markets** (see Chapter 7) with relatively few firms and a strong degree of known interdependence between those firms we would expect the value of $E_c$ to be positive if one of those firms were to initiate a price decrease. Retaliation from competitors would be expected and the recognition of such retaliation might discourage the firm from initiating that price decrease. However, the value of $E_c$ would be far lower were the firm to increase price, as that firm would be unlikely to anticipate rivals matching a price increase. In markets where there is little or no awareness of interdependence between firms the value of $E_c$ would be relatively low.

**oligopolistic markets** markets where a relatively small number of firms account for a large proportion of the total market

Although this elasticity contains a high degree of subjectivity, it is nevertheless relevant to a firm's decision-making strategy. Firms would also be aware that rivals might retaliate in reaction to the change in other sales variables, for instance a new advertising campaign or any new sales promotion (NB the link with game theory which is discussed in Chapter 7).

### The elasticities of demand for exports and imports

In open economies we are concerned with the international competitiveness of goods. A change in the price of UK goods relative to our competitors, perhaps brought about by a movement in our exchange rate, affects the demand for both exports and imports. We can measure the export price elasticity of demand as:

$$E_{ex} = \frac{\text{Percentage change in the demand for UK exports}}{\text{Percentage change in price of UK exports}}$$

and for imports:

$$E_{imp} = \frac{\text{Percentage change in the demand for UK imports}}{\text{Percentage change in price of UK imports}}$$

We can also consider the income elasticity of demand for UK imports and exports:
Income elasticity of demand for UK exports:

$$Ey_{exp} = \frac{\text{Percentage change in demand for UK exports}}{\text{Percentage change in disposable income abroad}}$$

and for imports:
Income elasticity of demand for UK imports:

$$Ey_{imp} = \frac{\text{Percentage change in demand for UK imports}}{\text{Percentage change in UK disposable income}}$$

The value of such trade elasticities is clearly of importance to our external trade balance. However, although price competitiveness and income changes play a major role in the fortunes of external trade, they are not the only factors affecting demand. As in all markets, consumers are also concerned with product characteristics, after-sales service, reliability, etc. UK firms must therefore pay attention to all such factors to secure success in competitive world markets.[6]

## 3.7 Criticisms of demand theory

### Are consumers perfectly informed and do they act rationally?

**utility** the satisfaction or pleasure derived from consuming a good

Demand theory tells us that consumers divide their disposable income between goods and services so as to maximise their satisfaction or **utility**. If the relative price of goods changes, the consumer adjusts expenditure between goods to maintain maximum satisfaction. If new goods come onto the market the consumer might reconsider their distribution of expenditure. Are consumers really so rational, and do they possess sufficient information about market conditions?

### Mini case    Telephones: which service is cheaper?

When faced with a choice of identical or near identical goods we would normally expect the consumer to purchase the cheapest alternative. However, comparisons can often be difficult, and obtaining the necessary information upon which to base the choice can be costly. A particular problem can emerge where rival firms have differing and complex pricing structures.

An example of such complexity can be found in UK domestic telephone services. At present, most consumers have a choice between British Telecom (BT); one of the cable operators; or a 'radio telephone' company. (There were a number of cable operators in 1998, only one being allowed to

▶

operate in a given geographical area.) Although different operators offer marginally different services, most customers place greatest emphasis upon price. However, the complexity of the differing tariffs charged by operators makes a comparison difficult. For example, to seek the cheapest provider you would have to compare the relative cost of such variables as:

- line rental
- additional lines
- call barring
- three-way calling
- call display
- last call return
- local call rates

- national rates
- international rates
- weekend, day and evening tariffs
- connection and disconnection charges
- internet services

etc.

Comparison is clearly difficult. One company might be cheaper as regards one service, yet more expensive on another. The consumer would therefore have to estimate their relative use of *each* service to identify the cheapest supplier. Cable firms may offer free evening and weekend calls yet only to other cable users. How many of your calls would go to other cable users? Additionally, companies might have a lower tariff, yet also have a 'minimum call' charge for each time you are connected. Including quality and range of service in the computation increases the problem.

The complexity of tariffs and the continual emergence of new offers and services clearly make comparison difficult. Indeed, firms in this and other industries may often deliberately engage in such practices with the aim of confusing the customer and making those comparisons near impossible. One firm might criticise another because of the apparent complexity of the rival's tariffs. For example, in the early summer of 1998, Diamond Cable launched an extensive poster and leaflet campaign featuring a picture of Albert Einstein with the wording. 'Albert Einstein discovered the theory of relativity . . . but could he figure out a BT discount scheme?' Diamond Cable went on to claim that its tariffs were both simpler and cheaper. Needless to say, BT would disagree.

Oftel, the Office of Telecommunications, regulates the industry. In May 1998, Oftel recognised the problem faced by consumers and called upon the industry to publish comparative data that would allow standardised comparison. It is anticipated that this might be introduced by the beginning of 1999. It will be interesting to see how this might be implemented, and how consumers would react. Price competition is already intense. Will a greater transparency lead to lower prices? Might this result in firms increasingly competing in terms of their range and quality of service?

We noted the general applicability of 'the law of demand' as illustrated by a downward sloping demand curve. In certain circumstances this 'law' might be broken, as with Giffen goods or speculative demand, although such cases are relatively rare. It is also possible that certain individuals might simply behave irrationally, but again we could argue that their actions are likely to be outweighed by the more normal behaviour of others. In short, we could speculate that overall market rationality is likely to remain intact.

Although the wide variety of goods in modern consumer markets provides consumers with a wealth of choice it can also create problems. For example, when buying a new computer the buyer is faced with an almost infinite choice of models and specifications. On what basis should he/she base their decision? Many follow the recommendation of friends, benefit from previous experience, or study information provided in consumer guides and advertisements. However, gaining such information can be costly in terms of time spent. It might therefore make sense to be less than fully informed. As a general principle, although the individual might have problems in making accurate measurements, the consumer should obtain information up to the point where the cost of doing so equals the resulting likely benefits. Generally, the more expensive and durable the good the greater the need to gain market information, as in the case of commissioning a structural survey on a house, or paying an independent mechanic to look over a second-hand car. With cheaper, less durable goods such expenditure appears less justified.

We also often find the same good priced differently in alternative locations. The rational consumer might be assumed to assiduously seek out the cheapest source. However, once again there is a cost involved, and such costs might outweigh the possible benefits. As above, it can make sense for the rational consumer to be less than fully informed.

Consumer attitude to risk is also relevant. Some might be unwilling to risk making an 'incorrect' consumer choice and therefore are prepared to spend time and money researching alternative products. Others might be more willing to take risks and therefore spend less on such research. Taking out an extended warranty on a consumer durable is one way of providing an insurance against risk.

The above observations are also of relevance to the producer as there are costs in obtaining information of market conditions, and such costs might outweigh possible benefits. As we will see in Chapter 16, although a firm benefits from forecasting future demand, the cost of doing so might be such that the firm would not consider this a worthwhile investment.

### An over-emphasis upon price?

Traditional demand analysis could be criticised for over-emphasising the importance of price in consumer choice, as the consumer might be more or equally interested in such **non-price factors** as quality, reliability, design, after-sales service, etc. Clearly, such factors are important, particularly in markets where goods are highly **differentiated** and it is important for non-price aspects to be considered alongside price factors. Certainly, an analysis of non-price factors would be similar to that of price. Thus an improvement in after-sales service, etc. (*ceteris paribus*) would be assumed to improve sales, and vice versa. We saw earlier that this would be illustrated by a shift in the demand curve.

When considering a purchase consumers may think in terms of a price range rather than seeking a good at a particular price. Thus when buying a new car the consumer might consider purchases within a set price range, most likely influenced by the trade-in value of an existing car and the cost of a future loan. They would now only seek information on cars within that price range. In so doing they might also seek particular product characteristics

**non-price factors** factors used by the firm to determine sales in addition to the sale price, for example, product design, quality, etc.

**differentiated goods** the creation of real or imagined differences in essentially similar goods by branding, packaging, advertising, quality, design, etc.

(e.g. it must be a four-door saloon capable of comfortably seating two adults and two children, be relatively fuel-efficient yet capable of acceptable acceleration; have at least a two-year warranty; and be available in a particular colour range). An individual might then be willing to trade off one characteristic against another. Additional passenger space might compensate for less fuel efficiency; other characteristics might not be negotiable such as never considering a two-door saloon whatever the compensations. This approach to consumer purchases certainly highlights both price and non-price factors and has particular relevance to the purchase of most consumer durables. An analysis of this **characteristics approach** will be included in Chapter 4.

**characteristics approach**
an approach to the determination of demand concentrating on the importance of the product characteristics inherent within the good

## 3.8   Conclusions

Within this chapter we have studied the main factors affecting the demand for a product, most particularly the influence of price and the 'law of demand'. The influence of these factors upon demand can be measured by the concept of an elasticity.

Although knowledge of such factors is of great importance to the firm this should not imply the firm is blessed with perfect knowledge. The firm might be strongly aware of the competition provided by rival firms without having a precise measure of the cross-price elasticity of demand. Further, our ability to draw a demand curve, and measure the value of price elasticity at any point along its length, should not imply that the firm has the same information at its disposal. Its knowledge of the demand curve is likely to be imperfect. Nevertheless, the firm requires an understanding of such factors, particularly the ability to identify the strength of the various factors determining the demand for its products. Armed with such information it can then make strategic decisions on pricing, product design and marketing.

As we will see, the basic concepts and tools we have developed will prove of great importance in subsequent chapters.

## Case study    The increasing price of football

At the end of each football season, professional football clubs announce the price of season tickets for the following year. Selling tickets in advance of games is clearly beneficial to the clubs as it provides an advanced source of income and acts as an insurance against poor performance.

In the 1997/98 season, Newcastle United was the only club to allow only season-ticket holders into the ground. Although other clubs might have been able to pursue such a policy, they chose instead to keep a proportion of tickets for sale to non-season-ticket holders and away supporters. Gates receipts for Premier League teams typically raise approximately 40 to 50 per cent of revenue, the remainder increasingly coming from sponsorship deals, merchandising and television receipts.

The football fan is by definition loyal to their club. Most would never consider changing their loyalty, and the fan is unlikely to switch clubs as a result of a relative price change. For instance, a Liverpool supporter would be unlikely to switch allegiance to Everton, a club in close geographical proximity within the city of Liverpool, because the price of admission to Everton fell relative to Liverpool. In short, although poor performances and the increasing cost of attending games can sorely test a fan's loyalty, their demand is generally price inelastic. Indeed, although there is often some complaint regarding the price of tickets, it is commonly difficult for supporters to obtain tickets for particular games. The supporter can avoid this uncertainty by purchasing a season ticket, although in many instances season tickets might also be difficult to secure. For example, as quoted in the *Guardian* on 18 February 1998, Manchester United received approximately 100,000 applications for its 40,000 season tickets (representing 70 per cent of capacity) for the 1997/98 season. This must imply that the club could have set higher prices, generated more revenue, and still sold the full allocation. Why didn't it do so? Perhaps it had objectives other than maximising immediate profits, including maintaining the good will of its supporters? (The objectives of firms are discussed in Chapter 6.)

It is interesting to note the price increases announced by many of the Premier League teams prior to the 1998/99 season as outlined in Table 3.5.

**Table 3.5  1997 final league positions and the price of season tickets for a selection of Premier League teams (most expensive tickets)**

| Premier League Club | 1997 season ticket (maximum price) | 1998 season ticket (maximum price) | % price increase (1997 to 1998) | Final league position (1997 season) |
|---|---|---|---|---|
| Arsenal | £702 | £806 | 15% | 1st |
| Aston Villa | £306 | £374 | 22% | 7th |
| Blackburn Rovers | £345 | £399 | 16% | 6th |
| Chelsea | £887 | £1025 | 16% | 4th |
| Coventry City | £355 | £393 | 11% | 11th |
| Derby County | £450 | £470 | 4% | 9th |
| Everton | £285 | £295 | 3% | 17th |
| Leeds United | £385 | £420 | 9% | 5th |
| Leicester City | £480 | £535 | 11% | 10th |
| Liverpool | £300 | £330 | 10% | 3rd |
| Manchester United | £380 | £399 | 5% | 2nd |
| Southampton | £360 | £396 | 10% | 12th |
| Tottenham Hotspur | £624 | £710 | 12% | 14th |
| Wimbledon | £480 | £500 | 4% | 15th |

Source: *The Times*, 21 May 1998.

The price increases in Table 3.5 were generally above the rate of inflation at that time (inflation was measured at 4.0 per cent in May 1998). The majority of price increases were therefore 'real' price rises.

The prices in Table 3.5 only represent the most expensive season tickets. Clubs actually sell a selection of season tickets at differing prices reflecting

▶

the position of the seat in the ground. Table 3.6 provides such information for Leicester City FC for the 1998 and 1999 seasons and the percentage prices increases. Note the different prices for the different locations (see the attached map of the ground). With the exception of the executive boxes, normally purchased by commercial organisations to entertain clients, the most expensive individual adult seats were in the Carling Executive Tier. It is more expensive in the Upper Tier of the South Stand than in the Lower Tier. The Upper Tier must give a better view. Also note, as with other clubs, Leicester charges differential prices to adults, juveniles, senior citizens and students, and the percentage price increases for those categories varied depending upon ground location. Not all categories of supporter are offered season tickets in all locations. For example, only adult season-ticket holders are allowed in the Lower

**Table 3.6  Season-ticket prices for Leicester City Football Club 1998 and 1999 seasons** (the figures in brackets show percentage price increases)

| Stand or Section | Adult | | Juvenile | | Senior Citizen | | Student | |
|---|---|---|---|---|---|---|---|---|
| | 1998 | 1999 | 1998 | 1999 | 1998 | 1999 | 1998 | 1999 |
| Carling Executive Tier | £480 | £535 (11%) | £240 | £265 (10%) | £240 | £265 (10%) | n/a | n/a |
| Carling Centre | £435 | £485 (11%) | £215 | £245 (14%) | £180 | £200 (11%) | £215 | £265 (23%) |
| Carling Wing | £380 | £425 (12%) | £195 | £215 (10%) | £180 | £200 (11%) | £195 | £215 (10%) |
| Carling Members Enclosure | £315 | £345 (10%) | n/a | n/a | £180 | n/a | n/a | n/a |
| Carling Family Enclosure | £315 | £345 (10%) | £160 | £170 (6%) | £160 | £175 (9%) | n/a | n/a |
| Family Club (North Stand) | £295 | £325 (10%) | £150 | £160 (7%) | £150 | £160 (7%) | n/a | n/a |
| East Stand | £295 | £325 (10%) | £150 | £160 (7%) | £150 | £160 (7%) | n/a | £160 |
| South Stand (Upper Tier) | £360 | £390 (8%) | £185 | £195 (5%) | £180 | £195 (8%) | £185 | £195 (5%) |
| South Stand (Lower Tier) | £295 | £325 (10%) | n/a | n/a | n/a | n/a | n/a | n/a |
| Supporters Club (Corner) | £295 | £325 (10%) | £150 | £160 (7%) | £150 | £160 (7%) | n/a | n/a |

Tier of the South Stand. The likely reason is that this is commonly seen as the most 'boisterous' area of the ground and 'less suitable' for non-adults. Such a pricing strategy is an example of discriminatory pricing, and will be examined further in Chapter 9. (Although season-ticket prices rose at Leicester City Football Club from 1998 to 1999, the club actually decreased prices for the 2000 season to maintain support and increase sales. It did this despite a successful club performance in the previous season.)

Clubs might charge different prices for different games: a premium price for a cup competition or when playing an attractive opponent. An individual club might know that a game against a club such as Manchester United is going to be an attractive proposition for its regular and less regular supporters, as well as attracting many Manchester United away supporters. There would certainly be scope for charging a higher price.

There are two commonly quoted reasons for the price increases noted in Tables 3.5 and 3.6:

1 the increased cost of players' salaries and transfer deals
2 the costs incurred by clubs to improve spectator facilities, including the introduction of 'all-seater' stadiums.

Additionally, and as noted above, the commitment of the supporters is also such that clubs are able to increase prices without this significantly affecting the level of demand (i.e. as demand is price inelastic, the increase in price results in an increase in gate receipts with relatively little impact upon attendance figures).

**Figure 3.13 Leicester City Football Club** (ground plan)

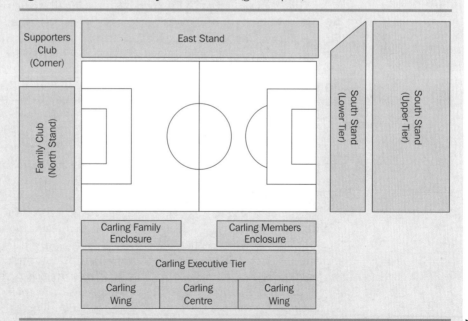

It is interesting to note the different price increases announced by clubs in Table 3.5. This might be rationalised on the grounds of their performance in the 1997 season. That is, a club performing well one year might be able to charge higher prices in the following year. However, the evidence for this observation is somewhat mixed. For example, as also noted in Table 3.5, Aston Villa, with the largest price increase, although arguably a lower starting price, finished seventh of the 20 clubs in the league, whereas Manchester United, with one of the smallest increases, finished second. However, the fact that Everton only felt able to increase prices by 3 per cent might certainly be partly explained by it having had one of its worst seasons, finishing seventeenth and only just missing relegation to a lower division.

Naturally, there are other factors apart from league position in the preceding season to explain price increases, such as the current financial position of the club. In this respect it could be argued that Manchester United, generally seen as a very wealthy and financially sound club, had less need to raise prices, although the nature of demand for its tickets, as noted above, could certainly have allowed the club to do so. In contrast, the large price increase imposed by Aston Villa, who had a 'mixed season' and eventually finished seventh, might be better explained by its financial situation. There may also be a regional bias in that clubs in relatively affluent areas can afford to increase prices more than others. This might certainly explain the relatively large increases by London-based clubs; an exception to this would be the London-based Wimbledon. However, in contrast to its 'more fashionable' London neighbours, it has never been able to attract large crowds and might appear reluctant to impose too high a price increase. Moreover, finishing fifteenth in the league would not have helped. In short, as noted, there are many factors that might influence the size of the price increase.

The current popularity of Premier League football would certainly seem able to sustain relatively high ticket prices. However, as noted in the *Guardian* (18 February 1998): 'the real fear of football supporters is that although increased prices might be sustained by the current crop of richer older supporters, clubs are pricing younger supporters out of the game'. Further, in the same article, Adam Brown (a member of the Football Supporters Association, and the government's Football Task Force set up in 1988 to monitor the national game) was quoted as saying: 'It's a long-term problem for the game. The habit of going to games is formed when you are 16, 17, 18. At a "Task Force" meeting recently, Roland Smith [Manchester United's Chairman] admitted that United has an ageing crowd. The great thing about football previously, and its strength as the national game, was its wide social base. Now that is narrowing both in social and age terms.' Is this really a problem and if so, what is the solution?

Although the Premier League can be looked upon as a very competitive market, at least in terms of the clubs competing for league positions, the effective hold that they have over their supporters certainly provides them with a degree of monopoly power. In support of this view Tony Banks, then Minister for Sport, was quoted in the *Observer*, on 31 May 1998 as saying: 'A number of clubs know that if they put up prices, they will sell them anyway. Football is a drug. But I am increasingly drawn to the conclusion that, sooner or later, a degree of regulation might be necessary.' Should football clubs have their powers regulated?

## Notes and references

1. Income and substitution effects, and the possibility of a Giffen good, can be further analysed through the use of indifference curves. See Chapter 4.

2. The original article by Harvey Leibenstein expounding the 'Bandwagon, snob and Veblen effects in the theory of consumers demand' appeared in the *Quarterly Journal of Economics*, February 1948. A further analysis of Leibenstein's approach can be found in Moschandreas, M. *Business Economics*, (1994), Routledge, London, pp. 182–184.

3. Such an approach to public investment decision-making is used within cost-benefit analysis (CBA). An introduction to the approach, and its application within road transport, can be found in Griffiths, A. and Wall, S. (1996), *Intermediate Microeconomics. Theory and Applications*, Longman, Harlow, pp. 445–450.

4. For a further analysis of how income elasticity of demand can affect industrial structure see Worthington and Britton (2000), *The Business Environment*, 3rd edition, Financial Times Prentice Hall, Harlow, pp. 268–270. Also see Griffiths, A. and Wall, S. (1999), *Applied Economics*, 8th edition, Longman, Harlow.

5. See Townsend, H. (1995), *Foundations of Business Economics*, Routledge, London, p. 26.

6. For further analysis and background see Worthington and Britton (2000), Chapter 13, and Griffiths, and Wall (1999), pp. 610–620.

## Review and discussion questions

**1** A new cinema complex is being planned to open on the outskirts of your town. Identify the main independent or explanatory variables that will determine its popularity.

**2** Why might you expect the demand for petrol to be more elastic in the long run than the short run? Name, with a brief explanation, two other goods that might share this characteristic. (These 'other goods' should not be in the general field of fuel or power.)

**3** As a long-term investment would you rather invest money in an industry that is income elastic or income inelastic? Provide an example of each, and indicate any provisos you might make with regards to your advice.

**4** A Premier League football club estimates that whilst the price elasticity of demand for its first-team fixtures is (–) 0.3, for second-team games the corresponding elasticity is (–) 2.2. Provide an explanation for this difference in elasticities and advise the club how this might influence its pricing strategy.

**5** In Section 3.6.7 we indicated how the concept of cross-elasticity of demand might be used to identify the goods that could be included in a particular segment of the automobile industry (e.g. the 'small car' market as opposed to the 'luxury car' market). Taking an example other than motor cars, indicate how you might use the same approach to identify the segmentation in that market and provide a broad indication of how that market is segmented. Would your analysis provide 'clear divisions'?

## Assignments

1 In the mini case entitled 'Telephones. Which service is cheaper?', it was noted that the consumer may have difficulties in identifying the cheapest alternative good or service. Such a situation is clearly not unique to telephone services. For example, if we imagine that the interest rate offered by a bank or building society to an investor is equivalent to the price the borrower (i.e. the bank or building society) pays the investor for the privilege of holding their money, then the rate on offer clearly differs relatively significantly between borrowers, being particularly dependent upon the 'terms and conditions' of the investment. In short, given the large choice of accounts on offer, the decision of the investor as to which account to choose can be relatively difficult, and particularly dependent upon the access that the investor seeks to their savings once placed in a particular account.

   Imagine that a relative seeks your advice on how best to place £6,000 in a savings account. Provide your relative with a written report that identifies the reasons for the different rates on offer (i.e. what are the variables that influence those rates?) and which also provides her with your recommendations as to which specific savings accounts she might consider.

2 It is commonly found that the same good (for example, a particular brand of baked beans) is priced differently in alternative retail locations.

   Identify such a good and investigate its price in a minimum of ten different locations. Analyse your results and provide a rationale for any price variations you might observe.

## Further reading

Atkinson, B. and Miller, R. (1998), *Business Economics,* Addison-Wesley, Harlow, Unit 6.

Dunnett, T. A. (1998), *Understanding the Market*, 3rd edition, Longman, Harlow, Chapter 2.

Griffiths, A. and Wall, S. (1996), *Intermediate Microeconomics: Theory and Applications*, Longman, Harlow, Chapter 2.

Nellis, J. G. and Parker, D. (1997), *The Essence of Business Economics*, 2nd edition, Prentice Hall, Hemel Hempstead, Chapter 2.

Worthington, I. and Britton, C. (2000), *The Business Environment*, 3rd edition, Financial Times Prentice Hall, Harlow, Chapter 11.

# CHAPTER 4

# Consumer behaviour: theory and applications

Andy Rees

1 To outline the major assumptions underlying theories of consumer behaviour.
2 To introduce the concept of 'utility'.
3 To examine the use of indifference curve analysis in understanding influences on consumption.
4 To apply indifference curve analysis to different areas of business.

## 4.1  Introduction

Microeconomic analysis deals fundamentally with how decision-makers react to scarcity. As incomes are finite, the consumer suffers a scarcity of income and must therefore choose carefully which goods to consume. Purchasing more of one good implies consuming less of another. The theory of consumer behaviour studies how individual consumers react to such scarcity. In this chapter we will develop a model of consumer choice. This will require us to make certain assumptions regarding the motivation of consumers.

The theory of consumer behaviour provides many valuable insights into the nature of choice and the basic model has many practical applications. As illustration we will look at a characteristics approach to consumer demand and an analysis of the individual's choice between work and leisure.

**indifference curve** a curve showing combinations of quantities of two goods such that the individual obtains equal satisfaction from those combinations and is therefore indifferent between them

The chapter looks at aspects of consumer behaviour using an **indifference curve** approach. To develop the model we must initially examine the basis of consumer choice including the concepts of consumer rationality, consistency and transitivity. The model shows how the consumer may obtain optimal satisfaction from their expenditure and how expenditure will be adjusted if there is a change in either the relative price of goods or in income. When price changes we will see how the change in expenditure can be broken down into a substitution and income effect.

It will be seen that the model can be used to analyse many real world situations.

## 4.2 Consumer preferences

Before analysing consumer behaviour we must make certain basic assumptions regarding the nature of consumer decision-making. These assumptions will form the basis of our analysis and include the following:

### 4.2.1 Rationality

**rational** consumers are assumed to be acting rationally by choosing those goods and services that yield maximum satisfaction

Consumers are assumed **rational** in the sense that they seek maximum **satisfaction** (or **utility**) from the goods and services they purchase with their fixed income.

This assumption appears reasonable, although we can imagine instances where consumers appear to act irrationally. This might be the case where we later regret purchasing an article of clothing, or having remained drinking at the bar instead of returning home to finish an essay. Nevertheless, it is reasonable to assume that consumers usually act rationally in their pursuit of maximum utility.

**goods** a physical commodity or service that the individual would prefer more of rather than less. Goods therefore yield positive satisfaction or utility to the consumer

We should always be careful of labelling individual actions as irrational. If a consumer freely chooses a good without coercion, the act of choice reveals preference. For example, where items A and B are the same price and A is chosen over B then A is assumed to be preferred to B and yields greater utility. (A different consumer might choose B over A.) It is also possible for a consumer to be indifferent between A and B. In this case we must assume that A and B provide the consumer with the same utility.

**bads** a physical commodity or service that an individual would prefer less of rather than more. Consuming a bad therefore yields negative satisfaction or utility

### 4.2.2 The consumer prefers more to less

**negative utility** obtained when by consuming a good the individual's satisfaction or pleasure diminishes

A consumer will generally prefer more rather than less of a given commodity. Commodities which share this common characteristic are referred to as **goods**. Not all commodities are goods. For example, society prefers less pollution to more; or, an individual might actively dislike broccoli and prefer no broccoli to even the smallest portion. Commodities which share this less usual characteristic are referred to as **bads**.

**total utility** the overall satisfaction or pleasure obtained from consuming a given quantity of a particular good or combination of goods

Needless to say, **goods** can become **bads**; although I might generally like broccoli, I will not always take extra portions. If forced to do so, the extra portion might give **negative utility**.

**marginal utility** the change in overall satisfaction from consuming an additional unit of a specific good. Marginal utility would be positive if that unit yields positive satisfaction and vice versa

### 4.2.3 Additional units yield decreasing utility

**Total utility** increases at a decreasing rate as an individual consumes additional units of a good. **Marginal utility** (the utility derived from the extra unit) declines. This proposition is illustrated in Figure 4.1.

**diminishing marginal utility** the observation that the consumer will generally obtain decreased satisfaction from each additional unit consumed of a specific good in a given time period

Diminishing marginal utility for commodity X is illustrated in Figure 4.1a. As consumption increases towards C, marginal utility declines. Additional units yield diminishing satisfaction. Beyond C commodity X becomes a **bad**. Further consumption yields increasing negative utility. The corresponding cumulative level of utility (total utility) is shown in Figure 4.1b. The slope of the total utility function illustrates **diminishing marginal utility**.

**Figure 4.1 The utility and marginal utility curves**

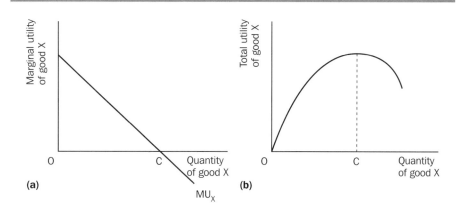

**(a)**  **(b)**

We implicitly assumed above that utility can be measured. We might imagine utility being measured in monetary units in the sense that the money a consumer pays for a good reflects the satisfaction gained. If this were the case the demand curve for commodity X would be identical to the positive section of the marginal utility curve. This is shown in Figure 4.2.

In Figure 4.2a the consumer gains a marginal utility of $MU_1$ from consuming the $X_1$ unit. $P_1$ reflects the price the consumer is willing to pay for that unit. In consuming the $X_2$ unit, marginal utility falls to $MU_2$. Price must therefore fall to $P_2$ to persuade the consumer to buy that additional unit. The concept of diminishing marginal utility therefore explains the downward slope of the demand curve.

The negative section of the marginal utility curve would not form part of the demand curve, as the consumer would not buy a good yielding negative utility. The relevance of the negative section might be seen in the sense that a consumer must be paid (or compensated) to consume a good yielding negative utility. For example, a person disliking broccoli might be willing to consume

**Figure 4.2 The marginal utility curve and the demand curve**

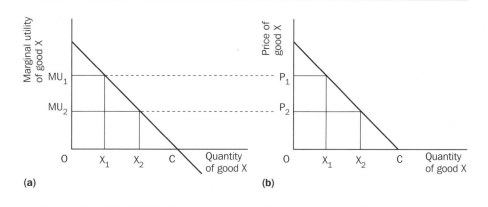

**(a)**  **(b)**

the vegetable if paid to do so. (This would be similar in principle to the parent bribing a child to eat their vegetables by the promise of a compensatory treat.)

In reality there are practical difficulties in objectively measuring utility. Although money might be used as a unit of measurement, to do so we must assume that money itself is subject to constant utility as any unit of measurement must be constant in value. However, it would be reasonable to assume that money is also subject to diminishing marginal utility. For instance, an extra £1 on top of a weekly income of £100 would be more valued than that same extra £1 on top of an income of £500. Nevertheless, despite problems of measurement the concept of diminishing marginal utility remains consistent with consumer experience.

### 4.2.4 Consistency and transitivity of choice

**consistent** consistency of choice implies that if a consumer currently chooses one good or combination of goods over another, they will not then change that choice unless some factor affecting demand, for example price, tastes, income, etc., were to change

Consumers are assumed **consistent** in their choices between goods (or bundles of goods) in the sense that if A is chosen over B in one time period, B would not later be chosen over A. To ensure this is the case we assume all factors affecting demand remain unaltered, or *ceteris paribus*.

Consistency also implies **transitivity**. For example, if A is preferred to B, and B is preferred to C, then A must be preferred to C. Transitivity can be represented symbolically as:

**transitivity** the relationship in which if a first element bears a relationship to a second and the second has a relationship to a third, then the first must have an implied relationship to the third

$$
\begin{aligned}
&\text{if} && A > B \\
&\text{and} && B > C \\
&\text{then} && A > C
\end{aligned}
$$

### 4.2.5 Diminishing marginal rate of substitution

Imagine a consumer possesses units of commodities X and Y. The consumer might now be willing to sacrifice units of Y to obtain additional units of X. The rate of exchange of X for Y will not, however, be constant and will depend upon the number of units of each good the consumer currently has. For example, if the consumer has a lot of Y and little X, the rate of exchange of X for Y will be relatively large. That is, a large amount of Y might be willingly sacrificed to obtain additional X. However, as Y becomes scarcer, and X more plentiful, the rate of exchange falls. Fewer Y would now be willingly sacrificed to obtain an extra unit of X.

**diminishing marginal rate of substitution** the rate at which one good is substituted for another as they move along an indifference curve is referred to as the marginal rate of substitution. The convexity to the origin of an indifference curve shows a diminishing marginal rate of substitution. That is, when moving down the indifference curve the consumer is only willing to sacrifice fewer and fewer units of one good to gain additional units of the other whilst maintaining the same level of satisfaction

This illustrates the principle of a **diminishing marginal rate of substitution** of one commodity for another. This would be consistent with our previous observation that additional units yield decreasing utility in that if X is scarce and Y plentiful an extra unit of X produces a relatively large amount of additional utility and the consumer should willingly sacrifice a number of units of Y (where the utility of those units would be relatively low) to gain an extra unit of X. The rate of exchange between the goods is such that the utility gained by consuming an extra unit of X is balanced by the utility lost in consuming less Y.

## 4.3    Indifference curve analysis

We have now assumed:

- rationality
- consumers prefer more to less
- additional units yield decreasing satisfaction
- consistency and transitivity of choice
- diminishing marginal rates of substitution

These assumptions can now be used to introduce **indifference curve analysis**.

An indifference curve shows combinations of two goods that yield the same total utility. Such an indifference curve ($IC_2$) is shown in Figure 4.3. The consumer is assumed indifferent between any combination of goods X and Y contained on that indifference curve.

Imagine point B on $IC_2$ in Figure 4.3. If we assume the consumer always prefers more of one good and no less of another, then any combination of goods above and to the right of B must yield greater utility. Such a combination might be represented by point C on indifference curve $IC_3$. All combinations on $IC_3$ therefore provide greater utility than those on $IC_2$. Similarly, point B would be preferred to any point below and to the left of that point. Point A therefore provides less utility than B and all combinations on $IC_1$ provide less utility than those on $IC_2$.

**indifference map** a set of indifference curves describing an individual's preferences concerning alternative combinations of two goods. Successively higher indifference curves denote higher levels of satisfaction

We have now developed an **indifference map** consisting of three indifference curves. We could imagine a larger number of curves, each curve denoting a different level of utility.

**Figure 4.3  An indifference curve**

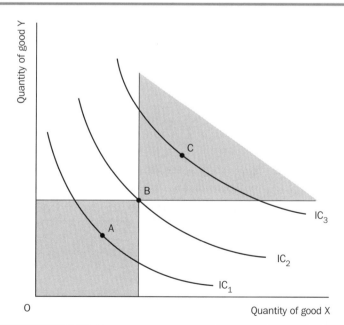

### 4.3.1 The properties of indifference curves

Indifference curves possess the following properties:

**They have a negative slope**

So long as both goods are desirable to the consumer (i.e. **goods** as opposed to **bads**), obtaining more of one good without a compensating reduction in the other makes the consumer better off. To maintain the same level of utility, the consumer must therefore sacrifice units of one good if obtaining additional units of the other. An indifference curve must therefore be downward sloping.

**Indifference curves are convex to the origin**

Convexity implies that the slope of the indifference curve falls as we move down the curve from left to right. This follows from our assumption of a diminishing marginal rate of substitution (see Section 4.2.5 above). This principle can be again illustrated in Figure 4.4.

As we move down the indifference curve in Figure 4.4, the consumer is willing to sacrifice fewer units of Y to obtain additional X.

The marginal rate of substitution of X for Y is defined as the number of units of Y that must be sacrificed to gain an extra unit of X when total utility remains constant. That is:

$$MRS_{XY} = \frac{\Delta Y}{\Delta X}$$

In moving from point a to point b on Figure 4.4, 5 units of Y must be exchanged for an extra unit of X. $MRS_{XY}$ therefore equals 5. If we then move

**Figure 4.4 The diminishing marginal rate of substitution on an indifference curve**

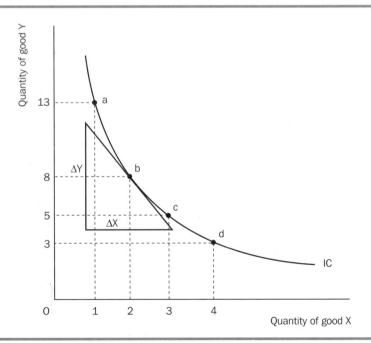

from point b to point c, and then from point c to point d, the marginal rate of substitution declines.

In moving up the indifference curve, the marginal rate of substitution of Y for X ($MRS_{YX}$) similarly declines.

$MRS_{XY}$ can be seen geometrically in Figure 4.4 as the slope of a line (or chord) between point a and point b. The slope of such chords diminishes as we move down the curve. The marginal rate of substitution is therefore determined by the slope of the indifference curve. At a single point on an indifference curve, the marginal rate of substitution would be represented by the slope of a tangent to the curve at that point. Such a tangent is shown at point b. As we move down the curve the slope of corresponding tangents declines.

The marginal rate of substitution changes if there is a shift in consumer preferences between the goods. For example, referring again to Figure 4.4, if the consumer were to develop an increased desire for X over Y the slope of the indifference curve would increase, illustrating the willingness of the consumer to sacrifice larger amounts of Y to obtain additional units of X. A shift in preference towards Y would cause the indifference curve to become more shallow.

We have noted the principle of diminishing marginal rate of substitution to be consistent with diminishing marginal utility. We may now show that $MRS_{XY}$ (the slope of indifference curve) is equal to the ratio of the marginal utilities of the corresponding goods at that point on the indifference curve.

Recall that:

$$MRS_{XY} = \frac{\Delta Y}{\Delta X}$$

and as total utility remains constant on an indifference curve then in moving from point a and point b on Figure 4.4 it must follow that:

$$\Delta Y . MU_Y = \Delta X . MU_X$$

i.e. the lost utility in consuming less Y is equal to the utility gained in consuming more X.

The above can be rearranged as:

$$\frac{MU_X}{MU_Y} = \frac{\Delta Y}{\Delta X}$$

therefore:

$$MRS_{XY} = \frac{MU_X}{MU_Y}$$

As we move down an indifference curve, $MU_X$ declines as more x is consumed, and $MU_Y$ increases as less Y is consumed. The ratio $MU_X/MU_Y$ therefore declines. This ratio represents the marginal rate of substitution between goods X and Y.

### Higher indifference curves denote greater utility

The further away from the origin an indifference curve lies, the greater the level of utility. This follows from the assumption that consumers always prefer more to less.

**Figure 4.5 The invalidity of intersecting indifference curves**

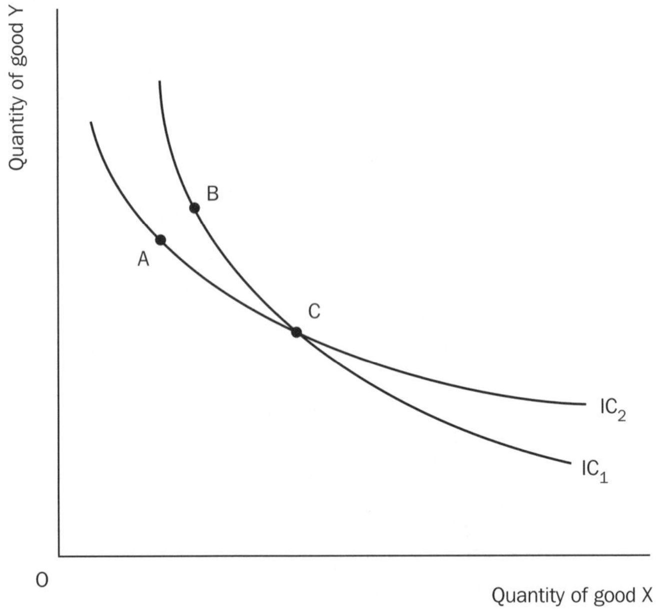

### Indifference curve cannot intersect

Transitivity of choice would be violated if indifference curves intersect.

If $IC_1$ and $IC_2$ intersected at C in Figure 4.5, this implies combination A is indifferent to C as they both lie on $IC_2$, and that combination B is also indifferent to C as they lie on $IC_1$. Under the assumption of transitivity, A should therefore be indifferent to B. However, this cannot be true since B contains more of both goods and must therefore yield greater utility. Transitivity must therefore have been violated.

The implication of the above is that only one indifference curve can pass through each point between the x and y axes.

### 4.3.2 The consumer's budget constraint

The indifference curve shows the willingness of a consumer to exchange one commodity for another. The ability to consume particular combinations of goods and trade one off against another will, however, depend upon the consumer's disposable income and the relative prices of those goods. The level of income and product prices therefore acts as a constraint upon consumer choice.

The relationship between a consumer's income, the prices of X and Y and the amount of each good that can be purchased is given by the equation:

$$I = P_X X + P_Y Y$$

where:

$I$ = income

$P_X$ = price of good X

**Figure 4.6  A budget line**

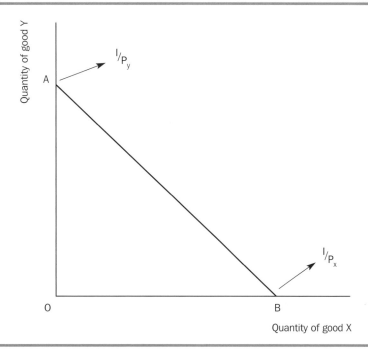

X   = quantity purchased of good X
$P_Y$  = price of good Y
Y   = quality purchased of good Y.

The above relationship, our budget constraint, is shown diagrammatically as a **budget line** in Figure 4.6.

**budget line** a budget line (or price-ratio line) shows the maximum combinations of two goods the consumer could buy from a given level of income

A budget line shows the maximum combinations of X and Y that can be purchased with a given income and the prices of the two goods. The budget line goes through every combination of the two goods that can be purchased when all income is expended. For example, if the consumer spent all their income on Y, they could purchase $I/P_Y$ units of Y and no units of X. This combination is shown at point A, the intercept of the budget constraint with the Y axis. Point B shows the intercept with the X axis, a consumption bundle of all X and no Y. Combinations of X and Y are contained along the budget line.

The budget line has a negative slope showing that more X can only be purchased by reducing the consumption of Y. Geometrically the slope of the budget line in Figure 4.6 is:

$$\frac{OA}{OB} = \frac{I/P_Y}{I/P_X} = \frac{P_X}{P_Y}$$

The slope of the budget line therefore equals the ratio of the prices of the two goods.

**Figure 4.7  Shift in the budget line following a change in income**

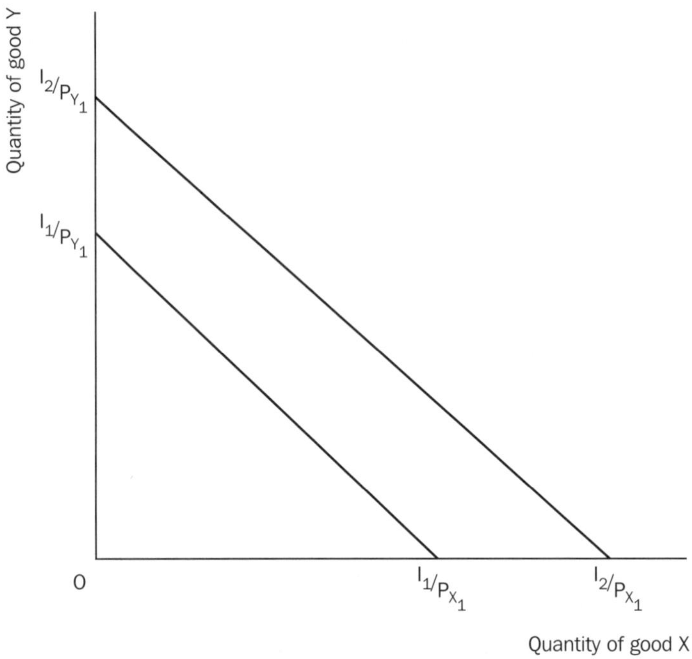

The budget line will shift following:

### A change in income

An increase in income allows the consumer to buy more of one good without consuming less of the other. The budget line therefore shifts to the right in Figure 4.7 following an increase in income from $I_1$ to $I_2$. With constant prices the shift will be parallel, the slope of the line remaining constant.

If income were to fall the budget line shifts to the left. The larger the change in income, the greater the shift.

### A change in price

If the price of good X falls but the price of good Y and income remains unchanged, the X intercept shifts to the right and the Y intercept remains intact. This is illustrated in Figure 4.8 for a fall in the price of X from $P_{X_1}$ to $P_{X_2}$. The slope of the budget line falls. That is: $P_{X_1}/P_{Y_1} > P_{X_2}/P_{Y_1}$.

If the price of X were to increase the intercept on the X axis shifts to the left. The slope of the budget line increases. If the price of Y were to change with the price of X and income constant, the budget line would pivot on the X intercept.

We could also imagine the effect on the budget line of an increase in the price of one good and a decrease in the price of the other, Or an increase (or decrease) in the price of both goods where one changes proportionally more than the other. If the price of both goods changes by the same proportion, relative prices remain the same and the budget line shifts inwards (for a price increase) or outwards (for a price decrease) in a parallel fashion, the slope of the budget line and the ratio $P_X/P_Y$ remaining constant.

**Figure 4.8  The effect of a price change on the budget line**

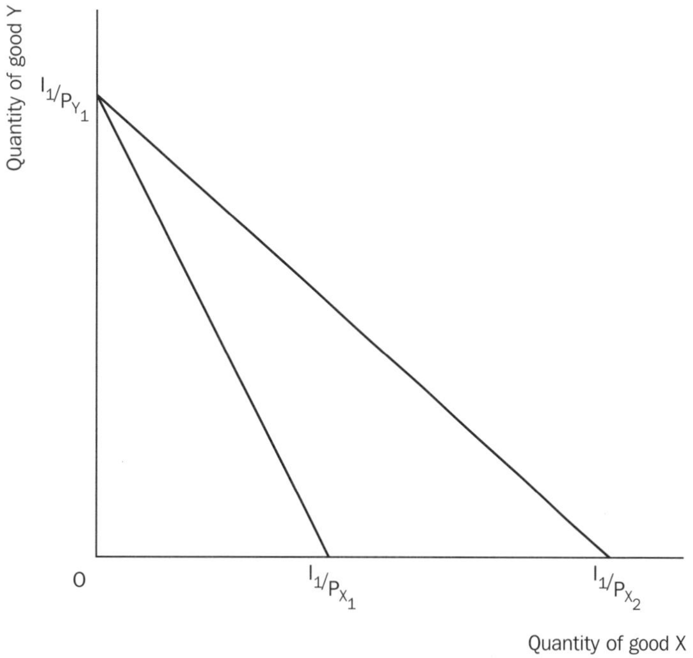

The above highlights the distinction between **money income** and **real income**. For example, a twofold increase in money income, *ceteris paribus*, shifts the budget line outwards. The consumer could now buy twice as many units of goods X and Y than previously. The value of money income and real income (the purchasing power of money) have doubled. Alternatively, imagine money income remains unchanged and the price of both goods halves. This has the same impact upon the budget line: the consumer could again buy twice the volume of X and Y than previously. Although money income is unchanged, real income has doubled. Finally, imagine a doubling of both money income and the price of both goods. The budget line now remains in place. Although money income increases, its real value (real income) stays constant.

The real value of income should therefore be seen in relation to its purchasing power. If money income rises by x per cent yet simultaneously the price of all goods rises by more than x per cent the purchasing power of your income falls. Real income has declined.

### 4.3.3 Consumer optimisation

**optimal** an optimal consumption pattern is achieved when the consumer buys that combination of goods that with given prices and fixed income results in maximum satisfaction

The consumer can choose any combination of goods along their budget line. Consumer rationality (see Section 4.2.1) dictates that the consumer will wish to reach the highest possible indifference curve. Given this information we can predict the consumer's **optimal** consumption pattern.

Figure 4.9 shows a consumer's budget line and three indifference curves. Combinations of goods along $IC_3$ are unavailable to the consumer as they lie

**Figure 4.9 Consumer equilibrium**

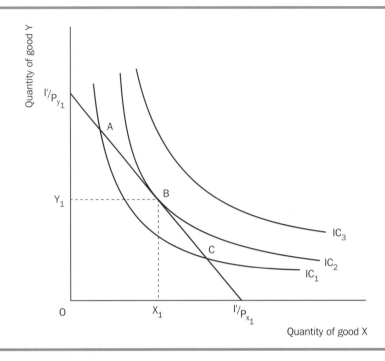

above the budget line. $IC_1$ is available for any combination between A and C. However, in choosing combination B ($Y_1$ of good Y and $X_1$ of good X) the consumer reaches the highest possible indifference curve, $IC_2$. This is a point of **consumer equilibrium**, occurring where the budget line is tangential to the highest indifference curve. At this point, the slope of the indifference curve (the rate at which the consumer is prepared to exchange one good for another and maintain satisfaction) is equal to the slope of the budget line (the market rate of exchange between the goods, determined by their price ratio).

The reason why the tangency solution at B in Figure 4.9 is optimal can be seen by considering the non-optimality of other combinations along the budget line. For example, at A the slope of the indifference curve is greater than the slope of the budget line. This implies that the market rate of exchange of X for Y is less than the rate of exchange of X for Y on the indifference curve. The consumer would therefore be better off moving down the budget line from A purchasing units of X in exchange for Y. This continues to be true up to combination B. Alternatively, if the consumer were at C the slope of the indifference curve is now less than the slope of the budget line, the inference being that the consumer would be willing to sacrifice more units of X than necessary to obtain an additional unit of Y. The consumer should therefore exchange X for Y along the budget line until reaching B. At B, the consumer's willingness to exchange one good for another (as given by the indifference curve) is equal to the market rate of exchange.

Tangency between the budget line and indifference curve requires that:

$$\frac{MU_X}{MU_Y} = \frac{P_X}{P_Y} (= MRS_{XY})$$

**consumer equilibrium**
consumer equilibrium is achieved where the budget line is tangential to the highest indifference curve. The consumption pattern is then optimal and satisfaction is maximised

By algebraic manipulation we can also obtain:

$$\frac{MU_X}{P_X} = \frac{MU_Y}{P_Y}$$

The implication of the above is that the rational consumer maximises utility by dividing income between the goods until the marginal utility per pound spent is the same for each good.

Imagine the above condition is not satisfied. For example:

$$\frac{MU_X}{P_X} > \frac{MU_Y}{P_Y}$$

This implies that the utility per pound spent on X is greater than on Y, and could correspond to combination A in Figure 4.9. The consumer would therefore be better off increasing consumption of X (and decreasing $MU_X$) and decreasing consumption of Y (and increasing $MU_Y$) until equality is regained.

A tangency solution might not always be achieved. For example, we could **corner solution** achieved have a **corner solution**. Consider the indifference map and budget line in where the consumer, when Figure 4.10. For the purpose of this diagram we could imagine good Y to represent all other goods.

**corner solution** achieved where the consumer, when faced with a choice of two goods, chooses to purchase units of only one good rather than a combination of both

The indifference curves in Figure 4.10 are relatively shallow, indicating a preference for Y over X. With the given budget line the consumer maximises utility at A, spending their entire income on Y, buying none of X. At A the indifference curve is shallower than the budget line, indicating that the amount of Y the consumer would be willing to sacrifice to obtain a unit of X is

**Figure 4.10 A corner solution with convex indifference curve**

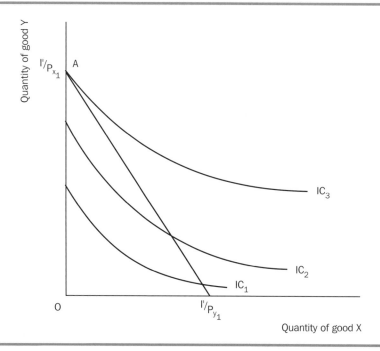

less than the amount required to be sacrificed given the relative prices of the two goods. The rational choice is therefore to consume only good Y.

Consumers commonly choose not to consume all available goods. From a limited income we can only consume a certain number of goods. Other goods that could be afforded are not purchased because to do so we would have to sacrifice others that are even more desirable. Goods currently not consumed might later become consumed (e.g. in Figure 4.10, the price of X might fall, or the price of Y increase, leading to a tangency solution with the consumer taking units of both X and Y). Or consumer preferences might change in favour of X, making the indifference map steeper. Finally, an increase in money income, and an outward shift in the budget line, might lead to the consumption of X.

### 4.3.4 Consumer response to a change in income

We can now use our analysis to examine how consumers react to changes in income or price. Firstly consider the impact of an income change.

As noted, an increase in money income, with constant prices, shifts the budget line outwards in a parallel fashion. The consumer could now buy more of both goods and reach a higher indifference curve. Real income has increased.

Figure 4.11 shows the effect of consecutive increases in income from $I_1$ to $I_5$. From an initial equilibrium at point a the consumer moves to a new equilibrium at b on a higher indifference curve. Further increases in income move the consumer to points c, d and e on progressively higher indifference curves.

**Figure 4.11 The effect of a change in real income**

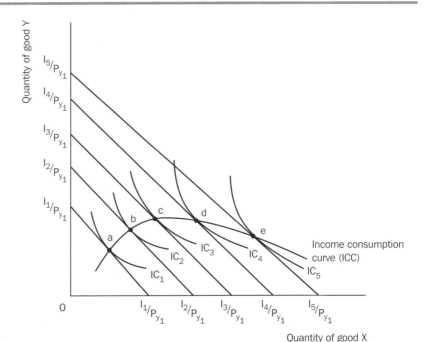

**income consumption
curve** a curve joining
points of tangency between
budget lines and
indifference curves when
the consumer
experiences successive
increases in income

A line joining the points of equilibrium in Figure 4.11 is known as an **income consumption curve (ICC)**. This is the locus of equilibrium points following a change in income when prices are held constant. The slope of the ICC shows how the consumer reacts to the change in income. In Figure 4.11 the ICC is positively sloped indicating that both goods are **normal**. A normal good is one that responds positively to an increase in income, and vice versa. Good Y becomes an **inferior** good from point c to point e. An inferior good responds negatively to an increase in income, and vice versa. Note that good y becomes an inferior good. When income increased from $I_1$ to $I_3$ it was normal although its income elasticity (the proportional change in quantity demanded divided by the proportional change in income) was declining.

### 4.3.5 Consumer response to a change in relative price

Following a decrease in the price of X from $P_{X_1}$ to $P_{X_2}$ in Figure 4.12 the consumer moves from point a on $IC_1$ to point b on the higher indifference curve $IC_2$. The falling price of X increases demand from $X_1$ to $X_2$. This is consistent with a downward sloping demand curve. In Figure 4.12 the demand for Y is not affected by the falling price of X and expenditure on Y must therefore be constant. Further, since money income is constant then expenditure on X must be the same following the price decrease. Price elasticity of demand for X is therefore of unitary elasticity, the proportional decrease in price leading to an equal

**Figure 4.12  The effect of a change in the real price of X** (Note that good Y could also represent expenditure on all other goods other than X)

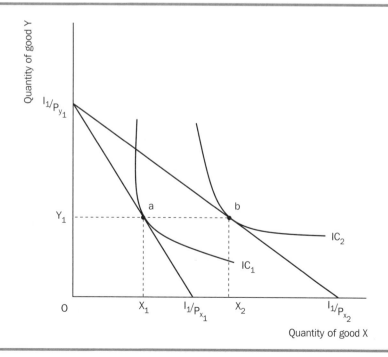

proportional increase in demand. This could also have been seen by imagining the vertical axis to represent expenditure on all other goods than X.

The outcome in Figure 4.12 is a special case. A fall in the price of X could result in the expenditure upon Y (or on all other goods) either increasing or decreasing. The outcome depends upon the slope of the indifference curves, reflecting the preferences of the consumer.

**Figure 4.13  Derivation of an individual demand curve**

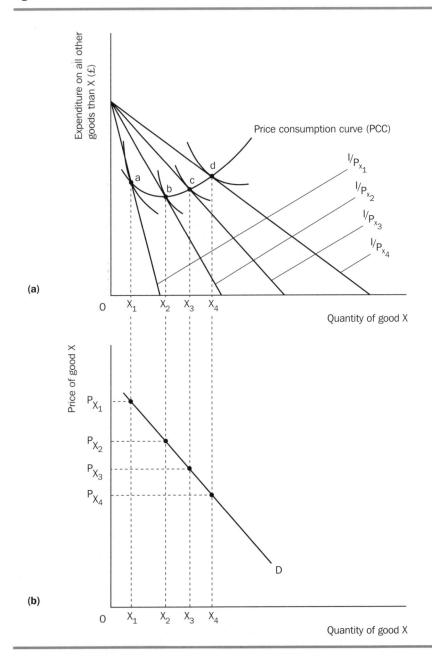

Figure 4.13a shows the effect of consecutive falls in the price of X from $P_{X_1}$ to $P_{X_4}$, income and the price of all other goods remaining constant. From an initial equilibrium at point a the consumer moves to new equilibrium points at b, c and d on progressively higher indifference curves. The line joining these points of equilibrium is known as a **price consumption curve (PCC)**. This is the locus of equilibrium points following a change in the price of a single good when income and the price of all other goods are held constant.

**price consumption curve**
a curve joining points of tangency between budget lines and indifference curves when the consumer experiences successive price changes in one of the goods

As the price falls from $P_{X_1}$ to $P_{X_2}$ in Figure 4.13a consumption of X increases from $X_1$ to $X_2$. The downward sloping PCC between points a and b shows that expenditure on goods apart from X has declined. Expenditure on X must therefore have increased and the price elasticity of demand for good X is elastic: the proportional fall in price leading to a greater than proportional increase in quantity demanded. However, when the price falls from $P_{X_2}$ to $P_{X_3}$, and then to $P_{X_4}$, the upward sloping PCC now shows that expenditure on goods apart from X is increasing. Although additional units of X are demanded ($X_2$ to $X_3$, and then $X_3$ to $X_4$) the price elasticity of demand for X is now inelastic: the proportional decrease in price leading to a less than proportional increase in demand.

The information contained in Figure 4.13a can be used to define the demand curve in Figure 4.13b.

| Mini case | **How the producer might capture consumer surplus** |
|---|---|

Indifference curve analysis can be used to analyse the concept of consumer surplus and show how a producer might use a dual pricing system to capture some of this surplus as additional revenue.

We first introduced the concept of consumer surplus in Chapter 3, defining it as the difference between what a consumer is willing to pay for a good and the amount they actually pay. This can be illustrated in Figure 4.14 where good X is measured on the horizontal axis and the money spent on all other goods apart from X on the vertical axis.

With a budget line AB the consumer maximises satisfaction on indifference curve $IC_2$, consuming $X_2$ units of good X and spending $Y_2$ on other goods. $Y_3 - Y_2$ must therefore be spent on the $X_2$ units of good X. How much would the consumer have been willing to spend to obtain $X_2$ units? This can be seen by drawing an indifference curve to touch the vertical axis at A. Such an indifference curve ($IC_1$) shows the consumer to be indifferent between either spending all their income on other goods and consuming no units of X, or spending $Y_1$ on other goods and $X_2$ upon X. The implication is that the consumer would consider spending $Y_3 - Y_1$ on $X_2$ units of X although only being required to spend $Y_3 - Y_2$. It therefore follows that $Y_2 - Y_1$ represents consumer surplus, the difference between the amount the consumer is willing to pay and the amount actually paid.

Consumer surplus represents a bonus to the consumer, yet a potential loss to the producer. How might the producer capture some of the consumer surplus as additional revenue?

Uniformly raising the price of X pivots the budget line AB downward from point A, and the consumer would be expected to consume fewer units. Total revenue only increases if price elasticity is inelastic. Alternatively, the producer might consider a dual pricing strategy whereby the consumer is allowed to buy a number of units at one price and additional units at a

▶

**Figure 4.14 Consumer surplus and dual pricing**

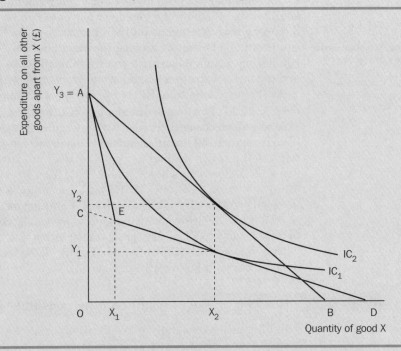

lower price. The advantage of this strategy to the firm is that it can increase total revenue by capturing some of the consumer surplus and yet maintain the level of consumption achieved with the original price.

The possibility of dual pricing is illustrated in Figure 4.14 whereby the first $X_1$ units are offered for sale at the relatively high price reflected by the budget line AE and units beyond $X_1$ at the lower price indicated by the budget ED.

The consumer therefore faces the kinked budget line AED and purchases $X_1$ units at the price indicated by AE and additional units at the lower price reflected by ED. The consumer would spend $Y_3 - Y_1$ to obtain $X_2$ units and the producer captures the entire consumer surplus as previously identified. (Note that in Figure 4.14 the consumer would actually be indifferent between purchasing zero units of X and $X_2$ units. However, the consumer would never buy less than $X_2$ and if the price of additional units were to fall slightly, then X would always be purchased.)

The above pricing strategy was specifically aimed at our individual consumer. As other consumers have different tastes, and therefore differing indifference maps, the same pricing strategy would not capture their entire consumer surplus. Nevertheless, such strategies allow producers to earn more revenue than could be achieved when setting a single price.

Examples of dual pricing are relatively common: for example, power companies charging consumers more for initial units up to a given volume and a lower price for subsequent units. Or, when renting DIY machinery, the rental agreement will commonly specify a lower daily rental for additional days above the minimum daily rate, and extra games of tenpin bowling will usually be charged at a lower rate than the first game.

### 4.3.6 The income and substitution effect of a price change

As we saw in Chapter 3, a price change affects the consumer for two reasons:

1 **The income effect**. A change in price directly influences the value of real income. A fall in price raises real income (and vice versa) as more of the cheaper good and/or other goods could now be purchased from existing money income. The consumer will respond to their increased purchasing power by redistributing their income between goods.

2 **The substitution effect**. A change in relative prices encourages the consumer to substitute towards the relatively cheaper good and away from those that are now relatively more expensive. This is our substitution effect.

The overall effect of a price change is therefore the combined influence of both the income and substitution effects. We can use indifference curve analysis to analyse and isolate these two effects.

In Figure 4.15 the decreased price of X pivots the budget from AB to AC and the consumer moves from an equilibrium at point a on $IC_1$ to point b on the higher indifference curve $IC_2$. The increased consumption from $X_1$ to $X_3$ is due to a combined income and substitution effect. We could assume that a consumer has a constant value of real income when they are able to achieve a constant level of satisfaction. Using this definition we can decrease the consumer's money income following the price decrease and pull budget line AC backwards in a parallel fashion until it is tangential to the original indifference curve, $IC_1$. Such a budget line is DE. As DE is parallel to AC it reflects the new price ratio. A decrease in money income of AD on the vertical axis just compensates the consumer for the increased real income brought about by the

**Figure 4.15  The income and substitution effects with a normal good**

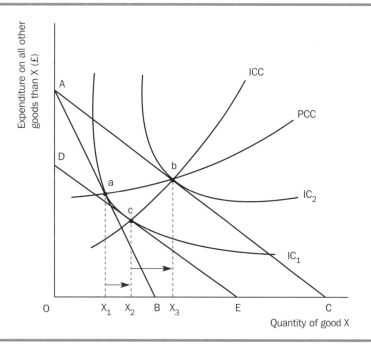

**compensating variation**
the necessary adjustment in money income to maintain the real purchasing power (or real income) of the consumer following a change in price. If price falls the compensating variation requires a compensating decrease in money income, and vice versa

fall in the price of X. This decrease in money income is called **compensating variation**. In reaching equilibrium at point c on indifference curve $IC_1$, the consumer regains their original level of real income and the movement from point a to point c is therefore brought about solely by a substitution effect. $X_1$ to $X_2$ therefore represents the substitution effect. The slope of the indifference curve ensures the substitution effect is positive.

If $X_1$ to $X_3$ in Figure 4.15 is the total effect of the price change and $X_1$ to $X_2$ represents the substitution effect, it follows that $X_2$ to $X_3$ is the income effect. In this case the income effect is positive. Good X must be a normal good. Where the good is normal the substitution and income reinforce each other.

We could also analyse the effect of an increase in the price of X. This would require an increase in money income to compensate the consumer for the decrease in real income brought about by the price rise. So long as the good is normal the substitution and income effects continue to reinforce each other.

Where the good is inferior the income effect works against the substitution effect. This is shown in Figure 4.16.

Using the same approach in Figure 4.16 as Figure 4.15, again assume a decrease in the price of X. Following the price decrease we compensate for the increase in real income by reducing money income by AD on the vertical axis. The movement from $X_1$ to $X_2$ represents the substitution effect. However, as good X is now inferior, the increased real income brought about by the price decrease has a negative impact upon consumption and the income effect is seen as a move from $X_2$ to $X_3$. The income effect therefore works against the substitution effect and we have a net impact of $X_1$ to $X_3$. In this case, the substitution effect is not strong enough to outweigh the income effect and the fall

**Figure 4.16 The income and substitution effects with an inferior good**

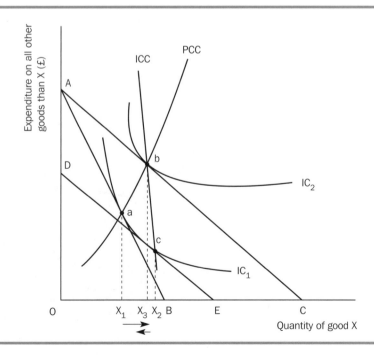

in price still results in an increased demand. However, if the good were strongly inferior the income effect could outweigh the substitution effect. If this were the case then point b on Figure 4.16 would lie to the left of point a and the decreased price of X would result in a lower level of demand. Such goods are referred to as Giffen goods (see Chapter 3).

We have so far conveniently defined constant real income as the ability of the consumer to gain a constant level of utility. There are, however, practical difficulties in this definition as we can only perform the necessary compensating variation where we have a precise knowledge of the shape of the original indifference curve. For example, in Figure 4.15 we only knew how far to pull back budget line AC because we assumed a knowledge of the shape of the indifference curve $IC_1$. If this indifference curve had been steeper we would have required a larger compensating reduction in money income to maintain utility. A shallow indifference curve requires a smaller reduction in money income. A lack of knowledge of the shape of the indifference curve therefore undermines the practicality of the approach. We could, however, avoid this problem by instead defining constant real income as the ability of the consumer to purchase a particular bundle of goods. We can illustrate this alternative definition of constant real income through a simple example.

Assume an increase in the price of student textbooks. This is illustrated in Figure 4.17 by the budget line pivoting from AB to AC. This diagram represents an average student. Book purchases now fall from $B_3$ to $B_1$, the result of a combined substitution and income effect. Imagine, however, that the government is concerned that the impact of the price increase will be a reduction in educa-

**Figure 4.17  The consumption of books following a price increase and a compensating variation** (using a 'given bundle of goods' concept of real income)

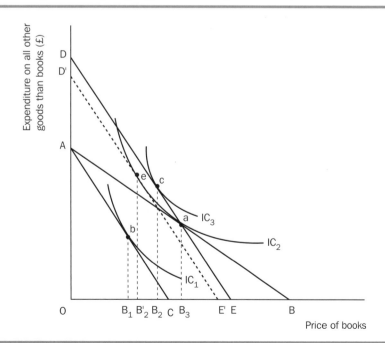

tional attainment and therefore proposes compensating students by providing an additional grant so that students are able to purchase the original number of books prior to the price increase. This involves an additional grant equal to the distance DA on the vertical axis. Such a compensating variation therefore maintains students' real income in the sense that they are able to purchase the original bundle of goods as represented by point a on budget line AB. This definition of real income is as acceptable as our previous definition and has the advantage that it does not involve any knowledge of the shape of the indifference curve. (Such an indifference curve is in fact shown in Figure 4.17 as $IC_2$.)

Although the compensating variation allows a student to regain bundle a in Figure 4.17 they would not wish to do so as the relative price of books has now decreased. The substitution effect comes into play and our student substitutes books for other goods and moves to point C on the higher indifference curve, $IC_3$. This approach again allows us to isolate the substitution and income effects of a price increase. The net effect of the price increase was to decrease consumption from $B_3$ to $B_1$. This can be divided into a substitution effect from $B_3$ to $B_2$ and an income effect from $B_2$ to $B_1$. In this case books are normal and the two effects reinforce each other. Were books regarded as an inferior product, the income effect would work against the substitution effect.

If the government had been able to identify the shape of the indifference curve in Figure 4.17 it might have considered a compensating variation in money income on the basis of constant utility. This involves a smaller compensating variation, AD' on the vertical axis as opposed to AD, and therefore involves less government expenditure. However, the student gains a lower level of satisfaction ($IC_2$ as opposed to $IC_3$) and the purchase of books would be lower ($B_2'$ as opposed to $B_2$) if books are assumed normal. If books were inferior, a compensating variation based upon constant utility results in the purchase of more books although still fewer than originally purchased prior to the price rise.[1]

## Mini case    Advertising and indifference curve analysis

Advertising can be generally thought of as being either informative (telling potential customers of a product's availability, characteristics or price) or as persuasive. A persuasive advert might portray a product as being in vogue, appealing to those of us wishing to be considered fashionable. Similarly, hiring a well-known sports or media personality to **endorse** a product might persuade consumers of the acceptability or quality of a product.

**endorsement**
recommendation of the purchase of a good to others. For example, a well-known footballer might endorse a brand of football boots

In reality it is difficult to categorise adverts as being either solely informative or persuasive. Most adverts contain elements of both, and what might be seen as informative could also be considered persuasive. For example, informing consumers that a new breakfast cereal has added fibre could be seen as persuasive, as there is an implicit message that the consumer should pay additional attention to their daily fibre intake.

In Chapter 3 we saw how advertising could move the demand curve to the right, allowing the firm to either sell the same quantity at a higher price, sell more at the same price, or a combination of the two. How may we illustrate the impact of advertising through indifference curve analysis?

**Figure 4.18 The impact of advertising**

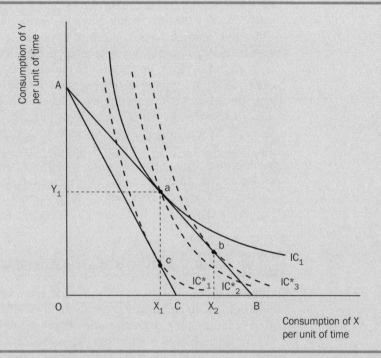

Figure 4.18 shows a budget line AB and the consumer reaching equilibrium at *point a* on indifference curve $IC_1$ consuming $X_1$ of good X and $Y_1$ of good Y. In equilibrium:

$$\frac{MU_X}{MU_Y} = \frac{P_X}{P_Y} = MRS_{XY}$$

Imagine that the producer of good X now embarks on an advertising campaign that successfully improves the product's image, shifting the demand curve to the right. This increases the relative attractiveness of X in terms of Y, the consumer now being willing to sacrifice additional units of Y to obtain X. In short, $MRS_{XY}$ increases for any value of X and we now have a new indifference map $IC^*_1$, $IC^*_2$, and $IC^*_3$.

The advertising campaign therefore increases the gradient of the indifference curves. The more effective the campaign the greater the increase in $MRS_{XY}$ and the steeper the gradient. *Point a* is no longer a point of equilibrium on $IC^*_2$ as $MRS_{XY}$ is greater than $P_X/P_Y$. The consumer regains equilibrium by moving to *point b* on $IC^*_3$. The advertising campaign therefore allows the firm to sell an additional $X_2 - X_1$ units at the original price.

Alternatively, the firm might wish to use the advertising to enable it to sell the original quantity $X_1$ at a higher price. On Figure 4.18 the price of X could be raised, pivoting the budget line to AC, allowing the consumer to obtain equilibrium at *point c* on the lower indifference curve $IC^*_1$. Finally, the firm might raise price less than the above and sell between $X_1$ and $X_2$. Note that in

▶

reality the firm might have difficulty in accurately predicting both the influence of advertising upon sales and the price increase necessary to maintain sales following the advertising. Nevertheless, our basic analysis remains valid.

We saw above how the firm uses advertising to increase consumer preference and raise MRS relative to others goods. In many instances, however, advertising might seek to maintain market position in the face of competitive advertising or other marketing initiatives from rival firms. For example, Firm X's advertising might have been in retaliation to a simultaneous campaign by Firm Y which could have tilted consumer preference towards Y and away from X, make the indifference map shallower, decrease $MRS_{XY}$ and increase the consumption of Y at the expense of X. Firm X's retaliatory advertising campaign might aim as a minimum to maintain the status quo and the original indifference map, or hopefully on balance shift preference toward X and increase $MRS_{XY}$.

## 4.4    Goods and their attributes

Indifference curve analysis can provide some interesting insights into consumer behaviour and business strategy. A specific application of the approach is Kelvin Lancaster's **characteristics approach to consumer demand**.[2]

This approach sees commodities as possessing specific attributes or characteristics. Competing products may possess different characteristics or similar characteristics in differing ratios. The consumer is then assumed to seek satisfaction from those characteristics rather than seeing the good as providing a single well-defined service or attribute. In short, it is the attributes that provide satisfaction rather than the good itself. For example, if purchasing a car the consumer gains satisfaction from the various characteristics possessed by that car including fuel economy, performance, safety, design, reliability, luggage space, number of passenger seats, etc. Such characteristics also act as a constraint upon choice. Thus a consumer might seek a certain degree of fuel economy but be willing to compromise on fuel economy if compensated by additional safety features.

The approach therefore sees utility being derived from bundles of attributes rather than bundles of goods and further the constraints upon consumption are set by incomes, prices and the characteristics of goods rather than just by incomes and prices.

Although commodities generally possess a number of key characteristics we may illustrate the approach by considering a single commodity with two characteristics. For example, the two key characteristics of nut chocolate are the amount of chocolate and the quantity of nuts; or the two characteristics of a daily newspaper might be the coverage of scandal or gossip relative to the reporting of serious news matters. Newspapers might also be seen as differing in their coverage of local as opposed to national/world news. In our example we will consider holiday destinations and assume the two key characteristics to be relaxation and cultural experience. Within our example we will also assume the consumer's expenditure on their holiday to be fixed.

**Figure 4.19  The characteristics approach to consumer demand: holiday destinations**

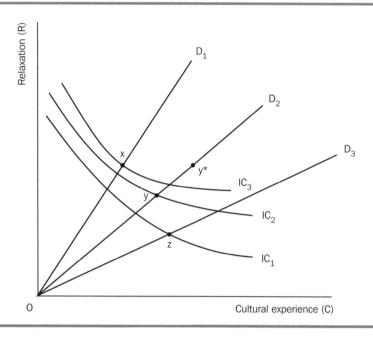

Figure 4.19 shows three different holiday destinations. We assume relaxation (R) and cultural experience (C) can each be measured as an index. They are shown respectively on the vertical and horizontal axes. Each destination has a different ratio of R to C. Destination $D_1$ is represented by the steeper ray, indicating a relatively high ratio of R to C. Destination $D_3$ has a high ratio of C to R and destination $D_2$ comes between the other two. The consumer increases their consumption of R and C in fixed proportions by moving from the origin along one of the three rays. The price of each destination is given by the daily average hotel price. We assume no discounts for additional days in a given location. With a fixed budget the consumer could reach a single point on each of the three rays, either x on $D_1$, y on $D_2$, or z on $D_3$. Each point represents a number of days in that location. If the consumer spent their holiday in only one location, these points represent a discontinuous budget constraint that includes the characteristics of the good, its price and the consumer's available expenditure.

The chosen destination depends upon the consumer's preferences between R and C. This is shown by the indifference map superimposed on Figure 4.19. Each indifference curve exhibits a diminishing marginal rate of substitution between the attributes. The optimal location is $D_1$ as it lies on the highest indifference curve, $IC_3$.

The consumer in Figure 4.19 might change their choice of destination if:

1  *There was a decrease in the price of an alternative location.* For example, as the price of $D_2$ falls, point y moves outwards along the ray. However, price must fall so that we reach y* before the consumer changes their choice of location. A smaller decrease in price has no impact.

This prediction is interesting in that a more conventional analysis predicts that as the price of a good falls the consumer gradually substitutes towards that good and away from other goods whose relative price has now increased. However, in this analysis, the shift is not gradual. It is only when price falls to the point that y* is reached that the consumer shifts, and the shift is then complete rather than gradual. This illustrates the notion of 'brand loyalty' – the practice of continuing to buy a particular brand even though its price has risen relative to other brands. However, brand loyalty can only go so far and if price continues to rise the consumer will eventually switch brands.

The individual's demand curve for $D_2$ would therefore not be a continuous downward sloping function. However, the market demand curve can be continuous as different consumers will have different indifference maps exhibiting their varying tastes. As the price of $D_2$ falls we would therefore anticipate a gradual substitution away from $D_1$ and $D_3$ and towards $D_2$.

2 *The consumer's tastes change.* Consumer tastes might change in favour of cultural experience (C). This increases the slope of individual indifference curves. The $MRS_{CR}$ increases. The optimal destination might now change from $D_1$ to either $D_2$ or $D_3$.

3 *A destination changes its mix of characteristics.* $D_2$ might experience a fall in popularity as consumers increasingly favour R over C. To maintain market share they might therefore persuade their local authority to convert their opera house or museum into a leisure centre. The gradient of the $D_2$ ray in Figure 4.19 therefore increases, encouraging holidaymakers to choose $D_2$. This can be achieved even though the ratio of R to C in $D_2$ is less than $D_1$. For example, in Figure 4.20 the increased ratio of R to C shifts to ray

**brand loyalty** a consumer's willingness to continue buying a specific brand of good despite, for example, an increase in its price or a fall in the price of a substitute. A firm creates brand loyalty by emphasising the differentiated nature of their product

**Figure 4.20 An increase in the ratio of R to C in destination $D_2$**

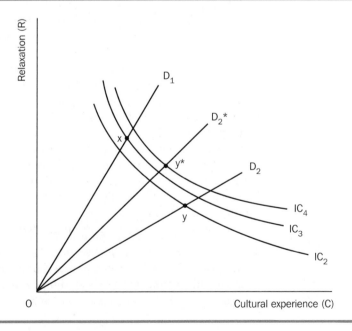

$D_2^*$. The consumer would now change their choice from x days in $D_1$ to $y^*$ days in $D_2^*$ and reach the higher indifference curve, $IC_4$.

$D_2$ could use a combination of the above to attract more holidaymakers. For example, they might decrease price and simultaneously provide a more attractive ratio of characteristics. A new higher ratio of R to C might even allow $D_2$ to increase the price of hotel accommodation and still attract more custom. Alternatively, $D_2$ might attempt to reverse the trend of holidaymakers favouring R over C by improving the quality of cultural experiences on offer at $D_2$.

Note the generality of the above analysis. For holiday destinations we could substitute our previous examples, nut chocolate or daily newspapers. For example, a newspaper might increase circulation by moving downmarket and increasing its coverage of scandal in relation to serious news reporting.

Supplying a large number of brands allows producers to cater for different consumer tastes. Individual producers commonly supply more than one brand, or a variety of a given brand; for example, News International publish both *The Times* and the more downmarket *Sun* and Coca Cola sell both traditional and diet coke.

## 4.5 Combining brands

So far we have assumed the consumer will make a choice between brands where the brand they choose has a fixed ratio of attributes. However, a consumer might be able to combine brands to obtain a more favourable ratio of attributes. For example, a connoisseur of freshly ground coffee might mix together different varieties of coffee bean to obtain a favoured combination of aroma and flavour; or one fruit cordial might taste too sweet and have an insufficiently fruity flavour, another might be too fruity and slightly bitter. Why not buy some of both, mix the brands and obtain a perfect combination of attributes? Finally, instead of spending a holiday in one destination, the holidaymaker could opt for a split-centre holiday, spending a number of days in two or more locations.

We may illustrate the possibility of combining brands through our holiday destination example. Consider Figure 4.21. We previously assumed the consumer to spend either x days in $D_1$, y in $D_2$ or z in $D_3$. Alternatively, a given expenditure could purchase any combinations of R and C on a line between x and y. Points on the line xy also represent combination of $D_1$ and $D_2$. Similarly, $D_2$ and $D_3$ could be combined along yz. Finally, $D_1$ and $D_3$ could be combined along xz. However, xz lies within the boundary xyz and would always be rejected as the same expenditure could buy more of both characteristics R and C. The locus xyz can therefore be considered an **efficiency characteristics frontier**. It is also a budget constraint.

**efficiency characteristics frontier** a locus showing maximum combinations of specific goods at fixed prices with differing ratios of product characteristics that could be purchased from a fixed income. Combining goods in this fashion allows the consumer to achieve a desired overall ratio of product characteristics

Utility is maximised at point k in Figure 4.21 where the efficiency characteristics frontier is a tangent to the highest indifference curve.

The ratio $R^*/C^*$ is achieved by dividing time between $D_1$ and $D_2$. The days spent in each location can be found by:

**Figure 4.21 Combining brands**

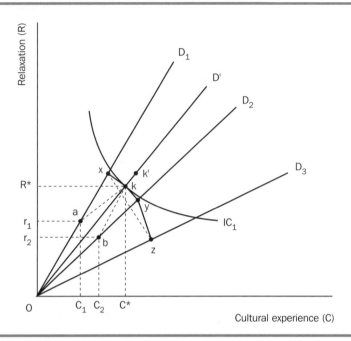

Cultural experience (C)

1 taking a line back from point k parallel to the $D_2$ ray until it cuts the $D_1$ ray at point a. The days spent in $D_1$ equal Oa;
2 taking a line back from point k parallel to the $D_1$ ray to point b on the $D_2$ ray. The days spend in $D_2$ equal Ob.

Therefore:

$$R^* = r_1 + r_2$$

and

$$C^* = c_1 + c_2$$

Figure 4.21 illustrates certain interesting marketing opportunities. For example:

1 If a majority of consumers favour the ratio $R^*/C^*$ our destinations might attempt to adjust their characteristics to achieve that ratio. This appears easier for $D_1$ and $D_2$ than $D_3$. However, although many might prefer the ratio $R^*/C^*$, there could remain a viable **niche market** for holidays providing the ratio of characteristics available at $D_3$. Providing a range of brands allows producers to cater for differing tastes.
2 Combining destinations is possible, yet involves more effort than booking a single destination. (It may also be more costly if the consumer loses any **economies of bulk purchase**.) Travel agencies might recognise the inconvenience of individuals booking such holidays and make available multisite holidays themselves providing an attractive combination of attributes (e.g. a largely cultural week in Rome and a second week in a nearby coastal resort). Where travel agencies book in bulk they might pass on such savings to customers.

**niche market** a specialised yet profitable segment of an overall market

**economies of bulk purchase** the economies or savings to be achieved when buying relatively large quantities of a given good. For example, a hotel might offer a cheaper nightly rate to persons willing to stay for a certain number of nights

3  Producers might see the marketing possibilities of producing a new brand with an attributes ratio R*/C*. For example, if $D_1$ and $D_2$ were two brands of fruit cordial, with R representing fruit flavour and C sweetness, a producer might introduce a new brand D'. If the price of D' was such that point k was attainable the consumer would not make a distinction between D' and combining $D_1$ and $D_2$. With a lower price the consumer shifts to D'. However, D' would not be purchased if point k was not attainable. This illustrates the importance of setting both an attractive mix of characteristics and an appropriate price.

If the price of a brand or destination changes, this represents a change in the price of the attributes that characterise the brand. The price change shifts the efficiency characteristics frontier: for example, the line xy shifts outwards to xy' in Figure 4.22 if the price of $D_2$ falls. We would then expect the consumer to make a smooth substitution towards attribute C, the relatively dominant attribute in $D_2$. The consumer could, however, move from point k to any point of tangency along xy'.

For example:

1  Moving to P results in a constant consumption of $D_1$, additional $D_2$ and an increase in the C/R ratio. Any point to the right of P leads to a fall in $D_1$, even greater $D_2$ and a still higher C/R ratio.
2  Moving to a point between P and N increases both $D_1$ and $D_2$, although $D_2$ increases more than $D_1$. The C/R ratio rises.
3  A move to N maintains the existing ratio of attributes. $D_1$ and $D_2$ increase in the same proportion.

**Figure 4.22  A fall in the price of $D_2$**

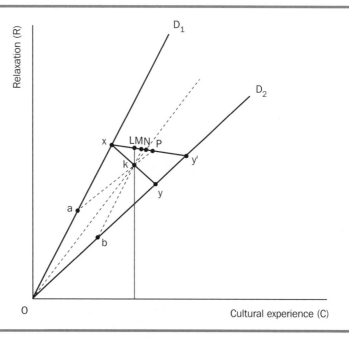

4 Moving between N and M increases the consumption of $D_1$ greater than $D_2$. The C/R ratio falls.

5 A move to M maintains the consumption of $D_2$, even though its price has fallen. The consumption of $D_1$ rises and the C/R ratio falls. However, although consumption of $D_2$ remains constant, the consumption of attribute C still rises.

6 Moving between M and L decreases the consumption of $D_2$ and increases $D_1$. The consumption of C still increases, although the C/R ratio falls.

7 Moving to L further decreases the consumption of $D_2$. Consumption of C remains constant.

8 Moving to the left of L decreases the consumption of $D_2$, the attribute C and the C/R ratio.

The above analysis is interesting, as it shows that following a price change a smooth substitution between brands is possible where the consumer is able to combine brands. When the individual was unable to do so, the response to the price change was either 'all or nothing'. Secondly, the approach shows that although the demand for a brand might fall following a decrease in its price (see point 6 above) the consumption of the attributes associated with that good can still increase. Therefore, although the good can be described as Giffen, the attributes cannot. This observation is interesting as it could be seen to increase the likelihood of Giffen goods and the existence of an upward sloping demand curve.

In conclusion, Lancaster's characteristics approach provides many additional insights into consumer behaviour that a more traditional theory ignores. Whilst a traditional analysis is less comfortable when dealing with brands, most generally treating either all brands as a single good or different brands as separate goods, Lancaster's analysis permits a useful analysis of branding, highlighting the advantage to the firm of aiming its products at particular consumer groups who desire product characteristics in a particular ratio. The analysis also stresses the importance of providing both an attractive ratio of product characteristics and an appropriate price. To identify such an appropriate mix of characteristics it is certainly worthwhile the firm investing time and money in market research. The differing tastes of consumers also provide a rationale for producing a range of brands, most likely at differing prices, each with a different ratio and range of characteristics.

### 4.5.1 The individual's supply of labour

A further application of indifference curve analysis can be seen in an analysis of an individual's choice between work and leisure.

Consider Figure 4.23. The horizontal axis measures the hours of leisure in a given day. Our individual could therefore take 24 hours of leisure and by inference zero hours of work. Alternatively, $L_2$ hours of leisure implies $W_1$ hours of work where:

$$W_1 = 24 \text{ hours} - L_2$$

Income is measured on the vertical axis. In sacrificing leisure in exchange for hours of work the individual receives income. Each hour of work increases income by the hourly wage rate and the hourly wage is therefore represented

**Figure 4.23  Optimal choice of hours worked with flexibility of hours**

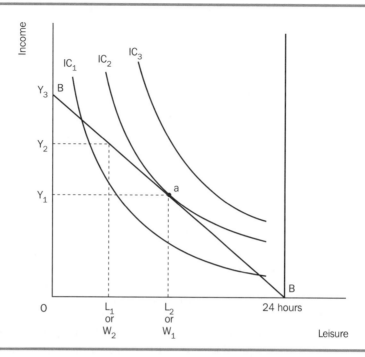

by the scope of the line BB in Figure 4.23. BB can also be considered an income–leisure constraint, and analogous to a budget constraint. BB is seen as cutting the vertical analysis, implying the possibility of working 24 hours in a given day. This is clearly unlikely. In reality, the worker would be restricted to working a maximum number of hours per day setting an upper limit to income. The diagram also implies that if an individual does not work they receive no income. In reality, this would be unlikely as our individual might be the beneficiary of unearned income from previous investments, and/or receive certain state benefits, although many of those benefits might then be forfeited upon employment. The continuity of the line BB also implies a worker's choice in the length of their working day. Once again, this might be unrealistic and we will later analyse situations where the working day is fixed, although additional hours (i.e. overtime) might then be offered at higher hourly rates of pay.

The individual's preferences between income and leisure are shown by the familiarly shaped indifference curves, $IC_1$ to $IC_3$ in Figure 4.23. Each indifference curve shows combinations of income and leisure that provide a given level of satisfaction. The convexity of the indifference curves shows a diminishing marginal rate of substitution between leisure and income. As leisure hours increase, progressively less income is willingly sacrificed. This is consistent with the observation that both income and leisure are goods subject to diminishing marginal utility.

Optimality in Figure 4.23 is found at 'point a' where the income–leisure constraint BB is at a tangent to the highest indifference curve. Our individual therefore chooses to work $W_1$ hours at the going wage rate, take $L_2$ hours of leisure and earn an income of $Y_1$. Hours of work would change if there were a shift in preferences between work and leisure. Thus, if the indifference map became steeper, indicating a willingness to sacrifice more income for an extra hour of leisure, fewer hours would be worked as leisure becomes more valued. This could be due to the worker gaining less job satisfaction, or having discovered more enjoyable sources of leisure. If the marginal rate of substitution of leisure for income continues to increase the individual might forgo all work, illustrated as a corner solution at point B on the leisure axis. Alternatively, if the indifference map became shallower, illustrating a decreased willingness to sacrifice income for leisure, more hours would be worked as leisure time becomes less valued. This might be due to a desire to earn and save more money in this time period in order to work fewer hours (and take more leisure time) in a later period.

Figure 4.23 assumed the worker to have a choice in the length of their working day. However, in most circumstances the offer of work entails an hourly wage rate for a fixed-hour day. In Figure 4.24 we assume an eight-hour day at a fixed wage rate given by the income–leisure constraint BB. The individual therefore chooses between an income of $Y_3$ and eight hours of work, or 24 hours leisure and no earned income. With the indifference curves in Figure 4.24 our individual chooses to work and reaches indifference curve $IC_2$. Not working results in the lower indifference curve $IC_1$. Ideally, this worker would prefer to work fewer hours, sacrifice income and reach a tangency position on $IC_3$.

Figure 4.24 shows the indifference curves being extended until they reach a line perpendicular to B on the leisure axis. This shows for $IC_2$ an indifference

**Figure 4.24 Fixed daily working hours**

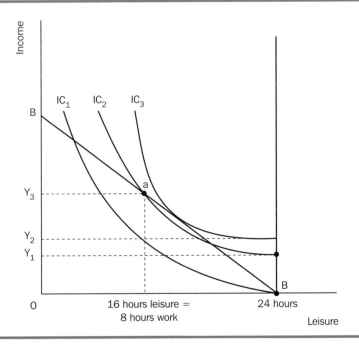

between an income of $Y_3$ and eight hours of work, or an unearned income of $Y_1$ and 24 hours of leisure. However, in not working the worker actually attains utility denoted by $IC_1$ with no unearned income. The gain in utility by working can therefore be seen as equivalent to $Y_1$ in unearned income. If the worker were able to choose the length of their working day and reach $IC_3$ the gain in utility compared to working an eight-hour day would be equivalent to $Y_2 - Y_1$ in unearned income.

As an exercise you should be able to redraw the indifference curves in Figure 4.24 to illustrate situations where either:

1 the worker refuses the offer of an eight-hour working day;
2 the offer of employment is accepted, although the worker ideally wishes to work in excess of an eight-hour day at the going hourly wage rate.

### Variations in the wage rate

A change in the hourly wage rate pivots the income–leisure constraint from the leisure axis. For example, in Figure 4.25a an increase in the hourly wage from $wr_1$ to $wr_2$ pivots the income–leisure constraint from BB to BB'.

The higher wage can be thought of as decreasing the price of income and the consumer will react by increasing their level of income. This would always be the case since income must be considered a normal good. It is, however, more interesting to consider the impact of the higher wage rate on the number of hours worked.

In Figure 4.25a the worker reacts to the higher wage by moving from point a on $IC_1$ to point b on $IC_2$, hours worked increasing from $W_1$ to $W_2$. This results in the upward sloping supply curve of labour in Figure 4.25b. More income yet less leisure is demanded. Income and leisure can therefore be considered substitutes.

**Figure 4.25 An increase in the hourly wage rate, flexibility of hours**

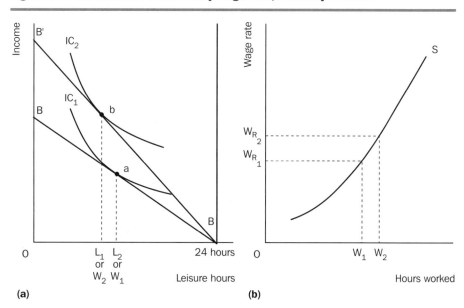

**Figure 4.26 An increase in the hourly wage rate, flexibility of hours, backwardbending supply curve**

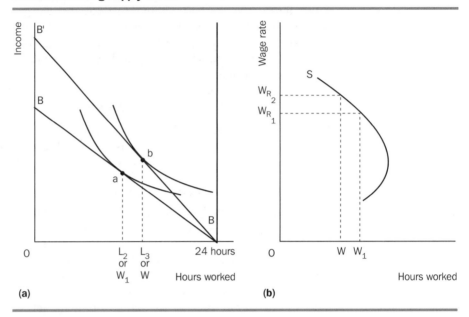

(a)

(b)

Figure 4.26a shows the same increased wage rate. In this case fewer hours are worked, the worker choosing to take more leisure hours though still achieving a higher income. This results in a backward bending supply curve as illustrated in Figure 4.26b. Income and leisure are now seen as complementary goods. (Note that the supply curve only becomes backward-bending at higher wage rates. At lower rates, it must have been upward sloping.)

We can analyse the impact of higher wages upon hours worked by breaking the reaction down into a substitution and income effect. The substitution effect is straightforward as the higher wage decreases the price of income and can also be thought of as increasing the price of leisure. In effect, the opportunity cost of leisure has increased as more income must now be sacrificed to undertake leisure. The substitution effect therefore increases the consumption of income and decreases leisure hours. If leisure were an inferior good the outcome of a change in the wage rate would now be certain as the substitution and income effect would reinforce each other and the supply curve must be upward sloping. However, it is unreasonable to consider leisure an inferior good. If it were, major winners of the lottery or football pools would react by decreasing their hours of leisure! Instead, leisure must be seen as a normal good and the outcome of an increased wage rate therefore becomes uncertain as the substitution effect encourages less leisure whilst the income effect encourages more and vice versa with a falling wage rate. Where the substitution effect outweighs the income effect, the supply curve for labour is upward-sloping. We have a backward-bending supply curve if the income effect outweighs the substitution effect.

We can isolate the income and substitution using the same diagrammatic approach developed previously (see Figure 4.27).

**Figure 4.27  The income and substitution effect of an increase in the wage rate**

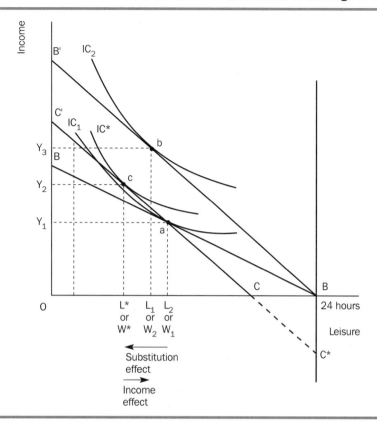

The increased wage rate in Figure 4.27 pivots the income–leisure constraint from BB to BB'. By defining constant real income as the ability to attain a particular combination of income and leisure we isolate the income and substitution effects by pulling BB' backwards until it passes through the original equilibrium at point a. The compensating income–leisure constraint appears as CC' and required a compensating decrease in money income of B'C' on the vertical axis, or the equivalent of a decrease in unearned income of BC* if this individual had been in possession of such unearned income. The movement from point a to c therefore represents the substitution effect, the movement from point c to b represents the income effect. In this case, the income effect fails to outweigh the substitution effect and the supply curve of labour remains upward sloping. The net effect is for hours worked to increase from $W_1$ to $W_2$ and income to rise from $Y_1$ to $Y_3$. If the income effect outweighed the substitution effect the supply curve would be backward-bending. Draw your own diagram to illustrate this possibility.

This analysis illustrates the possibility of workers reacting to a higher hourly wage by reducing the number of hours worked. The employer could, however, avoid this possibility by only offering the higher wage for additional hours worked. Such a practice is referred to as overtime payments, representing a form of price discrimination whereby the employer offers a different wage for different hours worked. For example, in Figure 4.27 the hourly wage rate shown by the income–leisure constraint BB could be offered for the first $W_1$ hours and the higher hourly overtime rate shown by CC' for hours worked in excess of $W_1$. In this instance the worker reacts by working $W^* - W_1$ hours of overtime, reaching equilibrium at point c on IC*. Overtime payments are analysed further in the case study below.

**4.6** ## Conclusions

Indifference curve analysis provides a valuable approach and insights into the study of consumer behaviour. The model can also be used to present a characteristics approach to consumer demand and in so doing provide additional insights into product branding and consumer loyalty unavailable through a more traditional approach. We also used the approach to analyse the individual's choice between work and leisure and show the advantage to the employer of offering overtime payments.

There are many other useful applications of the basic model: these include using it to analyse the relative merits of rewarding employees via either taxable income or extra possibly untaxed fringe benefits, or an analysis of how the consumer might seek to optimally allocate consumption and savings between different time periods.

The basics of the approach can also be extended into an analysis of production with the axes now measuring two factors of production, typically capital and labour. The production equivalent of the indifference curve is referred to as an **isoquant** showing different possible combinations of those factors that could produce a given output of a specified good. The equivalent of the budget line is the **isocost** line showing different ratios of the factors that can be purchased given their relative prices and a fixed productive expenditure. Equivalent conditions of optimality can then be developed to show how the producer can efficiently produce different levels of output and the likely reaction to changes in factor prices, factor productivity, etc.

**isoquant** the production equivalent of the indifference curve showing combinations of two factor inputs that would be required to produce a given level of output of a specific good

**isocost** the production equivalent of the budget line showing the maximum combinations of two factor inputs that could be purchased with a given cost outlay

**Case study** ### Overtime payments

Firms will commonly offer a higher hourly rate of pay for hours worked in excess of the standard contracted working day. This represents a form of price discrimination and can be advantageous to the employer as it can ensure workers will take on extra hours of work. We may illustrate this practice by adapting the analysis used in Figure 4.27. See also Figure 4.28.

With an hourly wage rate represented by BB in Figure 4.28 our worker takes on $W_1$ hours of work for an income of $Y_1$. Raising the wage rate pivots the income–leisure constraint to BB' and in this instance encourages the worker to increase their hours of work from $W_1$ to $W_2$. The employer pays additional wages of $Y_3 - Y_1$. However, instead of paying the higher wage for all hours worked the employer might only offer that rate for additional hours beyond $W_1$. The effect is to kink the income–leisure constraint at point

**Figure 4.28  Overtime payments**

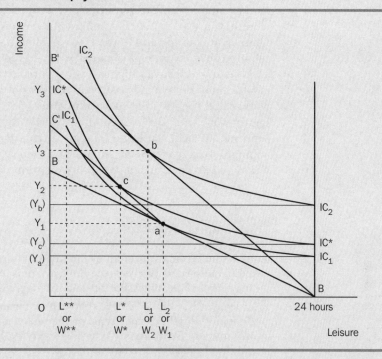

a, the constraint becoming steeper to the left of that point. The offer of over-time payments now encourages the worker to move to a new equilibrium along the steeper section of the income–leisure constraint (ac') where a higher level of satisfaction can be achieved. The new equilibrium is located at point c on IC*, $W^* - W_1$ hours of overtime undertaken for an additional wage of $Y_2 - Y_1$. The movement from point a to c is the substitution effect we previously isolated in Figure 4.27 when analysing the net effect of an increase in the wage rate that pivoted the income–leisure constraint from BB to BB'. The substitution effect therefore ensures the worker's positive response to the offer of overtime.

Through paying higher overtime rates rather than a uniform wage for all hours of work, management gains through a lower wages bill ($Y_2$ rather than $Y_3$) and obtains more hours of work ($W^*$ rather than $W_2$). Given the choice, workers clearly prefer uniformly higher wage rates as they can earn more for fewer hours. Indeed, using the analysis we introduced in Figure 4.24, whereas the movement from point a to b in Figure 4.28 could be seen as providing the worker with additional equivalent unearned income of $Y_b - Y_a$, the move from point a to c is only equivalent to $Y_c - Y_a$. The worker's loss is equivalent to $Y_b - Y_c$.

Our analysis so far assumes the worker to have a free choice in their hours of work, both overtime hours and regular hours. If management were to stipulate a fixed period of overtime hours per worker the offer would be refused if it placed the worker at a lower level of satisfaction. For example, having to take on $W^{**} - W_1$ hours of overtime in Figure 4.26 places the worker on a lower indifference curve than $IC_1$. It is also interesting to consider how a worker reacts to offers of overtime when working fixed regular hours. For example, in Figure 4.24 we noted a situation where the worker, if required to work an eight-hour day, would ideally have worked fewer hours and thereby attained a higher level of satisfaction. In such cases, the worker is less likely to respond positively to offers of overtime. Alternatively, if the worker had been willing to work in excess of an eight-hour day at the going hourly wage rate, they would almost certainly respond positively to offers of overtime. Indeed, you could imagine a situation where such a worker might willingly work overtime at an hourly wage less than the standard rate! How would you present such a possibility diagrammatically?

## Notes and references

1. For a similar analysis of an evaluation of alternative government policies using indifference curve analysis, see Koutsoyiannis, A. (1979), *Modern Microeconomics*, 2nd edition, Macmillan, Basingstoke, Chapter 2, pp. 36–38.

2. Lancaster, K. (1996), 'A new approach to consumer theory'. *Journal of Political Economy*. Further expositions of the analysis can be seen in Dobbs, I. (2000), *Managerial Economics*, Oxford University Press, Oxford pp. 125–127 and Laidler, D. (1974), *Introduction to Microeconomics* 2nd edition, Philip Allan, Oxford, Chapter 8.

## Review and discussion questions

1 Do you believe it reasonable to assume consumers normally act rationally? Can you provide any examples where you have acted irrationally?

2 Use an indifference curve approach to explain why if people generally prefer BMW cars to Ford cars it is nevertheless true that Ford sell more cars than BMW.

3 Draw an indifference map and a given budget line between two goods and show how a successful advertising campaign on one of those goods might impact upon sales.

4 Show how we may use the concept of indifference curves to measure consumer surplus.

5 Under what circumstances might an indifference curve be:
   (a) vertical
   (b) horizontal
   (c) downward-sloping and linear
   (d) upward-sloping.

## Assignments

1 Outline the 'additional insights into consumer behaviour' that can be achieved from Lancaster's characteristics approach to consumer demand compared to a more traditional approach.

2 Show the advantages to the employer of introducing a system of overtime payments. Need workers necessarily require the offer of such payments to induce them to work beyond the length of their normal working day?

## Further reading

Griffiths, A. and Wall, S. (1996), *Intermediate Microeconomics: Theory and Applications,* Longman, Harlow, Chapter 1.

Koutsoyiannis, A. (1979), *Modern Microeconomics,* 2nd edition, Macmillan, Basingstoke, Chapter 2, pp 13–44.

Lipsey, R. G. and Chrystal, K. A. (1995), *An Introduction to Positive Economics,* 8th edition, Oxford University Press, Oxford, Chapter 8.

# Supply, costs and profits

Andy Rees

1 To outline the factors affecting the supply of goods and services.

2 To consider how supply may vary with price and other factors.

3 To explain the notion of elasticity of supply.

4 To investigate the relationship between supply and costs in the short and long run.

5 To consider the notion of scale economies and other supply-related concepts.

6 To see how a firm might achieve maximum profit.

## 5.1 Introduction

**supply** the quantity of a good or service that producers are willing to supply to a market at a given price over a given period of time

**short run** the period of time when at least one factor of production is fixed

**long run** the time period when all factors of production are variable, although technology is assumed constant

In Chapter 3 we outlined the factors affecting the demand for goods and services and considered how demand may vary with price and other variables. In a similar fashion we may now analyse factors that determine the **supply** of those same goods and services and how changes in these factors will influence the level of supply. The time period over which a firm adjusts the level of production is of particular significance and we will distinguish between the **short run** where the firm is faced with at least one factor of production in fixed supply and the **long run** when all factors become variable. We will then see how the level of production in the short and long run affects the cost per unit of output.

Our analysis of consumer demand in Chapter 3 showed us how revenue earned by the firm varies with the level of output. A study of supply permits us to identify the cost associated with that output. By identifying values of revenue and cost at each level of output we can then identify different levels of profit and describe conditions whereby the firm might achieve maximum profit. Whether the firm really seeks a maximisation of profit, or is capable of doing so, is a matter of debate that will be discussed in Chapter 6. Nevertheless, a clear understanding of the factors involved in determining profit is of crucial importance to our understanding and analysis of the firm.

## 5.2    The supply curve

**market supply curve** the
curve illustrating the total
output of all firms in a
market at different prices

The quantity of a good supplied is defined as the quantity firms are willing
and able to supply to the market at a particular price over a specific time
period. Figure 5.1 shows a **market supply curve**.

The market supply curve represents the aggregate supply of all firms producing a given good at a range of prices. Such a curve would typically slope
upwards reflecting a profit motive and the firm's willingness to release more
output onto the market at higher prices. If production costs per unit were to
increase at higher levels of output, the firm would be compensated by the
higher sale price. At prices below $P_1$ it would not be considered profitable to
supply the market.

As in the case of demand there are a number of factors influencing supply
apart from price. The supply function could be presented as:

$$Q_{SX} = f(P, P_{S/C}, C, T, E, N)$$

where:

**contraction in supply** a
reduction in the quantity
supplied as a result of a
price change

- $Q_{SX}$ = quantity supplied per period of time of good X

- $P$ = the price of the good

**extension in supply** a rise
in the quantity supplied as a
result of a rise in price

As noted, due to a profit motive there should be a direct relationship between
price and quantity supplied. A change in price causes a movement up or down
an existing supply curve, known as an **extension** or **contraction in supply**.

### Figure 5.1  Market supply curve

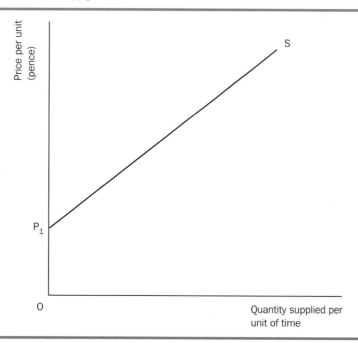

- $P_{S/C}$ = price of substitute and complementary goods

An increase in the price of a substitute would be assumed to decrease output of good X as producers move resources into production of the substitute. For example, if a brewer is producing both beer and lager and there is an increase in the price of lager then resources should flow into lager production and away from beer to take advantage of the increased relative profitability of lager. There is therefore an inverse relationship between the price of substitutes and the supply of good X. The supply curve for good X would shift to the right if the price of a substitute fell, and vice versa (see Figure 5.2).

If the price of a complementary good increased, then producers of this good would increase production, and the supply of good X would rise to match an anticipated increased demand. The goods might be complementary in the production process: for example, beef and leather hides. An increase in the price of beef would not only increase the supply of beef but also the supply of hides. There would therefore be a direct relationship between the price of complements and the supply of good X. The supply curve for good X would shift to the left if the price of a complement fell, and vice versa (see Figure 5.2).

- C = the cost of factor inputs

The consideration of such costs is pivotal to our study of supply. If costs rise, the producer would be assumed to decrease supply in anticipation of lower profits. There would therefore be an indirect relationship between the price of inputs and the supply of good X. The supply curve would shift to the left if the cost of inputs rose, and vice versa (see Figure 5.2). The degree of shift

**Figure 5.2 Shifting supply curves**

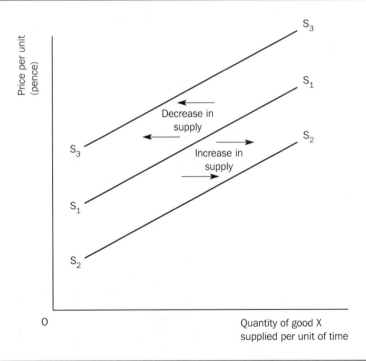

depends upon the size of a factor's price change, the relative importance of that factor in production, and the degree to which that factor could be substituted for others.

■ T = technology

An improvement in technology affects productivity and therefore decreases costs. As above, the reaction should be to increase output and the supply curve shifts to the right (see Figure 5.2). The impact of the technical change is likely to be biased towards increasing the productivity of a particular factor of production. For example, the introduction of robotic production increases the relative productivity of capital and should result in the substitution of labour for capital.

■ E = business expectations

As businesses become increasingly confident regarding the future they are likely to plan for and deliver an increase in supply. For example, a firm producing household furnishings might observe a recovery in the housing market, predict this will shortly result in increased demand for its products, and therefore increase supply in anticipation of future sales. The supply curve shifts to the right (see Figure 5.2) or to the left if firms becomes less optimistic of the future.

■ N = number of suppliers

**homogeneous goods**
where goods are undifferentiated and identical in the eyes of consumers

A market supply curve represents the combined supply of all producers. An increase in the number of suppliers shifts the curve to the right (see Figure 5.2) or to the left if suppliers leave the market. With a market supply curve we should assume those firms are producing an identical good. Whilst this might be a reasonable approach for relatively **homogeneous goods** such as potatoes or basic raw materials, we cannot meaningfully derive a market supply curve where firms are producing **differentiated goods**. For example, although we might measure total market car production, the derivation of a market supply curve presents difficulties.

## 5.3   The elasticity of supply

We noted in Chapter 3 that this could be measured as:

$$E_S = \frac{\text{Percentage change in quantity supplied}}{\text{Percentage change in price}}$$

The value of $E_S$ is positive, reflecting the upward-sloping supply curve. Figure 5.3a shows a supply curve where supply is price elastic, $E_S > 1$, a proportionate change in price leading to a greater than proportionate change in quantity supplied. Figure 5.3b illustrates a situation of inelastic supply, $E_S < 1$, a proportionate change in price leading to a less than proportionate change in supply.

If quantity supplied was not affected by a price change then supply would be perfectly inelastic, $E_S = O$, and the supply curve would be vertical. If any amount

**Figure 5.3 Price elasticity of supply**

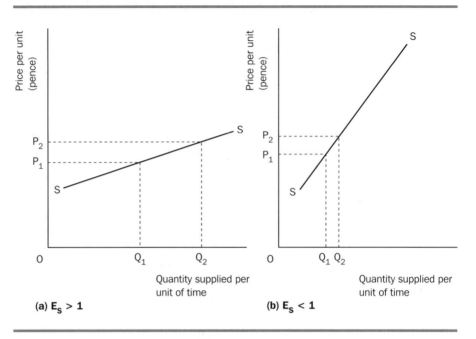

might be supplied at a given price, yet nothing below that price, then supply would be perfectly elastic, $E_S = \infty$, and the supply curve would be horizontal.

As with demand elasticities there is a time dimension to the responsiveness of supply to a change in price, referred to as a **supply lag**. Other things being equal, the longer the time period the greater the value of $E_S$. For example, immediately following a price increase existing producers might be incapable of increasing supply unless they have unsold stock and the value of $E_S$ might approach zero, the supply curve being nearly vertical. In the next period, the firm might hire extra workers to work with existing capacity, or use the existing workforce on overtime. Supply therefore increases. It may also be possible to shift resources from producing one commodity to another. Thus as the price of lager rises relative to beer, then beer-producing facilities might move over to lager. Eventually, supply might increase even further as new firms join the industry and existing firms fully adjust to new production plans. Certain firms might be able to adjust supply relatively quickly to price changes. However, particularly when using relatively specialised factors of production, which might immediately be in short supply, adjustments in supply might be more gradual. For example, an increase in the wages offered to dentists would have little immediate impact upon supply. However, in the longer time period this might encourage more persons to seek dental training, and allow dental schools the opportunity to provide extra places.

We will see in this chapter that the firm's ability to adjust production over the 'short' or 'long run' is a major consideration in our study of factors influencing supply.

**supply lag** the time required to allow supply to adjust to price changes

## 5.4 The production function

It was stated in Chapter 1 that organisations acquire resources – including labour, premises, technology, finance, materials – and transform those resources into the goods and services required by customers. In producing and selling output a firm hopes to earn sufficient revenue to maintain and replenish its resources, therefore facilitating further production which in turn requires further inputs to be purchased.

The production function shows a technical relationship between physical inputs and output. If we assume full productive efficiency within existing technology, then any combination of inputs prescribes a maximum volume of output. The possibility of inefficiency, resulting in less than maximum output, will be considered later in the chapter.

A production function could be presented as:

$$Q = f(K, L, La, M, ...)$$

where:
Q = output over a determined time period
K = capital
L = labour
La = land
M = materials.

For simplicity of exposition we usually present only two factors within the production function, and assume each factor to be homogeneous. For example, all units of labour would be assumed to possess equal skills and be equally efficient. Our production function would now appear as:

$$Q = f(K, L)$$

where K and L would be measured respectively as the units of capital and labour used in the time period of production.

There could be more than one combination of K and L that could efficiently produce a given level of output. For example, Table 5.1 shows how 100 units of Q could be produced using one of three processes.

**Table 5.1 Technical efficiency; three technically efficient methods of producing 100 units of output**

|                   | Process A | Process B | Process C |
|-------------------|-----------|-----------|-----------|
| Capital units (K) | 4         | 6         | 2         |
| Labour units (L)  | 6         | 4         | 8         |

**technical efficiency** a method of production which involves the minimum amount of a combination of different factors

These processes are all **technically efficient** because, although each uses more of one factor than another, it uses less of the other factor. If a fourth process used more of one factor and no less of another it would be deemed inefficient. For example, 3K and 8L would be technically inefficient compared to 'process C'.

As noted, the production function describes purely physical relationships. To see the cost of each process, and identify that process which minimises cost, we must consider the relative price of the factors. Table 5.2 shows the cost of the three processes with capital at £10 per unit and labour £4.

**Table 5.2 Economic efficiency: comparing the cost of three technically efficient methods of producing 100 units of output**

|  | Process A | Process B | Process C |
| --- | --- | --- | --- |
| Capital cost (K) (£10 per unit) | £40 | £60 | £20 |
| Labour units (L) (£4 per unit) | £24 | £16 | £32 |
| Total cost | £64 | £76 | £52 |

**economic efficiency**
economic efficiency in the use of resources requires any given output to be produced at minimum cost

In this case process C becomes the **economically efficient** process. However, the ratio of factors shown in 'process C' would not always be the chosen way of producing the good. For example, it is possible that:

- the price of factors might change (e.g. if factor prices were reversed with capital at £4 per unit and labour at £10, process B would now become economically efficient).
- the relative productivity of factors might change (e.g. if technical developments improved the productivity of capital, firms should substitute capital for labour to take advantage of its increased relative productivity).
- different technologies might become possible at output levels greater than 100 units. (e.g. at low output levels it might be unprofitable to consider high levels of automation, yet such productive methods could be introduced at higher levels of output. Highly automated car production lines provide an illustration).
- increasing output beyond 100 units requires the employment of more factors. In the short run (see below) it may be impossible to obtain more of both factors (e.g. additional capital may be unavailable and the firm can only increase output by employing more labour with a fixed supply of capital. If so, the ratio of capital to labour falls).

The variability of factors is an important concept. The economist defines three distinct time periods when the firm adjusts its productive capabilities:

### The short run

The time period when at least one factor is in fixed supply. Output can only be varied by using more or less variable factors with the fixed factor. With our simple production function containing only capital and labour it is usual to consider labour the variable factor and capital as the fixed factor. In other circumstances it might be land, premises or a particular category of skilled labour that is the fixed factor. The length of the short run would vary from firm to firm. For instance, a bus company might be able to extend the size of its fleet relatively quickly, particularly if bus manufacturers have unsold stock. In contrast, specialised machinery in the textile industry might take a matter of months to obtain and set up ready for production.

### The long run

The time period when all factors are variable, although technology is assumed constant. If capital were the fixed factor the firm may now receive and operate new capital. Note that once such capital is installed the firm moves into a new short-run situation, and can only vary output by using more or less of variable factors with the new volume of fixed factors. As such, the long run can be thought of as a series of short-run situations. It may also be thought of as a planning period as it is in the long run that the firm can plan to set up a new scale of plant.

### The very long run

The time period over which technology might change. It is likely that technical change is biased towards the productivity of particular factors. For example, more efficient machinery may be developed, or more efficient ways of motivating and utilising labour. Any given combination of capital and labour would now produce a higher level of output, or the same output could be produced using relatively fewer factors. As noted above, the firm should now orientate production towards those factors which have become relatively more productive.

We can now analyse production and cost under each of the above time periods.

## 5.5    Short-run production

Table 5.3 illustrates a productive situation where a single good is produced using variable amounts of labour with a fixed utilisation of capital at 15 units. This table introduces us to the concepts of **total product** (TP), **average product** (AP) and **marginal product** (MP). A clear understanding of these concepts, and their cost equivalents, is vital to our understanding of the firm's approach to an optimal production strategy.

**total product** the total output produced from using factor inputs

**average product** the output produced per unit of the variable factor of production

**marginal product** the additional output from employing one more unit of a variable factor of production

### Total product (TP)

Total product rises as more units of labour are employed with the fixed volume of capital. Figure 5.4 uses data obtained from Table 5.3 to draw a total product curve. It is interesting to observe the trend of the curve. As the employment of labour increases, total product first increases at an increasing rate, then at a decreasing rate. The explanation for this can be considered by introducing the concept of marginal product.

### Marginal product (MP)

Marginal product is defined as the change in total product when employing one more or one less unit of the variable factor. For example:

**Table 5.3 Short-run production, total, average, and marginal product**

| Labour (L) | Capital (K) | Total product (TP) | Marginal product (MP) | Average product (AP) |
|---|---|---|---|---|
| 1 | 15 | 10 | | 10 |
| 2 | 15 | 30 | 20 | 15 |
| 3 | 15 | 60 | 30 | 20 |
| 4 | 15 | 100 | 40 | 25 |
| 5 | 15 | 150 | 50 | 30 |
| 6 | 15 | 230 | 80 | 38 |
| 7 | 15 | 330 | 100 | 47 |
| 8 | 15 | 410 | 80 | 51 |
| 9 | 15 | 470 | 60 | 52 |
| 10 | 15 | 510 | 40 | 51 |
| 11 | 15 | 530 | 20 | 48 |
| 12 | 15 | 540 | 10 | |

MP of the fourth unit of labour = TP with 4 units of labour minus TP with 3 units of labour

$$= 100 - 60$$
$$= 40$$

or:

$$MP = \frac{\Delta TP}{\Delta L}$$

**Figure 5.4  Total, marginal and average product**

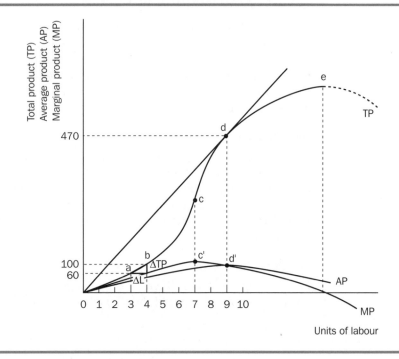

Where:

$\Delta$TP = the change in TP when using one more or less unit of the variable factor

$\Delta$L = the one unit change in the variable factor.

In moving from point a to point b on the TP curve in Figure 5.4, MP could be represented by the slope of the line (known as a **chord**) between a and b (= $\Delta$TP/$\Delta$L). If the units of labour on the horizontal axis were to increase, for example numbering 1 to 120 rather than 1 to 12, then the geometric distance $\Delta$L falls and the length of the chord diminishes. As $\Delta$L approaches zero, a continuation of the chord effectively becomes a tangent to the TP curve at that point. Therefore, a tangent drawn to the TP curve at any point approximates to the value of MP at that level of output. (Note: this is the same geometric approach used in Chapter 3 when estimating the value of marginal revenue (MR) from a corresponding total revenue (TR) curve.)

From our data marginal product increases up to the employment of the seventh worker. Whereas the second worker raises TP by 20 units, the third worker does so by 30 units, etc. It is not that the third worker works harder than the second: recall that we assumed workers to be homogeneous. The reason is due to the **spare capacity** in the fixed factor. In essence, there are too many units of capital relative to the employment of labour and capital is under-utilised. However, as more workers are employed, capital becomes more efficiently utilised and marginal product rises. Beyond the seventh worker MP falls, as there become too many people working with the fixed capital. Capital is now over-utilised, and becomes increasingly so.

A useful analogy might be a worker single-handedly cultivating a very large field. Productivity for this worker could be higher if only a relatively small part of the field were cultivated, yet it is assumed that all the fixed factor (in this case land) must be used. Although the worker tries their best, TP is relatively low. The field is barely dug, planting poor and it proves difficult to keep the weeds down and scare away the birds. The field is not used to its best potential. The fixed factor is severely under-utilised. Bringing in a second worker proves to be beneficial. The additional worker permits a better use of the fixed factor and TP more than doubles. It is possible that a degree of **specialisation** might be introduced, with the two workers fulfilling different tasks. Increasing marginal productivity might continue with the employment of additional labour. However, after a point MP starts to fall. The additional workers are still working hard, but the tasks they fulfil are less productive. For example, taking out relatively small weeds is a full-time job for the marginal worker, yet has little impact upon TP. It is even possible that excessive workers might decrease TP as workers get in each other's way and possibly damage the crop.

The same analogy could be seen in a manufacturing situation on a production line. Employing additional workers on that line could result in output increasing at a faster rate as the capital embodied within the production line becomes better utilised. Eventually, however, the capital becomes over-utilised and output increases at a lower rate than the rate of employment of additional labour.

Figure 5.4 shows the relationship between TP and MP. Up to point c the TP curve is increasing at an increasing rate and the return to the variable factor is increasing. MP is rising. (The slope of a tangent drawn to the TP curve would be rising.) At point c the curve is at its steepest and MP reaches a maximum. This point is referred to as the **point of inflection** of the curve. Beyond point c TP increases at a decreasing rate and MP falls. (The slope of a tangent would be falling.)

**chord** a straight line drawn between any two points on a curve

**spare capacity** spare or excess capacity exists when actual output is below the rate at which all inputs are fully employed. In the short run the fixed factor(s) may exhibit spare capacity in the sense that they are being under-utilised

**specialisation** the tendency to split a job into separate parts to allow individuals to specialise in particular tasks

**point of inflection** the point where the curve moves from increasing at an increasing rate to increasing at a decreasing rate

At point e, TP is maximised. A tangent drawn to this point has no slope and MP is therefore zero. Beyond point e MP is negative and becomes increasingly so. Economically, it makes no sense to employ workers if they have a negative effect upon production.

### Average product (AP)

Average product is shown in Table 5.3.

$$AP = \frac{TP}{L}$$

Average productivity rises up to the employment of the ninth unit of labour, then declines. Geometrically, the value of AP at any point on the TP curve in Figure 5.4 is represented by the slope of a line (referred to as a **ray**) drawn from the origin to the curve. At point d:

$$\text{Gradient Od} = TP / L = APL = 470/9$$

At point d the ray is tangential to the curve and AP is maximised. As the ray is also a tangent then AP must equal MP at this point. Prior to point d, MP exceeds AP as the slope of a tangent at any point exceeds the slope of a ray. Beyond point d AP exceeds MP. The ray is now steeper than the tangent at any point. There is therefore a clear relationship between the marginal and average values. If MP is rising, so must AP. Once MP equals AP then AP is at a maximum, and when MP falls below AP then AP must fall.

**principle of diminishing returns** the idea that as more units of a variable factor are combined with a given number of fixed factors there comes a point where the returns to the variable factor begin to decline

The above relationships are encapsulated in the **principle of diminishing returns**:

...as more of a variable factor is combined with a given volume of a fixed factor then eventually both marginal and average returns to the variable factor must decline.

Diminishing marginal returns set in after point c. Prior to this point marginal returns are increasing. Diminishing average returns set in after point d. Prior to this point average returns are rising.

This principle applies to all productive situations and ultimately the fixed factor places an upper limit on total production. For example, there must be a finite volume of car production from a given car plant, or a maximum number of people who could be served in a particular supermarket. As we approach these finite volumes the rate of increase of total product must decline. The only way of increasing maximum output is through either increasing the fixed factor ('the long run') and/or through technological improvements ('the very long run').

## 5.6 Short-run cost

**total cost** the total of a firm's fixed and variable costs incurred in production

We can now introduce corresponding short-run cost concepts.

**total fixed costs** those costs of production which do not vary with output

### Total cost (TC)

**Total cost** at each level of output is made up of **total fixed cost (TFC)** and **total variable cost (TVC)**:

**total variable cost** those costs of production which do vary with output

$$TC = TFC + TVC.$$

**overhead costs**
unavoidable costs in
a business

■ TFC remains constant at all levels of output. These are 'unavoidable' costs, and often referred to as **overhead costs**. In our example these were capital costs. Other fixed costs might include the rental a firm pays on its premises, the repayment costs of a loan, or money paid to a security firm to guard the premises. TFC is illustrated in Figure 5.5a as a horizontal line. The distance OF represents the value of fixed cost. If fixed costs were to rise, for example

**Figure 5.5 The derivation of short-run average cost curves from total cost curves**

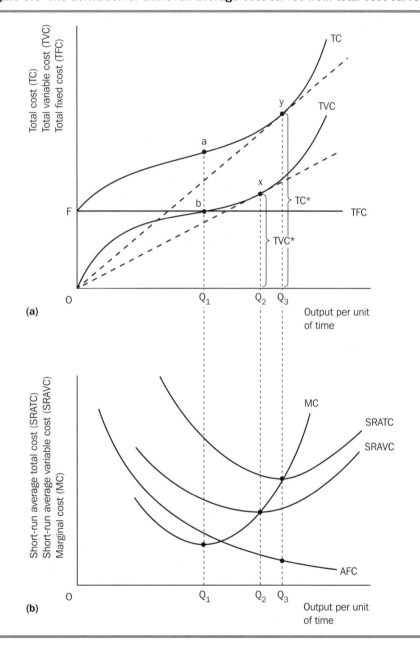

due to an increase in the price of capital, the curve would shift upwards, and vice versa.

■ TVC represents the cost of those factors that vary directly with output. In our example these are labour costs. Other variable costs could include the cost of raw materials and power. A TVC curve is illustrated in Figure 5.5a. The curve starts from the origin as there are no variable costs at zero output. As output rises, TVC rises. Note the connection between the shape of the TVC curve and the TP curve in Figure 5.4 in that if we assume labour the only variable cost, the axes on Figure 5.5 are the reverse of those in Figure 5.4. Output switches to the horizontal axis on Figure 5.5 and whereas labour units were plotted on the horizontal axis in Figure 5.4, labour costs (equal to TVC) are now plotted on the vertical axis on Figure 5.5. As the axes have switched, the TVC curve is the inverse shape of the TP curve. The rationale for the shape of the TVC curve is therefore the same as that of the TP curve. For example, with TP increasing at an increasing rate, TVC increases at a decreasing rate. That is, the increasing marginal productivity of labour means that additional units of output use proportionally less labour. Total labour costs (TVC) are therefore increasing at a decreasing rate. Once diminishing returns set in, and TP increases at a decreasing rate, additional units of output use proportionally more labour. The total wage bill (TVC), then increases at an increasing rate relative to the increase in output.

■ If the cost of variable factors were to rise, for example if wage rates were to increase, the TVC curve would pivot upwards and become steeper at all levels of output, and vice versa.

■ TC lies above TVC at a constant vertical distance equal to TFC. (i.e. TC = TFC + TVC). The TC curve in Figure 5.5 therefore starts from point F and is vertically parallel to TVC. The point of inflection of the two curves is at the same level of output, $Q_1$.

### Average total cost (ATC)

**average total cost** the cost per unit of output

**Average total cost (ATC)** at each level of output (Q) is equal to total cost divided by the corresponding level of output:

$$ATC = \frac{TC}{Q}$$

and as:

$$TC = TFC + TVC$$

then:

ATC = AFC (average fixed costs) + AVC ( average variable costs)

where:

$$AFC = \frac{TFC}{Q} \quad \text{and} \quad AVC = \frac{TVC}{Q}$$

Figure 5.5b shows how values of AFC, AVC and ATC correspond to TFC, TVC and TC.

**average fixed costs** the fixed costs per unit of output produced

- **Average fixed costs (AFC)** fall as output increases. At first, AFC fall rapidly. For example with output doubling from 5 to 10 units AFC per unit halves. At the higher levels of output the impact on AFC of an increase in output is less significant. This is illustrated in the shape of the AFC curve in Figure 5.5b. Although it is continually downward-sloping its slope becomes increasingly shallow at higher levels of outputs.

**average variable costs** the variable costs per unit of output produced

**average productivity of labour** the output per unit of labour utilised

- **Average variable costs (AVC)** first fall and then rise, as illustrated in Figure 5.5b. As the TVC curve was the inverse shape of the TP curve in Figure 5.4, AVC is the inverse of the AP curve. That is, as the **average productivity of labour (AP)** rises, then average labour costs (AVC) per unit of output must fall. When AP is maximised, AVC are at a minimum. As AP falls, AVC rise.

  The relationship between TVC and AVC is shown in Figure 5.5. The slope of a ray to the TVC curve at any point represents the value of AVC. For example, at point x, AVC = $TVC^*/Q_2$. The ray is tangential to the curve of this point and AVC is therefore at a minimum at output $Q_2$. A ray drawn to any other point of the TVC curve has a greater slope. AVC fall as we approached $Q_2$ and rise as we move away from $Q_2$. This is illustrated in the shape of AVC in Figure 5.5b.

- **Average total cost (ATC)** at each level of output is the sum of the corresponding values of AFC and AVC (i.e. ATC = AFC + AVC). ATC therefore lie vertically above AVC at a distance equal to AFC. As AFC fall at higher levels of output AVC and ATC therefore come closer together.

Although ATC has the same general shape as AVC it can be seen from Figure 5.5b to reach a minimum at a higher level of output. AVC are minimised at output $Q_2$, ATC minimised at $Q_3$. The reason is that although AVC increase from $Q_2$ to $Q_3$ the rate of increase is outweighed by falling AFC. As a result, ATC continues to fall. At $Q_3$ the rate of increase in AVC is matched by the decline in AFC, and ATC therefore reaches a minimum. Beyond $Q_3$, ATC rises because AVC are increasing faster than AFC are falling.

The slope of a ray drawn to the TC curve at each point represents the value of ATC. At point y, ATC = $TC^*/Q_3$, and ATC is minimised as the ray is tangential to the curve. At all other points the ray has a greater slope.

### Marginal cost (MC)

**marginal cost** the additional cost of producing one more unit of output

**Marginal cost (MC)** measures the change in total cost brought about by a one-unit change in production:

$$MC = \frac{\Delta TC}{\Delta Q}$$

The value of MC is determined by the degree of slope of the TC curve (see Figure 5.5). TC increases at a decreasing rate up to point a and MC therefore falls as additional units can be produced at less cost per unit. After point a, TC increases at an increasing rate and MC increases. Additional units now cost increasingly more to produce.

From our previous analysis (see MP above), the value of MC can be approximated by measuring the slope of a tangent drawn to the TC curve at each point. MC is therefore minimised at point a, the point of inflection of the TC curve, corresponding to an output of $Q_1$. As only variable costs change in the short run a change in total costs is equivalent to a change in variable costs (i.e. as noted, TC and TVC in Figure 5.5a are vertically parallel). MC might therefore be estimated from either the TC or TVC curves. For example, at output $Q_1$ in Figure 5.5a the slopes of tangents drawn to the TC curve (at point a) and to the TVC curve (at point b) are parallel. These are also the points of inflection of each curve; MC is therefore minimised.

Figure 5.5b shows the relationship between MC, AVC and ATC. If MC is less than AVC then AVC must be falling. When MC equals AVC then AVC is at a minimum, and once MC lies above AVC then AVC must increase. The same relationship holds between MC and ATC. (Note: this is the same relationship between marginal and average values initially illustrated between average product (AP) and marginal product (MP).)

Although MC is defined as the additional cost of producing an extra unit, firms may have difficulty in making such estimates. For example, imagine estimating the cost of producing an extra ball bearing when thousands might be produced in a given shift. Therefore, in practice we commonly talk of **incremental increases in production** and the corresponding 'incremental increase in cost'. This requires estimating the additional production costs associated with producing an extra 'batch' of production, for example an extra thousand ball bearings. Nevertheless, although we may distinguish between incremental cost and marginal cost our basic marginal analysis remains in place.

**incremental increases in production** small additional increases in output

### Short-run optimality

Figure 5.6 simplifies Figure 5.5b in showing only the MC and ATC curves. We may use this diagram to illustrate the concept of short-run efficiency.

Average total cost per unit is at a minimum in Figure 5.6 when the firm produce $Q_3$. This is achieved by combining an optimal combination of variable factors with our fixed factor or factors. This optimal level of output is often referred to as **full or optimum capacity**, i.e. the firm is producing at capacity. The firm can produce beyond capacity, yet in doing so uses a less than optimal combination of fixed and variable factors. The cost of moving beyond optimal output can be seen in terms of higher average costs of production. Similarly, producing less than $Q_3$ also proves less than fully efficient. The firm is now said to be producing with **reserve capacity**.

**full capacity** full or optimum capacity is achieved where all inputs are employed to their optimum efficiency

**reserve capacity** where the firm is not fully utilising its factors of production. By increasing production the firm could achieve increased efficiency

Firms may nevertheless plan to produce with a degree of reserve capacity to cater for variability in demand. Thus, if a lower division football club was planning a new stadium, it would be likely to specify a seating capacity in excess of current average attendance figures to cater for increased demand, particularly if it anticipated gaining promotion to a higher division. Manufacturers may similarly currently produce with spare capacity in anticipation of higher future levels of demand brought about by improving market conditions. Alternatively, the firm could cater for changing demand by stock inventory policy: building up or running down stock. Such a strategy can however, be less efficient than the ability to adjust output.

Although possessing a degree of spare capacity may appear attractive, our analysis, as demonstrated in Figure 5.6, indicates that the cost of doing so is higher average costs of production than if producing at capacity. However, the basic U-shaped cost curves of traditional theory have consistently been questioned on empirical grounds as firms are often observed to be able to vary

**Figure 5.6  Short-run efficiency**

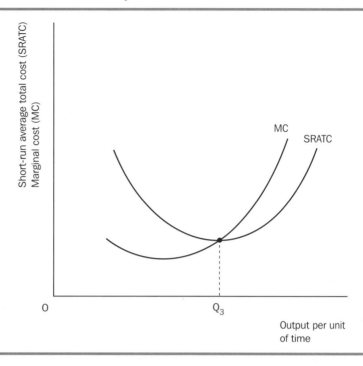

output over a given range of output at constant marginal cost, implying the short-run AVC curve to be 'saucer-shaped' over that range. This is illustrated in Figure 5.7.

Before considering Figure 5.7 it should be recalled that an important basic assumption of our original analysis was that all of the fixed factor was used in combination with the variable inputs (e.g. a single worker cultivating a large field or a relatively small number of workers operating a given production line). In such a case, the fixed factor is referred to as being **indivisible**.[1] However, in many productive situations the fixed factor might be **divisible**. Thus a single agricultural worker could avoid the under-utilisation of the fixed factor by only cultivating a portion of the available acreage and in so doing increase his or her productivity. Greater amounts of land only come under cultivation as the labour force increases. **Diminishing marginal returns** now only set in once the whole of the fixed factor is used.

Divisibility of the fixed factor can be observed in many productive situations. In a mail order business, for instance, a firm might employ one operative per telephone line linked to a computer terminal. Imagine there were ten such combinations, with each operative on average efficiently handling 50 calls per day. If business falls by 100 calls per day, management might lay off two employees and leave their telephones and computers idle. It would not be efficient to ask the remaining employees to cover those two telephone lines; instead business would be transferred to the remaining eight lines. If business were to return to 500 calls a day then two workers might be re-employed and the two capital units (telephones and computers) brought back into production. However, if demand increased beyond 500 calls this might necessitate

**indivisible** the impossibility of dividing a factor into smaller units

**divisible** a factor is seen to be divisible when it can be employed in discrete (small) units

**diminishing marginal returns** when one or more factors of production are fixed there comes a point when the extra output from using additional units of a variable factor starts to diminish

**Figure 5.7 Saucer-shaped cost curves: AVC and MC**

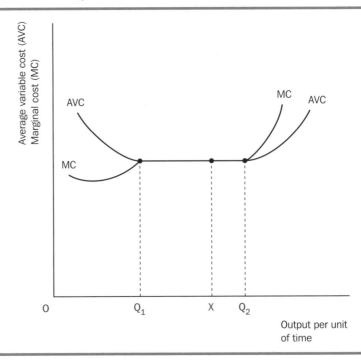

extending overtime for existing operatives. Or, although it would be difficult to employ more than one operative per telephone, the company might consider employing additional workers to cover the telephones when their operatives are taking breaks.

In the above example the divisibility of the fixed factor results in the proportion of fixed to variable factors remaining constant over a range from 50 to 500 calls. AVC and MC are therefore constant over that range of output.

Despite the simplicity of our mail order example, it nevertheless illustrates the possibility of fixed factor divisibility. In essence the firm plans to provide itself with a degree of reserve capacity to enhance flexible production. Such a situation is illustrated in Figure 5.7 where between $Q_1$ and $Q_2$ then AVC = MC. Over this range of output the firm is considered to have planned reserve capacity. Although the firm anticipates producing between $Q_1$ and $Q_2$, firms usually consider their **normal capacity utilisation** (or **load factor**) to be approximately two-thirds from $Q_1$ to $Q_2$ at output X in Figure 5.7.

**normal capacity utilisation** the level of output the firm would normally seek to produce at its current capacity. Also called the 'load factor'

The above reserve capacity is different in nature from that first referred to in Figure 5.6. In traditional theory, with inflexible fixed factors, the plant is designed to produce optimally at a single level of output and producing with excess capacity results in higher variable costs per unit produced.

Although divisibility of fixed factors can result in a horizontal section of the AVC curve, ATC continues to decline over this output range due to decreasing AFC. i.e.: although certain units of the fixed factor may not be used when the firm produces at normal capacity utilisation they nevertheless represent a cost to the firm. ATC still equals AFC + AVC, as illustrated in Figure 5.8. Note that MC intersects ATC at its lowest point, at an output to the right of $Q_2$.

**Figure 5.8  Saucer-shaped cost curves: AFC, AVC, ATC and MC**

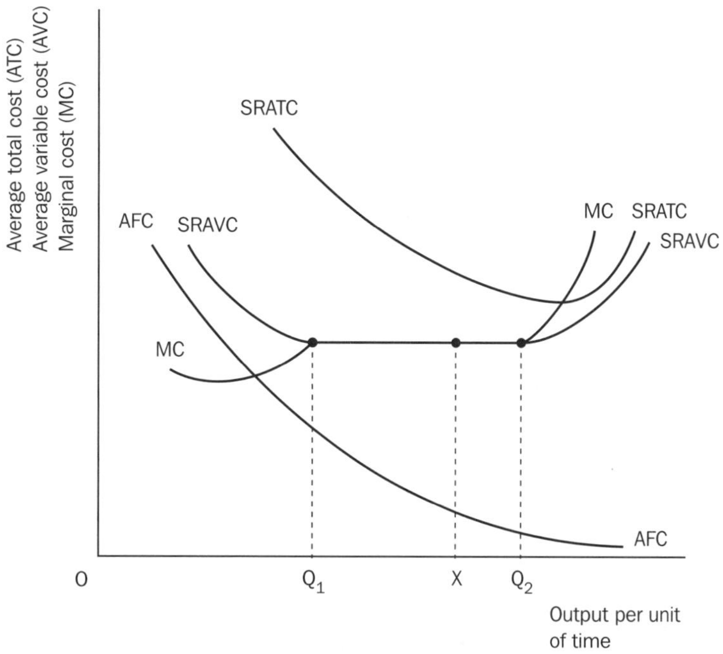

## 5.7  Long-run costs

Where the firm produces in excess of full capacity or normal capacity utilisation it may consider increasing its scale of operations. In the long run all factors become variable and the firm is able to change the scale of plant, for example by moving to a new production site. Alternatively, a business might consider decreasing its scale of operations if consistently producing at less than full capacity.

If firms were able to continually change all their factor inputs they might avoid diminishing returns to the variable factor and constantly ensure minimum production costs. However, the constant adjustment of all factors is not feasible, as it typically takes time to finance, order and install additional fixed factors. Therefore, having adjusted its fixed factors the firm is now in a new short-run situation and changes output by again employing more or less of the variable factors. As noted above, the long run in effect becomes a series of short-run situations and can be considered a planning period since it is in the long run that the business is able to plan a change in its scale of operations. Its decision to change the **scale of production** is clearly of importance, as it involves a significant further investment. If contemplating such an investment a firm should therefore be confident that current levels of demand will be maintained or the potential for higher future demand really exists.

Firms will also be aware that the scale of production can influence their average cost per unit produced. Changing the scale of production can also affect productive efficiency. There are three possibilities:

**scale of production** the amount a firm is able to produce in relation to its size

**constant returns to scale** where output increases in the same proportion as the employment of inputs

**increasing returns to scale** where output rises at a greater rate than the employment of inputs

**decreasing returns to scale** where output increases at a slower rate than the employment of inputs

- **constant returns to scale** – output increases in the same proportion as the employment of inputs. Average cost of production remains unaltered so long as factor prices remain constant.
- **increasing returns to scale** – output increases at a greater rate than the employment of inputs. Average cost of production falls with constant factor prices.
- **decreasing returns to scale** – output increases at a slower rate than the employment of inputs. Average cost of production increases with constant factor prices.

When measuring returns to scale we assume (as above) that all factor inputs are changed in the same proportion, i.e. maintaining the ratio between factor inputs. In reality (as seen in Section 5.4) this might not be the case since at higher output levels new technologies might become possible requiring a different ratio of factors. In our definition of returns to scale we will nevertheless maintain this assumption.

**short-run cost curve** a curve showing the relationship between a firm's output and costs in the short run

Each scale of plant is associated with a short-run cost curve. Changing the fixed factor allows a new scale of plant and a new **short-run cost curve**. The position of the new cost curve shows whether the firm is experiencing constant, increasing or decreasing returns to scale.

Figure 5.9 shows three short-run average cost curves, $SRAC_1$, $SRAC_2$ and $SRAC_3$, each successive curve denoting a larger scale of plant. These curves are of the 'traditional' type previously presented in Figure 5.6. As the scale of plant increases, the corresponding SRAC shifts downwards and to the right, indicating increasing returns to scale are being achieved.

If the firm wishes to produce output $Q_1$ then it could do so by either:

1 Using $SRAC_1$ with an average cost per unit of $C_3$, and producing above capacity;
2 Using $SRAC_2$ with an average cost of $C_2$, and producing at optimum capacity;
3 Using $SRAC_3$ with an average cost of $C_1$, and producing with excess capacity.

**long-run average cost curve** the curve showing the firm's average costs of production over the long run

The envelope of the short-run curves denotes the **long-run average cost curve** (LRAC). In this case the long-run curve has a scalloped shape. Increased divisibility of the fixed factors would provide a larger number of short-run curves and the LRAC becomes smooth, as illustrated in Figure 5.10.

**diseconomies of scale** where average costs of production begin to rise as the scale of production increases

From Figure 5.10 we observe that as the firm increases the scale of output to $Q_1$ then increasing returns to scale (or **economies of scale**) are achieved. Beyond $Q_1$ we have decreasing returns to scale (or **diseconomies of scale**). At $Q_1$ scale economies are exhausted and long-run average costs of production are minimised. At this point the corresponding SRAC is at optimum capacity. With a smooth LRAC any output less than $Q_1$ must correspond to a point on a SRAC with excess capacity, and beyond $Q_1$ to a point on a SRAC above capacity.

Figure 5.10 also shows the long-run marginal cost curve (LRMC) corresponding to the LRAC. This cuts the LRAC at its minimum point and has the same relationship to LRAC as a short-run MC to a corresponding SRAC. If the firm were to experience constant returns to scale over a given range of output (see Figure 5.11), LRAC and LRMC coincide.

If, in Figure 5.11, the firm produces at an output between $Q_1$ and $Q_2$ it is fully exploiting scale economies and producing optimally. Such optimality

**Figure 5.9  The relationship between short- and long-run average cost curves, increasing returns to scale**

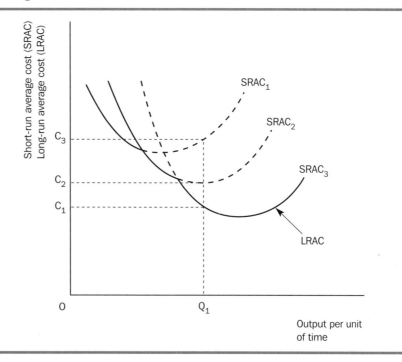

**Figure 5.10  The long-run average cost and long-run marginal cost curves**

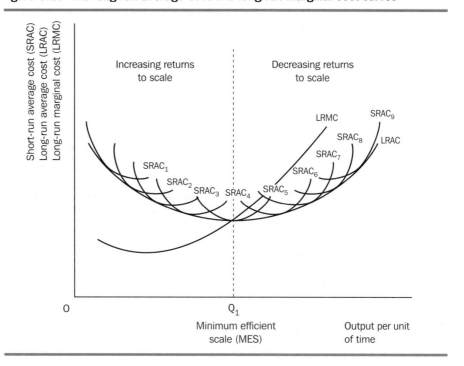

**Figure 5.11 Decreasing, constant and increasing returns to scale**

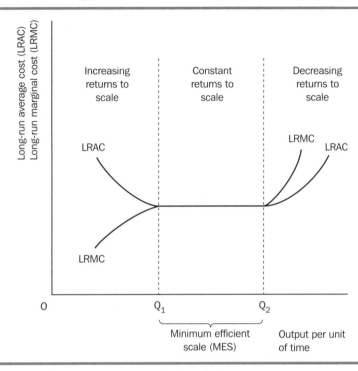

**minimum efficient scale**
the size of a firm or unit of a
firm beyond which there are
no additional economies of
scale to be obtained

could therefore be achieved with a range of plant sizes. With a U-shaped
LRAC (see Figure 5.10) there is a single optimal level of output and therefore
a single optimal scale of plant. When producing at minimum LRAC the firm is
said to be producing at **minimum efficient scale (MES)**.147

**internal economies of
scale** economies that arise
within the firm as it
increases its scale of
operations

## 5.8 The explanation for scale economies

We may distinguish between various types and sources of scale economy,
specifically:

**non-pecuniary economies**
economies resulting from a
proportional reduction in the
physical quantity of factor
inputs relative to output,
also known as technical
economies or real
economies

- **internal economies of scale** – economies internal to the firm resulting from
  a more efficient utilisation of resources. Can be pecuniary or non-pecuniary
  (see below).

**pecuniary economies**
savings available to the firm
which relate to the effect of
size on the price paid for
factor inputs

- **non-pecuniary economies** or **technical economies** or **real economies** –
  economies brought about by a proportional reduction in the physical quantity of factor inputs relative to output.
- **pecuniary economies to scale** – usually achieved at the firm level, referring
  to the effect of size on the price paid for factor inputs.

**external economies of
scale** where a firm's
average costs decrease as
the size of the industry in
which it operates grows

- **external economies of scale** – economies brought about by the growth or
  concentration of the industry.

The source and type of scale economy is exceedingly wide. Outlined below are
some of the main features.

### 5.8.1 **Non-pecuniary economies or 'technical economies' or 'real economies'**

#### Specialisation and 'flexible manufacturing'

At higher levels of output the firm can employ more specialised factors of production, both labour and capital. The advantages of such specialisation are well known and were analysed by Adam Smith as long ago as the eighteenth century, when he outlined the advantages of the 'division of labour' in the manufacture of pins. Specifically, with each worker undertaking just one of the tasks involved in production, productivity was enhanced. Workers did not need to move between tasks, repetition of a task improved performance, and management could allocate tasks relative to the inherent skills of individual workers. This same principle can be seen in modern production line technologies. Similar advantages are also found in the division of managerial tasks. For example, as a small firm expands, the owner/manager, who initially might undertake a general management function encompassing finance, production, marketing and personnel, is now able to employ specialists with specific management skills. The owner can now concentrate on that function, perhaps production design, where her or his comparative productivity is greatest.

The same advantages of specialisation can be seen in the employment of capital. Specialised capital equipment might only be economically justified at high volumes of output. For example, a small manufacturer might have to utilise a single average-sized fork lift truck which might be too large for certain tasks and too small for others. The firm could not justify the purchase of a range of trucks with differing capacities and capabilities as they would not be sufficiently utilised. However, a larger concern could justify such a purchase.

The epitome of capital specialisation is seen in production line technologies utilising highly specialised capital equipment dedicated to individual productive tasks. There can, however, be disadvantages in capital becoming too specialised as this might not allow the firm sufficient flexibility in production to cater for changing market demands. In fact, rather than producing large volumes of a standardised product, the firm may seek the ability to produce a variety of output, each batch of output possessing particular characteristics appealing to different consumer groups. For example, a car manufacturer will seek to use the same plant and equipment to produce various models of a particular car, including estates, hatchbacks, coupés, and cars with or without sun-roofs and in different colours, with a variety of engine sizes. Similarly, a firm producing electric elements for kettles will seek to use the same equipment to produce elements for deep-fat fryers, etc. To achieve productive flexibility the firm requires flexible capital that can be adapted to producing a range of commodities: capital becomes less 'dedicated' to a single product. This may also allow firms to avoid the cost of using capital below capacity since the same capital may be switched to producing a different product. It should be noted that **flexible production methods** also require a flexible, multiskilled workforce and there can be disadvantages in labour becoming over-specialised in so far as the possession of single skills might not lend itself to adaptability in production.

When firms achieve flexible production they are said to be benefiting from **economies of scope**. The firm now produces a range of output at volume rather than producing a single type of output at volume. The concept of economies of scale is therefore still relevant within flexible production.

**flexible production** a production process capable of responding to changes in consumer demand

**economies of scope** economies associated with producing a range of products rather than a single product

### Large initial outlays on individual projects

Modern mechanised production techniques are typically highly capital intensive, involving significant initial capital investment. Using such technologies at relatively low levels of output can be relatively expensive, for whilst variable costs might be low they would be offset by high average fixed costs. Such specialised equipment only really becomes profitable when working at full capacity (see also the concept of 'indivisibilities' referred to below.

Expenditure on research and development can be considered a fixed cost and can represent a considerable investment, as with the large sums involved in developing a new car engine or other car components or the cost of developing and testing a new pharmaceutical drug prior to commercial launch. The firm may therefore need to subsequently sell relatively large volumes to achieve an acceptably low research and development cost per unit. Advertising may also generally be considered a fixed cost and to be effective on a national basis may involve considerable outlay. Again, to justify such expenditure the firm must sell relatively large volumes.

### Increased dimensions

The basis of this principle can be best illustrated through a simple example as follows.

> Imagine an open-topped water tank 2 metres square made of a given thickness of galvanised metal. If the cost of the tank were seen purely in terms of its constituent materials then cost would be represented by the cost of 20 square metres of galvanised metal (i.e. five sides multiplied by 4 square metres). However, the productivity of the tank should be seen in terms of its cubic capacity, 8 cubic metres (i.e. 2 metres cubed).
>
> If we increase the size of the tank to 4 metres square then material cost rises to 80 square metres (a fourfold cost increase), yet cubic capacity rises to 64 cubic metres (an eight fold increase in productivity). The material in the large tank compared to the smaller therefore halves from 2.5 to 1.25 square metres of galvanised metal per cubic unit of capacity. So long as the large tank uses the same thickness of material, and construction costs are not dissimilar with large tanks, the relationship between surface area and volume represents a clear saving.

**economies of increased dimension** savings resulting from increasing the size of a product or process

The same **economies of increased dimension** can be seen in transport (e.g. the advantage of large oil tankers, juggernaut lorries, etc). It also helps to explain how heat loss is less per unit of capacity in larger buildings, as such a loss takes place through the outside walls. By the same principle, in a harsh winter small birds are more likely to die than larger birds as their heat loss per unit of body volume is greater. The principle of economies via increased dimension can be a significant source of scale economy.

**indivisibilities** indivisibilities in production exist where certain factors have to be employed as relatively large single units

**balanced production** balanced production is found when efficiency is achieved at each stage of production

### 'Balanced production' and 'indivisibilities'

Process-based industries typically involve inputs going through discrete stages of production where at each stage the firm may employ specialised machinery with differing capacities. **Indivisibilities** might then exist in the machinery at each stage, for although you could duplicate production by purchasing additional machines it is not efficient to run machines at less than full capacity. To promote efficiency the firm would then be concerned to promote **balanced production**.

For instance, assume a production process with three stages, each using different technologies such that:

|  | Stage 1 | Stage 2 | Stage 3 |
|---|---|---|---|
| Machine units per hour | 10 | 20 | 30 |

'Balanced production' could then be achieved by using machines in the following ratio:

|  | Stage 1 | Stage 2 | Stage 3 |
|---|---|---|---|
| Ratio of machines for balanced production | 6 | 3 | 2 |

Balance could therefore be achieved at 60, 120 or 180, etc. units per hour. Producing other levels of output results in idle capacity. Efficient production therefore requires a certain scale of production.

### Reserve capacity economies

Machinery breakdown is disruptive and the firm may keep machinery in reserve to substitute for others if they break down or require servicing. If the firm employs only one machine at each stage of production this may necessitate holding another in reserve. However, given some knowledge of the probability of machine breakdown, the firm should be able to proportionally reduce the number of reserve machines as the number of machines in use increases. For example, six active machines might still warrant only one in reserve.

To cater for unforeseen demand firms also hold stock (inventories) of materials and finished products. However, as with machines held in reserve, it is generally found that although the necessity to do so increases with the size of the firm it does so in decreasing proportion to the increase in output, since positive and negative 'random changes' in consumer demand tend to be 'smoothed out' or increasingly 'balanced' as the number of consumers increases, in effect allowing the firm to hold proportionally lower stocks. Thus if a newsagent sells an average of only four copies each week of *The Economist* he/she might consider holding a further copy in reserve for an unexpected purchase. However, with weekly sales of 20 this might only require a reserve of two copies, not five.

### 5.8.2 Pecuniary economies to scale

When deriving the LRAC we traditionally assume that factor prices and technology remain constant. A downward-sloping LRAC is therefore due to output increasing faster than the proportionate increase in inputs. (i.e. due to 'technical' or 'real economies' as outlined above). A change in factor prices or technology therefore shifts the entire LRAC. Further, a change in relative factor prices should result in factor substitution (e.g. an increase in the price of labour relative to capital should encourage a substitution of capital for labour).

There are various sources of pecuniary economy, including the following.

### Bulk buying of inputs

Larger firms can obtain discounts when purchasing large volumes of inputs: an example is the purchasing power exerted by the large supermarkets.

### External finance

Large firms can provide greater security and typically obtain finance at lower rates of interest and on more favourable terms. They are also likely to be public companies and have access to relatively cheaper sources of finance via the equity market. Further, when raising capital through a share issue the fixed administrative costs of doing so decrease proportionally the greater the size of the share issue.

### Sales and distribution

Firms advertising on a large scale can negotiate lower advertising rates. Large firms may also be able to negotiate preferential haulage rates from distribution companies or set up their own distribution network.

## 5.8.3 External economies of scale

Whereas economies referred to so far relate to the internal workings of the firm, **external economies** appear at the industry level. They are a function of the size of the industry and are available to all firms within that industry, most commonly where the industry is geographically concentrated. Such economies could include the following.

### Labour supply

Regional training centres might be set up and local traditions and culture can encourage and develop relevant skills. In a textile-producing area, for example, local colleges may supply relevant training programmes and family ties and connections encourage generations of workers to seek work in the local industry.

### Suppliers

Component suppliers, consultancy firms, specialised financial services, haulage firms, etc. are likely to locate in the close vicinity. Such proximity, and the specialised services provided, can prove advantageous.

### Social infrastructure

Governments and local authorities often encourage firms to relocate geographically by providing favourable social infrastructure such as good transport links. Other examples of social infrastructure include housing, schools and training facilities. The lack of adequate infrastructure can involve the firm in additional cost.

## 5.9    Learning effects

Whereas scale economy refers to the influence of a firm's size upon unit costs of production, it is also found that firms can achieve benefits from accumulated productive experience. In effect, learning by doing may lead the firm to introduce more efficient productive and managerial methods or change product design and benefit from fewer and cheaper components. The workforce can also become more efficient through its experience of the productive process.

Figure 5.12 illustrates the general principle, with the horizontal axis measuring accumulated output rather than a given volume of output. The firm achieves learning economies as it accumulates output over time.

**Figure 5.12  The learning curve, falling average cost as a function of cumulative output**

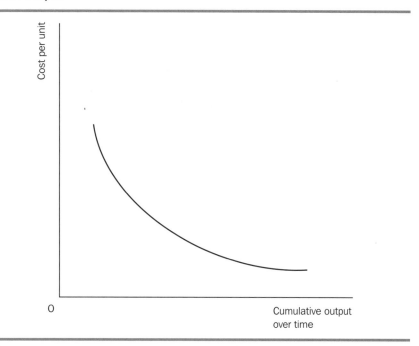

## 5.10    Scale diseconomies and 'minimum efficient size'

Figure 5.10 indicated decreasing returns to scale at levels of output beyond $Q_1$. It could be argued that there is no inherent reason why firms must experience such diseconomies, as technical scale economies could continue so long as the firm is able to employ more of all resources. However, the prime causes of scale diseconomy are said to be problems encountered in efficiently managing large organisations. Some of the concerns previously noted and addressed in a smaller firm might now go unnoticed or be only partially solved in a larger firm. Or the management structure might become overly bureaucratic, preventing swift and efficient decision-making: in effect, too much 'red tape'. It is even possible that with the additional management layers needed to organise an increasingly large and diverse workforce some staff might start to pursue their own objectives rather than promoting the firm's efficiency and profitability. The issue of managerial objectives will be addressed in Chapter 6.

**pecuniary diseconomies** a situation where the price paid for factor inputs begins to rise as the firm grows in size

**external diseconomies of scale** where a firm's average costs increase as a result of an increase in the size of the industry in which it operates

**Pecuniary diseconomies** and **external diseconomies of scale** might also emerge. For example, specific factors of production might become in short supply and, as a result, instead of benefiting from economies of bulk purchase the firm now starts to experience increasing factor prices. The industry might also become so concentrated in a given area that additional congestion costs are incurred.

It is management's responsibility to avoid scale diseconomy and continually strive for cost efficiency. This may necessitate the introduction of new management practice to counter managerial diseconomy. The emergence of external diseconomies might prompt geographical relocation. Such relocation could also help minimise transportation costs where the firm is producing bulky products and could also help avoid the effect of international trade barriers or quotas (e.g. Japanese car producers setting up in the UK). If scale diseconomies are unavoidable, the firm might consider replicating the plant in another location.

Even where scale diseconomies emerge, they might still be countered by continuing scale economies from another source and the LRAC could remain downward-sloping over all feasible levels of production. However, as production costs must remain positive, the slope of the LRAC will level out.

The firm would ideally wish to fully exploit scale economies and produce at minimum efficient scale (MES). In so doing it has a cost advantage over competitors failing to reach this output. The degree of disadvantage suffered by competitors depends upon the slope of the LRAC prior to MES, as illustrated in Figure 5.13.

Figure 5.13 shows two LRACs. Although both have the same MES, the gradient of their respective LRACs differs over other outputs. $LRAC_1$ shows a situation where economies and diseconomies of scale are less significant compared to $LRAC_2$. If a firm were producing Q* at one half of MES it would suffer a cost disadvantage compared to a rival producing at MES. However, the cost disadvantage on $LRAC_1$ is less than with $LRAC_2$. The size of MES relative to total market demand determines the number of firms that can fully efficiently produce within a given market. If scale economies are relatively significant and market demand relatively low, then no or few firms might reach MES. Alternatively, with a 'low' MES and high market demand a large number of firms might produce optimally.

**Figure 5.13  Minimum efficient size (MES) and cost advantage**

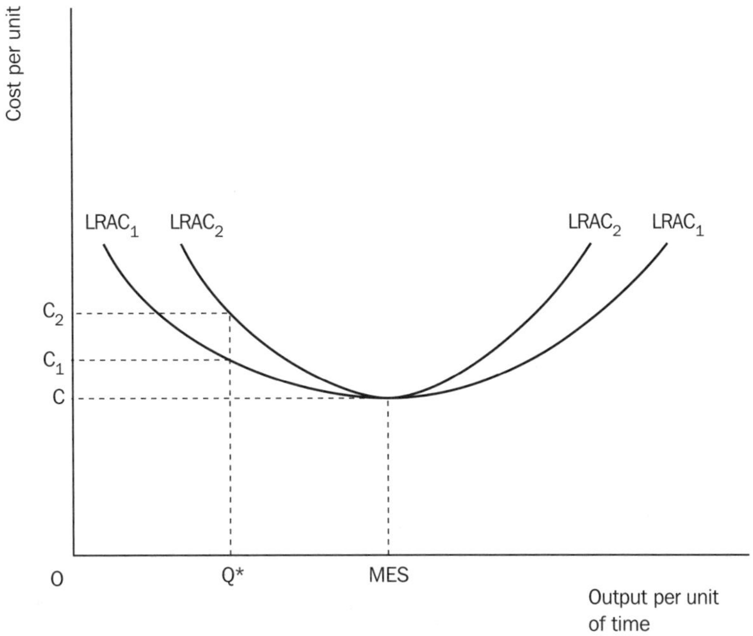

**Mini case** **Empirical estimates of MES**

Table 5.4 shows estimates of MES as a percentage of output in the UK and European Union (EU) and the cost penalties if producing at less than MES across a range of industries. C.F. Pratten collated these estimates in the 1980s from engineering studies of long-run costs where expected costs at differing outputs were estimated by production engineers assuming current technology and current factor prices.[2]

The value of MES as a percentage of output in either the UK or EU markets depends upon the absolute significance of MES in a given plant and the level of output in either market. MES as a proportion of domestic output in certain industries is relatively small. For example, the figure for glass bottle production in the UK is only 5 per cent, indicating the possibility of 20 fully efficient UK plants and a corresponding EU figure of 200. In other areas the percentage figure is relatively high suggesting only a small number of plants would be able to survive in each industry.

The third column shows the cost penalties incurred if producing below MES. As indicated in Figure 5.13 this depends upon the gradient of the cost curve at outputs below MES. The figures in our table show how the cost disadvantage at a third of MES varies from 26 per cent in cement production to only 2.2 per cent with cigarettes. Small plants in many areas do not therefore suffer severe cost disadvantages. Nevertheless it is generally found that economies of scale are usually most significant in areas associated with a significant technological input and growing demand: for

▶

**Table 5.4 Examples of single plant economies in manufacturing industries in the UK and the EU**

| Industry | MES as % of output | | % increase in costs at one-third MES* |
|---|---|---|---|
| | UK | EU | |
| Refrigerators | 85 | 11 | 6.5 |
| Integrated steel plants | 72 | 9.8 | 10 |
| Washing machines | 57 | 10 | 7.5 |
| Televisions | 40 | 9 | 15 |
| Cigarettes | 24 | 6 | 2.2 |
| Petrochemicals | 23 | 2.8 | 19 |
| Ball bearings | 20 | 2 | 8 to 10 |
| Tyres | 17 | 3 | 5 |
| Oil refining | 14 | 2.6 | 4 |
| Beer | 12 | 3 | 5 |
| Cement | 10 | 1 | 26 |
| Paint | 7 | 2 | 4.4 |
| Glass bottles | 5 | 0.5 | 11 |
| Nylon and acrylic | 4 | 1 | 9.5 to 12 |
| Cylinder blocks | 3 | 0.3 | 10 |
| Bricks | 1 | 0.2 | 25 |

*The final column shows the cost penalty suffered by a plant if producing at one-third of MES with the exception that for bricks, nylon and acrylic, cylinder blocks and tyres the cost penalty is at 50 per cent MES.

Source: Pratten (1984).

example, transport equipment, chemicals, machinery and instrument manufacture (office machines, etc.), and the paper and printing sectors. In contrast, those sectors with limited scale economies are typically associated with a lower technological input and less buoyant demand: for example, clothing, food, drink and tobacco, timber and leather goods.

Empirical study suggests the long-run average cost curve is generally L-shaped rather than U-shaped. Where this is the case the firm suffers no cost disadvantage in producing outputs beyond minimum MES.

## 5.11 X-inefficiency

Although firms may produce at levels other than MES, we nevertheless assume they are producing efficiently and achieve minimum production cost per unit at that level of output. That is, they are producing at a point on the relevant average total cost curve. It is possible, however, that the firm might not be fully efficient and therefore be incurring additional costs. In short, costs might be higher at a specific level of output than they need be. Such a situation is illustrated in Figure 5.14.

Imagine three firms, A, B and C, producing respectively at points a, b and c on Figure 5.14. Firm A is producing at MES and has a clear cost advantage

**Figure 5.14 X-inefficiency**

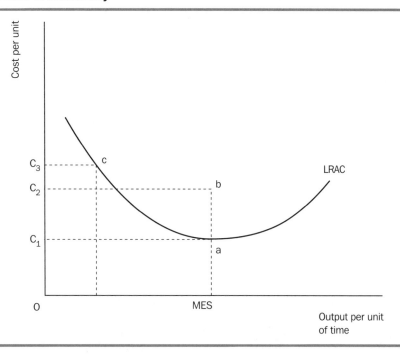

over both B and C. Although firm B is at MES, it is not producing efficiently and suffers a higher average cost per unit produced. The distance ab represents **X-inefficiency**, a measure of the degree to which costs are higher than they need be. Nevertheless, firm B still maintains a cost advantage over firm C. Firm C is fully efficient, yet suffers a cost disadvantage by producing at a relatively low level of output. If firm C could increase output and maintain efficiency it might gain a cost advantage over firm B.

**x-inefficiency** a term used to signify general managerial or technological inefficiency

X-inefficiency, or **organisational stock**, could not exist in the long run in fully competitive markets, as in such situations the firm must be fully efficient to survive. It can exist, however, in less competitive markets, where the firm may have the discretion not to minimise cost. In such circumstances it might even be found that management pursues its own goals and spends more than absolutely necessary to achieve a given level of output.

## 5.12 Profit maximisation

At first glance it appears reasonable to assume that firms seek maximum profit. In this section we identify how a firm might achieve this ambition. In Chapter 6 the validity of the assumption will be discussed, and alternative goals of the firm put forward.

In Chapter 3 we analysed consumer demand. The demand curve showed that to sell more output, other things remaining equal (i.e. *ceteris paribus*), price must fall. Total revenue then rises or falls relative to the value of price elasticity. The demand curve therefore specifies the price, total revenue and marginal revenue associated with each level of output. In this chapter we have seen how those same levels of output are associated with values of cost.

Therefore, given that:

**profit** the excess of revenue over costs

$$\textbf{Profit} = \begin{array}{c} \text{Revenue gained from selling a given level of output} \\ \text{minus} \\ \text{The total cost of producing that level of output} \end{array}$$

then the firm should be able to identify values of revenue and cost associated with each level of output and in so doing identify a profit-maximising position.

Figure 5.15a shows a total revenue and total cost curve for a given product. The demand curve (AR curve) and marginal revenue curve in Figure 5.15b correspond to the total revenue curve in Figure 5.15a. The total cost curve in Figure 5.15a is of a traditional shape, as analysed earlier in this chapter. The corresponding average total and marginal cost curves are presented in Figure 5.15b.

Firstly, observe Figure 5.15a. With output from zero to $Q_1$ then total cost (TC) exceeds total revenue (TR) and the firm makes a loss. At zero output the loss is equal to the distance Oa, representing fixed cost. At $Q_1$ and $Q_4$, TC equals TR and the firm breaks even. (We discuss below the implication of a firm 'breaking even'.) Between $Q_1$ and $Q_4$, TR exceeds TC and the firm earns a profit. Beyond $Q_4$ the firm makes a loss. Figure 5.15a includes a **profit function** showing the level of profit or loss at different levels of output. At $Q_2$, TC and TR are furthest apart and profit is maximised. Although TR continues to increase up to $Q_3$, TC increases at an even greater rate and profit falls.

**profit function** a line indicating the level of profit (or loss) at different levels of output

The above relationships are also shown in Figure 5.15b. For example, when TC equalled TR at $Q_1$ and $Q_2$ in Figure 5.15a then average cost (AC) equals average revenue (AR), equals price in Figure 5.15b. In Figure 5.15b at a price $P_1$, AR and AC are furthest apart, $Q_2$ units are sold and profit is maximised. Total profit is equal to the area efgh, representing the number of units sold multiplied by the difference between the price per unit sold and the average cost of producing each of those units.

At $Q_2$ in Figure 5.15b, marginal cost (MC) equals marginal revenue (MR), the implication being that, in maximising profit, the firm produces to the point where the revenue gained from selling the last unit (MR) is equal to the additional cost of producing that unit (MC). For units less than $Q_2$, MR exceeds MC and selling further units could increase profits. For units beyond $Q_2$, MC exceeds MR and a loss is made on those additional units. It therefore makes sense to decrease output to $Q_2$.

The profit maximising condition of equating MC to MR can also be seen in Figure 5.15a in that at $Q_2$ the slope of a tangent drawn to the TR function at point b (representing the value of MR as noted in Chapter 3) is parallel to a tangent drawn to the TC function at point c, representing MC. Where the corresponding tangents are parallel, then TC and TR are furthest apart. That is, MC equals MR at $Q_2$.

### Profit and opportunity cost

**normal profit** the amount of profit needed to keep a firm in a particular line of business

Although in equating TR to TC (i.e. 'breaking even') the firm makes zero profit, the economist refers to this as a situation of **normal profit**. The reason for so doing is that the economist uses a principle of **opportunity cost** in assigning cost to factor inputs, where opportunity cost represents the value of a resource

**Figure 5.15 Revenue and cost functions, profit maximisation**

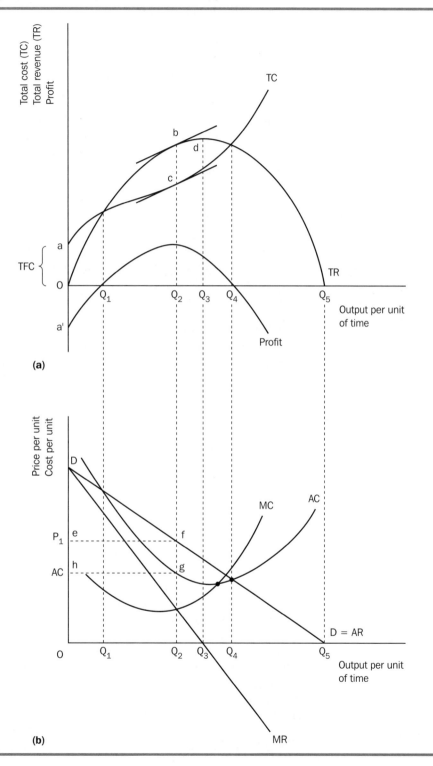

in its best alternative use. For example, if working for your own company the real cost of doing so should be seen in terms of the money you could earn in your most profitable alternative occupation. Similarly, the real cost of employing capital should include the sum that capital could earn in an alternative investment of similar risk.

**full economic cost** a calculation of costs which includes the opportunity costs of employing the factors of production

In essence, **full economic cost** includes the opportunity cost of all factors including capital. Therefore, when TR equals TC the firm earns the same return on capital that could have been made in a similar investment. It is in this sense that we refer to the firm as making 'normal profit', where 'normal profit' represents just sufficient return to compensate for risk and make it worthwhile continuing in that line of business. A variation in the degree of risk or the return available in an alternative investment changes the value of 'normal profit'.

**abnormal profit** profit over and above normal profit. Also called super-normal profit

If TR exceeds TC, for example at $Q_2$ in Figure 5.15a, the firm makes **abnormal** or **supernormal profit**. Abnormal profit implies a return in excess of that achievable when using those resources in the best alternative investment. In defining cost in terms of opportunity cost, then situations that might be judged profitable in pure monetary flows might now be seen as unprofitable if revenue earned fails to cover all opportunity costs. An allowance for 'normal' profit must be included as a component of economic cost.

### The firm's shut-down price

So long as the firm makes at least normal profit it is worthwhile staying in business. If making less than normal profit – a lower return than achievable in an alternative investment – the firm should close down. However, closing down cannot be undertaken immediately and in the short-run the firm may continue production so long as revenue earned helps pay the burden of fixed costs. In the meantime the firm should plan its closure and in the long run leave the industry.

**shut-down price** the minimum price at which the firm will continue to produce in the short run despite making a loss

In the short-run period we can identify a **shut-down price**, representing the minimum price at which the firm continues to produce despite making a loss. This is illustrated in Figure 5.16.

For simplicity of exposition we assume in Figure 5.16 the firm to be faced with a perfectly elastic demand curve. (We will see in Chapter 7 that this corresponds to a firm in **perfect competition** where each firm has no individual control over price and is assumed to take the market price.) With a perfectly elastic demand curve the firm can sell extra units without lowering price. The demand curve (average revenue curve) is therefore also a marginal revenue curve, as selling an extra unit increases total revenue at a constant rate equal to price. Figure 5.16 shows a series of such demand curves and also includes a short-run average total cost curve (ATC), a variable cost curve (AVC) and a corresponding marginal cost curve (MC).

With demand curve $D_5$, and a price of $P_5$ the firm equates MC to MR and sells $Q_5$. At $Q_5$ then average revenue (equals price) is greater than average total cost (ATC) and the firm earns abnormal profit. If demand falls and the demand curve shifts downwards to $D_4$, then with a price of $P_4$ the firm again equates MC to MR and decreases output to $Q_4$. ATC now equals average revenue and the firm makes normal profit. Imagine the demand falls again to $D_2$

**Figure 5.16 The shut-down position** (short run)

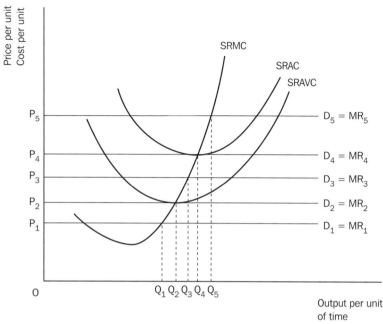

and a price of $P_2$. Equating MC to MR results in $Q_2$ and average revenue now equals AVC, with total revenue ($P_2$ multiplied by $Q_2$) just sufficient to cover total variable costs (AVC multiplied by $Q_2$). As total cost (TC) equals total variable cost (TVC) plus total fixed cost (TFC), the firm makes a loss equal to TFC. Revenue is now only sufficient to cover variable costs.

As we assume the firm remains in the industry in the short run it is faced with one of two choices: to produce and make either a profit or loss, or not produce and incur a loss equal to fixed costs. We can now see from Figure 5.16 that with demand curve $D_2$, a price of $P_2$ and an output of $Q_2$, the firm is indifferent to producing or not producing as in either case the firm makes a loss equal to fixed costs. However, if price fell below $P_2$, for example to $P_1$ and an output of $Q_1$, average revenue is now less than AVC and revenue from sales does not even cover variable costs. Losses would be in excess of fixed costs if the firm were to produce. It is therefore better to cease production and incur a loss of only fixed costs.

$P_2$ is therefore defined as the shut-down price. This is the minimum price the firm would accept to produce in the short run. If price fell below $P_2$ the firm should cease production in the short-run and incur a loss equal to fixed cost. With price between $P_2$ and $P_4$, for example at $P_3$ in Figure 5:16, then although the firm makes a loss the revenue earned more than pays the burden of fixed costs (i.e.: TR is greater than TVC). However, with prices below $P_4$ the firm makes less than normal profit and would cease production and leave the industry in the long run. The above relationships are summarised in Table 5.5.

In Section 5.2 we introduced the supply curve, showing how many units the firm supplies at different prices. From Figure 5.16 we may identify the short-

**Table 5.5 The short-run production decision**

| Relationship of price (AR) to cost | 'Short' and 'long-run' production decision | Level of profit |
|---|---|---|
| Price (AR) > ATC | ■ continue production in the short-run and long-run | profit > 'normal' |
| Price (AR) = ATC | ■ continue production in the short-run and long run | profit = 'normal' |
| Price (AR) > AVC < ATC | ■ continue production in the short run<br>■ leave industry in the long run | profit < 'normal' (losses are less than fixed costs) |
| Price (AR) = AVC | ■ make a loss equal to fixed costs whether producing or not<br>■ leave industry in the long run | profit < 'normal' (losses equal to fixed costs) |
| Price (AR) < AVC | ■ stop production in the short-run<br>■ leave industry in the long run | profit < 'normal' (if the firm produces in the short run, losses are greater than fixed costs. Therefore, cease to produce.) |

run supply curve for a firm in perfect competition as the marginal cost curve above the point where price (AR) equals the minimum point of AVC (i.e. as price rises the firm equates MC to MR and supplies the corresponding output). The industry supply curve would be the summation of the marginal cost curves of all the firms in the industry.

## 5.13 Conclusions

Our analysis of production in both the short and long run is clearly of great importance to our analysis and understanding of the firm. The effect of size upon the costs of production also has significant implications as regards the number of firms that may produce efficiently within a given industry. Nevertheless, this does not imply that large firms always have a productive advantage, as either scale economies might prove to be relatively insignificant in many industries, or large firms might become less efficient and bureaucratic with excessive size. It is, of course, the responsibility of management to promote efficiency in production and provide appropriate managerial organisation.

Our analysis of the conditions for profit maximisation is of particular importance to our understanding of the firm. In understanding the conditions and variables that determine the generation of revenue and the incurring of cost we can achieve a real understanding of the factors influencing the viability of the firm.

| Case study | ## Returning a loss-making firm to profit |

In this case study we use the profit-maximising model developed in the chapter to analyse options available to a loss-making firm. Imagine the following scenario.

Baldwin's Fashions is a small hosiery firm based in Manchester producing a range of ladies' underwear. (For the purpose of our case study we assume it produces a single garment, a specifically designed pair of cotton briefs.) Although in previous years the business has consistently made a profit, it now finds that with current plant and market demand it is making a loss at all conceivable levels of output and ranges of price. Previous work studies have shown the workforce to be fully efficient and the capital used to be of the latest design, incorporating the most modern technology and fully appropriate to the current range of output. Figure 5.17 shows the total cost and total revenue curves associated with the above garment.

The firm is considering closing down. What advice could you give the management to help them regain profit and remain in the industry. Use Figure 5.17 and the basic model developed in this chapter to illustrate your advice.

**Figure 5.17  Loss-making at all levels of output**

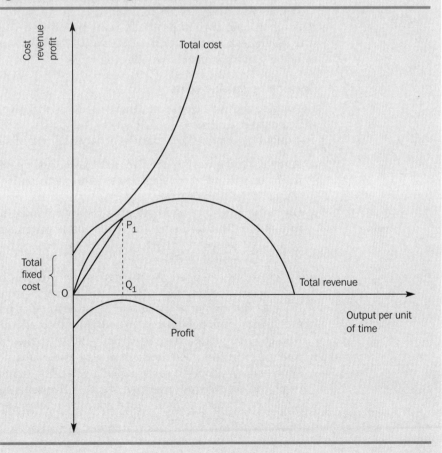

The current loss-making situation is illustrated in Figure 5.17. (This diagram is adapted from Figure 5.15a, Section 5.10 of this chapter.)

In Figure 5.17 the total cost (TC) curve lies above the total revenue (TR) curve at all levels of output. To minimise losses the firm should produce $Q_1$ where the difference between TC and TR is minimised. Marginal cost (MC) equals marginal revenue (MR) at this output as a tangent drawn to the TC curve (representing the value of MC) has the same slope as a tangent drawn to the TR curve (representing MR). The price required to sell $Q_1$ (i.e. $P_1$) is represented by the slope of the ray drawn from the origin to that point on the TR curve. Although the firm makes a loss at $Q_1$, (the profit function is below the horizontal axis) losses are greater at all other levels of output. In the short run the firm has the option of ceasing production, incurring a loss equal to total fixed cost (TFC). However, in selling $Q_1$ the revenue generated more than covers total variable cost (TVC) and therefore helps pay some of the burden of fixed cost.

The initial advice to the firm is therefore to set a price and output to minimise losses. Having done so, any temptation to then increase price (which at face value might appear to many observers a possible solution to a loss-making situation) only makes the situation worse, as would seeking a solution through lowering price to generate more sales.

It does not make sense to remain in business in the long run unless making at least normal profit. To remain in business we must now put forward policies to regain profit. Figure 5.17 would suggest that a solution could be sought in one of the following ways.

### Decreasing variable costs

Decreasing variable costs (and therefore MC), will pivot the TC curve downwards until it intersects the TR curve (see Figure 5.18). Decreasing variable cost might be achieved in a variety of ways. For example:

- Persuading the workforce to accept a lower hourly wage rate. The workers might be willing to consider lower remuneration if the alternative is the threat of the firm's closure.
- Changing suppliers and obtaining the cotton material at lower cost. (The firm might consider using a cheaper and lower-quality material, although this might adversely affect consumer preference for the good and cause the TR curve to shift downwards.)
- Although we assumed the workers to be working fully efficiently, if we could increase their productivity the TC curve would pivot downwards. Perhaps they might work harder if the method of payment changed from a 'flat rate', independent of an individual's productivity, to a 'piece rate' whereby individuals were rewarded relative to their own productivity.
- Redesigning the good in such a way that does not alter its physical appearance yet makes construction easier. For example, perhaps the garment currently requires sewing together five separate components. If this could be decreased to four components, then more garments could be sewn together in a given time period.

**Figure 5.18 Decreasing variable costs**

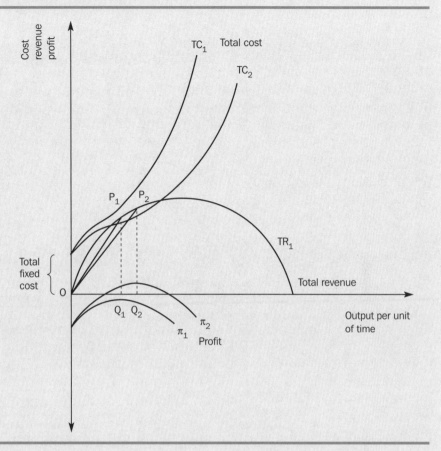

*Can you suggest other ways of decreasing variable cost?*

The successful implementation of one of the above strategies is illustrated in Figure 5.18. The total cost curve shifts from $TC_1$ to $TC_2$, the profit function moves upwards and profits are now maximised at an increased output of $Q_2$ and the lower price of $P_2$. A share of the cost saving is passed on to the consumer via the lower price, the producer benefiting through increased profit. The degree to which the cost saving is shared between producer and consumer depends upon the price elasticity of demand. The greater the price elasticity of demand, the greater the fall in price and the more of the cost saving passed on to the consumer. The lower the price elasticity the less the decrease in price and the greater the benefit to the producer via increased profit.

**Decreasing fixed costs**

Decreasing fixed costs pulls the TC curve downwards in a parallel fashion until the TR curve is intersected. (see Figure 5.19). A decrease in fixed cost could also be achieved in a variety of ways. For example:

▶

**Figure 5.19  Decreasing fixed costs**

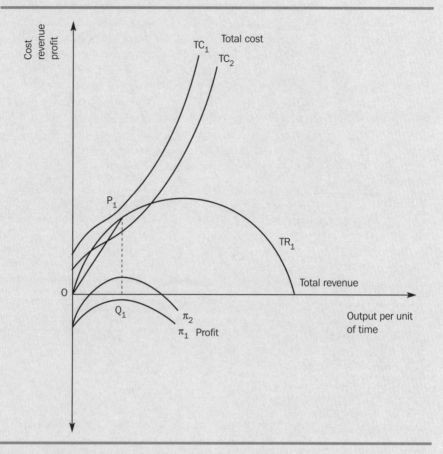

- We could imagine the firm's owner seeking to negotiate a lower interest rate with their bank manager on a loan originally taken out to purchase capital. Whilst this could be a possibility it might also be seen as a dangerous suggestion (e.g. if the bank sees its investment to be at risk due to the firm's current losses it may decide immediately to foreclose on its loan to ensure repayment).
- The firm could consider moving to cheaper premises. (The disadvantage of such a move is that it may cause disruption to production and the act of moving in itself involves additional expenditure.)
- Baldwin's currently uses outside contractors to clean office and factory space. This fixed cost could decrease by negotiating either a lower price or seeking a cheaper contractor.
- Decrease expenditure on research and development. Although such a cut might be considered short-sighted, it nevertheless achieves an immediate cost saving.

*Suggest other policies that could achieve a decrease in fixed costs.*

Figure 5.19 shows the successful implementation of one of the above strategies. The TC curve shifts down in a parallel fashion and the profit function shifts upwards. As marginal costs are unaffected by decreasing fixed costs, the output where marginal cost equals marginal revenue remains at $Q_1$ and price stays constant at $P_1$. The consumer does not therefore benefit from the cost saving, all the gain going to the producer as increased profit. (Note: see Baumol's model of sales revenue maximisation in Chapter 6.)

### Increasing the level of demand

Increasing the level of demand at each price causes the demand curve to shift outwards and the TR curve to shift upwards until it crosses the TC curve (see Figure 5.20). We will initially imagine how the firm might cause the total revenue function to shift upwards without at the same time having to increase overall expenditure. For example:

- The firm might increase demand by using its current advertising expenditure more productively. This might involve moving to a new advertising agency.
- Redesigning the product, at no additional cost, to appeal to additional consumers.

*How else might you propose increasing demand?*

**Figure 5.20  Increasing the level of demand**

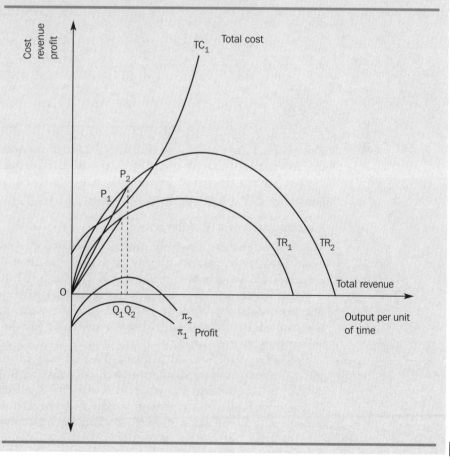

**Figure 5.21 Increasing advertising expenditure**

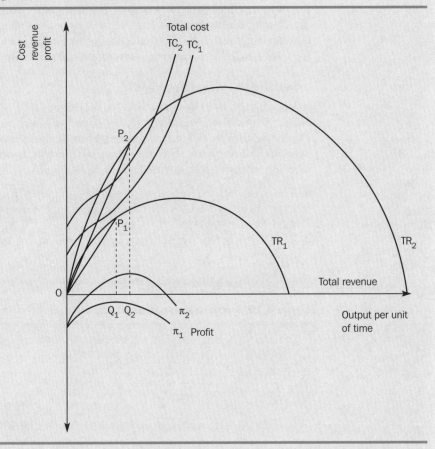

The effect of the above is to shift the TR function upwards. In Figure 5.20 maximum profit is now achieved at the higher output of $Q_2$ and a higher price of $P_2$. The degree to which price and output change depends upon the price elasticity of the new demand curve.

### A combination of any of the above

The firm might use a combination of the above proposals (e.g. simultaneously seeking a cheaper supply of materials, moving to less expensive premises and seeking to increase demand through redesigning the product).

We illustrate such a possibility in Figure 5.21 where we assume the firm decides to regain profitability by increasing advertising in the expectation that the additional expenditure will more than pay for itself by increasing sales revenue.

Production costs are independent of advertising costs, as advertising only affects demand conditions and not the production process of the firm as defined by its production function. It is also the case that advertising expenditures are made in a previous period and are therefore independent of current output and sales. As such, we may consider advertising expenditure as a fixed cost with a zero marginal cost in the current period. (Note that, as a general rule of thumb, the level of advertising for the next period is commonly set as a proportion of sales revenue in a previous period.)

Increasing advertising in Figure 5.21 therefore shifts the TC curve upwards to $TC_2$ and so long as the advertising is successful the demand curve shifts outwards and the TR curve upwards. In this case the TR curve shifts to $TR_2$ and the firm achieves maximum profit at an increased output of $Q_2$ and a price of $P_2$.

Successive increases in advertising should shift the demand curve further to the right, but due to diminishing returns to advertising these successive shifts will become smaller for equal increments in advertising. The optimal level of advertising would be determined where the additional revenue generated by the increased demand from advertising matches its extra cost.

The model we have developed therefore proves a valuable tool for analysing a realistic scenario.

## Notes and references

1. For a further discussion of indivisibilities see Koutsoyiannis, A. (1976), *Modern Microeconomics*, 2nd edition, Macmillan, Basingstoke, pp. 128–132 and Griffiths, A. and Wall, S. (1996), *Intermediate Microeconomics. Theory and Applications*, Longman, Harlow, pp. 174–175.
2. See Koutsoyiannis (1976, pp. 143–146).

## Review and discussion questions

1 Identify the fixed and variable factors of production associated with:
   (a) operating a professional football club
   (b) owning and running a private motorcar.

2 Although numerous methods of producing a given output of a particular good could be technically efficient, it is likely that only one of these methods will be economically efficient. Use an appropriate example to distinguish between technical efficiency and economic efficiency.

3 Draw a diagram showing an average fixed cost curve, marginal cost curve, average variable cost curve, and average total cost curve to explain why the average variable cost reaches a minimum at a lower level of output than average total cost.

4 Table 5.6 shows the output and corresponding total cost of a firm producing a particular good. The firm can sell this good at a constant price of £15 irrespective of the numbers sold.
   (a) Identify the firm's marginal cost and average cost curves.
   (b) At which output does the firm maximise profit?
   (c) How would the profit-maximising level of output be affected if fixed costs were to increase to £10?
   (d) How should the firm react if it could sell the good for only £10 per unit?

**Table 5.6**

| Output | Total cost (£) | Output | Total cost (£) |
|--------|----------------|--------|----------------|
| 0 | 5 | 6 | 65 |
| 1 | 19 | 7 | 78 |
| 2 | 30 | 8 | 94 |
| 3 | 39 | 9 | 112 |
| 4 | 46 | 10 | 133 |
| 5 | 55 | | |

5 Use the concept of an economy of increased dimension to explain how it can be seen to be cheaper to heat a large warehouse compared to a smaller warehouse.

6 Draw a diagram showing the total cost curve and the total revenue curve of a firm capable of making abnormal profit. (The total revenue curve should be one associated with a downward-sloping demand curve.) On this diagram identify the level or levels of output where:
   (a) profits are maximised.
   (b) the firm breaks even.
   (c) marginal revenue is zero.
   (d) average cost is minimised.
   (e) marginal cost is minimised.
   (f) there is the greatest gap between average cost and average revenue.

   Identify these same outputs using the corresponding average cost, marginal cost and demand curves.

## Assignments

1 Take an example of a small retailer selling a limited range of groceries.
   (a) Outline and explain the sources of scale economy such an enterprise might achieve if it were to grow in size.
   (b) Might any diseconomies emerge, and if so how might they be avoided?
   (c) How might the firm benefit from economies of scope?

2 A study of the concept of scale economy might indicate that large firms always dominate over smaller firms. Use current real world examples to explain why this will not always be so.

## Further reading

Chrystal, K. A. and Lipsey, R. G. (1997), *Economics for Business and Management*, Oxford University Press, Oxford, Chapter 4.

Dunnett, A. (1998), *Understanding the Market*, 3rd edition, Longman, Harlow, Chapter 5.

Griffiths, A. and Wall, S. (1996), *Intermediate Microeconomics, Theory and Applications*, Longman, Harlow, Chapter 4.

Hornby, W., Gammie, B. and Wall, S. (1997), *Business Economics*, Longman, Harlow, Chapter 7.

Nellis, J. G. and Parker, D. (1997), *The Essence of Business Economics*, 2nd edition, Prentice Hall, Hemel Hempstead, Chapter 3.

Pratten, C. F. (1989), *The Costs of Non Europe*, vol. 2,

Worthington, I. and Britton, C. (2000), *The Business Environment*, 3rd edition, Prentice Hall Financial Times, Harlow.

| Appendix 5.1 | **Market pricing by supply and demand** |

(This appendix is adapted from Worthington and Britton (2000). Pricing will be analysed further in Chapter 9.)

## 1 Introduction

In every market there will be a buyer and a seller who must be brought together so that a sale can take place. In a market economy this takes place through the market mechanism. In the product market the buyer is the household and the seller is the firm. Households demand the good or service that is supplied by a firm or firms.

The market is the place where buyers and sellers meet and demand and supply are brought together. Table 5.7 contains information on the level of supply and demand of a specific good. This information is presented graphically in Fig 5.22.

**Table 5.7  The supply and demand for 'Real Brew' draught beer**

| Price (£ per pint) | Quantity demanded (000s/wk) | quantity supplied (000s/wk) |
|---|---|---|
| 0.90 | 83 | 0 |
| 1.00 | 70 | 35 |
| 1.10 | 58 | 43 |
| 1.20 | 48 | 48 |
| 1.30 | 40 | 55 |
| 1.40 | 35 | 60 |
| 1.50 | 32 | 68 |

## 2 The equilibrium price

At a price of £1.20, the quantity demanded is the same as the quantity supplied at 48,000 pints per week. At this price the amount that consumers wish to buy is the same as the amount that producers wish to sell. This price is called the **equilibrium price** and the quantity being bought and sold is called the **equilibrium quantity**. The point of equilibrium can be seen on Figure 5.22 at the point where the demand and supply curves cross.

At price levels above £1.20 the quantity that producers wish to supply is greater than the quantity consumers wish to buy. There is **excess supply** and the market is a buyer's market. At prices less than £1.20 consumers wish to buy more than producers wish to supply. There is **excess demand** and the market is a seller's market.

In competitive markets, situations of excess demand or supply should not exist for long as forces are put into motion to move the market towards equilibrium. For example, if the price level is £1.30 per pint, there is excess supply and producers will be forced to reduce the price in order to sell their beer. Consumers may be aware that they are in a buyer's market and offer lower

**equilibrium price** the price at which the quantity demanded equals the quantity supplied

**equilibrium quantity** the market clearing quantity at the equilibrium price

**excess supply** a situation in which the amount supplied exceeds the amount demanded

**excess demand** a situation in which the amount demanded exceeds the amount supplied

**Figure 5.22 The market for 'Real Brew' draught beer**

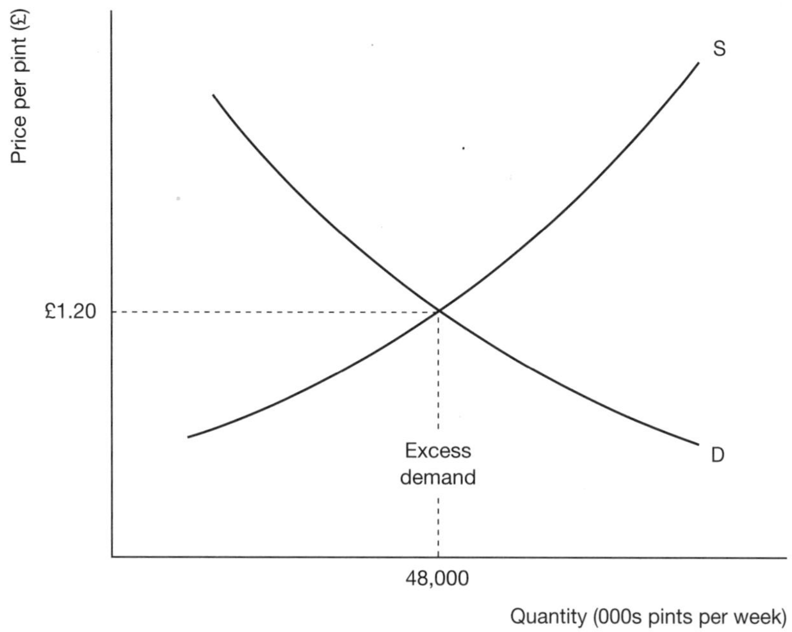

prices, which firms might accept. For one or both of these reasons, there will be a tendency for prices to be pushed back towards the equilibrium price. The opposite occurs at prices below equilibrium and price is pushed upwards towards equilibrium.

### Shifts in demand and supply

So long as the demand and supply curves in any market remain stationary, the equilibrium price should be maintained. However, as we have seen, there are numerous factors that could shift either or both of these curves. If this were to happen, then the old equilibrium would be destroyed and the market should work to a new equilibrium. How does this happen?

In Figure 5.23 the original equilibrium price for Real Brew draught beer is $P_1$. Assume that the demand curve moves from $D_1$ to $D_2$. This increase in demand could be due to a variety of factors. For example, the price of a rival drink may have increased; disposable income could have risen; or sales may have benefited from a successful advertising campaign. In any event, at the old equilibrium price there now exists an excess of demand over supply of $Q_1Q_3$. It is likely that price will be bid upwards in order to ration the shortage in supply. As price rises, demand is choked off and supply rises. Eventually there is a movement to a new equilibrium of $P_2$. At this new price both supply and demand at $Q_2$ are higher than they were at the previous equilibrium. If, alternatively, the demand curve had shifted to the left, then the process would have been reserved and the new equilibrium would have been at a level of demand and supply less that $Q_1$, with a price below $P_1$. Illustrate this process diagrammatically for yourself.

**Figure 5.23  A shift in the demand curve**

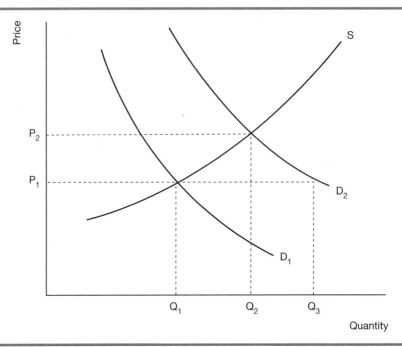

In Figure 5.24 there is a shift in the supply curve from $S_1$ to $S_2$. Refer back in this chapter to envisage specific reasons for a such a shift. At the original equilibrium price of $P_1$ there would now be an excess supply over demand of $Q_1Q_3$. Price would therefore fall in a free market. As it does so, demand will be encouraged and supply diminished. Eventually there will be a new equilibrium at P2 with a higher quantity demand and supply than at the previous equilibrium. If the supply curve had instead shifted to the left, then market forces would have resulted in a lower quantity supplied and demanded than before. Once again, illustrate this diagrammatically for yourself.

The analysis so far has been relatively straightforward; it has been assumed that either the demand or the supply curve moves. However, it is likely that in any given time period both curves could move in any direction and perhaps even more than once.

Given the many factors that may shift both the demand and the supply curves, it is easy to imagine that markets can be in a constant state of flux. Just as the market is moving towards a new equilibrium, some other factor may change, necessitating an adjustment in an opposite direction. Given that such adjustment is not immediate, and the market conditions are constantly changing, it may be the case that equilibrium is never actually attained. It is even possible that the very process of market adjustment can be destabilising (see cobweb theory in Chapter 9). The constant movement of price implied by the analysis may also be detrimental to business. The firm might prefer to keep price constant in the face of minor changes in demand and supply.

**Figure 5.24 A shift in the supply curve**

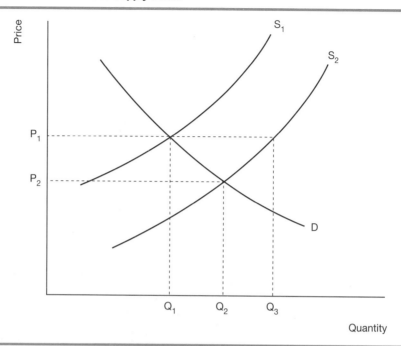

Mini case **BSE and the market mechanism**

(This mini case has been taken from Worthington and Britton (1997) and is included to illustrate the impact of shifts in demand and supply.)

The scare over bovine spongiform encephalopathy (BSE) in cattle and its links with Creutzfeldt-Jacob disease (CJD) in humans in 1996 demonstrates well the working of the market mechanism and the all-pervading power of market forces.

The announcement on Friday 22 March 1996 that there may be a link between BSE and CJD was followed very quickly by the boycotting of British beef by consumers. There was a spectacular drop of 50 per cent in consumer demand for beef over the following weekend. The large grocery retailers at first reduced prices in order to clear stock and eventually withdrew British beef from supermarket shelves for a period of time. The supermarkets also offered reimbursement to customers who had previously bought beef from them.

The drop in demand for beef (see Figure 5.25) led to a dramatic fall in the price of beef cattle. By the end of the first week of the crisis the market price for steers had fallen by 18p per kilo. This would have been more dramatic but farmers chose to hold back their cattle from market because of the crisis; there was a 97 per cent fall in the numbers of cattle sent to market in that week. There was an accompanying increase in the demand for substitutes (see Figure 5.26) like lamb (where sales rose by 7 per cent), pork (where sales rose by 18 per cent) and poultry (where prices increased

**Figure 5.25 The market for beef**

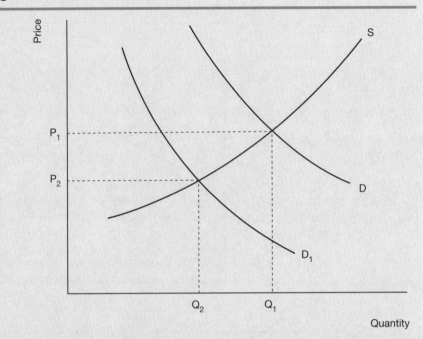

by 12 per cent) over the weekend. The poultry industry held emergency meetings to decide how to meet this extra demand and to decide whether to limit price increases to avoid the charge of profiting out of the crisis. There was also a search by consumers for other alternatives like vegetarianism and the first horsemeat shop to be opened since the Second World War began trading in the West Midlands on 9 April 1996.

There are various options open to the government, but at the time of writing the government had not decided on its response to the crisis and the debate within the EU continued. However, the implications and costs of destroying all 11.8 million British cattle are as follows. The cost of the slaughter and compensation to farmers and others is estimated to be around £17 billion, the cost of restocking British herds £5 billion. The loss of 11.8 million cattle would have a profound effect on the dairy industry, the UK would have to import much more of its milk and experts believe that our demand is too high to be met with increased imports and therefore there is likely to be an increase in prices. The fall in the price of beef will offset this slightly to begin with but the longer-term effect on inflation as other prices rise is estimated to be an increase of 1.5 per cent.

The trade deficit will worsen by an estimated £7 billion per year; the level of unemployment will rise by an estimated 500,000 (NFU estimate of the numbers employed in the beef industry) and this will cost the country £4.5 billion. The PSBR will rise by £20 billion and the possibility of tax cuts in the November 1996 Budget has been reduced dramatically. Indeed, many commentators expect that taxation will have to rise in 1997 to overcome the resulting fiscal crisis.

**Figure 5.26 The market for substitutes**

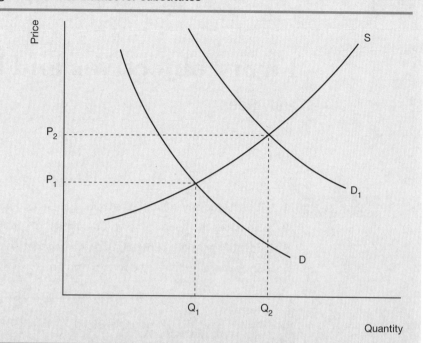

There has also been a wider threat to the UK's membership of the European Union, as a result of the British government's policy of non-co-operation and veto on European policies in an attempt to force the EU to lift the ban on British beef and beef derivatives.

Although this is a very extreme example of the impact of market forces, it clearly shows that demand and supply are powerful forces that have dramatic effects on markets, industries and whole economies.

# CHAPTER 6

# Firms' objectives and behaviour

Andy Rees

**Objectives**

1 To investigate key influences shaping the behaviour of business organisations.

2 To consider the usefulness of the concept of 'profit maximisation'.

3 To identify possible constraints on managerial decisions.

4 To examine alternative theories of the firm.

## 6.1 Introduction

To fully appreciate the game of football we need a clear understanding of the rules and aim of the game. Once we realise that the basic objective is for each team to place the ball in its opponent's goal we can start to appraise each team's performance. We may also propose improvements to a team's tactics to enhance its chance of achieving its objective. This sporting analogy has clear relevance to our study of the firm. To understand and appraise a firm's performance we must first find out what the firm is seeking to achieve.

We previously assumed that the sole aim of the firm is to maximise profit. Using this assumption we can then predict the price and output policy of firms under different market structures from perfect competition to monopoly (see Chapter 7). Is it reasonable to assume, however, that the firm will always seek to maximise profit? Perhaps the firm wishes to maximise something other than profit, or perhaps it has a range of goals and might feel it inappropriate to maximise any single goal at the expense of another.

Within this chapter we will question the applicability of profit maximisation and suggest alternative objectives for the firm.

## 6.2 The problems with profit maximisation

There are two basic questions:

1 *Does the firm have sufficient knowledge to maximise profit?*
2 *Would it wish to maximise profit?*

We will look at each question in turn.

### 6.2.1 **Does the firm have sufficient knowledge to maximise profit?**

In Chapter 5 we set out the conditions whereby a firm could maximise profit. This required the firm to identify the level of output where the revenue gained from selling the last unit (marginal revenue) was equal to the cost of producing that unit (marginal cost), and setting price accordingly. Identifying this level of output therefore implies a knowledge of the value of marginal revenue (MR) and marginal cost (MC) at all levels of output. This is clearly a difficult task.

To identify MR, the firm requires knowledge of the demand for its product at all prices, i.e. it should be able to identify its demand curve. However, as noted in Chapter 3, the large number of explanatory variables determining demand makes this difficult. Although the firm might be aware of its sales at the current price, it would be less sure of sales at alternative prices, and sales at previous prices might be a poor guide to future sales given that 'other conditions of demand' would be likely to have changed. For example, the prices charged by rival firms might now differ. In short, the firm is likely to possess less than **perfect knowledge**. There might, however, be a danger of exaggerating the problem in that the firm would only realistically be interested in the level of demand over a certain price range. Statistical and survey techniques also exist that allow the firm to estimate its demand curve. The firm may also gain knowledge through market experience. Nevertheless, the problem remains.

There are similar problems in identifying the value of marginal cost (MC) at different levels of output. Imagine a firm producing ball bearings. It is unrealistic to expect it to be able to estimate the additional cost of producing a single additional 'ball' when it might be producing many thousands in a given production shift. Many, if not most, firms would have a similar problem. However, firms are often better placed to estimate the cost of an extra batch or run of production. As we will see in Chapter 9, this is the approach used in **incremental pricing**, where instead of pricing on the basis of single unit changes of output, and the corresponding values of MC and MR, the firm instead looks at discrete (incremental) changes in output.

In many instances the firm produces more than one product. These products might have common or joint costs such as the cost of premises. These would be seen as fixed costs and such overheads should be allocated between the different products. (Note, however, that fixed costs do not influence MC as they do not change with output.) Variable costs might also be shared, as when using the same operative to produce more than one product, again necessitating the allocation of such costs between products. This would not prevent marginal costing, yet it does present a complication. Accounting theory provides a basis for the allocation of shared costs through the principle of **absorption costing**. The firm might nevertheless choose its own method of allocation. For example, a strategic decision might be made to under-allocate shared costs to a newly launched good in order that it might be competitively priced to gain immediate market share.

Irrespective of whether a firm can or cannot identify MC and MR, would it anyway use these concepts when setting price? An early empirical test of this question was carried out in the 1930s by two American economists, Hall and Hitch (1939), who questioned a range of 'well-organised' businesses on how they set price.[1] Their findings showed that most respondents were unfamiliar

**perfect knowledge** being aware of all aspects of the market in which the firm is operating

**incremental pricing** pricing decisions taken on the basis of larger changes in costs and revenues than those associated with strict marginal analysis

**absorption costing** a costing system whereby all overhead costs are apportioned first to cost centres and then to products

with marginal analysis, and anyway questioned whether firms would wish to maximise short-term profits on the grounds that too frequent price adjustments might alienate customers and lead to retaliation from competitors. Their results also questioned whether firms implicitly attempted to calculate elasticity or take it into account in price-setting.

Hall and Hitch's results have received a good deal of criticism over the years, particularly as it is naive to expect businesses to be familiar with economic jargon. If you were to ask a business whether it used a marginalist approach to pricing, its likely reaction would be 'no' as it has no familiarity with the approach. Nevertheless, it is still possible that its price-setting results in maximum profit, and if this is the case, then by definition MC must equal MR. It is possible that an established firm might approach a position of maximum profit through its experience of the market and through trial and error. We will also see in Chapter 9 that, under certain circumstances, profit maximisation can be achieved by cost-plus pricing, the favoured pricing method of many firms.

The complexity of the modern business organisation might also lead to difficulties in the firm achieving profit maximisation. Managers in different functional areas of the firm might start to pursue their own goals rather than profit. Co-ordination of common purpose can prove difficult in a large bureaucratic organisation. This will be further explored in Section 6.3.

In this debate, it is important to note that assuming the firm to be maximising profit does not imply it has no other goals, or that it will pursue profit to the ultimate degree in all circumstances. Instead, we assume profit to be so dominant an aim that for the purpose of our analysis and understanding of the firm other goals can be effectively ignored. That is, in assuming the firm has the sole aim of profit maximisation the results of our analysis are still seen to be viable and realistic.

We will now consider the possibility of alternative goals to profit maximisation.

### 6.2.2 Would a firm wish to maximise profit?

Even where the firm is able to maximise profit, would it always wish to do so?

The traditional neo-classical approach to the firm assumes the existence of an owner-manager. In such circumstances the rewards from the firm's performance come directly to the owner-manager and profit maximisation appears realistic. This assumption, however, could still be questioned. For example, an individual might set up in business on his or her own in order to provide customers with a valued service at minimal profit, at the same time maximising their opportunity to pursue such pleasures as golf or fishing.

The growth of large corporations and the dominance of public joint-stock companies brought the willingness of the firm to maximise profit into sharp focus due to the possibility of a separation of the ownership and management function. The implication was that although the firm was owned by its shareholders it essentially delegated the running of the business to professional managers, who may or may not have been shareholders. In short, there is a divorce of ownership from control and the goals of managers and shareholders might now be at variance. Under these circumstances it is easy to question the assumption of profit maximisation.

This situation can be illustrated by principal–agent theory (see Chapter 2), whereby the principals (in this case the shareholders) appoint agents (the professional managers) to operate the business on their behalf with the expectation that the business will be run in accordance with their wishes. If the shareholders' wish is to maximise profit, which would appear a reasonable assumption, they should monitor the behaviour of managers to ensure the firm is run accordingly. However, given the likelihood of there being a large number of shareholders, and shareholders usually only observing the outcome of managerial behaviour rather than the behaviour that resulted in the outcome, this is clearly a difficult task. There is now a clear possibility that management will be able to fulfil its own objectives which might be at variance with those of shareholders.

### 6.2.3 Constraints upon managerial behaviour?

Although managers may have different goals from shareholders they are still subject to control. At one extreme, legal constraints should prevent management defrauding the shareholders or running that company in a clearly negligent fashion. Other constraints would include the following:

#### Direct shareholder power

In theory, shareholders possess absolute power to appoint managers and dictate the direction and goals of the firm. Therefore, one might expect shareholders to act appropriately if the firm is not being run in their best interests. However, in practical terms they suffer from a lack of real information and the AGM is the only real opportunity to express their views. A further problem is the likely wide dispersion of share ownership in a given company and the ensuing difficulties that shareholders have in banding together to present their views.[2] Indeed, relatively few shareholders attend AGMs, many choosing to leave their proxy votes with the incumbent board of management. Although there are examples of shareholder power, such instances are relatively rare and usually brought about by extreme circumstances.

There can be a danger of under-estimating the power of shareholders as it is possible to exert control over a company with less than a majority of the shares. Indeed, the early work of Berle and Means (1934) in the United States in the 1930s assumed that given the wide distribution of shareholding within large companies,[3] an owner control situation could exist with a shareholding as low as 20 per cent, and further studies have estimated that effective control could be exercised with an even lower percentage share in most circumstances.[4]

#### Selling shares and the threat of takeover

If shareholders are dissatisfied with the firm's performance their likely reaction will be to sell their shares. If selling is widespread this will result in a falling share price. This may act as a control upon management as the falling share price will be seen in financial markets as a loss of confidence. It may also affect the prospects for further share issues and, importantly, increase the likelihood of **takeover** with the inherent risk of existing management losing its position.

**takeover** the process of acquiring another organisation or organisations

The risk of takeover increases due to the falling share price lowering the purchase price or market value of the firm relative to its asset value, the ratio of market value to asset value being the firm's **valuation ratio**, i.e.:

**valuation ratio** the ratio of a firm's market value to its asset value

Valuation ratio = market value/asset value

If we assume the asset value to be unaffected by low profit, then a falling share price lowers the valuation ratio and increases the chance of takeover. If the **asset value** were to exceed the **market value** the firm would lay itself open to **asset stripping**, i.e. a purchaser simply buying the firm to close it down and sell the assets.

**asset value** the value of the firm's assets as normally recorded in its balance sheet. The asset value per share is the total value of the firm's assets less its liabilities divided by the number of shares

The size of the valuation ratio does not in itself provide a complete explanation of takeover activity. There are other reasons for a takeover, for example to eliminate competition. In fact, in many instances it is found that a relatively high valuation ratio does not in itself deter takeover, and that it is often successful, well-managed firms that become targets for takeovers.[5]

**market value** the value of the firm as reflected in its share price

The ability of the threat of takeover to act as a constraint upon management can also be questioned on the grounds that potential bidders, like shareholders, do not have all the inside financial information that is available to management. The potential bidder might be unaware that the firm is failing to achieve its potential in terms of present or future profitability. Therefore, although a takeover might be warranted on the grounds that the present management is not achieving the firm's potential profitability, this might not be realised by outsiders. In other instances it might only be when the firm has been taken over, and the new owners become fully conversant with the company, that they realise they over-estimated the firm's potential. Current management might even attempt to disguise the well-being of the firm by boosting current dividend payments at the expense of future expenditure on research and development. In so doing they increase current share prices although this is likely to be at the expense of long-term growth and profits.

**asset stripping** where a purchaser buys an organisation in order to break up the firm and sell off some or all of its assets

In certain circumstances the value of a firm's assets can be under-valued as a result of a failure to include an appropriate valuation of the firm's brand name or names (see the mini case, 'The price of a brand name').

---

**Mini case** | **The price of a brand name**

When Nestlé took over Rowntree-Mackintosh in 1988 for £2.5 billion, it bought not only the physical assets of the company but also became owners of such valuable brand names as Kit-Kat, Smarties, Quality Street and Lion Bar. It was generally felt that Nestlé, in outbidding its rival Suchard, had obtained a bargain as the value of these brands was not properly reflected in Rowntree-Mackintosh's asset value.

At the time of the takeover comment was also made that Rowntree-Mackintosh had become prone to takeover due to its relatively low share price, brought about (according to Rowntree-Mackintosh's management and other observers) by the financial market's failure to correctly recognise the long-term potential of its plans to expand into European and overseas markets. Diverting investment into these overseas initiatives had affected profitability and diminished current share prices. Comment was made that this typified the financial market's concern with immediate performance rather than long-term potential. This accusation against UK financial markets is often referred to as **short-termism**.

**short-termism** a focus on immediate performance rather than long-term potential

The value of a brand was certainly not neglected in the case of the sale of Rolls-Royce Motor Cars to Volkswagen on 3 July 1998 for £479m. Although Vickers, the UK engineering group who owned both Rolls-Royce Motor Cars and Rolls-Royce plc (the aero-engine division), were willing to sell the motor car division to Volkswagen (VW) it purposely had not included the sale of the Rolls-Royce brand name, or marque (famously portrayed by the 'spirit of ecstasy' emblem and distinctive Rolls-Royce grille) in the deal. In fact, although Rolls-Royce Motor Cars owned the Bentley brand name, the Rolls-Royce brand name was separately owned by Rolls-Royce plc, a separate company. On 28 July 1998, Rolls-Royce plc sold the right to the Rolls-Royce name to BMW, one of VW's original rivals in its bid for Rolls-Royce Motor Cars. The Rolls-Royce brand name was sold for £40m.

Finally, in a deal brokered between BMW and VW, VW was allowed to use the Rolls-Royce and Bentley names until the end of 2002. From 2003, BMW would take over the Rolls-Royce name and produce cars of that name from a proposed new plant in the UK. VW will be left with the Bentley marque and its existing production plant at Crewe in the UK.

This relatively complicated takeover deal emphasises the value of a brand name in a company's assets.

### The power of banks and other financial institutions

Financial institutions and pension funds are increasingly major shareholders and will endeavour to influence firms, either as shareholders or by having a place on the board of directors. In either case they generally have greater expertise than the average shareholder and are more conversant with company practice and procedures. However, while such institutional investors can certainly act as a break on management they cannot guarantee profit-maximising behaviour.

### Managers as shareholders and linking pay to performance

The introduction of share option schemes whereby managers and workers are encouraged to obtain shares on preferential terms blurs the divide between owners and managers and goes some way to ensure that the interests of management and owners are common (see the mini case, 'Share options for company directors'). Nevertheless, the rewards to managers do not derive predominantly from their position as shareholders and the possible conflict between shareholder and management remains. Commonality of interest between shareholders and management could be influenced by the degree to which managers are also shareholders.

Directly linking managerial rewards to profit performance can induce management to work in the interest of shareholders. However, as indicated above, this may be only one determinant of managerial pay. Management might also seek to link its rewards to other performance measures such as company size and the growth of sales, although in certain circumstances these measures might not affect or might even conflict with profit and/or company efficiency. For example, sales might increase as a result of an overly expensive and inefficient promotional campaign; a gas company's sales will rise with lower than average winter temperatures; or the company might benefit from the demise or mistakes of rivals. Finally, although merger and takeover activity often provides a rationale for increased managerial salaries, it is often found that such activity does not in itself improve overall profitability. Such activity is, however, consistent with managerial motives for higher status.

---

| Mini case | **Share options for company directors** |

**share options** an option given to management to purchase shares in the organisation at some future date, usually at current prices

As part of their overall remuneration package most company directors are granted **share options** (a director's 'income package' typically comprises basic salary, performance-related or special bonuses including 'share options', additional allowances and benefits including pensions).

Share options allow directors at a future date to purchase a fixed number of the company's shares at a fixed price at or slightly above their current valuation. For example, a director might be given the option to buy 500,000 shares at 55p when the current price is 50p. If the price remains at or below 55p, the option is worthless. If the market price rises to 60p, the value of the option is worth $5p \times 500,000 = £25,000$. If the share price rises to 65p the value of the option rises to £50,000.

While the rationale behind such option schemes might be to reward directors for their contribution to company performance (as measured by the share price), a major deficiency with such a scheme is that a company's share price will most often rise or fall with the overall stock market index, which can fluctuate for all sorts of reasons due to the wider economic, international and political environment. The actual performance of the company might be only one determinant of the share price. For example, to quote from the *Observer* on 5 April 1998: 'National Westminster, which has been one of the poorest performers in the banking sector over the last year . . . was forced to sell its investment banking arm, has been involved in financial scandal and laid off thousands of staff. Yet Chief Executive Derek Wanless has seen the value of his share options soar by 216 per cent – more than £800,000 – to £1.2 million.'

Although the granting of share options has attracted criticism from certain circles, including trade unions and government spokespersons, the practice shows no sign of diminishing. Indeed, the rewards of such shares in the UK have been rising.

However, there is now an increasing trend to impose performance targets with certain schemes. For example (also quoted in the *Observer* on 5 April 1998): 'GEC's Managing Director George Simpson has received options to buy 1.25 million shares at 384p. With the company's share price at the end of March touching 473p it gives Simpson a potential profit of £1.2 million – but only if GEC hits a number of targets, such as outperforming the FTSE 100 index by 10 per cent over three years.'

Although share option schemes provide a link between managers and shareholders, they cannot in themselves guarantee managers acting in the best interests of shareholders.

The performance of a firm's managers affects their promotion prospects both within and outside the company. When seeking promotion management will therefore wish to be associated with success, as measured by their individual or company performance. Association with failure and/or poorly perceived market performance will lower a manager's future potential earnings. Therefore, a competitive market for managers, where their value is based upon the profitability and performance of their firm, might help ensure management works in the interest of shareholders. However, the question now arises as to the efficiency and competitiveness of such markets. A major problem is a lack of real information. For example, individual management performance might be difficult to identify and a 'poor' manager could be 'carried' by more efficient colleagues or subordinates, and vice versa. Where managers frequently change positions, the long- and medium-term impact of their performance might also not be immediately available. Further, even if performance data are available, this does not in itself guarantee an efficient market, as promotion may be gained on the basis of patronage or some other criterion. Nevertheless, the market still provides a 'control mechanism'. We may now consider the influence of the product market.

### Market forces in the product market

In perfectly competitive product markets the firm must be fully efficient to survive. In the long run, firms only earn normal profit (see Chapter 5). In these circumstances firms must pursue profit maximisation as any other policy results in the firm earning less than normal profit and being forced to leave the industry (note that long-run equilibrium in **monopolistic competition** is also characterised by firms only earning normal profit).

For a firm to pursue a non-profit-maximising goal it must therefore be in either an **oligopoly** or a **monopoly** and be capable of earning abnormal profit. In such circumstances the firm has the discretion to be less than fully efficient and still survive in the market (see the concepts of X-inefficiency in Section 5.11 and **organisational slack** below).

Market forces therefore act as a constraint upon management. In highly competitive markets management must achieve profit maximisation. The constraint is less where competitive forces are weaker. However, the dominance of oligopolistic markets in modern economies provides plenty of scope for non-profit-maximising behaviour. Nevertheless, competition is strong in all markets and firms cannot afford to neglect efficiency and profitability. However, as we will see below, profit now appears as a constraint upon behaviour rather than the sole or dominating goal of the firm.

**monopolistic competition** a market in which there are a large number of firms whose outputs are close but not perfect substitutes, either because of product differentiation or geographical fragmentation of the market

**monopoly** a market dominated by a single producer

## 6.3 · Alternative theories of the firm

Traditional theories of the firm broadly envisage a situation where the owner-manager (or entrepreneur), armed with perfect knowledge of the internal working of the firm and its competitive environment, pursues maximum profit by equating marginal cost to marginal revenue. The entrepreneur is assumed to have no objectives other than profit. All profit comes to the entrepreneur as the firm's owner.

This view cannot be seen as an accurate description of a typical modern enterprise. The question is, therefore, how do firms behave? New or alternative theories need to take into account current organisational structures and particularly the emergence of the public joint-stock company. The appearance of such companies and the separation of ownership from control has led to the development of alternative theories of the firm. Although profit plays an important role in such theories, it may no longer be seen as the sole or dominating goal of the firm.

There are two generic types of alternative theory, namely:

1 managerial theories
2 behavioural theories.

### 6.3.1 Managerial theories

**managerial theories** a school of thought in which organisational decision-making is generally related to the goals being pursued by senior managers

The starting point of all **managerial theories** is the assumption of a divorce of ownership from control. It is also assumed that top managers are able to dominate decision-making through their ability to determine company strategy, future investments, promotions and the appointment of persons to key company positions.

In common with the traditional neo-classical approach, these are also maximising theories. However, in place of profit, managers are now assumed to maximise their own utility or satisfaction subject to a minimum profit constraint. Managerial theories differ from one another in terms of the factors or objectives that determine managerial utility, and how those objectives might be achieved.

Although profit is no longer seen as the sole aim of the firm, its relevance remains in the sense that a firm's management can only pursue its own goals when shareholders receive an acceptable minimum level of profit. If this were not the case, managers would risk jeopardising their position, as shareholders will either collectively seek to replace them, or else sell their shares and increase the likelihood of takeover. In such theories profit therefore appears as a constraint upon managerial behaviour.

There are a number of management theories each associated with a particular economist and a specific maximising goal. We will examine three:

1 W. J. Baumol – 'sales revenue maximisation'
2 O. E. Williamson – 'managerial utility maximisation'
3 R. Marris – 'company growth maximisation'.

**Baumol's model of sales revenue maximisation**

As with all managerial theories, Baumol's (1959) starting point was the assumption of a divorce of ownership from control within oligopolistic markets.[6] From experience as a consultant to large corporations he proposed that rather than maximise profit, managers instead seek to maximise sales revenue, subject to an acceptable profit constraint. As we will see, in maximising sales revenue the firm will generally have higher sales and sales growth than a profit-maximising enterprise.

The preoccupation of management with sales revenue was largely rationalised on the grounds that managerial salaries, perks and status were more closely

linked to sales revenue than profit. Baumol also noted the favourable attitude
of banks and other financial institutions to sales growth and that growth
enhanced opportunities for promotion and higher salaries. Alternatively, with
declining sales revenue, employees might need to be laid off or have their
salaries reduced. Banks and other financial institutions would now look less
favourably upon financial provision, and retail outlets would become less willing to provide prime points of sale. Indeed, if sales fell below a certain
threshold, retailers might choose to cease trading a good altogether.

In his basic model, Baumol assumed the firm to produce a single product
and aim to maximise sales revenue (SR) over a single time period. There is no
consideration of the interdependence between the firm and others within and
outside the industry.

This model can be illustrated by Figure 6.1. The total revenue (TR) and
total cost (TC) curves are derived from conventional downward-sloping
demand curves and U-shaped cost curves. The profit function is also shown.
(This basic diagram was previously shown in Chapter 5 as Figure 5.15a).

To maximise profit the firm produces $Q_m$. To maximise SR, the firm increases
sales to $Q_b$ by charging a lower price, resulting in a lower level of profit.

As indicated, the model assumes a profit constraint. This represents the
minimum profit required to maintain the satisfaction of shareholders and
financial markets. This constraint might be either operative or inoperative.
For example, in maximising SR the firm would not achieve a constraint such
as $\pi_2$ and would be obliged to increase price and reduce output to $Q_b'$. This

**Figure 6.1 Baumol's sales revenue maximisation model**

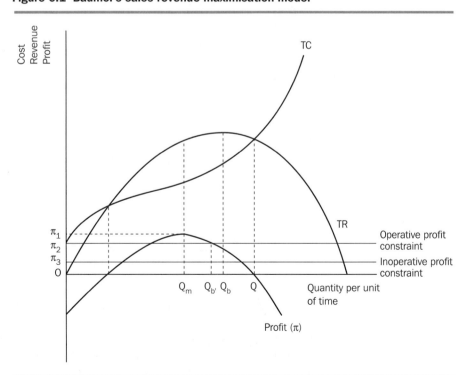

profit constraint would therefore be 'operative'. Alternatively, a constraint of $\pi_3$ would be 'inoperative' as the firm can still maximise SR and achieve a profit in excess of the constraint and more than satisfy the demands and aspirations of shareholders and financial markets.

Where the firm is faced with an inoperative profit constraint, the firm could be assumed to spend **surplus profit** (i.e. profit above the profit constraint) on any activity that would further enhance SR. For example, surplus profit could be spent on additional advertising, shifting the demand curve to the right and the TR curve upwards. The firm would continue spending more money on advertising (also shifting the TC upwards) until all surplus profit was exhausted and the profit constraint became operative. (The level of profit now equals the profit constraint.) Such a position must be reached if we assume there are diminishing returns to advertising: that is, increased expenditure upon advertising eventually having a diminishing impact upon SR.

Therefore, so long as the profit constraint is less than maximum profit, Baumol's firm will always produce more and charge a lower price than a profit maximiser. It is also likely that the firm will advertise more and generally invest more in any activity likely to increase demand.

An additional feature of Baumol's model is its prediction of how the firm reacts to a change in fixed or variable costs. Firstly imagine an increase in fixed costs. This would cause the total cost curve in Figure 6.1 to shift upwards in a parallel fashion and the profit curve to shift downwards. This is

**surplus profit** in this context profit above the profit constraint

**Figure 6.2 Impact of a change in fixed costs** (Baumol's model)

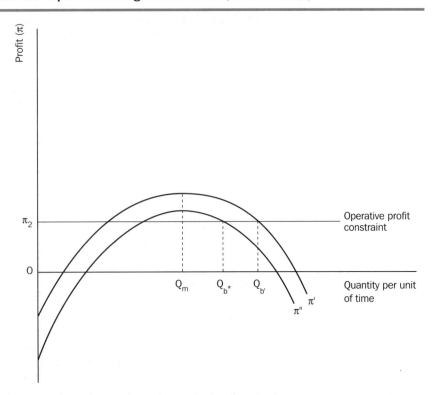

**Figure 6.3 Impact of a change in variable costs** (Baumol's model)

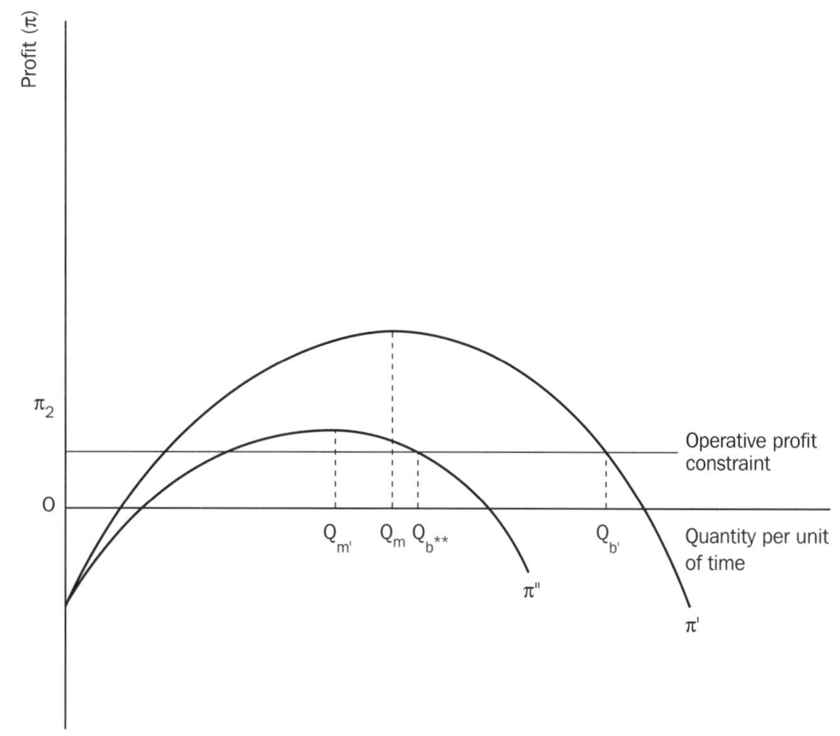

illustrated in Figure 6.2 with the profit curve shifting downwards from $\pi'$ to $\pi''$. With an 'operational profit' constraint of $\pi_2$ the sales maximiser would react to the increased cost by raising price and reducing output from $Q_b'$ to $Q_b^*$. This is in contrast to the prediction of the profit-maximising model where because a change in fixed cost does not affect marginal cost the profit-maximising output (where MC equals MR) is not affected. Therefore, price and output remain unchanged despite the increase in fixed cost. This can also be seen in Figure 6.2 by the profit-maximising output remaining at $Q_m$. The reaction of Baumol's firm appears more realistic.

Now, consider the impact of an increase in variable cost. This causes the total cost curve in Figure 6.1 to pivot upwards and become steeper at all levels of output (i.e. marginal cost has increased) and the profit function to shift downwards and to the left as illustrated in Figure 6.3. With an 'operative profit constraint' of $\pi_2$, the sales maximiser decreases output from $Q_b'$ to $Q_b^{**}$ and raises price. The increase in marginal cost also causes the 'profit maximiser' to increase price and reduce from $Q_m$ to $Q_m'$. Note, however, that the 'sales maximiser' reduces output more than the 'profit maximiser' and in consequence raises prices more, albeit from a lower initial level.

What might we say in conclusion regarding Baumol's basic model?

Firstly, although there is certainly some evidence to link managerial salaries and perks to sales revenue, the model fails to explicitly consider the interdependence and uncertainty within oligopolistic markets.[7] A further point involves the nature of the profit constraint. Would it really be so precise a figure as we have assumed and what might determine its size? In reality the constraint might better be seen as a band (or range), with management seeking to obtain profits within that band. Achieving profits at the lower end of the band increases the probability of shareholder dissatisfaction. In contrast, shareholders will almost certainly be satisfied with profits towards the top end of the band. This still leaves us with the question of what might determine the size of the profit constraint, or the range of the band. Various factors could determine this. These could include profits achieved in previous time periods, the current economic climate and the profit performance of close competitors.

The original model is also basically static in that the firm is assumed to maximise sales revenue in a single time period irrespective of the impact upon future time periods. However, Baumol later developed a dynamic multi-period model where the firm was assumed to maximise the rate of growth of sales over its lifetime. In this dynamic model, profit now appears as the main source of financing the growth of sales revenue and becomes an instrumental and determined variable within the model rather than an exogenous constraint upon managerial behaviour.

### O. E. Williamson's model of managerial utility maximisation

Williamson (1964), like Baumol, assumes managers have the discretion to maximise their own utility.[8] Profit is again seen as a necessary constraint to ensure managerial job security.

**U-form organisation** the unitary form of organisation with a strong management hierarchy and little decentralisation of decision-making

**M-form organisation** an organisation with a multi-divisional structure

Williamson in fact considered his model to be of more relevance to those firms operating with a strong management hierarchy and little decentralisation of decision-making, referred to as a **U-form (unitary-form)** of organisational structure (see Chapter 2). Alternatively, he believed managerial discretion would be better controlled (and profit maximisation maintained) in organisations with central control and a multidivision structure, with each division working as a separate profit centre with a strong degree of managerial independence. This is generally referred to as an **M-form (multi-form)** structure. Williamson therefore believed that managerial discretion was better explained by organisational structure rather than the existence of a separation of ownership from control. However, although M-form structures might be more efficient in certain circumstances, it remains in question whether managers would then by necessity always choose to act in accordance with the wishes of shareholders.

The variables within Williamson's managerial utility function include salaries, status, security, power and prestige. Of these variables only salary is directly measurable in monetary terms and therefore operational within the utility function. Other variables are deemed non-pecuniary and therefore non-operational. These variables then become operational by being measured by other pecuniary variables to which they are assumed correlated. These proxy variables are staff expenditures, emoluments and discretionary investment. Management is then assumed to have an expense preference for these variables: that is, a preference for expenditure on such variables above that required for the profit maximisation of the firm.

The utility function can be expressed as:

$$U = f(S, I_d, M) \quad \text{to be maximised subject to a minimum profit constraint.}$$

where:

- U = managerial utility or satisfaction

- S = staff expenditure, including managerial salaries, bonuses and share options.

It is assumed that management derives satisfaction from controlling and appointing additional members of staff: being in charge of more staff brings greater power, status and prestige. Obtaining more staff also implies the successful performance and future expansion of that manager's area of operation.

- $I_d$ = Discretionary investments

Managerial status and power is enhanced by the discretion managers have in undertaking additional investments in excess of those required for the normal operation of the firm. Such discretionary investment allows them to gain particular satisfaction by pursuing projects in line with their own interests. These might include expenditure on sports or arts sponsorship. For instance, although purchasing a hospitality box at a local Premier League football club could be rationalised on the grounds of enhancing the firm's public image and facilitating the entertainment of clients, it is also likely to provide additional utility to managers, particularly where the purchase coincides with their own sporting interests.

**discretionary investment** additional investment, undertaken by managers in excess of those required for the normal operation of the firm

The model assumes the source of **discretionary investment** to be 'discretionary profit', where 'discretionary profit' is the amount of profit remaining after subtracting from actual profit the minimum profit constraint and any tax liabilities. (Therefore, reported profits would normally be in excess of the minimum profit constraint.) This is in contrast to Baumol's model of sales revenue maximisation where the firm only aims to earn the minimum profit constraint.

- M = Expenditure on managerial emoluments (perks)

These could include managerial access to expense accounts, company cars, overseas business trips, luxurious offices, etc. and represent a major determinant of managerial prestige. Although such 'perks' might be included within the manager's overall employment package, by definition such emoluments represent payments in excess of opportunity costs, or **slack**. Their removal would not be assumed to cause management to seek employment elsewhere. Such 'perks' are possible due to the strategic position that management holds in controlling the firm.

Expenditures on S, $I_d$ and M are assumed to enhance managerial utility. However, the model assumes diminishing returns to each variable, implying that although total utility increases with the additional expenditure upon each variable it does so at a diminishing rate, i.e. the variables are subject to **diminishing managerial utility**. This assumption appears reasonable and in accordance with consumer theory where the consumer is assumed to gain diminishing satisfaction from additional units of a good consumed in a given time period.[9]

**diminishing managerial utility** the tendency for managerial satisfaction to rise at a diminishing rate with changes in other variables

To maximise utility (U), managers continue to consume S, $I_d$ and M to the point where each yields the same marginal utility (MU) per pound spent. This condition can be expressed as:

$$\frac{MU_s}{£s} = \frac{MUI_d}{£I_d} = \frac{MUM}{£m}$$

The above equation therefore states that to maximise overall utility each variable should have the same (marginal) benefit to (marginal) cost ratio.[10] The extra pound spent should yield the same additional utility (marginal utility) no matter which variable it is 'spent' on. If this were not the case then one variable would offer more 'marginal satisfaction per pound' than another, and the funds would not be optimally allocated. If the relative attractiveness to management of one of the variables increased, or its 'price of purchase' changed, management would be assumed to alter the distribution of expenditure between the variables until the above equality is regained.

Perhaps the most interesting implication of the model is the observation that managers do not have a neutral attitude to cost. Certain expenditures, for example discretionary investments or hiring additional staff, provide management with utility over and above the return achieved from the productivity of that expenditure. In contrast, a profit maximiser only values expenditure for its productivity. Managers in Williamson's model therefore have an 'expense preference' and will not minimise cost at each level of output. In essence, 'organisational slack' exists within the organisation. As a consequence, profit will be lower and costs higher than in a profit-maximising situation, as expenditures on staff (and staff numbers) together with other emoluments are higher than necessary.[11] However, in common with Baumol, the model does not explicitly take into account interdependence and rivalry.

### R. Marris's model of company growth maximisation

Marris (1964) assumed management to be motivated towards maximising the growth in demand for the firm's output.[12] The model is therefore dynamic in nature emphasising the proposition that management would rather be associated with a growing firm than simply a large firm, as growth brings financial rewards, job security, prestige and status. Association with a growing firm will also improve career prospects within and outside the existing firm.

A particular feature of the model is the assumption that shareholders are also interested in growth so long as the growth in sales is matched by a growth in the firm's capital (assets, stocks and liquidity), as shareholders will then also gain through the increased value of their shares. Marris therefore proposed that the goals of management and shareholders could be reconciled through the growth of the firm, reconciliation coming about through the firm achieving **balanced growth** whereby productive capacity (the firm's capital) and market demand grow at the same rate. Reconciliation of interests therefore ensures the firm avoids either excess demand over productive capacity or excess capacity over demand.

**balanced growth** a situation in which the firms productive capacity and market demand grow at the same rate

In line with other managerial theories, management is faced with a profit constraint. To maintain job security, which is assumed a major aim, management must keep the market price of shares and the share dividend at a satisfactory level. With share prices falling relative to the capital value of the firm there is a risk of takeover and a loss of job security.

The basis of the model can be illustrated in Figure 6.4.

**Figure 6.4  Marris's growth model**

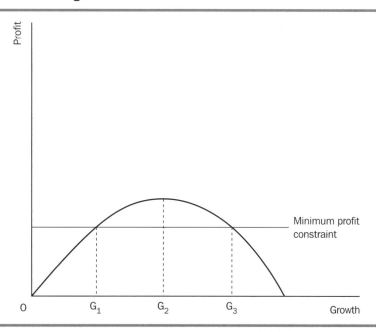

As growth increases in Figure 6.4 towards $G_2$, the rate of profit is assumed to increase, although at a decreasing rate. At this stage the firm is benefiting from increased scale economies and profits can be reinvested in productive new investments to promote further growth. However, the rate of profit eventually declines as growth can only be maintained by further price reductions and spending excessive amounts on other activities including advertising to promote further growth. It is also likely that, in an attempt to maintain growth, the firm increasingly moves into less profitable sidelines and investments, including takeovers. Such diversification is likely to be at the expense of profit. So long as the rate of profit is increasing it is likely that the ratio of the share price to the firm's capital value will also rise. Once the profit rate starts to fall then the ratio will eventually decline, increasing the possibility of takeover and endangering job security.

Figure 6.4 shows a minimum profit constraint. Management therefore runs the risk of either growing at too slow or too fast a rate. That is, at a rate of growth below $G_1$ or above $G_3$ managers risk job insecurity. Given that managers are assumed to gain satisfaction from growth rather than profit we can assume a growth rate closer to $G_3$.

The model emphasises profit as a source of investment to promote growth. It is therefore in the interest of management to reinvest a high proportion of profit rather than provide shareholders with high dividends. Management therefore seeks a high **retention ratio** of realised to distributed profit. However, in so doing this may diminish the share price and increase the risk of takeover. To ensure security, management therefore seeks a retention ratio that is acceptable to shareholders.

We therefore have an overall principle of balance in that the firm is assumed to seek a balance between the rate of growth of demand and the rate

**retention ratio** the ratio of retained to distributed profits

of growth of the firm's assets subject to providing shareholders with an acceptable dividend payment or retention ratio. In satisfying shareholders, and ensuring job security, management may therefore be willing to sacrifice a degree of growth.

A major feature of Marris's model is the observation that the goals of management and shareholders are not so wide as implied by other managerial theories, as both parties are interested in growth. That is, management is concerned with the growth of sales and shareholders with the growth of the firm's capital; reconciliation can be achieved through balanced growth.

A further significant feature of the model is the inclusion of the firm's financial policies into the decision-making process. However, Marris does not clearly specify why shareholders should necessarily prefer capital growth rather than profit, and in line with other managerial theories there is no real analysis of the influence of oligopolistic interdependence.[13]

### 6.3.2 Behavioural or satisficing theories

Once again it is assumed that there is a divorce of ownership from control. However, whereas managerial theories see management as having a single maximising goal, **behaviouralists** focus on the complexity of business organisations and see the organisation as being made up of various groups or **stakeholders** (managers, workers, shareholders, customers, suppliers, trade unions, etc.) with each group having differing and possibly conflicting objectives and demands.

**behaviouralists** a school of thought which generally focuses on the human aspects of organisations in explaining organisational behaviour

The behaviouralist then studies the nature of such conflict between the groups and how it might be resolved. In so doing it is recognised that the firm may only seek 'satisfactory' levels of performance. In short, rather than maximise, the firm **satisfices**.

**satisfices** a situation which organisational (or personal) goals are set at a satisfactory and sufficient level rather than being maximised

The concept of 'satisficing' was introduced by H. A. Simon (1959) who proposed that managers were unable and unwilling to set themselves maximising goals and instead sought satisfactory levels of achievement or goals.[14] It was then recognised that there would be a tendency not to set objectives too high since failure to achieve an objective might bring censure; setting too low a goal might also bring criticism. Where goals were achieved this would then be likely to result in the setting of marginally higher goals. This general approach is often referred to as **management by objectives**.

**management by objectives** the idea that managerial performance can be measured in relation to pre-specified objectives

**coalition** the idea that a firm comprises a collection of groups with particular needs and requirements

Cyert and March (1965) extended Simon's analysis by focusing upon the different groups within the organisation.[15] In so doing they introduced the concept of the **coalition** to include all those groups who place demands upon the firm at a given time, for example:

- workers seek high wages, good working conditions and security of employment;
- managers seek high salaries, power and prestige;
- shareholders wish for healthy share dividends and the increased value of their shares;
- the customer demands value for money, prompt delivery and good after-sales service;
- suppliers hope for regular orders without too many changes of specification;
- trade unions demand negotiation rights and full means of address for their members, etc.

Cyert and March suggested that most groups remain relatively passive so long as they receive satisfactory compensation (see also the concept of slack payments below) such as workers receiving adequate payment or shareholders receiving satisfactory dividends. However, although parts of the coalition might be bought off in this fashion, management is assumed to seek specific policy commitments and rewards.

Interestingly this approach does not see management as a single homogeneous group with common goals. Instead, it is seen as fulfilling different functional roles within the organisation. For example, we may have marketing managers and personnel managers; each of these managers, and the area of the firm in which they operate, may then have different goals and demands. The firm is commonly divided into the following functional departments:

- production and production development
- sales and marketing
- personnel
- finance

**top management** the most senior managers within the organisation

Within the management group we can distinguish **top management**. It is the role of top management ultimately to set the goals of the firm. The firm is seen to have five main goals:

1 *The product goal*. This goal is of direct concern to the production department. It will wish for smooth and continuous production and the avoidance of either excess capacity (necessitating the lay-off of workers) or working above capacity and the inherent problems of overworking fixed capital, machinery breakdowns, etc. It may also be reluctant to implement too many design modifications to the product.

2 *The inventory goal*. Whilst holding inventories (stocks) of raw materials and finished products may satisfy the production and the sales/marketing departments respectively by avoiding the risk of running short of stock, it will displease the financial department who regard the holding of excessive stock as wasteful in tying up working capital.

3 *The sales goal*. This originates from the sales/marketing department and may be defined in terms of either sales revenue or sales volume. In either case there might be a conflict with profitability as these goals might, for example, be achieved through excessive advertising and/or price reductions. The need for more output to satisfy increased demand, and for increasingly innovative products to create demand, might cause conflict with the production and design departments.

4 *The market share goal*. The firm is clearly concerned with its market share and outperforming its rivals. Although this goal may be contained within the sales goal, it is likely to be a pivotal goal within the firm's strategic planning.

5 *The profit goal*. Profit is clearly essential to satisfy shareholders and financial institutions. It also serves as a source of investment and growth, and as a fund for 'slack' payments and 'policy commitments' (see below). Excessive profit might not be viewed so positively by customers, suppliers, shop-floor workers and outside agencies including government.

The setting of targets for the above goals will necessitate senior managers bargaining with the various groups within the coalition, and they will attempt to satisfy as many demands as possible. Certain basic goals (for example, the sales goal) may be acceptable to virtually the whole coalition, since without sales the firm will cease to exist. As we have seen, other goals can cause conflict. It is also interesting to note that over different time periods certain goals may be given more prominence. For example, the firm might become more sales or marketing orientated due to the current state of the market or the dominance within top management of those with a marketing background. At other times the firm might become more production orientated.

Where conflicts persist, top management might seek a degree of resolution by providing rewards to individuals above their opportunity cost. A manager, for instance, might receive a salary in excess of that required to keep them in the firm. Or the manager of a department might become reconciled by the provision of more luxurious office space, recreational facilities, expense accounts, etc. Such additional payments are referred to as slack payments.

**policy commitments**
undertakings made by
senior decision-makers

Reconciliation might be also sought via **policy commitments** to provide additional resources to particular sections of the coalition, such as through upgrading computing facilities in the finance department, or purchasing a new fleet of cars for the sales department. Such policy commitments might be sequential in the sense that a department might not receive immediate funding yet be told it has been prioritised for future funding. Priority should be given to the most immediate problems. For example, the breakdown of machinery might necessitate immediate investment in production.

In essence, the firm is not seeking to maximise any of its goals. Instead, it has aspiration levels with regard to these goals and seeks 'satisfactory' overall performance: 'satisfactory' levels of production, inventories, sales, market-share and profit. The firm is therefore seen as a 'satisficer' rather than a 'maximiser'.

The undoubted strength of the behavioural approach is to concentrate upon the nature of decision-making (and compromise) within a complex business organisation. In that sense there is certainly a strong degree of realism. A consideration of the influence of the whole range of stakeholders, both internal and external to the firm, upon decision-making is also welcome and timely, given the recent emphasis upon stakeholders in business practice. However, the need to include such a wide range of variables makes the model difficult to test, and as with other alternative theories there is no real concentration upon the interdependence of firms within oligopolistic markets.

## 6.4 Conclusions

The traditional assumption of profit maximisation can certainly be questioned as regards the ability and willingness of firms to pursue such an objective. This question was brought particularly into focus with the divorce of ownership from control in modern joint-stock companies and the unlikelihood that constraints upon managers would force them to retain profit as their sole objective. Managerial theories set out alternative models of behaviour with management assumed to seek the maximisation of its own utility through, for example, the maximisation of either sales revenue or growth. The choice of such an objective then impacts upon the firm's price and output. In contrast, the behaviouralists focus upon the complexity of a modern business organisation and question whether the firm should be seen to have a single goal. Instead, there emerge a number of goals, with top management seeking satisfactory levels of attainment for each goal rather than a strategy of maximisation.

Nevertheless, in all our alternative theories profit still plays an important role as a constraint upon managerial behaviour. It is also an important source of investment and future growth. Profit therefore remains pivotal in explaining the strategic decisions of the business organisation.

It is also relevant to distinguish between short- and long-run behavioural objectives of the firm. For example, although the firm might pursue a short run strategy of sales revenue maximisation as a means of increasing market share (and in the short run be willing to sacrifice profit to do so), the long-term strategy might be to maximise profit. Specifically, having captured a larger share of the market and having eliminated, or taken over, much of the competition, the firm can then achieve the benefits of greater profitability. Profit-maximising behaviour could therefore remain as a long-term objective.

---

**Case study**   ## 'Name and shame' policy to curb the 'fat cats'?

Since the privatisation of the majority of the UK's public utilities in the 1980's, successive government and public opinion has been concerned with the high salaries paid to the top management of some of Britain's best-known companies. Whilst the media branded such persons as 'fat cats', the defence was made that salaries had been kept artificially low pre-privatis-ation and that current levels were warranted given the market demand for top managers and their achievements in securing high profits and performance. In fact, since privatisation, not only have such managers consistently received high basic pay, they have additionally received relatively large bonuses and share options on the basis of company performance. For example, the *Independent* on 28 July 1998 reported the current chief executive of National Grid as earning £355,000 including an £88,000 bonus, and the managing director of Thames Water with a corresponding £277,000 including a £47,000 bonus. (However, as we will see below, such salaries might appear relatively modest in comparison to others outside the utilities sector.)

Rather than directly controlling the pay of utility company executives, the Labour government in July 1998 announced its intention to create a greater degree of 'transparency'. To this end, future legislation was promised to provide a closer link between bonuses awarded to executives and the standards of performance achieved by companies in the water, gas, electricity and telecommunications industries. The new legislation would require companies in their annual accounts to set out clearly the link between directors' pay and service standards, indicating the weight given to their achievement when setting salaries and bonuses. Additionally, the current utility regulators (see Chapter 11) would attempt to influence companies by writing an 'open letter' each year to company remuneration committees setting out how, in their belief, such companies had performed with regards to customer service in a bid to influence bonus and salary decisions.

▶

It remains to be seen how effective such a 'name and shame' strategy will be. Will utility bosses who might be appearing to pay themselves more than their performance warrants really be constrained by finding themselves 'pilloried in public!?' Many believe this might not be the case given the existing 'thick hides' of many such executives. It should also be noted that the government regulation of utilities is confined to their 'regulated businesses' and not their growing non-regulated business. For example, only 22 per cent of BT revenues in 1998 was covered by regulatory controls.

If the above initiative proves ineffective it is possible that the government might counter by introducing further regulatory pricing controls. However, many believe that ultimate market control will only really be achieved through increased competition in utility markets, on the grounds that the allegedly currently inflated salaries and bonuses are primarily a function of the current 'monopoly' position within the major utilities. In the absence of such competition, Stephen Byers, the UK Chief Secretary to the Treasury, was quoted in August 1998 as stressing that boardroom pay was particularly crucial in monopoly utilities where customers had no other choices. In such circumstances, he believed directors' pay should be linked to levels of service.

Although there has been much emphasis paid to boardroom pay at the privatised utility companies, an index of top executive pay published and commissioned by the *Guardian* in July 1998 indicated that the utility company directors were relatively modestly rewarded compared to their peers. Indeed, whereas the study indicated an average annual pay for utility chiefs at £439,000, this was only just above half the average received by the bosses of companies listed in the FTSE 100 Index.

The findings of the *Guardian* survey were later supported by a survey published by Incomes Data Services and Arthur Andersen, the accountancy and consultancy firm, on 6 August 1998. They reported that 49 directors from Britain's 350 largest companies received more than £1 million in pay and bonuses in the previous year, representing about one in 40 leading executives, 13 of whom received more than £2 million. The research also indicated that most of the largest packages came in the financial sector, and that the average annual pay increase for the highest-paid directors was 18 per cent at a time when average earnings were rising at just over 4 per cent. In this context, rather than appearing to concentrate upon the utilities, perhaps the government should seek moderation from the wider executive business community.

The recent initiative into the pay of executives in the major utilities should also be seen in the context of three relatively recent committees that were set up to consider boardroom remuneration and behaviour (see also Chapter 2).

1 Sir Adrian Cadbury's committee at the beginning of the 1990s was set up initially to recommend checks and balances in the light of corporate scandals involving such companies as Maxwell Communications, Polly Peck and British and Commonwealth. Although Sir Adrian's committee was largely concerned with corporate governance, it also recommended that there be more meaningful disclosure of executive pay and that boardrooms should

establish independent remuneration committees. Further, quoted in the *Guardian* on 22 July 1998, he stated that: 'We set out the guidelines. Boardrooms address them and institutions have the responsibility to take action and exert influence. But this is where the debate ought to be: between directors and shareholders.'

2 The Greenbury Committee was set up later in the 1990s in the wake of the much publicised and criticised 75 per cent pay award to Cedric Brown, the then chief executive of British Gas and the distribution of various share windfalls to the executives of other privatised utilities. Although the Greenbury Committee did make various recommendations it rejected the suggestion that boardroom pay increases should match those further down the company hierarchy. (Note, however, that even if executives were receiving the same basic pay award as all other workers it is still likely that they would receive other additional bonuses.)

3 The Hampel Committee on corporate governance reported in 1998. This committee rejected the suggestion from Margaret Beckett, then the Trade and Industry Secretary, that shareholders should be provided with the right to vote directly on executive pay packages. Nevertheless, Sir Ronnie Hampel was quoted in the *Guardian* on 22 July 1998 as saying: 'the existence of law or codes does not of itself ensure they are followed'. He was further quoted: 'as far as remuneration specifically is concerned, it cannot be controlled in a free market except by government action. But the full disclosure of directors' pay in the UK does enable judgements to be made by all relevant parties and any excesses to become obvious.'

This is clearly a lively debate. Does the government have a role in controlling the pay of company executives, or should it be left to market forces and the supervision and discretion of shareholders? Are company executives really worth such large salaries? Why should a company executive receive a pay award of 18 per cent whilst those on the shop floor only receive 4 per cent?

## Notes and references

1. Hall, R. L. and Hitch, C. J. (1939), 'Price theory and business behaviour', Oxford Economic Papers. Also reprinted in Andrews, P. W. S. and Wilson, T. (eds), (1952), *Oxford Studies in the Price Mechanism*, Oxford University Press, Oxford.

2. There is evidence from both the USA and UK economics that the dispersion of shares within companies has steadily increased since the 1930s. See Moschandreas, M. (1994), *Business Economics*, Routledge, London, Chapter 9, pp. 269–272.

3. Berle, A. A. and Means, G. C. (1934), *The Modern Corporation and Private Property*, Macmillan, New York.

4. For example, Nyman, S. and Silberston, A. (1978), in 'The ownership and control of industry', Oxford Economic Papers, suggested that control in certain circumstances might be exercised with only a 5 per cent shareholding. In addition to such arguments, it is also often pointed out that many large companies are family-owned and controlled and that in such circumstances there is no effective separation of ownership from control (e.g. in UK retailing, Sainsbury and Dixons).

5. For an interesting and informative discussion of 'economic theory and merger activity' see Griffiths, A. and Wall, S. (1999), *Applied Economics: An Introductory Text*, 8th edition, Longman, Harlow, Chapter 3, pp. 87–93.

6. Baumol, W. J. (1959), *Business Behaviour, Value and Growth*, Macmillan, New York; revised edition, Harcourt, Brace and World, Inc., 1967.

7. See Griffiths, A. and Wall, S. (1996), *Intermediate Microeconomics, Theory and Applications*, Longman, Harlow, Chapter 5, pp. 223–234. For example, as cited in Griffiths and Wall, a study by Conyon, M. and Gregg, P. (1994), 'Pay at the top: A study of the sensitivity of a top director remuneration to company specific shocks', *National Institute Economic Review*, 3, found the pay of top UK executives to be closely related to 'relative sales revenue growth, that is, sales growth relative to that of close competitors.

8. Williamson, O. E. (1964), *The Economics of Discretionary Behaviour: Managerial Objectives in the Theory of the Firm*, Prentice Hall, Englewood Cliffs, NJ.

9. Most introductory economic texts include an analysis of the 'utility theory of demand'. For example, see Lipsey, R. G. and Chrystal, K. A. (1995), 'An Introduction to Positive Economics, 8th edition, Oxford University Press, Oxford, Part 3, pp. 128–132.

10. The rationale behind this utility–maximising equation is also presented in the section of Lipsey and Chrystal (1995).

11. Further predictions of Williamson's model can be seen in Moschandreas, M. (1994), *Business Economics*, Routledge, London, pp. 283–285. This section includes an analysis of how the 'managerial utility maximiser' is assumed to react to changes in demand and different types of tax. Moschandreas (pp. 281–283), also illustrates how the model can be presented utilising an indifference curve approach that we introduced in Chapter 4.

12. Marris, R. (1964), *Theory of Managerial Capitalism,* Macmillan, Basingstoke.

13. A further analysis of Marris's model can be found in Koutsoyiannis, A. (1979), *Modern Microeconomics,* 2nd edition, Macmillan, Basingstoke. Also see Griffiths and Wall (1996), pp. 211–214.

14. Simon, H. A. (1959), 'Theories of decision making in economics and behavioural science', *American Economic Review*, June.

15. Cyert, R. M. and March, C. J. (1965), *A Behavioural Theory of the Firm*, Prentice Hall, Englewood Cliffs, NJ.

## Review and discussion questions

1 Outline the main difficulties faced by a firm seeking to maximise profit.

2 Examine the problems faced by shareholders in controlling the behaviour of a firm.

3 Baumol's model of sales revenue maximisation assumes managers to be faced by a profit constraint. What determines the size of this constraint and would it be a precise figure?

4 Use an appropriate diagram to show the distinction between an operational and a non-operational profit constraint in Baumol's model.

5 Managers in Williamson's model of managerial utility maximisation are assumed not to have a neutral attitude towards cost. What does this mean and how does it impact upon the firm?

6 Provide examples of how short-run non-profit-maximising behaviour can often be consistent with maximising long-run profits.

## Assignments

1 Find and analyse any recent evidence in financial newspapers and reports supporting the proposition that shareholders, acting either individually or collectively, can have a real impact upon the behaviour of the firm.

2 Do you believe that behavioural theories of the firm are intrinsically more realistic and provide greater insights into the behaviour of firms than other theories?

## Further reading

Dobbs, I. (2000), *Managerial Economics*, Oxford University Press, Oxford, Chapter 17.

Griffiths, A. and Wall, S. (1996), *Intermediate Microeconomics Theory*, Longman, Harlow, Chapter 5.

Griffiths, A. and Wall, S. (1999), *Applied Economics*, 8th edition, Longman, Harlow, Chapter 3.

Koutsoyiannis, A (1979), *Modern Microeconomics*, 2nd edition, Macmillan, Basingstoke, Chapters 15, 17 and 18.

Moschandreas, M. (1994), *Business Economics*, Routledge, London, Chapter 9.

# Market structures

Chris Britton

## 7.1 Introduction

It is important to look at the structure of markets or industries for at least two reasons. Firstly, structure affects the way in which firms behave and their performance. For example, the behaviour of firms in a highly competitive market will be quite different from that of firms which face little or no competition. Thus it is important for firms themselves to know and understand the **market structure** in which they operate. Secondly, an assessment of market structure is also important in the formulation of strategic policies. This chapter starts with a consideration of two approaches which have been used to characterise and analyse markets or industries: the Structure–Conduct–Performance approach and Porter's five forces model. The chapter then goes on to look at alternative market structures from both a theoretical and an empirical viewpoint.

## 7.2 The Structure–Conduct–Performance approach

**structure-conduct-performance model** an economic model of how markets and industries operate

The **Structure–Conduct–Performance (S-C-P)** approach was first proposed by Mason (1939) as a means of analysing firms and markets;[1] his ideas were later modified by his student, Bain (1956).[2] The S-C-P approach is clearly rooted in neo-classical economics, where firms are assumed to maximise profits, consumers are assumed to maximise utility and markets tend towards a position of equilibrium. The traditional S-C-P model argues that basic market conditions and structural factors in an industry will determine the conduct of

**Figure 7.1  The simple Structure–Conduct–Performance approach**

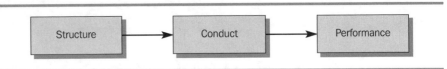

firms in that industry and these in turn will determine the performance of the industry's businesses. Figure 7.1 illustrates the simple S-C-P approach.

Basic market conditions and **structural factors** include:

**structural factors**  the underlying factors which determine the competitive relations between sellers

- the nature of the product, e.g. is it a good or a service, is it homogeneous or differentiated?
- cost conditions
- the existence of economies of scale and scope
- the number of sellers and their relative sizes, i.e. seller concentration
- the number of buyers and their relative sizes, i.e. buyer concentration
- entry and exit conditions in the market
- demand conditions in the market.

**Conduct factors** would include:

**conduct factors**  factors which are under the control of the firm, such as advertising

- pricing policies
- marketing and advertising strategies
- financing policies
- the degree of competition or co-operation between firms
- output decisions
- extent of research and development and innovation
- growth and merger behaviour.

**Performance factors** include:

**performance factors**  are those indicators which measure the performance of the organisation, for example profitability

- productive efficiency
- profitability
- the size and growth of industry output
- the development of products and technology.

Some basic market conditions, such as demand and cost factors, have already been considered (see Chapters 3 and 5). Other structural factors will be considered in more detail in this chapter. Conduct and performance factors will be examined in Chapter 8.

There are many criticisms of the S-C-P approach (see below), but despite these it remains a much used and useful framework for the classification and analysis of industries. Its main advantages are that it is a simple framework, easy to understand and apply, and it is not industry-specific and can therefore be used on different industries and for comparative purposes.

### 7.2.1  Criticisms and alternatives to the S-C-P approach

**exogenously determined**  a factor determined by forces outside of the model being considered

The simple monocausal S-C-P approach assumes that structure determines conduct which in turn determines performance. Structure is **exogenously determined** and so the S-C-P approach tells us nothing about what shapes

**Figure 7.2  The S-C-P approach with reverse linkages**

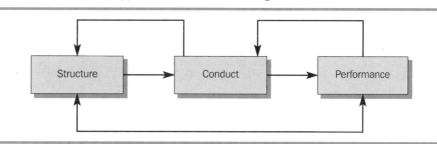

market structure. It is evident that this approach is a simplification of the real world since past conduct and performance will clearly affect present structure: for example, if the level of merger activity in an industry is high, then concentration will be rising and market structure will change. Thus there will be reverse linkages (see Figure 7.2).

Some factors could be regarded as both conduct and structural factors: for instance, advertising is a conduct variable since firms decide what level of advertising they should have, but it also constitutes a **barrier to entry** for new firms and therefore could also be included under the heading of structure.

**barriers to entry** factors which prevent or deter a firm from entering a market

The S-C-P approach is only useful for analysing single-product firms since it is market/industry-specific. Many firms are multi-product, diversified firms.

There have been a great number of empirical studies of the S-C-P approach over the years. These have mainly concentrated on testing the link between structure (measured by the concentration ratio[3] or barriers to entry[4] or product differentiation[5]) and performance (nearly always measured by profitability). These studies and others have indicated a link between structure and performance but they have not been totally conclusive. The choice of only one performance indicator does not tell the whole story and, like all econometric studies, suffers from **econometric** problems such as omitted variables and mis-specification of functional forms. Profitability is chosen because of the ease of measurement but also because it is in keeping with the neo-classical theory of the firm where the main objective of the firm is profit maximisation. Once some discretion is allowed in the setting of objectives by the firm, the link between structure and profitability will be weakened.

**econometrics** the application of mathematical and statistical techniques to economic problems

The concentration on the empirical testing of the link between structure and performance has served to downgrade the importance of conduct within the S-C-P approach. Although this is entirely in keeping with the neo-classical approach, which sees the firm as powerless in the face of market forces, it runs contrary to more recent developments in the area of strategic management (see Chapter 15). The new industrial organisation approach reverses the S-C-P approach completely by postulating that conduct is the main determinant of structure and performance, and that conduct is exogenously determined.

**contestable markets** markets in which there are no (or very few) barriers to entry and exit

A further critique of the S-C-P approach comes from **contestable markets** theory.[6] This argues that it is *potential* competition which influences conduct and performance not the *actual* level of competition in a market. The threat of entry can force incumbent firms to behave in a certain manner even if the potential entrants do not enter. Thus actual market structure is not that important in the determination of conduct and performance.

Despite these not inconsiderable problems, the S-C-P model has endured and is still used in the industrial economics literature to analyse and classify industries.

## 7.3 Porter's five-forces model

Porter's **five-forces model** can also be used to classify and analyse industries.[7] It incorporates the same factors as the S-C-P model but characterises them under different headings. The model posits that the structure of an industry and the ability of firms in that industry to act strategically depend upon the relative strengths of five forces: current competition, potential competition, threat of substitutes, the power of buyers and the power of suppliers. Thus it is a tool which can be used both to analyse current market position and in the formulation of strategic policies (see Chapter 15).

### 7.3.1 Current competition

This refers to the amount of competition which exists in the market at the present time – in business economics this is most commonly measured by the number of firms which operate in the market/industry. The higher the number of firms in a particular market the higher will be the level of current competition. In the same way as in the S-C-P approach this will impact upon the conduct and performance of the firms in the industry. Current competition is considered fully later in this chapter but it should be remembered that even in industries where there is a small number of firms, the existing firms might act in a competitive way simply because of the threat of competition.

### 7.3.2 Potential competition

It is possible that firms in an **oligopolistic market** (see below) may act in a way more consistent with **perfect competition** (see below) because of the threat from potential competition. This threat will be determined by the existence of and the height of barriers to entry and exit. **Barriers to entry** are factors which prevent or deter new firms from entering the industry. **Barriers to exit** refer mainly to the cost of leaving an industry. The higher the barriers to entry and exit, the lower will be the threat of entry and therefore the effect of potential competition.

**barriers to exit** factors which prevent or deter a firm from leaving a market

Barriers to entry can be 'innocent' or can be deliberately erected. Economies of scale can be regarded as innocent barriers to entry since they are inherent in the production process. Advertising or branding could be seen as deliberately erected barriers since they increase the expense of any firm wishing to enter the industry. When innocent barriers to entry and exit are low, potential competition will be high and firms within such a market are faced with the choice of accepting entry or deliberately erecting some barriers. This is an example of strategic behaviour on the part of firms; whether it is attempted or not depends upon the likelihood of success and the relative costs and benefits. **Game theory** can be used to evaluate such strategic possibilities (see Chapters 8 and 14 and also the case study at the end of this chapter).

**game theory** a mathematical theory which looks at situations where decision-making is interdependent

### 7.3.3 **Threat of substitute products**

This largely depends upon the nature of the good being traded in the market and the extent of product differentiation. It has a clear impact upon market structure because if there are no substitutes for a good the producer of that good will face little competition and have a great deal of market power. Much of the expenditure by firms on differentiating their products is designed to reduce the threat from substitute products.

### 7.3.4 **The power of buyers**

The power of buyers will vary from market to market. There will be some markets with many buyers as in retailing and there will be some (e.g. car parts manufacture) where there are few buyers. A market in which there is only one buyer is called a **monopsony**, and it is the buyer who will have a great deal of market power rather than the seller. It is possible to put together the seller and buyer characteristics of a market in order to predict conduct and performance. For example, a market which consists of a single buyer and a single seller will have quite different characteristics from a market which has many buyers and sellers. In markets where there are strong sellers and weak buyers the producers' power can be offset by the establishment of consumer advice centres or watchdog bodies, as in the privatised former public utilities.

**monopsony** where there is a single buyer in a market

### 7.3.5 **The power of suppliers**

As with the power of buyers this is likely to vary a great deal between markets, depending upon the nature of the product being supplied. For example, is the product highly specialised? Is the same or a similar product available from elsewhere? How important is the product in the production process? Is it possible to produce the product in house? The importance of good and reliable supplies has assumed greater significance since firms have started to adopt **just-in-time** production methods. Reducing stock levels to reduce costs can only be effective if firms can depend upon their suppliers; hence there has been the development of **partnership sourcing** as firms develop long-term relationships with their suppliers.

**just-in-time** a manufacturing system which reduces the need for holding stocks and inventories

**partnership sourcing** the development of long-term relationships between firms and their suppliers

## 7.4 **Market structure in theory**

In neo-classical economics, market structure essentially means the number of firms which operate in an industry. There could be many firms, where the level of competition will be very high, or very few, where the level of competition is low. Clearly such markets will have different characteristics and give rise to quite different behaviour. It is important for businesses to know as much as they can about the market structure in which they operate, both in order to understand current market conditions and to formulate strategic policy in the future. The two extremes of market structure are perfect competition (where there are many firms) and monopoly (where there is only one). Between these two extremes lie other market structures, two of which – monopolistic competition and oligopoly – are also considered in this chapter (see Figure 7.3).

**Figure 7.3  Market structures in theory**

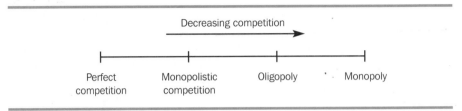

The characteristics of each of these market structures and the implications of structure for behaviour and conduct will be examined. Since oligopoly is the most realistic and common market structure it will be considered in more detail than the others. In the whole of this section, it is assumed that the objective of the firm is to maximise profit, in keeping with neo-classical economic theory.

### 7.4.1 Perfect competition

This theoretical market structure lies at one end of the continuum of competition – the most competitive end. The conditions which are necessary for **perfect competition** to exist are as follows:

- There must be many buyers and sellers: therefore no one buyer or seller has any **market power**.
- The product is **homogeneous**, i.e. each firm in the industry sells an identical product.
- Everyone has **perfect knowledge** in the industry: consumers know that the product is homogeneous, firms know the cost conditions of all other firms, etc.
- There is **perfect mobility** in the market – for consumers and factors of production.
- There must be **free entry and exit** to and from the market.

These conditions mean that although the total demand curve for the product will be downward-sloping, the demand curve facing each individual firm is horizontal – it can sell as much as it likes at the prevailing market price ($P_m$ in Figure 7.4). It cannot charge a higher price since perfect knowledge would mean that consumers would go elsewhere to buy the product. The price would not be lower since, if the firm can sell all it wants at the prevailing price, there is no point in reducing price below this level. Therefore the demand curve facing the firm is perfectly elastic (see Figure 7.4) – the firm is a **price-taker**.

The individual firm does not have the power to affect prices since its supply is small in comparison to the total market supply. It therefore only has to decide what level of output it should produce. Even this decision is largely a foregone conclusion since this depends upon the costs of the firm. If the organisation is attempting to maximise profits it will produce the level of output at which marginal cost equals marginal revenue (see Chapter 5). Figure 7.5 shows the short-term and the long-term equilibrium positions of the firm in perfect competition.

Our analysis in Chapter 5 is appropriate at this point. As the market price is fixed, marginal revenue (the revenue gained from selling one more unit) will be equal to price, therefore the demand curve is also the MR curve.

**market power** the ability of the firm to alter market variables such as price

**perfect mobility** where the factors of production have complete freedom of movement, either between jobs or regions

**free market entry and exit** where there are no barriers to prevent entry to or exit from a market by a firm

**price-taker** a firm that does not have the power to influence the price of its product

**Figure 7.4 The demand curve in perfect competition: (a) the industry; (b) the firm**

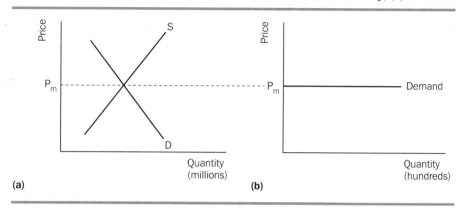

**(a)**   **(b)**

**Figure 7.5 Equilibrium position of the firm in perfect competition**

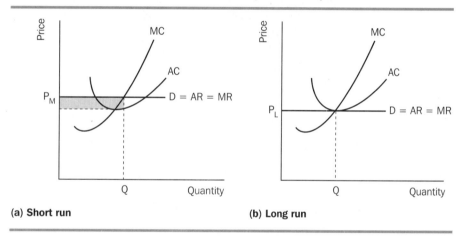

**(a) Short run**   **(b) Long run**

Superimposed on this are the firm's average cost and marginal cost curves which are assumed to have the normal U-shape. The firm will set MR = MC and the resultant output will be Q. In the short run the firm will be making abnormal profits, since AR is higher than AC – the shaded area in Figure 7.5. This position cannot be sustained in the long run, however, because there is perfect knowledge in the market. Other firms will see these abnormal profits, and as there are no barriers to entry they are free to join the market. Market supply will be increased, price will fall ($P_L$) and abnormal profits will be competed away. The long-run position of equilibrium is also shown in Figure 7.5. Price will not fall to a level lower than $P_L$ as this would incur losses and, using the same line of argument, this would cause firms to leave the industry. Market supply would fall this time and price would rise.

So far it has been assumed that cost curves are identical for each firm, which goes back to the neo-classical idea that there is such a thing as a 'representative' firm. If this highly unrealistic assumption is relaxed, the long-run equilibrium position is where the **marginal firm** is just making normal profits.

**marginal firm** the last firm to enter the market

The implications for behaviour and performance in perfectly competitive markets are as follows:

- no advertising, as the product is homogeneous and everyone knows this
- no product differentiation
- one prevailing market price determined by market demand and supply
- no market power over price on the part of any individual buyer or seller
- no abnormal profits in the long run – they will be competed away.

Clearly in practice the concept of perfect competition is highly unrealistic; it is impossible to think of a market where all of the conditions hold. The foreign exchange markets could be an example – the product (currencies) is homogeneous, there are many buyers and sellers (although some are very powerful) around the world, it is relatively easy to get information but there is not perfect mobility and there are barriers to entry and exit. A fruit and vegetable market is again a close example of perfect competition, since the product will be relatively homogeneous, there is a high degree of mobility and knowledge, but again there are barriers to entry and exit. Although unrealistic, the theory does provide a benchmark in the spectrum of competition. It also has implications for the direction of government competition policy (see Chapter 11), since the implications of perfect competition for the behaviour and performance of firms compared to other market structures appear very desirable from the viewpoint of the consumer.

### 7.4.2 Monopoly

**Monopoly** as a market structure lies at the other end of the spectrum of competition: it is the least competitive market structure. The characteristics of monopoly in its purest (or **absolute**) form are:

**absolute monopoly** a market with only one possible supplier

- only one supplier of the product in the market
- no substitutes for the product
- the existence of barriers to entry and exit.

**price-maker** a firm that has the power to influence the price of its product

The monopolist firm has the power to fix the price of the product (i.e. be a **price-maker**) or the quantity offered for sale, but it cannot determine both since it cannot determine the demand for its product. As there is only one producer in the market the market demand and the demand curve for the monopolist is the same and it is downward-sloping (see Figure 7.6).

Equilibrium is shown in the diagram at point A where marginal cost equals marginal revenue. This determines the price at which the product is sold ($P_0$) and the quantity sold ($Q_0$). Abnormal profits are being made (the shaded area) which are not competed away because of the existence of barriers to entry which prevent other firms from entering the market. The power of the monopolist depends upon the availability of substitutes and the existence and height of barriers to entry.

In a pure monopoly there would be:

- *no spending on advertising* – a waste of resources since there is only one supplier and no substitutes
- *a great deal of market power* – to determine either price or quantity produced

**Figure 7.6  Monopoly as a market structure**

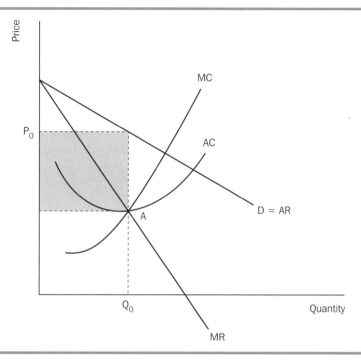

■ *price discrimination* – since different customers can be charged different prices for the same product

■ *abnormal profits* – which can persist in the long run because of barriers to entry.

As with perfect competition it is again hard to think of examples of pure monopolies since most products have substitutes. For example, British Rail at one time had the monopoly on rail travel in the UK but there are other forms of transport. The old public utilities are perhaps the closest examples of monopolies – the barriers to entry are the massive economies of scale which make these industries naturally monopolistic.

### 7.4.3 Monopolistic competition

This was a model proposed by Chamberlain and Robinson in the 1930s.[8] It was an attempt to make economic theory more realistic since it is a market structure which combines elements of both perfect competition and monopoly. The conditions for **monopolistic competition** are the same as for perfect competition except that the product is no longer homogeneous; there is some **product differentiation**. This may be real or imagined.

**product differentiation**
the creation of real or imagined differences between products

Each producer is therefore a 'monopolist' in their own product and will face a downward-sloping demand curve, but because of the availability of close substitutes this will be fairly elastic. The greater the level of product differentiation the more inelastic will be the demand curve. The short-run and long-run positions of the industry are shown in Figure 7.7.

**Figure 7.7 Monopolistic competition as a market structure**

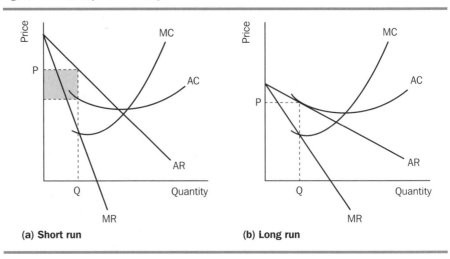

**(a) Short run**  **(b) Long run**

In the short run abnormal profits are being made (the shaded area) but as there is perfect knowledge and no barriers to entry, new firms can enter the market. This pushes the demand curve to the left and it becomes more elastic due to greater competition so that in the long run no abnormal profits are being made.

The implications of this type of market structure for behaviour and performance of firms is as follows:

■ some spending on product differentiation
■ some spending on advertising and branding
■ some small differences in price
■ no abnormal profits in the long run.

### 7.4.4 Oligopoly

An **oligopolistic market** is one where there is a small number of large producers. A small number is usually regarded as anything between two and ten firms – a market where there are only two producers is called a **duopoly**. Oligopolies are very common as market structures; they dominate the manufacturing sector of the economy. For example, both the soap powder and the tobacco industries are duopolies. Oligopolies are characterised by high **interdependence** in decision-making between the firms which makes theoretical analysis difficult. Firms in oligopolies cannot take decisions without taking into account the possible reactions of their competition. Pricing decisions, for example, will therefore depend upon demand conditions, cost conditions and also the pricing strategies of competitors (see Chapter 9). As the reactions of competitors are not known beforehand, there is a degree of uncertainty which makes precise determination of equilibrium price and output impossible. **Non-collusive oligopoly** is where decisions are taken independently by firms, although they do need to take into account the possible reactions of their competitors. **Collusive oligopoly** is where firms collude in some way to determine price and/or output. Collusion can either

**duopoly** a market in which there are two suppliers

**interdependence** when the decisions of one firm are influenced by the decisions of others

**non-collusive oligopoly** an oligopolistic market in which decisions are made independently by firms

**collusive oligopoly** refers to oligopolistic markets where decisions are made through collusion between firms

**cartel** a group of firms or countries acting together to set prices and/or output in a market

be explicit, through formal arrangements like a **cartel** or implicit, as in price leadership. Both of these are considered later.

Oligopolistic markets tend to have high barriers to entry which protect the position of the incumbent firms – as indicated previously these barriers can be 'innocent' or deliberately erected. The observed characteristics of oligopolies are:

- interdependence in decision-making
- 'sticky' prices
- much non-price competition.

**kinked demand curve** a perversely shaped demand curve which results from the interdependence of decision-making present in oligopolies

**sticky price** a price which has a tendency to prevail over time

The '**kinked demand curve**' was developed by Hall and Hitch (1939)[9] and Sweezy (1939)[10] to try to explain the '**sticky' price** level often observed in oligopolistic markets (see Figure 7.8).

Assume that the market price is P. A firm in an oligopolistic market is unlikely to increase the price of its product above P since it assumes that its competitors will not increase their price and therefore it will lose customers to the firms where price is now relatively lower. It will also lose market share. The firm therefore faces a fairly elastic demand curve at prices above P – any increase in price will result in a more than proportionate fall in quantity demanded since consumers will buy from the other firms who have not increased their price. At prices below P the firm assumes the opposite – if it reduces price it assumes that the other firms in the market will follow suit and all firms will be worse off since market share will be unchanged but with a lower price. Thus in oligopoly, once determined, price tends to be 'sticky' as firms will

**price war** the undercutting of price between rivals in an attempt to increase sales

not increase price and lose market share or reduce price and start a **price war**.

The kinked demand curve recognises the interdependence which exists in oligopoly and explains why prices tend to be sticky but tells us nothing about

**Figure 7.8  The kinked demand curve**

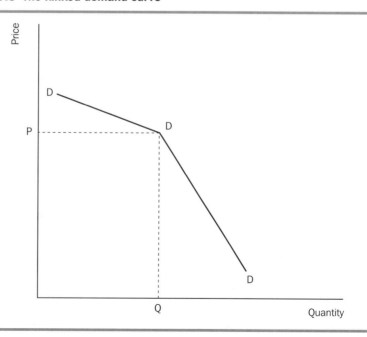

**Figure 7.9 The operation of a cartel**

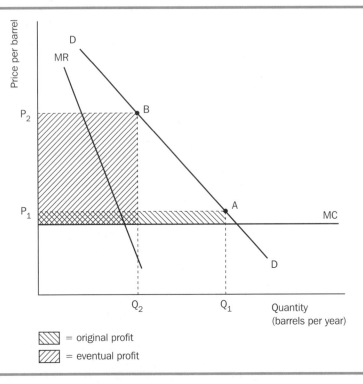

☒ = original profit

▨ = eventual profit

**collusion** the overt
agreement between firms to
set common policies

what determines price in the first place. As suggested above, price could be determined by **collusion** between firms either explicitly or implicity.

**Cartels** are where firms come together and make an agreement on prices to be charged and/or output to be produced. In effect the firms are working together as though they were a monopolist – by restricting output and increasing prices they can earn maximum profits. Cartels are illegal in most countries and so the best examples tend to be international organisations which transcend national laws – e.g. the Organisation of Petroleum Exporting Countries (OPEC). OPEC was formed in 1960 as a cartel of the major producers and exporters of crude petroleum. It did not have much impact upon the market until the 1970s when it enforced massive increases in the price of oil. By restricting the output of oil it was possible to force up the price and maximise the profit of OPEC, as Figure 7.9 shows.

In Figure 7.9, DD is the market demand for oil and, as expected, is fairly inelastic in shape. MC is the marginal cost curve of oil and is assumed to be constant over all levels of output. Point A represents the pre-1973 equilibrium point and the corresponding price of oil was $0P_1$ – this is slightly above the competitive level but far below the monopoly price level. In 1973 OPEC exercised its market power by restricting output to $Q_2$. As a result, the price of oil rose to $0P_2$, close to the monopoly price (not up to the monopoly price since there were other oil-producing non-members). The price of oil rose from around $2.50 per barrel to $12.00 per barrel. The shaded areas represent the pre- and post-1973 profit levels. It can be seen that the successful operation of a cartel can substantially increase profits to members.

**Mini case**    ## OPEC

The power of OPEC to raise price depends upon its ability to restrict the supply of oil to $Q_2$. If there are non-members of OPEC who produce and export oil then supply cannot be restricted to $Q_2$ and the higher price therefore cannot be maintained. The same thing will happen if any members of OPEC cheat and increase their production levels above their specified quotas. The problem with cartels is that there is an inherent incentive to cheat, since if one country exceeds their quota their profitability will be increased at the expense of other countries. Such cheating was commonplace in OPEC from the late 1970s onwards. In addition to these internal disagreements, the very success of OPEC in raising prices in 1973 sowed the seeds of its own demise, as higher prices encouraged energy-saving and the search for alternative sources and forms of energy. As a result of these two forces, since the 1980s the price of oil has fluctuated considerably. In January 1999 the price of oil stood at less than $9.00 per barrel.

In 1999 OPEC once again exercised its power over the market by announcing restrictions in the supply of oil. At the Vienna conference in March 1999, OPEC agreed to cut back on the production of oil by 4.3 million barrels of oil per day for one year. With a world supply of oil of around 75 million barrels per day, such a cutback in supply can have dramatic effects on the price of oil. Almost immediately after the announcement (and even before the cutback in supply had been made) the price of oil rose from $9 per barrel in January 1999 to $15 per barrel in May 1999 and peaked at $32 per barrel in 2000 – the highest price for over ten years.

During late 1999 and early 2000 there was great international pressure put on OPEC to increase production quotas. In the USA, where petrol carries relatively low tax and therefore oil price increases are quickly seen in higher petrol prices, there were demands for OPEC to increase oil production by between 2 and 2.5 million barrels per day. Within OPEC itself there was disagreement between the hard-liners like Iran who wanted to keep increases in production to 1 million barrels per day and countries like Saudi Arabia who were proposing increases of 1.7 million barrels per day. At the Vienna meeting in March 2000, OPEC finally settled on an increase of 1.5 million barrels per day. This is part of an attempt to keep the price of oil within a target band of $22–28 per barrel. If the price of oil goes below this band for a period of time, OPEC will reintroduce quotas and if the price strays above this band production will be increased.

If OPEC is successful in this strategy there will be stability in oil prices, but there are already signs that the agreement might falter. There is much internal disagreement about the quotas within OPEC. Quotas are not the same as production and in the past there has been widespread quota-breaking. Iraq, which is not party to the OPEC agreement, is threatening to increase production in an attempt to capture market share and this will upset the production quotas. At the time of writing the situation on oil prices still remains uncertain.

The success of OPEC in the 1970s sowed the seeds of its own downfall. On the one hand, higher prices of oil encouraged energy-saving and the search for alternative sources of energy. On the other hand, although cartels increase the profits of the group as a whole, there is an inherent incentive to cheat. If any one member of the cartel produced more than their agreed quota, their profitability would be increased, but at the expense of other members of the cartel. This is exactly what happened in OPEC and as a result the price of oil has fluctuated considerably since the 1980s.

**price leadership** when one firm's pricing policies are followed by other firms

Price could also be determined through **price leadership**, where the biggest, most powerful or lowest-cost firm sets a price and all other firms in the industry follow suit. To a large extent prices will depend upon the barriers to entry which exist. If these are low and the threat of entry is therefore high, the prevailing price might be little higher than the competitive price would be.

**non-price competition** policies used by the firm to increase sales other than by changing price

In oligopolies there is little price competition; the product is sold mainly through **non-price competition** such as branding, advertising, special offers and free gifts. The implications of oligopoly for behaviour and performance are as follows:

- high advertising and branding
- a tendency to price rigidity
- much non-price competition
- abnormal profits can exist.

## 7.5 Market structure in practice

### 7.5.1 Seller concentration

Market structure as defined by economic theory can be measured in several ways. The **concentration ratio** measures the percentage of a market or industry accounted for by the $n$ largest firms. It can be measured for employment, output or value-added. The choice of $n$ is arbitrary but commonly three or five is used. A three firm concentration ratio of 0.5 (or 50 per cent) means that the biggest three firms in the market or industry together account for 50 per cent of employment/output/value-added in that industry. In the UK, for instance, five-firm concentration ratios were published by the Office for National Statistics in the Annual Census of Production up to 1992 by industry. Table 7.1 shows selected five-firm concentration ratios for 1992 for illustrative purposes.

**concentration ratio** a measure of market share among the firms supplying the market

Although concentration ratios are only shown for a small selection of industries, it can be seen that there is a great deal of variation in the degree of concentration across industries. Only one service industry is listed because of the unavailability of data relating to the service sector.

The $n$ firm concentration ratio is simple to calculate, easy to understand and is readily available for many industries from the Census of Production. It does, however, have some problems. Firstly, the choice of $n$ is entirely arbitrary – it is possible that three or five is inappropriate for certain industries. Secondly, the concentration ratio tells us nothing about the number of other firms in the industry – are there only two or are there 100? Similarly, the concentration ratio tells us nothing about the market shares of the biggest $n$

**Table 7.1  Five-firm concentration ratios for selected industries in the UK (1992)**

| Industry | Employment (%) | Output (%) |
| --- | --- | --- |
| Sugar and sugar by-products | 100.0 | 100.0 |
| Tobacco | 97.7 | 99.5 |
| Asbestos goods | 90.5 | 89.8 |
| Production of manmade fibres | 88.6 | 92.7 |
| Spirit distilling and compounding | 74.9 | 63.1 |
| Ice cream, cocoa, chocolate and sugar confectionery | 61.4 | 69.8 |
| Domestic-type electrical appliances | 56.2 | 55.2 |
| Pharmaceutical goods | 31.5 | 43.5 |
| Leather goods | 12.4 | 16.1 |
| Executive recruitment[11] | 5.0 | 10.0 |

*Source*: Adapted from Census of Production, National Statistics © Crown copyright (1992).

firms. For example, if the five-firm concentration ratio is 0.5, does each firm have 10 per cent of the market or does one firm have 45 per cent of the market and the other four firms share the remaining 5 per cent? Clearly the two latter points are important when predicting conduct and performance. Thirdly, the general scarcity of any sort of data on the service sector means that concentration ratios are not published for many service industries.

A measure of concentration which overcomes some of these problems is the **Herfindahl index** (HI). This measures concentration by summing the squared market shares of all of the firms in the industry. This has the benefit of including all firms in the industry and as the market shares are squared it gives increased importance to the larger firms. The HI is shown as a decimal: the largest value it can take is 1 where there is a single producer in the industry and the smallest value is $1/n$ where $n$ is the number of firms in the industry. This would be where there are a large number of firms which are exactly the same size. Although this measure overcomes the problems of the simple concentration it is much more difficult to calculate and to understand. Other ways of measuring concentration include the **Lorenz curve** and the **Gini coefficient**[12]. A general problem which applies to all measures of concentration is that if the level of imports in a market is high, measuring domestic concentration tells us little about market structure. A prime example of this would be the car industry in the UK – to look only at UK car producers would give a very unrealistic picture of the level of competition in the market.

The level of concentration in an industry is important because concentration gives firms market power and has implications for the conduct and performance of firms in the industry, as we have seen above. It would be expected that high levels of concentration would mean that the firms in those industries have greater market power, prices would be higher, abnormal profits would be likely and there would be greater interdependence in decision-making. It is, however, an imperfect measure of market structure since it only looks at one side of the equation – the number of sellers in a market. There are other things which are equally important in determining what conduct and performance will be. In Porter's model there are five forces which determine the structure of the market. **Seller concentration** is a

**Herfindahl index** a measure of the level of concentration in a market

**Lorenz curve** a curve which shows the relationship between the cumulative percentage of firms in the industry and the cumulative percentage of market share

**Gini coefficient** a measure of concentration in a market

**seller concentration** the number of firms supplying a market

measure of the number of firms in a market (or inter-firm rivalry) and it is only one of the forces. To look only at seller concentration is to ignore the other four forces, all of which can have an impact. These have already been considered briefly; further consideration is given below.

### 7.5.2 The threat of new entry

**threat of entry** the likelihood of new firms entering the market

The second of Porter's five forces is the **threat of new entry**. The measures of concentration considered above gauge the degree of actual competition in the market place but this might not be a good indicator of the behaviour of firms in the industry. If the threat of new entry is high, firms in an oligopoly might act in a way consistent with perfect competition because of the threat of potential competition. Thus potential competition as well as actual competition affects conduct and performance. The threat of new entry is largely determined by the presence and height of barriers to entry and exit.

As indicated previously, entry barriers are obstacles which prevent or deter the entry of firms into an industry. There are several sources of barriers to entry:

*Economies of scale*

Scale economies have been discussed in some detail in Chapter 5 but are worth mentioning here. As we have seen, some production processes are subject to economies of scale. As firms grow in size, or as the scale of production increases, certain economies occur which serve to reduce the average cost of production. In Figure 7.11 the downward-sloping part of the curve shows economies of scale or falling average cost. Economies of scale reduce average cost and therefore benefit the producer and also the consumer if they are passed on in lower prices (see also Figure 5.11).

---

**Mini case** | **The long-run average cost curve**

Business economics makes the distinction between the short run and the long run (see Chapter 5). The difference between these is that in the short run only some of the factors of production can be varied in quantity while in the long run they can all be varied in quantity. This means that in the long run the firm can increase production by using more labour, by buying more machines or by building new plant. This is called increasing the **scale of production**. The long-run average cost curve (LRAC) shows the least cost methods of producing each level of output.

In Figure 7.10 the short-run average cost curves (SRAC) show the average cost curves which face the firm at three different levels of capacity. The lowest point on each of these represents the lowest cost (or most efficient) way of producing that level of output. The LRAC is tangential to each of the SRAC curves as it represents the lowest cost methods of producing each level of output. It shows what happens to average cost as the scale of production rises.

As Figure 7.10 shows, at least to begin with, as capacity increases, costs will fall. This is because of the presence of economies of scale which are dis-

**Figure 7.10 The long-run average cost curve**

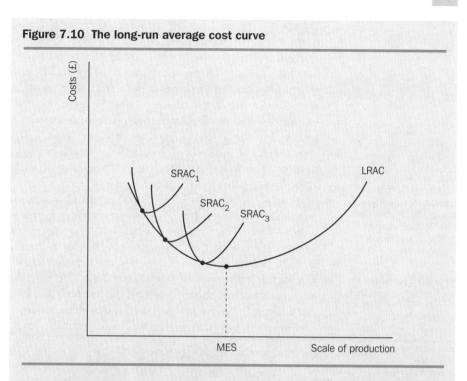

cussed at length in the text. The lowest point of the LRAC curve shows the minimum efficient scale of production (MES) – the level of output at which all economies of scale have been exhausted. The upward-sloping part of the LRAC curve represents diseconomies of scale, which are factors which give rise to increasing average costs as output increases beyond a certain scale of production. Diseconomies of scale mainly stem from the problems associated with managing a large organisation. As size increases, communication is more problematic, it is harder to monitor and exercise control over the workforce and it becomes more difficult to co-ordinate and motivate them.

As indicated above, economies of scale are normally divided into the categories of **internal** and **external**. Internal economies of scale result from the increased size of the firm itself – they are internal to the firm. External economies of scale result from the growth of the industry in which the firm operates and are therefore external to the firm. Internal economies of scale are frequently classified under four headings – technical, financial, marketing and risk-bearing. You should compare these with the terms used in Chapter 5; either is appropriate.

■ **Technical economies** come from increased specialisation and indivisibilities which are only possible in larger firms. In large firms the production process can be broken down into its component parts and there can be greater division of labour and specialisation. This will increase productivity and therefore reduce average costs of production. Greater functional specialism can take place in a large firm with dedicated departments for such things as finance, marketing and purchasing. Large firms can also make more intensive use of machinery and plant. With greater numbers of workers and machines the implication of one being absent or breaking down is less significant. There are certain indivisibilities involved in production which only large firms can benefit from. For example, a small firm cannot have half a production line as that is meaningless, but might not be big enough to use a whole production line. Another type of indivisibility is involved in the notion of fixed costs. Fixed costs (e.g. rates) remain the same irrespective of the level of production. Therefore the greater the level of production, the lower will be the average cost of such items, as it is being spread over a larger amount of output.

**marketing economies** economies of scale which result from spreading the cost of marketing over a higher output

- **Marketing economies** come from spreading marketing costs over a larger output, so that even though total advertising spend is higher, average costs will be lower. The firm will probably have a specialised department devoted to marketing which will be more effective at things like negotiating preferential advertising rates and special deals for purchasing in bulk.

**financial economies** the economies that large firms can obtain in the financing of the firm because of their size

- **Financial economies** of scale come from the fact that larger firms find it easier and often cheaper to borrow capital. Again the fact that they are more likely to have a specialised finance department will help.

**risk-bearing economies** economies which result from the ability of large firms to diversify production

- **Risk-bearing economies** of scale result from the diversification that is possible with larger firms, as they may well have interests in other industries. Therefore any fluctuations in demand in one market will not have a large effect overall on the firm's profitability.

As suggested in Chapter 5, all of these economies of scale give rise to falling average cost and therefore explain the downward-sloping part of the average cost curve shown in Figure 7.10. Economies of scale are a very effective barrier to entry. If the incumbent firms in an industry are operating at a lower cost than a potential new entrant, it will be hard for the newcomer to compete effectively at a small scale of output, since it will have to charge a higher price than existing firms in order to cover its costs. The new entrant will have to enter the market at a very large scale of production to be able to compete. Two points can be made about this. Firstly, establishing a plant that big may not be possible because the cost may be prohibitive. Secondly, if the MES of output is large in comparison with the total industry output, entry on such a scale may not be profitable since the increased output will push down market price.

Gas, electricity and water are examples of industries with high economies of scale. This makes it difficult for others to come into the market in competition with existing firms and this is why these industries are called '**natural monopolies**'.

**natural monopoly** where the market can be supplied at lowest cost by one firm only

There are also external economies of scale which stem from the growth of the industry as a whole (see Chapter 5). These often result from the concentration of producers in one locality which may be accompanied by the growth of a local infrastructure to support that industry. There are likely to be training courses at local colleges tailored to the industry's needs and a readily available trained labour force. Commercial services, including banks and solicitors, will have a greater understanding of the needs of the local industry. It is also likely that suppliers of components to the industry will locate nearby and thus distribution costs will be less. There will often be the interchange of ideas through formal networks (like local Chambers of Commerce) and informal networks (like golf clubs).

**Figure 7.11 Long-run average cost curves**

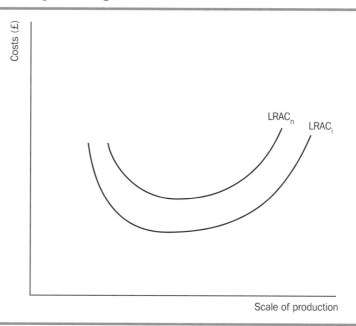

### Cost advantages

It is possible that incumbent firms have lower costs (LRAC$_i$) than new entrants (LRAC$_n$) at all levels of output as shown in Figure 7.11.

It is not profitable for the new entrant to enter at any scale since they cannot cover costs at the prevailing market price. Cost advantages could be due to the experience effects gained from operating in the industry, good location of plant, good access to well-trained labour, the negotiation of exclusive deals with suppliers and distributors and so on.

### Legal barriers to entry

**patents** exclusive licences to exploit an invention for a given length of time

**franchises** licences given to an individual or a company to manufacture or sell a named product in a certain area for a certain length of time

There can be legal barriers to entry, as in the case of **patents** and **franchises** which serve to restrict competition and prevent new firms from entering the industry. There may be government restrictions on competition as when a government nationalises an industry. Many industries operate a licensing system where firms have to be licensed in order to operate. Such licences may be government-imposed, industry-imposed or peer-imposed.

### Advertising and branding

These can be very effective barriers to entry. Industries where brand names are well established are difficult for a newcomer to enter without massive expenditure on advertising. Strong product differentiation and product proliferation will also limit the ability of any newcomer to successfully enter a market and capture sufficiently large market share.

### Initial capital requirements

Some industries require a high initial capital investment to enter, for example dry cleaning where the machinery needed is very expensive, and this is a barrier to entry.

### Switching costs

If the consumer incurs a cost in switching from one good to another that might be enough to deter the consumer from doing so and therefore serve as a barrier to entry. The recent practice of the building societies and banks offering low fixed-rate mortgages with penalties for early withdrawal can be seen as an example of the introduction of switching costs into the market.

### Lack of distribution channels

It is likely that there are established distribution channels in the industry which might be difficult or impossible to break into. The alternative for potential new entrants would be to establish their own channels for distribution but this again might be difficult and would increase the initial capital requirements.

### Restrictive practices

Incumbent firms may act either singly or in conjunction with one another to restrict entry into a market. This would include predatory pricing, carrying spare capacity, etc. Many of these practices are against the law.

### Barriers to exit

Apart from the entry barriers discussed above, firms often face exit barriers. These are obstacles which prevent or deter a firm from quitting an industry, and are mainly related to the cost of leaving the industry. The cost of exit depends upon how industry-specific the assets of the firm are. Physical assets such as, say, a printing press tend to be highly specific to the printing industry and could not be used for anything other than printing. Although there will be a second-hand market for printing presses it would be limited to other printing firms and would probably have to be sold at a loss, thereby incurring a cost. A van, however, would be different since it is not specific to a particular industry. Therefore although the sale of it would incur a loss it is likely to be smaller. Generally the more industry-specific an asset the lower will be the second-hand value and the higher will be the cost of exit. An intangible asset such as knowledge of the market or expenditure on research and development cannot be resold and must be left in the market, and is therefore a **sunk cost** (see below).

**sunk cost** a cost that cannot be recovered if a firm leaves an industry

    A contestable market is defined as one where there are: no barriers to entry, no barriers to exit and no sunk costs.[13] Sunk costs are costs which cannot be recovered if a firm should cease production and, as indicated above, they will vary with the specificity of the asset. The printing press carries high sunk costs, while the van carries lower sunk costs. Sunk costs represent a barrier both to entry and to exit since high sunk costs increase the risk involved in entering a market and also make an incumbent firm more reluctant to leave a market since it cannot recover its costs. It could be worth a firm carrying on in the face of losses in the hope that things will improve in the future.

    A contestable market can produce results similar to perfect competition in terms of pricing and output decisions but without the restrictive conditions of perfect competition. For example, a large number of sellers is not needed – even a monopoly could be a contestable market. A firm in a contestable market would not charge high prices since it knows that this would encourage new entrants, so price will tend towards its competitive level and there will be no abnormal profits. Potential competition as well as actual competition is regulating the behaviour of firms.

The theory of contestability has implications for government competition policy (see Chapter 11). Contestability produces similar results to perfect competition in terms of price, output and abnormal profits. A government, wishing to achieve such results, can do so by making markets more contestable rather than more competitive. This would involve policies designed to reduce the size and scope of barriers to entry and exit rather than breaking up monopolies. Baumol *et al.* have produced a list of guidelines to determine whether a market is contestable or not.[14] If a market is contestable government intervention is not needed. If a market is not contestable the government needs to look at the barriers which exist and how they can be reduced in size. Although it is difficult to think of a pure example of a contestable market (there are likely to be sunk costs in most types of production), government policy could be designed to make markets more contestable.

### 7.5.3 Buyer concentration

Buyer concentration could be measured in the same way as seller concentration but lack of data means that these are not calculated or available in the same way as for seller concentration. Buyer concentration is clearly important, as a reduction in the number of buyers will severely curtail the ability of firms in the industry to make abnormal profits. In markets where there are a small number of powerful sellers the grouping together of buyers into larger units can be seen as a manifestation of **countervailing power**.[15] The buyers are grouping together to exert market power which counteracts the power of the sellers. Retailers' associations are an example of the exercise of countervailing power, as are trade unions, which evolved to counteract powerful employers. Another factor which gives buyers greater market power is increased knowledge. Consumer rights organisations, publications like *Which?* and TV programmes like *Watchdog* all serve to increase the knowledge and therefore the power of buyers in the market place. It is not surprising, given the naturally monopolistic nature of the privatised public utilities, that regulatory bodies have been set up to protect the interests of consumers (see Chapter 11).

A distinction can be made between existing and potential customers. Existing customers are particularly significant to firms in industries where repeat orders are important or where goods are supplied on a regular basis, as in grocery retailing. The power of existing customers is much lower where the firm supplies goods on a one-off basis, although it cannot disregard existing customers, as this will affect its reputation and the ability to attract potential customers. Potential customers may be new to the market or may be buying from a competitor at present.

The importance of existing customers has received a great deal of attention recently in the marketing literature under the name of **relationship marketing**. It is recognised that it is more cost-effective to keep existing customers

**countervailing power**
where excessive power held by one group can be balanced by the power held by another group

**relationship marketing**
marketing policies which are designed to build and maintain long-term relationships

than it is to attract new customers. Therefore much of what firms do is directed at forging long-term relationships with customers and keeping existing customers happy. The tools of relationship marketing include after-sales service, the loyalty cards used by all major retailers and so on.

### 7.5.4 Substitute products

The **threat from substitutes**, will vary from market to market. Monopoly power often comes from a lack of available substitutes – if there are no substitutes for a good the producer of that good will face little competition and have a great deal of market power. However, as was seen earlier, even industries which appear to be pure monopolies (e.g. the former British Rail) normally face competition from substitutes (e.g. alternative forms of travel).

### 7.5.5 Supplier power

**supplier power** the power exerted over a company by its suppliers of raw materials or components

Similarly the **power of suppliers** will vary between markets depending upon the nature of the product being supplied, whether or not it is specialised, whether or nor it is available from elsewhere and its relative importance in the production process. Transactions cost economics (see Chapter 2) looks at the make or buy decision faced by the firm.

**flexible manufacturing system** a system which utilises automated techniques and robotics

The traditional methods of mass production required the holding of large inventories of raw materials and parts, so that production could take place continuously. The increased adoption of **flexible manufacturing systems** has reduced this requirement and made good relationships with suppliers much more important. As part of the movement towards flexibility in production, many firms have turned to **just-in-time (JIT)** methods of inventory control. If raw materials and parts can be delivered as they are needed in the production process, the storage space needed for holding inventories and the associated costs are reduced. JIT enables firms to react more quickly to changes in demand and might also increase reliability since defective stock can be identified more quickly. In order that JIT methods are effective, good relationships with suppliers are necessary – supplies must be reliable and delivered on time. Up-to-date and accurate information is needed on stockholdings so that orders can be quickly made. Advances in information technology and the use of barcodes has helped this process; many retailers now have direct computer links with their suppliers so that orders are automatically triggered. JIT production methods shift the burden of stockholding to suppliers and this should be recognised by the firm and not just seen as a cost-cutting exercise.

## 7.6   Conclusion

This chapter has looked at the concept of market structures. Economic theory identifies four theoretical market structures – perfect competition, monopolistic competition, oligopoly and monopoly – which differ according to the level of competition present. Each of these models was discussed and although economic theory makes some unrealistic assumptions, it does provide a framework for looking at market structures and makes useful predictions about the conduct and performance of firms under different market conditions. These predictions have been used by 'free marketeers' to argue that competitive markets produce better results than monopolistic markets and have been used as the basis for formulating government competition policy.

More discussion was devoted to oligopoly as a market structure because it is a much more realistic and common market structure. Game theory is used to analyse pricing in oligopolistic markets in the case study at the end of the chapter.

Market structures were then considered in practice, using Porter's five-forces model, and reasons for high (and low) levels of concentration were discussed. Although traditional economic theory concentrates on current market structure as the most important determinant of conduct and performance, it is clear from this chapter that there are other factors at work such as the level of potential competition, which is considered by contestable market theory. In government competition policy in the UK there is now a greater acceptance that markets should be 'contestable' rather than competitive.

## Case study    Game theory and oligopoly

Game theory has become a popular tool in business economics to model behaviour including the operation of oligopolistic markets. It can be used to demonstrate many of the characteristics observed in oligopolies. The following model is an adaptation of the Prisoners' Dilemma (see the Appendix to this chapter). Assume that there are two firms in an industry, A and B, and there are two possible prices that can be charged by these firms, high or low. The effect of the choice made by one firm will depend upon the choices made by the other firm. Hence there is interdependence in their decision-making. Table 7.2 shows the pay-off matrix for both firms for both strategies.

**Table 7.2  A pay-off matrix for a duopoly**

|  |  | Firm B | |
|---|---|---|---|
|  |  | Low price | High price |
| Firm A | Low price | 3  3 | 10  0 |
|  | High price | 0  10 | 5  5 |

The pay-offs represent the profits of the two firms; the first figure in each cell refers to firm A and the second to firm B.

When both firms have low prices, profit equals 3 for each firm; when price is high profit equals 5 for each firm. Each firm does best (profit equals 10) when it has low price and the other has high price since it captures market share at the expense of the other firm. Consider the choice faced by firm A first – it is better off having a low price if firm B has a high price, but it is also better off having a low price if firm B has a low price. Therefore firm A is better off by choosing a low price irrespective of what B chooses to do – thus low price is a dominant strategy. Exactly the same is true for firm B. Therefore the equilibrium position would be low price for both firms and a profit of 3 for each of them. Both firms are reluctant to increase price since if the other firm maintains the lower price they will lose market share. Thus game theory can be used to illustrate the sticky price often observed in oligopoly.

This game also shows the benefits from collusion, since both firms would be better off if they agreed that price should be set at the higher level – they would then be earning profits of 5. The inherent incentive to cheat is also demonstrated here since if both firms have agreed to charge the higher price, it would benefit one firm to reduce its price provided the other firm maintain the higher price level. If both firms choose to reduce their prices there is the possibility of a price war. In an oligopolistic market it is likely that any increases in price would come from the price leader, but reductions in price will not come from the price leader, since if they have biggest market share they have the most to lose and they could be accused of predatory pricing (see Chapter 8).

## Notes and references

1. Mason, E. S. (1939), 'Price and production policies of large-scale enterprises', *American Economic Review*, 29, pp. 61–74.

2. Bain, J. S. (1956), *Barriers to New Competition*, Harvard University Press, Cambridge, MA.

3. Bain, J. S. (1968), *Industrial Organisation*, John Wiley, New York.

4. Bain (1956, 1968).

5. Singh, A. (1971), *Takeovers: Their Relevance to the Stock Market and the Theory of the Firm*, Cambridge University Press, Cambridge; Utton, M. A. (1974), 'On measuring the effects of industrial mergers', *Scottish Journal of Economics*, 21, pp. 13–28.

6. Baumol, W. J., Panzar, J. C. and Willig, R. D. (1988), *Contestable Markets and the Theory of Industrial Structure*, Harcourt Brace Jovanovich, San Diego.

7. Porter, M. E. (1980), *Competitive Strategy: Techniques for Analysing Industries and Competitors*, Free Press, New York.

8. Chamberlain, E. H. (1933), *The Theory of Monopolistic Competition*, Harvard University Press Cambridge, MA; Robinson, J., (1933), *The Economics of Imperfect Competition*, Macmillan, Basingstoke.

9. Hall, R. L. and Hitch, C. J. (1939), 'Price theory and business behaviour', *Oxford Economic Papers*, 2, pp. 12–45.

10. Sweezy, F. M. (1939), 'Demand under conditions of oligopoly', *Journal of Political Economy*, 47, pp. 568–573.

11. From Britton, L. C., Doherty, C. and Ball, D. F. (1997), 'The changing international scope of executive search and selection', *Small Business and Enterprise Development*, 4(3), November, pp. 137–146.

12. Ferguson, P. R. and Ferguson, G. J. (1994), *Industrial Economics – Issues and Perspectives*, Macmillan, Basingstoke.

13. Baumol *et al.* (1988).

14. Baumol *et al.* (1988).

15. Galbraith, J. K. (1977), *The Affluent Society*, André Deutsch, London.

## Review and discussion questions

1 Can the game theory approach used in the case study explain why you tend to see high non-price competition in oligopolistic industries?

2 Select some markets for different goods and services. How do these markets meet the expectations of economic theory with respect to conduct and performance?

3 What are the barriers to entry in the cinema industry?

4 If contestability is accepted as the basis for government competition policy, what kind of policies might the government use?

## Assignments

1 You have been asked to make a presentation to some overseas visitors on the level of concentration in the UK. Go to the most recent Census of Production published by the Office for National Statistics for data and prepare your presentation. (You could look for differences over time in 'average' concentration as shown by the share of the largest 100 enterprises in the UK or the differences in concentration levels between markets.)

2 Your organisation is considering entry into a new market. Select an industry and investigate the barriers to entry which exist. Produce a report on your findings with recommendations, making any assumptions you have made clear.

## Further reading

Cook, M. and Farquharson, C. (1998), *Business Economics: Strategy and Applications*, Pitman Publishing, London.

Ferguson, P. R. and Ferguson, G. J. (1994), *Industrial Economics – Issues and Perspectives*, Macmillan, Basingstoke.

Worthington, I. and Britton, C. (2000) *The Business Environment*, 3rd edition, Financial Times Prentice Hall, Harlow.

**The prisoners' dilemma**

Game theory, which is used in the mathematical literature to evaluate games like poker or chess, can also be used to evaluate the strategic choices which face the firm as the text demonstrates. The most famous non-economic example of the application of game theory is the Prisoners' Dilemma. Two people X and Y are arrested for a joint crime; they are interrogated separately and given the following information:

- If both say nothing, the courts have enough evidence to convict and they will get a prison sentence of one year each.
- If only one confesses to the crime, while the other does not, the one that confesses will receive a prison sentence of three months, while the other will receive a sentence of ten years.
- If both confess to the crime they will each receive a prison sentence of three years.

Table 7.3 shows these sentences or 'pay-offs'.

**Table 7.3 The Prisoners' Dilemma**

|  |  | Individual X | |
| --- | --- | --- | --- |
|  |  | Not confess | Confess |
| Individual Y | Not confess | Both get one year | Y gets ten years, X gets three months |
|  | Confess | Y gets three months, X gets ten years | Both get three years |

The optimal joint position is the top left-hand cell – where the two individuals X and Y collude and say nothing and where each receives a sentence of one year. However, because they are being questioned separately, they do not know what the other is doing, and the best solution for each individual is to confess. Consider the choice faced by individual X – if X confesses he will receive at best a three-month sentence (if Y does not confess) or at worst a three year sentence (if Y also confesses). If X does not confess but Y does, X faces a prison sentence of ten years. Therefore, it is in the best interests of individual X to confess. However, the same is also true for individual Y. Therefore the equilibrium position will be the bottom right-hand cell where both confess and both receive a prison sentence of three years.

# CHAPTER 8

# Conduct and performance

## Chris Britton

| Objectives | 1 To consider important conduct factors including product differentiation, advertising, invention and innovation. |
| --- | --- |
| | 2 To recognise the effects of the firm's conduct on market structure and performance. |
| | 3 To use game theory to analyse the effects of entry deterrence behaviour. |
| | 4 To consider performance factors such as profitability and productivity. |
| | 5 To recognise the interlinkages between conduct and performance. |

## 8.1 Introduction

This chapter considers conduct and performance factors – the ways in which organisations behave and their performance. The original Structure–Conduct–Performance model (see Chapter 7) portrayed market/industry structure as determined by factors such as minimum efficient scale, demand and cost conditions, all of which were beyond the control of the firm. **Structure** then was seen to influence the **conduct** of the organisation and in turn to determine the **performance** of these enterprises. In this model the firm is seen as passive – it attempts to achieve its objectives subject to certain constraints: for example, maximising profits subject to existing cost and demand conditions or maximising sales subject to earning a satisfactory level of profits. This is a very crude view of the operation of firms; in reality businesses are active rather than passive, they can and do make decisions which will change the constraints under which they operate. Later versions of the Structure–Conduct–Performance model accepted that market structure is not exogenously determined but could be affected by strategic behaviour on the part of firms. Even in neo-classical economic theory it is only in perfect competition that the firm is completely powerless in the face of market forces. In all other market structures the firm can make choices which will impact upon the structure of the market in which it operates.

Thus conduct takes on a pivotal role in the analysis of markets since to a large extent it determines how well the firm performs and it also impacts upon market structure (see Figure 7.2). The same line of argument can be applied to performance factors. Rather than being the passive result of the initial market structure and conduct, performance factors such as profitability impact upon both structure and conduct. High profitability will encourage new entry and thus influence the structure of the market/industry. Similarly, high profitability will give firms the means to behave in a certain way, for example by providing the finance for advertising. This chapter accepts this view of conduct and performance and considers the following conduct and performance factors:

- entry deterrence behaviour
- product differentiation
- product proliferation
- advertising
- innovation
- co-operation between firms
- profitability
- investment
- productivity.

## 8.2   Conduct factors

Why do firms behave in a certain way? Sometimes their behaviour will be passive as they react to market conditions which are beyond their control; at other times, however, their behaviour will be designed to achieve specific strategic goals. For example:

1 *A firm could deter or prevent the entry of other firms into the market*, thereby protecting its market position. Its pricing or advertising policies could be such that they form an effective barrier to entry and deter the entry of new firms. Game theory is often used to analyse the feasibility of **entry deterrence measures** (see below).

**entry deterrence measures** policies which are designed to deter new firms from entering the market

2 *A firm can influence existing market conditions*, to protect or improve its market position. Once other firms have entered the market, the incumbent firm could use policies such as price-cutting or merger/takeover to capture market share.

3 *A firm can reduce the uncertainty under which it operates* through collusive behaviour. The formation of a cartel, for example, greatly reduces the trading uncertainty for member firms and gives the firms more control over market conditions.

Any or all of these three may be the objectives of the firm's strategic decision-making, but many of the policies mentioned are considered to be anti-competitive and would therefore come under the jurisdiction of government competition policy (see Chapter 11). Competition policy acts as a constraint on the conduct of firms, and it is a constraint that firms attempt to change through the lobbying of government either individually or as members of pressure groups designed to influence government policy (see mini case on newspaper pricing).

In addition to government policy, there are other factors which influence the firm's ability to act strategically. Many of these factors are considered in detail elsewhere in this book but they include:

- *the objectives of the firm* (Chapter 6) – clearly the firm that is attempting to maximise profits will behave quite differently in terms of its pricing and advertising policies from a firm that is only trying to achieve a certain satisfactory level of profits;
- *the market structure in which the firm operates* (Chapter 7) – although this appears to be a circular argument, as much of a firm's behaviour is designed to influence structure, the initial market structure is important in determining the scope for strategic policy-making;
- *general macroeconomic conditions* (Chapter 12) – this will have an impact upon demand conditions and therefore on the firm's ability to vary price;
- *the size of the firm* – generally it would be expected that larger firms have more scope for acting strategically than smaller firms;
- *the time horizon* – in the short term it might be very difficult for the firm to change anything, while in the long term it is much easier.

### 8.2.1 Entry deterrence

**cross-entry** the entry into a market by firms already established in another industry

'Entry' was defined by Bain (1956) as the establishment of new productive capacity in an industry by a new firm.[1] This definition could exclude **cross-entry** (entry by firms established in another industry) and takeovers as a form of entry. As both of these result in the formation of new productive capacity and bypass many of the barriers to entry which exist, this is a serious omission. In addition, as the theory of contestability shows, actual entry is not necessary – potential entry can affect behaviour. A better definition of entry is as a process which changes the existing balance of market conditions. Barriers to entry are then those obstacles which prevent the disturbance to the market.

A distinction has already been made between innocent barriers to entry such as economies of scale, which exist independently of any actions by firms, and deliberately erected barriers. This section concentrates upon the latter – barriers to entry which are deliberately erected as part of the firm's strategic behaviour designed to discourage entry.

**mark-up pricing** where a margin is added to the cost in setting price

Bain measured the height of the barriers to entry by the extent to which incumbent firms were able to raise price above the perfectly competitive level without attracting entry. He identified industries where barriers were very high (a mark-up of 10 per cent in price) to substantial (a mark-up of 5–9 per cent) to moderate to low (a mark-up of 1–4 per cent). It is interesting to note that in some markets (cosmetics, for instance) the mark-up in price can be in excess of 100 per cent! (NB: **mark-up pricing** is discussed in detail in Chapter 9.) Thus in Figure 8.1 the competitive price is $P_C$ (i.e. the price that would prevail under perfect competition in the long run) and the prevalent price is $P_L$, which is higher than the competitive level. In the absence of barriers to entry, such a price level would encourage new entry, supply would increase, price would be forced down to its competitive level and any abnormal profits would be competed away. It is only the presence of barriers to entry which enable price to be maintained above its competitive level. Bain identified four main barriers to entry which have all been considered briefly along with others in Chapter 7. The four were product differentiation (which is further considered below), absolute cost advantage, economies of scale and initial capital requirements.

**Figure 8.1 Long-run average cost curve for incumbents and new entrants**

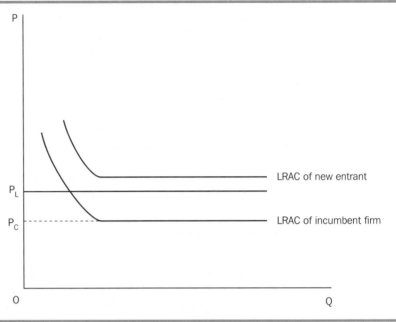

### 8.2.2 Spare capacity as entry deterrent

**Game theory** is a very useful vehicle for illustrating and evaluating entry deterrence behaviour. Consider an industry in which there is one incumbent firm and one potential entrant. The entrant is faced with the choice of attempting to enter or not. If the entrant decides to enter, the incumbent firm is then faced with the choice of accepting this and sharing the market or fighting entry. Assume that this is a 'two stage' game where these choices take place in two successive stages. Figure 8.2 show the pay-offs at each stage in terms of profits for each firm (**bold** for incumbent and ***bold italic*** for new entrant).

Figure 8.2 shows that the best outcome for the incumbent firm is if new entry does not take place. The new entrant makes a profit of 0 since it has not entered and the incumbent firm makes a profit of 50. If the new entrant does attempt to enter, the best solution for the incumbent firm is to accept entry and the accompanying lower profits. If the incumbent decides to resist entry the resultant price war means that both firms end up making losses. Since the new entrant knows this, it will enter the market and the equilibrium position will be in the left-hand box, both firms making profits of 10.

Now assume that the incumbent had previously acted strategically to deter entry by carrying excess capacity. A new row has to be added to the pay-off matrix in Figure 8.2 to take account of the cost of carrying spare capacity (see Figure 8.3).

The pay-offs to the new entrant are unchanged but for the incumbent firm profit is lower in the absence of being challenged, since carrying spare capacity carries a cost. Similarly, if the incumbent firm accepts the new entry, its profits are correspondingly lower. If there is a price war, total output must be high and the spare capacity is being used and is therefore not wasted. The best solution for the incumbent firm is still to remain unchallenged, but in the

**Figure 8.2 Profits without deterrence**

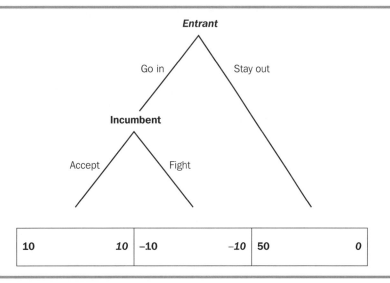

| 10 | 10 | −10 | −10 | 50 | 0 |

**Figure 8.3 Profits with deterrence**

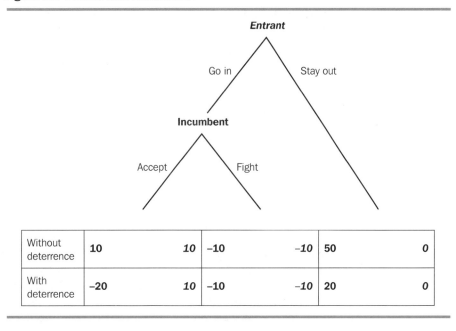

| | | | | | | |
|---|---|---|---|---|---|---|
| Without deterrence | 10 | 10 | −10 | −10 | 50 | 0 |
| With deterrence | −20 | 10 | −10 | −10 | 20 | 0 |

event of entry its best solution now is to fight since the cost is less in terms of lost profit. Previously there was no incentive for the incumbent firm to resist entry but now there is and the new entrant knows that – resisting entry is a 'credible threat' since it is in the incumbent firm's best interest. The new entrant is deterred and equilibrium occurs in the bottom right-hand box.

This is an example of successful entry deterrence; the outcome, however, depends upon two critical assumptions. Firstly, the result depends on the numbers used in the pay-off matrix; had these been different the resultant equilibrium would have been different. Secondly, perfect (or at least sufficient) knowledge is being assumed – the entrant and the incumbent must both be aware of the pay-offs resulting from their behaviour. This is clearly a simplification, information is incomplete and actors sometimes get it wrong; the incumbent firm may react differently post-entry from the way the entrant expected. However, it does illustrate the principle involved in entry deterring behaviour and the use of game theory for evaluating the outcome of such behaviour.

Other types of entry deterring behaviour as well as spare capacity can be analysed using game theory. For example, advertising, product proliferation, product differentiation, sunk costs and limit pricing which all carry a cost can be seen as credible threats to a potential entrant.

### 8.2.3 Product differentiation

**Product differentiation** can be used strategically by firms to deter new entry into their industry and also to increase competitive advantage over existing producers. Product differentiation refers to the degree to which consumers distinguish between products or have preferences towards particular products. Product differentiation may be based on real differences between products in their technical attributes or imagined differences which are introduced through branding and advertising. Products do not actually have to be different; they just have to be perceived as different in the minds of consumers. In the case of homogeneous products like milk or petrol, for example, where technical differences are small or even non-existent, product differentiation can be done through branding. Some of the sources of product differentiation are:

- location of the firm
- differing quality
- advertising and branding
- product prestige
- consumer ignorance.

Product differentiation can be an effective barrier to entry since, to overcome the preference consumers have for existing products, the new entrant would either have to offer its product at a much lower price or be forced to spend a great deal on advertising to persuade consumers to buy its product. Both of these would have the effect of making the costs of the new entrant higher than incumbent firms and therefore would deter entry (see Figure 7.11).

Bain looked at product differentiation in 20 different industries and found that, although the importance of product differentiation varied between industries, overall it was the biggest barrier to new entry. The height of the barrier depended upon factors such as the amount of advertising, the durability of the product and the extent to which the reputation of the producer was important in the buying process. Again it should be stressed that Bain's conclusions apply only to entry by completely new firms. In the case of cross-entry, the height of the barrier might well be reduced.

Product differentiation can also be used as part of a strategy to influence market conditions and as a means of gaining competitive advantage over other producers in an industry. If a firm can successfully differentiate its products in the minds of consumers it brings itself more market power. It becomes a **'price-maker'** in the sense that it can increase its price without losing custom since consumers do not see other products as competitors. Product differentiation influences both the firm's costs and its demand. Costs will rise since product differentiation through advertising or increased research and development will incur real costs to the firm. At the same time the demand curve will shift and it will become more inelastic. This means that price becomes less important in a consumer's decision to buy, and **non-price factors** assume greater importance.

Product differentiation is based on the proposition that when buying a product consumers take into account many factors including colour, design, after-sales service and image of product as well as technical attributes. Products are a mixture of tangibles and intangibles. Three levels of a product are often identified (see Figure 8.4).

The **core product** is the fundamental service or benefit the consumer is buying: for example, a jacket is purchased because it gives coverage and warmth, a car brings transportation. In addition to these basic benefits, products are purchased because they bring other benefits. The second level of the product – the **tangible product** – would include such factors as design, quality and packaging. A designer label jacket would have a certain cut and style. The third level is the **augmented product** which would include such factors as after-sales service, guarantees, image and brand name. Kotler (1994) adds an extra two levels – the **generic product**, which comes after the core product and refers to a basic version of the product, and the **potential product** after the augmented product which includes all of the possible augmentations that the product could go through in the future.[2]

The above is a useful way to view products since it is clear that the three levels will assume differing levels of importance for different products. In the case of fairly homogeneous products (e.g. milk) it would be expected that the core product would be most important. For durable goods, like washing machines, the augmented product is important because of guarantees and after-sales service. For fashion items the tangible product will be important, as will the augmented product through image and brand name. This gives the marketer important clues about where to direct the tools of product differentiation and which tools to use. In the purchase of cosmetics, for example,

**core product** the bundle of core benefits that the consumer is buying in a product

**tangible product** the product features that combine to deliver the core product benefits

**augmented product** the additional consumer services added to the core product

**generic product** the basic version of a product

**potential product** all possible augmentations that could take place in the future

**Figure 8.4  The three levels of a product**

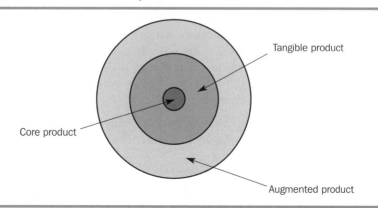

offering after-sales service and guarantees will have little relevance but the building of image and brand names would be much more effective. In the purchase of a car, however, after-sales service and guarantees would be very important to the consumer.

**market segmentation** the creation of subdivisions in a market on the basis of some common characteristic

The three levels of the product can also be used in the **segmentation** of markets, as they will assume differing importance in different market segments. The car market, for example, could be segmented into three – the economy, the family car and the luxury segments. Although the core product is important in all three of these market segments, it will assume greater importance for the economy car segment which is likely to be less concerned by the tangible and augmented product. As each of these segments will have different characteristics, they will therefore respond differently to the tools of product differentiation. This highlights the importance of market research in the process of product differentiation.

Product differentiation is an important conduct factor since it influences market structure through changing market shares and it gives firms a degree of market power over price. If successful it can lead to abnormal profits, since the consumer does not regard other products as substitutes.

---

**Mini case** **The market for trainers**

The market for designer trainers is one which has experienced rapid growth in the 1990s but is now forecast to even out. Nike, market leaders with 33 per cent of the market, was forecasting a 20 per cent drop in sales in 1998. Reebok, with 14 per cent of the market, was forecasting a similar trend. What are the causes of this reversal of the trend?

Many reasons are put forward as follows:

- There has been a growth in the adventure shoe market. The fashionable item of the moment for young people is the adventure shoe produced by such companies as Timberland which are a cross between trainers and walking boots.
- Although continued growth is forecast in the European market, the American market appears to be saturated. In the USA it is common for people to buy a different type of trainer for each sport played, while in Europe it is common for individuals to have one type of trainer for all sports.
- The patent on Nike Air expired in 1997 and there has been increased competition as a result of this.
- There has been increased competition in this market from the designer footwear industry with the entry of companies like Tommy Hilfiger. These were expected to increase their share of the market by 5 per cent in 1998.

In addition to these, it is argued that Nike and Reebok took a deliberate step from the 'performance end' of the trainer market into the fashionable end. By doing this Nike and Reebok have lost 'authenticity' with respect to the sports performance of their trainers. Authenticity is important to sportswear companies and this partly explains why Nike chooses to use sportsmen to advertise its trainers – it is adding authenticity to the product through '**endorsement**'.

In terms of the three levels of the product shown in Figure 8.4, it could be argued that by moving into the fashionable end of the trainer market both Nike and Reebok have concentrated too much on the **tangible product** and the **augmented product** to the detriment of the **core product.** Although this might have been a successful strategy in the short term, perhaps in the long term it will not have been quite so successful.

### 8.2.4 Product proliferation

**niche marketing** entering the market by concentrating on a very small specialised segment of the market

Product proliferation is an effective barrier to entry since it reduces the scope for product differentiation and **niche marketing** by a new entrant. It is common in markets like detergents and breakfast cereals, where existing producers manufacture a whole range of different brands in a market to meet the needs of each part of the market. This means there will be little or no scope for a new producer to find a market niche. In the markets for detergents and soap powders the only competition has come from the major grocery retailers who have introduced 'own-brand' products.

### 8.2.5 Advertising

Advertising is an important conduct variable for the firm which does two things – it provides information on the product to the consumer and it also persuades consumers to buy a particular product. Advertising can be used in the process of product differentiation either to inform consumers of real differences in the technical attributes of products or to create imagined differences in the minds of consumers through the establishment of brand names. It is an important element of non-price competition and is therefore particularly important in oligopolistic markets as an alternative to price warfare.

Figure 8.5 shows the total advertising spending in the UK between 1985 and 1998. The level of spending for 1998 represents a 4.1 per cent real increase over 1997 and it is the seventh successive year of increase. It represents 1.9 per cent of GDP in 1998, about the same percentage of GDP that is spent on research and development. It can seen from Figure 8.5 that advertising expenditure is related to the **trade cycle**, with downturns occurring in adspend both in total and as a percentage of GDP in the early 1990s. Figure 8.6 shows the breakdown of advertising according to media for 1998. The press accounts for the largest category and there has been little change in the patterns of advertising between these types over the last ten years.

There is a continuing debate on the pros and cons of advertising and the effect it has on the economy. Many argue that in a world with incomplete and **asymmetric information**, the informative aspect of advertising has a positive influence on the market. By keeping the consumer informed of developments in the product and the introduction of any new products, the consumer is in a better position to be able to make informed rational decisions. In addition to this, if advertising is successful in increasing sales, the firm could experience

**Figure 8.5 Total advertising spending at constant (1990) prices and as a percentage of GDP, UK** (from *Advertising Statistics Yearbook*, 1999)

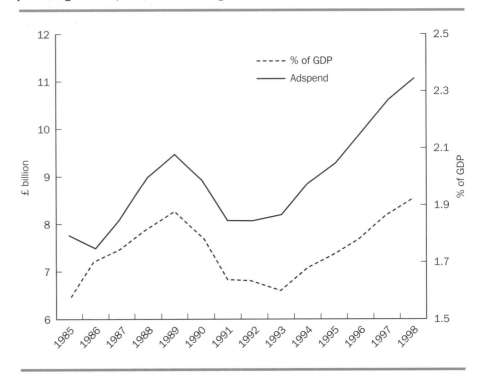

**Figure 8.6 Total advertising expenditure in 1998 by type at current prices, UK** (from *Advertising Statistics Yearbook*, 1999)

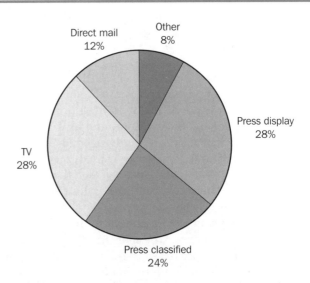

economies of scale which will lead to lower costs and therefore lower prices to the consumer. In contrast many argue that expenditure on advertising is a waste of resources, as firms tend to exaggerate the differences in their products over those of other firms. This form of product differentiation creates a barrier to entry which serves to reduce the level of potential competition in the market. As advertising is regarded as a selling cost, it is likely to be reflected in higher prices to the consumer. It seems that the situation is not clear cut and as there are arguments both for and against advertising, there is little government regulation of the level of advertising. In addition to this it is difficult in practice to separate out the persuasive aspects of advertising from the informative and if all firms in an industry are advertising the persuasive effects of advertising tend to cancel out. The exception to this is in the case of harmful goods such as cigarettes, where there are restrictions on advertising set by the government.

Advertising can be for individual products or markets as a whole. The purpose of advertising individual products from the firm's point of view is to shift the demand curve to the right and therefore to increase the level of sales and capture market share or, if sales are expected to fall for some reason, to maintain sales at the original level. The purpose of advertising the whole market is to raise public awareness of the product and to increase the total level of demand for it. Advertising expenditure is a barrier to entry, since any new entrant would have to match or exceed the incumbent firms' level of advertising. This will increase the costs of entry and therefore might make entry prohibitive. The level of advertising varies greatly between different types of products (see case study at the end of the chapter).

### 8.2.6 Pricing

Pricing is a conduct variable for firms. Even in neo-classical economics, there is only one market structure where the firm has no power over price – in perfect competition the firm is seen as a **'price-taker'** (see Chapter 7). Pricing is considered in more detail in Chapter 9, including its use in deterring entry into the market.

**limit price** the maximum price that can be set by an incumbent firm without attracting new entry to the market

For our purpose we should note that the **limit price** is the maximum price that can be set by an incumbent firm (or firms acting together) without attracting new entrants into the market. In the market illustrated in Figure 8.1 entry will not occur because the prevailing price of $P_L$ is lower than the long-run average cost (LAC) of the potential new entrant and therefore entry is not profitable for the potential new entrant. The barrier to entry illustrated in Figure 8.1 is the cost advantage experienced by the incumbent firm which means that its LAC is below the LAC of the new entrant at every possible level of output (see Chapter 7).

**predatory pricing** when incumbent firms force the price of the product down to such a level that other firms cannot enter the market and make a profit

Limit pricing is a pricing strategy which is designed to deter potential entrants and it is only the existence of barriers to entry which enables price to be maintained above its competitive price level. If a new entrant does manage to enter the market the incumbent firms could use predatory pricing to force a new entrant out of the market and return the market to some sort of balance. **Predatory pricing** is where incumbent firms increase output and therefore

**Newspaper pricing**

The price war which has raged in the newspaper industry for a number of years was started in 1993 by Rupert Murdoch's News International when it reduced the price of the *Sun* from 25p to 20p and the cover price of *The Times* from 45p to 30p. Details of the price war and its effects have been considered elsewhere.[3] In the broadsheet newspaper market there was a mixed response to the price cuts – the *Independent* joined in the price war and reduced its cover price while others (the *Guardian*, for example) did not and maintained price levels. The *Financial Times* has even managed to increase its cover price over the seven-year period without losing circulation. The stated motivation for the price cut was Murdoch's belief that newspapers were over-priced, but it is also about market share. *The Times* has increased its market share over this period. For example, in 1993 circulation stood at 360,000; in November 1996 circulation peaked at 862,000. Is this all due to reduced prices?

Clearly price has had an impact but there are other forces at work too. Indeed there were signs that the circulation of *The Times* was increasing even before the start of the price war. As well as price reductions over the years, there have been great changes in *The Times*. It has become more focused and contains more sections and supplements than previously. It is argued that each newspaper has its natural population which is finite in size. It could be that *The Times* has found its market niche and its natural readership. Evidence on circulation seems to support this idea. At present the circulation of *The Times* is bobbing along at around 720,000. The introduction of the 10p on Monday's *Times* between June 1996 and January 1998 increased circulation above this but only temporarily.

It appears that price cuts increase circulation for a while but not for ever. Readers quickly get used to the new price and other things become more important. The price cuts attract footloose readers who have not found their 'natural' newspaper yet. Product differentiation is more important than price. Evidence for this is provided by the *Financial Times* which has increased its price from 50p in 1990 to 85p in 2000 without any loss of circulation. It is a premium people are willing to pay for a specialism.

These price cuts can be seen as a strategic move designed to increase market share at the expense of competitors. In 1998 the *Telegraph* and the *Guardian* accused News International of predatory pricing and made a complaint to the Office of Fair Trading. In May 1999, after a 15-month investigation, the OFT found that although News International had acted uncompetitively by reducing the price of *The Times* to 10p on Mondays it was not guilty of predatory pricing. News International was required to justify any future reductions in price to the OFT.

force down market price so that all firms make a loss. Only the largest will be able to withstand this and the market would return to the previous balance. If this sort of behaviour was expected prior to entry, the new entrant might not have entered in the first place.

### 8.2.7 Innovation

Innovation is usually defined as the introduction of new products or new processes of production in an industry. Schumpeter (1943) adopted a very broad definition of innovation and located it in the middle of a three-stage process:[4]

**invention** the discovery of a new product or production process

**innovation** the introduction of a new product or new production processes

**diffusion** the widespread adoption of an innovation

1 **invention** – of a new idea;
2 **innovation** – the commercialisation of the new idea. It could be a new product or a change in existing product, a new method of production or a change in an existing method of production or the development of a new market;[5]
3 **diffusion** – the general acceptance and widespread adoption of the innovation.

It is extremely difficult to measure the level of innovation in a market/industry. The level of research and development is often used as a proxy for innovation since there is a strong relationship between R&D spending and innovation, but it must be remembered that R&D is the input into the process, while innovation is the output. Innovation is seen as a conduct factor for firms since it depends upon the amount of R&D firms choose to carry out. The level of R&D expenditure and innovation will depend upon the nature of the product and will vary greatly between industries. It will also depend upon the stage of the product in its life cycle. Invention and innovation are high-risk activities which are encouraged by the government through the patent system which reduces the risk involved in R&D. Table 8.1 shows the breakdown of R&D spending in the UK for 1997 by broad sector. The total of £9,657 million represents around 2 per cent of GDP.

In many markets invention and innovation are important competitive tools, more important than traditional tools of competition like price or advertising. The commonly quoted example is of pharmaceuticals, where the level of R&D and innovation is very high. The introduction of a new drug can have dramatic effects on markets. Although pharmaceuticals is not shown as a separate category in Table 8.1, it accounted for 20 per cent of total R&D spending in 1997.

There has been a long-running debate about which type of market structure best encourages innovation. Many argue that competitive markets are most conducive to innovation because the threat of competition means that unless firms

**Table 8.1  Spending on R&D in 1997, 1997 prices**

| Product group | £ million | % of total |
|---|---|---|
| All product groups | 9,657 | 100 |
| All products of manufacturing industry | 7,360 | 76 |
| Chemicals | 2.831 | 29 |
| Mechanical engineering | 709 | 12 |
| Electrical machinery | 1,181 | 9 |
| Aerospace | 893 | 10 |
| Transport | 966 | 10 |
| Other manufacturing | 779 | 8 |
| Services | 2,297 | 24 |

*Source*: Adapted from Table 19.4, *Annual Abstract of Statistics*, National Statistics © Crown copyright 2000

innovate they will be forced out of business. Others, including Galbraith (1974), argue that oligopolies are better because the large firms in the industry have the resources to finance research and development and are better able to bear the risks involved in R&D.[6] They will also be more motivated to innovate than firms in perfect competition, since they will reap the benefits of innovation in the form of abnormal profits. As there is less price competition in an oligopolistic market there will be more reliance on other forms of competition, including innovation.

### 8.2.8 Co-operation between firms

In competitive markets firms face uncertainty and risk. How will economic forces operate? How will competitors react? What will happen to the level of demand? This uncertainty can be partly reduced through planning and control of output and supplies through co-operation with other firms. There is a whole range of co-operative behaviour ranging from special relationships with suppliers and distributors through collusion with competitors and integration. Included under the heading of co-operative behaviour would be the relatively new phenomena of **networking** and **franchising** (all of these are discussed at length in Worthington and Britton 2000). Such relationships reduce the uncertainty faced by firms and once in operation can operate as a barrier to entry which would need to be addressed by any new entrant.

**networking** the formal and informal relationships which exist between organisations and the people employed in those organisations

#### Collusion

This refers to co-operation between independent firms which serves to modify the behaviour of the firms. Agreements or 'understandings' could be reached on price-fixing, output quotas or the segmentation of markets. Collusion can be tacit (or informal) as in the case of price leadership in oligopolistic markets, where one firm takes the lead in setting prices and the others follow suit; or formal as in the case of a cartel (see Chapter 7). By forming or joining a cartel firms can operate like a monopolist – they can exercise some control over price or output and therefore reduce some of the uncertainty under which they operate.

Collusion is illegal in the UK, unless the collusive arrangement can be argued as being in the public interest (see Chapter 11).

#### Integration

Where collusion between competitors is not possible or practical, one solution is for firms to integrate their activities either through merger or takeover. Such integration is called **horizontal integration**, since it involves two firms at the same level of the production process. There are a number of reasons why firms in an industry might wish to integrate:

**horizontal integration** integration between two firms at the same level of the production process

- If there is a fall in demand for the product and therefore excess capacity, integration might be necessary in order to rationalise supply.
- Integration with other producers should lead to bigger economies of scale in production.
- Such integration might be an effective way of combating increased international competition.
- As an aggressive move, it is a way to increase market share.
- As a passive move, it could be done as a reaction to the activities of other firms in the industry.

Horizontal integration will affect the structure of an industry through an increase in the level of concentration. If the resulting economies of scale are large it will also increase the height of the barriers to entry and reduce the level of potential competition.

Integration between firms at different stages of the production process is called **vertical integration**. This can take place 'forwards' as in the case of a car manufacturer taking over a car showroom or 'backwards' if the car manufacturer takes over a supplier of parts. The motivations for this type of integration are:

**vertical integration forwards** integration with a firm further forwards in the production process

**vertical integration backwards** integration with a firm at a previous stage of the production process

- The possible economies of scale which result from the two activities being brought together.
- In the case of backwards integration, the increased control over the supplies of raw materials or parts brings much greater security to the acquiring firm. Such integration also allows the acquiring firm to control or restrict the supplies of the parts to its competitors.
- In the case of forwards integration, the firm gains greater control over the distribution or retailing of the finished product. Again this could serve as a barrier to entry since any new entrant would have to break into an existing distribution chain or set up their own.

**conglomerate integration** a merger or takeover of a company in a completely different industry which results in diversification in production

**diversification** the production of goods or services by a firm which are not related to the goods and services already being produced

The third type of integration is **conglomerate integration**, which refers to a merger or takeover between firms in different industries. The main reason for this type of integration is the **diversification** of risk which follows from not having to rely on only one market. It is also possible that there may be **economies of scope** from combining two different activities.

It should be stated that integration is only one of the ways of doing all this. It is possible and is very common for firms to have strong relationships with suppliers and distributors without having to resort to integration. All such relationships will have an impact on market structure and performance.

## 8.3   Performance

The assessment of the performance of firms is problematic, initially because of the choice of performance indicators and subsequently in the measurement of these indicators. A number of variables could be considered as a gauge of performance. These would include:

- profitability
- the growth of organisations
- the technical progressiveness of organisations
- levels of investment
- efficiency
- social performance
- productivity levels.

Of these, profitability remains the main performance indicator used in empirical studies of the relationships between structure, conduct and performance and it is considered in more detail below along with investment and productivity. The choice of performance indicators is problematic because there is a blurring of the distinction between performance and conduct variables. For example **growth** is included in the list because growth, either of the organisation or the industry, may indicate good performance since high growth implies that the organisation/industry is producing what consumers want, thereby increasing their share of consumer expenditure. However, takeover and merger behaviour (two of the ways in which organisations grow in size) have already been considered as conduct factors. So growth can be used both as a measure of performance and of conduct. A further complication is that growth may not be an explicit objective of the organisation (see Chapter 6) and it is therefore unfair to assess the performance of the organisation according to its growth rates. Although it is relatively easy to find information on the growth rates of industries and sectors of the economy it is much more difficult to find information at the micro level about individual firms.[7]

**technical progressiveness**
the extent to which new technology has been adopted in an industry

**level of investment** the amount of investment carried out by firms over a given time period

A similar line of argument can be applied to **technical progressiveness** or the extent to which new technology is adopted in an industry. The higher the level of technical progressiveness in an industry, the more responsive the organisation can be to market changes and the higher can be growth and profitability. The level of technical progressiveness in an industry is related to the **level of investment** (see below) and the level of innovation and invention. Both invention and innovation have already been considered as conduct factors. Furthermore there are obvious problems involved in measuring the level of technical progressiveness of an organisation or industry and in making comparisons between industries since they differ in their ability or need to adopt new technology.

**allocative efficiency (or Pareto efficiency)** where resources are allocated such that no-one could be made better off without making someone else worse off

Another measure of performance of organisations and industries is their efficiency. **Economic efficiency** is said to exist when there is **technical efficiency** – i.e. firms are operating at the lowest possible cost given the current state of technology and **allocative efficiency** – resources are devoted to producing the goods and services that society wants. Allocative (or Pareto) efficiency is said to exist when resources cannot be redistributed between products to make anyone better off without making someone else worse off. Theoretically, economic efficiency occurs in perfectly competitive markets. Empirically, it is very difficult to measure technical efficiency, since most organisations will not have sufficient information to be able to plot their cost curve and therefore its proximity to lowest cost cannot be ascertained. A possible way of assessing efficiency is to conduct an efficiency audit, either internally by management or externally by regulatory bodies. The efficiency of the organisation can be assessed either by comparing its actual performance with theory or with other organisations in the same industry in this or other countries.

**social performance** a wider assessment of performance which looks at the company's impact on society as a whole

All of the factors mentioned above are connected with the economic performance of the organisation. A popular view which is gaining a degree of acceptance in the business world is that (as well as the traditional measures of economic performance) the organisation should be concerned with much wider issues of **social performance**. Stakeholder theory, as mentioned previously, implies that there are many groups with very diverse interests in the activities of the organisation.[8] The actions of the organisation might impact upon the environment in terms of pollution or the local community in terms of employment opportunities or quality of life. So firms contribute to social welfare as well as economic welfare and a measure of social performance would encapture this. This might be done through a social audit which would look at the costs and benefits of an organisation's activities to society as a whole. The social audit would include many factors like the impact on the environment and the local community as well as measures such as profitability and productivity (see e.g. Chapter 14).

### 8.3.1 Profitability

This is the most commonly used measure of performance. According to economic theory, in order to maximise profits firms should be producing up to the level where marginal cost is equal to marginal revenue (see Chapter 5), in other words operating at the point of lowest average cost. If all firms in a market face the same demand conditions, but one is operating at lower cost than the others, it will be earning higher profits. Therefore profitability can be used as a measure of performance. There are, however, a number of problems with the use of profitability as a measure of performance which are both theoretical and empirical. These problems will be considered later after a discussion of the concept of profit (see also Chapter 5 which looks at supply, costs and profit).

There is a difference between the economist's view and the accountant's view of profit. The economist sees profit as a payment to a factor of production – a reward to the entrepreneur for risk-taking. The accountant has no such view of profit. As previously stated, the economist would measure profit as the excess of the revenue derived from using resources over the opportunity cost of using those resources. Furthermore, as we have seen in Chapter 5, the economist identifies two types of profit. **Normal profit** is the minimum profit that the entrepreneur would expect to earn in an industry to remain in production. This will vary between industries and is largely dependent on the level of risk involved in production. If the level of profit falls below the normal level the entrepreneur will cease production and leave the industry. This will cause supply of the product to fall and market price to rise so that the remaining firms in the industry will once again be earning normal profits and equilibrium is re-established. If profits are above this level, then **abnormal or supernormal profits** are being earned. This will encourage entry into the industry, supply of the product will increase, price will fall and profits will be competed back down to the normal level. Again equilibrium has been re-established. According to economic theory, abnormal profits can only exist in the long run if there are barriers to entry.

**net profit** gross profit minus interest on loans and depreciation

The accountant has several different definitions of profit. **Net profit** is the residual of revenue over money costs, which includes wages and salaries, rent, fuel and raw materials, etc. and fixed interest payments, stock valuation and depreciation. This can be measured before tax or after tax when corporation or income tax have been deducted. **Gross profit** is net profit before the deduction of depreciation and interest payments. In the calculation of profit rates accountants use different conventions for calculating depreciation or valuation of stock which makes a comparison of figures very difficult between firms, industries and countries. Changing accounting conventions means that even for the same organisation over a period of time meaningful comparisons are problematic. Added to this, costs can be measured on a **historic cost basis** or a

**gross profit** the revenue from sales minus the cost of sales

**historic cost** the cost of an asset when it was purchased

**replacement cost** the cost of replacing a capital good

**replacement cost basis**, both of which will give different figures. The accountant usually expresses profit as a ratio – the return on capital employed or the return on equity, for example.

The measures of profit used by the economist and the accountant are likely to diverge for a number of reasons. As the economist is concerned with the opportunity cost of production, allowance will need to be made for the use of retained earnings since they could have yielded a revenue if they had been used outside the business. This would be ignored by the accountant. The same is true of the time devoted to the business by the entrepreneur, since the opportunity cost of that time is the wage that could have been earned if the entrepreneur had worked outside the business. Both this and the cost of retained earnings would have to be imputed costs, but they would need to be allowed for in the calculation of true economic profit. In addition to this, accountants tend to base their calculations on historic cost, whereas the relevant concept for the economist would be the replacement cost. As a result of these factors, the accountant's measure of profit will tend to overstate the economist's measure of profit. It is possible for a firm which shows an accounting profit to actually be making an economic loss.

**return on capital employed** an accounting ratio of profit as a percentage of capital employed

A ratio commonly used to measure profitability is **return on capital employed**, where the measure of profit used is shown as a percentage of the average capital employed in a firm. Figure 8.7 shows the return on capital employed for listed companies over a period of time. It can be seen that, as with most other economic variables it is affected by the trade cycle and moves in a cyclical way.

The problems discussed so far concentrate on the practical aspects of calculating profit rates. They are important when empirical studies use published (accounting) profit figures to test economic theories about relationships

**Figure 8.7 Rates of return on capital employed in the business sector, UK 1981–1999**

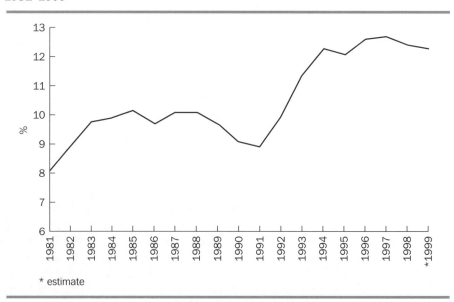

* estimate

*Source: OECD, Economic Outlook, No. 62, December 1997, copyright OECD*

between structural and conduct factors and profitability. Added to these practical problems there are also significant theoretical problems in using profitability as a measure of performance. It is possible that high profits might not be the result of efficiency in production, but the opposite – high profits could be due to the existence and the abuse of monopoly power. Conversely, low profitability might not be due to poor performance if the firm's objective is sales or growth maximisation. In this case the firm will be attempting to **satisfice** rather than maximise profits and therefore its performance should not be judged on the basis of its profit levels. Clearly more than one indicator should be used to measure performance but, as will be seen later, many of these suffer from similar theoretical and empirical problems.

Despite these problems, many tests have been made of the relationships between structural and conduct factors and profitability. In testing the link between market power and the level of profits, concentration ratios have been used as a proxy for market power. The S-C-P model predicts that the more concentrated an industry is the greater would be the level of abnormal profits. Many empirical tests of this hypothesis have been carried out over the years and early studies supported this proposition; the results of later studies, however, have been contradictory.[9] Economic theory suggests that one of the characteristics of oligopoly and monopoly is the persistence of abnormal profits in the long run. Tests have been carried out of this hypothesis but again the results are contradictory; there seems to be no stable relationship between concentration and the endurance of abnormal profits.

Empirical studies of the relationship between advertising and profit have also been undertaken. The S-C-P model predicts that there would be a positive relationship between the level of advertising and profits. This is because on the one hand successful advertising leads to increased sales and therefore economies of scale, and on the other high advertising expenditure is a barrier to entry. Both of these would enable the firm to enjoy higher profitability. The results of these empirical studies have been equally inconclusive.

Many empirical studies have used regression analysis to estimate relationships between variables. This means that they suffer the same econometric problems discussed below in Chapter 16. Perhaps the relationships are not linear. Some attempts have been made at non-linear estimation but the results are no clearer. A major problem here is the route of causality assumed by the S-C-P model which underlies the empirical testing of these relationships. It could be that high profitability leads to higher levels of concentration rather than the reverse. The numerous problems discussed in this section make it very difficult to come to any conclusions about the relationships between structure, conduct and profitability and to accept or reject the predictions of the S-C-P model.

### 8.3.2 Investment levels

**investment** expenditure by firms on investment goods

**Investment** by firms in capital assets is important for many reasons – it is necessary to increase output of products and to facilitate growth and higher profitability and it is especially important in the process of invention and innovation. High investment can also be used as a tool of entry deterrence through the erection of barriers to entry. The wrong investment decisions by

**Table 8.2 Investment in fixed assets in the UK by sector, at current prices 1995, £ million**

| | Gross investment | Net investment |
|---|---|---|
| Agriculture, hunting, forestry and fishing | 933 | −661 |
| Mining and quarrying | 4,463 | 143 |
| Manufacturing | 15,237 | 327 |
| Electricity, gas and water supply | 4,802 | 288 |
| Construction | 770 | −209 |
| Wholesale and retail trade; repairs; hotels and restaurants | 10,642 | 5,126 |
| Transport, storage and communication | 10,483 | 2,339 |
| Financial intermediation, real estate, renting and business activities | 15,061 | 6,849 |
| Other services | 17,675 | 10,590 |
| Dwellings | 21,837 | 7,709 |
| Total | 105,385 | 32,501 |

*Source*: Adapted from Table 14.4, UK National Accounts, National Statistics © Crown copyright (1996).

**fixed assets** assets which are retained for the long term benefit and use of the firm

**gross investment** the total level of investment by the firm

**replacement investment** investment in capital goods needed to replace worn out or obsolete machinery

**net investment** new investment over and above the level required to replace worn out and obsolete capital

**capital widening** investment which accompanies an increase in labour and therefore leaves the capital/labour ratio unchanged

**capital deepening** investment which is labour saving and serves to increase the capital/labour ratio

the firm can have disastrous results on the operation of the organisation, as can the wrong choice of finance for the investment.

Investment in **fixed assets** refers to expenditure on new buildings, plant and machinery, vehicles, ships and aircraft. The level of investment is subject to cyclical movements, increasing in times of boom and falling in times of recession. The total level of investment is called **gross investment** and this can be subdivided into **replacement investment**, for replacing worn-out and obsolete machines and **net or new investment**, which is any investment over and above the replacement level. Table 8.2 shows the breakdown of investment in the UK for 1995, and it can be seen that net investment accounted for only 31 per cent of gross investment in that year so that nearly 70 per cent of investment was for replacement purposes. The most important sector for net investment in 1995 was the service sector which accounted for 76 per cent of the total. The two negative values for net investment imply contractions in those sectors. In the UK there has been a decrease in the size of the agriculture, hunting, forestry and fishing sector while the construction sector is notoriously susceptible to cyclical movements and is sometimes negative and sometimes positive. It is difficult to say whether low investment causes low growth or vice versa, as in the case of the primary sector in the UK.

In the measurement of performance it is net investment which is important as it leads to a growth in the productive potential of organisations. It can be of two types: **capital widening**, which involves the use of more capital but with the same capital/labour ratio; or capital **deepening**, which increases the capital/labour ratio. A replication of a production line would be an example of the former and increased mechanisation of a production line would be an example of the latter. Table 8.3 shows net investment as a percentage of gross investment over a specified period of time.

From Table 8.3 it can be seen that, like gross investment, the level of replacement investment is cyclical. It rose as a percentage of gross investment in the boom of the late 1980s and fell in the recession of the early 1990s. In

**Table 8.3  Net investment as a percentage of gross investment in the UK, 1985 to 1995**

| Year | % | Year | % |
|------|------|------|------|
| 1985 | 31   | 1991 | 35   |
| 1986 | 30.7 | 1992 | 33   |
| 1987 | 36   | 1993 | 30.7 |
| 1988 | 42   | 1994 | 31.2 |
| 1989 | 46   | 1995 | 30.8 |
| 1990 | 43   |      |      |

*Source:* Adapted from Table 14.4 UK National Accounts 1996j National Statistics © Crown copyright.

1995, net investment was nearly 31 per cent of gross investment, so that nearly 70 per cent of investment that took place in that year was for replacement purposes.

### 8.3.3 Productivity

**Productivity** measures the relationship between inputs used and outputs produced. It can be used as a measure of performance since two organisations (or industries) could produce different quantities of output with the same quantities of inputs because of differences in productivity level. The organisation (or industry) with higher productivity levels will be operating at lower cost and therefore more efficiently than the other. The use of productivity as a performance measure overcomes the problems involved in plotting and finding the lowest point of the cost curves of organisations in the determination of efficiency.

The main problems in the use of productivity levels are to do with measurement. Firstly the output of organisations is heterogeneous and therefore has to be measured in monetary terms. But some outputs are transferred within or between firms without a price being attached to them; also many of the outputs of the public sector are not priced. There are two main inputs into the production process and these too are subject to measurement difficulties. As far as labour is concerned, a common measure of productivity is output per person employed (see Figure 8.8), but this does not take into account the number of hours worked or the quantity of capital used or the skill of the workforce. These problems make comparisons very difficult both between industries in one country or internationally. The measurement problems for capital are even greater than for labour; how can the measurement of different machines be standardised other than merely counting the number of machines? For this reason the measure of productivity usually used is output per person employed, as shown in Figure 8.8.

Figure 8.8 shows the trend in productivity for the whole economy and the manufacturing sector over a 20-year period. There was a fairly sharp increase in productivity levels in the manufacturing sector in the UK over the 1980s. Productivity growth in the UK compared favourably with that of other countries in the 1980s and 1990s but research by the Department of Trade and Industry in 1998 found that much of this improvement was due to longer

**Figure 8.8 Productivity in the UK, output per person employed**

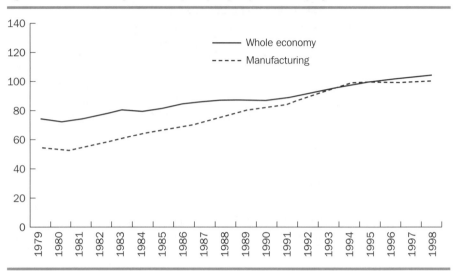

Source: Table 3.8, *Economic Trends 2000*, National Statistics © Crown copyright

working hours rather than increased efficiency of labour. In 1997 British workers worked 9 per cent more hours than German workers and 5 per cent more than French workers.

A major study on productivity differences was carried out by the McKinsey management consultancy in 1998.[10] It used output per hour worked to measure **labour productivity**; this is a better measure since it removes the effects of increases in the number of hours worked. The results are summarised in Table 8.4.

**labour productivity** the relationship between the quantity of labour inputs and the output produced

**Table 8.4 Labour productivity in selected countries, 1997 measured by output per hour worked (UK = 100)**

| Country | Labour productivity |
| --- | --- |
| UK | 100 |
| France | 126 |
| West Germany | 126 |
| USA | 137 |

Source: McKinsey Global Institute (1998).

In terms of output per hour worked, labour productivity in the USA is 37 per cent ahead of the UK while France and Germany are both 26 per cent ahead. This is an average which is variable across sectors of the economy (the UK has performed fairly well in the manufacturing sector but badly in services) and across industries (both the chemical industry and paper products and printing have exceptionally high productivities in the UK).

The McKinsey Report also looked at another measure of productivity called 'total factor productivity' which measures the efficiency of both labour and

**Table 8.5  Total factor productivity in selected countries, 1997 (UK = 100)**

| Country | Factor productivity |
| --- | --- |
| UK | 100 |
| France | 112 |
| West Germany | 114 |
| USA | 127 |

Source: McKinsey Global Institute (1998).

capital. Table 8.5 summarises the survey results for the same four countries. As can be seen, the UK does rather better on this measure of productivity.

Although many reasons are put forward for the relatively low productivity levels in the UK, including the educational system, the activities of trade unions, the high value of the pound and low levels of research and development, the major reason given is lack of investment. The McKinsey Report concluded that as far as capital productivity is concerned, the UK performs better than France and Germany and not far behind the USA. It would seem that the investment that does take place is used efficiently enough but that there is not enough of it. Two major factors identified by the report which inhibit productivity growth in the UK are the effects of regulations (which govern markets and land use) and skill shortages.

Low productivity has implications for the performance of organisations and industries but also for wider factors like international competitiveness, growth prospects and inflation.

## 8.4  Conclusion

This chapter has considered important conduct and performance factors. The way in which firms behave is affected by many factors including the market structure in which they operate, the objectives of firms and general macroeconomic conditions. A distinction is made between passive behaviour and strategic behaviour. Strategically firms could be trying to deter entry through the erection of barriers to entry like advertising and product differentiation; they could be attempting to influence existing market conditions through pricing policy or through mergers and takeovers; or they could be attempting to reduce the level of uncertainty they face through co-operation with other firms. All of these conduct factors and more have been considered in this chapter. In the basic Structure–Conduct–Performance model conduct is a result of market structure which then goes on to determine performance. A more sophisticated model allows reverse linkages and this is the view that has been adopted above. The effects that conduct has on performance and structure were also discussed.

Several performance indicators have been considered and a similar view has been taken of these – that they are not the passive result of conduct but that they impact upon both conduct and market structure and the dividing line between conduct and performance is often blurred. Although neo-classical economics uses profitability as the main measure of the performance, it is clear from the discussion in this chapter that the measure of performance of firms and industries cannot be based on a single indicator but on a balanced set of indicators like profitability, growth, productivity and investment and other more diverse social indicators.

**Case study**

## Advertising

**advertising intensity**
the ratio of advertising to sales

The **advertising intensity** in a market can be measured by the advertising to sales ratio. Table 8.6 shows advertising to sales ratios for a selection of industries and it can be seen that there are significant differences between the products shown.

**Table 8.6  Selected advertising to sales ratios, 1997, UK**

| Product category | Advertising to sales ratio (%) |
| --- | --- |
| Shampoo | 24.76 |
| Soap | 14.43 |
| Washing powder | 7.97 |
| Baby-care products | 3.85 |
| Dishwashers | 1.99 |
| Refrigerators | 0.75 |
| Beer | 0.62 |
| TV sets | 0.41 |
| Vegetables | 0.23 |

*Source: Advertising Statistics Yearbook (1999).*

Why should the level of advertising vary so much between products? There is not one single explanation but instead a number of factors are put forward to explain the differing levels of advertising intensity.

- The first factor comes directly from the Structure–Conduct–Performance model which sees the level of advertising as a conduct factor which will be influenced by **market structure**. Oligopolistic markets are characterised by high levels of advertising and Table 8.6 shows that soap and soap powder have relatively high advertising to sales ratios.

**search qualities** the characteristics of a product which can be objectively described prior to purchase

**experience qualities** qualities of the product which can only be evaluated after the consumption of a product

- The second explanation concentrates on the qualities of the product. Nelson (1974) talks about two qualities of goods – **search qualities** and **experience qualities**.[11] Search qualities are characteristics that can be described in an objective way prior to purchase, e.g. a computer or a car will be high in search qualities. Experience qualities are characteristics that can only be evaluated after they have been consumed, e.g. the taste of something or how comfortable something is to wear. The advertising of goods with high search qualities will mainly concentrate on providing consumers with the information needed to make a decision and consequently the demand for such a good will be more price sensitive than those high in experience qualities. In the case of goods high in experience qualities, the level of advertising is likely to be higher since this might be the only source of information which is available and it will tend to be much more persuasive in nature. In Table 8.6 the top three products are high in experience qualities while goods high in search qualities like dishwashers and TVs have much lower advertising intensities. Empirical evidence seems to support the thesis that goods with high experience qualities are advertised more heavily.[12] In the literature on the marketing of services a third quality has been added to the above – **credence qualities**[13] – these are qualities which the consumer may find impossible to evaluate even after purchase and consumption. The intensity of advertising is affected by several factors:

**credence qualities** qualities inherent in a product that are hard to evaluate even after purchase and consumption

- *The frequency of purchase.* If a good (e.g. vegetables) is purchased frequently, the consumer does not have to rely on advertising to find out about it: there exists up-to-date and reliable information.
- *The durability of the product.* A large durable purchase like a dishwasher or a refrigerator carries a high penalty for a mistake and so the consumer will seek out as much information as possible from other sources like consumer magazines and is less likely to rely on advertising.

**consumer goods** goods purchased by consumers for consumption as opposed to consumption by firms for production purposes

**producer goods** goods that are used by firms in the production of other goods

- Empirical evidence shows that there is much more advertising for **consumer goods** than there is for **producer goods**. The reasons for this are that the market for producer goods is likely to be fairly small and therefore advertising through mass communication is not necessary. The purchaser of producer goods is likely to be very knowledgeable about the product and their requirement for very specialised information is better met by a sales representative than through advertising. It should be remembered that advertising is just one of a whole range of promotional activities including sales representation. It could be that certain products (e.g. producer goods) are better sold by sales reps than advertising.

**product life cycle** the course of a product's sales and profitability over its lifetime

- *The characteristics of the market.* In markets where there is a high level of product innovation high levels of advertising are necessary to keep consumers informed of these changes. Similarly, in the market for baby products, there will be a continual change in the consumer base and therefore high levels of advertising are needed to keep the new consumers informed. The position in a product's life cycle is likely to have a bearing on the level of advertising in an industry (see Chapter 9). In the birth and growth phases of the **product's life cycle** informative advertising is likely to be high in order make consumers aware of the product. In the maturity phase of the life cycle advertising will be more persuasive as firms attempt to increase their market share. In the decline phase, the level of advertising will be low.

## Notes and references

1. Bain, J. S. (1956), *Barriers to New Competition*, Harvard University Press, Cambridge, MA.

2. Kotler, P. (1994), *Marketing Management: Analysis, Planning, Implementation and Control*, Prentice Hall, Englewood Cliffs, N.J.

3. Worthington, I. and Britton, C. (2000), *The Business Environment*, 3rd edition, Financial Times Prentice Hall, Harlow.

4. Schumpeter, J. A. (1943), *Capitalism, Socialism and Democracy*, Allen and Unwin, London.

5. See Chapter 5 in Worthington and Britton (2000).

6. Galbraith, J. K. (1974), *The New Industrial State*, Penguin, Harmondsworth.

7. Ways of measuring growth include growth in sales, growth in employment, growth in value added and growth in capital employed. Data on these can be found in government publications like *Annual Abstract of Statistics, Economic Trends* and *UK National Accounts* (www.ons.gov.uk).

8. Worthington and Britton (2000).

9. See Ferguson, P. R. and Ferguson, G. J. (1994), *Industrial Economics: Issues and Perspectives*, Macmillan, Basingstoke for a full discussion of empirical tests.

10. McKinsey Global Institute (1998), *Driving Productivity and Growth in the UK Economy*, Washington DC.

11. Nelson, P. (1974), 'Advertising as information', *Journal of Political Economy*, 82, pp. 729–754.

12. Ferguson and Ferguson (1994).

13. Darby, M. and Karni, E. (1973), 'Free competition and the optimal amount of fraud', *Journal of Law and Economics*, April, pp. 67–88.

## Review and discussion questions

1 Why is the level of advertising high in the market for designer trainers?

2 Use the model in Figure 8.4 to determine the three levels of the product for the following goods: painkillers, beer, CDs. How might this information help in marketing the product?

3 In the relationship between the firm and its suppliers, what are the advantages and disadvantages of the following three possibilities:
- remaining independent of suppliers, buying supplies as and when needed,
- having a 'special relationship' with suppliers?
- taking over or merging with suppliers?

## Assignments

1 You work for a regional newspaper which is worried about falling circulation levels. You have been asked to come up with some ideas which might help promote loyalty amongst its readers. Produce a short report outlining your ideas.

**2** The organisation you work for is producing some PR material on its activities. The managing director has heard of the notion of the social audit and wishes to stress the concept of social responsibility in the PR material. She has asked you to research the factors which would be included in the social audit. Produce a briefing for your MD (hint – start with a list of stakeholders for the organisation of your choice).

## Further reading

Ferguson, P. R. and Ferguson, G. J. (1994), *Industrial Economics: Issues and Perspectives*, MacMillan, Basingstoke.

Worthington, I. and Britton, C. (2000), *The Business Environment*, 3rd edition, Financial Times Prentice Hall, Harlow.

# CHAPTER 9

# Pricing in theory and practice

Andy Rees

**Objectives**

1 To review the concept of equilibrium price.

2 To investigate supply lags and cobweb theory in relation to price formation.

3 To examine pricing in different competitive markets.

4 To consider different pricing strategies used by business organisations.

5 To discuss the notion of 'price discrimination'.

## 9.1 Introduction

In Chapter 3 we presented a **demand function** containing the explanatory variables determining the level of demand for any particular good. Although we noted a tendency in traditional analysis to over-emphasise the importance of price, as consumers might be more or equally interested in **non-price factors** such as quality, reliability, design, after-sales service etc. (often referred to as the **marketing mix**), price nevertheless remains a significant factor in determining demand and ultimately serves as the firm's source of revenue.

**marketing mix** the combination of both price and non-price factors that a firm might use to influence the sale of a good. Attention is often paid to the 'Four Ps: produce, place, promotion and price

We also noted (see Chapter 5) price to be an important determinant of supply. Thus, if price rises, the firm will consider it profitable to supply additional units. If it is confident that high prices will be maintained, it may then increase productive capacity through additional investment. To calculate the return to such an investment requires an estimate of prices and levels of demand over the lifetime of the investment.

Price is therefore of paramount importance to the firm as a determinant of both supply and demand. To ensure continued success the firm must pay particular attention to its **pricing strategy**. The purpose of this chapter is to investigate the basis of pricing and outline differing pricing strategies that might be used by business organisations.

**pricing strategy** the firm's consideration of how best to set price to determine sales both in the present time period and in future time periods. This should take into account the firm's competitive environment and its overall goals

## 9.2 Setting an equilibrium price

In the appendix to Chapter 5 we considered how market price is determined by the forces of supply and demand. From this appendix consider Figure 5.22, here represented and adapted as Figure 9.1.

**Figure 9.1 The market for 'Real Brew' draught beer**

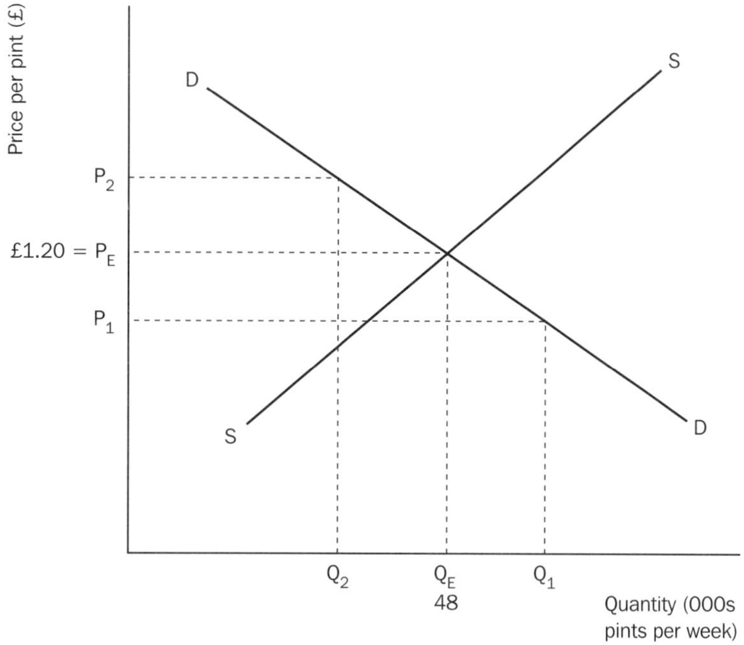

Real Brew (depicted in Figure 9.1) can be assumed to be one of a number of brands currently available on the market. Real Brew will attempt to create brand loyalty through, for example, innovative advertising and providing a quality product sold in a convivial environment. Nevertheless, due to the competitive nature of the market, the demand curve is likely to remain **relatively elastic**. Therefore, if the firm was to lower price from $P_E$ to $P_1$ this would result in a relatively significant increase in demand ($Q_E$ to $Q_1$) as the product becomes more price competitive compared to rivals whose prices are assumed to have remained constant. Similarly, increasing price from $P_E$ to $P_2$ would significantly reduce demand from $Q_E$ to $Q_2$. If the firm was able to increase **brand loyalty**, and therefore decrease price elasticity, the fall in demand following a price increase would be less.

It is important for the firm to have an **equilibrium price**: a price where supply is equal to demand ($P_E$ in Figure 9.1). Consider the problems of setting a price in excess of $P_E$. The cost would be in terms of unsold stock and inherent **cash flow** problems as production costs are unlikely to be covered by sales revenue. The high price could also result in a loss of both market share and consumer loyalty, which might not be regained were price later to be reduced. Retail outlets might also decide to stop selling the good if sales were to fall below a critical level. Alternatively, if price is set too low (for example, below $P_E$ in Figure 9.1) the cost could be seen in terms of excess demand and the frustration of existing and potential customers unable to obtain the good. In their frustration, customers might consume elsewhere and having sampled a rival good might permanently switch their consumer loyalty. Unfulfilled

**cash flow** the flow of money payments to or from a firm. The firm requires an adequate cash flow to cover costs

demand also represents a loss of potential sales revenue and leads to unhappy retailers who bear the brunt of consumer dissatisfaction.

### 9.2.1 Price-takers and price-makers

Can the firm set an equilibrium price? We traditionally see firms as either **price-takers** or **price-makers**. You might find it useful at this point to revisit Chapter 7.

#### Price-takers

As we have seen in perfectly competitive markets with large numbers of buyers and sellers and a homogeneous product the firm has no individual control over price and simply takes the market price. The firm is a **price-taker**. For example, if we assume a perfectly competitive market for carrot growers, the individual carrot farmer has no control over price and is assumed to take the price as determined in the market by the interaction of market supply (made up of the combined efforts of numerous individual carrot farmers) and total market demand. In such a market, price adjusts to ensure market equilibrium and the individual farmer is always able to sell their product at the going market price. An increase in market demand raises the price at which farmers could sell their existing crop; a bumper harvest lowers market price. The producer is unable to charge more than the market price, as the consumers would then buy the good from a cheaper source. (The known homogeneity of goods ensures consumers always buy from that cheapest supplier.) Due to the large number of producers no single farmer can influence price by producing more or less of the product, as the effect upon overall supply would be insignificant and market price would remain unaltered.[1]

#### Price-makers

Non-perfectly competitive markets are typified by firms producing products that are differentiated, yet sufficiently similar in the eyes of the consumer to be included in the same product group or market. The firm therefore has the ability to set its own price which helps determine its competitive position and market share.

The firm is now referred to as a **price-maker** and administers the prices of the goods it produces. However, although it has the discretion to set its own price, the level of demand is determined by market forces. Alternatively, a firm might release a given supply on to the market and allow the market to determine a **market clearing price**. This can often be seen in an auction where items are sold to the highest bidder. Nevertheless, the norm is for the firm to set a price and then adjust supply to meet the level of demand. If it has a target supply it might adjust price until that supply is sold.

**market clearing price** the market price that results in the sale of all current supply of a specific good – the price that clears the market

It is again in the interest of the firm to set an equilibrium price, although locating and maintaining such equilibrium can pose certain problems for the enterprise. For example, imagine a situation (illustrated in Figure 9.2) where a firm is currently in equilibrium (sales per period of time matching current production). The business now decides to increase demand and market share through a revamped advertising campaign, its aim being to sell more at the existing price. If the new campaign were to increase cost, then those extra costs might be absorbed

**Figure 9.2 Maintaining equilibrium following a shift in the demand curve**

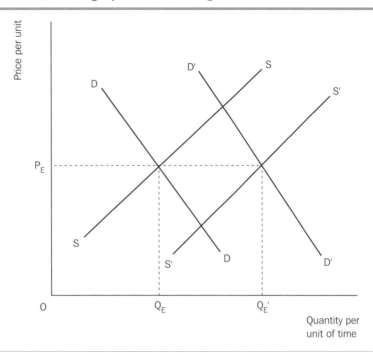

by a lower profit margin. It is also possible that increased sales could allow the firm to gain further **scale economies** that might balance out additional advertising costs. Or, as we will assume, the firm might not be spending additional money upon advertising but instead spending the same money on a revamped and more effective campaign. (Note: if the firm incurs additional cost this should shift the supply curve to the left. That is, given the additional cost, the firm now requires a higher price to supply any given level of supply.)

In Figure 9.2 we initially assume the firm in equilibrium at a price of $P_E$. The revamped advertising campaign shifts the demand curve to the right from DD to D'D'. To maintain an equilibrium at the initial price the firm should therefore increase production from $Q_E$ to $Q_E'$.

From the diagram this appears straightforward. However, in practice it can be more problematic. Prior to the launch of the new advertising campaign, the marketing and sales division of the firm would need to consult with the production team to request additional production to satisfy the anticipated extra demand. If it is seen to be difficult or perhaps excessively costly to increase production the campaign might have to be cancelled or delayed. If the campaign goes ahead then sales representatives might be dispatched to retailers to persuade them to increase stock in anticipation of increased demand. For example, the publisher of a popular novel soon to be serialised on BBC television would ask its sales representatives to contact book retailers prior to televising, requesting them to increase orders in anticipation of additional consumer interest.

In practice, preventing either excess demand or supply (and therefore maintaining an equilibrium) can be difficult. For instance, a new advertising initiative might fail to generate the anticipated extra demand; it might be affected by a downturn in the economy or by the reactions of competitors. The result is an excess of supply. Alternatively, the campaign might generate more demand than anticipated. In the case of our television serial, the quality of the production might captivate the public and generate higher than expected viewing figures. In both cases, this results in excess demand at the price set.

Despite these problems, it is in the interest of the producer (and retailer) to approach an equilibrium. This might finally be achieved by increasing production to match higher than expected demand or by selling off surplus supplies at discounted prices.

**Stability of an equilibrium**

If an equilibrium is achieved it is unlikely to remain stable due to the fluctuations in supply and demand. Thus, in foreign exchange markets the supply and demand for a currency might constantly change reflecting the collective desires of individuals to buy and sell a particular currency. Equilibrium is ensured by the price of a currency (its **exchange rate**) which adjusts many times in a given trading period. Prices in competitive markets are therefore likely to fluctuate constantly to maintain equilibrium.

**exchange rate** the price or rate at which one currency is exchanged for another

In non-competitive markets (with administered prices) we generally observe greater **price stability** as producers usually regain equilibrium by adjusting supply rather than price. For example, if a car manufacturer experiences declining sales for one of its models its initial reaction would be to cut back on production. If demand increases, the producer reacts by expanding supply. The result is that price remains relatively stable despite changing demand conditions. Even where supply changes (e.g. through a loss of production due to labour problems), the manufacturer is likely to maintain price and ask the consumer to await delivery.

**price stability** the degree to which the price of a good might vary through time. Stability implies constant or relatively constant prices

It might not be sensible for the price-maker to constantly adjust price as the act of changing price can be expensive, involving the re-pricing of existing goods, changing catalogue prices, and so on. Constantly changing prices can also create consumer uncertainty, making buyers reluctant to commit themselves to purchases on the expectation that prices might imminently fall. We have also seen in Chapter 7 that the interdependence between firms in non-competitive markets – highlighted in oligopolies – can result in a firm's reluctance to change price due to its uncertainty as to the reaction from its rivals.

In summary, although price-makers will adjust prices (for example, to reflect cost changes brought about by technological advance, changing consumer tastes and incomes, or a change in the competitive structure of the market), they generally fluctuate less than in competitive markets where firms are price-takers.

We should finally note that in such non-competitive markets we do not actually have a market price in the sense that individual firms administer the price of each good. Although price is influenced by market conditions it is not set by those conditions as it is in competitive markets. As stated, the firm is a price-maker as opposed to a price-taker.

### 9.2.2 Supply lags and cobweb theory

How can competitive markets regain equilibrium once it has been disturbed?

We presented a traditional analysis of this question in the appendix to Chapter 5. For example, if the supply curve shifts to the right there would be an

**Mini case**

## Setting price by auction: the UK sells off mobile phone licences

An equilibrium price could be determined by selling goods by auction. When the UK Labour government had the opportunity to sell the radio spectrum required for firms to operate the next (third, or 3G) generation of mobile phone services it decided to sell the five available licences by auction. Interest in obtaining the licences was intense, as this provided the opportunity for marrying together two of the fastest growing technologies, mobile phones and worldwide web access. The big players could not bear the prospect of exclusion. The auction eventually lasted for almost eight weeks, went through 150 rounds of bidding and concluded on 27 April 2000 when the sixth remaining bidder dropped out. Original government estimates of the likely proceeds had included an estimate of £3 billion. In the event, the auction raised £22.48 billion, the winners for the five licenses being TIW, Vodafone, BT Cellnet, Orange and One 2 One.

The auction proceeds eclipsed those achieved in privatisation sell-offs by previous Conservative governments where the sale of British Telecom, the most lucrative of those privatisations, raised £16 billion.

By collecting together all possible bidders, auctions should secure the maximum price from the most eager bidder, therefore representing an efficient method of allocating a scarce good. It is also an efficient method of determining price when the seller is unsure of a good's market value. This was clearly the case for the UK government when selling the mobile phone licences.

The amount bid in a commercial auction should reflect the eventual profit each bidder anticipates making. When bidders join an auction they should therefore know the maximum sum they can bid, although clearly wishing to secure the good for the lowest possible price. Bidders should therefore carefully analyse the likely behaviour of other players, whose actions in turn depend upon how those other bidders believe others will bid. This is clearly analogous to the interdependence, conjecture and uncertainty of oligopoly theory and is of particular relevance to game theory. Tactical bidding was certainly in evidence in the auction for the five mobile phone licences, each company employing its own team of tacticians and game theorists. Vodafone, the eventual successful bidder for the second licence was said to have paid more than it might have done owing to tactical bidding by British Telecom, whose strategy involved switching its bids between licences in what appears in hindsight to have been a relatively unsuccessful attempt to keep prices down.

Despite the high prices paid by the five successful bidders, they later claimed not to have exceeded the limits of their respective business models, although admitting to have come close.

There are a number of auction methods, including:

**ascending price auction**
an auction where bidders offer sequentially higher bids until the good is sold to the highest bidder

- **ascending price auction**, where bidders offer sequentially higher bids until there is only one bidder left. Often referred to as an English auction. This was the method used above.

▶

**descending price auction**
an auction where price falls from an initial high level until an individual denotes their willingness to purchase the good

**sealed bid auction** an auction where individuals submit their bids in secret without a knowledge of the size of other bids. The highest bidder wins the good or contract

- **descending price auction**, commonly referred to as a Dutch auction. Prices start high and fall until a buyer is found.
- **sealed bid auction**, where each bidder makes one bid without knowledge of what its rivals might be bidding. A common method when firms tender for government contracts.

Two principal problems are associated with auctions, namely:

1  The victor might secure the bid by being over-optimistic in their estimate of future profit and therefore pay too much, possibly leading to future bankruptcy. This is often referred to as the 'winner's curse'.
2  Collusion between bidders. This can emerge in sealed bid auctions where bidders might actively collude and take turns in winning tenders for alternate contracts. Collusion can also take place in ascending bid auctions. For example, cases have been found in antique auctions where specialist dealers agree between themselves not to bid against each other, so keeping prices down, and then distributing the lots between themselves in a private deal after the auction.

The apparent success of the UK auction may cause other countries to reassess how to allocate their own licences. It also remains to be seen what the impact might be of the relatively high prices paid by companies for their UK licences. Despite denials, have they paid too much, will they need to charge very high prices to recover initial outlays, and how might this affect consumer take-up of the new technology? In the meantime, the UK government is debating how to spend its windfall.

excess supply at the existing price. Price should fall, demand will extend and the quantity supplied diminishes until equilibrium is regained at a higher quantity demanded and supplied than at the original equilibrium. In short, as illustrated in Figure 9.3, we move from point a to a new stable equilibrium at point b.

The downward slope of the demand curve, the upward-sloping supply curve and the resulting market forces brings about the adjustment to a new equilibrium. It is possible, however, that this basic analysis might exaggerate the ease and manner through which competitive markets regain equilibrium. In certain markets the adjustment mechanism might be slowed, and even prevented, by the time it takes supply to adjust to a change in market price. As noted in Chapter 5, **supply lags** might exist. That is, rather than supply adjusting to a price change in the same time period, supply might only adjust in the next or future time period. For example, an increase in the price of an agricultural product might encourage farmers to increase output. However, they can only do so in the next growing season; we therefore have a one-year time lag.

Specifically, rather than:

$S_t = f(P_t)$    implying that supply in the current time period $_t$ is a function of the price in that same time period. Instead:

$S_t = f(P_{t-1})$  that is, supply in the current time period depends upon the price in the previous time period. Whereas:

**Figure 9.3  Movement to a new equilibrium**

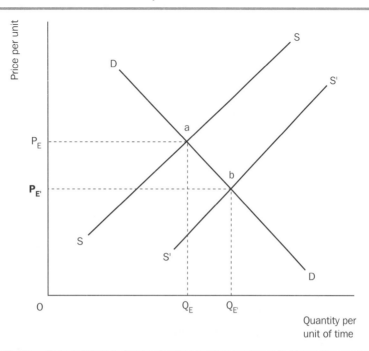

$D_t = f(P_t)$   that is, demand in the current period depends upon the price in the same time period. However, as noted in Chapter 3, there is often a time dimension to demand in that generally speaking demand is more price elastic in the long run than the short run.

In certain industries the supply lag might be longer than a single time period. For example, if there was an increase in the wages paid to computer programmers this might encourage more people to consider such a career. However, gaining the necessary qualification might take many years of study and the increased supply might only become evident after a number of years.

Introducing supply lags into the analysis has an interesting effect upon the way in which market forces seek to regain equilibrium. The process is explained through **cobweb theory** (see Figure 9.4).

As an illustration, assume a perfectly competitive market for a specific agricultural crop, such as potatoes. For simplicity of analysis assume there is a one-year supply lag, output in the current year being dependent upon price in the previous year. In contrast, demand in the current year depends upon price in that same year. As this is a perfectly competitive market we assume there to be a large number of producers all taking independent decisions on the volume of crops to plant in a given year. This would generally be in accord with the agricultural industry. In our example we preclude any market intervention (e.g. as with the agricultural policies currently in force in the European Union) whereby farmers might receive production quotas for individual products.

**cobweb theory** an analysis of whether in a market where current supply depends upon price in a previous time period, price will either move towards or away from an equilibrium

**Figure 9.4 Unstable cobweb**

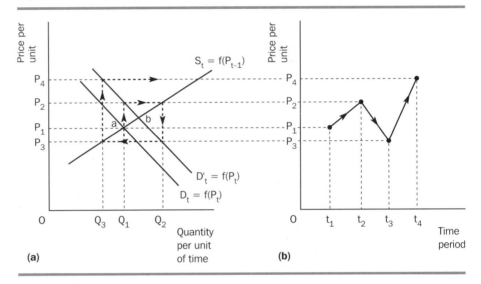

(a)

(b)

## Unstable cobweb

**unstable cobweb**
situation where prices do
not converge towards an
equilibrium and instead
become increasingly
unstable, oscillating from
high to low

Firstly consider the necessary conditions for an **unstable cobweb**: that is, a position where instead of the market converging towards an equilibrium, prices become increasingly unstable, oscillating from high to low, and exploding away from equilibrium.

Imagine in Figure 9.4a that we are initially in equilibrium with a price of $P_1$ and a quantity demanded and supplied of $Q_1$. This equilibrium is now disturbed by an increase in market demand, perhaps as a result of new research extolling the beneficial effects of consuming potatoes. As a consequence the demand curve shifts outwards from $D_t$ to $D_t'$ and in the initial time period $(t_1)$ current market supply $Q_1$ commands a price of $P_2$. How will farmers react to this news? Those currently producing potatoes will be particularly pleased and if possible might independently decide to produce more potatoes next year $(t_2)$ in anticipation of a continued price of $P_2$. Farmers not currently producing potatoes will plan to do so next year. (It is the nature of such competitive markets that producers make their decisions independently of each other. That is, they do not consider the total effect upon the market of the combined decisions of other producers.) The result is that in the following year $(t_2)$ total market supply rises to $Q_2$. However, to sell $Q_2$ market price falls to $P_3$, this lower price leading to a market supply of $Q_3$ in the next year $(t_3)$ and a high price of $P_4$ in that year to ration the limited supply. The high price of $P_4$ would then lead to a large rise in supply in the following year $(t_4)$, necessitating in a very low market clearing price.

Observe the path traced out in Figure 9.4a (note why this is called a **cobweb**). Instead of regaining equilibrium, price and quantity oscillations increase. Market forces move us away from equilibrium. The situation is **unstable** or **explosive**. The increasing price oscillations are also shown in Figure 9.4b.

The instability is caused by the supply curve being shallower (or more elastic) at all prices than the demand curve. The relatively elastic supply curve leads to exaggerated changes in market supply as price changes, whilst the less elastic demand curve means that changes in supply require relatively large price movements to clear the market. The reaction of supply is stronger than the response of demand.

## Stable cobweb

**stable cobweb** a situation where price fluctuations become smaller and smaller, converging towards an equilibrium where the amount placed on the market equals the amount consumers are willing to buy at the price which existed in the last period

Consider Figure 9.5. We now have a situation where the supply curve is steeper (less elastic) at all prices than the demand curve. The reaction of supply is weaker than the response of demand. That is, the initial price increase brought about by the shift in demand from $D_t$ to $D'_t$ brings about a relatively small increase in market supply, and this supply can be cleared from the market with a relatively small fall in price, etc. Price fluctuations therefore diminish over time (see Figure 9.5b) and the market moves towards a new equilibrium.

Introducing time lags into the analysis illustrates that market forces need not necessarily lead to an equilibrium. However, in reality, the price oscillations observed with an unstable cobweb must reach a limit. We could not imagine prices in alternate years of the cycle going from ridiculously low to ridiculously high, implying that in one year huge areas of agricultural land are given over to a particular crop and in the following year production falls to a minuscule scale. Eventually, individual farmers would gain from experience and start to react differently to price changes, or perhaps government agencies might intervene in the markets to create stability. Nevertheless, oscillations of price and quantity are certainly observed in many competitive markets, particularly in agricultural products. The pig market is often cited as an example.

Note that although the market might be out of equilibrium, market price adjustments ensure that farmers sell their entire crop, albeit not at prices they had anticipated. Price adjustments ensure the market is cleared and suppliers are not faced with unsold stock or excess demand.

**Figure 9.5  Stable cobweb**

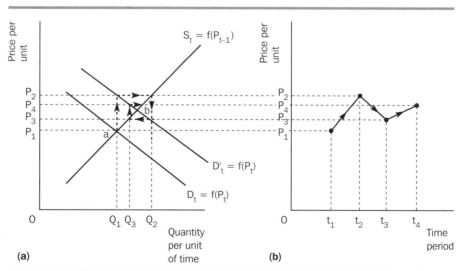

(a)

(b)

### 9.2.3 **Black markets**

We have noted the advantage to the firm of setting price at or very near equilibrium. Nevertheless, we can imagine situations where price might be set in the knowledge that this will result in excess demand and consumers are thwarted in their desire to purchase the good at the stated price. This is often the case in the sale of tickets to prestigious sporting events, for example the World Cup or the annual Football Association Cup Final in England (see Figure 9.6).

Figure 9.6 illustrates the supply and demand curves for the FA Cup Final, played annually at Wembley Stadium in London. For the purpose of this analysis assume all tickets are sold at a single price. The capacity of the stadium is approximately 90,000 and the supply curve is vertical to the quantity axis at this point, as whatever the ticket price this has no immediate impact upon capacity. If the Football Association was to expand capacity, either at Wembley Stadium, or by moving to a new stadium, this could be illustrated by the vertical supply curve shifting to the right.

The demand curve DD is relatively inelastic, reflecting the strong desire of each team's supporters (and other neutral football fans) to obtain tickets irrespective of the price set. The position and relative elasticity of the demand curve will be determined by the perceived attractiveness of the final and the support for each club. For example, a final between Manchester United and Chelsea (currently well-supported and attractive teams) would be certain to create a huge level of interest, perhaps resulting in the demand curve DD in Figure 9.6. Alternatively, a final involving two less attractive clubs, perhaps

**Figure 9.6 The market for Football Association Cup Final tickets**

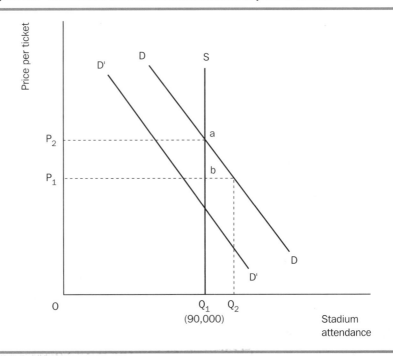

from a lower division with lower levels of support, would cause the demand curve to shift to the left, perhaps as far as D'D', although all FA Cup Finals are generally sell-outs.

Imagine the FA sets the ticket price at $P_1$, resulting in excess demand for tickets of $Q_2 - Q_1$. Note this is below the free market equilibrium price of $P_2$. In setting the price of $P_1$ the FA only raises revenue equivalent to the area $OP_1bQ_1$ as opposed to a maximum of $OP_2aQ_1$ if it set the equilibrium price of $P_2$. The sum lost to the FA is therefore $P_1P_2ab$.

Why would the FA set a price $P_1$ in the knowledge that it is creating excess demand and sacrificing revenue? The traditional explanation is that loyal fans should not be exploited and that others, perhaps with high incomes who might seldom attend other games, should not be able to outbid true and loyal fans for this showpiece occasion. In fact, to reward loyal fans, the FA allocates a proportion of the seats (although arguably never a sufficient share) to the finalists and these tickets are then distributed to the most loyal fans, giving priority to season-ticket holders and those who can prove through match vouchers to have attended most games through the season. Nevertheless, the popularity of the occasion still results in many disappointed supporters. The allocation to the two finalists is never enough to satisfy their supporters.

**black markets** alternative markets that might appear when there is an impediment to the running of a free market

When demand is in excess of supply, it is often found that alternative or **black markets** appear: markets where prices rise above the official price as consumers bid to obtain a good in short supply. In the case of the FA Cup Final, those who obtained tickets at the official price see the possibility of reselling their tickets at a profit to those less fortunate. Middlemen or ticket touts commonly appear who obtain tickets from various sources and sell them on at a profit. Frustrated fans will commonly place advertisements in newspapers offering to buy tickets at inflated prices. Many fans without tickets will go to the stadium before the game in the expectation of approaching a ticket tout to purchase a ticket.

Despite the efforts of the FA and the legal authorities to prevent such practices, the sale of tickets on black markets remains common. If the entire allocation of $Q_1$ in Figure 9.6 were sold at a price of $P_2$ the black market would realise a surplus of $P_2abP_1$, representing a net loss of revenue to the FA. In fact, the black market could make even more as certain supporters would willingly pay in excess of $P_2$. That is, as noted in our discussion of **consumer surplus** (see Chapter 3), $P_2$ can be thought of as representing the price required to sell the last ticket. Intra-marginal consumers might be willing to pay higher prices. In short, the black marketeers might seek to capture some of the consumer surplus through **discriminatory pricing** (see below).

We might imagine other situations whereby a firm or organisation appears to knowingly set a price where demand exceeds supply. For example, it might be awaiting increases in supply (perhaps due to unforeseen or mismanaged production problems) and would not wish in the short term to increase price from its current position. In the short term the firm might take orders, promising to deliver at a later date.

It is even possible to imagine a situation where it is a positive marketing decision to deliberately set price and production at such levels that the consumer has difficulty in obtaining the good. The shortage of the good can create a certain cachet, with consumers priding themselves on their ability to obtain the good, or the period they had to wait to receive the good. An example could be seen with the Morgan sports car. This is a relatively rare and classic British sports car produced largely through non-production-line techniques. The company prides itself on hand finishing and a degree of uniqueness. The car is sufficiently popular within its **niche market** that at the price charged there is a persistently long waiting list of customers. Economic theory might therefore predict that Morgan should either increase price and/or increase production. However, the company has been generally reluctant to do either on the basis that drastically increasing supply might lead to a lowering of quality standards. The current price is also seen as appropriate for the firm's market positioning. Further, as noted, the company and customers also benefit from the perceived rarity and resulting attractiveness of the car. The typical Morgan owner would not like to be seen driving a mass-produced and commonly seen car.

Despite the above observations it still generally remains in the interest of the firm to seek an equilibrium price. Firms that do so, adjusting price and production in line with changing market conditions, are likely to remain the most successful over time.

## 9.3    Pricing in different competitive markets

We have seen how profit-maximising firms produce to the point where marginal cost equals marginal revenue (see Chapter 5). In so doing a unique price emerges. However, we also noted that identifying such a position is in reality somewhat difficult. Would the firm have the necessary knowledge of marginal cost and marginal revenue?

As observed previously a business might only be aware of the additional cost of producing an extra batch of output rather than the extra cost of a single unit. It might then estimate the change in total revenue of selling that extra batch. This forms the basis of **incremental pricing**. That is, rather than pricing based upon strict marginal rules, we instead more reasonably deal with larger changes in cost and revenue. The basis of the marginal approach still remains intact, the profit-maximising firm now producing to the point where the incremental change in total cost equals the incremental change in total revenue.

In Chapter 5 we also introduced the concept of the **shut-down price**, and noted that in the short run a firm might continue to produce so long as the revenue generated at least helped to pay the burden of fixed cost. In short, the firm compares the costs of not producing (fixed cost) against the losses incurred through producing. So long as total revenue earned is greater than total variable cost the firm then produces in the short run as the loss incurred would be less than fixed cost. We will refer to this concept under **peak load pricing** in Section 9.4.6.

**peak load pricing** price setting to reflect the level of demand at different times of the day or year for a specific product or service in an attempt to even out demand between those periods. At times of peak demand, price should be set to reflect all costs, both fixed and variable

Competitive market share will influence price. As indicated in Chapter 7, traditionally we identify four market structures, namely:

1 perfect competition
2 monopolistic competition

3 oligopoly

4 monopoly.

The discussion below briefly reviews these market structures and examines the forces underlying pricing behaviour in each type of market.

### 9.3.1 Perfect competition

Under perfect competition, as we have seen, firms are **price-takers**. Price is determined in the market by the interaction of market demand and market supply and the firm has no individual say in the determination of price and therefore no meaningful pricing strategy. The producer is unable to sell above market price and all firms charge that same price. In this situation, a firm must remain fully efficient to survive and therefore by definition will always maximise profit. It has no discretion to pursue alternative policies. Examples of such markets are difficult to find, yet are approximated by many agricultural markets and situations where there is co-ordinated trading with clear lines of communication and near perfect information.

### 9.3.2 Monopolistic competition

The monopolistically competitive market (often referred to as **imperfect competition**) is similar to perfect competition with the exception that goods are heterogeneous rather than homogeneous. Firms attempt to differentiate their goods from competitors through branding, often supported by extensive advertising.

Although the products might be essentially similar, it is only important that they appear different in the eyes of the consumer. In so doing, the firm seeks to create a degree of brand loyalty and its demand curve will be downward-sloping. The more successful the branding, the lower the price elasticity. The firm is therefore no longer a price-taker and can, for example, raise price without losing all custom. The lower the price elasticity, the fewer the customers it will lose.

The freedom of new firms to enter the market, and the high degree of substitutability between competing products, ensures that firms are continuously in a highly competitive environment. As in perfect competition they must remain efficient to survive. They therefore have no real discretion to pursue anything but profit maximisation.

### 9.3.3 Oligopoly

The essential features of oligopoly are uncertainty and interdependence. Firms are aware that if they change price this might have an unpredictable effect upon sales as they cannot be sure of the reaction of competitors. For example, if there were three fast-food outlets in a given location, then each outlet would believe that if it individually was to change its prices (or perhaps extend its opening hours) this would almost certainly bring forth a competitive reaction. As a result, firms might be reluctant to change prices (perhaps, as in monopolistic competition, choosing to compete through non-price competition), or else they might seek to create a degree of market certainty through collusion or other non-competitive practices.

An essential feature of oligopoly therefore is that the firm (in contrast to firms in monopolistic competition) sets price and other marketing variables in full awareness of its interdependence with other firms. It will also be aware of potential competitors, who might seek to join the industry if potential profits appear sufficiently attractive. Existing firms seek to prevent such entry by collectively setting prices sufficiently low to discourage entry. This practice is referred to as **entry preventing pricing** (see below).

**entry preventing pricing**
pricing by current firms to
exclude or discourage new
firms joining the market

Oligopoly is therefore an indeterminate market structure in that there is no single model of oligopolistic behaviour. An individual oligopoly might be characterised by either competition or collusion, and pricing strategy might include price competition, price rigidity, price leadership or other forms of price collusion.

Barriers to entry result in firms typically earning abnormal profit in both the short and long run. Therefore, in contrast to both perfect competition and monopolistic competition, firms have the discretion to earn less than maximum profit and pursue non-profit-maximising goals: in effect they can achieve less than maximum profit and still survive in the market. Further, given that oligopolistic markets are characterised by there being a relatively small number of firms (hence the strong interdependence) those firms are likely to be relatively large and typically set up as joint-stock companies with managers and shareholders. We now have (as outlined in Chapter 6) the probability of a divorce of ownership from control, with managers able to pursue non-profit-maximising goals subject to the constraints of shareholders.

Managerial objectives clearly have an impact upon pricing strategy. For example, as we saw in Baumol's model of sales revenue maximisation (see Chapter 6), firms seeking maximum sales revenue (subject to a profit constraint) typically set a lower price, and consequently sell more, than a profit-maximising firm. If the firm were a utility maximiser (see Williamson's model), a corporate growth maximiser (see Marris's model), or a satisficer (see our behavioural model), this would similarly impact upon pricing. In short, different managerial goals, and any change in these, will impact upon price. Thus, a firm might decide to maximise growth and market share in the short run through relatively low pricing and later capitalise on increased market power by raising prices in the long run.

### 9.3.4 Monopoly

As with oligopoly the monopolist is a **price-maker**, although a lack of competitors means that the monopolist has complete discretion (subject to possible government control) over pricing. Unless absolute entry barriers exist, the monopolist might still be wary of the emergence of potential competitors and set an **entry preventing price**.

It would also be unreasonable to imagine the monopolist having absolute power over consumers. If this were the case, it might be illustrated by the monopolist's demand curve being either:

(a) **perfectly inelastic** (i.e. implying that consumers will always buy a fixed volume independent of price), or

(b) of **unitary elasticity** (i.e. implying that the monopolist will capture the same total revenue or total expenditure no matter what price is set. Such a demand curve could exist if we imagined the monopolist to have complete control over all goods and services, i.e. monopoly over all supply in the economy. We might imagine the demand curve representing the demand for a composite product sold at a single price.

What might be the pricing strategy in either of the above extremes?

With **perfect inelasticity** it is impossible to imagine an optimum price, as the monopolist could theoretically raise price indefinitely and keep increasing total revenue and profit. To reach equilibrium we could imagine there is a finite price above which consumers would not purchase any units, or perhaps the demand curve becomes less than perfectly inelastic above that price.

With **unitary elasticity** no matter what price is set the firm earns constant total revenue. To maximise profit it makes sense to minimise cost by setting price where demand (and output) is limited to a single unit. However, the flaw with this proposition is that this level of output necessitates a minimum level of employment, and therefore in the next time period factor incomes and consumer purchasing power would be exceedingly low, limiting the potential for further profit. The implication is that maximising profit over a period of time involves setting price to achieve an optimal balance between output and factor incomes – hardly a straightforward proposition.

In reality the monopolist's power is less than absolute and the demand curve is downward-sloping with an elasticity dependent upon the substitutability of that good against those supplied by firms in other markets. For example, although a single company might have a monopoly over bus travel in a given location, it still faces competition from other modes of transport including train, private car, taxis and bicycles. In setting bus fares the company will be constantly aware of the pricing strategy and attractiveness to consumers of those alternatives. As the degree of monopoly power increases, the monopolist has a greater opportunity to charge high prices. If monopoly power falls, then demand becomes more price-sensitive and the monopolist has less ability to charge high prices.

If the monopolist seeks profit maximisation then our marginal analysis (MC = MR) provides the basis of pricing strategy. However, as in oligopoly, the likelihood of abnormal profit allows the monopolist to choose non-profit-maximising objectives (subject to the constraints of shareholders) and still survive in the market. Whatever the objective, the monopolist's market power will assist its achievement.

The monopoly might engage in **price discrimination**, charging different prices to different consumers (or different prices for different units to the same consumers) for the same good. This practice is most common where the producer has control over the supply of a given commodity and is therefore most associated with monopoly or strong oligopoly situations (see below).

## 9.4 Alternative pricing strategies

We have outlined pricing strategies within the context of a traditional profit-maximising model, and indicated how different managerial objectives might impact upon pricing. We will now take the analysis further and examine a number of other key pricing strategies and issues. Specifically, we will consider:

- entry preventing pricing
- mark-up pricing
- product life cycle pricing (including new product pricing)
- price discrimination
-  joint-product pricing
- peak load pricing
- transfer pricing.

### 9.4.1 Entry preventing pricing

It was originally observed by J. Bain (1947)[2] that traditional economic analysis failed to consider the impact of potential competition in pricing strategy as it was assumed that price was set to maximise short-run profits irrespective of whether this might encourage other firms to enter the market. Firms were only concerned with actual competition between established firms rather than including an awareness of potential competition. Bain, however, stressed the probability of a dual **recognised interdependence** between existing and potential firms. Firms might then set a short-run non-profit-maximising price that nevertheless maximises long-run profitability by preventing entry.

**recognised interdependence** where firms fully realise that their competitive situation and fortune depend upon the actions and reactions of other firms within the market and of firms who might consider joining the market

**Entry preventing pricing** is likely in oligopolies and monopolies where the existence of entry barriers brings the possibility of abnormal profit which existing firms are eager to protect. In perfect competition and monopolistic competition, the assumption of freedom of entry ensures that in the long run firms earn only normal profit.

We will develop a basic model of entry preventing prices based upon Bain's original analysis. This is illustrated in Figure 9.7.

Assume:

1 Existing and potential firms face the same long-run average cost curve (LRAC) depicted in Figure 9.7a. This shows increasing returns to scale up to

**Figure 9.7 Entry preventing pricing**

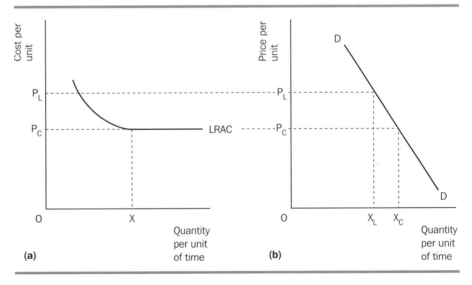

an MES (minimum efficient size) of X and then constant returns to scale. As all firms (existing and potential) face the same LRAC, no firm possesses a cost advantage over another and there are no barriers to entry due to a cost advantage existing over potential firms. (If this were the case the LRAC of the potential firm would lie above that of existing firms.) The only cost disadvantage a firm might face would be in producing less than X. Potential firms will not enter the market unless they can produce at least X.

2 The demand curve in Figure 9.7b is the market demand curve. Existing and potential firms are assumed to know the position and elasticity of this curve.

3 Existing and potential firms produce such similar products that there are no barriers to entry due to the reluctance of customers to consider purchasing the product of a new entrant. Indeed, the model assumes that existing and potential firms all charge the same price, implying either product homogeneity or that products are such close substitutes that consumer preferences are evenly distributed between producers. As a consequence the total market is shared equally between producers and a new entrant would gain the same market share as existing firms.

4 $P_C$ in Figure 9.7a represents the competitive price, where $P_C$ = LRAC. $X_C$ in Figure 9.7b is the competitive market output.

5 The potential entrant believes existing producers will maintain their current output following entry. Existing firms believe the potential firm will only enter if they can bring X on to the market. There is therefore a **double conjecture**: one on behalf of the entrant, another on behalf of existing firms. This is generally referred as the **Sylos postulate**.[3]

**double conjecture** where existing firms and potential entrants each have a clear expectation as to how they assume the other will behave as regards entry strategy

**Sylos postulate** the presumption that the potential entrant believes existing producers will maintain their current output if entry occurs and that existing firms believe the potential entrant world only enter the market at minimum efficient size

**entry premium** the degree to which price can exceed the competitive price without allowing new firms to join the market

The Sylos postulate provides an entry preventing price. That is, existing firms collectively decide to produce $X_L$ in Figure 9.7b in the belief that if a potential firm were to enter the market with an output of X (where $X = X_C - X_L$ and therefore $X_L = X_C - X$) market price would fall to (or just below) $P_C$. As the potential firm believes that existing firms will maintain output they know that $P_L$ is an entry preventing price. With a post-entry price just below $P_C$ they make a loss. The distance $P_L - P_C$ is referred to as the **entry premium** – the degree to which price can exceed the competitive price without allowing entry.

The size of the entry premium will depend significantly upon the following:

1 *The size of MES*. The larger the minimum efficient size the higher the entry premium. With a large MES the extra output brought onto the market by the entrant leads to a relatively large fall in pre-entry price. Consequently $P_L$ and the entry premium can be relatively large without attracting entry. The converse would be the case with a relatively small MES.

2 *The total size of the market at the competitive price ($X_C$)*. The larger $X_C$ the lower the entry premium, and vice versa. With a large total market the extra output contributed by the entrant would result in a small fall in pre-entry price. Therefore, $P_C$ and the entry premium can be relatively low to preclude entry. The opposite would be the case if $X_C$ were relatively small.

3 *Price elasticity of market demand*. The lower the elasticity the higher the entry premium, and vice versa. For example, with a relatively low price elasticity extra output can only be cleared with a relatively large decrease in price. $P_L$ can therefore be set relatively high.

From a consideration of the above points we note that $P_L$ and the entry premium will be greatest where market demand is inelastic and MES and the size of the competitive market ($X_C$) are relatively large.

The basic model has, however, certain weaknesses. Most particularly, the assumption that existing firms maintain output post-entry is a rather accommodating and defensive reaction on the part of those firms. As Bain pointed out, other reactions are likely. For example, by acting more aggressively, existing firms might initiate a **price war** and force post-entry price down further by increasing output. Although this places existing firms in a loss-making situation they are likely, in contrast to the entrant, to have sufficient financial reserves to sustain losses. In reality, entrance into an existing market is a risky business. The entrant can never be sure of the reception they will receive. The climate of uncertainty might itself act as a deterrent.

The model also assumes the entrant to be a new firm. Alternatively, we might have **cross-entry** where the entrant is a firm already producing in another industry, such as Virgin moving into rail transport or financial services. Entry could also be via **vertical integration**, or **takeover**. The entrant might now be capable of sustaining short-term losses and bearing the cost of producing below MES.

Economies to scale are assumed the only barrier to entry within the model in that the firm must be capable of producing up to MES. In reality, other barriers to entry are possible. These could include:

- *produce differentiation barriers:* existing customers are likely to have a preference for current brands. The new entrant has the problem of attracting new customers. This might involve costly advertising or low pricing.
- *high initial investment requirements:* setting up a new business can be expensive, often involving large initial capital outlay. The new entrant might not have access to such funds, or only at higher interest rates than charged to existing firms. If the entrant were forced to pay a higher interest rate then they would also suffer an absolute cost disadvantage.
- *absolute cost advantages*: existing firms might have **absolute cost advantages** due to their production and managerial know-how; their control of raw materials; the need for the entrant to expend large sums on staff training, etc. Where this is the case the LRAC of established firms would be below that of existing firms.

**absolute cost advantage**
the cost advantage that existing firms in a market might have over a potential entrant

The above barriers to entry can further influence the size of the entry preventing price. For example, absolute cost advantages can allow existing firms to prevent entry by keeping price below the LRAC of the potential entrant.

However, once again, these barriers are less significant with cross-entry (e.g. Virgin using their brand name to break down a product differentiation barrier, or their access to capital can solve problems associated with high initial capital requirements). A new entrant might actually have an absolute cost advantage over existing firms by introducing new technology and ideas, or by having access to cheaper sources of supply. Accordingly their LRAC might be lower than that of existing firms.

Finally, we should note that alternative pricing strategies to those implied in our basic model also exist. A business, for instance, might set price to maximise profits in the short run and revert to a **limit price** upon the threat of entry. Or it might maximise short-run profit irrespective of the known threat of entry in the knowledge that it plans to exit the market once new entrants emerge. Alternatively, in continually expanding markets, existing firms may be unconcerned with entry; they might only seek to control the number of entrants rather than pursue absolute exclusion.

### 9.4.2 Mark-up pricing

If you were to ask a business how it determines price, what answer might you expect? Could you imagine those responsible constructing a graph of average costs, marginal cost, demand (average revenue) and marginal revenue and then – *eureka!* – equating marginal cost and marginal revenue and announcing that time period's optimal price and production level. It hardly seems likely. In fact, the most likely response is that they use a form of **mark-up pricing** whereby they simply add a mark-up for profit on top of average cost (average variable plus average fixed). That is:

**mark-up** the profit margin that is added to cost to determine price

$$P = AVC + AFC + \text{mark-up}$$

Once price is determined the firm sells all it can at that price. There is no assumed knowledge of the demand curve.

The approach raises a number of questions as follows.

**How does the firm determine the level of output at which to estimate cost?**

Traditional pricing (MC = MR) provides a determinate level of output. Mark-up pricing assumes the firm places a profit mark-up in addition to cost, yet does not specify the level of output at which to estimate cost.

We saw in Chapter 5 how output affects average cost per unit produced. In the long-run this was explained by the concepts of increasing, constant and decreasing returns to scale. In the short run it was determined by whether the firm produced above or below optimum capacity – that level of output where short-run average cost (SRAC) is at a minimum. We also noted that short-run average variable cost (SRAVC) might be saucer-shaped due to the divisibility of the fixed factor(s), and that SRAVC and marginal cost (MC) would be equal over that range of output. This was illustrated in Figures 5.7 and 5.8 of Chapter 5 and is presented here as Figure 9.8.

It is usual for firms to base their mark-up upon short-run rather than long-run cost. Short-run data is more reliable as long-run involves estimates of future factor prices and the impact of technical change. Figure 9.8 illustrates a short-run situation. Between points x and y the firm has **reserve capacity** due to the divisibility of the fixed factor(s). Average total costs (ATC) continue to fall up to point z due to falling average fixed costs (AFC).

With reserve capacity the firm can produce between points x and y in Figure 9.8 with constant AVC per unit. Although the firm might produce at any point between x and y it is usual for firms to consider their normal utilisation of capacity to be approximately two-thirds to three-quarters towards y, approximately at point a. In so doing they benefit from lower ATC and maintain a degree of reserve capacity. This normal level of utilisation is also referred to as the plant's **load factor**.

**Figure 9.8 Short-run average cost curves and the price mark-up**

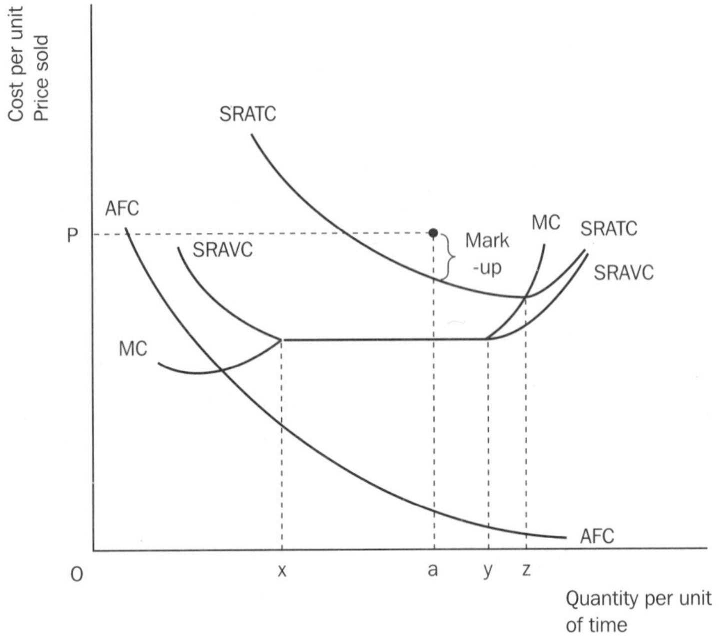

A firm therefore determines its **mark-up** from point a. It is usual for it to firstly estimate AVC (equal to MC in our example), add a charge for overheads (AFC) and then add a percentage mark-up, or profit margin. Our mark-up price is therefore P in Figure 9.8. The firm then sells all it can at that price. Actual sales are determined by the firm's demand curve although the firm is assumed to have no knowledge of its position. If it fails to sell a, it should consider decreasing output. If excess demand exists, then it might increase output and possibly consider increasing the size of plant.

At its crudest, mark-up pricing appears to assume no consideration of demand: the mark-up is simply placed upon cost. However, as we will see below, the size of the mark-up is likely to be closely influenced by the nature of demand.

### How might fixed costs be allocated where the firm produces more than one product?

Where fixed costs are shared between a number of products, those costs should be apportioned to each product. For example, when a private hospital costs its various services, from heart surgery to the removal of an appendix, it must allocate fixed costs (overheads) between individual activities including surgical procedures.

A general principle is to allocate fixed costs amongst products in proportion to their variable cost. For example, if total fixed costs are estimated at £2 million and total variable cost for a particular product at £0.5 million, the firm might add a charge for overheads at 400 per cent of variable cost. Therefore, if AVC were estimated at £1.00, the addition for overheads would be £4.00, leading to a full cost figure of £5.00. The mark-up would then be charged to obtain market price. (The principles involved in allocated fixed costs are the subject of **absorption costing** in accountancy.)

Despite recognised conventions and accounting rules firms might nevertheless choose their own methods. For example, a new product might be under-allocated overheads to provide an early opportunity to gain market share. Successful or mature products might receive an over-allocation despite this creating artificially low profit margins. Relatively price inelastic products may be allocated more overheads than those with a high price elasticity on the grounds that price inelastic goods can sustain relatively high prices. However, where overheads are apportioned without true consideration of their true contribution to the total cost of a product, this can lead to inappropriate resource allocation and decision-making within the firm. Thus, over-allocating overheads to previously successful products might result in their losing market share and possibly being withdrawn from the market.

**full cost pricing** price determination whereby the firm takes fully into account both fixed and variable costs. That is, the firm uses a principle of fully allocated costs

By including both fixed and variable cost in pricing, the firm is using a principle of **fully allocated costs**. The approach is also referred to as **full cost pricing**. Such a pricing strategy is most appropriate where the firm is operating at full capacity, in a period of peak demand. In an off-peak period where the firm has excess capacity, it can be more appropriate to consider only incremental costs (variable costs) in price-setting. This will be considered in Section 9.4.6.

### What determines the size of the mark-up?

The size of the mark-up will be determined by a number of factors such as the margin required to achieve an acceptable level of profit. This could be the level of profit earned in a comparable alternative investment.

Where the firm has a profit target we may distinguish between a profit target per unit of output as opposed to a target profit volume from total sales. In the first case, the mark-up would be constant and independent of output (see Figure 9.9a). In contrast, the mark-up to achieve a target profit volume varies according to sales. Low sales require a high mark-up; high sales need only a low mark-up. This is illustrated in Figure 9.9b. Note, however, that there is a degree of circular causation in this argument as the high mark-up (and therefore high price) required to achieve a particular target profit volume may itself cause the low sales. A lower mark-up (and therefore lower price) could generate higher sales. This illustrates the dilemma of the small trader in that low sales may necessitate large mark-ups to generate profit targets, yet those high mark-ups could be a major reason for low sales.

The firm should be sensitive to demand considerations when setting a mark-up and may arrive at an appropriate mark-up through trial and error. If an initial mark-up results in unsold stock, this might necessitate a reduction in mark-up, decreased production, or a combination of both. If a mark-up creates excess demand then either the mark-up or output could be increased, or an appropriate combination of both. A knowledge of the demand curve would clearly help, although, as noted, the firm might readjust its mark-up and output to achieve sales and profit targets.

The mark-up should be sensitive to competitive market pressures. Where the product faces strong competition we would expect a relatively low mark-up. A high mark-up would cause customers to buy cheaper alternatives. In less

**Figure 9.9  Mark-up to achieve profit targets: (a) profit target per unit of sales; (b) profit target volume from total sales**

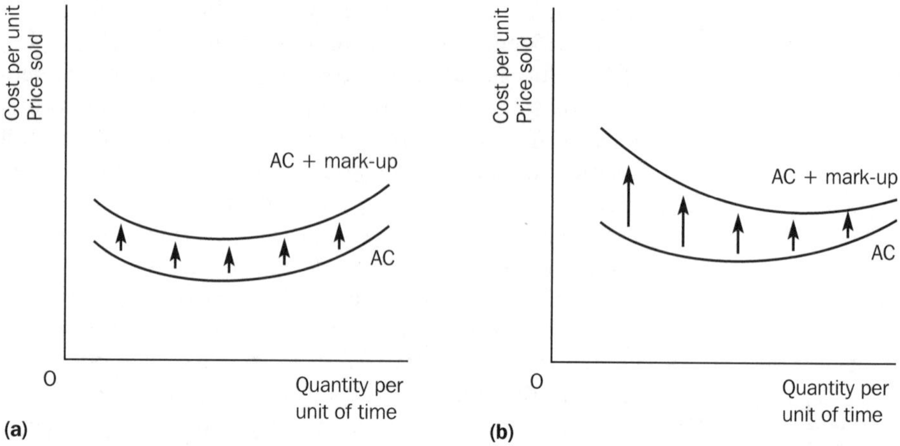

(a)

(b)

competitive situations, the mark-up could be higher. The size of the mark-up should therefore be inversely related to the value of price elasticity. High price elasticity, low mark-up: low price elasticity, high mark-up.

A firm selling a range of products might charge a different mark-up for each good depending on its relative price elasticity.

The firm should also be willing to alter the mark-up and target profit to reflect changing market conditions. For example, if the economy moves into or towards a recession then market demand will be relatively low and firms may have to adjust their profit mark-up downwards. The mark-up can be increased when the economy recovers.

The mark-up might also be set to discourage the entry of new firms and we would expect a higher mark-up with more significant barriers to entry. The firm will also be likely to take into account the reaction and behaviour of rivals. In oligopolistic markets, for example, firms might be unwilling to increase price when faced with increased costs for fear of losing market shares to their rivals. They would therefore maintain price and charge a lower mark-up.

### Can mark-up pricing lead to profit maximisation?

The size of the mark-up should be sensitive to demand and firms should adjust their mark-up in reaction to new demand conditions. However, they might not make adjustments as a consequence of relatively small changes in demand due to the administrative costs of constantly (or marginally) changing list prices. Continuous price changing can also create uncertainty for the consumer. Also (as noted above) prices might not change due to the uncertainty of oligopolistic interdependence. (Such observations and reservations could, however, also be made with regards to the profit maximiser.)

The mark-up pricer should also adjust price in recognition of cost changes in a similar fashion to the profit maximiser. Once again, adjustments might not be made as a result of relatively small changes in cost for the reasons noted above. (The same might also be said for the profit maximiser.) However, note that the mark-up is made from the level of output associated with normal capacity, or load factor. In contrast, the profit maximiser calculates optimum output by consideration of both marginal cost and marginal revenue.

Where does this leave us? It is probably fair to say that there is less conflict between mark-up pricing and profit-maximising pricing than originally supposed. Mark-up pricing, particularly where an experienced firm sets its mark-up (possibly by trial and error) in sensitivity to demand conditions, and adjusts price in relation to cost changes, might approximate profit maximisation.

### 9.4.3 Produce life cycle pricing

Products and brands typically have a finite market life and during the various stages of that life the firm might employ different and appropriate pricing strategies. We may identify four stages in a **product's life cycle:**

1  product launch
2  product growth
3  product maturity
4  product decline.

The stages are illustrated in Figure 9.10.

#### Product launch

Determining price for a genuinely new product (as opposed to a new variant of an existing product) is problematic when there is little real knowledge of the potential market. Estimates of demand might be widely inaccurate. Price will

**Figure 9.10  The stages of a product's life cycle**

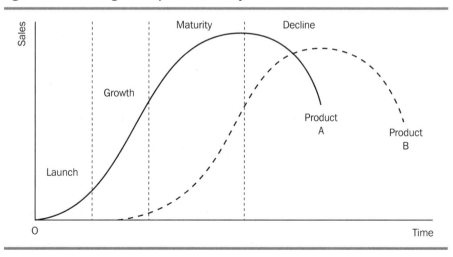

clearly be influenced by cost, with the firm needing to raise revenue to cover production, promotional and development costs. Where the firm is already selling other goods these might subsidise the cost of the new product. Where overheads are shared between products, the firm might decide to under-allocate overheads to the new product (see the discussion above).

The firm must decide a pricing strategy. Two general strategies can be identified, a **skimming** and a **penetration pricing** strategy.

**skimming strategy**
a pricing strategy where the firm initially sets a high price for a new product in the expectation of gaining high profits

**penetration pricing**
a strategy whereby price is initially set low so as to attract customers to the new product and immediately gain market share

### Skimming

With a skimming strategy the firm sets a high launch price with the expectation of high initial profits and of recovering costs (including development costs and the high promotional costs that are likely to accompany the strategy) as soon as possible. This strategy might be most appropriate where the firm is taking advantage of a monopoly situation (and low price elasticity) when introducing a genuinely unique product or product variant. A high price may also help create a quality image for a new product. Customers purchasing innovatory new products are also likely to be less price-sensitive and to be willing to pay relatively high prices.

A skimming strategy would be less appropriate where the new product already faces competition from other firms. A high-price/low-volume strategy would also be less appropriate where a firm might gain significant scale economies through producing at greater volume. The firm should also consider the impact of a high price upon entry and may wish to lower price to discourage entry. Alternatively, it may ignore entry either believing this to be inevitable, or anyway intending to cease production once competition emerges. This might be the case with the originator of a new clothing fashion; once imitations appear, it plans its next fashion launch.

### Penetration

This strategy implies a low initial price in the expectation of gaining significant market share and creating **brand loyalty** in advance of emergent competition. It therefore implies the firm intends to remain in the market for a significant time period. The strategy might also be appropriate where significant cost efficiencies can be gained by producing at high volume and price where elasticity is relatively high.

The firm might set its launch price at or even below cost in an attempt to quickly gain market share, and could use the revenue from established goods to finance short-term losses. Where other sources of sales revenue are not available it should include an allowance for short-term losses in its strategic calculation of long-term viability. Once market share and a consumer base are established it may feel able to increase price.

The firm might adjust price early into the launch phase once it has gained better knowledge of the price elasticity of demand and the likelihood of the entry of competitors. For example, the probability of entry might now be seen to have been exaggerated and the firm might feel able to increase price. Alternatively, a high price might have been chosen in the belief that price elasticity was relatively low. In the event, disappointing sales might now indicate higher price elasticity and the need to lower price.

## Product growth

Consumer resistance to the new product has now been overcome and a mass market is approached. New customers are likely to be more price-conscious than those bolder customers who were willing to buy at the launch phase. This will necessitate a lower price to encourage consumption. Increased sales and production may also allow firms to benefit from scale economies.

Rival brands are now likely to join the market leading to oligopolistic interdependence. However, despite competition, the growing market allows firms to experience sales growth. New firms may compete through introducing product variants rather than lower prices. The market becomes more **segmented** (an increased range of product variations).

## Product maturity

Maturity is achieved when most households who realistically aspire to a good now own one. This is now the case with colour televisions in a developed economy. Most demand is now determined by consumers replacing their existing product as it either breaks down, becomes unreliable, or is seen to be out-of-date compared to new product variants available in the market. The rate of replacement will be influenced by such factors as the cost of repair relative to the cost of renewal and the attractiveness of new variants. For example, the consumer might be persuaded to replace their existing television with a wide-screen model.

Demand will also be influenced by the state of the economy. In general, job insecurity in a recession causes households to delay exchanging their old car for a new model. Company fleet buyers might similarly delay replacement of their sales representatives' cars. Replacement eventually takes place as the economy improves.

Competition is now intense with a number of firms competing to maintain sales and market share in the face of slow market growth. Competition increasingly emerges through the development and promotion of new product variants and the updating and replacing of existing products. Individual firms might produce a range of variants, although generally competing in a specific quality segment of the market. An example would be Sony producing a range of relatively expensive high-quality televisions, whilst Matsui (the brand name sold by the British retailer Dixons) competes with lower prices at the lower-quality end of the market.

Firms producing high-quality goods will be able to charge high prices and also usually invest heavily in product development and marketing. Firms at the other end of the quality spectrum may compete through lower prices and are more likely to replicate than initiate innovation. The intensity of competition may result in the periodic outbreak of price wars, although oligopolistic interdependence can also be characterised by price stability due to rival firms' awareness that price decreases will almost certainly provoke retaliation.

## Product decline

A product might decline following the launch of a new or superior alternative brought about by technological advance as with the decline of the manual or electric typewriter and the launch of the personal computer and word processor, or, in previous decades, the decline of the horse-drawn carriage and the launch of the motor car. Products might also decline due to a change in consumer tastes (e.g. the general decline in cigarette smoking in developed economies over recent years).

Faced with product decline we might at first witness intense competition between suppliers in an attempt to retain sales in a declining market, involving both **price** and **non-price competition**, such as more attractive credit facilities, extended warranties, etc. Less successful firms might withdraw from the market at an early stage. Market leaders might retain relatively high prices in the expectation of continued consumer loyalty, although now being less likely to invest in product development and instead using increased profit to promote alternative products.

Eventually, the market might go into continued or terminal decline with the product becoming virtually obsolete. Alternatively, the decline might slow, leaving a smaller number of producers largely catering for replacement demand.

We have now seen how pricing strategy might vary through the stages of a product's life cycle. The length of the cycle and its component stages will vary from product to product, exemplified by the short life cycle of a clothing fashion, music style or pop group. However, certain goods that go into decline might later be reinvented and relaunched; hence, the yo-yo's return as a craze for a new generation of children in the United Kingdom in 1998 and into 1999. The craze quickly took off again, matured and declined. New crazes took over. Nevertheless, the yo-yo will return; it is expected to bounce back at some stage!

The life cycle of other goods (prolonged by the introduction of new product variants) might last for decades. The market matures yet fails to decline. This would be the case with the motor car, although individual models clearly go through their own life cycle. In 1998 Ford announced that after 20 years' production and a great many different model variants it planned to phase out the Ford Escort by the year 2000. The Escort had originally replaced the Ford Anglia in 1968 and was now to be replaced by the Ford Focus, introduced in 1998. The Escort had been the best-selling model in Ford's history, selling around 20 million cars. Will the basic motor car go on forever? Perhaps, yet that was the expectation in the late nineteenth and early twentieth century for the horse-drawn carriage. Nothing lasts forever!

Figure 9.10 shows the product life cycle of products A and B. Following the launch and growth of product A, the firm might anticipate its eventual maturity and decline and plan to launch product B as its replacement. In so doing, the firm's strategy is to possess a **portfolio of products** at different stages of the cycle, the profits from maturing products being used to develop and launch new products.

**portfolio of products** the range of products currently produced by the firm. It is likely that these products will be at different stages of the product life cycle

### 9.4.4 Price discrimination

So far we have assumed that firms charge the same price to each consumer, and the same price for each unit sold to a single consumer. This might not always be the case in that a firm might engage in **price discrimination**.

Price discrimination involves charging different prices for the same good for reasons other than differences in the cost of supply, as when a football club changes juvenile supporters a lower entrance fee than adults. However,

**Mini case** | **BOGOF pricing**

There are clearly further pricing strategies than those outlined in this section. For example, in addition to offering price reductions in their competitive pricing strategies, supermarkets appear particularly fond of multibuy offers, e.g. 'buy one, get one free' or BOGOF for short; or, 'buy two and get the third one free' (BTGTOF); or even 'buy one, get one half price' (BOGOHP). Such offers often appeal to customers as it appears, particularly with BOGOF and BTGTOF offers, that they are getting something for nothing. In reality the offers represent a per unit price cut of 50 per cent, 33 per cent and 25 per cent respectively and could be seen as a form of second-degree price discrimination.

This practice is not confined to supermarkets; book retailers occasionally offer three books for the price of two over a given range of books.

To take advantage of such offers the consumer is likely to buy more units than originally planned and therefore spend more on that particular shopping bill. As such offers cover only a limited range of goods, and possibly not the goods or brand usually purchased by the consumer, it is possible that an offer might persuade the consumer to purchase goods they might later regret buying.

Whilst the true value of BOGOF, BTGTOF or BOGOHP offers might be relatively easily understood by the majority of consumers, other offers might be less easy. For example, ASDA stores in May 2000 were offering seven tins of their branded cat food for the price of six, or 24 cans of Banks's beer for the price of 16. Estimating the real worth of these and similar offers is slightly more difficult.

Although consumers generally welcome such offers, a case could be made for supermarkets simply lowering their overall prices instead. This could certainly avoid consumers having to purchase more units of a good than originally planned and it would not disadvantage those on limited budgets; for example, many pensioners might be unable to afford multibuy offers. Nevertheless, their popularity as a promotional tool and their appeal to consumers ensures their continued existence.

Multibuy pricing provides an example of the complexity of choice facing the supermarket shopper. Indeed, research published in April 2000 by the Future Foundation in conjunction with Abbey National suggests that many shoppers are becoming 'confused and bewildered' by the large array of lines and choices in the modern supermarket. The research noted that whereas two decades ago the typical supermarket stocked 5,000 different lines, it now handles 40,000 separate products, including 400 brands of shampoo and nearly 100 different types of toothbrush. Such expansion in choices available is also evident elsewhere: for example, the explosion in the number of television and radio channels, the variety of foods available when eating out, etc. The founder of the Future Foundation noted: 'Individual choice can be very empowering but, as this new research demonstrates, it brings hassles too. Consumers are feeling over-whelmed and it is starting to have a negative effect on people, making them feel anxious and stressed about making the right choice.' However, he further noted: 'our research shows that consumers are finding their own solutions to cope with this situation. Choosing well-known brands is one, but some people are starting to employ less obvious strategies like buying only organic products.'

*Do you feel overwhelmed by the variety of goods on offer?*

charging a higher price for a pint of beer in central London than the suburbs might not be price discrimination if the price differential were justified by higher costs. Price discrimination exists if not all the price differential can be explained by differential cost.

It is possible to imagine price discrimination where there are differences in the cost of supply yet price is uniform. Thus, the Post Office in the United Kingdom charges the same price for a first-class stamp and service whether the letter is delivered over one mile or one hundred miles. It could now be argued that those using the postal service for deliveries over a short distance are discriminated against compared to those posting letters over a longer distance where a greater cost is incurred. Despite this observation, we will confine ourselves to instances of discrimination where actual price differences exist.

The advantage of price discrimination to the firm is that it may earn higher revenue from any given volume of sales than when charging a uniform price. The firm would also be likely to sell additional units. These points will be illustrated below.

There are three basic types (or degrees) of price discrimination:

1. first-degree price discrimination
2. second-degree price discrimination
3. third-degree price discrimination.

### First-degree price discrimination

This is the most extreme form of discrimination and involves charging each consumer the maximum price they would be willing to pay for each individual unit consumed. Imagine a vendor selling ice cream in a city park. Instead of selling ice cream cones at a given price, each consumer is required to pay the maximum they would be willing to pay for each ice cream (i.e. the maximum sum rather than do without the ice cream). This price could be arrived at through barter. Different consumers would be willing to pay higher or lower prices depending upon their individual desires and levels of disposable income. Where a consumer might wish to purchase a second ice cream they would only be willing to do so at a lower price.

The impact of first-degree price discrimination would be for the firm to capture each consumer's entire **consumer surplus** (see Chapter 3). This can be illustrated in Figure 9.11. $P_1$ represents the price required to sell the 200th unit, the marginal unit. However, rather than charge this price for intra-marginal units the firm instead charges the maximum price possible for each individual unit as indicated by the demand curve. In so doing, total revenue is represented by the area acdO rather than bcdO if a single price of $P_1$ were charged, and the area acd (consumer surplus if a price of $P_1$ were charged) is taken by the firm as additional revenue.

The firm also has an incentive to sell more units than when charging a single price because an extra unit can now be sold without lowering the price of intra-marginal units. The revenue gained is therefore a net addition to total revenue. In selling an extra unit total revenue increases by the price at which the unit is sold. Marginal revenue (MR) now equals price and the demand curve is also an MR curve. However, the demand curve is no longer an average revenue (AR) curve; in fact AR will now be in excess of price at all levels of output.

**Figure 9.11 First-degree price discrimination**

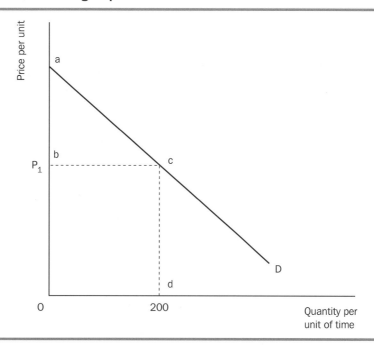

The firm maximises profit by equating MC to MR (see Figure 9.12) at output $Q_2$, charging $P_1$ (= MC) for the last unit. In contrast, a firm charging the same price for all units sells only $Q_1$ at a uniform price of $P_2$. This illustrates our observation that firms engaged in price discrimination will generally sell more units.

First-degree price discrimination is the most extreme form of discrimination and in reality has little practical application. It would require the firm to have a perfect knowledge of each consumer's demand curve, or to obtain such information (as with our ice cream vendor) through a system of barter. It is hard to imagine a firm attempting to practice such extreme discrimination.

**Second-degree price discrimination**

This is a more practical form of price discrimination. Rather than charge a different price for each unit sold the firm charges a different price for different blocks or portions of consumption.

This is illustrated in Figure 9.13. For all units up to $Q_1$ a uniform price of $P_3$ is charged, for units between $Q_1$ and $Q_2$ a price of $P_2$, and for units from $Q_2$ to $Q_3$ a price of $P_3$. In so doing, consumer surplus diminishes and the firm's revenue increases compared to when a single price of $P_1$ is charged. If $Q_3$ were to be divided into four blocks with four prices rather than three, then consumer surplus would decrease further and the firm would gain even more revenue.

Examples of such discrimination are commonly found in the utility industries. The same principle can be observed in the hire of DIY tools or car rental when the consumer who agrees to hire a tool or car for an extra day is charged a lower rate for the additional time period. Similarly, a wine merchant might offer a 10 per cent discount per bottle for purchases of 12 or more bottles.

**Figure 9.12  Profit maximisation with first-degree price discrimination**

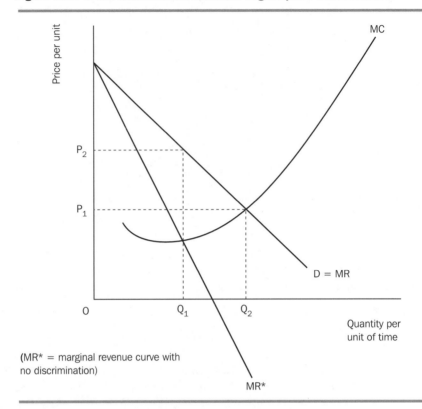

(MR* = marginal revenue curve with
no discrimination)

**Figure 9.13  Second-degree price discrimination**

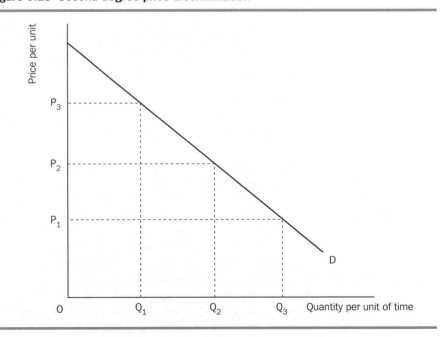

### Third-degree price discrimination

This is the most common form of price discrimination and involves charging different prices for the same good in different markets. Markets might be separated by either geography, time or nature of demand. For example:

- Car manufacturers might sell the same car at different prices in different countries.
- Units of electricity consumed off-peak are usually sold cheaper than in peak hours. The same principle is used by telephone and rail companies. Public houses might have a happy hour in the early evening when drinks are sold at discounted prices.
- Football clubs commonly charge lower admission to children and senior citizens. Such discriminatory pricing is also common with rail and bus companies and might extend to concessionary fares for students. Hairdressers also use such pricing.

Figure 9.14 illustrates price discrimination between two markets, X and Y. The demand curves and corresponding marginal revenue curves are assumed to be known in each market. The demand curves have a differing price elasticity. Figure 9.14c shows total market demand obtained by a horizontal summation of the corresponding curves in markets X and Y.

The profit-maximising market output can be seen in Figure 9.14c at an output of $Q_m$ units. This is the point where market marginal revenue equals marginal cost. The firm then decides how to distribute this output between the two markets.

Optimal allocation is achieved by dividing output between the markets so that the revenue gained from the sale of the last unit in either market is equal (i.e. MR is equal in markets X and Y). As illustrated, this is achieved by selling $Q_X$ units in market X and $Q_Y$ units in Y. Any other allocation would yield less revenue and therefore less profit. For example, if one more unit were sold in X and one less unit in Y, the revenue gained (MR) in X would be less than the

**Figure 9.14 Profit maximisation under third-degree price discrimination**

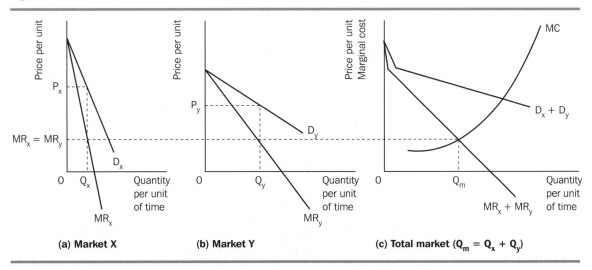

(a) Market X          (b) Market Y          (c) Total market ($Q_m = Q_x + Q_y$)

revenue lost in Y. Reallocating that unit back to Y would increase revenue and regain maximum profit.

The optimal allocation between the markets results in differential pricing, $P_X$ per unit in X and $P_Y$ in Y. Market X, with the lower price elasticity charges a higher price than Y.

We have assumed the firm aims to maximise profit. If this were not the case and the firm had a non-profit-maximising goal or were using a method of mark-up pricing which might not result in profit maximisation we would be unable to predict the discriminatory prices. Nevertheless, such firms still have an incentive to engage in discrimination as the strategy results in higher returns than would otherwise be the case.

A further reason to engage in such discrimination might be to prevent or remove competition in a particular market. Thus, if a bus company was planning to extend its services into a new area it might charge lower prices than on its existing services to break into this new market. It might in the short term charge prices below cost in an attempt to gain advantage over existing competition. This is referred to as **predatory pricing**.

### Conditions necessary for successful price discrimination

Successful price discrimination requires the following conditions:

1 The seller should have a significant degree of monopoly power to control supply and determine price in the different markets. Discriminatory pricing is incompatible with competitive markets and is generally associated with monopolies or oligopolies where firms are working closely together.

2 Where a firm charges a different price for different units to the same consumer (as in first- and second-degree discrimination) it should be capable of monitoring consumption to identify how many units have been consumed. This is certainly possible with gas or electricity where consumption is metered. With non-metered goods, the seller would require proof of existing purchase before offering a discount for additional consumption. This might be achieved by providing the consumer with a voucher with their first purchase allowing a second purchase to be made at a lower price in a given time period. Alternatively, supermarkets may offer, three tins of baked beans for the price of two! In effect, the second and third tins are sold at half price.

3 The firm should be able to prevent resale between markets. Thus, in Figure 9.14 the seller would not wish consumers in market X to purchase the good in market Y, or persons in market Y to make a private profit by reselling the good to consumers in market X. The ability of the firm to isolate markets and prevent resale is easier with certain goods than others. The resale of services is generally difficult; if a hairdresser charges lower prices to senior citizens, it is impossible for the senior citizen to resell their haircut to others. Nevertheless, the hairdresser might have a problem with customers trying to pass themselves off as senior citizens and may require proof of senior citizen status.

The resale of tangible goods is more likely. It would be difficult for a garden centre to charge higher prices to customers from the more affluent side of town. Those customers would either refuse to divulge their domestic location or pay others to purchase the goods for them.

Geographical isolation clearly discourages the possibility of resale, although consumers might be willing to travel long distances and incur additional expense if the price differential is sufficiently wide; hence some British consumers travel to mainland Europe to purchase cars at lower prices (see mini case Chapter 11).

4  For third-degree price discrimination to be worthwhile each market should have a different price elasticity of demand. It is on the basis of different conditions of demand between markets that it is profitable to charge different prices.

5  Any costs incurred in pursuing price discrimination must be exceeded by the potential return. The act of discrimination might not be costless to the firm (e.g. market research costs in identifying the demand characteristics of market segments and the cost of preventing resale). Discrimination might also reflect adversely on the firm and even result in legal redress.

### Is price discrimination beneficial?

This is a difficult question and for the consumer depends upon whether they feel discriminated against or in favour. Discrimination might allow those on low incomes to purchase goods that might otherwise be beyond their means. We have also noted that it will generally lead to increased sales and therefore higher levels of consumption. However, we have also noted the transfer of consumer surplus to the producer.

It is possible that it is only through price discrimination that a firm is capable of making a profit. This is illustrated in Figure 9.15 where with a single price of $P_1$ (MC = MR) and output $Q_2$ the firm makes a loss equal to $abcP_1$. However, if the firm were able to sell the first $Q_1$ units at a price of $P_2$ and the remaining units up to $Q_2$ at $P_1$ the firm makes a profit so long as the area $P_2deP_1$ (the additional revenue gained via price discrimination) exceeds the area $abcP_1$.

### 9.4.5  Joint-product pricing

When a firm produces a single commodity its concern is to maximise the return on that good, and set price accordingly. However, where it produces a range of goods its pricing strategy should consider the interdependence between those goods. That is, the firm should engage a strategy of **full-range pricing** and aim to maximise overall performance rather than the returns on a single good.

**full-range pricing** where a pricing strategy recognises the interdependence between the range of goods the firm is selling and/or producing

**loss leader** when a product is priced below cost in order to tempt customers also to buy other goods which are priced above cost

**cherry pickers** a term often used by supermarkets to describe those who largely confine themselves to purchasing goods with very low or negative profit margins

Full-range pricing can be illustrated by supermarkets in their use of **loss leaders**, backed by heavy advertising to tempt shoppers into the store. In themselves these loss leaders earn little or negative returns, yet the supermarket gains when additional shoppers also purchase goods with higher mark-ups, ideally placed in close proximity to the loss leaders. An appropriate loss leader would be one with a low price elasticity of demand as this will generate a large number of customers. Common examples are such staple commodities as bread, milk and sugar. Customers who confine themselves to loss leaders, disdaining to also buy other goods with a higher mark-up, are often referred to as **cherry pickers** by the supermarkets.

A firm might produce a range of either substitute or complementary goods. For example, Cadbury markets a wide range of chocolate bars that are in clear

**Figure 9.15  Price discrimination allowing a firm to make a profit**

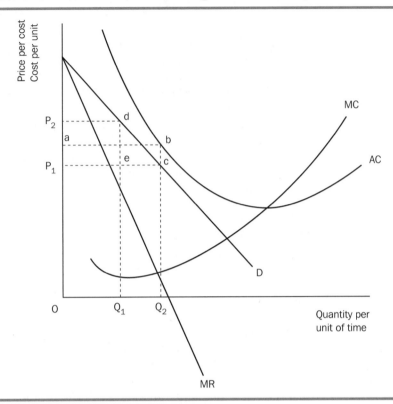

competition with each other. The increased sales of one brand might be at the expense of another. Similarly, Nescafé markets a range of instant coffees. Alternatively, with regards to complementary production, Gillette sell both razors and replacement blades and many supermarkets combine grocery sales with the sale of petrol from their own on-site service stations. In such cases, the firm must consider **complementary pricing**. Gillette might price its razors relatively cheaply to ensure a continued demand for the more highly priced blades. Providing discount petrol at supermarket service stations encourages shoppers and makes the journey by car to the out-of-town site appear worthwhile.

Full-range pricing should therefore take into account the complementary and substitute relationships between a firm's product range. This necessitates a knowledge of the cross-price elasticities of demand between goods.

Multiproduct firms might also have production interdependencies in addition to demand interdependencies. **Production interdependence** is a situation where it is impossible to produce one commodity without also producing a quantity of another commodity, and is referred to as **joint production**. Such products might either be produced in fixed proportions (for example, beef and hides) or in variable proportions (for example when refining crude oil, petrol, diesel, heating oil and other products are produced in variable proportions).

Joint production might specifically result in the production of a **by-product**. That is, a product that appears purely as a consequence of the production of another good and only therefore comes about as a result of the demand for the

**complementary pricing** where pricing strategy takes into account the complementary relationship between goods

**production interdependence/joint production** a situation where one commodity by necessity results in the simultaneous production of another

**by-product** a material or product that is the outcome of a process primarily designed to produce another product

original good. For example, whey is a by-product of cheese; horse manure could be considered a by-product of the stabling of horses.

Let us consider horse manure. The firm must decide whether to sell this by-product and if so at what price. As the manure is by definition a by-product, it is often common practice to allocate all costs to the main business, the stabling of horses. In that case the only real costs associated with the sale of manure would be those associated with advertising, bagging and delivery. So long as price at least covers these costs, it would be common practice to proceed with the sale of the by-product.

Whilst the above might be common practice, it would not necessarily be the best strategy. In reality, the two products have joints costs and consideration should be given to an appropriate allocation of those costs between the products. The outcome of an allocation might be to set appropriate prices for both stabling and manure to the benefit of the overall business.

The significant point with joint production is that any change in the price or output of one of the products will influence the price and output of the other products. The firm should therefore simultaneously calculate an optimal price and output strategy for all its joint products.[4]

### 9.4.6 Peak load pricing

The demand for many products varies at differing times of the day or year, as in the case of the off-peak demand for public transport or demand for holidays out of season. In such circumstances, it can pay the firm to set differential prices at peak as opposed to **off-peak** periods to reflect the differences in the costs of supply at these periods and to even out consumer demand between those periods.

**off-peak pricing** price setting in recognition that demand is below the capacity of current supply. Price might be set to only cover variable or incremental costs

During peak periods when facilities are fully utilised, it may only be possible to increase supply by investing in more capacity. Thus, if a hotel is already full, the ability to take additional guests may require building a further extension. In such a situation it would be appropriate to use a principle of **fully allocated costs** when setting price to include both fixed and variable cost.

Alternatively, in off-peak periods it would be more appropriate to consider only those costs that rise with production (incremental or marginal costs) when setting price. For example, to persuade holidaymakers to book out of season a hotel might be willing to offer significantly discounted prices. So long as the revenue received at least covers the variable costs of operating, it will be worthwhile opening. If variable costs cannot be covered then the hotel would be better closing down out of season and simply incurring fixed costs.

Peak load pricing is commonly used in the transport, telecommunications and power supply industries. British Telecom, for example, charges different rates in relation to daytime (Monday to Friday, 8am to 6pm), evenings and night-time (Mondays to Friday, before 8am and after 6pm) and weekend (midnight Friday to midnight Sunday). Such differential pricing certainly influences consumer behaviour.

### 9.4.7 Transfer pricing

Large businesses are often based on a multidivisional structure (see Chapter 2) where component divisions may have a degree of autonomy within the overall company structure. Each division may control the production of an individual good or specific range of goods, service a particular geographical area, or produce components for the overall company.

**Transfer pricing** refers to the price charged for goods or services that are traded between divisions of a company. It would therefore be particularly relevant where components or intermediate products are traded between divisions, the goods produced by one division being used as inputs by another. In a car company various components might be produced in different divisions before coming together in final assembly. The transfer price therefore represents a cost to the buying division and revenue to the selling division. Hence prices charged have a significant impact upon the profitability of each division, the volume of trade between divisions and the company's overall profitability.

Conflict might arise, in that individual divisional heads might pursue their own divisional interests to the detriment of the company as a whole. This might involve individual divisions exploiting their monopoly position and charging high transfer prices in pursuit of profit to enhance their division's standing within the company. Purchasing divisions would have to either absorb these high costs and show a low profit or pass the costs on. Alternatively the purchasing division might use its own monopoly power as a buyer to persuade the supplying division to charge a low transfer price and itself seek to earn high profit at the expense of the supplier.

Independent and unco-ordinated action is likely to be detrimental to overall company performance. Top management within the company must therefore provide leadership and determine an appropriate strategy for transfer pricing. The relationship between top management and their divisional heads is therefore similar to the **principal–agent relationship** we identified in Chapter 2. In this case, top management (the principal) delegates authority to the divisions (the agents) and must now ensure that the self-motivated divisions work to achieve the objectives of the company as a whole. This will involve providing incentives and rewards, including methods of censure and control if divisional targets are not achieved.

Appropriate transfer prices might be identified by comparison to the external market. That is, the company might expect the transfer price to be compatible with or below the external market price of the component. If this cannot be achieved, it could make sense to close the division and source from outside. An external market certainly provides an incentive to divisional performance. Where an external market does not exist, cost-based pricing can be used, usually based upon marginal cost. This would allow the marginal cost of the final product to be based upon real overall marginal cost and enable the firm to maximise profit by equating this marginal cost to the marginal revenue of the final product. In the pursuit of company profit, the divisions should minimise their marginal costs. The company's profit-maximising output determines the required output from each division. Where the company has non-profit-maximisation goals, there is the same need for co-ordinated control to ensure divisional performance is compatible with company goals.

Where a company's divisions are located in different countries with different rates of tax, pricing might also be used to minimise the company's overall tax burden. For example, imagine a supplying division is in a country with a low corporation tax providing a component to a division in a country with a higher corporate tax. It would make commercial sense for the supplier in the

**transfer pricing** the consideration given by the firm to pricing when goods or services are traded between divisions of a company low-tax country to charge an inflated transfer price and thereby increase the cost and reduce the profitability and tax liability of the buying division in the higher-tax country. The overall tax burden of the company is therefore reduced. Although such activity might be illegal under an individual country's fiscal laws, such practices are difficult to detect. The growth of **multinational** activity provides an increased scope for such practice.

## 9.5   Conclusions

We have looked in some detail at the concept of an equilibrium price and the problems of an individual firm achieving and maintaining equilibrium. In this context we have distinguished between the firm as a **price-taker** and as a **price-maker**. Despite the problems, we noted the advantage to the firm of achieving equilibrium so as to avoid the disadvantages associated with either excess supply or demand. Nevertheless, in certain circumstances an equilibrium will not exist due to either the innate instability of the market, the pricing strategy of the firm, or government interference in the market. Where persistent excess demand exists we often observe the emergence of **black markets**.

Following a review of pricing within a traditional profit-maximising model and a review of how different managerial objectives might impact upon pricing, we examined a number of other key pricing strategies and issues.

We referred to these other key pricing strategies as 'alternative strategies' on the basis that they were alternative to our traditional profit-maximising strategy based upon the firm setting a single price irrespective of the impact upon entry, the position of the product within its **product life cycle** or the possible interdependence between products in both demand and production. Our 'alternative strategies' included an analysis of these and other issues. In so doing, we noted the importance and subtlety of a firm's pricing strategy in different market situations.

**cost-based pricing** a method of pricing primarily based upon costs. For example, mark-up pricing

In practice, it would appear that firms generally favour a **cost-based pricing** procedure whereby they identify their normal level of capacity utilisation and then add a profit mark-up to average cost. The size of the mark-up would be sensitive to market pressures and generally inversely related to the value of price elasticity. Given the sensitivity of such cost-based procedures to market conditions and the state of competition it is possible that there is less conflict with profit-maximising pricing than might have been originally supposed.

Finally, despite the breadth and relative complexity of different pricing procedures, we should always stress that price is only one of the variables at the disposal of the firm in determining demand. Other non-price variables including product design, after-sales service and the quality and degree of advertising should always be considered.

# Pricing on the internet

**e-tailers** a term used to denote retailers selling directly to consumers via the internet

British high-street retailers are now facing increased competition from businesses selling directly from the internet, often referred to as on-line retailers or **e-tailers**. Competition is increasingly fierce with electrical goods, including computers and their accessories, music, games, DVDs and videos, although the whole range of goods is available via the internet from cars and books to groceries.

Such competition is having an impact upon prices charged by high-street retailers. For example, Dixons, the UK's leading electrical retailer felt itself under particular pressure when Buy.com, America's second-largest internet retailer introduced a UK site in March 2000 and launched a hard-hitting advertising campaign and low prices aimed specifically at Dixons and its subsidiary, PC World. Dixons reacted with a series of retaliatory price cuts. For example, Buy.com's offer to sell the Kodak DC240 digital camera at a price one-third cheaper than Dixons was immediately countered by Dixons who lowered its price below that offered by Buy.com.

High-street retailers may themselves also offer an e-mail service (e.g. the British high-street catalogue firm Argos also has an website allowing customers to purchase directly from its catalogue, offering delivery for most areas within three days). Most large supermarkets also offer an e-mail and delivery service. In the case of supermarkets the advantage to the consumer is one of added convenience rather than obtaining the goods more cheaply.

Buying books off the internet is becoming increasingly popular although the service does not allow the customer to browse in the same way they might in their local bookshop. Nevertheless, perhaps having browsed in a more traditional way, the customer can then browse the e-tailers to compare prices and make their purchase accordingly. It should nevertheless be remembered that e-mail browsing is not necessarily costless, given the cost of the telephone call to connect to the internet. However, with many e-mail goods, including books, the customer can connect to an 'internet shopping guide' linked to various retailers. For example, in October 1999 the website shopguide.co.uk linked to approximately 40 internet book sites and using their 'bargain finder' facility customers can save the time and expense of individually searching each website to find the cheapest source. Similarly, shopsmart.com, ranked in February 2000 as the number one electrical retailer with 288,000 unique visitors to its website is not actually a shop that sells anything; instead it is a website allowing customers to compare prices in more than 1,600 on-line shops, generating commission from those on-line retailers and advertising revenue on the site. It should be remembered that when comparing prices for all internet purchases, the customer should take delivery cost into account, which in many instances could counter perceived savings. Delivery time could also be seen as an additional cost.

E-tailers not only offer added convenience to many customers, they can also (as noted above) typically sell at lower prices than high-street retailers. The e-tailer can have specific advantages. For example, to quote the website of one particular e-tailer, LetsBuyIT.com (also see below):

> When buying from the high-street store, the price that you're paying (at or near the recommended retail price) includes the overheads of the manufacturer, distributors, suppliers and so on, plus a healthy mark-up margin.

> LetsBuyIT.com is a member driven company that sources co-buy products and services directly from suppliers and manufacturers, thus enabling us to deliver brand-name merchandise at much lower prices.

Although the above statement clearly includes an element of promotional hype the e-tailer can certainly avoid many of the overheads of the high-street trader.

The pricing strategy of LetsBuyIT.com is particularly interesting. LetsBuyIT.com is a Swedish-based internet company which in April 2000 operated in Europe with sales concentrated in Scandinavia, Germany and the UK. The firm describes itself as a form of shopping co-operative where groups of consumers join together to purchase goods collectively and drive prices down according to the number of units they collectively buy. Rather than set a fixed discounted price, the norm for most e-tailers, the final price is therefore dependent on sales volume.

An example of LetsBuyIT.com's pricing strategy is found in Figure 9.16.

Figure 9.16 is adapted from LetsBuyIT.com's website and helps explain its basic pricing strategy. £1,100 is defined as the **benchmark price** for a specific good and is either the recommended retail price or the suggested price established by the manufacturer. If such a price is not available, LetsBuyIT.com establishes the benchmark price by taking the average price currently set by three large resellers. The good is then initially offered for sale to registered members at the benchmark price for a specified time period. The more members join the co-buy, the lower the price. For example, in Figure 9.16, once 24 members come forward, the price drops to £850. The price at any given time is referred to as the **current price**, which in our example would be £850 as the number of co-buyers is currently between 24 and 39. The **best price** is the lowest possible price, representing the lowest step on the price scale, reached in our example when the 39th co-buyer comes forward. This price can be reached before the offer's closing date if sufficient numbers of co-buyers come forward. The offer is then closed. This therefore creates an incentive for customers to bid early to avoid disappointment.

When the good is advertised on the website, potential customers are informed of the good's characteristics, the threshold price, the best price, the

**benchmark price** the recommended retail price or price suggested by the manufacturer

**current price** the price ruling at any given time

**best price** the lowest possible price that can be attained

**Figure 9.16 LetsBuyIt.com's pricing strategy**

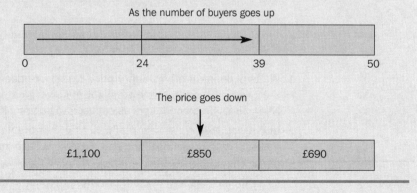

number of co-buyers needed to reach each price step, the maximum number of units available and the closing date of the offer. By accessing the site, potential and existing bidders can be updated as to the number of bids and the current price. When joining a co-buy the customer decides whether they want the good at the best price only or at the current price, the price when the co-buy closes and which can also be the best price. However, where only the best price has been selected the customer only receives the good if the final price is reached when the co-buy closes.

In April 2000 LetsBuyIT.com claimed to deal with 150 brands, including Kodak, Hewlett Packard and Psion and to be providing its members with price savings of between 10 per cent and 60 per cent. It also planned geographical expansion and further extension of its product range. The impact of on-line retailers on UK markets is clearly likely to increase as consumers become increasingly willing to consider purchasing goods through the internet and the number of households with internet connections increases. The challenge for many major high-street retailers could be to compete through both traditional retail networks and by providing their own on-line service.

## Notes and references

1. As previously indicated, the foreign exchange market can also be seen as a perfectly competitive market in that the individual private seller or buyer of a currency has no individual control over price, given their insignificance as an individual buyer or seller in the context of the total market. In short, the individual is a price-taker and the flexibility of price (that is, the rate of exchange) maintains equilibrium.

2. Bain, J. (1947), 'Oligopoly and entry prevention', *American Economic Review*.

3. This conjecture, originally proposed by Bain (1947) as one of a range of possible conjectures, was included by P. Sylos-Labini (1957) in his model of limit pricing, *Oligopoly and Technical Progress*, Harvard University Press, Cambridge, MA. For a critique of the Sylos postulate, see Koutsoyiannis, A. (1979), *Modern Microeconomics*, 2nd edition, Macmillan, Basingstoke, pp. 312–313.

4. The profit-maximising solution differs, depending upon whether the products are produced in fixed or variable proportions. See Brewster, D. (1997), *Business Economics*, Dryden Press, Chapter 10, pp. 202–204.

## Review and discussion questions

1 We may define firms as either price-takers or price-makers. Distinguish between the two and examine why we might observe greater price instability in markets where firms are price-takers as opposed to price-makers.

2 In cobweb theory we saw markets as either stable or unstable. What is it that makes a market unstable and how extreme is such instability likely to be?

3 What determines the size of the mark-up in mark-up pricing? Provide examples to illustrate how the size of mark-up differs between firms in different markets.

4 Examine the relative merits of a skimming or penetration pricing strategy within the launch phase of the product life cycle.

5 Provide an example of the different types of price discrimination and indicate the necessary conditions for each to exist.

## Assignments

1 Tickets for major sporting events or concerts by popular artists are traditionally hard to come by and often result in the emergence of black markets and persons commonly referred to as ticket touts. Take a real example of such an event and using appropriate diagrams illustrate:
   (a) how a black-market may emerge;
   (b) the potential gain to ticket touts and loss in revenue to the organisers of the event;
   (c) your own recommendations to the organisers of the event as to how they might regulate the market.

2 'Go Rail Plc' recently obtained a franchise to provide a passenger railway service between Leicester and London. Whilst initially deciding to charge a standard fare to all customers at any time of day, the appropriateness of this strategy has now come into doubt given heavy financial losses in the first year of operation. Propose an alternative pricing strategy to the firm together with guidelines as to how they might determine the degree of any differentials in price.

## Further reading

Atkinson, B., Livesey, F. and Milward, B. (1998), *Applied Economics*, Macmillan, Basingstoke, Chapter 1.

Brewster, D. (1997), *Business Economics*, Dryden Press, Chapter 10.

Griffiths, A. and Wall, S. (1999), *Applied Economics,* 8th edition, Longman, Harlow, Chapter 9.

Nellis, J. G. and Parker, D. (1997), *The Essence of Business Economics*, Prentice Hall, Hemel Hempstead, Chapter 6.

# International markets

## Chris Britton

**Objectives**

1 To understand why international trade takes place.

2 To look at the effects of the European Union on trade.

3 To survey the balance of payments position in the UK.

4 To understand the working of the foreign exchange markets and its implications for business.

5 To consider the operation of multinationals and their link with foreign direct investment.

## 10.1 Introduction

International markets are important to most firms; even if they do not produce for the export market they may well be dependent upon raw materials which are imported and they will almost definitely be affected by movements in **exchange rates**. Great Britain, like all other advanced industrial countries, is highly dependent upon international markets and that dependence has grown over the years. What makes international trade different from trade within a country is that the former needs a system for international payments. It is essential for businesses to have an understanding of international markets, exchange rates and the balance of payments. In this chapter we start with a standard theoretical view of international trade and why trade takes place, before concentrating on practical issues such as exchange rates, their effects on business and the operation of multinationals. This chapter concludes with a discussion of the process of globalisation.

## 10.2 International trade – why it takes place

Trade between countries takes place because resources are unevenly distributed through the world and the mobility of the factors of production is limited; consequently some countries are better at producing certain goods than others. Some countries could not actually produce a particular good: for example, Britain cannot produce minerals that are not indigenous or fruit that can only be grown in tropical weather conditions. If there is a demand for these goods in Britain, there are a number of possibilities: either the British could do without these goods; or an attempt could be made to grow them (in the case of the fruit) despite the climatic conditions; or Britain could buy the goods from other countries that can produce them. In other words it can trade for them.

It is easy to see that if country A can produce video cameras more cheaply than country B and that B can produce wheat more cheaply than A then specialisation should occur and A should produce video cameras and B should produce wheat and they should trade with one another. Complete **specialisation** however is unlikely for strategic reasons. It is also true that even if country A can produce both goods more cheaply than country B there is scope for benefits from trade. As this may not be so easy to imagine, Table 10.1 gives a numerical example.

**Table 10.1  Production of video cameras and wheat**

|  | Number of units that 100 workers can produce | |
| --- | --- | --- |
|  | Video cameras | Wheat |
| Country A | 100 | 100 |
| Country B | 20 | 40 |

Country A can produce 100 video cameras or 100 units of wheat using 100 workers. Country B can produce 20 video cameras or 40 units of wheat with the same number of workers. Country A can therefore produce both goods at lower cost than country B. To show that even in this situation trade will benefit the world, assume that both countries produce both goods and that they each devote half of their workforce to each good.

**Table 10.2  Production of video cameras and wheat**

|  | Video cameras | Wheat |
| --- | --- | --- |
| Country A | 50 | 50 |
| Country B | 10 | 20 |
| Total | 60 | 70 |

The total output of video cameras is 60 units and of wheat is 70 units. Country A is five times more efficient at producing video cameras than country B, but only 2.5 times more efficient that B in producing wheat. It would therefore benefit both countries if production was rearranged. If B specialised completely in wheat and A produced 35 units of wheat and 65 video cameras, world output would be as indicated in Table 10.3.

In short, world output has been increased and everyone is better off provided that trade takes place. This simplified example illustrates the basic

**Table 10.3 Production of video cameras and wheat**

|  | Video cameras | Wheat |
|---|---|---|
| Country A | 65 | 35 |
| Country B | 0 | 40 |
| Total | 65 | 75 |

argument for free trade. Free trade brings the advantages of higher world output and higher standards of living. Countries will produce the goods in which they have a cost advantage and trade with other countries for other goods. So countries can buy goods at lower prices than they could be produced at home. Where economies of scale are present, the savings as a result of specialisation can be substantial.

Theoretically free trade brings most benefit; however, there are often restrictions to such trade and it is unlikely that complete specialisation will take place. Most countries would regard being totally dependent on another country for a particular good as a risky proposition.

**import quotas** physical limitations placed on the quantity of imports

**voluntary export restraints** agreements made with other countries where they voluntarily agree to limit the level of exports into the country

**import tariffs** taxes imposed on imported goods

**exchange controls** limits placed on the purchase of foreign currencies

**export subsidies** payments made to export-producing firms which reduce their costs of production and make them more competitive internationally

**qualitative controls** controls placed on imports which specify qualitative standards

**administrative controls** bureaucratic procedures which are designed to reduce the level of imports

**import controls** controls on the level of imports into a country

**infant industries** new industries that might need protecting against foreign competition in the short term

## 10.3 Restrictions to international trade

There are a number of things that governments do to restrict international trade. These restrictions include:

- **quotas** – a physical limitation on the import of certain goods into a country, sometimes by mutual agreement (e.g. **voluntary export restraints**);
- **tariffs** – a tax placed on imported goods;
- **exchange controls** – a limit to the amount of a currency that can be bought, which will limit the import of goods;
- **subsidies** – payments made to domestic producers to reduce their costs and therefore make them more competitive on world markets;
- **qualitative controls** – controls on the quality of goods rather than on quantity or price;
- **administrative controls** – complicated bureaucratic procedures to discourage exporters.

All of these serve to restrict international trade and therefore reduce specialisation on a world level. They invite retaliation and could lead to inefficiencies. **Import controls** can have a wide effect on industry. The 200 per cent tariffs that the Americans threatened to impose on French cheeses and wines at the end of 1992 if the GATT talks were not successful would have impacted on many other industries like the bottle-making industry or the insurance industry. But there are powerful arguments used in support of import controls. For example, they can be used to protect industries, whether these industries are **'infant' industries** or strategic industries. In the recent debate within the EU on bananas, it was argued by the African, Caribbean and Pacific countries who receive preferential treatment in the EU for their bananas that the relaxation of these preferential terms might lead to the complete devastation of their economies. Import controls can also be used to improve the **balance of payments** position in the case where a deficit exists.

The UK is a member of a number of international organisations which serve to promote free trade and control the restrictions to free trade, like the World Trade Organisation.

### 10.3.1 The European Union (EU)

The EU was established in 1958 by the Treaty of Rome. The six original members, France, West Germany, Italy, Holland, Belgium and Luxembourg were joined in 1972 by the United Kingdom, Ireland and Denmark. Greece joined in 1981, followed by Spain and Portugal in 1986 and Austria, Finland and Sweden on 1 January 1995. These countries, along with the former East Germany, currently constitute the 15 member states of the community, a number which is likely to grow further in the next few years. Many of the former Eastern Bloc countries have applied to join, and negotiations were started in November 1998 over the formal accession of the first six of these – Poland, Hungary, Slovenia, Estonia, the Czech Republic and Cyprus. Other countries which are waiting to join could bring the number of member states to 27. The accession of these countries will bring fundamental changes to the nature of Europe.

**common market** a market characterised by an absence of internal trade barriers but a common external tariff to regulate external trade

**single market** where member countries operate as if they were a single market, a concept which underlies trading in the European Union

**customs union** a group of countries that has set up a free trade area

The primary aim of the Treaty of Rome was to create a '**common market**' in which member states were encouraged to trade freely and to bring their economies closer together, ultimately culminating in the creation of a '**single market**' within the community. To bring this about, a protected free trade area or '**customs union**' was established which involved the removal of tariff barriers between member states and the institution of a common external tariff (CET) on goods from outside the community. Institutional structures and community policies – most notably the Common Agricultural Policy (CAP) – also contributed to this end and to the creation of a trading bloc of immense proportions. Within this bloc, member states were expected to gain numerous advantages including increased trade and investment, huge economies of scale and improvements in productivity and cost reductions. To support the goal of increased trade and co-operation between community members, a European monetary system was established in 1979 in which a majority of member states undertook to fix their exchange rates within agreed limits (see below).

A major step towards the creation of a single market – capable of competing effectively with the United States and Japan – was taken in 1986 when the then 12 community members signed the Single European Act. This Act established 31 December 1992 as the target date for the creation of a Single European Market: an area (comprising the 12 EU countries) without internal frontiers, in which the free movement of goods, services, people and capital was to be ensured within the provisions contained in the treaty. Amongst the measures for making the single market a reality were agreements on:

■ the removal or reduction in obstacles to cross-border travel and trade (e.g. customs checks)
■ the harmonisation or approximation of technical and safety standards on a large number of products

- closer approximation of excise duties and other fiscal barriers (e.g. VAT)
- the removal of legal obstacles to trade (e.g. discriminatory purchasing policies)
- the mutual recognition of qualifications.

The overall programme has involved hundreds of changes to each country's national laws – a majority of which have now been introduced, though not always exactly as originally envisaged.

The benefits expected to flow from the creation of the single market can be viewed in both macro and micro terms. At the macro level, for instance, it was suggested by the Cecchini Report[1] that, at the worst, the new measures would increase the EU's gross domestic product by 4.5 per cent and would create 1.8 million jobs – a prediction which, given the economic climate in Europe in the early 1990s, was rather ambitious.

In micro terms, it is generally accepted that despite some additional costs for firms who have to implement the new requirements (e.g. safety standards), many businesses are likely to gain from increased trade and efficiency (e.g. through greater economies of scale), although this will vary between firms and across sectors within and between each member state. Likely beneficiaries are those larger firms which have adopted a European approach to business development and have put in place structures and procedures to cope with the threats as well as the opportunities of the single market (e.g. by establishing joint ventures; by modifying personnel policies; by adapting marketing strategies; by modifying products). The sectors which arguably have the greatest potential are those where technical barriers are high or where a company has a distinct cost advantage over its rivals. In the UK, these would include the food and drink industry, pharmaceuticals, insurance and a number of other service industries.

Further steps in the development of the EU came with the decision to establish a **European Economic Area (EEA)**, which permits members of the **European Free Trade Area (EFTA)** to benefit from many of the single market measures and, in particular, from the Treaty on European Union, agreed by the 12 in December 1991 at Maastricht. In addition to some institutional changes, the Maastricht Treaty contained provisions for:

**European Economic Area** formed in 1992 between members of the EU and EFTA to promote free trade

**European Free Trade Area** a trade association initially formed in the 1960s which concerns itself with reducing trade barriers

- increased economic and monetary union between member states
- a single currency
- a social charter to protect workers' rights
- a common foreign and security policy
- community citizenship.

These various measures have been introduced over a number of years, although in some cases – most notably the UK – specially negotiated 'opt-out' clauses have meant that some provisions were not initially implemented by all member states (e.g. the single currency; the social charter).

Maastricht set out a three-stage plan towards **economic and monetary union (EMU)**:

**economic and monetary union** the introduction of a common economic and monetary framework across member countries

- Stage 1 – the creation of the single European market by January 1993
- Stage 2 – exchange rates to be fixed within narrow bands, inflation rates to be matched and targets set for government budget deficits and interest rates by January 1994
- Stage 3 – an intergovernmental conference to be set for 1996 to review progress towards EMU and the progress towards a single European currency.

**Euroland** the group of 11 members of the EU which have a common currency

European monetary union was finally achieved on 1 January 1999 with the creation of what has become known as 'Euroland'. Eleven members of the EU are included – the UK, Denmark and Sweden chose not to participate, while Greece failed the convergence criteria for membership. Euroland is effectively a single economic zone since it operates with a single currency – the **euro** (see later) and members have given up sovereignty over monetary policy which is now to be determined by the European Central Bank. National sovereignty over fiscal policy has been retained, so there can be some differences in tax rates and government spending, but this is to operate in a framework of 'harmonisation'. The creation of Euroland enables increased specialisation across the whole of Europe and bigger economies of scale. Euroland embraces more than 300 million people and is responsible for one-fifth of the world's output and as such comes a close second to the USA as an economic superpower.

The UK has chosen not to join Euroland and the single currency until a referendum has been held after the next general election. In 1997 the Chancellor of the Exchequer set out five economic tests of whether the UK should join Euroland or not. These are:

**business cycle** the periodic fluctuations of national output around its long-term trend. Also known as the trade cycle

1  Are **business cycles** and economic structures of the UK and Euroland compatible and sustainable?
2  If problems emerge, is there sufficient flexibility to deal with them?
3  Would joining EMU encourage long-term investment in the UK?
4  What impact would it have on the competitive position of the UK's financial services industry?
5  Will joining EMU promote higher growth, stability and employment?

In the last analysis it is likely that political rather than economic factors will determine whether the UK decides to adopt the euro.

## 10.4  The balance of payments

Foreign trade is essentially about movements of goods, services and capital. The balance of payments is a record of one country's international trade with other countries over a period of time, usually a year. It records the flows of money rather than goods, so that an import will be recorded as a negative amount since the money is flowing out of the country to pay for the good, and an export is recorded as a positive amount. Money flows into and out of countries for two basic reasons, firstly in exchange for goods and services (current transactions) and secondly for investment purposes (capital transactions). In the UK, for example, these two flows are recorded separately in the balance of payments accounts which are produced by the government. Since 1992 when customs points were abolished the UK balance of payments figures have been collected by Intrastat, and are based on VAT returns. Sections 10.4.1 and 10.4.2. below examine how the UK records trade flows.

**current account** a country's record of international flows of money in exchange for goods and services

**visible trade** trade in goods

### 10.4.1 Current transactions

The **current account** records the flows of money received and paid out in exchange for goods and services. It is subdivided into **visible trade** (the import

**invisible trade** trade in services

and export of goods) and **invisible trade** (the import and export of services). Invisible trade includes:

- services like banking, insurance, tourism
- interest, profits and dividends
- transfers, which include grants to developing countries, payments to international organisations like the EU and private transfers such as gifts.

**balance of trade** a country's record of international flows of money in exchange for goods only

The balance of these flows on visible trade is called the **balance of trade** and the balance on the current account overall is called the **current balance**. It is one of these balances that newspapers and politicians are usually referring to when they talk about the balance of payments. Table 10.4 shows the balance of payments for the UK in 1999. It can be seen that the balance of trade was –£26,767 million, the invisible balance was +£15,786 million and the current balance was –£10,981 million. More will be said later about the history of the balance of payments in the UK.

**Table 10.4  UK balance of payments, 1999 (£ million)**

| | | |
|---|---:|---:|
| Visible balance | | −26,767 |
| Invisible trade | | |
| Services | 11,538 | |
| Interest, profits and dividends | 8,332 | |
| Transfers | −4,084 | |
| Invisible trade balance | | 15,786 |
| **Current account balance** | | **−10,981** |
| **Capital account balance** | | **776** |
| Financial account | | |
| Direct investment | −72,962 | |
| Equity capital | | |
| Reinvested earnings | | |
| Other capital transactions | | |
| Portfolio investment | 110,170 | |
| Equity Securities | | |
| Debt securities | | |
| Other investments | −31,994 | |
| Reserve assets | 639 | |
| **Net transactions on financial account** | | **5,853** |
| Balancing item | | 4,352 |

*Source:* National Statistics © Crown copyright 2000 (internet).

### 10.4.2  Capital transactions

As well as these current transactions there are flows of money for investment purposes. This includes funds from both the public and private sectors and long-term and short-term monetary movements.

Long-term capital transactions include:

- overseas investment in the UK (e.g. purchase of shares, acquisition of real assets, purchase of government securities by non-residents);
- UK private investment overseas, where UK residents buy shares, acquire real assets, etc. in overseas countries. The capital account does not include interest, dividends or profits but only flows of money for investment purposes. A capital transaction can give rise to a current flow in the future. If a non-resident bought shares in a UK company the initial amount would appear on the capital account. The resulting flow of dividends paid in the future would be recorded as a flow on the invisible account;
- official long-term capital, i.e. loans from the UK government to other governments.

Short-term transactions include:

- trade credit – as goods are often not paid for as they are received, the physical export and import of goods is not matched with an inflow or outflow of money. In order that the balance of payments balances, these amounts would be included here as trade credit;
- foreign currency borrowing and lending abroad by UK banks;
- exchange reserves held by other countries and other organisations in sterling;
- other external banking and money market liabilities in sterling.

These capital transactions are recorded in the UK balance of payments as changes from the previous year; they are not a record of all the transactions that have taken place over time. If money is flowing into the UK for investment purposes there is an increase in the UK's liabilities and these are shown as positive amounts on the balance of payments. If money is flowing out of the UK there is an increase in the UK's assets and these are shown as negative amounts in the balance of payments.

Up until 1986, capital flows to/from the public sector and capital flows to/from the private sector were shown in two separate accounts. In 1986 the format of the balance of payments was then changed to show all capital transactions in one account under the heading of 'UK transactions in external assets and liabilities'. In 1998 the format of the balance of payments was changed once more to bring it in line with the standards published in the fifth edition of the IMF *Balance of Payments Manual*. The UK balance of payments now comprises three sections :

**capital account** a country's record of international flows of money for investment purposes

- the **current account** as before;
- the **capital account** which records capital transfers and transfers of non-financial assets into and out of the UK; as Table 10.4, shows the balance on this account was +£776 million in 1999;

**financial account (balance of payments)** a country's record of international flows of money in exchange for financial assets

- the **financial account** which gives the balance of trade in financial assets. This section of the balance of payments is itself subdivided between direct investment, portfolio investment, other investments and reserve assets. The balance on the financial account for 1999 was +£5,853 million.

**speculative currency flows** international flows of currencies for speculation purposes

**Speculative flows** of currencies would appear in the financial account of the balance of payments. Portfolio investment is the purchasing of shares in companies while direct investment is the setting up of subsidiaries. The main difference between these two elements of the financial account is the nature of the implied relationship. The purchase of shares implies a relatively passive relationship while foreign direct investment implies a more active, long-term role. More will be said about foreign direct investment later in this chapter. Reserve assets show the change in official reserves – an increase in official reserves is shown as a negative amount and a decrease is shown as a positive amount.

The balance of payments overall should balance, as negative flows will be balanced by positive flows. As this is often hard to understand, two examples will be given.

*Example 1*

If a UK resident buys foreign goods there will be a negative entry in the current account equal to the value of those goods. That individual has to pay for those goods in foreign currency and could do this by using money from a foreign currency bank account if he has one, or by borrowing the foreign currency from a bank in that country. Either way there is an increase in the amount of liabilities and the same amount would be shown as a positive amount in the capital account.

*Example 2*

If a foreign investor purchased shares in a UK company, there would be a positive amount recorded in the capital account. The investor might pay for these shares by using sterling from a sterling bank account and so there would be an equal negative amount shown in the capital account.

The balance of payments should therefore always balance but invariably fails to do so owing to errors and omissions in the recording process, and so a balancing item is included to ensure it balances. As can be seen from Tables 10.4 and 10.5, the balancing item can be very large, and this calls into question the accuracy of the figures.

### 10.4.3 Equilibrium in the balance of payments

If the balance of payments always balances how can there be a deficit? The answer is that the media and politicians are referring to the current balance

**Table 10.5  UK balance of payments** (£ million)

|  | 1990 | 1991 | 1992 | 1993 | 1994 | 1995 | 1996 | 1997 | 1998 | 1999 |
|---|---|---|---|---|---|---|---|---|---|---|
| Visible balance | −18,707 | −10,223 | −13,050 | −13,319 | −11,091 | −11,724 | −13,086 | −11,910 | −20,598 | −26,767 |
| Invisible balance | −806 | 1,849 | 2,968 | 2,701 | 9,633 | 7,979 | 12,486 | 18,213 | 22,072 | 15,786 |
| Current account | −19,513 | −8,374 | −10,082 | −10,618 | −1,458 | −3,745 | −600 | 6,303 | 1,474 | −10,981 |
| Capital account | 497 | 290 | 421 | 309 | 33 | 534 | 736 | 837 | 438 | 776 |
| Financial account | 17,529 | 9,990 | 5,716 | 9,447 | −6,082 | 937 | 1,781 | −8,620 | −9,094 | 5,853 |
| Balancing item | 1,487 | −1,906 | 3,945 | 862 | 7,507 | 2,274 | −1,917 | 1,480 | 7,182 | 639 |
| Drawings on (+) or additions to (−) official reserves |  | −76 | −2,679 | 1,407 | −698 | −1,045 | 200 | 510 | 2,380 | 165 | 4,352 |

*Source:* National Statistics © Crown copyright 2000.

or the balance of trade rather than the overall balance of payments position. A balance of payments surplus on the current account is where the value of exports exceeds the value of imports. A deficit is where the value of imports exceeds the value of exports. As explained above, if there is a surplus on the current account, this will be matched by an outflow in the capital account, for example a reduction in the size of sterling bank balances, or an increase in official reserves. The opposite is true for a deficit. This implies that there cannot be a balance of payments problem. However, persistent surpluses or deficits on the current account are considered to be problematic. A persistent deficit has to be financed in some way, either through borrowing, to increase the external liabilities, or by selling more assets. A deficit will also lead to pressure on the exchange rate, as will be shown later. A continued surplus is also a problem, since one country's surplus must mean that other countries are experiencing a deficit, and they will be faced with the problem of financing the deficit. Political pressure will be brought to bear, and there is the possibility of the introduction of tariffs or other import controls in order to reduce a deficit.

### 10.4.4 Methods of correcting balance of payments deficits

Since surpluses are not regarded as being such a problem as deficits, this section will concentrate on action needed to overcome a deficit, although the actions would be reversed for a surplus. When there is a current account deficit, the outflow of funds is greater than the inflow of funds from international trade. The authorities therefore need to increase exports and/or reduce imports. There are a number of ways in which this might be achieved.

1  A fall in the exchange rate will have the double effect of making exports cheaper abroad and imports dearer at home, thus encouraging exports and discouraging imports. This will be explained fully later.
2  To increase exports British companies that produce for the export market could be subsidised. This would have the effect of reducing the price of UK goods abroad, making them more competitive.
3  Import controls could be imposed to restrict the level of imports coming into the country.
4  A rise in the rate of interest would make Britain more attractive to investors and therefore increase capital flows into Britain and help offset the current account deficit.

## 10.5 The history of the balance of payments in the UK

A country's trade performance can change over time. Its balance of payments figures can help to provide an indication of where an economy's strengths and weaknesses might lie and which might ultimately require governmental action (e.g. import controls or export subsidies). Table 10.5 gives a summary of the balance of payments in the United Kingdom over the last ten years. The table shows that the current account was in deficit from 1990 until 1997, when it went into surplus for two years before returning to deficit in 1999. The weaknesses on the current account predate this and are somewhat hidden in the overall figures. The current account deficits started in 1987; the visible balance has been in deficit (and still is) since 1983 and within this the non-oil balance has been in deficit since 1982. This did not show in the overall current account figures until 1987 because of the offsetting effect of invisibles and oil. The United Kingdom's underlying weaknesses on the current account came from several sources:

**propensity to import** the relationship between income and the level of imports

1 While exports rose during this period, imports have risen faster. In the UK there has been a high **propensity to import** goods.

2 The collapse of oil prices reduced the value of the UK's oil exports

3 The recession of the early 1980s left the UK's manufacturing base in an extremely weak position. This meant that it was difficult to produce enough goods for export or even to meet domestic demand so the balance of payments was hit from both directions. Changes in the **industrial structure** of the UK have implications for the balance of payments, as services are less exportable than goods.

**industrial structure** the relative sizes of the different sectors of the economy

4 The consumer boom that occurred in the late 1980s after the budget of 1986 led to an increase in the level of imports.

5 The impact of oil was twofold. Firstly as the UK had become an oil exporting country it brought in revenue which improved the balance of payments. On the other hand, it kept the exchange rate higher than it would have been and, as will be shown in the next section, made the UK's goods less competitive in world markets, therefore resulting in a worsening of the balance of payments.

6 The high value of the pound in the late 1990s hit the UK's export market.

7 The most recent deterioration was due to a fall in the level of non-European exports especially to Asia and Russia which were experiencing serious economic problems.

The recent surpluses on the current account stem from good performances on invisibles – services and income on investments (interest, profits and dividends). Figure 10.1 shows the breakdown of the current account between the balance in goods, services and interest, profits and dividends. It is clear that in recent years the invisible balance has compensated for weak trade in goods. According to the Office for National Statistics the surpluses in 1997 and 1998 were largely due to the huge losses made by foreign-owned banks in the City of London because of global financial turmoil. This had the effect of reducing the profits they sent out of the country compared with previous years. At the same time the overseas profits of British companies increased. Again this serves to hide in the overall figures a further deterioration in the visible balance which worsened to –£26,767 million in 1999.

### 10.5.1 Patterns of trade

Over time, patterns of trade change for many reasons, Table 10.6 shows UK patterns of trade by destination/source and Table 10.7 shows UK trade by type of good (see page 313). From these tables it is possible to look at how the country's patterns of trade have changed.

**Figure 10.1 Components of the current account, UK, 1990–1999**

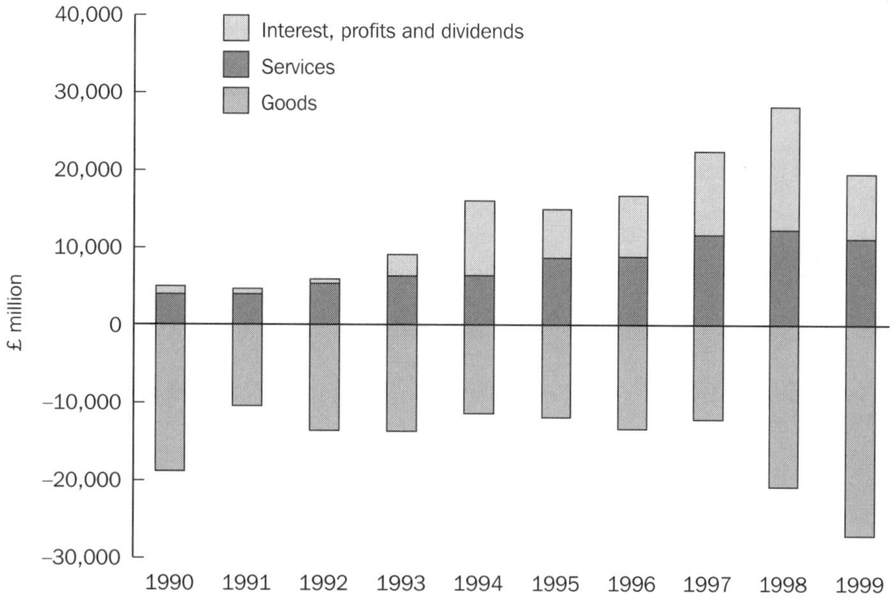

*Source:* National Statistics © Crown copyright 2000.

Mini case **The current account of the balance of payments**

Figures on the balance of payments are produced every month by the government in the UK and are often seized upon by commentators as indications of either an improvement in the UK's economic performance or a deterioration, depending upon the details of the figures. There are a number of reasons why this is incorrect. First, balance of payments figures are notoriously unreliable, and are often revised by very large amounts. In June 1996, for example, the estimated deficit on the balance of payments for 1995 was revised from £6.7 billion to £2.9 billion because of the discovery of large investment flows. Second – and this applies to all short-term economic indicators – there are very short-term changes in economic variables which are not translated into long-term trends. So the balance of payments can vary quite dramatically each month due to short-term factors which are evened out over the course of the year. In addition, the balance of payments like other indicators often does not behave as expected. As late as December 1998, the Treasury was predicting a current account deficit of £1.75 billion for 1998, but higher than average investment income flows resulted in a surplus overall of £1.5 billion.

Figure 10.2 shows the UK current balance for the period 1970 to 1999. Two points can immediately be made about the behaviour of the balance of payments. First, the data moves in a cyclical way and is therefore affected by the trade cycle. Second, the balance of payments generally improves in times of recession (e.g. the early 1980s and early 1990s) and worsens in times of boom. The reasons for this are twofold – in a recession the level of imports falls as income falls and the level of exports is unlikely to fall unless other countries are experiencing the same level of economic downturn. The balance

▶

**Figure 10.2  UK current balance, 1970–1999** (£ million)

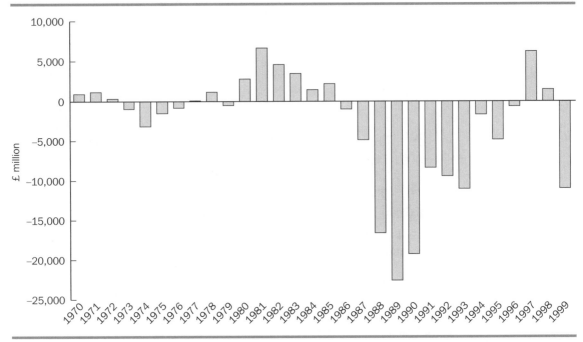

*Source:* National Statistics © Crown copyright 2000.

of payments therefore improves. Usually the balance of payments improves enough in a recession to push it into surplus, although this did not happen in the early 1990s when the UK's current account remained in the red.

The unpredictability of the balance of payments is very evident in the figures for the 1990s. In 1994 the balance of payments improved, despite the recovery in economic conditions which would have been expected to worsen the balance of payments. This improvement continued in the late 1990s despite economic conditions which implied the opposite. The balance of payments should have suffered as a result of the high value of the pound and the economic turmoil in Asia and Russia. One possible explanation for the apparently contrary behaviour of the balance of payments is the J-curve effect (see Figure 10.7). It could be that the improvement in the balance of payments in the mid-1990s was caused by the fall in the value of the pound after the UK left the ERM, even though that happened in 1992, because of the time lags involved. Similarly, the effects of the high value of the pound had only just started to show in the balance of payments in 1999. The effects of the Asian crisis have been felt in the balance of payments figures – in 1998 exports to South-East Asia were less than a third of their 1997 level. Exports to Russia were down to a half of 1997 levels. However, at the same time, there was an improvement in our trading position with EU countries and a record performance on invisibles – in particular interest, profits and dividends, as previously noted.

The multitude of factors which impact upon the balance of payments and the difficulties involved in accurate data collection make the balance of payments figures unreliable and very difficult to predict. The use of one month's figures by commentators to prove either that recovery is underway or that a recession is imminent is unsound.

**Table 10.6  UK's imports and exports by destination/source (%)**

| | 1970 Exports | 1970 Imports | 1980 Exports | 1980 Imports | 1990 Exports | 1990 Imports | 1997 Exports | 1997 Imports |
|---|---|---|---|---|---|---|---|---|
| EU | 32 | 32 | 46 | 44 | 53 | 52 | 56 | 54 |
| Other W. Europe | 13 | 12 | 12 | 12 | 9 | 13 | 5 | 6 |
| USA | 12 | 11 | 10 | 12 | 13 | 11 | 12 | 13 |
| Other OECD countries | 11 | 10 | 6 | 7 | 5 | 7 | 8 | 10 |
| (of which Japan) | 2 | 2 | 1 | 4 | 2 | 6 | 2 | 5 |
| Oil exporting countries | 6 | 11 | 10 | 9 | 6 | 2 | 6 | 2 |
| Rest of the world | 18 | 14 | 12 | 11 | 10 | 10 | 14 | 15 |

*Source*: Adapted from Table 18.6, *Annual Abstract of Statistics* National Statistics © Crown copyright (1999, 1992, 1982, 1972).

The most obvious change that can be seen in Table 10.6 is that trade with the EU has become more important over the last 30 years while trade with the rest of Western Europe has declined. More than half of our imports in 1990 came from the EU, more than half of our exports went to the EU, the proportions increased further up to 1997. Despite this, the USA is still important to Britain. There has been a decline in our trade with other OECD countries over the whole period, although the importance of Japan within that has increased, particularly with respect to imports. Our trade with the oil-exporting countries has declined in importance, as has our trade with the rest of the world, although this increased between 1990 and 1997. The rest of the world includes many Commonwealth countries, which at one time were our biggest markets.

Since 1970 the UK has imported less food and fewer animals for consumption. The impact of oil can be seen in Table 10.7 as the quantities of oil-related products imported into the UK have fallen over the period. Manufacturing is clearly the most important category of good as far as the balance of payments is concerned. Manufacturing has retained its importance for exports, accounting

**Table 10.7  Pattern of trade by type of good (%)**

| | 1970 Export | 1970 Import | 1990 Export | 1990 Import | 1997 Export | 1997 Import |
|---|---|---|---|---|---|---|
| Food and animals | 3 | 20 | 4 | 8 | 4 | 7 |
| Beverages and tobacco | 3 | 2 | 3 | 1 | 3 | 2 |
| Crude materials except fuels | 3 | 12 | 2 | 5 | 2 | 3 |
| Minerals, fuels | 3 | 14 | 8 | 7 | 6 | 4 |
| Chemicals and related products | 9 | 6 | 13 | 9 | 13 | 10 |
| Manufactured goods | 24 | 20 | 15 | 17 | 13 | 15 |
| Machinery | 43 | 19 | 41 | 38 | 46 | 44 |
| Miscellaneous manufacturing | 9 | 7 | 13 | 15 | 13 | 15 |
| Total manufacturing | 85 | 51 | 81 | 78 | 72 | 72 |
| Others | 3 | 2 | 2 | 1 | 1 | 1 |

*Source*: Adapted from Table 18.4, *Annual Abstract of Statistics* National Statistics © Crown copyright (1972, 1999)

**Table 10.8 Import penetration[a] in manufacturing in the UK (%)**

| | 1970 | 1980 | 1990 | 1994 | 1996 |
|---|---|---|---|---|---|
| | 16.6 | 26.2 | 36.7 | 48[b] | 56 |

[a] measured as $\dfrac{\text{import value}}{\text{home demand}} \times 100$

[b] new Standard Industrial Classification definition

*Source*: Adapted from Table 18.2, *Annual Abstract of Statistics,* National Statistics © Crown copyright (1972, 1982, 1992, 1996, 1999).

for 76 per cent of exports in 1970 and 72 per cent in 1997. As far as imports are concerned the percentage increased a great deal over 27 years. The UK is now a net importer of manufactured goods. In 1997 the value of imported manufactured goods was £139,073 million, and the value of exported manufactured goods was £124,591 million. One reason for this is the increased **import penetration** in the UK. Table 10.8 shows import penetration in UK manufacturing for 1970, 1980, 1990, 1994 and 1996. It can be seen that import penetration has increased over this time period.

**import penetration** the proportion of domestic consumption accounted for by imports

### 10.6 Exchange rates

The **exchange rate** of a currency is the price of that currency in terms of other currencies. If each country has its own currency and international trade is to take place, an exchange of currencies needs to occur. For example, when a UK resident buys goods from France, these must be paid for in francs. The individual will probably purchase francs from a bank in exchange for sterling in order to carry out the transaction. There must therefore be an exchange rate between sterling and francs. Likewise, there will be exchange rates between sterling and other currencies acceptable for trade purposes.

**floating exchange rate** an exchange rate which is determined within a free market

Basically, there are two types of exchange rate: the **floating exchange rate**; and the **fixed exchange rate**. There are also hybrid exchange rate systems which combine the characteristics of the two main types.

**fixed exchange rate** an exchange rate which is fixed and maintained at a certain level by the government

#### 10.6.1 The floating exchange rate

This type of exchange rate is determined within a free market, there is no government intervention, and the exchange rate is free to fluctuate according to market conditions. The exchange rate is determined by the demand for and the supply of the currency in question.

If we take sterling as an example, the demand for the currency comes from exports, i.e. overseas residents buying pounds either to buy British goods and services or for investment purposes. The supply of pounds comes from imports, i.e. UK residents who are buying foreign currencies to purchase goods and services or for investment purposes and who are therefore at the same time supplying pounds to the market. The market for sterling can then be drawn using simple demand and supply diagrams.

In Figure 10.3, the price axis shows the price of £1 in terms of US dollars and the quantity axis shows the quantity of pounds being bought and sold.

**Figure 10.3 The determination of the exchange rate of £ to $**

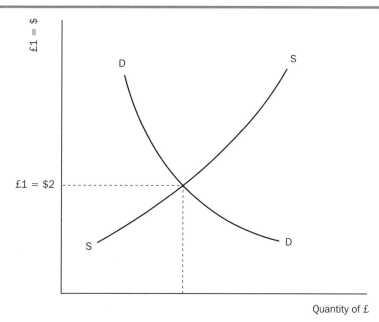

The equilibrium exchange rate is determined by the intersection of demand and supply at £1 = $2. As this is a totally free market, if any of the conditions in the market change the exchange rate will also change.

The demand for and supply of sterling and therefore the exchange rate is affected by:

1  changes in the balance of payments
2  changes in investment flows
3  speculation in the foreign exchange markets.

This analysis can be applied to other currencies.

### Changes in the balance of payments

Figure 10.4 shows the effect on the exchange rate of changes in the balance of payments. The original demand curve is DD and the original supply curve is SS. At the equilibrium exchange rate of £1 = $2 the demand for pounds is equal to the supply of pounds. In other words, if the demand for pounds comes from exports and the supply of pounds comes from imports, imports and exports are equal and the balance of payments is in equilibrium. Now it is assumed that a balance of payments deficit is caused by the level of imports rising while the level of exports stays the same. If exports remain the same there will be no change in the demand curve for pounds. As imports rise there will be a rise in the supply of pounds to the market and the supply curve will move to the right to S̀S̀. At the old exchange rate of £1 = $2, there is now an excess supply of pounds, and as this is a free market there will be downward pressure on the value of the pound until equilibrium is re-established at the new lower exchange rate of £1 = $1. At this exchange rate the demand for

**Figure 10.4 The effect of changes in the balance of payments on the exchange rate**

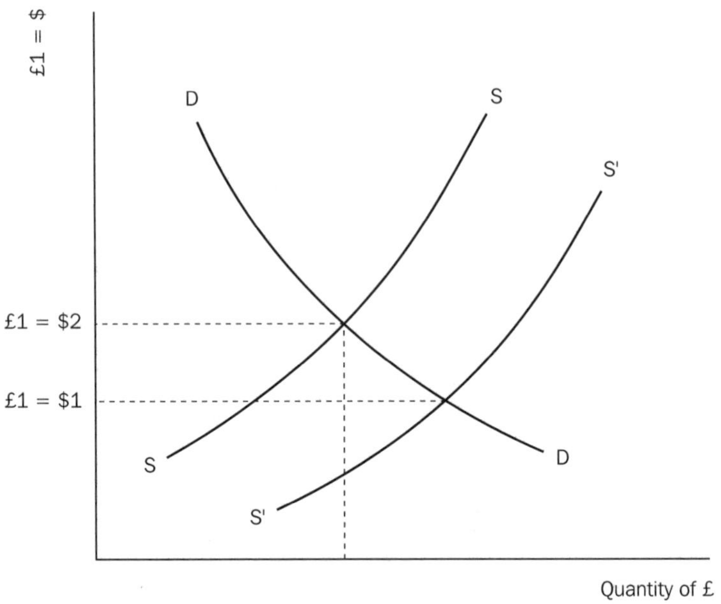

pounds is again equal to the increased supply of pounds and the balance between imports and exports is re-established.

How does this happen? When the value of the pound falls two things happen: the price of imports rises and the price of exports falls. Thus the level of imports falls and the level of exports rises and the deficit is eradicated. A simple numerical example illustrates this point:

- At old exchange rate £1 = $2, an American car which costs $20,000 in the USA costs £10,000 in the UK and a British car which costs £10,000 in the UK costs $20,000 in the USA
- If the exchange rate falls to £1 = $1, the American car still costs $20,000 in the USA but now costs £20,000 in the UK and the British car still costs £10,000 in the UK but now costs $10,000 in the USA

Therefore a depreciation in the exchange rate has made imports dearer (the American car) and exports cheaper (the British car). Thus a fall in the value of the pound helps to re-establish equilibrium in the balance of payments.

In the case of a surplus on the balance of payments, the exchange rate will rise, making exports more expensive and imports cheaper and thereby re-establishing equilibrium in the balance of payments. You should test your understanding of the working of the foreign exchange markets by working through what happens if a surplus develops.

A fall in the value of the pound in a free market is called a **depreciation** in the value of the pound; a rise in its value is called an **appreciation**.

**currency depreciation** a decrease in the value of a currency brought about by market forces

**currency appreciation** an increase in the value of a currency brought about by market forces

### Changes in investment flows

In Figure 10.5, the original equilibrium exchange rate is £1 = $2. If there is an increase in the level of investment in the UK from overseas, there will be an

**Figure 10.5 The effect of changes in investment flows on the exchange rate**

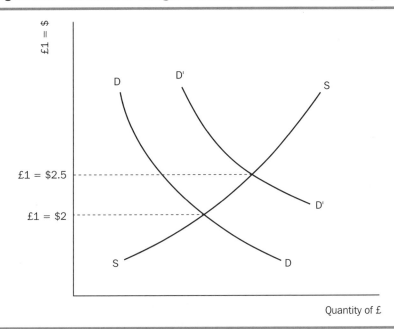

increase in the demand for pounds. The demand curve moves to the right (to D'D'), and the exchange rate rises to £1 = $2.5.

### The effect of speculation

**currency speculators** individuals or groups of individuals who buy and sell currencies in order to make a capital gain

If the exchange rate of sterling is expected to rise, **speculators** will buy sterling in order to make a capital gain by selling the currency later at a higher exchange rate. There will be an increase in the demand for pounds and the exchange rate will rise. If the exchange rate is expected to fall, speculators will sell sterling in order to avoid a capital loss, and there will be an increase in the supply of sterling and therefore a fall in the exchange rate. Illustrate these changes yourself using demand and supply diagrams.

The important thing about speculation is that it tends to be self-fulfilling. If enough people believe that the exchange rate is going to rise and act accordingly, the exchange rate will rise.

The main advantage of the floating exchange rate is the automatic mechanism it provides to overcome a balance of payments deficit or surplus. Theoretically, if a deficit develops, the exchange rate will fall and the balance of payments is brought back into equilibrium. The opposite occurs in the case of a surplus. Of course in reality it does not work as smoothly or as quickly as the theory suggests. A depreciation is supposed to work as demonstrated in Figure 10.6.

There are a number of problems which may occur to prevent this self-correcting mechanism working properly. Firstly, if in the UK the goods which are imported are necessities that cannot be produced at home, then even if their price goes up as a result of a depreciation, they will continue to be demanded. Thus not only will the balance of payments deficit not be automatically rectified, another economic problem will result, that of **inflation**. The UK

**inflation** a widespread and persistent rise in the general price level

**Figure 10.6 The effect of a depreciation**

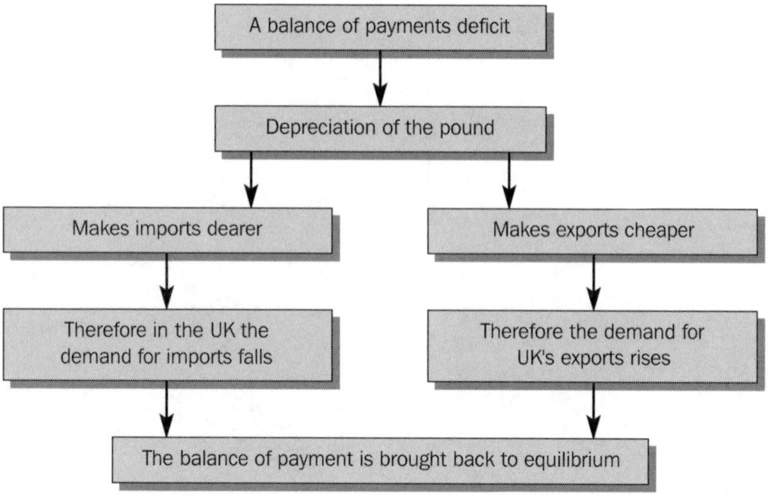

will continue to buy the imported goods at the new higher price. A second problem occurs on the other side of the equation. It is assumed above that as the price of exports falls more exports are sold. This presupposes that in the UK the capacity is there to meet this increased demand, but this may not be the case, especially if the economy is fully employed already or if the export-producing industries are not in a healthy enough state to produce more.

**J-curve effect** the relationship between the devaluation of a currency and its effects on the balance of payments

These problems give rise to what is called the '**J-curve effect**'. A fall in the exchange rate may well lead to a deterioration in the balance of payments in the short term, until domestic production can be increased to meet the extra demand for exports and as substitutes for imported goods. Once this can be done there will be an improvement in the balance of payments, hence the J-curve effect pictured in Figure 10.7. The effect of a fall in the exchange rate is limited and the curve levels off after a certain time period. The depreciation in the value of the pound seen when Britain left the exchange rate mechanism (ERM) did not have an immediate effect on the balance of payments and many argued that this was due to the J-curve effect.

One major disadvantage of the floating exchange rate is that it introduces uncertainty into the market, and for firms that operate internationally this introduces another variable which needs to be considered when planning. Moreover, since the possibility of speculation exists with the floating exchange rate, this can be destabilising and unsettling to markets – something which businesses do not welcome.

### 10.6.2 The fixed exchange rate

The **fixed exchange rate** is one that is fixed and maintained by the government. An exchange rate can be fixed in terms of other currencies, gold or a basket of other currencies. In order to maintain a fixed exchange rate the government has to actively intervene in the market, either buying or selling

**Figure 10.7 The J-curve**

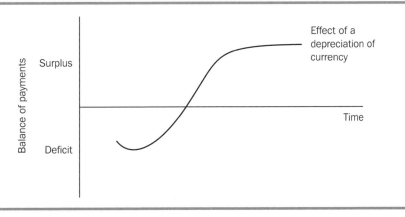

**Figure 10.8 The effect of changes in the balance of payments on a fixed exchange rate**

currencies. Figure 10.8 shows the action needed by the UK authorities in the case of downward pressure on the value of the pound. Again, this analysis can be applied to other currencies.

The exchange rate is fixed at £1 = $2, and the government wants to maintain that rate. If a balance of payments deficit develops, brought about by an increase in imports, exports remaining the same, there will be an excess supply of pounds at the fixed exchange rate. In a free market the value of the pound would fall until the excess supply had disappeared. However, this is not a free market, and the government must buy up the excess supply of pounds in

**Figure 10.8 The effect of changes in the balance of payments on a fixed exchange rate**

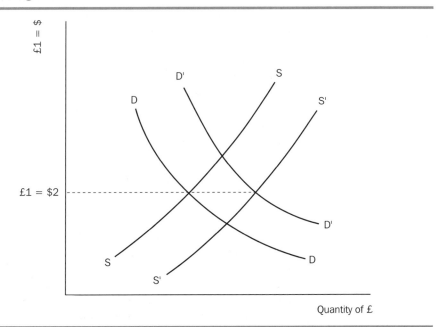

order to maintain the exchange rate at £1 = \$2. Thus the demand curve moves to the right and the exchange rate has been maintained at the same level. Alternatively if there is excess demand for pounds, the government has to supply pounds to the market in order to maintain the fixed exchange rate.

A prime advantage of a fixed exchange rate is that there is less uncertainty in the market, everyone knows what the exchange rate will be in a year's time, and long-term planning is made easier. It also reduces the likelihood of speculation in the foreign exchange markets. One major disadvantage, however, is that there is no longer an automatic mechanism for rectifying any balance of payments problems as there is in the case of the floating exchange rate and this means that government intervention is necessary, not just to support the exchange rate, but also to overcome any balance of payments problems. Added to this, a fixed exchange rate is not sustainable in the case of persistent deficits or surpluses. In the event of a surplus, the government must supply pounds to the market and if the surplus persists then eventually the government will exhaust its reserves and might well have to **revalue** the pound, i.e. increase the exchange rate of the pound. In the case of a persistent deficit, the size of the government's reserves will be increasing over time and the government may have to **devalue** the pound, to correct the problem.

There are, then, advantages and disadvantages to both types of exchange rate and there have been hybrid exchange rate systems that serve to combine the advantages of both systems. In such an exchange rate system the exchange rate is basically fixed but is allowed to fluctuate by a small amount either side of the central value. The exchange rate mechanism of the European Union was an example of this. When the UK entered the ERM the exchange rate was fixed against other member currencies but allowed to vary by 6 per cent either side of the central value before action was needed.

Over the years the UK has had a variety of different types of exchange rate. Before the First World War and for some time between the wars, the exchange rate was fixed in terms of gold – the **gold standard**. From the Second World War until 1972, the UK was part of the Bretton Woods system of fixed exchange rates, where the pound was fixed in terms of dollars. From 1972 to 1990, the UK had a floating exchange rate. In 1990 Britain joined the exchange rate mechanism of the European Union, which was a fixed exchange rate. In September 1992, the pound left the ERM and was allowed to float. The key question for the British government now is whether the UK should adopt the euro, thereby replacing sterling with the single currency. This is an issue to which we now turn.

### 10.6.3 The single European currency

On 1 January 1999 the **single European currency** – the **euro** – was introduced. In order to qualify for membership of the single currency, EU members have to fulfil strict criteria with respect to inflation rates, budget deficits and rates of interest.[2] In the end all members qualified with the exception of Greece, where there were problems with high inflation rates. The UK, Denmark and Sweden decided not to join the single currency, so Euroland comprises 11 members. Each of the currencies of these members is fixed to the euro at a specified rate, but are sub-units of the euro rather than separate currencies.

**currency revaluation** an increase in the value of a currency brought about by government intervention

**currency devaluation** a decrease in the value of a currency brought about by government intervention

**gold standard** a system where the value of a currency is fixed in terms of gold

**euro** the single European currency introduced in 1999

Initially the euro will only be a paper and electronic currency. Financial and government transactions can take place in the new currency, but the only currency in circulation will be national currencies. Although UK membership is still in abeyance, it is already possible to open euro bank accounts and UK banks and building societies are offering euro savings accounts and mortgages. Euro notes and coins are scheduled to be put into circulation on 1 January 2002 and will circulate alongside national currencies until 31 July 2002 after which national currencies will cease to be legal tender. There will be euro-cent coins in 1, 2, 10, 20 and 50 cent denominations, plus 1 and 2 euro coins. Notes will be issued in denominations of 5, 10, 20, 50, 100, 200 and 500 euros.

The first weekend in January 1999 was designated 'conversion weekend' and across Europe 100,000 financial service workers converted computer systems and bank accounts. More than £1,300 billion worth of government securities and £300 million worth of bank accounts were converted from 11 currencies to one. The bill for conversion is estimated to be around £30 billion. In London, even though the UK has not joined, there was similar activity over the conversion weekend, as the City is the largest foreign exchange market in the world. Around 30,000 City staff worked to convert computer systems so that trading in euros could commence on 4 January.

Even though the UK has not joined the euro, many businesses in the UK have already adapted to the existence of the euro. Many large companies are using the euro for accounting purposes; ICI is already invoicing in euros, Marks and Spencer stores are fully equipped to accept euros and BT has plans to convert 40,000 call boxes to accept both sterling and euro coins when they are introduced. This is patchy though, as recent research shows that less than a quarter of small and medium enterprises (SMEs) had started to prepare for the euro by January 1999, despite the fact that around half of them trade with other European countries. Preparation is necessary for practical reasons, since many large companies will start to invoice and pay bills in euros. Computer systems will need to be adapted to allow for this. There will also be a cost involved in the UK as banks are charging fairly high commissions for converting euros, particularly for small users. Preparation is also a strategic issue for business. Firstly, EMU will result in greater competition and price differences will be more obvious to customers. The cost of converting currencies serves to increase the costs of UK businesses and make them less competitive. Secondly, EMU will probably result in more mergers and acquisitions across Europe and this will have dramatic effects on the structure of industries.

In the UK the debate over the single European currency continues. The pro single currency camp claim that the UK will be further marginalised in Europe if it does not join in the single currency. It also argues that there are great advantages to membership – a reduction in transaction costs like the costs of currency exchange, a reduction in the instability caused by changing exchange rates, lower rates of interest and the maintenance of London as a financial centre in currencies. It argues that the UK is imperilling **foreign direct investment** by staying out of the euro, although there is little evidence of this (see later in this chapter). The anti camp argue just as vociferously that all of this would be at the expense of loss of sovereignty – the UK would be unable to change its exchange rate in order to boost the competitiveness of UK goods. They are afraid that EMU would be followed by political union, and are calling for a referendum on the issue.

**foreign direct investment**
the establishment of production facilities in an overseas country

Even in the first three months of the new single currency there were some problems. When it was first introduced one euro was worth 70p, and commentators were expecting the value to rise because of the size of the currency to around 78p by the end of 1999. In fact by April 2000 the euro had lost about 15 per cent of its value and the fall is expected to continue. The two main reasons for this were weaker than expected economic performance by the members of Euroland and internal political arguments between the European Central Bank and national finance ministers over monetary policy and the rate of interest. As the section on exchange rates shows, once a currency starts to slide, speculation serves to push its value down further and make the situation worse. This rather weak start for the new currency has strengthened the anti-European case in the UK and has also caused problems for UK exporters as it has given rise to an increase in the value of the pound.

## 10.7 Exchange rates and business

Reference has already been made to the fact that changes in exchange rates can affect businesses in several ways. These would include:

- making it easier or harder to export (as prices change)
- making it easier or harder for foreign competitors to penetrate the domestic market (again through the price effect)
- causing uncertainty in both trading and investment terms
- adding to or reducing the cost of imported raw materials and component parts.

In addition, if a falling exchange rate causes inflationary pressures within the economy, this could add to a firm's production costs (e.g. through higher wage bills) and could encourage the government to introduce counter-inflationary policies which might subsequently depress demand in the home market.

For businesses regularly involved in currency dealing and/or multinational activities, changing currency values can also bring other gains or losses. Shell and Allied Lyons, for example, lost over £100 million each on currency gambles in the early 1990s by entering into deals when the exchange rate between currencies was not fixed in advance. In contrast, Unilever's record profits for the financial year 1992/3 included substantial overseas earnings, some of which were the direct result of a weaker pound which meant that remitted profits increased when converted back into sterling. Clearly the introduction of the single European currency will impact upon such gains or losses.

## 10.8 Multinationals and foreign direct investment

Substantial amounts of foreign trade and hence movements of currency result from the activities of very large multinational companies or enterprises. **Multinational enterprises (MNEs)**, strictly defined, are enterprises operating in a number of countries and having production or service facilities outside the country of their origin. These multinationals usually have their headquarters in a developed country – with two exceptions (Daewoo and Petróleos de Venezuela), the largest 100 MNEs are based in the developed world. Typically,

MNEs still employ two-thirds of their workforce and produce two-thirds of their output in their home country. A relatively new concept is the **transnational enterprise**. Often used interchangeably with multinational enterprise, this refers to enterprises which do not have a national base – they are truly international companies. More will be said about this concept later, but as they are still relatively rare, this section will concentrate on MNEs. Multinationals are often well-known household names, as Table 10.9 shows.

**Table 10.9  The world's ten largest MNEs, ranked by foreign assets, 1997**

| Rank | Company | Country | Transnationality index* % |
|------|---------|---------|---------------------------|
| 1 | General Electric | United States | 33.1 |
| 2 | Ford Motor Company | United States | 35.2 |
| 3 | Shell, Royal Dutch | Netherlands/UK | 58.9 |
| 4 | General Motors | United States | 29.3 |
| 5 | Exxon Corporation | United States | 65.9 |
| 6 | Toyota | Japan | 40.0 |
| 7 | IBM | United States | 53.7 |
| 8 | Volkswagen Group | Germany | 56.8 |
| 9 | Nestlé SA | Switzerland | 93.2 |
| 10 | Daimler-Benz | Germany | 44.1 |

\* Measured as the average of three ratios: foreign assets to total assets, foreign sales to total sales and foreign employment to total employment.

*Source: World Investment Report*, UNCTAD (1999).

The transnationality index gives a measure of an MNE's involvement abroad by looking at three ratios – foreign asset/total asset, foreign sales/total sales and foreign employment/total employment. As such it captures the importance of foreign activities in its overall activities. In Table 10.9 Nestlé has the highest index – this is because in all three ratios it has a high proportion of foreign involvement. Since 1990 the average index of transnationality for the top 100 MNEs has increased[3] from 51 per cent to 55 per cent, but the rate of increase slowed slightly in 1998, mainly reflecting a decline in the ratio of foreign to total assets.

These multinational are huge organisations and their market values often exceed the GNP of many of the countries in which they operate. There are over 60,000 MNEs around the world and they are estimated to account for a quarter of the world's output. The growth in MNEs is due to relaxation of exchange controls, making it easier to move money between countries, and the improvements in communication which makes it possible to run a worldwide business from one country. The importance of multinationals varies from country to country as Table 10.10 shows.

As can be seen, foreign affiliates are very important for some countries and not so important for others: in the case of Japan there is hardly any foreign presence at all. For all of the countries except Finland foreign affiliates have a bigger impact upon production than employment.

**Table 10.10 Percentage share of foreign affiliates in manufacturing production and employment, 1997**

| Country | Share of foreign affiliates in manufacturing production | Share of foreign affiliates in manufacturing employment |
| --- | --- | --- |
| Hungary | 67 | 43 |
| Ireland | 66 | 47 |
| UK | 34 | 19 |
| Czech Republic | 31 | 18 |
| Netherlands | 29.5 | 18 |
| France | 28.5 | 26 |
| Sweden | 21 | 20 |
| Norway | 20 | 16 |
| USA | 16 | 12 |
| Finland | 13 | 14 |
| Germany | 12 | 8 |
| Turkey | 12 | 6 |
| Italy | 11 | 10 |
| Japan | 1 | 1 |

Source: *Measuring Globalisation: The Role of Multinationals in OECD Economies.* Copyright OECD (1999).[4]

### 10.8.1 Foreign direct investment.

An important aspect of MNE activity is **foreign direct investment (FDI)**. Between 1990 and 1999 the value of FDI worldwide more than doubled. The two biggest donors and recipients were the USA and the UK. The wave of FDI in the 1980s brought new companies and jobs – in the USA, for example, the number of Americans employed by foreign companies more than doubled between 1980 and 1990. This changed in the 1990s, when FDI was directed towards mergers and acquisitions rather than the opening of new factories or subsidiaries. In 1997 it is estimated that 90 per cent of FDI took the form of mergers and acquisitions.[5]

In the UK, despite protestations that the failure of the UK to join the single European currency would lead to a fall in direct investment from overseas, FDI remains high. Between 1987 and 1998 26 per cent of all FDI into the EU went into the UK. In the year to March 2000, the stock of foreign investment rose by 23 per cent to stand at £252.4 billion. It seems that non-membership of the euro has not damaged inward investment into the UK yet. However, it could be argued that what is happening now is the outcome of past investment decisions and that the expectation is that the UK will eventually join the single currency. It is also the case that the majority of inward investment to the UK comes from the USA and that language and historical ties are more important than membership of the single European currency. The biggest recipient of FDI in the UK is the financial services sector.

At one time economists thought of international trade and FDI as alternatives to one another – instead of trading with a country a company could enter that country by opening a subsidiary. These days, however, the two are seen as complementary. A major study by the OECD[6] found that for donors of FDI each outward investment of $1 produces additional exports of $2. For recipients of FDI, the short-term effect is an increase in imports; an increase in exports is not seen until the longer term.

### 10.8.2 The operation of MNEs

Multinationals can diversify operations across different countries. This brings them great benefits:

1  MNEs can locate their activities in the countries which are best suited for them. For example, production planning can be carried out in the parent country, the production itself can be carried out in one of the newly industrialised countries where labour is relatively cheap and marketing can be done in the parent country where such activities are well developed. The relocation of production may go some way to explaining the decline in the manufacturing sector in the developed nations.[7]

**cross-subsidisation** when a company subsidises a loss-making activity with revenue from a profit-making activity

2  An MNE can **cross-subsidise** its operations. Profits from one market can be used to support operations in another one. The cross-subsidisation could take the form of price cutting, increasing productive capacity or heavy advertising.

3  The risk involved in production is spread, not just over different markets but also over different countries.

**tax holidays** a way of encouraging foreign direct investment by excusing the payment of corporation tax for a set period of time

4  MNEs can avoid tax by negotiating special tax arrangements in one of their host countries (**tax holidays**) or through careful use of **transfer pricing** (see Chapter 9). Transfer prices are the prices at which internal transactions take place. These can be altered so that high profits can be shown in countries where the tax rate is lower. For example, in the USA in 1999 two-thirds of foreign-based multinationals paid no federal income tax. The loss to US taxpayers from this has been estimated to be in excess of $40 billion per year in unpaid taxes.

5  MNEs can take advantage of subsidies and tax exemptions offered by governments to encourage start-ups in their country.

The very size of MNEs gives rise to concern as their operations can have a substantial impact upon the economy. For example, the activities of MNEs will affect the labour market of host countries (see mini case) and the balance of payments. If a subsidiary is started in one country there will be an inflow of capital to that country. Once it is up and running, however, there will be outflows of dividends and profits which will affect the invisible balance. Also there will be flows of goods within the company and therefore between countries, in the form of semi-finished goods and raw materials. These movements will affect the exchange rate as well as the balance of payments and it is likely that the effects will be greater for developing countries than for developed countries.

There is also the possibility of exploitation of less-developed countries, and it is debatable whether such footloose industries form a viable basis for economic development. Added to this, MNEs take their decisions in terms of their overall operations rather than with any consideration of their effects on the host economy. There is therefore a loss of economic sovereignty for national governments (see Chapter 12).

The main problem with multinationals is the lack of control that can be exerted by national governments. In June 2000 the OECD updated its Guidelines for Multinational Enterprises, which are not legally binding but are promoted by OECD members governments. These seek to provide a balanced framework for international investment that clarifies both the rights and responsibilities of the business community. It contains guidelines on business ethics, employment relations, information disclosure and taxation, among other things. Against all this is the fact that without the presence of MNEs, output in host countries would be lower, and as the mini case shows, there is evidence that on labour market issues the multinationals do not perform badly.

---

**Mini case** | **MNEs**

Multinational enterprises have often been criticised for the effects they have on local labour markets. They have been accused of destroying jobs, limiting their overseas operations to low-skill, low-technology functions so that the jobs that are created are low paid and exploiting the local workforce by pushing down wages. A major OECD study of the activities of multinationals found little evidence for these claims.[8] It found that multinationals play an increasingly important role in terms of output and employment in OECD countries, but that the degree of involvement varied between countries, as Table 10.10 shows.

The report found that in all member countries foreign affiliates paid their employees more than the national average wage and for the vast majority of countries the gap is widening. In the UK, for example, foreign affiliates paid their employees an average of 29 per cent more than national firms in 1996 while in 1989 this figure was 22 per cent. For the USA, the comparable figures are 6 per cent in 1996 and 4 per cent in 1989. The study also found that MNEs were creating jobs at a faster rate than domestic companies in all member countries except for one – Germany. The report found that multinational enterprises spent heavily on research and development: in 1996 they accounted for 40 per cent of R&D spending in the UK, for example, and 12 per cent in the USA. This seems to contradict the argument that MNEs limit their overseas operations on low-technology jobs.

The main problem with MNEs is their size and the fact that they can take decisions without recourse to national governments. For a country like Ireland, where 66 per cent of output and 47 per cent of employment is accounted for by multinationals, this is worrying.

### 10.8.3 Globalisation

**globalisation** the internationalisation of goods and services by large firms

**Globalisation** is a term used to describe the process of integration on a worldwide scale of markets and production. The world is moving away from a system of national markets that are isolated from one another by trade barriers, distance or culture towards one where there is one huge global market place. This is certainly true for goods such as Coca-Cola or McDonald's although it is not true for all products. The globalisation of markets has been intensified by the globalisation of production where firms disperse parts of their production process to different parts of the world. It is not just the large multinational enterprises that are becoming global; many small and medium-sized enterprises are also engaged in global production and marketing.

The two main reasons for the increased globalisation of both markets and production are:

- the decline in barriers to trade and investment that has occurred over the last half-century. Each day over $1.5 trillion are exchanged in foreign exchanges and international trade accounts for one-third of the world's output. New markets that were formerly protected, like the Soviet bloc, have opened up for competition.
- the dramatic developments in communication and information technologies which not only facilitate global production through the transfer of information between different parts of a company, but also allow the transfer of ideas and beliefs around the world. The so-called '**global culture**' makes it appear as if the same trends occur in many parts of the world at the same time. Developments in transportation technology, such as the jet engine, have also served to make the world a smaller place.

**global culture** the replacement of traditional cultural differences between countries with one common universal culture

Globalisation has meant that firms face an increasingly complex environment. For example, there are new markets to be captured, increased competition to be faced from abroad, an understanding needed of the workings of foreign exchange markets, and a knowledge of the differences which exist between countries. Despite what has been said about globalisation, there still remains a great diversity in the world – different countries have different cultures, political systems and legal systems. Global production and marketing require a knowledge of all of these.

## 10.9  Conclusion

The importance of international markets will vary between firms and industries but most businesses do not operate solely within national boundaries. Businesses which operate in the export market will obviously need an understanding of international markets but even the sole proprietor producing for a small local market may well use imported raw materials or components in the production process and so will be influenced by changes that take place internationally. Other than people who are totally self-sufficient, we are all affected directly or indirectly by foreign trade.

 This chapter has looked at the international market place and in particular the benefits that derive from international trade. Consideration has also been given to some of the restrictions that exist to free trade and to the role of the EU in promoting a single European market for goods and services. Patterns of trade in the UK have been examined, as well as the recent history of the balance of payments position. Exchange rates have been discussed, including an analysis of how businesses are affected by changes in the value of currencies. Finally, the role and the operation of multinational enterprises has been considered since MNEs are key players in the international market place.

## Case study

## The euro and the car industry in the UK

In January 1999 £1 sterling was worth 1.4236 euros; in July 2000 the value of the pound against the euro had risen to 1.6052 euros, an appreciation of 13 per cent. Figure 10.9 shows that the rise in the value of the pound has been consistent over the period with slight falls in July and August 1999 and more recently in May and June 2000. At the time of writing there was no sign that the strength of the pound would falter.

Many economic commentators have argued that the strong pound is having a detrimental effect on foreign direct investment in the UK, but as the text of the chapter shows there is little evidence of this yet in the overall FDI figures. What is undoubtedly true is that the manufacturing sector suffers at the hands of strong currencies.

The strong pound against the euro hits the car industry in particular since Europe is the world's largest car market – 16 million cars are sold each year in Europe against 12 million in the USA. As a result of the high exchange rate it becomes more difficult for companies to sell cars manufactured in the UK to the domestic market (since imported cars will be cheaper) or to sell them abroad (since high exchange rates make exports more expensive). The same is also true of the cost of components, and many car manufacturers are sourcing components from outside the UK to keep costs down. Any fall-off in investment has long-term implications for the car industry as plant becomes old, outdated and less productive. This contributed towards Ford's decision to close its Dagenham plant in May 2000.

Two of the three Japanese car producers present in the UK have warned that the strength of the pound might affect their future investment de-

**Figure 10.9 Exchange rate of sterling with the euro** (from Bank of England 2000 (internet))

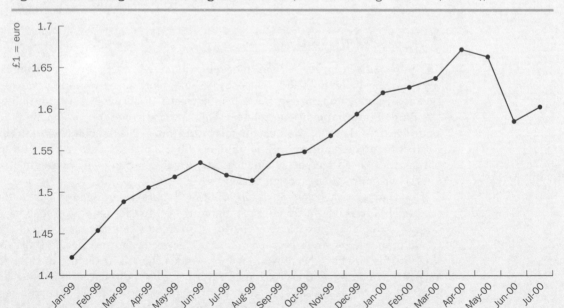

cisions. In July 2000, Nissan announced that the contract to produce the new Micra might be awarded to France instead of the UK because of the high value of the pound. Such a decision would affect the £150 million investment needed to facilitate production of the Micra. In August 2000, Toyota announced that its UK suppliers would be paid for all components in euros. This has the effects of shifting the risk of currency changes onto suppliers as their costs will be in sterling. Nissan and Honda have not followed suit as yet, but it is likely that they will. Given the importance of Europe for the world car industry, it is expected that the euro will become the world currency for car supplies in the same way that the aerospace industry costs in terms of dollars the whole world over.

There is evidence that many UK manufacturers are turning away from parts produced in the UK in an attempt to keep their costs down. It is only the decisions made by the big multinationals that make the headlines. Clearly such trends are disturbing for the manufacturing sector in general and the car industry in particular, but it is true that the manufacturing sector is not the whole economy. In terms of the stock of FDI in the UK, the car industry accounts for only £3 billion, while the financial services sector accounts for £35 billion. Even within the car industry itself, the picture is not clear, since in August 2000 Honda announced the building of a new factory in the UK and a doubling of output. Honda argues that investment decisions are long-term decisions which should not be based on currency levels which can easily and quickly change. In addition, the car industry is currently undergoing structural change on a world scale, so not all of the problems experienced by UK car manufacturers can be ascribed to the high exchange rate.

## Notes and references

1. Cecchini, P. (1988), *The European Challenge 1992: The Benefits of a Single Market*, Wildwood House, Aldershot.

2. See Chapter 13 of Worthington, I. and Britton, C. (1997), *The Business Environment*, 2nd edition, Pitman, London.

3. UNCTAD (1999), *World Investment Report*, UNCTAD, Geneva.

4. OECD (1999), *Measuring Globalisation: The Role of Multinationals in OECD Countries*, OECD, Paris.

5. Office for National Statistics (2000), *Survey of Current Business*, ONS, London.

6. Fontagné, L. (1999), *Foreign Direct Investment and International Trade: Complements or Substitutes?*, OECD, Paris.

7. See e.g. Dicken, P. (1998), *Global Shift: Transforming the World Economy*, 3rd edition, Paul Chapman, London.

8. OECD (1999).

## Review and discussion questions

1 For a business considering expansion into Europe, what methods of expansion are available?

2 Using demand and supply diagrams show the effects on the market for foreign exchange of the following:
- a decreased level of imports
- a fall in the rate of interest
- the development of a balance of payments surplus.

3 What is the likely effect on a system of fixed exchange rates of continued speculation on one of the member currencies?

4 Explain why businesses generally prefer fixed rather than floating exchange rates.

## Assignments

1 You work for a local chamber of commerce and have been asked to make a presentation to its members on the arguments for and against UK membership of the single European currency. The audience is likely to be mixed in its attitude to the single currency. Prepare this presentation anticipating and answering any possible questions the audience may have.

2 You work for a trade union in the hosiery industry which strongly supports the use of import restrictions to protect its workers from competition from countries where wage rates are much lower. You have been asked to take part in a debate on the issue by your local Conservative MP, who is a champion of the free market. Present a set of arguments that will counter any points that your opponent is likely to make.

## Further reading

Dicken, P. (1998), *Global Shift: Transforming the World Economy*, 3rd edition, Paul Chapman, London.

Ellis, J. and Williams, D. (1995), *International Business Strategy*, Pitman, London.

Griffiths, A. and Wall, S. (1999), *Applied Economics: An Introductory Course*, 8th edition, Longman, Harlow.

# CHAPTER 11

# Government and business

Ian Worthington

**Objectives**

1 To consider the broad rationale for government intervention in the economy.

2 To examine government intervention at a variety of spatial levels.

3 To investigate the rationale, background and implementation of key government policies which affect the business community.

4 To examine UK government attempts to nurture the small firms' sector.

5 To highlight the concept of a 'negotiated environment'.

## 11.1  Introduction

As we have seen, the essence of business activity is producing goods and services to satisfy consumer needs and wants. The previous sections of this book have focused on how in an economy firms (as suppliers) interact with individuals (as consumers) to bring about the allocation of scarce productive resources to satisfy society's demands. In what we have described as a market-based economic system there is, however, a third key actor which plays an influential role in resource allocation. That actor is the state or what we call here the 'government'. When we consider that in most advanced industrial economies government activity constitutes between 30 per cent and 40 per cent of a country's gross domestic product, it follows that the state and its agencies have a significant influence on private sector business organisations and on the markets in which they purchase their inputs and sell their output. In this and the following chapter we examine the interface between the public and the private sectors and, in particular, the way in which government policy decisions can impact on the operations of both firms and markets, whether by legislation and regulation or by influencing consumer behaviour.

## 11.2  An overview

As a prelude to examining the policy aspect of the business relationship it is useful to begin by recalling the various key roles that government can (and does) play in a modern economy. A typical list would include the following:

- consumer of resources (e.g. employer, landowner)
- supplier of resources (e.g. infrastructure, information/data)
- consumer of goods and services (e.g. via government spending)
- supplier of goods and services (e.g. nationalised industries)
- regulator of business activity (e.g. consumer laws, employment laws)
- redistributor of income and wealth (e.g. via the taxation system)
- promoter of economic development (e.g. via aid to industry)
- regulator of the economy (e.g. via fiscal and monetary policy).

Government, in other words, not only assists in the functioning of the private sector but is also a major business itself, with the unique capacity both to spend huge sums of money raised predominantly through taxation and the ability to pass laws and introduce policies that impact on the different sectors of the economy and/or on the economy as a whole.

But why should a government become involved at all in the operations of a market economy and in particular in the relationship between consumers and producers? Why not allow the free market to determine the most appropriate allocation of productive resources?

The answer to this question depends to a large extent on the person or organisation to whom it is addressed. An individual consumer, for example, might see the government largely as an agency for guaranteeing and protecting consumer rights; a firm is likely to be more interested in how the government manages the economy or creates a more competitive environment or stimulates innovation and enterprise. The government itself might justify intervention on all these grounds, as well as pursuing a number of normative goals such as a more equitable distribution of resources or protecting the weakest and most vulnerable members of society.

But how might an economist justify state intervention? The conventional reply offered by economists is that the market mechanism left to its own devices does not always deliver what might be described as the optimum solution to the problem of resource allocation. As we saw in Chapter 8, one of the key measures of performance of both firms and the economy is **economic efficiency,** which is deemed to be a characteristic of competitive markets.[1] To the extent that 'real' (as opposed to theoretical) markets may not always be efficient in either the technical or allocative sense they can be deemed to have failed. For many economists this idea of **market failure** provides a rationale for government intervention whether it be for economic and/or social reasons.[2]

The key areas of market failure are well known but are worth repeating here. Primary concerns include:

- the unwillingness of markets to produce goods and services which are either unprofitable or which it is not practical to provide through private means (i.e. **public goods** such as defence, social services, and so on);
- the likely under-provision of certain goods and services felt to be of general benefit to the community (i.e. **merit goods** such as education, libraries, and so on);
- the failure to take into account the external costs and benefits of production or consumption (i.e. **externalities** such as pollution, congestion, and so on which are discussed in Chapter 14);
- the danger of monopoly power if businesses can be freely bought and sold;

**market failure** the idea that left to their own devices markets sometimes fail to deliver desirable economic and/or social outcomes

**public goods** goods which, because they cannot be withheld from one person without withholding them from all, must be supplied communally, e.g. street lighting or defence

**merit goods** goods or services which the government feels are likely to be under-produced or under-consumed in a free market and which the government wishes to encourage

**externalities** side effects from economic choices that are not reflected in market prices, e.g. pollution

- the tendency for output to be determined and distributed on the ability to pay rather than on the basis of need or equity;
- the under-utilisation of economic resources (e.g. unemployment resulting from demand deficiency, new technology, or structural or frictional problems – see Chapter 12).

As the above list illustrates, governments not only seek to encourage (or discourage) different forms of consumption but they are also concerned with the broader questions of how the economy operates overall. Since the Great Depression of the 1930s, most economists and politicians have come to accept that market forces alone cannot be the sole determinant of the overall level of economic activity and that government intervention may be required from time to time to tackle problems such as inflation, unemployment, low growth or balance of payments crises. While views about the amount and type of state intervention have tended to vary over time and according to political persuasion, few have questioned the need for government action in the economy. The critical question, in short, is not whether an economic role for government should exist, but what that role should be and where the boundaries should be drawn between private and public (i.e. collective) action.

## 11.3    Levels of analysis

While all forms of government intervention in the economy invariably have direct or indirect consequences for business, it is possible to distinguish certain policies which are designed specifically to influence the industrial and commercial environment. These range from economy-wide approaches as in the case of government macroeconomic policy, to policies which are targeted at specific problems (e.g. anti-competitive practices) or groups (e.g. job creation measures) or areas (e.g. regional policy) or sectors (e.g. small firms' policies) within the economy. Many of the latter, more targeted policies are sometimes grouped together and described as **industrial policies**, though it is questionable whether in countries such as the United Kingdom historically such measures have ever amounted to a single and coherent policy for business.

**industrial policies**
government policies
designed to assist industry

In examining the policy dimension of the government/business interface, this chapter focuses on four specific policy areas, using UK experience to illustrate the various forms intervention can take. These are:

- privatisation policy
- competition policy
- regional policy
- small firms' policy.

It examines the rationale and background to each and identifies some of the key measures introduced by recent UK governments to achieve their objectives. It points in particular to the increasing level of intervention that is taking place at supranational level (e.g. within the European Union) to tackle such problems as anti-competitive practices and market structures. The broader question of government macroeconomic policy is discussed in Chapter 12.

## 11.4  Privatisation policy

### 11.4.1 Background

**public sector** the state or government sector of the economy

**centrally planned economies** an economic system in which the state makes most of the decisions on resource allocation. Also known as command economies

**free market economies** economic systems in which decisions on resource allocation are determined by market forces

**capitalist economies** economies based on the existence of private property and on the profit motive

**nationalisation** the process of bringing a firm or an industry under state ownership and control

In all countries whatever their economic and political systems, certain goods and services are provided by the state (i.e. the **public sector**). One of the main ways in which state provision has traditionally taken place is through public (i.e. state) ownership of productive assets, normally in key areas of the economy (e.g. energy, transport, telecommunications, the media). In **centrally planned economies** (e.g. Cuba), the degree of public ownership is substantial (though never total) and the private sector usually remains limited in size and influence. In contrast in **free market** or **capitalist economies**, ownership of the means of production, distribution and exchange lies predominantly in private hands, except for those areas of activity which the state (via the decisions of the governing authorities) chooses to **nationalise** and, in some cases, monopolise.

Government decisions on which assets the state should own (and/or acquire) is as much a political as it is an economic question and needs to be seen within the appropriate historical context. For example, in Britain the heyday of nationalisation was in the period 1945–51 when the new Labour government took into public ownership the coal, gas, electricity, rail and steel industries. Coming immediately after the end of a highly destructive World War, this was a time when the British government was seeking to rebuild the peacetime economy with the ultimate goal of achieving full employment and economic prosperity. Under what was then clause 4 of the Labour Party constitution, public ownership was seen as a desirable policy objective and one which would provide a Labour government with control over the 'commanding heights of the economy', thereby ensuring that the country's key strategic industries would receive the huge level of investment they needed in the immediate post-Second World War period.

Looking back at this point in history, it seems fair to suggest that economic justifications also added considerable weight to the government's political predispositions. Apart from the question of safeguarding vital industries and ensuring much-needed investment, nationalisation appeared to provide a means of guaranteeing that the general public would benefit from the huge economies of scale available to what were effectively natural monopolies. Through public ownership, it was felt that unnecessary duplication of assets could be avoided, costs lowered and efficiency increased, thereby potentially promising lower prices for consumers rather than monopoly profits for private individuals. Since the country's firms were also a major consumer of the output of these key industries, controlling factor input prices also promised to be of substantial benefit to the wider economy, particularly from a counter-inflationary point of view.

It ought to be said that these arguments are of more than merely historical interest, for they underline how fashions can change in economic thinking and how different economists can come to different conclusions about apparently the same situation. To most present-day economists, and the governments they advise, 'nationalisation' tends to be a dirty word and associated with higher costs, inefficiency, lack or absence of competition, under-investment and a stifling of enterprise. The private sector rather than the state is seen as the key to economic prosperity and wealth creation and **privatisation** as a means of shifting the balance away from public and towards private provision.[3]

### 11.4.2 The roots of privatisation policy

In its broadest sense 'privatisation' involves the transfer of assets or different forms of economic activity from the public to the private sector. In countries such as the United Kingdom this has taken a number of forms including:

- the sale of state-owned assets, especially nationalised industries (e.g. British Gas) or industries in which the government had a substantial share-holding, (e.g. BP);
- the contracting-out of services normally provided by the public sector (e.g. school meals, hospital cleaning);
- the deregulation or liberalisation of activities over which the state had previously placed some restriction (e.g. the deregulation of bus routes or postal services);
- the injection of private capital into areas traditionally financed by the public sector (e.g. the road system);
- the sale of local-authority-owned property to private citizens or organisations (e.g. council houses, school playing fields);
- the privatisation of government agencies (e.g. Her Majesty's Inspectors for Education).

Of these, the sale of state assets – particularly state-owned corporations or nationalised industries – has tended to be the one to evoke the most public and media interest and hence in the discussion below attention is focused on this aspect of privatisation policy.

To understand the case for 'privatisation' it is useful to return briefly to Chapter 7. Here it was suggested that, on the whole, in market structures which are uncompetitive (e.g. monopoly) firms had little (if any) incentive to be efficient, with the result that consumers face not only reduced choice but also higher prices than is likely to be the case in a competitive market. Competition, in effect, is seen to be the key to efficient resource allocation and a mechanism for protecting consumers from potential exploitation by producers.

**monetarism** an economic approach that generally believes that government intervention in the economy should be kept to a minimum

**Keynesianism** an economic approach based on the ideas of John Maynard Keynes who basically supported government intervention in the economy in pursuit of particular macroeconomic objectives

This belief in the virtue of competition and in the need to develop competitive market structures is a central theme in **monetarism**, an economic philosophy which has largely dominated official thinking in capitalist economies for much of the latter part of the twentieth century. Broadly speaking, monetarists argue that levels of output and employment in an economy are supply-determined, in contrast to the **Keynesian** view which emphasises the importance of demand in shaping economic activity. To the monetarist it follows that government economic policy in a capitalist economic system ought to be directed towards improving the output responsiveness of the economy, by focusing on the workings of markets and in particular on removing obstacles which prevent markets from functioning efficiently. One way of doing this is by reducing the state's involvement in business activity, most notably as a monopoly supplier and/or regulatory authority in key areas of economic life.

A good example of the interplay between economic theory and practice can be seen by examining privatisation policy in the UK in the period 1979–90. Under the leadership of Prime Minister Margaret Thatcher, the Conservative government of the day set about reducing the size and influence of the public sector in an effort to improve the supply side of the British economy. In addition to a sustained attempt at labour market reforms via legislation, the government embarked on a huge programme of divestment of state assets, which was subsequently emulated by many other countries (see below). Concepts such as 'rolling back the frontiers of the state' and 'selling the family silver' became part of everyday language and underlined the fundamental shift in economic thinking that had taken place from about the mid-1970s onwards.

The government's case for privatisation centred round the claim that the sale of state-owned businesses would improve their efficiency and general performance, and would give rise to increased competition that would broaden consumer choice. Under state control, it was argued that businesses had no incentive to strive for efficiency or to respond to consumer preferences, since many of them lacked any direct competition and all of them could turn to government for financial support if revenue was insufficient to meet operating costs. In contrast, firms which were exposed to the 'test' of the market would have to satisfy both the consumer and the financial markets if they were to survive or to avoid take over by more efficient and competitive organisations.

Allied to this argument was the proposition that privatisation would improve the performance of an organisation's management and workers. Freed from the need to meet objectives laid down by government, management could concentrate on commercial goals such as profitability, improved productivity and cost reduction, and on encouraging greater flexibility and technical innovation within the organisation. Implicit in these claims was the acceptance that a considerable degree of restructuring would need to occur within each privatised company and that this was likely to act as an incentive to the workforce to improve its performance. Additional encouragement was also expected to derive from the use of **employee share-ownership schemes**, under which current employees within a newly privatised company were offered a proportion of the equity, thus giving them a vested interest in the organisation's fortunes.

**employee share-ownership schemes**
schemes to provide employees of a company with shares in the organisation

**share-owning democracy**
the idea that a large number of a country's citizens have a stake of company shares

The sale of shares to employees and to the public generally was also presented as a benefit of privatisation in that it helped to encourage wider share ownership and to create a **share-owning democracy**, with increased sympathies towards capitalist modes of production (and possibly the Conservative Party!). Concomitantly, the sale of state assets also served to reduce the size of the public sector borrowing requirement – since revenue from sales was counted as negative public expenditure – and this helped to reduce the government's debt burden and to take some of the pressure off interest rates, as well as releasing funds for use by the private sector.

### 11.4.3 Privatisation in practice: UK experience

Privatisation has not been simply restricted to the leading capitalist economies: most countries irrespective of their size, ideology and level of economic development (including China, Spain, Jamaica, France, South Africa) have experimented with various forms of state divestment and deregulation

**transition economies**
those economies that are in
the process of changing
from being centrally planned
economies to being market-
based economies

and major privatisation programmes are currently underway in the so-called **transition economies**. Students wishing to find information on developments in a particular country can use as a starting point the very useful publications by Ernst and Young and PriceWaterhouse Cooper which are referred to in the latter part of Chapter 15.

As far as the UK is concerned a number of discernible phases can be identified in the privatisation process that has spanned the last two decades or so. In the first phase, between 1979 and 1983, government asset sales tended to generate relatively small sums of money compared with later years and generally involved the sale of government shares in companies such as British Aerospace, Britoil, BP, ICL and Ferranti. Between 1983 and 1988, the government disposed of a number of its largest industrial and commercial undertakings, including British Telecom, British Gas and British Airways, along with Rolls-Royce and Jaguar. These were followed by the sale of British Steel and the Rover Group, the National Bus Company and, more significantly, by the regional water authorities and the electricity industry in the late 1980s and early 1990s. In the most recent phase, major sales have included British Coal, British Rail, the flotation of the National Grid and the privatisation of the nuclear industry.

In disposing of its assets the government used a number of different methods including selling shares to a single buyer, usually another company (e.g. the sale of Rover); selling shares to the company's management and workers (e.g. the management buy-out of the National Freight Corporation); selling shares on the open market for purchase by individuals and institutions (e.g. the stock market flotation of British Telecom). In some cases the process took place in several stages, as a proportion of shares was released onto the market over several years (e.g. BP); in other cases a one-off sale occurred, with investors invited to subscribe for the whole of the equity (e.g. British Steel). As Figure 11.1 indicates, proceeds from privatisation sales between 1979 and 1991 exceeded £34 billion, with most of the revenue being raised in the mid- to late 1980s. Estimates for the period 1991–94 suggest that privatisation yielded a further £25–30 billion for the Exchequer. According to the Office of National Statistics, between 1984 and 1996 privatisation revenues were equal to around 1–2 per cent per annum of GDP.

A further and paradoxical feature of the UK privatisation programme was the development of a regulatory system to oversee certain aspects of the operations of the newly privatised utilities in telecommunications, gas, water and electricity. Faced with the problem of how to regulate the behaviour of firms which provided vital services and which had been given a significant amount of monopoly power, the government set up a number of **regulatory agencies** to consider issues such as pricing and levels of service (see Table 11.1). By acting as a kind of proxy for competition, the regulatory system was intended to protect the consumer from possible monopoly abuse until true competition could be introduced into the industry. Opinions are divided on how effective this system has proved in practice, particularly since the incoming Labour government in 1997 decided to levy a special tax on the windfall profits of the privatised utilities to help fund its New Deal programme.

**Figure 11.1  Proceeds from privatisation**

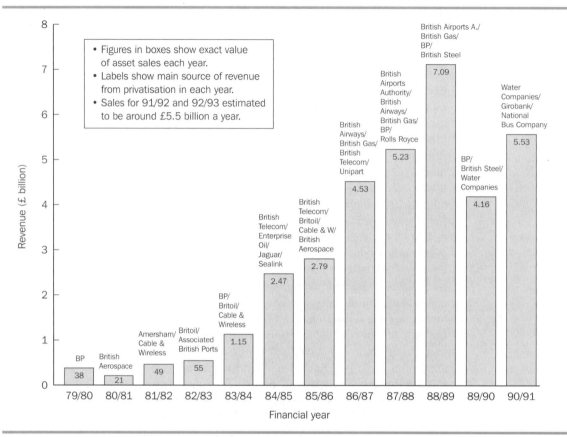

*Source:* Cook, G. C., *Privatisation in the 1980s and 1990s*, Hidcote Press, 1992.

**Table 11.1  Regulatory bodies for key privatised utilities**

| Name | Date established | Main activities |
|---|---|---|
| Office of telecommunications (OFTEL) | 1984 | Regulates BT – especially line rentals, inland calls, overseas calls; provides conditions for new entrants; licenses new forms of service; regulates equipment market. |
| Office of Gas Supply (OFGAS) | 1986 | Regulates gas supplies to domestic users – including average price per therm. |
| Office of Water (OFWAT) | 1989 | Regulates domestic and non-domestic supply by water and sewerage companies. Regulates price increases to customers. |
| Office of Electricity Regulation (OFFER) | 1990 | Regulates prices of transmission distribution and supply to regional electricity companies and overall electricity costs for smaller customers. |

### 11.4.4 Assessment

Has privatisation in the UK proved successful and/or beneficial?

Viewed from a stakeholder point of view there have clearly been some discernible benefits. The government, for example, has received substantial revenues from the sales of public assets and from increased profits taxes and has removed utility borrowing requirements from the public sector.[4] Customers are said to have gained from an improved level of services (in most cases) and from lower prices, while many shareholders in privatised utility stocks have made windfall gains from share transactions. As for employees in privatised companies the evidence is somewhat ambiguous: a substantial number lost their jobs in the run-up to privatisation and of those who remained the main 'gainers' in terms of salary and other benefits appear to have been senior executives rather than ordinary personnel (e.g. the controversy over the salary increases of the heads of privatised utilities).

Measured against some of the government's stated (or apparent) objectives, a number of studies have suggested that privatisation has helped to:

- improve the supply side of the economy (e.g. Oulton 1995; Crafts 1998)
- increase efficiency in many privatised industries (e.g. Martin and Parker 1997)
- promote wider share ownership (e.g. Ernst and Young 1994)
- benefit the public finances (e.g. NERA 1996)
- produce gains in consumer welfare (e.g. Miller 1995).[5]

However, as indicated elsewhere, findings such as these are by no means unequivocal and any evaluation tends to be fraught with conceptual and methodological difficulties (see e.g. Worthington and Britton 2000). In the last analysis, we may be tempted to argue that the greatest impact of the privatisation programme has proved to be at a cultural level: in promoting the idea of the superiority of private enterprise. If emulation is the sincerest form of flattery, then the number of countries following the UK's lead in selling off state assets suggests that promoting free enterprise may have been one of the country's most significant exports over recent years.

## 11.5 Competition policy

### 11.5.1 Why intervene?

As previous chapters have indicated, large firms can often achieve economies of scale which may benefit the consumer in the form of reduced prices. At the same time scale economies represent an important barrier to entry which can restrict competition in a market, thereby helping to reduce consumer choice, and, in some cases, allowing firms to make abnormal profits. To proponents of the idea of 'contestable markets', it is entry barriers rather than market structure which are the key to consumer exploitation and this provides a rationale for government intervention to promote greater competition. A contrary view is that there is little, if any, need for government to intervene in markets since consumers will ultimately benefit from market dominance if high profits help to increase the speed of technical innovation and encourage some firms to be efficient *vis-à-vis* their competitors.[6]

For policy-makers seeking to promote free markets, the question of government intervention raises an important philosophical issue. If goods and services and resources should be freely traded, why should firms not be allowed to buy and sell other firms free from government control and regulation? For most political decision-makers the answer to this problem lies in the previously mentioned idea of **market failure** – the need to intervene to reduce or prevent undesirable economic and/or social consequences emanating from free market operations. For most people the question is not 'whether' to intervene but 'when' and 'how'; should it be discretionary or non-discretionary? That being the case, government intervention in the form of competition policy is as much a political as it is an economic problem and one which is subject to external as well as national influences.

---

**Mini case**    **UK car prices**

It has long been known that on the whole the price of new cars in the UK is higher than their equivalent in other parts of Europe (see e.g. Worthington and Britton 2000, pp. 76–7). Price comparisons compiled by the European Commission in November 1999, for example, indicated that on certain models UK manufacturers' list prices could be between 40 per cent and 60 per cent higher than in the cheapest EU country. Inevitably, claims that UK consumers were being overcharged led to an investigation by the UK competition authorities which was asked to examine the relationship between car makers and their exclusive dealerships. For many observers, including the Consumers' Association, this was a case where government intervention into the operation of markets was wholly justified.

Published in the early part of 2000, the Competition Commission's report upheld the view that UK private motorists were on average paying around 10 per cent more for their vehicles than their counterparts in countries such as France, Germany and Italy. According to the Director General of Fair Trading the overall cost of this differential to UK private car buyers could be as much as £1 billion a year.

The report highlighted the selective and exclusive distribution system – under which all new cars are sold through manufacturers' franchised dealerships – as the root of the problem. It suggested that such a system gave the car manufacturers excessive power to influence the market and should ideally be abolished. Responding to the report's findings, the Trade and Industry Secretary promised a number of new measures designed to reduce car prices and to stimulate competition (see e.g. the *Guardian,* 11 April 2000) in the UK car market. He also indicated that he intended to press the European Commission to remove the European block exemption mechanism which governs car distribution within the European Union. This mechanism – which was renewed for seven years in 1995 – gives the car industry exemption from the competition provisions within the Treaty of Rome and permits car manufacturers to sell vehicles solely through their own dealer networks.

Current evidence suggests (see e.g. the *Guardian*, 12 May, 2000, p. 27) that the EU Competition Commissioner is favourably disposed to ending the block exemption scheme after 2002 in the hope of bringing more competition and price transparency into the European car market. Whether he ultimately succeeds in bringing about significant market reforms is likely to be as much a political as an economic problem. It would be wrong to under-estimate the power of the multinational car manufacturers to influence the decision of the EU competition authorities. Whatever the outcome, this is likely to have an important bearing on what happens in the UK car market.

### 11.5.2 UK competition policy: the evolving legislative framework

Whereas privatisation has focused on the balance between public and private provision within the overall economy, UK government competition policy has largely been concerned with regulating market behaviour and in particular with controlling potential abuses of market power by firms acting singly or in concert in specific markets. To achieve these aims, successive British governments have relied mainly on legislation, as well as on a measure of self-regulation and persuasion, and have generally taken a more liberal view of market structures than in the United States, where monopolies have been deemed illegal for over a century. This legislative framework to regulate market activity, and the institutional arrangements established to support it, are considered below.

Official attempts to control market behaviour through statutory means date back to the late 1940s with the passage of the Monopolies and Restrictive Practices Act 1948. This Act, which established the Monopolies Commission (later the Monopolies and Mergers Commission), empowered it to investigate industries in which any single firm (a **unitary monopoly**), or a group of firms acting together, could restrict competition by controlling at least one-third of the market. Following such an investigation, the Commission would publish a report which was either factual or advisory and it was then the responsibility of the relevant government department to decide what course of action, if any, to take to remove practices regarded as contrary to the public interest. In the event, the majority of the Commission's recommendations tended to be ignored, though it did have some success in highlighting the extent of monopoly power in the United Kingdom in the early post-war period.

**unitary monopoly** where a single firm can restrict competition in a market by holding a significant market share

In 1956 investigations into unitary monopolies were separated from those into **restrictive practices** operated by a group of firms, with the enactment of the Restrictive Trade Practices Act. This Act, which outlawed the widespread custom of manufacturers jointly enforcing the retail prices at which their products could be sold, also required firms to register any form of restrictive agreement that they were operating (e.g. concerning prices, sales, production) with the Registrar of Restrictive Practices. It was the latter's responsibility to bring such agreements before the Restrictive Practices Court and they were automatically deemed 'against the public interest' unless they could be justified in one of a number of ways (e.g. benefiting consumers, employment, exports). Further extensions to the Act in 1968 (to cover 'information agreements') and in 1973 (to cover services) were ultimately consolidated in the Restrictive Practices Act 1976. This new Act vested the responsibility for

**restrictive practices** agreements between traders that are not felt to be in the public interest

bringing restrictive practices before the court in the recently established Director General of Fair Trading (see below).

A further extension of legislative control came with passage of the Monopolies and Mergers Act 1965. The Act allowed the Monopolies Commission to investigate actual or proposed mergers or acquisitions which looked likely to enhance monopoly power and which involved at that time the takeover of assets in excess of £5 million. The aim of the Act was to provide a means of regulating activities which threatened to be contrary to the public interest, by permitting government to decide which mergers and acquisitions should be prohibited and which should be allowed to proceed and, if necessary, under what terms. Additional steps in this direction were taken with the passage of the Fair Trading Act 1973 and the Competition Act 1980, the main provisions of which are summarised below.

- A scale monopoly exists where at least 25 per cent of a market is controlled by a single buyer or seller; this can be applied to sales at local as well as national level and can include monopolies resulting from nationalisation.
- Investigations can occur when two related companies (e.g. a parent and a subsidiary) control 25 per cent of a market or when separate companies operate to restrict competition even without a formal agreement (e.g. tacit collusion).
- Mergers involving gross world-wide assets over £70 million or a market share over 25 per cent can be investigated.

Responsibility for overseeing consumer affairs, and competition policy generally, lies with the Director General of Fair Trading (DGFT), operating from the Office of Fair Trading (OFT). The DGFT has the power to make monopoly references to the renamed Monopolies and Mergers Commission (MMC) and to advise the relevant government minister on whether merger proposals should be investigated by the MMC.

In the latter context, it is worth noting that while there was no legal obligation for companies to inform OFT of their merger plans, the Companies Act 1989 introduced a formal procedure enabling them to pre-notify the DGFT of merger proposals, in the expectation that such pre-notification would enhance the prospects for rapid clearance in cases which are deemed straightforward.

While the question of market share still remains an important influence on official attitudes to proposed mergers or takeovers, there is no doubt that in recent years increasing attention has focused on anti-competitive practices and under the Competition Act 1980 such practices by individuals or firms – as opposed to whole markets – could be referred to the MMC for investigation. In addition the Act allowed the Commission to scrutinise the work of certain public sector agencies and to consider the efficiency and costs of the service they provided and any possible abuses of monopoly power, and similar references could also be made in the case of public utilities which had been privatised (e.g. under the Telecommunication Act 1984, the Gas Act 1986, the Water Industry Act 1991).

Additional statutory control also comes in the form of EU legislation governing activities which have cross-border implications. Article 85 of the Treaty of Rome prohibits agreements between enterprises which result in a restriction or distortion in competition within the Union (e.g. price-fixing, market-sharing). Article 86 prohibits a dominant firm, or group of firms, from using their market power to exploit consumers; while Articles 92–4 prohibit the provision of government subsidies if they distort, or threaten to distort, competition between industries or individual firms.

Moreover, under Regulation 4064/89 which came into force in September 1990, concentrations or mergers which have a 'Community dimension' have become the subject of exclusive jurisdiction by the European Commission. Broadly speaking, this means that mergers involving firms with a combined worldwide turnover of more than five billion ECU are subject to Commission control, provided that the EU turnover of each of at least two companies involved exceeds 250 million ECU and the companies concerned do not have more than two-thirds of their EU turnover within one and the same member state. Mergers which do not qualify under the regulation remain, of course, subject to national competition law.

In the most recent phase of evolution the UK government has acted to bring UK competition policy into line with EU law under the Competition Act 1998 – which came into force on 1 March 2000. Two basic prohibitions have been introduced: (1) a prohibition of anti-competitive agreements, based closely on Article 85 of the Treaty of Rome, (2) a prohibition of abuse of dominant position in a market, based on Article 86. These prohibitions which replace a number of other pieces of legislation (e.g. the Restrictive Trade Practices Act 1976; the Resale Prices Act 1976; most of the Competition Act 1980) will be enforced primarily by the DGFT, together with the utility regulators who will have concurrent powers in their own sphere of operations. Companies breaching either or both of the prohibitions will be liable to fines and may be required to pay compensation to third parties affected by their anti-competitive behaviour.

<table>
<tr><td>Mini case</td><td>**The law and competition**</td></tr>
</table>

In market-based economies governments are keen to promote competition and, where necessary, to prevent apparent abuses of market power. Legislation to regulate the operation of firms and markets is a common feature of capitalist economies and can be invoked when a situation appears to be against the interest of consumers and/or competitors.

In a recent highly-publicised case (April 2000) a US district court judge ruled that Microsoft had abused its hold on personal computer operating systems in violation of US anti-trust laws. In essence the judge argued that Microsoft's bundling of its internet browser with Windows – which is used on more than 90 per cent of the world's PC's – was a violation of legislation which had been designed to curb monopolistic power. Prior to the judgement Microsoft had faced investigations into its position in the software market and a number of law suits claiming that it was in breach of anti-trust laws. In accepting the arguments put forward by the federal and a number of state governments, District Judge Thomas Jackson ultimately ruled against Microsoft, following attempts to reach a settlement through an independent mediator.

The uncertainty over possible further lawsuits and demands for changes in the future shape of the organisation has had an impact on Microsoft's share price but as yet it remains unclear what the final out-

▶

come of the judgement will be. Some economists have argued that technological monopolies tend to have relatively short lives as new companies
rise up to challenge them, so there may be no real need to take action to
promote competition. Others claim that breaking up an organisation like
Microsoft into competing units is likely to prove beneficial for both the consumer and the company itself, by encouraging the release of innovative
forces currently tied up in a dominant organisation. The future – including
(possibly) the result of the US presidential election in November 2000 –
will decide which of these two views will hold sway.

### 11.5.3 The institutional framework

The formulation and implementation of UK competition policy involves a variety of agencies including the Department of Trade and Industry, the Office of
Fair Trading, the Monopolies and Mergers Commission and the Mergers
Panel. Of these, the MMC (now the Competition Commission) and OFT
deserve special attention.

From its foundation in 1948 until its replacement in 1999, the Monopolies
and Mergers Commission remained a statutory body, independent of government both in the conduct of its inquiries and in its conclusions which were
published in report form. Funded by the DTI, the Commission had a full-time
chairperson, and around 35 other part-time members, three of whom were
deputy chairpeople and all of whom were appointed by the Secretary of State
for Trade and Industry. Such appointments normally lasted for three years at
the outset and included individuals drawn from business, the professions, the
trade unions and the universities. To support the work of the appointed members, the Commission had a staff of about 80 officials, two-thirds of whom it
employed directly, with the remainder being on loan from government departments (especially the DTI) and increasingly from the private sector.

It is important to note that the Commission had no legal power to initiate
its own investigations; instead, references – requests for it to carry out particular inquiries – came from either the Secretary of State for Trade and
Industry, the Director General of Fair Trading, or from the appropriate regulator in the case of privatised industries and the broadcasting media. Where a
possible merger reference was concerned, the initial evaluation of a proposal
was made by a panel of civil servants (the Mergers Panel) who considered
whether the merger should be referred to the MMC for further consideration.
The decision then rested with the Secretary of State, who took advice from the
Director General of Fair Trading before deciding whether the proposal should
be investigated or should be allowed to proceed.

Under the legislation, references to the Commission could be made on a
number of grounds. As indicated above, these included not only monopoly and
merger references but also references concerned with the performance of
public sector bodies and privatised industries and with anti-competitive practices by individual firms (i.e. competition references). In addition, the
Commission was empowered to consider general references (involving practices in industry), restrictive labour practices and references under the

Broadcasting Act 1990, as well as questions of proposed newspaper mergers, where special provisions apply.

On receipt of a reference, the Commission's chairman appointed a small group of members to carry out the relevant inquiry and to report on whether the company (or companies) concerned was operating – or could be expected to operate – against the public interest. Supported by a team of officials, and in some cases including members appointed to specialist panels (e.g. newspaper, telecommunications, water and electricity), the investigating group gathered a wide range of written and oral evidence from both the party or parties concerned and from others likely to have an interest in the outcome of the inquiry. In reaching its conclusions, which tended to take several months, the group had to take into account the 'public interest', as defined under Section 84 of the Fair Trading Act 1973, which stressed the importance of competition, the protection of consumer interests and the need to consider issues related to employment, trade and the overall industrial structure. While in most references issues relating to competition were the primary concern, the Commission was able to take wider public interest issues into account and could rule in favour of a proposal on these grounds, even if the measure appeared anti-competitive.

The culmination of the Commission's enquiry was its report which, in most cases, was submitted to the Secretary of State for consideration and was normally laid before Parliament, where it often formed the basis of a debate or parliamentary questions. In the case of monopoly references judged to be against the public interest, the Secretary of State – with the advice of the DGFT – decided on an appropriate course of action which could involve an order to prevent or remedy the particular adverse effects identified by the Commission. In the case of merger references, a similar procedure occurred in the event of an adverse judgement by the Commission. The Secretary of State, however, was not bound to accept the Commission's recommendations; nor was he or she able to overrule the conclusion that a merger does not operate, or may be expected not to operate, against the public interest.

It is important to note that at all stages of this multistage process a considerable degree of lobbying occurred by the various interested parties, either in an attempt to influence the outcome of the investigations or the subsequent course of action decided upon. Moreover, considerable pressure tended to occur, even before a decision was taken as to whether or not to make a reference to the MMC. As a number of recent cases have shown, lobbying *against* a reference can represent a key step in justifying a proposed merger. By the same token, lobbying *for* a reference has tended to become an important weapon used by companies wishing to resist an unwelcome takeover, particularly where matters of public interest appear paramount.

With the passage of the Competition Act 1998, the MMC has been replaced (on 1 April 1999) by the Competition Commission, a public body which has taken on the MMC's former reporting role and which will also hear appeals against decisions made under the prohibition provisions of the new legislation. The chairperson (full-time) and members (part-time) of the Commission are appointed and – as in the case of the MMC – will be drawn from a variety of backgrounds and will initially serve for a period of three years. Organised into a series of panels, the Commission will be supported by a staff of about 90 which will include administrators, specialists and individuals engaged in support services. Most of these will be direct employees; the remainder will be seconded from government departments.

Turning very briefly to the Office of Fair Trading, this is a non-ministerial government department headed by a Director General, who is appointed by the Secretary of State for Trade and Industry. Under the Fair Trading Act 1973, the DGFT was given the responsibility of overseeing consumer affairs as well as competition policy and this includes administering various pieces of consumer legislation, including the Consumer Credit Act 1974 and the Estates Agents Act 1979. In carrying out his or her responsibilities in both these areas, the Director General is supported by a team of administrative, legal, economic and accountancy staff and has a Mergers Secretariat to co-ordinate the Office's work in this field.

With regard to competition policy, the OFT's duties were originally governed primarily by the Fair Trading Act and the Competition Act 1980; in addition, under the Restrictive Trade Practices Act 1976 the Director General had responsibility for bringing cases of restrictive practices before the Restrictive Practices Court. With the passage of the Competition Act 1998, the new prohibition regime is to be applied and enforced by the DGFT, and the OFT is to be given additional resources to root out cartels and restrictive behaviour. The legislation gives the Director General considerable powers to investigate if he/she has a reasonable suspicion that either of the prohibitions is being infringed. Under certain circumstances the DGFT can also grant exemptions from the scope of the two prohibitions and may be called upon to defend her/his decisions before the Competition Commission.

## 11.6 Spatial policies

### 11.6.1 The spatial dimension of business activity

Firms have a spatial and temporal as well as a legal existence. Over time their success or failure as economic units can have implications not only for different stakeholder groups (e.g. employees, suppliers, investors) but also for the geographical area in which a particular enterprise (and possibly that of its suppliers) is located. As economic history readily demonstrates, factors as varied as changing demands, new technology, demography and cultural change can affect the fortunes of a country's business organisation and can ultimately help to alter its **industrial structure**, with some firms and industries and sectors growing and developing while others are facing decline and possibly extinction.

The spatial consequences of structural change are easy to imagine: within an economy over time one would expect to see patterns of unequal development, with some areas prospering in economic, social and environmental terms (e.g. jobs, income, infrastructural development) while others are experiencing less favourable conditions. This being the case, it is reasonable to ask whether a government should intervene to correct any spatial imbalance that might occur within the economy and if so how this intervention might occur.

### 11.6.2 Is government intervention necessary?

As previous sections have illustrated, economists tend to be divided over the question of state intervention in the workings of the market economy. Free marketers generally argue that in a dynamic economy problems such as spatial disparities in income, output and employment are usually short-term and will eventually be corrected by market forces, as firms and individuals acting rationally seek to improve their positions within the economy (see Figure 11.2). For the firm, for example, an area with high unemployment and lower wage costs (area A) will be commercially attractive and this will cause businesses to migrate to such locations in search of cheaper labour.[7] At the same time individuals will tend to be keen to improve their job and wage prospects by moving to a more prosperous area (area B), which results in an outward migration of labour. On the assumption that both labour and capital are perfectly mobile, spatial disparities should logically start to disappear as the prosperous area (area B) experiences rising unemployment and falling wages while the less prosperous area (area A) finds both employment and wage levels rising. Given time and perfect mobility, the free market view is that the economies of different localities will tend to converge, making government intervention unnecessary.

The counter view calls into question free market assumptions of rationality and factor mobility, based on observations of behaviour in the real world. Whatever their current job prospects some individuals may be unwilling or unable to move to another locality because of social ties or the cost of moving or inappropriate skills or a lack of knowledge of job opportunities. Firms similarly may be reluctant to relocate because of the costs involved or the preferences of the owner(s) or some other imperfection in the market place. This being the case, pro-interventionists question the degree to which convergence will occur as a result of labour and capital migration and generally support government action to enhance the workings of the market mech-anisms. Some economists go even further, arguing that government intervention may be necessary to prevent a growing divergence between localities that stems essentially from market forces. Under this view, the more prosperous areas are likely to act as a magnet for successful firms and the best elements of the labour force, leaving the disadvantaged localities with fewer jobs, less income, less output, fewer resources and a decaying infrastructure, thereby perpetuating a downward spiral of decline. To the proponents of this view, nothing short of purposive government action to counteract the market is likely to arrest this cumulative divergence between localities.

**Figure 11.2 The migration of firms and employees**

### 11.6.3 The when and how of intervention

If one accepts the case for government intervention, then three main questions arise: (1) in what situation is government intervention necessary? (2) at what level does and should this intervention take place? (3) what form(s) should it take? These three questions are considered in this and the subsequent sections of this chapter.

With regard to question 1 it is probably fair to say that there is a general consensus on when a situation of spatial imbalance becomes a 'problem' requiring a governmental response. In essence areas which are significantly and persistently under-performing on a range of socio-economic indicators (especially unemployment, income and growth), compared to the national average, tend to be designated 'problem areas' recommending themselves for governmental action. As most of the data on which decisions are made are routinely collected by government agencies, regular comparisons can be made in performance between different locations and where necessary adjustments made in government policy and/or implementation over time.

The question of the appropriate level of governmental intervention is arguably more contentious, but in effect the choices boil down to three main possibilities: supranational, national and sub-national (e.g. regional and/or local). What happens in any particular country tends to be dictated largely by history, politics and constitutional arrangements and these can change over time. In the United Kingdom, for instance, the absence (until recently) of a regional system of government has meant that the focus of governmental action has traditionally been at national and local level, with national government responsible for regional aspects of policy and for delegating authority to local government to promote local economic development. With the UK's membership of the European Union, policy and action after 1972 also became subject to supranational influence and support under a system currently (2000) undergoing reform. It remains to be seen how far structural reform of funding within the EU and the move towards greater regional devolution of power within the UK will affect the locus of decision-making in the future.

As far as methods of intervention are concerned, a variety of possibilities exist, ranging from grant aid to businesses to stimulate investment and growth to schemes to promote enterprise through the deregulation of business or the creation of a favourable fiscal climate. In the United Kingdom such schemes have largely formed the core of what have become known as **regional policy** and **urban policy**: in effect the spatial targeting of aid to sub national areas which are designated as requiring government assistance. It is to these two forms of government intervention that we now turn.

**regional policy**
government policies designed to reduce regional disparities in income, wealth, unemployment, etc.

### 11.6.4 UK regional policy

A region is a geographical area that possesses certain characteristics (e.g. political, economic, physical) which give it a measure of unity that allows boundaries to be drawn round it, thus differentiating it from surrounding areas. In the United Kingdom the standard planning regions have traditionally been the North, North-West, Yorkshire/Humberside, East Midlands, West Midlands, South-West, East Anglia, South-East, Wales, Scotland and Northern Ireland. Each of these is further divided into sub-regions based on administrative counties and on designated metropolitan areas. These planning regions and sub-regions form the units of classification for a wide range of official government statistics.

The idea of providing government assistance to particular areas of the country experiencing substantial economic and/or social problems can be traced back to the 1930s when the incumbent government first began to provide help to a number of depressed areas in the form of low-interest loans, subsidised rents and the establishment of government trading estates. Over the next 50 years the system gradually evolved into one in which central government delineated a number of types of **assisted area** which became eligible for regional assistance. Figure 11.3 indicates the main types of assisted area in mainland UK from 1993 to 2000, the majority of which were in the north and the west and largely

**assisted area**  a part of the country designated for government assistance under government regional policy

**Figure 11.3  Assisted areas from August 1993 (DTI).** (Crown copyright is reproduced with the permission of HMSO)

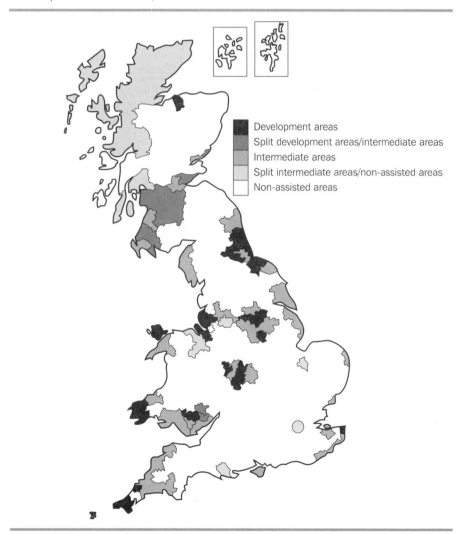

corresponded with the older industrial conurbations (e.g. Manchester, Liverpool, Glasgow, South Wales). Under new rules published by the European Commission in early 1999 all member states were required to revise their assisted areas maps by 1 January 2000. The new guidelines have essentially meant a reduction in the areas eligible for regional industrial assistance as the EU undergoes a process of enlargement.

Over the last decade the main focus of government regional policy has been on business creation and expansion, with the Department of Trade and Industry providing two main forms of grant assistance which have been administered by the regional government offices.

### Regional Selective Assistance (RSA)

This is a discretionary form of assistance available to businesses of all sizes which reside in or are planning to set up in development and intermediate areas. Designed to help with investment projects in manufacturing and some service sectors that might not otherwise go ahead, RSA is the main form of regional aid available to firms to find plant and machinery and associated project costs (e.g. professional fees, site preparation). To be eligible for assistance, businesses must demonstrate that a proposed project is viable, creates or safeguards employment, makes a contribution to both the regional and the national economy and needs assistance to proceed in its present form. The expectation is that firms will find most of the finance from their own or other private sector sources and hence grants are negotiated as the minimum necessary to ensure a project proceeds.

### Regional Enterprise Grants

This is a scheme specially designed to help small firms to get started, modernise, expand or diversify. Under this scheme, two types of discretionary assistance were originally available for viable projects:

- *Regional Investment Grants* for manufacturing and some service sectors under which the government paid 15 per cent of the costs of fixed assets (to a maximum of £15,000 in 1996) for firms in development areas with no more than 25 employees which could demonstrate a need for assistance. Grants were also available in localities affected by colliery closure and businesses could gain assistance under a number of European programmes (e.g. the European Union Programme for Shipbuilding – called RENAVAL).
- *Regional Innovation Grants* under which the government paid 50 per cent of the costs of development and introduction of new or improved processes (to a maximum of £25,000 in 1996). To be eligible a firm had to have no more than 50 employees and the project had to take place in development, intermediate, Task Force, City Challenge or European Commission Objective 2 areas or in certain Scottish inner urban areas eligible for assistance.

Regional Enterprise Grants are now only available in the East and West Midlands coal closure areas which fall outside the assisted area. Regional Innovation Grants are available throughout Wales to encourage the development of new products and processes.

Firms in assisted areas and Urban Programme areas (see below) have also been able to approach the DTI for help with the arrangement and costs of consultancy projects in fields such as design, marketing, quality, business planning, manufacturing and services systems, and the government has contributed up to two-thirds of the costs as long as a firm has fewer than 500 employees. In addition, through membership of the European Union, United Kingdom businesses have access to EU funds, particularly from the European Regional Development Fund (ERDF) which was established in 1975. Using money from the EU provides finance for regional support with the expectation that funds will be used to supplement a government's existing package of regional aid. Understandably most of these funds tend to go to the EU's poorer regions in southern Europe, although the United Kingdom has also benefited from such funding, particularly in the declining industrial areas.

**European Structural Funds** European Union funding arrangements designed to support investment in infrastructure, industry and agriculture in the less well-developed regions of Europe

It should be noted that the ERDF is one element of **European Structural Funds** which are designed to support investment in infrastructure, industry and agriculture in the less-developed regions of Europe. As Table 11.2 indicates, within the ERDF funds have been targeted at particular problems of structural decline (e.g. industrial decline, rural depopulation etc.). Of the six so-called objective areas, three have been identified for regional enterprise initiatives (Objective 1, 2, 5b) and additional funds are frequently available under specific Community initiatives, tailored to alleviate specific problems or to meet certain needs (e.g. RECHAR programmes in declining coal mining areas; LEADER funding for areas of rural decline). In total the amount available under EU Structural Funds in the period 1995–99 was estimated to be ECU141 billion. Under the Agenda 2000 negotiations the scale of future funding and areas of eligibility are currently being discussed and argued over by member states.

Despite the variety of policy instruments it is clear that the extent of regional assistance has been significantly reduced since 1979, in terms of both the amount of resources committed to the programme and the areas receiving

**Table 11.2  European structural funds**

| Fund | Main focus | Typical support |
|---|---|---|
| European Regional Development Fund | Redevelopment and structural adjustment of less-developed and declining industrial regions. Funds are concentrated in: (a) least-favoured regions (Objective 1 areas); (b) regions/areas suffering industrial decline (Objective 2); (c) rural areas (Objective 5b). | Industrial investment Infrastructure Local initiatives Environmental |
| European Social Fund | Funding for organisations running vocational training schemes and job creation. Responsibility for implementing Objectives 3 and 4. | Schemes which have funding from a public authority. |
| European Agricultural Guidance and Guarantee Fund | Funding designed to guarantee farm incomes within the EU and to guide farm production. | Support for farm agricultural prices and to encourage farm rationalisation. |

assistance. Moreover, aid has increasingly been targeted at small and medium-sized enterprises and has been progressively extended to include service as well as manufacturing industries. In part these changes represent a desire by successive governments to control public expenditure and to reduce the influence of the state in the working of the market economy by withdrawing from some areas of public support for industry. At the same time, government attempts to encourage 'enterprise' and to attract more private sector funding into business development has given rise to a number of new forms of government intervention aimed specifically at urban or inner city areas. This spatially selective approach to business creation and expansion has become known as 'urban policy'.

### 11.6.5 UK urban policy

**urban policy** government policy aimed at tackling urban problems

**Urban policy** focuses on those inner-city and urban areas which have experienced progressive decay and decline, largely as a result of long-term shifts in employment and population. This 'problem', with its disproportionate effects on the low-paid, unskilled and ethnic members of the population, first came to prominence in the 1960s and gave rise to an urban programme aimed predominantly at funding capital projects and education schemes in deprived inner-city locations. Working in partnership with the local authorities, the government's aim under the programme was to channel central government funds into projects designed to regenerate economic activity (e.g. by land clearance) and meet social needs (e.g. by providing community facilities for deprived groups) in designated urban areas. This role was further enhanced by the Inner Urban Areas Act (1978) which conferred wide powers on certain local authorities to assist industry wherever a need was felt to exist and where government help was seen to be appropriate. Central to the government's strategy was its attempt to regenerate inner-city areas through capital investment and through environmental improvement, some of which was to be funded from the private sector. To encourage private sector investment, local authorities in the designated areas were allowed to declare industrial and commercial improvement areas and to give financial assistance to companies which located in such areas.

With the election of the Conservative government in 1979, a number of new initiatives were introduced which indicated a move towards an even more spatially selective policy for urban areas. These initiatives – which included Enterprise Zones, Urban Development Corporations, free ports and City Action Teams (see Table 11.3) – frequently bypassed local authorities or reduced their powers over the allocation of resources and/or land use, and were seen by many commentators as a vote of no confidence in local government's ability to stimulate urban regeneration. At the heart of the new approach lay an attempt by central government to turn inner-city areas into investment opportunities for the private sector by clearing dereliction and improving infrastructure. The basic idea, as the *Financial Times* (30 October 1990) pointed out, was to reduce downside risk to a level where private investors would see enough potential to develop in cities rather than take softer profits elsewhere.

In March 1988 the government launched its 'Action for Cities' initiative which covered a range of programmes administered by different government departments that were designed to promote industrial and commercial investment and

**Table 11.3 Some major urban policy initiatives**

| Initiative | Primary aim(s) | Examples |
|---|---|---|
| Urban Development Corporations (UDC's) | To oversee inner-city development within designated areas. Specifically to (1) bring land and buildings into effective use; (2) encourage industrial and commercial development; (3) encourage people to live and work in the area. | London Docklands Development Corporation Trafford Park Development Corporation Cardiff Bay Development Corporation |
| Enterprise Zones (EZs) | To encourage industrial and commercial activity in designated local areas by removing certain tax burdens and other impediments to enterprise. | Isle of Dogs Wakefield Corby Rotherham Dudley |
| City Action Teams (CATs) | To co-ordinate a range of agencies within inner cities in order to provide information, advice and assistance to businesses. | Liverpool Manchester Birmingham Cleveland Newcastle |
| City Challenge | Public/private/partnerships designed to help regenerate inner urban areas through the design and implementation of local development projects. | Bradford Lewisham Manchester Nottingham Wolverhampton |

hence create employment in the inner-city area. Programmes under this initiative were co-ordinated by a special unit located at the Department of the Environment and local co-ordination occurred through City Action Teams. After 1994, in an attempt to achieve greater co-ordination in policy and to introduce competition for resources, the government began to amalgamate a wide range of inner-city programmes under the **Single Regeneration Budget (SRB)**, with the funds being administered by the newly integrated regional government offices which brought together the existing regional offices of a number of major government departments (e.g. Environment, Trade and Industry, Transport, Employment). It also established a new development agency (English Partnerships), which now draws its public funding from the SRB. From April 1999 English Partnerships' regional functions and the SRB Challenge Fund have become the responsibility of the newly established **Regional Development Agencies**. The latter are expected to take the lead in delivering more effective and integrated regeneration programmes, thereby promoting sustainable economic, social and physical regeneration with the regions.

With the change of government in 1997, urban policy in the UK appears to have taken on a more targeted and focused approach, with funding increasingly being directed towards a range of economic, social and environmental initiatives. Key recent developments include:

**Single Regeneration Budget** a government funding mechanism to support inner city regeneration proposals put forward by local partnerships under a competitive bidding process

**Regional Development Agencies** agencies set up in the regions of the UK to promote regional development and growth

- *the New Deal for Communities programme* – designed to combat social exclusion through focused and intensive neighbourhood renewal projects in the most deprived neighbourhoods;
- *SRB Challenge Rounds 5 and 6* – which include a more regional focus and an increased emphasis on partnership capacity building. The majority of new resources are to be concentrated in the most deprived areas;
- *housing estate regeneration* – through Housing Action Trusts and Estate Action;
- *coalfields initiatives* – especially the Coalfields Regeneration Trust and the Enterprise Fund.

In addition, the government has announced a range of area-based and non-area-based initiatives to tackle a variety of problems (e.g. crime, health, drugs education, employment) and has set up an Urban Task Force to identify ways of encouraging the regeneration of urban areas. In its report published in mid-1999 and entitled *Towards an Urban Renaissance*, the Task Force suggested a number of approaches including tax-breaks for inner-city areas, an urban fund to tackle eyesores and a system of cleaning up contaminated land. It remains to be seen how far the various ideas will be politically acceptable, especially if the proposals on public transport threaten to antagonise motorists.

## 11.7 UK small firms' policy

### 11.7.1 The importance of the small firm sector

**small firm** a business deemed to be small on the basis of predetermined criteria such as number of employees, annual turnover or capital employed

While economists may disagree over what precisely constitutes a **small firm**, few, if any, observers of the business world would deny the importance of a healthy small firm sector to the well-being of a capitalist economy. In the late 1990s, for example, it was estimated that small businesses with fewer than 50 employees accounted for 99 per cent of all UK businesses, almost 50 per cent of non-government employment and 42 per cent of turnover (excluding the financial sector). These, and other small firms, have made and continue to make important contributions to output and growth in the economy, exports, investment and research and development as well as enhancing consumer choice. By any measure, the small business is clearly a vital component of competitive and dynamic market-based economy.[8]

UK government attempts to support and nurture the small firm sector have grown in importance in the last two decades or so and reflect the shift in emphasis to the supply side of the economy which occurred from the late 1970s onwards. Under the leadership of Margaret Thatcher the Conservative government after 1979 actively promoted the idea of a culture of 'enterprise' and sought to encourage small business creation and expansion as a means of reducing the growing level of unemployment in the UK economy. Some 20 years later, under more favourable economic conditions, the Labour government's 1998 White Paper Our *Competitive Future: Building the Knowledge Driven Economy* stated that its aim was to 'create a broadly-based entrepreneurial culture, in which more people of all ages and backgrounds start their own business'. As the White Paper indicated, developing such a culture in which entrepreneurship, innovation and creativity could flourish required, at least in part, purposive action by government at both the macro and micro level.

At the risk of over-simplification, it seems fair to suggest that the focus of recent UK government policy for small firms has been on tackling those problems which appear to impact on small business creation, development, growth and survival. These have included questions of over-regulation, access to finance, lack of knowledge and/or skills, a changing business environment, market development and bad debts. Examples of government initiatives designed to help small businesses to overcome these problems are outlined below.

### 11.7.2 Improving the regulatory framework/business environment

Deregulating and simplifying the environment in which small businesses exist and operate remains a key stated objective of recent UK governments. To this end various developments have occurred since 1990. These include the following.

■ A *deregulation initiative* was launched in 1993 in an effort to reduce the number of unnecessary rules and to simplify and improve those which had to remain. A Deregulation Unit staffed by civil servants was set up to co-ordinate the attack on bureaucracy to ensure that business views were fed into the decision-making process.

■ A *Better Regulation Task Force* was launched in September 1997 to give smaller businesses a greater voice in shaping regulations which are single, helpful and fair.

■ *Direct Access Government* was established in 1997 as a 'one-stop shop' on the internet to provide firms (including SMEs) with access to regulatory guidance and forms.

■ *Small Business Service* was set up in 1999 to give SMEs a more powerful voice at the heart of government. It is expected to become a focal point within government for communication with SMEs on regulation requirements and will assist new employers with their regulation obligations by offering an automated payroll service from April 2000.

■ The administration of tax and National Insurance contributions was brought together in April 1999.

■ Fiscal changes to encourage the SME sector were announced in the 1998 and 1999 Budgets (e.g. a cut in the small companies' rate of corporation tax to 20 per cent; reduced starting rates of corporation tax for the smallest firms; tax credits for SMEs against investment in research and development).

### 11.7.3 Finance and the financial environment

Creating a more favourable environment and improving access to finance have been persistent themes in small firms policy over the years and a number of schemes have been introduced to help small businesses in these areas.

■ The *Loan Guarantee Scheme (LGS)* was first introduced in 1981 to cover situations where potential borrowers were unable to provide sufficient collateral or where the banks deemed the risk of lending unacceptable. The scheme provides a government guarantee for loans by approved lenders up to certain limits.

**business angels**
successful practitioners in
business who provide
investment finance for small
enterprises

- The *Enterprise Investment Scheme (EIS)* began in 1994 as a replacement for the Business Expansion Scheme. It is designed to help small, unquoted companies to raise equity finance from **business angels** (outside investors with a background in business) by offering the latter tax relief on their investment. The 1998 Budget announced a new unified EIS and capital gains tax reinvestment relief to increase the supply of equity capital for smaller, high-risk trading companies.

- The *Venture Capital Trust (VCT)* was introduced in 1995 with the aim of encouraging individuals to invest in smaller, unlisted trading companies. Individuals who invest in VCT gain certain tax advantages.

- The *Enterprise Fund (EF)* was announced in the Competitiveness White Paper (1998) and is designed to help the financing of small businesses with growth potential. It builds on support already available under the Loan Guarantee Scheme.

- The *National Business Angels Network (NBAN)* was launched in 1999 to connect 'business angels' with companies seeking equity capital. A similar scheme in Wales, entitled 'Xenos' is part of the Business Connect initiative.

- The *Small Firms Merit Award for Research and Technology (SMART)* is a national government award scheme which began in 1986 to support innovative projects at the technical feasibility stage. From April 1997 SMART was merged with SPUR (Support for Products Under Research), SPUR plus (for very large development projects) and the innovation element of Regional Enterprise Grants. During 1999 further elements were added to the scheme to help SMEs develop and acquire the technologies needed to bring innovative products and processes to the market.

- The *Scottish Technology Fund* was launched in 1997 as a partnership between Scottish Enterprise and 3i to provide pre-start finance for science and high-technology businesses across the region.

- The *University Challenge fund* was a partnership arrangement set up in 1998 to make awards available to UK universities on a competitive basis to set up their own seed venture capital funds to finance the commercialisation of good research ideas.

- The *Late Payment of Commercial Debts (Interest) Act 1998* gives certain small businesses a statutory right to claim interest from large businesses and the public sector on late payment of commercial debts. All businesses will eventually be brought under the terms of the Act.

### 11.7.4 Help and advice to small businesses

Lack of information, help and advice is recognised as a major barrier to small firm development, particularly in the field of exporting. Recent initiatives in this sphere include the following.

- The *Business Link network* – set up from 1993 to act as a 'one-stop' shop for information and advice to SMEs. It brings together the services of the major business development services in a single accessible location.

- The *Enterprise Zone (EZ)* – launched in 1997 as a definitive internet site for business information. It provides help on a whole range of business issues such as regulation, finance, exporting, innovation, technology and managing a business.

- The *Information Society Initiative (ISI)* – set up in 1996 as a partnership between industry and government to encourage both the development and informed usage of information and communication technologies in the UK. A key element of the ISI is the system of Local Support Centres normally based in Business Links (or in Local Enterprise Companies in Scotland).
- *ISI/Interforum E-Commerce Award* – launched in 1999 as part of the government's E-Commerce strategy. It is essentially an award scheme to recognise and reward best practice in the use of electronic trading among smaller firms (employing fewer than 250 people).
- The *Software Business Network (SBN)* – established in 1998 as an internet-based self-help network to provide information on finance, marketing and management for young software companies.
- *Export Explorer* – a programme to introduce new and inexperienced exporters to Western European markets.
- The *Sales Lead Service* – an internet-based service to link UK exporters to potential overseas buyers.

### 11.7.5 Promoting innovation, research and development and training

Promoting innovation, R&D activity and labour flexibility remain central to UK government SME policy and has given rise to a variety of initiatives, some of which have already been referred to in previous sections (e.g. SMART awards, tax credits, measures to encourage 'business angels'). Others include:

- The *National Endowment for Science Technology and the Arts (NESTA)* – aimed at talented individuals who need support to see their ideas and skills transferred into successful commercial enterprises;
- *patents costs* – measures to reduce the costs of filing patent applications;
- *Centres of Excellence for IT* – to help boost local skills training and reduce skills shortages;
- *Individual learning accounts* – part of the governments' strategy for 'life-long learning';
- The *Foresight Programme* – launched in 1994 as a means of bringing together government, industry and the science base to explore emerging opportunities in technologies and markets. Since 1997 the emphasis has been on doing more to help SMEs (e.g. by establishing SMART Foresight Awards);
- The *UK Business Incubation Centre* – launched in 1998 and based at Aston Science Park. Its aim is to help gain maximum benefit from **business incubation** activity in the UK by promoting best incubation practices, encouraging uptake of business incubation and aiding better networking between incubations.

**business incubation** the fostering, development and growth of new small businesses

### 11.7.6 Fostering enterprise and an enterprise culture

This has been a persistent theme in government policy since 1979 and has most recently found expression in the idea of 'life-long learning'. The concept of Individual Learning Accounts (see above) is one part of the approach to developing education and skills throughout a person's lifetime. Other key developments are:

- The *University for Industry (UfI)* – set to be launched in 2000 and designed to stimulate learning among individuals and businesses and to improve availability and access to high-quality learning programmes. The scheme involves extensive use of new technology and a network of learning centres to promote basic skills;
- *National Vocational Qualifications (NVQs)* and *General National Vocational Qualifications (GNVQs)* – designed to make learning at schools and colleges more relevant to the world of work;
- The *Teaching Company Scheme (TCS)* – seen as the government's premier technology transfer mechanism for linking businesses and UK higher-education establishments. Provides firms (especially SMEs) with access to high-quality graduates on a project basis;
- The *College–Business Partnerships (CBP) initiative* – similar to TCS but promoting technology transfer between smaller firms and further education institutions.

### 11.7.7 A final comment

It is worth noting that many of the above initiatives could be allocated to more than one area of interest and some of them are not specifically restricted to just small and medium-sized enterprises. That said, it is clear from government policy statements that over recent years SME policy has become an increasingly vital component in governmental attempts to create a competitive economy capable of achieving sustainable economic growth. While SME-related policies and initiatives in recent years have largely been part of general economic policy, current evidence suggests a move to a more multi-agency approach (e.g. including different government departments and regional agencies) and one which is becoming substantially focused on the small firm sector. The latter development is exemplified by the government's announcement (in February 1999) that it supported a 'think small first' approach to company law reform. This could entail a revised Companies Act – following consultation – organised around the needs of small companies, with clearly identified add-on provisions for larger enterprises.

## 11.8  The 'negotiated environment'

The above reference to 'consultation' on potential changes to company legislation highlights a key fact: in democratic states government policy and legislation which affect businesses usually emanate from a political process in which the business community and government interact. Whether it be general macro-economic policy as outlined below or policies and laws targeted at specific sectors (e.g. SME policy), democratically elected governments regularly consult, negotiate, bargain and (sometimes) compromise with businesses and their representative organisations prior to making a final decision. At Budget time, for instance, UK Chancellors of the Exchequer and their senior civil servants at the Treasury are invariably lobbied by a range of interests, including the 'drinks lobby', the tobacco industry, the oil industry, the Federation of Small Businesses, the Institute of Directors, the Confederation

**negotiated environment**
an environment in which the government negotiates with different interests over the shape of government policy

**professional lobbyist** a person, often an ex-politician or civil servant, who is paid to lobby government on behalf of a particular interest group or groups

of British Industry (CBI) and the Association of British Chambers of Commerce. There is, in short, a **negotiated environment** in which individuals and groups bargain with one another and with government over the form of regulation of the environment that a government may be seeking to impose.[9]

At an individual level, it tends to be large companies – and in particular multinational corporations – that are in the strongest position to influence government thinking, by dint of their economic and political power, and many of them have direct contacts with government ministers and officials for a variety of reasons (e.g. large defence contractors supply equipment to the Ministry of Defence). In addition, many large businesses use **professional lobbyists**, or create their own specialist units, whose role is to liaise directly with government agencies and to represent the interest of the organisation at national and/or supranational level (e.g. in Brussels). While such activities do not ensure that governments will abandon or amend their proposals or will pursue policies favourable to a particular company's position, they normally guarantee that the views of the organisation are considered alongside those of the other vested interests. Added weight tends to be given to these views when they are supported by all the leading firms in an industry (e.g. the tobacco lobby's fight against a complete ban on tobacco advertising).

As indicated above, the voice of business is also heard in political circles through various voluntary representative organisations such as Chambers of Commerce, employers' associations, trade associations and the CBI. Chambers of Commerce, for example, largely represent the views and interests of small businesses at local level, but also have a national organisation that lobbies in Whitehall and Brussels. In contrast, trade associations – which are sometimes combined with employers' associations – are usually organised on an industry basis (e.g. the Society of Motor Manufacturers and Traders) and handle consultations with appropriate government agencies, as well as providing information and advice to members about legislation and administration pertinent to the industry concerned.

### 11.8.1 The Confederation of British Industry (CBI)

The largest employers' association overall, representing thousands of companies employing millions of workers, is the CBI, whose members are drawn from businesses of all types and sizes and from all sectors, but especially manufacturing. Through its director general and council – and supported by a permanent staff which has representation in Brussels – the organisation promotes the interests of the business community in discussions with governments and with national and international organisations, as well as seeking to shape public opinion. Part of its influence stems from its regular contacts with politicians, the media and leading academics and from the encouragement it gives to businesses to take a proactive approach to government legislation and policy. Additionally, through its authoritative publications – including the Industrial Trends Surveys and reports – the CBI has become an important part of the debate on government economic policy generally, as well as a central influence on legislation affecting the interests of its members.

A good illustration of its more proactive approach in recent years has been its attempts to shape government thinking on environmental policy and to harmonise the work of both government and businesses in this area by promoting its own 'Action Plan' for the 1990s. To this end the CBI established a group of staff specially dedicated to work on environmental issues of interest to business and set up a policy unit and a management unit to provide information, contacts and advice to the various parties involved. The policy unit's role was to monitor developments in legislation, liaise with government departments and enforcement agencies (e.g. the former National Rivers Authority), lobby government and other organisations, provide information and advice, and help to formulate CBI policy on vital environmental issues. The management unit produced promotional literature for businesses, organised conferences and seminars on specific topics, conducted surveys and provided advice on financial and other assistance available to its members to help them develop good environmental management practices within their organisation.

In a report published in late 1998, entitled *Worth the Risk – Improving Environmental Legislation*, the CBI launched an attack on what it called an over-prescriptive approach to environmental laws. It called upon government to listen to industry and to concentrate pollution control on the biggest risk areas. According to the chairman of the CBI's environmental protection panel, the existing approach to legislation did not take account of the cost of regulation and its impact on the competitiveness of industry. By using a risk-based approach, the CBI argued that the government could achieve a better system of regulation without compromising business competitiveness.

While it is impossible to say with any degree of certainty how influential industry has been in shaping government policy in this or other areas, there is little doubt that the views of leading industrialists and their representative bodies and associations have received increased attention, particularly under recent Conservative administrations. Regular pronouncements by senior government ministers, including the former Prime Minister and Chancellor of the Exchequer, frequently refer to the fact that a particular policy or piece of legislation has been framed 'with industry in mind'. The signs are that the current Labour administration under Tony Blair has sympathies in the same direction.

## 11.9 Conclusions

As the chapter has demonstrated, in market-based economies governments can exercise considerable influence over firms, sectors and markets. A combination of forces, operating at differential spatial levels, can help to fashion government policies and decisions and these will invariably impact either directly or indirectly on business organisations. Whether it is the regulation of market structure and conduct through legislation on monopolies and mergers, or policies designed to promote small firm creation and development, governments play a central role in shaping the business environment. This role is normally carried out in consultation and collaboration with the private sector and its representative organisations and associations who form part of what can be described as a 'negotiated environment'.

## Mega-mergers: a prescription for success?

Firms grow in two main ways: internally and/or externally. **Internal growth** occurs where a business expands its existing capacity by such methods as increasing the size of its premises, acquiring new plant and equipment, taking on more staff and increasing its product range. **External growth** is where firms grow in size by either **merging** with or **taking over** other businesses. These latter two processes are sometimes referred to as growth by **integration** or **acquisition**.

Economists traditionally distinguish between three major forms of external growth:

- **Horizontal merger/takeover** involves the coming together of competitive firms in the same industry at the same stage of the production process (e.g. two car manufacturers; two banks; two oil companies).
- **Vertical merger/takeover** is between firms in the same industry but at different stages of the production process. A **forwards vertical merger**, for example, would occur where a producer merges with the distributor or retailer of its product; a **backwards vertical merger** would involve the manufacturer and the supplier. Some industries can be entirely vertically integrated (e.g. oil).
- **Conglomerate merger/takeover** involves firms in different (i.e. unrelated), industries, although synergistic benefits might be available.

Of these the horizontal merger/takeover tends to be the most common and is often a favoured strategy for firms attempting to increase their market share. By joining together with a competitor in the same industry a business is likely to increase its market power and influence and reap the kind of **economies of scale** referred to in previous chapters. Simultaneously it might also help to increase the **barriers to entry** for other firms seeking to join the market.

One major international industry in which horizontal mergers and takeovers have been particularly prevalent in recent years is the pharmaceutical industry where they are increasingly being seen as a key to future growth and profitability and, in some cases, survival. Given the huge research and development costs and long lead times in this industry, together with new discoveries in science and the financial advantages of patenting new treatments, many pharmaceutical companies have been looking to mergers to create the critical mass to exploit the rapidly evolving technologies. Recent examples include:

- Astra (Sweden) and Zeneca (UK) now AstraZeneca
- Hoechst (Germany) and Rhone Poulenc (France) now Aventis
- Pharmacia Upjohn (US/Sweden) and Monsanto (US).

Arguably the industry's most significant consolidation is that proposed between Glaxo Wellcome and Smithkline Beecham which, if it goes ahead as seems likely, will create the largest global drugs company in the world. Announced in January 2000, the proposed merger received European Commission approval in May following an investigation by the EU competition authorities and a target date for completion of the deal was set for late

▶

August. Despite shareholder approval at the end of July, the merger was delayed because of regulatory inquiries in the United States by the Federal Trade Commission (FTC). By September it emerged that the deal was likely to be held up further pending additional investigations by the FTC which was evidently concerned that the combined group might have an excessive share of the market for 'smoking cessation products'. While it seems unlikely that the fresh delay will prevent the merger taking place by the end of 2000, it does illustrate the level of anti-competitive scrutiny that may be faced by large international companies seeking to combine their activities. A cynic might be tempted to add that demonstrating a robust US regulatory regime could be politically advantageous to the incumbent government in the run-up to the US presidential elections in November.

(Postscript: The Glaxo Wellcome and Smithkline Beecham merger has subsequently taken place)

## Notes and references

1 See Chrystal, K. A. and Lipsey, R. G. (1997), *Economics for Business and Management*, Oxford University Press, Oxford, Chapter 9 for a good discussion of economic efficiency.

2 It is worth noting that where market failure occurs government intervention is not a guarantee of success. Some economists argue that state intervention makes matters worse.

3 But see *The Economist,* 13 June 1998, 'The end of privatisation', which argues that under the current Labour government 'privatisation' has also become a 'dirty' word.

4 See e.g. NERA (1996), *The Performance of Privatised Industries*, vol. 2: *Finance*, NERA, London.

5 These references can be found in Further reading at the end of this chapter.

6 This view is associated with the Austrian School of Economics. See e.g. Atkinson, B. and Miller, R. (1998), *Business Economics*, Addison Wesley Longman, Harlow, Unit 11.

7 This process is similar to the increasing business practice of sourcing products from lower-wage countries. This is usually referred to as one of the key features of 'globalisation'.

8 See e.g. Griffiths and Wall (1999), Chapter 4.

9 See Thomas, R. E. (1987), *The Government of Business*, 3rd edition, Philip Allan, London.

## Review and discussion questions

1 In the 1940s the UK government argued that nationalisation would make certain industries more efficient but by the 1980s the incumbent government was claiming that denationalisation (i.e. privatisation) was the key to greater efficiency. How do you explain this apparent contradiction?

2  If governments support the idea of 'free markets', why should they sometimes prevent free trade in businesses (e.g. takeovers)?

3  To what extent do you think that increasing labour mobility would help to solve regional 'problems'?

## Assignments

1  Imagine you are employed in the public relations section of the Knitwear, Footwear and Apparel Trades Union. The organisation is seriously concerned about job losses in the UK textile, clothing and footwear industry as a result of the combined effect of foreign competition and a strong pound and is determined to lobby the UK government to take action. Draft a press release calling for government intervention on cheap imports and the exchange rate to prevent further job losses in the industries you represent (maximum 400 words).

   Draft a counter press release (maximum 400 words) on behalf of the Department of Trade and Industry explaining why the government is currently against such intervention.

2  As a small firms adviser in your local Business Link you are regularly asked about what sources of government financial support are available for new start-up businesses. Produce a simple leaflet explaining what schemes are currently in operation to support new small firms.

## Further reading

Cook, G. C. (1992), *Privatisation in the 1980s and 1990s*, Hidcote Press, Leicester.

Cook, M. and Farquharson, C. (1998), *Business Economics: Strategy and Applications*, Pitman Publishing, London, Chapter 22.

Crafts, N. R. (1998), *The Conservative Government's Economic Record: An End of Term Report*, IEA, London.

Ernst and Young (1994), *Privatization in the UK*, Ernst and Young, London.

Griffiths, A. and Wall, S. (1999), *Applied Economics: An Introductory Course*, 8th edition, Longman, Harlow, Chapters 4, 8, 21.

Hornby, W., Gammie, R. and Wall, S. (1997), *Business Economics*, Longman, Harlow, Chapter 12.

Martin, S. and Parker, S. (1997), *The Impact of Privatisation: Ownership and Corporate Performance in the UK*, Routledge, London.

McKeown, P. (1998), 'Regional policy', in Atkinson, B, Livesy, F. and Milward, B., *Applied Economics*, Macmillan, Basingstoke.

Miller, A. N. (1995), 'British Privatization: Evaluating the Results', *Columbia Journal of World Business*, 30(4), pp. 82–98.

NERA (1996), *The performance of Privatised Industries*, vol. 2: Finance, NERA, London.

Oulton, N. (1995), 'Supply side reform and UK economic growth: what happened to the miracle?' *National Institute Economic Review*, 154, pp. 3–70.

Thomas, R. E. (1987), *The Government of Business*, 3rd edition, Philip Allan, London.

Worthington, I. and Britton, C. (2000), *The Business Environment*, 3rd edition, Financial Times Prentice Hall, Harlow, Chapters 10 and 14.

# CHAPTER 12

# The macroeconomic environment of the firm

Ian Worthington

**Objectives**

1 To outline the basic features of a market-based economic system.

2 To examine flows of income, output and expenditure in a market economy and to account for changes in the level and pattern of economic activity.

3 To analyse the role of government in the macroeconomy, including government macroeconomic policies and the objectives on which they are based.

4 To consider the role of financial institutions.

5 To survey the key international economic institutions and organisations which influence the business environment in open, market economies.

## 12.1 Introduction

State intervention which affects individual firms (e.g. privatisation) or sectors (e.g. small firms' policy) or markets (e.g. competition policy) occurs at what economists describe as the micro level. Here the focus is on the component parts of the economy and on the way in which government policies and decisions seek to improve on the workings of the free market. Governments, in addition, have an interest in how the economy is performing as a whole (e.g. levels of growth, inflation, unemployment) and the effects this might have on the business community's prospects both now and in the future. As this chapter will demonstrate, the **macroeconomic environment** within which firms exist and operate has an impact upon their activities and behaviour and this environment can be shaped by governments and other agencies operating at different spatial levels. It is worth remembering that just as the macroeconomy can affect the decisions of individual firms and consumers regarding production and consumption, so those individual producers and consumers help to shape the economy as a whole by their behaviour in the market place.

## 12.2  The market-based economy

We saw in Chapter 1 that economic scarcity gives rise to the key problem of resource allocation and particularly the question of how a society should utilise its limited resources. In tackling this dilemma it was suggested that a society had to choose between two broad approaches which we characterised as a **centrally planned economic system** (i.e. where the government decides on how resources will be used) and a **free market economic system** (i.e. one where individual buyers and sellers determined how resources are deployed). In practice, all countries have aspects of both systems (i.e. a **mixed economy**), with some favouring a large element of state planning (e.g. Cuba) while others have a preference for a free market approach combined with a significant level of government activity in the economy (e.g. USA, Japan, UK, etc.). This latter approach we have described as a **market-based economy** which is now the dominant form of economic system following the collapse of the old-style planned economies in Eastern Europe and elsewhere. It is appropriate, therefore, to look in more detail at how such an economy works and its underlying principles.

Put at its simplest a market-based economy is one in which most economic decisions are made by private individuals (sometimes called **households**) and by firms who interact in free markets, through a system of prices, to determine the allocation of resources. The key features of this type of economic system are as follows:

- Resources are in private ownership and the individuals owning them are free to use them as they wish.
- Firms, also in private ownership, are equally able to make decisions on production, free from state interference.
- No blueprint (or master plan) exists to direct production and consumption.
- Decisions on resource allocation are the result of a **decentralised system** of markets and prices, in which the decisions of millions of consumers and hundreds of thousands of firms are automatically co-ordinated.
- The **consumer is sovereign**, i.e. dictates the pattern of supply and hence the pattern of resource allocation.

In short, the three fundamental choices regarding what to produce, how to produce and how to distribute are solved by market forces.

The diagram in Figure 12.1 illustrates the basic operation of a market economy. In essence individuals are owners of resources (e.g. labour) and consumers of products; firms are users of resources and producers of products. What products are produced – and hence how resources are used – depends on consumers, who indicate their demands by purchasing (i.e. paying the price) or not purchasing, and this acts as a signal to producers to acquire the resources necessary (i.e. pay the price) to meet the preferences of consumers. If consumer demands change, for whatever reason, this will cause an automatic reallocation of resources, as firms respond to the new market conditions. Equally, competition between producers seeking to gain or retain customers is said to guarantee that resources are used efficiently and to ensure that the most appropriate production methods (i.e. how to produce) are employed in the pursuit of profits.

**mixed economy**  an economic system which contains elements of both state enterprise and free enterprise

**households**  an economic unit involved in consumption and frequently referred to in economic statistics (e.g. the number of households with televisions)

**decentralised system**  a system of markets and prices influenced by millions of individual decisions on consumption and production

**consumer sovereignty** the idea that consumer preferences determine the allocation of resources

**Figure 12.1 The market economy**

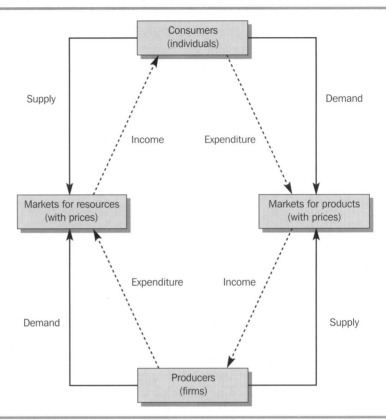

The distribution of output is also determined by market forces, in this case operating in the markets for productive services. Individuals supplying a resource (e.g. labour) receive an income (i.e. a price) from the firms using that resource and this allows them to purchase goods and services in the markets for products, which in turn provides an income for firms that can be spent on the purchase of further resources (see below). Should the demand for a particular type of productive resource increase – say, as a result of an increase in the demand for the product produced by that resource – the price paid to the provider of the resource will tend to rise and hence, other things being equal, allow more output to be purchased. Concomitantly, it is also likely to result in a shift of resources from uses which are relatively less lucrative to those which are relatively more rewarding.

This matching of supply and demand through prices in markets has been described in detail in previous chapters and the analysis has also been applied to the market for foreign currencies (see Chapter 10). In practice, of course, no economy operates entirely in the manner suggested above; firms after all are influenced by costs and supply decisions as well as by demand, and generally seek to shape that demand, as well as simply responding to it. Nor for that matter is a market-based economy devoid of government involvement in the process of resource allocation, as evidenced by the existence of a public sector responsible for substantial levels of consumption and output and for helping to shape the conditions under which the private sector operates. In short, any study of the market economy needs to incorporate the macroeconomic role of government and to examine, in particular, its influence on the activities of both firms and households. These are issues to which we now turn.

## 12.3  Modelling the macroeconomy

### 12.3.1 The 'flows' of economic activity

As we saw in the opening chapter of this book, economic activity can be portrayed as a flow of economic resources into firms (i.e. productive organisations), which are used to produce output for consumption. This flow gives rise to a corresponding flow of payments from firms to the providers of those resources, who use them primarily to purchase the goods and services produced. These flows of resources, production, income and expenditure accordingly represent the fundamental activities of an economy at work. Figure 12.2 illustrates the flow of resources and of goods and services in the economy – what economists describe as **real flows**.

In effect, firms use economic resources to produce goods and services, which are consumed by private individuals (private domestic consumption) or government (government consumption) or by overseas purchasers (foreign consumption) or by other firms (**capital formation**). This consumption gives rise to a flow of expenditures that represents an income for firms, which they

**real flows** the flows of goods and services and resources in the economy

**capital formation** additions to the stock of real capital or net investment in fixed assets

**Figure 12.2  Real flows in the economy**

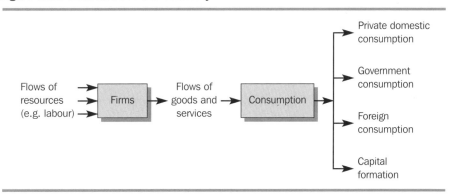

**Figure 12.3  Income flows in the economy**

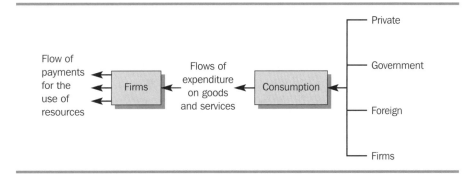

**Figure 12.4  A simplified model of real flows and income flows**

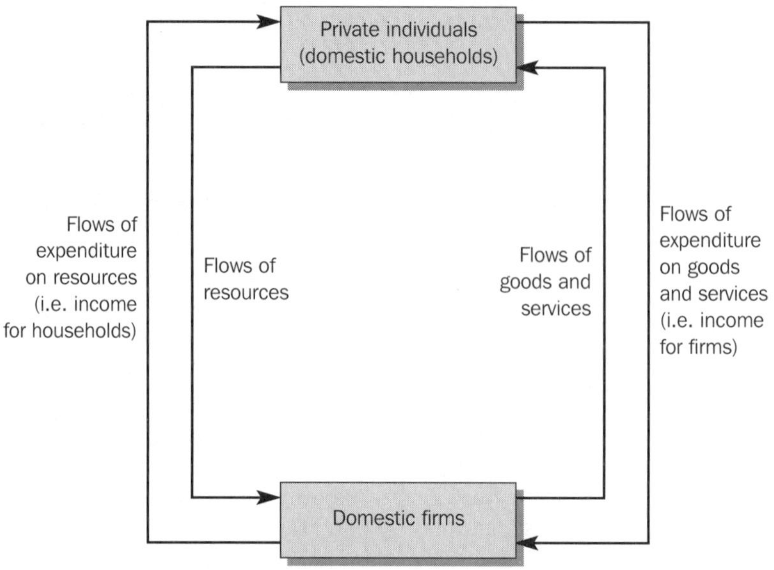

use to purchase further resources in order to produce further output for consumption. This flow of income and expenditures is shown in Figure 12.3.

The interrelationship between **income flows** and **real flows** can be seen by combining the two diagrams into one, which for the sake of simplification assumes only two groups operate in the economy: firms as producers and users of resources, and private individuals as consumers and providers of those resources (see Figure 12.4). Real flows are shown by the arrows moving in an anti-clockwise direction; income flows by the arrows flowing in a clockwise direction.

Despite a degree of over-simplification, the model of the economy illustrated in Figure 12.4 is a useful analytical tool which highlights some vitally important aspects of economic activity which are of direct relevance to the study of business. The model shows, for example, that:

- income flows around the economy, passing from households to firms and back to households and on to firms, and so on; hence the **circular flow of income (cfi) model**;
- these income flows have corresponding real flows of resources, goods and services;
- what constitutes an income to one group (e.g. firms) represents an expenditure to another (e.g. households), indicating that income generation in the economy is related to spending on consumption of goods and services and on resources (e.g. the use of labour);
- The output of firms must be related to expenditure by households on goods and services, which in turn is related to the income the households receive from supplying resources;
- the use of resources (including the number of jobs created in the economy) must also be related to expenditure by households on consumption, given that resources are used to produce output for sale to households;

**income flows** movements of income and expenditure in the economy

**circular flow of income model** a simplified model of the economic system to show how income flows round the economy in relation to production and consumption decisions

- levels of income, output, expenditure and employment in the economy are, in effect, interrelated.

From the point of view of firms, it is clear from the model that their fortunes are intimately connected with the spending decisions of households and any changes in the level of spending can have repercussions for business activity at the micro as well as the macro level. In the late 1980s, for instance, the British economy went into **recession**, largely as a result of a reduction in the level of consumption that was brought about by a combination of high interest rates, a growing burden of debt from previous bouts of consumer spending, and a decline in demand from some overseas markets also suffering from recession. While many businesses managed to survive the recession, either by drawing from their reserves or slimming down their operations, large numbers of firms went out of business, as orders fell and costs began to exceed revenue. As a result, output in the economy fell, unemployment grew, investment by firms declined, and house prices fell to a point where some houseowners owed more on their mortgage than the value of their property (known as **negative equity**). The combined effect of these outcomes was to further depress demand, as individuals became either unwilling or unable to increase spending and as firms continued to shed labour and to hold back on investment. By late 1992, few real signs of growth in the economy could be detected, unemployment stood at almost 3 million, and business confidence remained persistently low.

The gradual recovery of the British economy from mid-1993 – brought about by a return in consumer confidence in the wake of a cut in interest rates – further emphasises the key link between consumption and entrepreneurial activity highlighted in the model. Equally, it shows, as did the discussion on the recession, that a variety of factors can affect spending (e.g. government policy on interest rates) and that spending by households is only one type of consumption in the real economy. In order to gain a clearer view of how the economy works and why changes occur over time, it is necessary to refine the basic model by incorporating a number of other key variables influencing economic activity. These variables – which include savings, investment spending, government spending, taxation and overseas trade – are discussed below.

### 12.3.2 **Changes in economic activity**

The level of spending by consumers on goods and services produced by indigenous firms is influenced by a variety of factors. For a start, most households pay tax on income earned which has the effect of reducing the level of income available for **consumption**. Added to this, some consumers prefer to **save** (i.e. not spend) a proportion of their income or to spend it on imported products, both of which mean that the income of domestic firms is less than it would have been had the income been spent with them. Circumstances such as these represent what economists call a **leakage** (or **withdrawal**) from the circular flow of income and help to explain why the revenue of businesses can fluctuate over time (see Figure 12.5).

At the same time as such leakages are occurring, additional forms of spending in the economy are helping to boost the potential income of domestic firms. Savings by some consumers are often borrowed by firms to spend on

**economic recession** a situation of little or no growth and possibly a decline in output in the economy

**negative equity** a situation in which falling property prices mean that a person's mortgage on a property is greater than the value of the property

**saving** not spending income on consumption

**leakage** factors which cause a decrease in the flow of income in the economy

**Figure 12.5 The circular flow of income with 'leakages'**

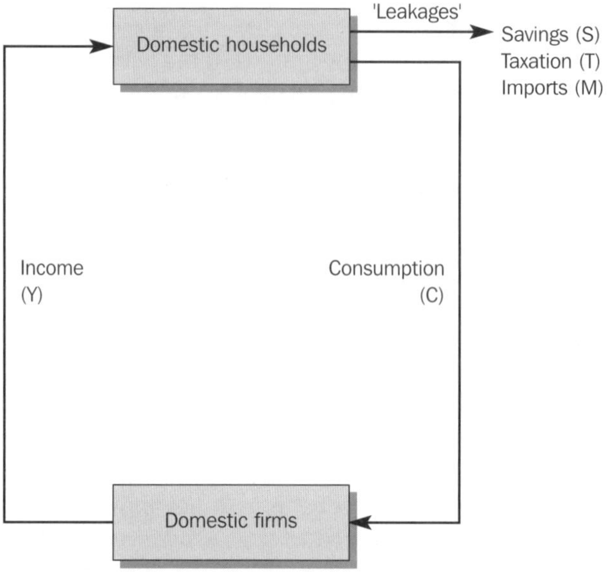

**investment spending**
spending by businesses on
the acquisition of assets

**public expenditure**
spending by government
on providing public goods
and services

**injection** factors which
help to increase the flow of
income in the economy

**autonomous change**
change that is independent
of other variables in the
model

**external shock** a
significant and often
unanticipated event which
has a major impact on the
economy (e.g. an oil crisis)

investment in capital equipment or plant or premises (known as **investment spending**) and this generates income for firms producing **capital goods**. Similarly, governments use taxation to spend on the provision of public goods and services (**public** or **government expenditure**) and overseas buyers purchase products produced by indigenous firms (export spending). Together, these additional forms of spending represent an **injection** of income into the circular flow (see Figure 12.6).

While the revised model of the economy illustrated in Figure 12.6 is still highly simplified (e.g. consumers also borrow savings to spend on consumption or imports; firms also save and buy imports; governments also invest in capital projects), it demonstrates quite clearly that fluctuations in the level of economic activity are the result of changes in a number of variables, many of which are outside the control of firms or governments. Some of these changes are **autonomous** (i.e. spontaneous), as in the case of an increased demand for imports, while others may be deliberate or overt, as when the government decides to increase its own spending or to reduce taxation in order to stimulate demand. Equally, from time to time an economy may be subject to **external shocks**, such as the onset of recession among its principal trading partners or a significant price rise in a key commodity (e.g. the oil price rise in the 1970s), which can have an important effect on internal income flows. Taken together, these and other changes help to explain why demand for goods and services constantly fluctuates and why changes occur not only in an economy's capacity to produce output, but also in its structure and performance over time (see mini case: Global economic crisis).

It is important to recognise that where changes in spending do occur, these invariably have consequences for the economy that go beyond the initial 'injec-

**Figure 12.6  The circular flow in income with 'injections' added**

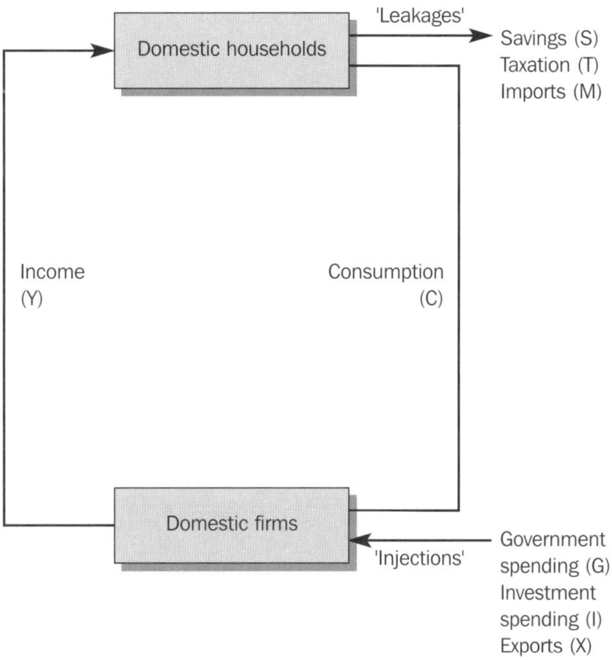

tion' or 'withdrawal' of income. For example, a decision by government to increase spending on infrastructure would benefit the firms involved in the various projects and some of the additional income they receive would undoubtedly be spent on hiring labour. The additional workers employed would have more income to spend on consumption and this would boost the income for firms producing consumer goods, which in turn may hire more staff, generating further consumption and so on. In short, the initial increase in spending by government will have additional effects on income and spending in the economy, as the extra spending circulates from households to firms and back again. Economists refer to this as the **multiplier effect** to emphasise the reverberative consequences of any increase or decrease in spending by consumers, firms, governments or overseas buyers.

**multiplier effect** where the eventual change in the level of income in circulation is greater than the initial change in the injection or leakage

Multiple increases in income and consumption can also give rise to an **accelerator effect**, which is the term used to describe a change in investment spending by firms as a result of a change in consumer spending. In the example above it is possible that the increase in consumption caused by the increase in government spending may persuade some firms to invest in more stock and capital equipment to meet increased consumer demands. Demand for capital goods will therefore rise, and this could cause further increases in the demand for industrial products (e.g. components, machinery) and also for consumer goods, as firms seek to increase their output to meet the changing market conditions. Should consumer spending fall, a reverse accelerator may occur and the same would apply to the multiplier as the reduction in consumption reverberates through the economy and causes further cuts in both consumption and investment. As Peter

**accelerator effect** an increase in investment expenditure as a result of an increase in sales or output

Donaldson has suggested, everything in the economy affects everything else; the economy is dynamic, interactive and mobile and is far more complex than implied by the model used in the analysis above.[1]

---

**Mini case**    ## Global economic crisis

**Asian Tiger economies**
those Far Eastern economies with high annual levels of economic growth and high per capita GDP

**economic growth** annual increases in the productive capacity of the economy giving rise to increases in national income

Throughout the 1980s and early 1990s the **Asian Tiger economies** – Indonesia, Hong Kong, Malaysia, Singapore, South Korea, Taiwan and Thailand – were widely regarded as an unqualified success story, with their rapid rates of **growth** and booming stock markets. As exemplars of free market capitalism, these economies had an enviable reputation in the West and attracted considerable funds from foreign investors. This miracle began to unravel in 1997 with the onset of an economic crisis in the Far East which sent shock waves throughout the world financial system.

The roots of the crisis appear to lie in unregulated investment decisions which ultimately resulted in the inability of the tiger economies to protect their currencies, which at the time were pegged against the US dollar. Following the collapse of a number of Thai property companies, which had over-extended themselves in the boom times and the subsequent withdrawal of loans by an increasing number of foreign investors, the Thai government was forced to let the currency (the baht) float. As the speculators gathered, other currencies came under pressure and were ultimately forced to give up the dollar peg. As currency values collapsed and forced up the size of multibillion-dollar loans, foreign investors rapidly withdrew their funds, resulting in a collapse on Asian stock markets which spread to London, New York and elsewhere, provoking fears of a worldwide recession.

The Asian crisis was followed in 1998 by the collapse of the Russian rouble which also came under speculative attack. The subsequent announcement by the Russian government that it was to devalue the currency and to suspend repaying its foreign debts simply convinced investors that emerging markets were too risky an investment and other countries' currencies came under pressure, particularly Brazil. Understandably the American stock market reacted very unfavourably to the problem in Latin America and share prices plummeted, sparking off similar falls on other stock exchanges across the globe.

Fears that the global economic crisis could plunge the whole world into recession thankfully soon subsided, but we should not under-estimate the human cost of the problems in the countries affected by economic collapse, particularly widespread job loss and growing poverty. Nor should we forget that our own economy and its businesses have felt the effect, whether it be from deferred investment by Far Eastern companies, lost trade, bad debts or reduced overseas earnings for UK multinationals. As economies across the globe become increasingly interlinked, economic collapse in one country or region spreads to other parts of the world. Arguably this makes the role of international institutions such as the IMF and the World Bank (see below) more rather than less relevant as we enter the next millennium.

## 12.4    Government and the macroeconomy: objectives

Notwithstanding the complexities of the real economy, the link between business activity and spending is clear to see. This spending, as indicated above, comes from consumers, firms, governments and external sources and collectively can be said to represent total demand in the economy for goods and services. Economists frequently indicate this with the following notation:

**aggregate monetary demand** the total spending on goods and services within the economy by consumers, firms and government and net overseas trade

**consumer spending** total spending by individuals (or households) on goods and services for immediate consumption

**Aggregate monetary demand** = Consumer spending + Investment spending + Government spending + Export spending − Import spending

or **AMD** = C + I + G + X − M

Within this equation, **consumer spending** (C) is regarded as by far the most important factor in determining the level of total demand.

While economists might disagree about what are the most significant influences on the component elements of AMD,[2] it is widely accepted that governments have a crucial role to play in shaping demand, not only in their own sector, but also on the market side of the economy. Government policies on spending and taxation or on interest rates clearly have both direct and indirect influences on the behaviour of individuals and firms, which can affect both the demand and supply side of the economy in a variety of ways. Underlying these policies are a number of key objectives which are pursued by government as a prerequisite to a healthy economy and which help to guide the choice of policy options. Understanding the broad choice of policies available to government, and the objectives associated with them, is of prime importance to students of business economics.

In practice most governments tend to share a number of key economic objectives, the most important of which are normally the control of inflation, the pursuit of economic growth, a reduction in unemployment, the achievement of an acceptable balance of payments situation, controlling public (i.e. government) borrowing, and a relatively stable exchange rate. These are discussed below.

### 12.4.1 Controlling inflation

**value of money** what money can buy in terms of goods and services. Inflation causes the value of money to fall

**retail price index** a measure used for indicating the rate of inflation, frequently referred to as the 'cost of living index'

**underlying inflation** inflation excluding the effect of mortgage interest payments

**Inflation** is usually defined as an upward and persistent movement in the general level of prices over a given period of time; it can also be characterised as a fall in the **value of money**. For governments of all political complexions reducing such movements to a minimum is seen as a primary economic objective (e.g. the current UK government's target for **underlying inflation** is 2.5 per cent).

Monitoring trends in periodic price movements tends to take a number of forms; in the UK, for example, these include:

1  the use of a **retail price index (RPI)**, which measures how an average family's spending on goods and services is affected by price changes;
2  an examination of the **underlying rate of inflation**, which excludes the effects of mortgage payments (known as RPIX in the UK);
3  measuring 'factory gate prices', to indicate likely future changes in consumer prices;

4  comparing domestic inflation rates with those of the United Kingdom's chief overseas competitors, as an indication of the international competitiveness of UK firms.

In addition, changes in monetary aggregates, which measure the amount of money (and therefore potential spending power) in circulation in the economy, and movements of exchange rates (especially a depreciating currency – see Chapter 10) are also seen as a guide to possible future price increases, as their effects work through the economy.

Explanations as to why prices tend to rise over time vary considerably, but broadly speaking fall into two main categories. First, supply-siders tend to focus on rising production costs – particularly wages, energy and imported materials – as a major reason for inflation, with firms passing on increased costs to the consumer in the form of higher wholesale and/or retail prices. Second, demand-siders, in contrast, tend to emphasise the importance of excessive demand in the economy, brought about, for example, by tax cuts, cheaper borrowing or excessive government spending, which encourages firms to take advantage of the consumer's willingness to spend money by increasing their prices. Where indigenous firms are unable to satisfy all the additional demand, the tendency is for imports to increase. This not only may cause further price rises, particularly if imported goods are more expensive or if exchange rate movements become unfavourable, but also can herald a deteriorating balance of payments situation and difficult trading conditions for domestic businesses.

Government concern with inflation – which crosses both party and state boundaries – reflects the fact that rising price levels can have serious consequences for the economy in general and for businesses in particular, especially if a country's domestic inflation rates are significantly higher than those of its main competitors. In markets where price is an important determinant of demand, rising prices may result in some businesses losing sales, and this can affect turnover and may ultimately affect employment if firms reduce their labour force in order to reduce their costs. Added to this, the uncertainty caused by a difficult trading environment may make some businesses unwilling to invest in new plant and equipment, particularly if interest rates are high and if inflation looks unlikely to fall for some time. Such a response, while understandable, is unlikely to improve a firm's future competitiveness or its ability to exploit any possible increases in demand as market conditions change.

Rising prices may also affect businesses by encouraging employees to seek higher wages in order to maintain or increase their living standards. Where firms agree to such wage increases, the temptation, of course, is to pass this on to the consumer in the form of a price rise, especially if demand looks unlikely to be affected to any great extent. Should this process occur generally in the economy, the result may be a **wages/prices inflationary spiral**, in which wage increases push up prices, which push up wage increases, which further push up prices and so on. From an international competitive point of view, such an occurrence, if allowed to continue unchecked, could be disastrous for both firms and the economy.

**wages/prices inflationary spiral** a situation in which rising wages cause rising prices which in turn cause further wage rises causing price rises, and so on

### 12.4.2. Economic growth

**Growth** is an objective shared by governments and organisations alike. For governments, the aim is usually to achieve steady and sustained levels of non-

**export-led growth**
economic growth resulting
from an increased demand
for a country's exports

**real national income**
national income excluding
the impact of inflation

**gross domestic product**
the value of the output
produced by the economy
over a twelve-month period

inflationary growth, preferably led by exports (i.e. **export-led growth**). Such growth is normally indicated by annual increases in **real national income** or **gross domestic product** (where 'real' = allowing for inflation, and 'gross domestic product, (GDP) = the economy's annual output of goods and services measured in monetary terms).[3] To compensate for changes in the size of the population, growth rates tend to be expressed in terms of real national income per capita (i.e. real GDP divided by population).

Exactly what constitutes desirable levels of growth is difficult to say, except in very broad terms. If given a choice, governments would basically prefer:

- steady levels of real growth (e.g. 3–4 per cent p.a.), rather than annual increases in output which vary widely over the **business cycle** (see mini case);
- growth rates higher than those of one's chief competitors; and
- growth based on investment in technology and on increased export sales, rather than on excessive government spending or current consumption.

It is worth remembering that, when measured on a monthly or quarterly basis, increases in output can occur at a declining rate and GDP growth can become negative. In the United Kingdom, for instance, a **recession** is said to exist following two consecutive quarters of negative GDP.

| Mini case | **The business cycle** |

**actual growth** the annual
percentage increase in
output produced by the
economy

**potential growth** the
speed at which the
economy could grow i.e. the
rate of growth in potential
output

Economists draw an important distinction between how much an economy is actually growing and how much it *could* grow. The former (**actual growth**) refers to the rate of growth in actual output as measured by annual changes in national income or gross domestic product. The latter (**potential growth**) is the annual change in the economy's capacity to produce goods and services as a result of factors such as increases in the availability of resources or improvements in efficiency in the use of existing resources. Potential growth is normally portrayed as increasing steadily over time and is generally drawn as a slowing rising potential output function. In comparison, actual growth is characterised as fluctuating – sometimes rising, sometimes falling – around the long-term trend.

**Figure 12.7 The business cycle**

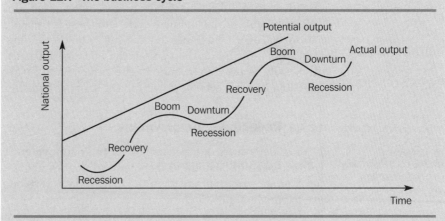

This pattern of changes in the economy's actual output is known as the **business cycle** or **trade cycle**.

A business cycle typically has four main phases, illustrated in Figure 12.7. In the **recovery** (or **upturn**) phase, the economy starts to recover from a recession or depression and output starts to grow as business and consumer confidence begin to return. This phase leads on to a **boom**, when economic growth is rising and the gap between actual output and potential output has narrowed as fuller use is made of the available resources. Once a boom reaches its height, growth tends to slow down or cease and the economy experiences a **downturn** in economic activity, culminating in a **recession** or **slump**. Ultimately the cycle begins again as a recovery starts to take place.

Note that the business cycle shows an upward trend of actual output and a regular pattern of phases. In practice the picture tends to be more complex.

**economic recovery** that phase of the business cycle when the economy begins to recover from a recession and output starts to increase

**economic boom** a situation of rapid economic growth and increased utilisation of resources

**economic downturn** the phase of the business cycle when economic growth starts to slow down

**economic slump** an extended or severe period of recession in the economy

From a business point of view, the fact that increases in output are related to increases in consumption suggests that economic growth is good for business prospects and hence for investment and employment, and by and large this is the case. The rising living standards normally associated with such growth may, however, encourage increased consumption of imported goods and services at the expense of indigenous producers, to a point where some domestic firms are forced out of business and the economy's manufacturing base becomes significantly reduced (often called **deindustrialisation**).[4] Equally, if increased consumption is based largely on excessive state spending, the potential gains for businesses may be offset by the need to increase interest rates to fund that spending (where government borrowing is involved) and by the tendency of government demands for funding to '**crowd out**' the private sector's search for investment capital. In such cases, the short-term benefits from government-induced consumption may be more than offset by the medium- and long-term problems for the economy that are likely to arise.

**deindustrialisation** a term usually used to denote the decline of a country's manufacturing industry

**crowding out** the idea that the growth of the public sector was in part responsible for the decline of the market sector

Where growth prospects for the economy look good, business confidence tends to increase, and this is often reflected in increased levels of investment and stockholding and ultimately in levels of employment. In Britain, for example, the monthly and quarterly surveys by the Confederation of British Industry (CBI) provide a good indication of how output, investment and stock levels change at different points of the business cycle and these are generally seen as a good indication of future business trends, as interpreted by entrepreneurs. Other indicators – including the state of the housing market and construction generally – help to provide a guide to the current and future state of the economy, including its prospects for growth in the short and medium term.

### 12.4.3 Reducing unemployment

**full employment** when resources in the economy are being fully utilised, especially the labour force

In most democratic states the goal of **full employment** is no longer part of the political agenda; instead government pronouncements on employment tend to focus on job creation and maintenance and on developing the skills appropriate to the demands of the early twenty-first century. The consensus seems to be that in technologically advanced market-based economies some unemployment is inevitable and that the basic aim should be to reduce unemployment to a level which is both politically and socially acceptable.

As with growth and inflation, unemployment levels tend to be measured at regular intervals (e.g. monthly, quarterly, annually) and the figures are often adjusted to take into account seasonal influences (e.g. school-leavers entering the job market). In addition, the statistics usually provide information on trends in long-term unemployment, areas of skill shortage and on international comparisons, as well as sectoral changes within the economy (see also Chapter 13). All of these indicators provide clues to the current state of the economy and to the prospects for businesses in the coming months and years, but need to be used with care. Unemployment, for example, tends to continue rising for a time even when a recession is over; equally, it is not uncommon for government definitions of unemployment to change or for international unemployment data to be based on different criteria.

The broader social and economic consequences of high levels of unemployment are well documented: it is a waste of resources, it puts pressure on the public services and on the Exchequer (e.g. by reducing tax yields and increasing public expenditure on welfare provision), and it is frequently linked with growing social and health problems. Its implication for businesses, however, tends to be less clear cut. On the one hand, a high level of unemployment implies a pool of labour available for firms seeking workers (though not necessarily with the right skills), generally at wage levels lower than when a shortage of labour occurs. On the other hand, it can also give rise to a fall in overall demand for goods and services which could exacerbate any existing deflationary forces in the economy, causing further unemployment and with it further reductions in demand. Where this occurs, economists tend to describe it as **cyclical unemployment** (i.e. caused by a general deficiency in demand), in order to differentiate it from unemployment caused by a deficiency in demand for the goods produced by a particular industry (**structural unemployment**) or by the introduction of new technology which replaces labour (**technological unemployment**) or frictions in the labour market (**frictional unemployment**).

**cyclical unemployment**
unemployment related to downturns in the level of economic activity

**structural unemployment**
unemployment resulting from a change in the structure of the economy, particularly the decline of particular industries

**technological unemployment**
unemployment associated with the introduction and use of technology

**frictional unemployment**
unemployment resulting from frictions in the labour market (e.g. time lags in the redeployment of workers)

### 12.4.4 A favourable balance of payments

As we saw in Chapter 10 a country's **balance of payments** is essentially the net balance of credits (earnings) and debits (payments) arising from its international trade over a given period of time. Where credits exceed debits a balance of payments surplus exists; the opposite is described as a deficit. Understandably governments tend to prefer either equilibrium in the balance of payments or surpluses, rather than deficits. However, it would be fair to say that for some governments facing persistent balance of payments deficits, a sustained reduction in the size of the deficit may be regarded as signifying a 'favourable' balance of payments situation.

Like other economic indicators, the balance of payments statistics come in a variety of forms and at different levels of disaggregation, allowing useful comparisons to be made not only on a country's comparative trading performance, but also on the international competitiveness of particular industries and commodity groups or on the development or decline of specific external markets. Particular emphasis tends to be given to the **balance of payments on current**

**account**, which measures imports and exports of goods and services and is thus seen as an indicator of the competitiveness of an economy's firms and industries. Sustained current account surpluses tend to suggest favourable trading conditions, which can help to boost growth, increase employment and investment and create a general feeling of confidence amongst the business community. They may also give rise to surpluses which domestic firms can use to finance overseas lending and investment, thus helping to generate higher levels of corporate foreign earnings in future years.

While it does not follow that a sustained current account deficit is inevitably bad for the country concerned, it often implies structural problems in particular sectors of its economy or possibly an exchange rate which favours importers rather than exporters. Many observers believe, for instance, that the progressive decline of Britain's visible trading position after 1983 was an indication of the growing uncompetitiveness of its firms, particularly those producing finished manufactured goods for consumer markets at home and abroad. By the same token, Japan's current account trade surplus of around $120 billion in late 1995 was portrayed as a sign of the cut-throat competition of Japanese firms, particularly those involved in producing cars, electrical and electronic products, and photographic equipment.

### 12.4.5 Controlling public borrowing

Governments raise large amounts of revenue annually, mainly through taxation, and use this income to spend on a wide variety of public goods and services (see below). Where annual revenue exceeds government spending, a **budget surplus** occurs and the excess is often used to repay past debt (known in the United Kingdom as the **public sector debt repayment** or **PSDR**). The accumulated debt of past and present governments represents a country's **National Debt**.

In practice, most governments face annual budget deficits rather than **budget surpluses** and hence have a **public sector borrowing requirement** or **PSBR** (recently renamed in the UK as **public sector net borrowing** or **PSNB**). While such deficits are not inevitably a problem, in the same way that a small personal overdraft is not necessarily critical for an individual, large-scale and persistent deficits are generally seen as a sign of an economy facing current and future difficulties which require urgent government action. The overriding concern over high levels of public borrowing tends to be focused on:

1 its impact on **interest rates**, given that higher interest rates tend to be needed to attract funds from private sector uses to public sector uses;
2 the impact of high interest rates on consumption and investment and hence on the prospects of businesses;
3 the danger of the public sector 'crowding out' the private sector's search for funds for investment;
4 the opportunity cost of debt interest, especially in terms of other forms of public spending;
5 the general lack of confidence in the markets about the government's ability to control the economy and the likely effect this might have on inflation, growth and the balance of payments;
6 the need to meet any agreed external requirements (e.g. the '**convergence criteria**' laid down at Maastricht for entry to the single European currency).

**budget surplus** where annual government revenue exceeds annual government expenditure

**public sector debt repayment** a situation in which government revenue exceeds annual government spending, thereby allowing the government to pay back some of its debt

**National Debt** the accumulated debt of past and present governments who have borrowed to finance some elements of public expenditure

**public sector borrowing requirement** the annual amount the government needs to borrow to finance its spending when government spending is in excess of revenue

**public sector net borrowing** the government's annual net borrowing requirement in the light of government spending and revenue

**interest rates** the price of borrowing money

**convergence criteria** the criteria laid down at Maastricht to determine whether member states of the EU qualify for membership of the single European currency

The consensus seems to be that controlling public borrowing is best tackled by restraining the rate of growth of public spending rather than by increasing revenue through changes in taxation, since the latter could depress demand.

### 12.4.6 A stable exchange rate

A country's currency has two values: an internal value and an external value. Internally, its value is expressed in terms of the goods and services it can buy and hence it is affected by changes in domestic prices. Externally, its value is expressed as an **exchange rate** which governs how much of another country's currency it can purchase (e.g. £1 = $1.50 or DM2.35 or FF9.60). Since foreign trade normally involves an exchange of currencies, fluctuations in the external value of a currency will influence the price of imports and exports and hence can affect the trading prospects for business, as well as a country's balance of payments and its rate of inflation (see Chapter 10).

On the whole, governments and businesses involved in international trade tend to prefer exchange rates to remain relatively stable, because of the greater degree of certainty this brings to the trading environment; it also tends to make overseas investors more confident that their funds are likely to hold their value. To this extent, schemes which seek to fix exchange rates within predetermined levels (e.g. the ERM), or which encourage the use of a common currency (e.g. the euro), tend to have the support of the business community, which prefers predictability to uncertainty where trading conditions are concerned.

## 12.5 Government and the macroeconomy: policies

Government macroeconomic objectives represent the 'goals' or 'ends' which a government pursues within the framework of a market-based economy. Since there is no guarantee that the free market will automatically deliver these objectives to the satisfaction of a country's political decision-makers, all governments at times intervene in the workings of the economy to push it in a direction consistent with their stated aims. In broad terms, this intervention usually takes three main forms, described as fiscal policy, monetary policy and direct controls. These policy instruments – or instrumental variables – and their effects on the business community are discussed below, using the UK as our example.

### 12.5.1 Fiscal policy

Each year governments raise and spend huge amounts of money. Recent UK government estimates for 1999/2000 suggest that government spending will be about £349 billion and is to be allocated in the manner illustrated in Figure 12.8. This spending will be funded mainly from **taxation** (**direct** and **indirect**), and social security contributions (see Figure 12.9). The PSNB is estimated at £3 billion.

**direct taxation** taxation levied on the earnings of individuals or businesses. They are taxes on income or wealth rather than on expenditure

**indirect taxation** government taxes imposed on spending (e.g. VAT)

**Fiscal policy** involves the use of changes in government spending and taxation to influence the level and composition of aggregate demand in the economy and, given the amounts involved, this clearly has important implications for business. Elementary circular flow analysis suggests, for instance,

**Figure 12.8 The allocation of UK government spending, 1999/2000**

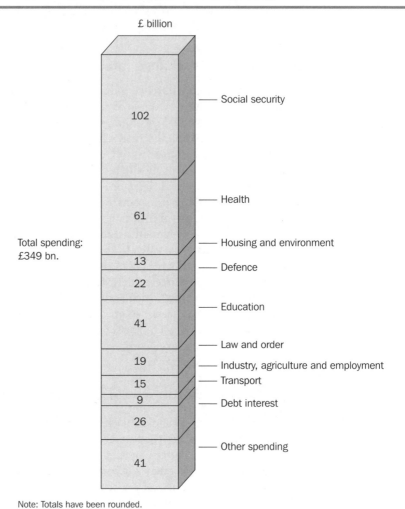

£ billion

Total spending:
£349 bn.

- 102 — Social security
- 61 — Health
- 13 — Housing and environment
- 22 — Defence
- 41 — Education
- 19 — Law and order
- 15 — Industry, agriculture and employment
- 9 — Transport
- 26 — Debt interest
- 41 — Other spending

Note: Totals have been rounded.

that reductions in taxation and/or increases in government spending will inject additional income into the economy and will, via the **multiplier effect**, increase the demand for goods and services, with favourable consequences for business. Reductions in government spending and/or increases in taxation will have the opposite effect, depressing business prospects and probably discouraging investment and causing a rise in unemployment.

Apart from their overall impact on aggregate demand, fiscal changes can be used to achieve specific objectives, some of which will be of direct or indirect benefit to the business community. Reductions in taxes on company profits and/or increases in tax allowances for investment in capital equipment can be used to encourage business to increase investment spending, hence boosting the income of firms producing industrial products and causing some additional spending on consumption. Similarly, increased government spending targeted at firms involved in exporting, or at the creation of new business, will encour-

**Figure 12.9  Sources of government revenue, 1999/2000**

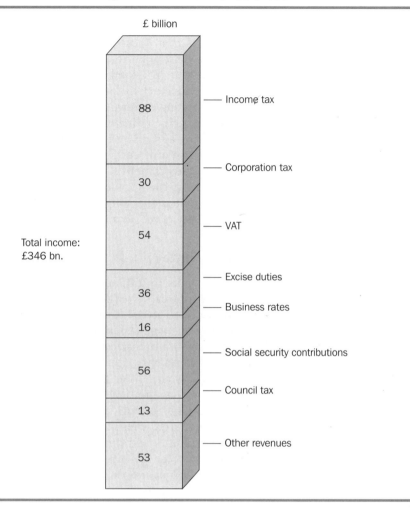

age increased business activity and additionally may lead to more output and employment in the economy.

In considering the use of fiscal policy to achieve their objectives, governments tend to be faced with a large number of practical problems that generally limit their room for manoeuvre. Boosting the economy through increases in spending or reductions in taxation could cause inflationary pressures, as well as encouraging an inflow of imports and increasing the public sector deficit, none of which would be particularly welcomed by entrepreneurs or by the financial markets. By the same token, fiscal attempts to restrain demand in order to reduce inflation will generally depress the economy, causing a fall in output and employment and encouraging firms to abandon or defer investment projects until business prospects improve.

Added to this, it should not be forgotten that government decision-makers are politicians who need to consider the political as well as the economic implications of their chosen courses of action. Thus while cuts in taxation may receive public approval, increases may not, and, if implemented, the latter may encourage higher wage demands. Similarly, the redistribution of government spending from one programme area to another is likely to give rise to widespread protests from those on the receiving end of any cuts; so much so that governments tend to be restricted for the most part to changes at the margin, rather than undertaking a radical reallocation of resources and may be tempted to fix budgetary allocations for a number of years ahead (e.g. the **comprehensive spending review** in the UK).

**comprehensive spending review** a system designed to fix budgetary allocations in the UK for a number of years ahead rather than for just one year

Other factors too – including changes in economic thinking, external constraints on borrowing and international agreements – can also play their part in restraining the use of fiscal policy as an instrument of demand management, whatever a government's preferred course of action may be. Simple prescriptions to boost the economy through large-scale cuts in taxation or increases in government spending often fail to take into account the political and economic realities of the situation faced by most governments.

### 12.5.2 Monetary policy

**money supply** the amount of money which exists in an economy at a given time. Different measures of money supply exist

**Monetary policy** seeks to influence monetary variables such as the **money supply** or **rates of interest** in order to regulate the economy. While the supply of money and interest rates (i.e. the cost of borrowing) are interrelated, it is convenient to consider them separately.

As far as changes in interest rates are concerned, these clearly have implications for business activity, as circular flow analysis demonstrates. Lower interest rates not only encourage firms to invest as the cost of borrowing falls, but also encourage consumption as disposable incomes rise (predominantly through the **mortgage effect**) and as the cost of loans and overdrafts decreases. Such increased consumption tends to be an added spur to investment, particularly if inflation rates (and, therefore **'real' interest rates**) are low and this can help to boost the economy in the short term, as well as improving the supply side in the longer term.[5]

**mortgage effect** normally taken to mean the impact on a person's consumption resulting from a change in interest rates which affects a person's mortgage payments

Raising interest rates tends to have the opposite effect – causing a fall in consumption as mortgages and other prices rise, and deferring investment because of the additional cost of borrowing and the decline in business confidence as consumer spending falls. If interest rates remain persistently high, the encouragement given to savers and the discouragement given to borrowers and spenders may help to generate a recession, characterised by falling output, income, spending and employment and by increasing business failure.

Changes in the money stock (especially credit) affect the capacity of individuals and firms to borrow and, therefore, to spend. Increases in money supply are generally related to increases in spending and this tends to be good for business prospects, particularly if interest rates are falling as the money supply rises. Restrictions on monetary growth normally work in the opposite direction, especially if such restrictions help to generate increases in interest rates which feed through to both consumption and investment, both of which will tend to decline.

As in the case of fiscal policy, government is usually able to manipulate monetary variables in a variety of ways, including taking action in the money markets to influence interest rates and controlling its own spending to influence monetary growth. Once again, however, circumstances tend to dictate how far and in what way government is free to operate. Attempting to boost the economy by allowing the money supply to grow substantially, for instance, threatens to cause inflationary pressures and to increase spending on imports, both of which run counter to government objectives and do little to assist domestic firms. Similarly, policies to boost consumption and investment through lower interest rates, while welcomed generally by industry, offer no guarantee that any additional spending will be on domestically produced goods and services, and also tend to make the financial markets nervous about government commitments to control inflation in the longer term (see below, Section 12.7.2).

This nervousness among market dealers reflects the fact that in modern market economies a government's policies on interest rates and monetary growth cannot be taken in isolation from those of its major trading partners and this operates as an important constraint on government action. The fact is that a reduction in interest rates to boost output and growth in an economy also tends to be reflected in the exchange rate; this usually falls as foreign exchange dealers move funds into those currencies which yield a better return and which also appear a safer investment if the market believes a government is abandoning its counter-inflationary policy. As the UK government found in the early 1990s, persistently high rates of interest in Germany severely restricted its room for manoeuvre on interest rates for fear of the consequences for sterling if relative interest rates got too far out of line.

### 12.5.3 Direct controls

Fiscal and monetary policies currently represent the chief policy instruments used in modern market economies and hence they have been discussed in some detail. Governments, however, also use a number of other weapons from time to time in their attempts to achieve their macroeconomic objectives. Such weapons, which are designed essentially to achieve a specific objective – such as limiting imports or controlling wage increases – tend to be known as **direct controls**. Examples of such policies include:

**direct controls**
government policies targeted at particular economic problems such as rising wages or increases in imports

- incomes policies, which seek to control inflationary pressures by influencing the rate at which wages and salaries rise (see Chapter 13);
- import controls, which attempt to improve a country's balance of payments situation, by reducing either the supply of, or the demand for, imported goods and services (see Chapter 10);
- regional and urban policies, which are aimed at alleviating urban and regional problems, particularly differences in income, output, employment, and local and regional decline (see Chapter 11).

## 12.6 Government and the macroeconomy: a comment

The macroeconomic model of the market-based economy described above demonstrates how governments can apply macroeconomic policies in pursuit of their objectives. Since these policies, as we have seen, impact both directly and indirectly on firms and/or their customers, a country's decision-makers can clearly play a significant role in shaping the environment within which businesses operate. Can we assume therefore that a government is in an all-powerful position to determine economic success or failure through its actions?

While there is no doubt that governments can have an impact on the business cycle, it is debatable how far an individual government is able to push the economy in the direction it wishes it to go. Apart from international and supranational developments (e.g. see Chapter 10 on the single European currency), which can limit a government's freedom of economic decision-making, a growing number of observers now believe that **globalisation** threatens to reduce the power of the nation-state significantly. As capital becomes ever more mobile, decisions concerning the movement of assets and the location of production increasingly rest in the hands of big corporations, particularly huge **multinational enterprises** (see Chapter 10). In these circumstances the impact of government in shaping a favourable economic climate within which businesses can flourish must, by definition, remain limited.

## 12.7 The role of financial institutions

Interactions in the macroeconomy between governments, businesses and consumers take place within an institutional environment that includes a large number of **financial intermediaries**. These range from banks and building societies to pension funds, insurance companies, investment trusts and issuing houses, all of which provide a number of services of both direct and indirect benefit to businesses. As part of the **financial system** within a market-based economy, these institutions fulfil a vital role in channelling funds from those able and willing to lend, to those individuals and organisations wishing to borrow in order to consume or invest. It is appropriate to consider briefly this role of financial intermediation and the supervision exercised over the financial system by the central bank, before concluding the chapter with a review of important international economic institutions.

**financial intermediaries** institutions that channel spare funds from lenders to borrowers

**financial system** the individuals, agencies and markets involved in raising and borrowing funds for different purposes

### 12.7.1 Elements of the financial system

A financial system tends to have three main elements:

1 *Lenders and borrowers* – these may be individuals, organisations or governments;
2 *Financial institutions*, of various kinds, which act as intermediaries between lenders and borrowers and which manage their own asset portfolios in the interest of their shareholders and/or depositors;
3 *financial markets*, in which lending and borrowing takes place through the transfer of money and/or other types of asset, including paper assets such as shares and stock.

**money markets** the markets for short-term finance in an economy

**capital market** market for longer-term loanable funds for industry and commerce

**stock exchanges** markets in which securities are bought and sold, thereby facilitating saving and investment

Financial institutions, as indicated above, comprise a wide variety of organisations, many of which are public companies with shareholders. Markets include the markets for short-term funds of various types (usually termed **money markets**) and those for long-term finance for both the private and public sectors (usually called the **capital market**). **Stock exchanges** normally

**Figure 12.10 The role of financial intermediaries**

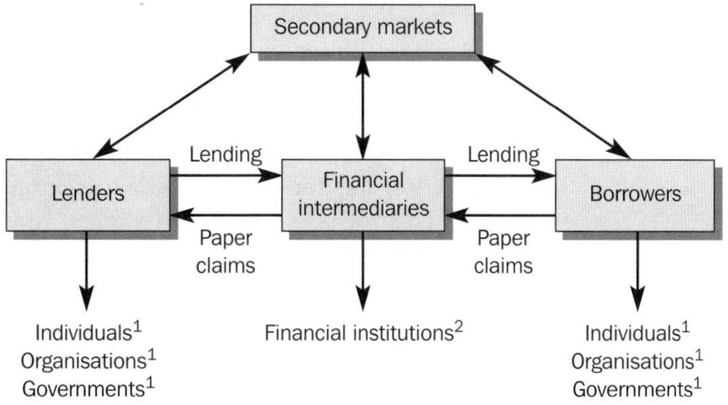

Notes: [1] both domestic and foreign.
[2] including retail and wholesale banks, building societies, overseas banks, pension funds, and so on.

lie at the centre of the latter, and constitute an important market for existing securities issued by both companies and government.

The vital role played by financial intermediaries in the operation of the financial system is illustrated in Figure 12.10 and reflects the various benefits which derive from using an intermediary rather than lending direct to a borrower (e.g. creating a large pool of savings; spreading risk; transferring short-term lending into longer-term borrowing; providing various types of fund transfer services). Lenders on the whole prefer low risk, high returns, flexibility and **liquidity**; while borrowers prefer to minimise the cost of borrowing and to use the funds in a way that is best suited to their needs. Companies, for example, may borrow to finance stock or work-in-progress or to meet short-term debts and such borrowing may need to be as flexible as possible. Alternatively, they may wish to borrow in order to replace plant and equipment or to buy new premises – borrowing which needs to be over a much longer term and which hopefully will yield a rate of return which makes the use of the funds and the cost of borrowing worthwhile.

The process of channelling funds from lenders to borrowers often gives rise to paper claims, which are generated either by the financial intermediary issuing a claim to the lender (e.g. when a bank borrows by issuing a certificate of deposit) or by the borrower issuing a claim to the financial intermediary (e.g. when government sells stock to a financial institution). These paper claims represent a liability to the issuer and an asset to the holder and can be traded on a secondary market (i.e. a market for existing securities), according to the needs of the individual or organisation holding the paper claim. At any point, financial intermediaries tend to hold a wide range of such assets (claims on borrowers), which they buy or sell ('manage') in order to yield a profit and/or improve their liquidity position. Decisions of this kind, taken on a daily basis, invariably affect the position of investors (e.g. shareholders) and customers (e.g. depositors) and can, under certain circumstances, have serious

**liquidity** the ease with which assets can be turned into spending power

consequences for the financial intermediary and its stakeholders (e.g. the bad debts faced by Western banks in the late 1980s and early 1990s).

Given the element of risk, it is perhaps not surprising that some financial institutions tend to be conservative in their attitude towards lending on funds deposited with them, especially in view of their responsibilities to their various stakeholders. UK retail banks, for instance, have a long-standing preference for financing industry's working capital rather than investment spending, and hence the latter has tended to be financed largely by internally generated funds (e.g. retained profits) or by share issues. In comparison, banks in Germany, France, the United States and Japan tend to be more ready to meet industry's medium- and longer-term needs and are often directly involved in regular discussions with their clients concerning corporate strategy, in contrast to the arm's length approach favoured by many of their UK counterparts.[6]

### 12.7.2 The role of the central bank

**central bank** the state or national bank of a country

A critical element in a country's financial system is its **central** or **state bank**; in the United Kingdom this is the Bank of England. Like most of its overseas counterparts, the Bank of England exercises overall supervision of the banking sector, and its activities have a significant influence in the financial markets (especially the foreign exchange market, the gilts market and the sterling money market). These activities include the following roles:

- banker to the government;
- banker to the clearing banks;
- manager of the country's foreign reserves;
- manager of the national debt;
- manager of the issue of notes and coins;
- supervisor of the monetary sector; and
- implementer of the government's monetary policy.

In the last case, the Bank's powers were significantly enhanced following the decision by the new Labour government (1997) to grant it 'operational independence' to set interest rates and to conduct other aspects of monetary policy free from Treasury interference. This historic decision has given the Bank's Monetary Policy Committee the kind of independence experienced by the US Federal Reserve and the Deutsche Bundesbank and has been designed to ensure that monetary policy is conducted according to the needs of the economy overall, particularly the need to control inflation.

## 12.8 International economic institutions and organisations

Given that external factors constrain the ability of governments to regulate their economy, it is appropriate to conclude this analysis of the macroeconomic context of business with a brief review of a number of important international economic institutions and organisations which affect the trading environment. One of these, the European Union, was discussed in Chapter 10. In the analysis below, attention is focused on the International Monetary Fund (IMF), the

Organisation for Economic Co-operation and Development (OECD), the European Bank for Reconstruction and Development (EBRD), the World Trade Organisation (WTO) and the World Bank (IBRD).

### 12.8.1 The International Monetary Fund (IMF)

The IMF came into being in 1946 following discussions at Bretton Woods in the USA which sought to agree a world financial order for the post-Second World War period that would avoid the problems associated with the world-wide depression in the inter-war years. In essence, the original role of the institution – which today incorporates most countries in the world – was to provide a pool of foreign currencies from its member states that would be used to smooth out trade imbalances between countries, thereby promoting a struc-tured growth in world trade and encouraging exchange rate stability. In this way, the architects of the Fund believed that the danger of international pro-tectionism would be reduced and that all countries would consequently benefit from the boost given to world trade and the greater stability of the inter-national trading environment.

**lender of last resort** a function of a country's central bank designed to ensure adequate liquidity in the banking system

While this role as international '**lender of last resort**' still exists, the IMF's focus in recent years has tended to switch towards helping the developing economies with their mounting debt problems and in assisting Eastern Europe with reconstruction, following the break-up of the Soviet empire.[7] It has also been recently involved in trying to restore international stability following the global economic turmoil in Asia and elsewhere (see mini case earlier in this chapter). To some extent its role as an international decision-making body has been diminished by the tendency of the world's leading economic countries to deal with global economic problems outside the IMF's institutional framework. The United States, Japan, Germany, France, Italy, Canada and Britain now meet regularly as the **Group of Seven (G7)** leading industrial economies to dis-cuss issues of mutual interest (e.g. the environment, Eastern Europe). These world economic summits, as they are frequently called, have tended to supersede discussions in the IMF and as a result normally attract greater media attention.

**Group of Seven** the world's seven leading industrial economies, i.e. the USA, Japan, Germany, France, the UK, Italy and Canada

### 12.8.2 The Organisation for Economic Co-operation and Development (OECD)

The OECD came into being in 1961, but its roots go back to 1948 when the Organisation for European Economic Co-operation (OEEC) was established to co-ordinate the distribution of Marshall Aid to the war-torn economies of Western Europe. Today it comprises nearly 30 members, drawn from the rich industrial countries and including the G7 nations, Australia, New Zealand and most other European states. Collectively, these countries account for less than 20 per cent of the world's population, but produce around two-thirds of its output – hence the tendency of commentators to refer to the OECD as the 'rich man's club'. Not surprisingly other countries are keen to join the organisation and a number have recently been allowed to attend part of its annual minist-erial meeting for the first time (e.g. Russia, China and India in 1999).

In essence the OECD is the main forum in which the governments of the world's leading industrial economies meet to discuss economic matters, particularly questions concerned with promoting stable growth and freer trade and with supporting development in poorer non-member countries. Through its council and committees, and backed by an independent secretariat, the organisation is able to take decisions which set out an agreed view and/or course of action on important social and economic issues of common concern. While it does not have the authority to impose ideas, its influence lies in its capacity for intellectual persuasion, particularly its ability through discussion to promote convergent thinking on international economic problems. To assist in the task, the OECD provides a wide variety of economic data on member countries, using standardised measures for national accounting, unemployment and purchasing-power parities. It is for these data – and especially its economic forecasts and surveys – that the organisation is perhaps best known.

### 12.8.3 The European Bank for Reconstruction and Development (EBRD)

The aims of the EBRD, which was inaugurated in April 1991, are to facilitate the transformation of the states of Central and Eastern Europe from centrally planned to free market economies and to promote political and economic democracy, respect for human rights and respect for the environment. It is particularly involved with the privatisation process, technical assistance, training, investment in upgrading infrastructure and in facilitating economic, legal and financial restructuring. It works in co-operation with its members, private companies and organisations such as the IMF, OECD, the World Bank and the United Nations.

### 12.8.4 The World Trade Organisation (WTO)

The World Trade Organisation, which came into being on 1 January 1995, superseded the General Agreement on Tariffs and Trade (the GATT), which dated back to 1947. Like the IMF and the International Bank for Reconstruction and Development (see below), which were established at the same time, the GATT was part of an attempt to reconstruct the international politico-economic environment in the period after the end of the Second World War. Its replacement by the WTO can be said to mark an attempt to put the question of liberalising world trade higher up the international political agenda.

With a membership of over 100 states – and many more waiting to join – the WTO is a permanent international organisation charged with the task of liberalising world trade within an agreed legal and institutional framework. In addition it administers and implements a number of multilateral agreements in fields such as agriculture, textiles and services and is responsible for dealing with disputes arising from the Uruguay Round Final Act. It also provides a forum for the debate, negotiation and adjudication of trade problems and in the latter context is said to have a much stronger and quicker trade compliance and enforcement mechanism than existed under the GATT. At the time of writing, its credibility as a conciliation organisation is likely to be severely tested by a number of ongoing disputes between the USA and the EU over certain traded products (e.g. bananas, hormone-treated beef).

### 12.8.5 The World Bank (IBRD)

Established in 1945, the World Bank (more formally known as the International Bank for Reconstruction and Development or IBRD) is a specialised agency of the United Nations, set up to encourage economic growth in developing countries through the provision of loans and technical assistance. The IBRD currently has around 180 members.

## 12.9    Conclusions

Business and economics are inextricably linked. Economics is concerned with the problem of allocating scarce productive resources to alternative uses – a fundamental aspect of business activity. In market-based economies, this problem of resource allocation is largely solved through the operation of free markets, in which price is a vital ingredient. The existence of such markets tends to be associated primarily, though not exclusively, with democratic political regimes.

In all democratic states, government is a key component of the market economy and exercises considerable influence over the level and pattern of business activity – a point illustrated by the use of elementary circular flow analysis. A government's aims for the economy help to shape the policies it uses and these policies have both direct and indirect consequences for business organisations of all kinds.

In examining the economic context in which firms exist, due attention needs to be paid to the influence of a wide range of institutions and organisations, some of which operate at international level. Equally, as markets become more open and business becomes more global, the fortunes of firms in trading economies become increasingly connected and hence subject to fluctuations that go beyond the boundaries or control of any individual state.

## Case study    Perceptions of fiscal prudence

The UK Chancellor of the Exchequer's Budget in March 2000 will probably be remembered for the extra spending announced on health and education. Bolstered by a significant improvement in the public finances, Chancellor Gordon Brown was able to add an extra £1 billion to spending on schools and colleges and to pledge that expenditure on health care would rise by over 6 per cent more than the rate of inflation over the next four years. While these and a number of other planned spending increases looked set to loosen the government's fairly tight 'fiscal stance', Brown nevertheless described his budget strategy as 'prudent' and 'disciplined'. He was, he suggested, determined not to return to the familiar pattern of 'boom and bust' in the UK economy that had plagued successive post-Second World War administrations.

While many of the individual measures in the Budget were broadly welcomed, not everyone was convinced by the Chancellor's overall strategy. The International Monetary Fund in its half-yearly health check of the global economy (see the IMF's *World Economic Outlook*) described the decision to increase public spending as 'regrettable' and a 'step in the wrong direction'

▶

and warned that this would put extra pressure on monetary policy (i.e. interest rates) and on the exchange rate (i.e. the strength of sterling). The fear was that boosting economic activity through additional government spending could threaten higher inflation and higher interest rates and this would have adverse effects on businesses, especially exporters. According to *The Economist* (25 March 2000, p. 30), City analysts were surprised by the scale of the Chancellor's spending plans and many were convinced that the Bank of England's Monetary Policy Committee (MPC) would be forced to raise interest rates in order to dampen down inflationary pressures to the UK economy.

The government's own view was that the increases in public spending were justified by the larger than anticipated surplus in the government's finances that had accumulated over the previous fiscal year, largely as a result of an undershoot on planned public expenditure and an unexpected rise in government revenue from taxation. According to the Chancellor, fiscal policy was set to remain 'tight' over the next two years in line with previous budget forecasts and hence it was unlikely that either interest rates or inflation would be significantly affected.

To reassure the City and the markets, the Bank of England signalled that it would be examining the Chancellor's Budget in case it threatened upward pressure on prices and interest rates (see e.g. the *Guardian,* 23 March 2000, p. 28). The concern in some quarters – including the Confederation of British Industry – was that the government's budgetary strategy was being driven by political rather than economic considerations (i.e. the electoral cycle) and that the costs of the Chancellor's fiscal largesse may ultimately have to be borne by industry. Should inflation threaten, the MPC would undoubtedly be forced to raise interest rates and this would increase borrowing costs and strengthen the pound on the foreign exchanges to the disadvantage of exporters. In the view of *The Economist* (25 March 2000) the primary macroeconomic objection to the Chancellor's Budget was that he had left the Bank of England to deal with the existing inflationary pressures in the economy through interest rates rather than through a further tightening of fiscal policy (p. 30). Had he taken the latter course of dealing with them himself, *The Economist* suggested that the Bank might have been able to cut borrowing costs and this would have helped exporters by weakening sterling. It might equally have added that a weaker pound also increases import prices, thereby adding to inflationary price rises in the economy, something both the government and the Bank of England are keen to avoid.

You pay your money and take your choice!

## Notes and references

1. Donaldson, P. and Farquhar, J. (1988), *Understanding the British Economy*, Penguin, Harmondsworth, p. 84.

2. See, for example, Griffiths, A. and Wall, S. (1999), *Applied Economics*, 8th edition, Longman, Harlow.

3. See, for example, Morris, H. and Willey, B. (1996), *The Corporate Environment*, Pitman Publishing, London, pp. 117–22.

4. See, for example, Griffiths and Wall (1999), Chapter 1.

5. Real interest rates allow for inflation.

6. See, for example, Neale, A. and Haslam, C. (1991), *Economics in a Business Context*, Chapman and Hall, London, p. 141.

7. The role of assisting reconstruction in Eastern Europe is also undertaken by the European Bank for Reconstruction and Development (EBRD).

## Review and discussion questions

1 To what extent do you agree with the proposition that the market economy is the 'best' form of economic system? Do you have any reservations?

2 Explain how interest rates could be used to boost the economy. Why, then, do governments frequently hesitate to take such steps?

3 Using circular flow analysis, suggest why a large programme of capital expenditure by government (e.g. on new motorways, roads, railways) will benefit businesses. How could such a programme be financed?

4 Which businesses are likely to benefit from a recovery in a country's housing market?

## Assignments

1 Illustrate how circular flow analysis can be applied to the case study to explain the the IMFs concern over the UK government's budgetary strategy.

2 You are a trainee journalist on a regional or national newspaper. As part of your first big assignment, you have been asked to provide information on the 'privatisation' of eastern European economies. Using journals and newspapers, provide a scrapbook of information indicating the different ways in which Western companies have sought to exploit business opportunities in the '**transition economies**'.

## Further reading

Donaldson, P. and Farquhar, J. (1988), *Understanding the British Economy*, Penguin, Harmondsworth.

Griffiths, A. and Wall, S. (1999), *Applied Economics*, 8th edition, Longman, Harlow.

Macdonald, N. T. (1999), *Macroeconomics and Business: An Interactive Approach*, International Thomson Publishing, Andover.

Neale, A. and Haslam, C. (1995), *Economics in a Business Context*, 2nd edition, Chapman and Hall, London.

# CHAPTER 13

# Human resource issues

Chris Britton

| Objectives | 1 To investigate recent trends in the labour market in the UK. |
| --- | --- |
| | 2 To look at different theoretical approaches to the labour market which attempt to analyse and explain these trends. |
| | 3 To give students a grounding in the traditional economic theory of the labour market and the impact of investment in human capital on the labour market. |
| | 4 To consider a range of other theories which can be applied to the labour market, particularly segmented labour markets, the flexible firm, transactions cost economics and principal–agent theory. |
| | 5 To examine the role of trade unions and government in the labour market and developments in the area of human resource management. |

## 13.1 Introduction

Neo-classical economics sees labour as one of the factors of production, exchanged in markets like other commodities and governed by the laws of demand and supply. People, however, are important in the economy both as producers and consumers of goods and services. For most products people are the most important input into the production process; therefore the quantity and quality of labour available in an economy will have a considerable impact upon the economy's ability to produce. The quantity and quality of labour available depends upon many factors including total population size, participation rates and the level of education and training.[1]

In this chapter we start by defining basic terms and looking at trends in the labour market in the UK and the EU. The neo-classical theory of the labour market is then considered along with other more modern theories. Our analysis concludes with an examination of a range of contemporary issues relevant to the organisation.

## 13.2 Labour market trends

**workforce** the number of people in a country who are eligible and available for work

The **workforce** is the number of people who are eligible and available to work and offer themselves up as such. The size of the workforce will be determined by cultural and political factors such as the age at which people can enter employment (which in the UK is 16) and the age at which they leave employment. In the UK the retirement age for men is 65 years, and for women will be 65 years by the year 2020. Those included in the definition of the workforce are:

- those in paid employment, even if they are over retirement age
- part-time workers
- the claimant unemployed
- members of the armed forces
- the self-employed.

**economically active** in the UK it refers to those in paid employment, the claimant unemployed, members of the armed forces and the self-employed

These are the **economically active.** The size of the workforce in the UK in 1999 was 27.8 million, which represents just over 47 per cent of the whole population.

Those excluded from the definition of the workforce are:

- students
- housewives
- the sick
- those in prison
- those who have taken early retirement.

**economically inactive** in the UK it refers to students, housewives, the sick, those in prison and those who have taken early retirement

**participation rate** the proportion of the population who are economically active

These are classed as **economically inactive**. Table 13.1 shows the breakdown of the workforce for 1999 in the UK.

An important determinant of the size of the workforce is the **participation rate** or the proportion of the population who are economically active. Table 13.2 shows participation rates in the UK over the period 1979–99.

Two trends are visible – an increasing participation of women in the workforce and a falling participation rate amongst men. A major factor which has contributed to both trends is the change that has taken place in the industrial structure of the UK and similar trends are visible in most other industrialised

**Table 13.1 Population of working age by gender and employment status, spring 1999, UK** (millions)

|  | Males | Females | All |
|---|---|---|---|
| Full-time employees | 11.4 | 6.2 | 17.7 |
| Part-time employees | 0.9 | 4.6 | 5.6 |
| Self-employed | 2.2 | 0.7 | 3.0 |
| Others in employment* | 0.1 | 0.1 | 0.2 |
| All in employment | 14.7 | 11.7 | 26.4 |
| ILO unemployed | 1.1 | 0.6 | 1.7 |
| **All economically active** | **15.8** | **12.3** | **28.2** |
| **Economically inactive** | **3.0** | **4.8** | **7.8** |
| **Population of working age** | **18.6** | **17.1** | **35.9** |

\* Those on government employment and training schemes and training programmes

*Source: Social Trends* 30, National Statistics © Crown copyright, 2000

**Table 13.2 Participation rates by gender, UK, selected years (percentage of 16–59/64-year-olds)**

| Year | Men | Women | All |
|------|------|-------|------|
| 1979 | 91 | 63 | 77.2 |
| 1991 | 88 | 71 | 80 |
| 1992 | 86.7 | 71 | 79.2 |
| 1993 | 86 | 71 | 78.7 |
| 1994 | 85.6 | 71 | 78.6 |
| 1995 | 85.1 | 71 | 78.3 |
| 1996 | 85 | 71.4 | 78.5 |
| 1997 | 84.8 | 71.8 | 78.6 |
| 1998 | 84.3 | 71.9 | 78.4 |
| 1999 | 84.6 | 72.5 | 78.8 |

*Source:* Adapted from Table A.1, *Labour Market Trends*, March 2000, National Statistics © Crown copyright

economies.[2] There has been a decline in the size of the manufacturing sector and consequently a loss of jobs in that sector – these were traditionally full-time male jobs – and at the same time a growth in the service sector where jobs are typically female and part-time. In addition to this there are other factors which have specifically raised the participation rate of women – cultural factors such as smaller family sizes and the changing role of women in society and political factors like legislation to promote equal pay and treatment.

An economist would define **unemployment** as all of those able and willing to work but who are unable to find work. In the UK there are at present two commonly used measures of unemployment both of which are reported in government statistical publications – the claimant count and the Labour Force Survey definition. The claimant count was adopted as a measure of unemployment in 1982 and counts unemployment as all those registered as able and willing to work and in receipt of benefit. It has long been argued that this is an inaccurate measure of unemployment since it will overstate true unemployment (as it will include those who are working but fraudulently receiving benefit) and at the same time understate unemployment by excluding many who would regard themselves as unemployed but who are not eligible for benefit (many married women, for example). In recognition of these problems an additional measure of unemployment has become accepted which is derived from the Labour Force Survey (LFS). This defines unemployment on the basis of a survey of 150,000 people each quarter as:

**unemployment** those able and willing to work but unable to find work

- those who were without a job at the time of the survey
- *and* were available to start work within two weeks
- *and* actively looked for work in the last four weeks
- *or* had found a job and were waiting to start.

Table 13.3 gives a comparison of the two measures for selected years and shows that the LFS measure is consistently higher than the claimant count. The LFS definition is the one which is accepted by the International Labour Office for international comparisons. Unemployment tends to move in a cyclical way, rising in times of recession and falling in times of boom. From Table 13.3 it can be seen

**Table 13.3 Unemployment in the UK, third quarter, selected years**

| | Labour Force Survey | | Claimant count | |
| --- | --- | --- | --- | --- |
| | Number (000s) | % of workforce | Number (000s) | % of workforce |
| 1990 | 1988 | 6.9 | 1614 | 5.6 |
| 1994 | 2704 | 9.6 | 2643.1 | 9.4 |
| 1995 | 2487 | 8.9 | 2336.1 | 8.3 |
| 1996 | 2316 | 8.2 | 2158.1 | 7.7 |
| 1997 | 1971 | 7.0 | 1585.3 | 5.6 |
| 1998 | 1807 | 6.5 | 1334.3 | 4.6 |
| 1999 | 1771 | 5.9 | 1224 | 4.3 |

Source: Adapted from Table 3.19, *Monthly Digest of Statistics* (March 2000) National Statistics © Crown copyright

that the level of unemployment has fallen rapidly according to both definitions over the last seven years in the UK, and that the downward trend continues.

Like unemployment, the level of employment also moves in a cyclical way. There is not, however, an exact negative relationship between the level of unemployment and the level of employment. It is possible that when a job is filled (and therefore the level of employment goes up) that it is taken by someone who is not counted as unemployed (and there will not therefore be a corresponding drop in unemployment). This could either be because they are not included in the definition of unemployment or perhaps because they are already employed. In spring 1999 there were 1.3 million people in the UK with more than one job. Figure 13.1 shows what has happened to the level of employment in the UK over the period 1987–99.

**Figure 13.1 The level of employment in the UK, 1987 to 1999**

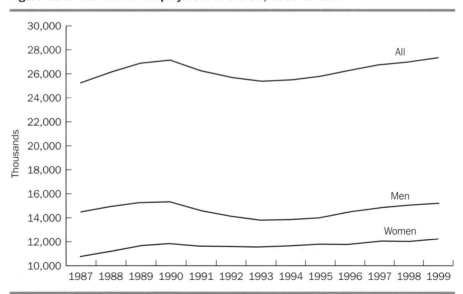

Source: Table A.1, *Labour Market Trends* (March 2000), National Statistics © Crown copyright

The total level of employment has risen over the 12-year period for both men and women. The total number of men employed has increased by around 4 per cent while for women the increase is around 14 per cent. This illustrates the changes that have taken place in the participation rates of men and women. It is forecast that if present trends continue the number of women in the workforce will exceed the number of men by the year 2010. Figure 13.1 makes no distinction between full-time and part-time jobs. Table 13.4 gives a more detailed breakdown of employment for four selected years in this time period.

**Table 13.4  Breakdown of total employment by gender (16–59/64), UK**
(000s, percentages in brackets)

| | 1987 | | 1992 | | 1997 | | 1999 | |
|---|---|---|---|---|---|---|---|---|
| **Men** | | | | | | | | |
| In employment | 14,065 | | 14,021 | | 14,451 | | 15,100 | |
| Part-time | 635 | (5%) | 816 | (6%) | 1,150 | (8%) | 1,361 | (9%) |
| Full-time | 13,407 | (95%) | 13,197 | (94%) | 13,294 | (92%) | 13,735 | (91%) |
| | | | | | | | | |
| **Women** | | | | | | | | |
| In employment | 10,205 | | 10,975 | | 11,429 | | 12,262 | |
| Part-time | 4,335 | (43%) | 4,668 | (43%) | 4,977 | (46%) | 5,438 | (44%) |
| Full-time | 5,854 | (57%) | 6,301 | (57%) | 6,449 | (54%) | 6,822 | (56%) |

*Source:* Adapted from Table B.1, *Labour Market Trends* (March 2000) National Statistics © Crown copyright.

This table shows a quite different pattern for employment between the genders. In 1997 women represented 33 per cent of all those working full-time and 81 per cent of those working part-time. For men the percentage working part-time has increased over the time period from 5 per cent in 1987 to 9 per cent in 1999. The number of full-time jobs over the period has risen by 2.5 per cent while the number of part-time jobs has risen by just over 23 per cent in the same time period. This, together with other evidence has been used to argue that there has been a fundamental change in the way we organise our working lives.

Further evidence on flexibility is provided by looking at the incidence of temporary employment. Since 1990 there has been an increase in both the numbers of employees and the proportion of the workforce who were classed as temporary – 5.5 per cent in the mid-1980s to 6.9 per cent in 1999. In 1999 7.6 per cent of female employees and 6.3 per cent of male employees were on temporary contracts. Although this does not appear to be a dramatic increase, temporary jobs have accounted for a third of the new jobs created since 1984. A large minority of each gender (38.4 per cent of men and 29.4 per cent of women) said that they had taken temporary employment because they could not find permanent employment.[3]

In 1999, 6 per cent of the workforce belonged to ethnic minority groups and, as Table 13.5 shows, there are great differences in economic activity rates between ethnic origins.

| Mini case | **The new world of work** |

The world of work is changing – there has been an increase in flexible working practices in the UK and elsewhere – and these changes will have much wider implications for every part of our lives. A report published in April 1998 by the Royal Society for the Encouragement of Arts, Manufactures and Commerce[4] projects current trends forward in order to predict what work will be like in the future:

■ There will be more short-term, fixed-term and part-time work.
■ The 40-hour working week and the 40-year working life will come to an end.
■ People will have more than one job.
■ Career breaks between jobs will become as common for men as they are for women.
■ People will have work but not jobs.
■ More organisations will become 'virtual organisations'.
■ More people will work from home.

The rapid changes in information technology will facilitate and accelerate this flexibility. Individuals will not go out to work, they will be linked together globally via the internet. In such a world the concept of 'employability' becomes crucially important – the individual needs to acquire and maintain a portfolio of skills which will enable new employment to be found.

These changes have massive implications for the way in which individuals live their lives. Lifetime earnings might fall and the pattern of income flows will change. Banks and building societies will have to change their practices with respect to the granting of mortgages. There will be implications for pensions which are still based on an individual paying contributions for a period of 40 years. The benefit system which is based on the traditional pattern of employment will need to change. At the present time work is not only important as a source of income but also as a source of status, but in the future this will have less to do with a person's occupation. For men the changes will be particularly acute – the number of households where women are the top earner has risen from one in 12 to one in five. The gap between work-rich and work-poor families will widen – the number of households in which no adult is working has doubled over the last 20 years to stand at one in five.

The white population has higher employment rates than ethnic minority groups and lower unemployment rates, but there are also big differences between ethnic minority groups. Although not shown, these differences are most pronounced among women. Some of the explanation for these differences lie with the demographic characteristics of each ethnic group, the qualifications held, and the geographical and occupational location of ethnic groups.[5]

Differences in wages exist both between and within occupations, and some of the theoretical explanations for these are considered in this chapter. Table 13.6 shows that median wages are higher for those with educational qualifications and the higher the highest qualification, the higher the median income.

**Table 13.5 Economic status by ethnic origin, Winter 1998, UK, percentage of over 16 year olds in each ethnic group**

|  | In employment | ILO unemployed | Economically active | Economically inactive |
|---|---|---|---|---|
| White | 59.5 | 5.8 | 79.7 | 20.3 |
| Black | 57.3 | 15.0 | 73.0 | 27 |
| Indian | 57.1 | 11.0 | 72.0 | 28 |
| Pakistani and Bangladeshi | 39.9 | 17.0 | 51.0 | 49 |
| Chinese | 48.1 | n/a | 66.0 | 34 |
| Other/mixed origin | 57.1 | 14.0 | 69.0 | 31 |

ILO = International Labour Organisation
*Source:* Adapted from Table 1, *Labour Market Trends* (June 1999) National Statistics © Crown copyright.

Table 13.6 also shows that on average men earned more than equally qualified women. Explanations for this are also considered in this chapter.

**Table 13.6 Wages and education – median weekly earnings (£) by highest qualifications and sex, full-time employees, GB, 1996**

| * | Degree or equivalent | HE below degree level | GCE A level or equiv. | GCSE grades A–C or equiv. | GCSE grades D–G or equiv. | No qualifications |
|---|---|---|---|---|---|---|
| Men | 485 | 375 | 337 | 288 | 255 | 251 |
| Women | 353 | 309 | 216 | 217 | 298 | 117 |

*Source: General Household Survey*, National Statistics 1996 © Crown copyright 2000.

## 13.3 Traditional labour market economics

We now turn to more theoretical considerations. Neo-classical economics sees labour as one of the factors of production, and in the short run it is the only variable factor. If the firm wishes to increase production in the short run, it can only do so by using more labour. In the longer run the firm can also use more capital and/or land. Labour is exchanged in the **labour market** according to the laws of demand and supply. **Wages** are seen as the price which responds to changing market conditions. In short, we return, yet again, to basic demand and supply analysis.

**labour market** a market where the commodity being exchanged is labour

**wages** the price paid for labour

### 13.3.1 The demand for labour

**derived demand** the demand for a factor of production which arises from the demand for the product it produces

The demand for labour is seen as a '**derived demand**' – it is only demanded by firms because it produces something that is in demand. The greater the demand for a product the greater will be the demand for the labour which produces it. The **elasticity of the demand** for a particular type of labour will depend upon the elasticity of demand for the product and its relative importance in the production process. The easier it is to substitute capital for labour in the production process, the more elastic will be the demand for that type of

**marginal product of labour** the output produced by each additional worker employed

**marginal revenue product** the revenue added by each additional worker employed

**average revenue product** the average revenue produced by each worker employed

labour. The demand that firms have for labour will depend upon its **productivity** – more particularly the **marginal product of labour**. This has been fully discussed in Chapter 5, but will be further developed here.

The **principle of diminishing returns** tells us that as more labour is used eventually the marginal product of labour will fall. This was illustrated in Table 5.3. So how can the firm determine the optimal number of workers to employ? To do this the firm needs to know the marginal product of each worker and from that the revenue derived from each worker. Assuming that the product being produced in Table 5.3 sells for £20 per unit, Table 5.3 can be recalculated in terms of money rather than physical units of output (see Table 13.7). Columns (1) and (2) appear in Table 5.3. Column (3) is the **marginal revenue product** or the revenue added by each additional worker, and is obtained by multiplying the marginal (physical) product of labour by the price at which that output sells, £20. Column (4) is the **average revenue product** per worker, obtained by multiplying column 2 by £20.

**Table 13.7  The marginal revenue and average revenue of labour**

| No. of workers | (1) Marginal product | (2) Average product | (3) Marginal revenue product (£) | (4) Average revenue product (£) |
|---|---|---|---|---|
| 1 | 10 | 10 | 200 | 200 |
| 2 | 20 | 15 | 400 | 300 |
| 3 | 30 | 20 | 600 | 400 |
| 4 | 40 | 25 | 800 | 500 |
| 5 | 50 | 30 | 100 | 600 |
| 6 | 80 | 38 | 1,600 | 760 |
| 7 | 100 | 47 | 2,000 | 940 |
| 8 | 80 | 51 | 1,600 | 1,020 |
| 9 | 60 | 52 | 1,200 | 1,040 |
| 10 | 40 | 51 | 800 | 1,020 |
| 11 | 20 | 48 | 400 | 960 |
| 12 | 10 | 45 | 200 | 900 |

Average revenue product and marginal revenue product are plotted in Figure 13.2. It should be remembered that in constructing this figure (and in keeping with the spirit of neo-classical economics) it has been assumed that the product is being sold in a perfectly competitive market where the firm can sell as much as it likes at the going market price.

If this information is available to the firm it is possible to determine the optimal number of workers to hire. As long as the workers are bringing in more revenue than it costs to hire those workers (i.e. the marginal revenue product is greater than the wage) it will pay the firm to employ more workers. If the cost of hiring exceeds the marginal revenue product the firm will be incurring losses. Therefore the firm will hire workers up to the point where the wage rate is equal to the marginal revenue product (note that this is another way of expressing the marginal cost = marginal revenue rule). In

**Figure 13.2 Average and marginal revenue products of labour**

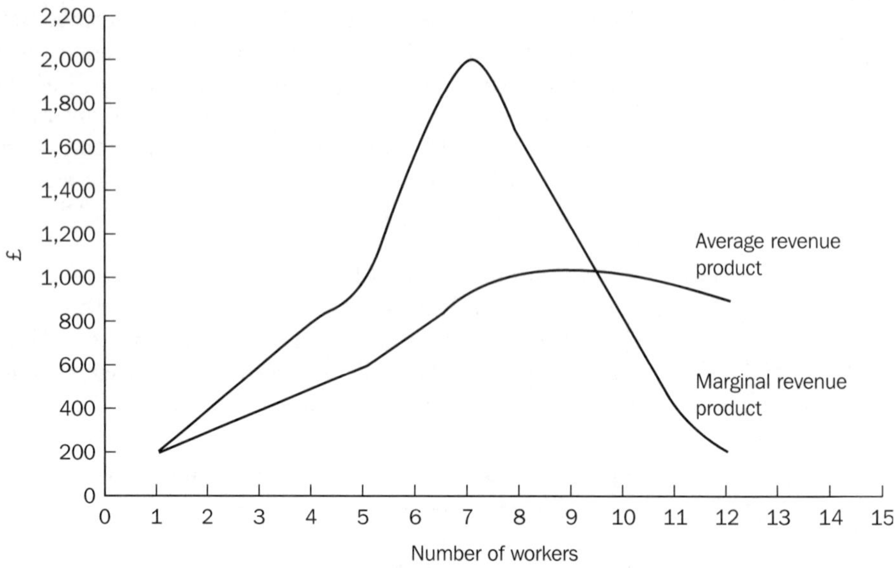

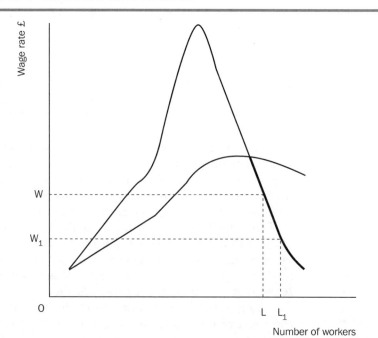

Figure 13.3 at wage rate equal to £W the farmer will hire OL workers, if the wage rate falls to £$W_1$ the farmer will hire more workers (O$L_1$).

The marginal revenue product curve shows the relationship between wages (or price) and the quantity demanded of labour. It is therefore the demand

**Figure 13.3 The demand curve for labour**

curve for labour but only the downward sloping part which lies below the average revenue product curve. Where the average revenue product is below the wage rate, the firm would not hire workers since it would not be covering average costs and would therefore be incurring losses on each worker employed.

In deriving this demand curve many assumptions have been made:

■ The firm is a profit maximiser.
■ The product is being sold in a perfectly competitive market.
■ Labour is available freely and at a constant wage rate.
■ No changes occur in the productivity of labour.

All of these are unrealistic assumptions but can largely be incorporated into the theory. For example, if the product is being sold in an imperfectly competitive market, there will not be a constant price for the product but marginal revenue product will still be obtained in the same way. If the productivity of labour changes there will be a shift in the MRP curve. Despite the drawbacks of neo-classical theory, it has established that the firm will hire labour up to the point where the cost of hiring is equal to the revenue derived from hiring.

The demand curve for labour for the whole industry is not the summation of the individual firm's demand curves, since the MRP curve is derived on the assumption that the price of the product remains constant. This will not be the case for the whole industry. As firms use more labour, there will be an increase in the output of the product which will lead to a fall in the price of the product and therefore there will be a different MRP curve for every possible price. The industry demand curve will still be downward-sloping but will be more inelastic than the individual MRP curves.[6]

### 13.3.2 The supply of labour

The total supply of labour in an economy depends upon factors such as the total population, participation rates and the number of hours worked. In this section the supply of labour is considered from the point of view of the individual and for occupations as a whole. As far as the individual is concerned, if they have freedom over the number of hours worked, they are faced with a choice between work or leisure (see Chapter 5 for a further discussion).

As the hourly wage rate increases the individual at first chooses to work more hours – the supply curve for labour is normally shaped (AB) (see Figure 13.4). After a certain point, however, the supply curve bends backwards on itself indicating that fewer hours are worked (BC). This is because the individual is choosing leisure time rather than work.[7] The individual will not necessarily be experiencing a drop in income since the lower number of hours worked might be compensated by a higher hourly wage rate. As income levels in an economy increase there is generally an increase in the demand for leisure. Except for the self-employed, however, there are not many jobs where individuals have complete control over the number of hours worked. The majority work contractual hours which are determined by employers, possibly in conjunction with trade unions.

Although the labour supply curve of the individual may be backwards-sloping after a certain point, this will not be true for a particular occupation. The supply curve of labour to a particular occupation will be normally shaped

**Figure 13.4 The individual's supply curve for labour**

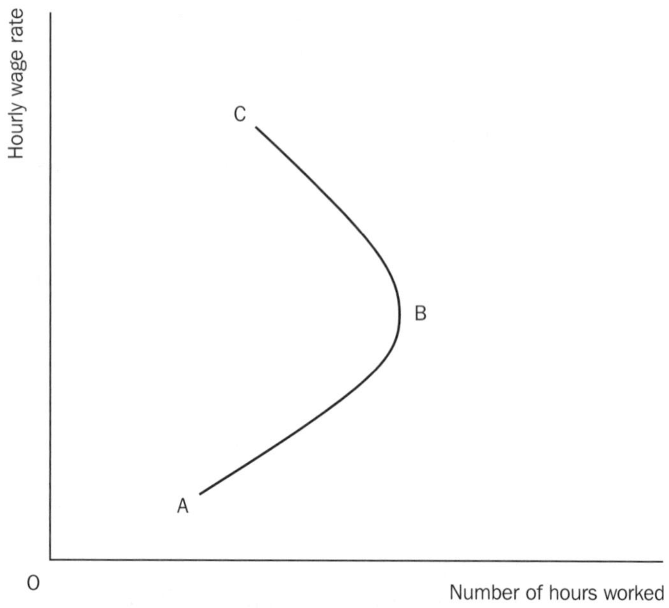

since increasing wages will encourage workers into particular occupations and so there will be an increase in the quantity of labour supplied.

### 13.3.3 The determination of wages in a particular occupation

According to neo-classical economic theory, the wage rate will be determined by the interaction of demand and supply (see Figure 13.5). The equilibrium wage rate is £OW; any changes in demand or supply will lead to a change in the equilibrium wage rate. If the demand for labour increases to $D_1$, at the old wage rate there will be a shortage of labour. The equilibrium wage rate will rise to $£OW_1$ to clear the market. As the wage rate for this occupation is now higher than previously, in the longer term more labour will be attracted into this industry, the supply of labour will rise ($S_1$) and the wage rate will fall. Thus the equilibrium wage rate changes in response to changes in demand and supply factors.

If some occupations command higher wages, labour will be encouraged to move into these occupations from lower-paid ones. Thus in a perfect labour market with no barriers to mobility and no differences in productivities wage rates across occupations will eventually converge. Clearly this is not the case in practice; large differentials in wages exist between occupations. How can this happen? In neo-classical economics the explanation for wage differentials lies in differences between marginal productivities of workers. The focus therefore is on the characteristics of individual participants in the labour markets.

There are a number of shortcomings in the neo-classical theory of the labour market:

**Figure 13.5  The labour market**

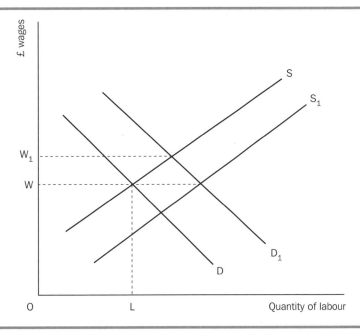

1 It is very difficult in practice to measure the marginal productivity of workers.

2 The theory implies that wages will be flexible both upwards and downwards in the face of changing market conditions. In reality this is not usually the case. In times of labour shortage, it is common for firms to make greater use of overtime rather than offer higher wages. Similarly in times of excess labour supply, in the short term at least the firm is likely to use less overtime and more short-time working. Firms adjust quantities rather than wages.

3 The fundamental assumption of neo-classical theory is that markets clear, and therefore in the case of labour markets there can be no unemployment. Again this is not in keeping with reality as unemployment does exist, and often it co-exists with unfilled vacancies!

4 Neo-classical economics predicts that workers in the same occupation with the same level of ability will be paid the same wages. This is often not the case; there are differentials both between and within occupations. In an attempt to explain differentials between occupations neo-classical economics can be made more realistic by relaxing the assumption of perfect **mobility of labour.**

**mobility of labour**  the extent to which workers are willing or able to move between jobs or areas

**geographical immobility** the inability of workers to move between geographical areas

The labour supply curve is drawn on the assumption that labour is perfectly mobile. Again this is open to dispute. People are frequently **geographically immobile** for a variety of reasons:

■ The cost of moving. It is an expensive business to move to another part of the country, particularly to areas where housing costs are high, like London.

■ There may be shortages of housing in certain areas, or it may be difficult or even impossible to sell a house in other areas.

■ There may be social ties in the form of family and friends that people may be reluctant to leave.

■ For people with children, schooling will be important. For example, parents are reluctant to relocate when their children are working for GCSE or A level examinations.

**occupational immobility**
the inability of workers to move between occupations

People are also **occupationally immobile** for the following reasons:

■ Some jobs require a natural ability that an individual might not possess (e.g. entertainers, footballers).
■ Training is required by many occupations (e.g. doctors, engineers). Without this training an individual could not do the job and the length of training may be a deterrent.
■ To enter some occupations (e.g. starting up your own business), a certain amount of capital is required. In some cases the amount of capital needed will be very high and for many this may be a barrier to entry.

In addition to these barriers many occupations have strong professional bodies (accountancy, for example) or strong trade unions (the closed shop, for example) which regulate entry to an occupation. The higher these barriers are to mobility in an occupation, the more inelastic will be the supply of labour to that occupation. The supply of brain surgeons is likely to be highly inelastic due to the qualifications and skill needed and the length of training. If there is a shortage of brain surgeons, it would be very difficult to increase supply quickly because of these factors. Unskilled labour is likely to have a much more elastic supply.

Figure 13.6 shows two labour markets with differing supply curves: (a) has inelastic supply (e.g. doctors or engineers) and (b) has elastic supply (unskilled workers). In both cases it is assumed that the demand curves are identical, as are the shifts in the demand curves.

In Figure 13.6 the wage rate starts at £OW in both occupations. Assuming that demand increases in each market by the same amount (D to $D_1$) the wage rate will increase to £$OW_1$. For occupation (a) this will be higher than for occupation (b). A differential has opened up in wages. The qualifications and length

**Figure 13.6 Wage differentials: (a) inelastic supply (b) elastic supply**

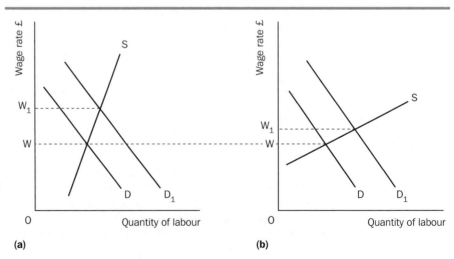

of training needed to become a doctor have influenced the supply curve of labour such that this occupation commands a higher salary than unskilled occupations. This differential will not be competed away because of the barriers to mobility which exist and in fact this differential has an important role to play in persuading individuals to go through the long and demanding training process to become a doctor (see Section 13.4 below). Differentials also exist for jobs which are dirty or dangerous, as supply might not be forthcoming if wages did not reflect these factors.

Differing levels of productivity of labour and barriers to mobility, insofar as they affect the demand and the supply of labour, go a long way to explaining wage differentials between occupations. There are also wage differentials within occupations which could be due to the incremental scales which are common within organisations, the influence of performance-related pay or regional differences in the availability of labour or in the cost of living. The existence of incremental scales is largely based on an acceptance of the idea that with time and experience workers become more productive.

## 13.4 Human capital approach

**human capital** the stock of expertise accumulated by a worker

**Human capital** refers to the stock of expertise accumulated by a worker. This stock of expertise partly stems from natural ability, but also comes from experience and from investment in education and training. As with investment in machinery, the purpose of investment in human capital is to increase the productivity. Neo-classical economic theory implies that wages are related to productivities, so that skilled labour is paid more than unskilled. The human capital approach argues that education and training make people more productive and therefore eligible for higher returns. So differentials in wages are due to different productivities, which in turn are due to different investment levels in human capital.

### 13.4.1 The evidence: education

Investment in education helps the individual to find employment. The General Household Survey (1996) found that men aged 16–64 with no educational qualifications were nearly twice as likely to be unemployed as those with a qualification (11 per cent compared with 6 per cent) and nearly four times as likely to be unemployed as those with higher education qualifications (11 per cent compared with 3 per cent). The relationship between unemployment and education was less marked for women, who were more likely to be classified as economically inactive. Investment in education also helps the individual to enter internal labour markets (see Section 13.5). In addition, Table 13.6 shows that there is a premium to education – the higher the level of educational achievement the higher the average salary. Evidence shows that this additional earning power only applies to traditional academic qualifications and not to vocational qualifications. In the UK, for example, an advanced GNVQ is supposed to be equivalent to two A levels but in earning power only appears to be worth as much as five good grade GCSEs.

Like investment in machinery, investment in human capital involves a financial outlay now in order to generate future income. How does the individ-

**cost-benefit analysis**
a decision-making aid which compares the costs and benefits of undertaking a project

ual decide how much to invest in education? A useful technique used in investment appraisal is **cost-benefit analysis** which compares the costs and benefits of a project (see also Chapter 14).[8] All of the costs and all of the benefits of a project need to be identified and quantified in monetary terms. Consider the choice faced by an 18-year-old on leaving school – to go on to higher education or to get a job. The costs of going on to higher education are all incurred now – the cost of the course, the cost of books, living expenses and also the *opportunity cost* of staying on in education – the salary that would have been earned if the individual had entered employment. The benefits are mostly in the future – a greater likelihood of securing a good job and the increased earnings that can be expected. These costs and benefits cannot be directly compared since the value of money is not the same now as in the future because of the impact of inflation. Future flows of money need to be **discounted** at an appropriate rate of interest. Once this has been done the costs and benefits can be compared and the **net present value** can be calculated. If this is positive the benefits outweigh the costs and it is worth the individual staying on in education.

**discounting** the process of applying a discount rate to reduce future flows of money to a present value

**net present value** the present value of a project obtained by offsetting the discounted flows of money in the future with present cost

As with any cost-benefit analysis there are problems in the identification and quantification of all costs and benefits. Future benefits are expected future benefits and are therefore not certain. The choice of appropriate discount rate is also problematic since the future flows might stretch some time into the future and long-term forecasting of inflation will be necessary. It is extremely unlikely that an 18-year-old will sit down and carry out a detailed cost-benefit analysis on entry into higher education. But the fact that the introduction of tuition fees for higher education courses in 1998 has led to a 2.5 per cent fall in applications to university implies that some sort of evaluation of relative costs and benefits does take place, albeit on an ad hoc basis. The fall is greater for mature students for whom the opportunity cost will be higher.

### 13.4.2 The evidence: training

**on-the-job training**
training given to an employee as part of their job

The same sort of analysis can be applied to **on-the-job training** which represents an investment in human capital which increases productivity. The decision on how much training to invest in is complicated by the fact that training can be financed by the firm as well as the individual. Two types of training can be identified:

- general training which involves the acquisition of skills which are widely applicable like the use of word-processors. Although such skills will enhance the productivity of the individual and therefore benefit the firm too, there is little incentive for the firm to finance the cost of training since these skills are highly transferable and will increase the potential earning power of the individual outside the firm. An organisation which spends a great deal on training its employees in general skills runs the risk of losing these employees to firms which are able to pay higher wages simply because they do not finance such training.
- specific training which involves the acquisition of skills which are highly specific to the firm – knowledge of a particular filing system for example. This type of training also increases productivity but there is much more incentive for the firm to finance this type of training since the skills would

be virtually useless to the individual outside of the firm and would not increase the possibility of poaching.

This distinction raises the question of who should finance on-the-job training. If both firms and individuals benefit as a result of such training the cost should be shared between them. An example of the sharing of costs of training is provided by the apprenticeship system where apprentices are gaining general skills in a particular field. Employers make the apprentices bear some of the cost of training by paying them low wages to begin with (below their current marginal productivity) on the understanding that their wages will rise fairly rapidly during the apprenticeship. There are also social benefits involved in education and training since the country as a whole benefits from having an educated and well-trained workforce. For this reason the government has also become involved in the finance of education and training.

The underlying assumption made so far is that education make individuals more productive; therefore graduates receive higher returns than those without educational qualifications. However, there is another way of looking at this. It is easy to see why a degree in accounting and finance would be helpful in the banking sector but is the same true for a degree in philosophy? It could be that a degree does not actually increase productivity but it acts as a signal to employers that this individual has a high level of innate ability and the potential for high productivity.[9] Higher education is performing a screening function for firms by identifying individuals with higher potential productivity levels.

## 13.5    Segmented labour market theory

**segmented labour market**
the notion that labour markets are fragmented into non-competing groups

**Segmented labour market** theory takes the view that the traditional neoclassical view of the working of the labour market is inadequate. It sees the labour market as fragmented into numerous non-competing groups – the markets for unskilled manual workers in the car industry and doctors, for example. The wages of unskilled manual car workers in the car industry are likely to respond to the forces of demand and supply (as outlined in Section 13.3), since the emergence of a wage differential is likely to encourage unskilled manual workers from other sectors. Such movement, however, is not possible into highly skilled occupations like medicine and engineering. Therefore there is not likely to be such a relationship between wage levels – the labour market is segmented.

**core production**
production for mass markets using capital intensive methods of production

**peripheral production**
production that is not core to the purpose of the firm

Segmented labour market theory stems from divisions within production which have given rise to a 'core' and a 'periphery'. Core production is for mass markets using capital-intensive, large-scale production techniques. Profitability in this sector depends upon a high and stable level of output which firms seek to achieve by protecting themselves from competitive market forces. This can be accomplished by securing monopolistic positions within markets and by creating a sector of firms dependent on the core (through things like subcontracting), which bears the risks of fluctuations in output. These dependent firms, together with firms engaged in small-scale or specialised production, form the periphery – a sector fully exposed to competitive market forces.

This dualism in production is reflected in the labour market and employment. Peripheral firms, being at the mercy of core firms and market forces, require a

**internal labour market**
the demand and supply of
labour which is sourced
from within the firm

cheap and flexible workforce. Because their technology is labour-intensive and productivity and profitability low, employment in peripheral firms is often poorly paid, unskilled and insecure. In marked contrast, core firms require a stable and usually skilled workforce. One response to this need is the creation of **internal labour markets (ILMs)** which by regulating recruitment, promotion, pay and conditions will reduce labour turnover and secure a stable labour force for the firm.[10] Access to ILMs is often limited to one or two 'ports of entry' with subsequent progression up a job ladder being dependent upon the acquisition of skills and experience. Thus employment in core firms is characterised by good pay and conditions, security of employment and a career structure.

**external labour market**
the hiring of labour from
outside the firm

Workers unable to gain access to ILMs will be forced to compete on open or **external labour markets (ELMs)** for jobs in peripheral firms where the stability of employment is not crucial or where a ready supply of labour is always available, as is the case with unskilled labour. Such jobs will inevitably tend to be low-paid, insecure and will offer little by way of a career. The labour market thus becomes divided into two: a primary sector consisting of 'good jobs' in ILMs and a secondary sector comprising 'poor jobs' in ELMs. Internal labour markets are not necessarily internal to an organisation but can apply to occupations: for example, in the medical profession there are rules and regulations that apply to inter-hospital transfers of doctors.

One of the criticisms of segmented labour market theory is that it is overly simplistic and that there are additional segmentations which exist, especially among primary workers where segmentation may occur on the basis of the extent to which jobs involve decision-making. Differences in ILMs will reflect variations in technology, industrial structure and corporate organisation. Table 13.8 attempts to catch some of this complex pattern.

**Table 13.8 Labour market structure**

| Labour market dimension | Internal | External |
|---|---|---|
| **Primary** | High wages<br>Good conditions<br>Strong unionisation<br>Skilled work<br>Advanced technology<br>Autonomous work control<br>Substantial promotion | High wages<br>Good conditions<br>Variable unionisation<br>Advanced technology<br><br>Relatively autonomous work control<br>Little promotion |
| | *Examples*<br>Oil, electricity, higher-order services | *Examples*<br>Engineering assembly, lower-order banking |
| **Secondary** | Variable wages<br>Poor conditions<br>Low unionisation<br>Advanced technology<br>Supervised work control<br>Little promotion | Low wages<br>Primiitive workshop conditions<br>Little unionisation<br>Simple technology<br>Rigid work rules<br>Little promotion |
| | *Examples*<br>Engineering components, retailing | *Examples*<br>Textiles, footwear, food-processing |

*Adapted from*: Loveridge and Mok (1979).[11]

**Figure 13.7 The flexible firm**

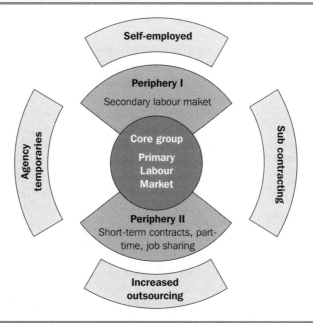

*Source:* Atkinson, *Personnel Management*, August 1984

Segmented labour market theory has implications for groups that do not possess (or are not believed to possess) the characteristics required by primary jobs – skills, above average productivity, career commitment. These groups will tend to be excluded from entry into the ILMs of the primary sector. Thus, there will be differential access to good jobs. This contributes towards an explanation of wage differentials between gender and ethnic origin and the increased incidence of female part-time workers. Part-time work is usually lower-paid and less secure. Craig *et al.* (1985) argue that the causation can run from the characteristics of the workforce to the status of the job.[12] Jobs that are predominantly done by women will tend to be regarded as unskilled and of low status simply because they are done by women.

This theory has been further extended into the debate about the **flexible firm**.[13] It is argued that increased risk caused by greater uncertainty and rapidly changing business conditions has led firms to seek organisational arrangements which allow the maximum scope for the adjustment of production. The flexible firm is illustrated in Figure 13.7.

Firms will attempt to reduce the number of jobs which are essential to their activities to the irreducible '**core**'. The distinguishing feature of core jobs is that they require skills which are specific to the firm and in which the firm often has an investment through training. Core employees will be drawn from primary labour markets and they will have relatively high wages and job security. Even within the core, however, firms will seek **functional flexibility** in the form of arrangements which allow labour to be switched from one activity to another.

Beyond the core is the **periphery** which is where the firm can achieve **numerical flexibility**. As Figure 13.7 shows this is subdivided into a number of categories. Periphery I refers to employees of the organisation who carry out

**flexible firm** the predisposition of a firm to change its organisation structure in order to distinguish between core and peripheral activities with a view to achieving cost savings

**functional flexibility** the flexibility the firm enjoys from being able to move individuals between jobs and functions

**numerical flexibility** the flexibility a firm has over the quantity of labour it uses

low-level tasks which involve little or no decision-making and who receive lower rewards than core employees. These employees are drawn from the secondary labour market and although they have a degree of job security (fixed-term contracts, for example) it is not as high as for core workers. Periphery II would include those who find it difficult to break into the ILM and would include those on temporary, often part-time, contracts. In some cases numerical flexibility is achieved through the hiring and firing of peripheral employees.

**subcontracting** the outsourcing of part of the production process (e.g. the manufacture of a component) to another firm

In addition to these peripheral employees, firms can cease to employ labour at all in some activities, preferring instead to shed risk by **subcontracting** or using agency staff. The flexible firm can terminate these arrangements more cheaply than if it were to hire and fire corresponding labour itself. Workers in subcontracting firms or in agencies are peripheral workers because their employment is 'risky' and dependent upon the custom of the core firm. Such peripheral firms often reflect this by poor working conditions, low pay and insecurity of employment. In some cases, however, this is not true – there are some subcontractors (accountants or management consultants, for example) who have the working conditions and rewards commensurate with core workers. For these workers the decision to remain outside the firm is a deliberate one. To explain this apparent contradiction Figure 13.8 has been drawn to bring together Table 13.8 and Figure 13.7. It can be seen that the self-employed subcontractor like the accountant or management consultant would fall into the primary/external cell and have all of the corresponding characteristics of the primary workforce. In fact, better accountants or management consultants could quickly exploit their market power and command higher wages than core workers.

The search by firms for flexible modes of production may have the effect of discriminating against certain groups. Overtime and temporary employment is likely to be taken by those whose attachment to the labour market is marginal or who have difficulty in reconciling work and domestic commitments and whose market position is therefore weak. Over the last 20 years there has been a massive expansion in the employment of women, nearly all in part-time employment.

A number of critiques of the flexible firm model have been put forward.[14] One problem is how to define the core and the periphery. Although this sounds easy in practice, an organisation will have a variety of employment contracts with different groups and distinctions become blurred. Although there is evidence that

**Figure 13.8 The flexible firm (2)**

| Labour market dimension | Internal | External |
|---|---|---|
| **Primary** | Core group | Self-employed and subcontractors |
| **Secondary** | Periphery I | Periphery II |

organisations are making more use of flexible working,[15] it is debatable whether this is the result of strategic decisions on the part of the firm in order to increase efficiency. More often it is about cutting costs and in some cases it is a response to a particular problem. In the National Health Service, for example, the old rigid shift system for nurses has caused major recruitment and retention problems. The response has been the introduction of more flexible working hours, temporary contracts, part-time hours and a return to nights-only contracts. Another possible reason for increased flexibility in the labour force is that most of the growth in industrialised economies over recent years has been through the service sector where part-time jobs are much more common. The flexible firm model was originally applied to the manufacturing sector. There are also costs involved in flexibility: the cost of training temporary staff; a possible lack of commitment on the part of temporary staff; and possible conflicts between temporary and permanent employees. A recent report which throws doubt on the benefits of flexibility in the workplace identifies these factors as counterproductive to the aims of flexibility.[16]

## 13.6    Other theoretical approaches to labour markets

The three relatively new approaches in business economics discussed in Chapter 2 – transactions cost economics, principal-agent theory and team production – can all be used in the analysis of labour markets.

As indicated above, neo-classical economics sees wage differentials as largely caused by differences in the marginal productivities of workers. This presupposes that the firm has some way of measuring the marginal productivity of each worker. As has been observed, in practice this is extremely difficult because of information deficiencies:

- In the case of services even the definition and measurement of output itself is problematic because of the intangible nature of services.
- The production of anything is usually the result of team activities and there will be problems involved in assigning the individual contribution of each worker to the total level of output. This means that the marginal productivity of an employee will depend partly on how hard others work.

Principal–agent theory involves the search for a payment system which aligns the interests of the principal and the agent such that the agent will exert maximum effort on behalf of the principal. In the case of the employment relationship the firm is the principal and the employees are the agents and there is no inherent reason why the interests of these two groups should coincide. The objective of the firm might be to maximise profits, but employees will only benefit from profit maximisation if they are also shareholders in the company. The majority of employees are not shareholders and therefore their objectives might be quite different. Furthermore, given the difficulties involved in defining output and then allocating it to individual employees, why should the employees exert maximum effort on behalf of the firm? Effort cannot usually be observed and measured so there is an incentive to shirk.

Where output is easily measurable maximum effort might be encouraged by the use of **piece rates**, where employees are rewarded directly according to

**piece rates** where payment is directly dependent on output

**fixed salary** that part of salary which is independent of output

**hybrid pay systems** a payment system which contains a fixed element and an element dependent on performance

**performance-related pay** is where a person is rewarded partly or wholly on the basis of their performance against set targets

their output. But this does not overcome the inherent problem of team production and there will be factors beyond the control of the employee which will affect their output levels. Piece rates have the undesirable effect of shifting all of the risk involved in production to the employee, and this may be unacceptable. In cases where output is either unobservable or difficult to measure employees could be paid a **fixed salary** which is not dependent on their output. Now the firm is bearing all of the risk and the incentive to shirk has not been removed. Instead the firm could monitor inputs – employees could be monitored to ensure that they were not having too many breaks from work and that they were present at their work stations at other times. But of course the monitors themselves will have the same incentive to shirk as those they are monitoring; thus the monitors need to be monitored, and so on.

Organisations will have different reward systems for different workers in recognition of some of these problems. **Hybrid systems** are common – where employees are paid a fixed salary and in addition to this a performance-related element. This has the effect of sharing the risk between principal and agent. The offering of share options to managers is a way of creating incentives for maximum effort and so is **performance-related pay (PRP)**. Production line operatives, where output is easily observable, are often paid by piece rates. Sales staff are often on small fixed salaries with large commissions which are related to their performance.

Transactions cost economics looks at the structure of organisations (e.g. which production takes place in house and which will be externalised?) and offers some explanation for the flexible firm. In Figure 13.7 the core group of employees has highly transaction-specific skills, crucial for the firm and in which the firm has probably made an investment in training. The higher the level of human asset specificity the greater will be the advantages of the firm over the market in both production and governance costs. The same is true for periphery I but to a lesser degree – this group possesses skills which are still important to the firm but are less transaction-specific and so again the firm has the advantage over the market. For both of these groups the transactions costs will be lower for the firm to employ them in internal labour markets, but the importance of core workers means that they are offered better employment conditions.

Workers without specific skills are likely to be employed on the external labour market; these would include the self-employed and subcontractors and the periphery II. The choice of employment contract is governed by the transactions cost involved. For some workers the market will give the lowest transactions cost while for others it will be internal labour markets. Thus transactions cost economics can be used to explain the myriad of different employment contracts which exist in the workplace.

## 13.7 Labour market policies

### 13.7.1 Trade unions

In the UK we traditionally distinguish between four different types of trades union:

1 *Craft unions* represent one particular craft or skill, like the Boilermakers' Union, which was formed in 1834 and was the longest-lived craft union in

the Trades Union Congress when it merged with the GMB in 1982. These were the earliest type of union.

2 *Industrial unions* have members doing different jobs but in the same industry. Industrial unions are more common in other countries, but some UK unions come close to this type; the National Union of Mineworkers for example.

3 *General unions* contain members doing different jobs in different industries, like the Transport and General Workers' Union.

4 *White-collar unions* represent non-manual workers like teachers, social workers and so forth. An example is UNISON.

**collective bargaining**
where bargaining over wages or working conditions takes place between representatives of the employers and representatives of the employees

One of the main aims of all types of union has been to counteract, and protect their members from, the power of the employer. They are an integral part of **collective bargaining** – the process of negotiation between representatives of the employers and employees over such things as working conditions and wages. Initially collective bargaining to determine conditions of employment took place at the local level, but with the growth of the trade union movement increasingly most negotiations took place at a national level between employers and trade unions. Before they were abolished, the wages councils undertook collective bargaining on behalf of the lowest-paid workers. More recently in the UK there has been a trend away from collective bargaining because of a decline in the membership and power of the trade unions and a range of anti-trade union legislation passed during the 1980s. In 1999 an estimated 37 per cent of all employees were covered by collective bargaining. It is much more common in the public sector and in large workplaces.

It is argued that the actions of trade unions through collective bargaining of wages have served to increase the wage rate above its equilibrium level and thus cause unemployment. Figure 13.9 demonstrates this effect. Assume that

**Figure 13.9 Trade unions and the labour market**

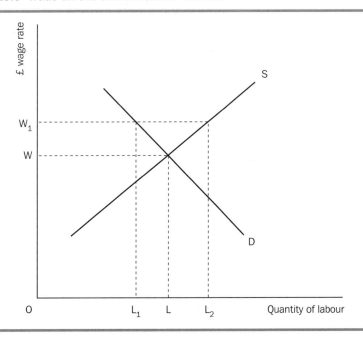

the market clearing wage rate is £W and the quantity of labour used is L. Assume that a trade union enters this market and has the power to raise the wage rate above this level to £$W_1$. At this wage rate the demand for labour is $L_1$ while the supply is $L_2$ – the market does not clear. There is excess supply of labour or unemployment.

How does this happen? To begin with the trade union must be able to control the supply of labour to have the ability to enforce the higher wage rate. If it does not control the supply of labour then workers can offer themselves to the firm for work at less than £$W_1$ and this wage rate is undermined. One way for the trade unions to control supply is to have a **closed shop** – where only union members can be employed. Once a higher wage rate has been enforced the firm has two options: it could take a drop in profits to pay for the increased wage bill; or it could attempt to pass the increased wage costs onto the consumer in the form of higher prices. Both of these are likely to lead to lower demand for labour. Furthermore if increased wages are passed on in higher prices to the consumer the whole process may be self-defeating, because although money wages have gone up the resulting increase in prices might leave real wages unchanged or even lower. If increased wages are accompanied by increases in productivity there will be no inflationary impact.

The process of higher wages leading to higher prices leading to higher wages and so on is called the '**wage–price spiral**' and some governments have used prices and incomes policies in an attempt to break this cycle. During the 1970s a variety of prices and incomes policies were used in the UK, ranging from statutory to voluntary. An example of a statutory incomes policy was the wages freeze introduced by the Conservative government in 1972. The main problem with this approach is that although it may be effective while in place, as soon as conditions are relaxed there tends to be a 'catching-up' period when wages rise very quickly and the whole process is set in motion once more. An example of a voluntary incomes policy in the UK was the 'social contract' introduced by the Labour government in 1974. In exchange for wage restraint the government pledged itself to a range of policies. The main problem with a voluntary policy is that it cannot be enforced and although the social contract continued for four years it finally fell in the 'winter of discontent' of 1978/79. In 1979 there was the election of a Conservative government headed by Margaret Thatcher which did not believe in government intervention. During the 1980s and 1990s there were no formal prices and incomes policies in the UK but successive governments controlled wages in the public sector and called for voluntary restraint over wages in the private sector.

Wage inflation is one of the factors considered by the Monetary Policy Committee of the Bank of England in its deliberations over the setting of interest rates (see Chapter 12). The accepted view is that wage rises of 4.5 per cent are inflationary. In June 1998 the rate of interest was increased because wage inflation was standing at 4.9 per cent, but this figure hides sectoral differences in wage rises. In the public sector wage rises were running at 2.6 per cent while in the private sector the figure was 5.6 per cent and within this pay rises for company directors averaged at 7 per cent

Table 13.9 shows the trend in trades union membership since 1989. The decline in **union density** has been especially marked among male employees,

**closed shop** an organisation where only union members can be employed

**trade union density** the percentage of employees who are members of trades unions

**Table 13.9 Membership of trades unions, Great Britain, 1989–1998**

|  | Number of members (000) | Union density of employees (%) |
|---|---|---|
| 1989 | 8,964 | 39.0 |
| 1990 | 8,854 | 38.1 |
| 1991 | 8,633 | 37.5 |
| 1992 | 7,999 | 35.8 |
| 1993 | 7,808 | 35.1 |
| 1994 | 7,553 | 33.6 |
| 1995 | 7,275 | 32.1 |
| 1996 | 7,215 | 31.3 |
| 1997 | 7,117 | 30.2 |
| 1998 | 7,087 | 30.0 |
| Change since 1989 | −1,877 | −9.0 |

*Source:* Adapted from Table 1, *Labour Market Trends* (March 2000) National Statistics © Crown copyright.

manual employees and those in production areas, where it has traditionally been higher. Union density varies a great deal between industries, the lowest is 7 per cent in hotels and restaurants and the highest is 75 per cent in the rail transport industry. The decline in membership is due to many factors including:

- structural change in the UK economy which has led to a decline in the number of manufacturing jobs (traditionally highly unionised) and a growth in the service sector (traditionally less unionised);
- the number of women in the workforce who are less likely to join a trade union;
- the fact that young workers are not joining trades unions – the average age of trade unionists is 45 years while the average age of the workforce is 31 years;
- a growth in the number of part-time jobs where the incidence of trade union membership is lower;
- anti-trade-union legislation enforced during the 1980s (see next section).

### 13.7.2 The government and the labour market

During the 1980s governments' policies on the labour market became polarised. On the one hand was the USA model of flexibility and on the other was the European model of **regulated labour markets**.

**regulated labour markets** labour markets where there is a great deal of government intervention and regulation

With the election of the Conservative government in the UK in 1979 there came a general belief in the operation of the free market which permeated every walk of economic life including the labour market. Factors which interfered with the operation of the free market (like the trade unions, for example) only served to reduce the efficiency of the market. The UK government took the American approach of labour market flexibility as its model. In the USA there was less employment protection, lower unemployment benefits (which made low-paid employment more attractive), more flexible wages and fewer social overheads. Many measures were introduced to make labour markets more flexible and responsive to market conditions.

### Reductions in the power of the trade unions

This was based on the idea that trade unions had become too powerful and that they were interfering with the operation of the labour market – their actions were generating inflationary pressures and unemployment. A number of Acts were passed which restricted the power and rights of trade unions. The Employment Acts of 1980 and 1982 and the Trade Union Act of 1984 were introduced to curb union power. Secondary action by trades unions was declared illegal, as was the picketing of places other than a member's own place of work. The possibility of closed shops was limited and it was ruled that ballots had to be held for strike action. Strikes were allowed only if a majority of union members voted in favour of such action and a time limit of four weeks was imposed from the time of the ballot. The Employment Acts of 1988, 1989 and 1990 virtually outlawed the closed shop and allowed grounds for dismissal of employees engaged in unofficial action. The Trade Union Reform and Employment Rights Act of 1993 made it harder for trade unions to collect subscriptions and ruled that ballots for strike action had to be carried out through the post to reduce the pressure which could be brought to bear on individuals at a union meeting. These laws have almost certainly contributed to the fall in membership of the trade unions evident in the UK over the last 20 years and the reduction in their power.

### The abolition of the wages councils

In the UK in 1993 all wages councils except the one for agriculture were abolished. They negotiated wages for the lowest-paid occupations and represented 3.5 million employees. The purpose of this legislation was to remove the impediment to the working of the free market and make wages more flexible.

### A weakening of employment protection

Throughout the 1980s there was a weakening of employment protection, although this was partially counteracted by rulings from the European Union and the House of Lords in 1994 which gave part-timers the same employment and pension rights as full-time employees.

### Opting out of the Social Chapter of the Maastricht Agreement

The Maastricht Agreement was made in December 1991 by the leaders of the 12 members states of the European Union and contained clauses on political union, economic and monetary union and social policy. The Social Chapter put forward minimum requirements for EU members and was an attempt to introduce measures which would harmonise social policies across Europe. These included the minimum wage, the length of the working week and health and safety legislation. The Conservative government under the leadership of John Major refused to accept the Social Chapter because of the expense of introducing these changes and the imperfections in the market that would be introduced.

### No national minimum wage

Until 1999 there was no national minimum wage in the UK.

Since the election of the Labour government in 1997, there has been a change of emphasis in labour market policies. Tony Blair has talked about the

**third way** an approach to government which is a compromise between free market policies and government intervention

**re-skilling** the acquisition of new skills by workers

'third way' between the USA free market approach and the regulated approach of the European Union.

- For the labour market the Labour government has two stated aims: to **re-skill** the UK workforce; and at the same time to retain the flexibility which has been built up over the 1980s and 1990s. There is evidence that these two aims may be incompatible, as flexibility seems to be a disincentive for employers to train workers. Government data show that workers on part-time or temporary contracts are less likely to receive work-related training than those on full-time or permanent contracts.

- The Fairness at Work White Paper was published in May 1998 and restores some of the rights lost by the trade unions over the previous two decades including: companies with more than 20 employees will be forced to recognise a trade union if the majority of its workforce wishes it; employees will be able to bring union representatives to grievance hearings; it will be illegal for employers to discriminate against employees for being members of a trades union; employees will be able to claim unfair dismissal after one year's service instead of two. Although this is a reversal of the approach towards trades unions, there are some rights which have not been reinstated. There will be no return to the closed shop, strikes without secret ballots or mass picketing.

- The Welfare to Work programme pledged to take 250,000 under-25-year-olds off benefit and place them into work by offering employers £60 per week for each job given to an individual under the age of 25 years who had been unemployed for more than six months. A similar new deal for older people who have been unemployed for two years or more started in June 1998.

- The new deal for lone parents was launched in October 1998 which offers advice, training and childcare.

- The UK has now signed up to the Social Chapter of the EU, although not all of the directives have been enacted at the time of writing.

- A national minimum wage has been accepted (see mini case).

- a new definition of full employment has gained widespread acceptance which means employment *opportunity* for all rather than employment for all. The Welfare to Work programme is aimed at ensuring 'full employability' – that individuals remain in touch with the labour market and have saleable skills. It is argued by many that increased employability will lead to increased employment through increased skill levels of the workforce.

These policies represent a change of emphasis in the labour market and the results of these policies should be watched with interest.

### 13.7.3 Human resource management

**human resource management** a managerial perspective which looks at the management of human resources to enhance the performance of the organisation

The theoretical approaches discussed in this chapter have contributions to make in the area of **human resource management (HRM)**. It is generally accepted that HRM as a discipline developed out of personnel management and industrial relations in the 1980s in the USA and spread to the UK. Personnel management was concerned with finding the right person for the job at the right time while HRM takes the employment relationship and its management right into the heart of the organisation's corporate objectives.

**Mini case**    ## The minimum wage

In the UK the Low Pay Commission recommendations for a minimum wage were accepted in a slightly amended form by the government. The main provisions were:

- a minimum wage of £3.60 per hour introduced in April 1999
- 16- and 17-year-olds, and those on apprenticeships to be exempt
- a 'development rate' of £3 per hour for 18- to 21-year-olds, rising to £3.20 by the year 2000.

The Low Pay Commission wanted the lower rate to be paid to 18- to 20-years-olds, but the government increased this age band on the argument that it might hinder the Welfare to Work programme. It is estimated that it will affect around 2 million people, who will receive an average wage increase of 20 per cent.

What have been some of the main arguments for and against the imposition of a minimum wage?

1 It will create unemployment. This can be illustrated using a simple demand and supply diagram – Figure 13.10. The market clearing wage rate is £OW per hour. If a minimum wage is set above this level (£OW$_1$) there will be excess supply of labour or unemployment. The minimum wage is a rigidity introduced into the market which is preventing the market from clearing

    *BUT* Figure 13.10 tells us little about the effect of a particular minimum wage. For some occupations a minimum wage of £3.60 per hour will be well below the market clearing rate of £OW and therefore will

**Figure 13.10 The minimum wage**

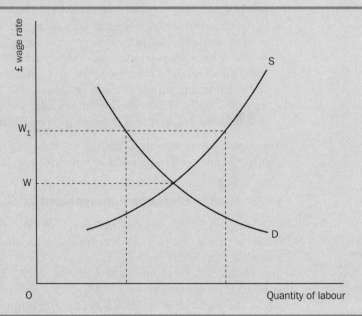

have no impact on the market at all. It will only affect the low-paid occupations. The actual effect of a minimum wage will depend upon the shapes of the demand and supply curves shown in Figure 13.10. There may be other factors like the elasticity of demand which will influence the impact of the minimum wage. If the very low paid receive an increase in their wages, they will have greater spending power and so the demand for goods and services will rise. As the demand for labour is a derived demand, there will be a corresponding increase in the demand for labour – thus using up the excess supply of labour.

2  It will increase costs to the employers who will pass these increased costs on to the consumer in the form of higher prices. It has been estimated that a minimum wage of £3.60 would add around 0.75 per cent to the national wage bill, and about 1 per cent to the annual rate of inflation.

   *BUT* employers are faced with a choice – instead of increasing prices to consumers they could accept lower profits or attempt to increase productivity in line with wage increases.

3  A minimum wage might encourage employers to cut back spending on training.

   *BUT* one way of increasing the productivity of workers so that the minimum wage does not have inflationary consequences is to train workers, so the minimum wage might actually increase the provision of training.

One year after its introduction, it is possible to evaluate some of these arguments for and against the minimum wage. A Low Pay Commission report published in February 2000 concluded that the introduction of the minimum wage had increased the wages of the lowest paid without hurting employment. Women, in particular, have gained – in April 1998 14 per cent of part-time females earned less than £3.60 per hour while by April 2000 this had fallen to only 4.4 per cent. Total employment has not fallen and the number of jobs in low-paying sectors has actually increased over the period. There is also no evidence that the introduction of the minimum wage has increased inflation, either through the cost effects or through attempts to maintain wage differentials.

Most of the opponents to the minimum wage have now accepted that the pessimistic view of its effects have not been realised and accept it. The minimum wage rose by 10p in October 2000.

HRM came from a recognition that people are important in organisations as a potential source of competitive advantage. This was important at that time because of the increasingly competitive product markets of the 1980s and because of the success stories of cultures and organisations which gave HRM a high priority.

Aspects of HRM would include:

■ *Managing the employment relationship*. The employment relationship is central to the role of HRM and takes into account the individual's characteristics, the activities of trade unions, and the needs of the firm and the economy. All of these contribute to the exact form of the employment relationship. The decline in trade union membership and the consequent reduction in the role of collective bargaining has shifted the emphasis more towards the management of individual employment relationships and the managerial prerogative to manage.

■ *Employee resourcing*. This refers to the internal and external resourcing of the organisation which would include manpower planning, recruitment and selection and performance measurement. The HR manager needs to have information on factors which influence the demand and supply of labour – the organisation's need for labour, changes in educational patterns, the skill levels of the local workforce, employment protection legislation and local unemployment rates, for example.

■ *Employee development*. Successful HRM is not only about successful recruitment and selection but also about the development of employees through training. The Investors in People initiative established by the government in 1990 in the UK is built on the premise that focused training and good communication is good for the organisation.

■ *Employee reward*. An important role of the HRM function lies in the motivation and reward strategy of the organisation. There has been a trend towards individualised pay bargaining through increased use of performance-related pay and the decline in the incidence of collective bargaining. The concept of '**empowerment**' is relatively new in this area – where employees are encouraged to have a wider involvement in the running of the organisation.

**empowerment** the process of taking a wider involvement in the running of the organisation

Business economics provides insight and guidance into many of these areas. Although the neo-classical theory of the labour market is highly theoretical, it incorporates many factors that the HR manager needs to know for employee resourcing. Human capital theory considers the importance of developing human skills through the education and training involved in employee development. Internal labour markets theory points to the importance of such development in the retaining of highly skilled core workers. The adoption of flexible production methods has great implications for employee resourcing. Although flexibility helps to synchronise more closely the level of demand with the workforce it can create some HRM problems which need to be dealt with – a lack of commitment from temporary or part-time workers and possible conflict between different categories of employee, for example.

**hard HRM** policies designed to secure full utilisation of labour resources

**soft HRM** the use of policies designed to elicit commitment and develop resourceful humans

A distinction is often made between '**hard**' HRM and '**soft**' HRM.[17] The hard approach assumes that people are an economic resource to be used like any other resource – it is to do with numbers and the notion of flexibility. Soft HRM policies have more to do with the development of employees and they stress the importance of communication and the involvement of the workforce. Soft HRM would be more relevant to internal labour markets where investment in skill and retention of employees is of paramount importance. Writers often try to define 'best practice' with respect to HRM policies. Hard HRM policies, however, are better suited to the external labour markets where numerical flexibility is important.

The more recent theoretical approaches of transactions cost economics and principal–agent theory have a great deal to offer in explaining the nature of the employment relationship and why an organisation typically has many different types of employment relationships with its employees.

## 13.8    Conclusion

This chapter has investigated recent trends in the labour market and finds that there have been fundamental changes in the make-up of the workforce and the nature of employment in the UK over the last 20 years. These changes have been mirrored by most other industrialised nations. There is evidence of increased flexibility in the workforce in the form of higher levels of temporary and part-time employees. These changes have implications for all aspects of our lives as the mini case study shows.

A number of theoretical approaches have been considered which help to enhance our understanding of the employment relationships which exist within an organisation. Although traditional neo-classical economics is abstract in its approach, it does yield some useful conclusions and serves as a basis for the analysis of labour markets. Human capital theory is an extension of this. Both approaches see the characteristics of the individual as the most important defining factor in the labour market.

The segmented labour market approach takes rather a different view. It does not see individual characteristics as important but instead the (perceived) characteristics of groups. Occupational differences and wage differentials are the results of barriers which exist in labour markets which prevent members of these groups gaining access to internal labour markets in the first place and then restricting movement upwards once in the internal labour market. Thus particular groups become segregated into certain occupations and certain hierarchical levels. The case study on the position of women in the labour market uses the different theoretical approaches to try to explain why there are gender differentials in wages.

The last section of the chapter looked at the role of trade unions and the government in the labour market and the response of HRM to these changes.

**Case study**    ## Women in the labour market

### The evidence

Table 13.10 shows that on average men are paid more than women for the same broad group of occupations. Why should this be the case?

### Possible explanations

#### Differing levels of education and training

Traditional economic theory suggests that wage differentials can be explained by differences in marginal productivities. Marginal productivities can be increased (or signalled to employers) by investment in human capital

▶

**Table 13.10  Average hourly earnings excluding overtime pay for full-time employees, Great Britain, April 1999**

|  | Men | Women |
|---|---|---|
| All | £ 10.68 | £ 8.71 |
| Manual occupations | £ 7.54 | £ 5.56 |
| Non-manual occupations | £13.49 | £ 9.37 |

*Source*: Adapted from Table 7.20, *Annual Abstract of Statistics* (2000) National Statistics © Crown copyright.

in the form of education and training. Table 13.6 indicates that there is a premium to education in the form of higher wages, so perhaps gender differences in average earnings can be explained by differential levels of investment in human capital.

Figure 13.11 shows that a higher percentage of men have some sort of educational qualification than women (73 per cent against 66 per cent in 1996), although the gap has narrowed slightly over the time period. This implies that women make less investment than men in their human capital. Why should this be the case? There are a number of possible explanations – it could be that boys are encouraged more than girls at school or it could be that girls have different tastes from boys with respect to education. Using a cost-benefit approach it would seem that the benefits derived from the increased time spent obtaining educational qualifications are not perceived to be as high by girls as they are by boys. This could be because the per-

**Figure 13.11  Percentage of men and women with some educational qualification, 16–69, Great Britain, selected years**

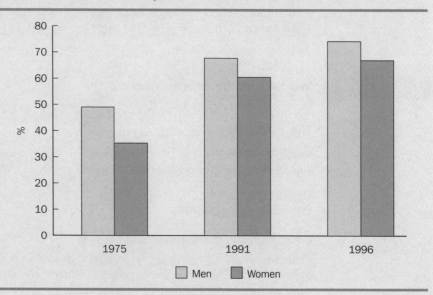

*Source: General Household Survey* (1996) National Statistics © Crown copyright

ceived typical working pattern for many women includes a career break for children, and this will give rise to lower income flows to be offset against the costs. It could also be that girls see that observed wages for women are lower, therefore higher investment in human capital is not cost-effective. Thus the process becomes a vicious circle which is difficult to break.

Once this pattern is set it is further intensified because those with higher educational qualifications are much more likely to receive on-the-job training than those without, as Table 13.11 shows.

**Table 13.11 Job-related training by highest qualification, spring 1996, UK, percentages**

|  | Economically active workforce |
|---|---|
| Degree or equivalent | 22.9 |
| Higher education below degree level | 23.0 |
| GCE A level or equivalent | 12.8 |
| GCSE grade C and above or equivalent | 14.5 |
| Other qualification | 9.7 |
| No qualification | 4.0 |

Source: Adapted from Table 3.24, Social Trends (1997), National Statistics © Crown copyright 2000.

Wage differentials could therefore be due to differences in investment in human capital, for whatever reason. But this cannot be the whole explanation, since for each level of education there is a wage differential between men and women. Table 13.6 has been reproduced as Table 13.12 with an additional row showing women's wages relative to men's for each level of education.

**Table 13.12 Wages and education – median weekly earnings by highest qualifications and sex, full-time employees, GB, 1996**

|  | Degree or equivalent | HE below degree level | GCE A level or equiv. | GCSE grades A–C or equiv. | GCSE grades D–G or equiv. | No qualifications |
|---|---|---|---|---|---|---|
| Men | 485 | 375 | 337 | 288 | 255 | 251 |
| Women | 353 | 309 | 216 | 217 | 208 | 177 |
| Earnings of women relative to men (%) | 73 | 82 | 64 | 75 | 82 | 71 |

Source: Adapted from Table 7.7, General Household Survey (1996), National Statistics © Crown copyright 2000.

It can be seen that women educated to degree level earn only 73 per cent of the salary of men educated to the same level, and this pattern is reproduced across the board. Therefore investment in human capital alone is not sufficient to explain gender differentials in wages.

### Different jobs

Another possible explanation for wage differentials is that men and women with the same level of educational qualifications might do different jobs which pay different salaries so that women end up concentrated in low-paid occupations.

**Table 13.13  Employees by gender and occupation, UK (%)**

|  | Men | | Women | |
| --- | --- | --- | --- | --- |
|  | *1991* | *1999* | *1991* | *1999* |
| Professional | 10 | 11 | 8 | 10 |
| Managers and administrators | 16 | 19 | 8 | 11 |
| Associate professional and technical | 8 | 9 | 10 | 11 |
| Clerical and secretarial | 8 | 8 | 29 | 26 |
| Personal and protective services | 7 | 8 | 14 | 17 |
| Sales | 6 | 6 | 12 | 12 |
| Craft and related | 21 | 17 | 4 | 2 |
| Plant and machines operatives | 15 | 15 | 5 | 4 |
| Other occupations | 8 | 8 | 11 | 8 |
| All employees | 100 | 100 | 100 | 100 |

*Source*: Adapted from Table 4.13, *Social Trends* (2000), National Statistics © Crown copyright.

Table 13.13 shows that there are gender differences in occupation. In 1999 over 25 per cent of women worked in clerical and secretarial occupations compared to only 8 per cent of men. Thirty per cent of men were in professional, managerial and administrative occupations compared to only 21 per cent of women. This is called **horizontal segregation** – that certain occupations are seen as male and others as female. The occupations into which women are concentrated are the ones where the incidence of part-time and temporary working is much higher. Again this pattern, once set, is exacerbated by the fact that part-time and temporary employees are less likely to receive work-related training and there are differential training rates between occupations. Nearly a quarter of professional, managerial and administrative employees receive work-related training, while only 13 per cent of those in clerical and secretarial occupations receive training.[18] Even in industries where women predominate there tends to be **vertical segregation** – women are in less senior positions. In 1996 only 11 per cent of women were managers and only 3 per cent were directors. There has been much discussion of the '**glass ceiling**' in organisations – an invisible barrier which limits the progress of women up the managerial ladder.

So why are women horizontally and vertically segregated? It cannot only be due to differences in educational levels, since men with a degree are more likely to be in the professional, managerial and administrative groups than women with a degree – 70 per cent compared with 41 per cent.[19] The segmented labour market approach sees occupational choice and the resulting

**horizontal segregation** when certain occupations are seen as female and others are seen as male

**vertical segregation** where different groups within an organisation are not represented at all levels of seniority

**glass ceiling** an invisible barrier which limits the progress of women up the managerial ladder

wage differentials as determined by the barriers which exist – either to enter the internal labour market in the first place or to progress up the managerial ladder once in the internal labour market. According to this approach, the characteristics required by internal labour markets are high skill levels, commitment, ability to work long hours, etc. If women are not perceived to have these characteristics they will be prevented from entering internal labour markets. The reason why women might be perceived as not having these characteristics could stem from the domestic division of labour. Many women experience an interruption to their working lives to raise children and this interruption, and employers' expectations of it, places women at a disadvantage. Re-entry into the workforce after a break can be difficult to achieve and to reconcile with continuing domestic responsibilities – hence the importance of part-time employment. Yet part-time employment is generally viewed as a secondary mode of employment offering convenience at the expense of low pay, insecurity and little prospect of career advancement.

Even when women do enter the internal labour market they are often not allowed to progress up the managerial ladder. There could be a number of reasons for this. It is possible that women do not want to be promoted. It is possible that they lack (or feel they lack) the skills, training or experience. Again it could be perceived by the organisation that women do not have the required characteristics to be promoted. Where organisations bear some of the cost of training they may not think it worthwhile to train women because of the possibility of career breaks. This has nothing to do with the characteristics of an individual woman but the perceived characteristics of women in general. The fact that women are prevented from progressing up the managerial ladder serves to lower their expectations for career advancement and leads to a weakening of the resolve to try.

## The future

There are signs of change. The gap in hourly earnings of full-time employees shown in Table 13.10 has narrowed considerably since 1974. In 1974 women's average hourly rate was 66 per cent of men's while in 1999 it was 82 per cent. Three main reasons are given for this: the effects of the Sex Discrimination Act and the Equal Pay Act; greater competitive pressures which reduce the scope for discrimination; and a rise in the demand for the goods and services women typically produce. A recent study by the London Chamber of Commerce found that between 1981 and 1996 almost 70 per cent of new professional jobs in the UK went to women. So it is likely that occupational patterns will change.

Many of the new initiatives coming from the government and the European Union might also have the effect of changing the pattern of inequality. The granting of parental leave to fathers and the provision of childcare in the workplace may shift the balance of domestic work away from women and therefore make employers take a different view on the training of women.

## Notes and references

1. See Worthington, I. and Britton, C. (2000), *The Business Environment*, 3rd edition, Financial Times Prentice Hall, Harlow, Chapter 5.
2. See Worthington and Britton (2000), Chapter 9.
3. Labour Force Survey, April 2000.
4. *Redefining Work* (1998), The Royal Society for the Encouragement of Arts, Manufactures and Commerce, London.
5. *Social Focus on Ethnic Minorities* (1996), HMSO, London.
6. Begg, D., Fischer, S. and Dornbusch, R. (1997), *Economics*, McGraw-Hill, London.
7. This can be explained in terms of income and substitution effects – see Begg, Fischer and Dornbusch (1997), Chapter 10.
8. Griffiths, A. and Wall, S. (1999), *Applied Economics: An Introductory Course*, 8th edition, Longman, Harlow.
9. Spence, M. (1972), Market Signalling: *The Informal Structure of Job Markets and Related Phenomena*, Harvard University Press, Cambridge, MA.
10. Kerr, C. (1954), 'The Balkanisation of labour markets', in Bakke, E. (ed.), *Labour Mobility and Economic Opportunity*, Greenwood Press, Westport, CT.
11. Loveridge, R. and Mok, A. (1979), *Theories of Labour Market Segmentation: A Critique*, Martinus Nijhoff, The Hague.
12. Craig, C., Garnsey, E. and Rubery, J. (1985), 'Labour market segmentation and women's employment: a case study from the UK', *International Labour Review*, 124(3), pp. 267–280.
13. Atkinson, J. (1984), 'Manpower strategies for flexible organisations', *Personnel Management*, August, pp. 28–31.
14. Beardwell, I. and Holden, L. (1997), *Human Resource Management: A Contemporary Perspective*, 2nd edition, Pitman Publishing, London.
15. See case study in this chapter and case study in Chapter 5 of Worthington, I. and Britton, C. (1997), *The Business Environment*, 2nd edition, Pitman Publishing, London.
16. Guest, D., Mackenzie Davy, K. and Smewing, C. (1998), *Innovative Employment Contracts: A Flexible Friend?*, Birkbeck College, University of London.
17. Guest, D. (1989), 'Personnel management and human resource management: can you spot the difference?', *Personnel Management*, 21(1) pp. 48–51.
18. See ONS (1997), *Social Trends*, Office of National Statistics, London, Table 3.23.
19. See ONS (1996), *General Household Survey*, Office of National Statistics, Table 7.4b.

## Review and discussion questions

1 What is the 'glass ceiling'? What barriers might there be to the upward progression of women in an organisation and what can be done to overcome these barriers?

2 What are the wider effects of increased flexibility in the workforce?

3 Give some examples of the kinds of issues and policies which would be included under the headings of 'soft' and 'hard' HRM.

4 What are the arguments for and against the imposition of a minimum wage?

## Assignments

1 Your managing director has read an article about the 'flexible firm' and is interested to find out more. You have been asked to produce a short briefing document outlining the main forms of flexibility which exist, the arguments in favour of increased flexibility and any drawbacks to flexibility.

2 You work in the Low Pay Unit of the local council and have been asked to give a presentation to a group of sixth-form students of economics on the reasons for wage differentials between occupations. Prepare the presentation on the assumption that the audience have a good grounding in basic economics.

## Further reading

Beardwell, I. and Holden, L. (1997), *Human Resource Management: A Contemporary Perspective*, 2nd edition, Pitman Publishing, London.

Marchington, M. and Wilkinson, A. (1996), *Core Personnel and Development*, Institute of Personnel and Development, London.

# CHAPTER 14

# Business, government and the natural environment

Ian Worthington

**Objectives**

1 To incorporate environmental considerations into the study of business activity.

2 To examine government and market-based approaches to environmental problems and their consequences.

3 To illustrate some of the key techniques and approaches available to government and business when assessing the environmental impact of projects, plans, programmes and policies.

4 To discuss the notion of 'sustainable development' and 'corporate social responsibility'.

5 To identify potential benefits to businesses which adopt a more environmentally responsible approach to their activities and operations.

## 14.1 Introduction

In Chapter 1 business activity was portrayed as an essentially linear process in which firms and other organisations, operating against a background of multiple external influences, acquire and transform inputs into outputs for consumption purposes. While this approach has much to recommend it – not least its emphasis on the interaction between an organisation's internal and external contexts – it does not entirely capture the complexity of business activity in the real world; nor does it always highlight the constraints placed upon the economic system by the natural environment or the full costs to society of production and consumption processes. For a start, natural resources provided by the environment are not limitless and it is important to recognise that their exploitation has implications that go far beyond the level of the individual enterprise. Equally, in focusing on entrepreneurial activity we should not forget that waste and pollution are also outputs of the business system, requiring a response by government and/or the market. Extending the open systems approach to take account of such links between the business community and the natural environment is the primary purpose of this chapter.

## 14.2  Linking the firm and the natural environment

In beginning to explore some of the important interactions between firms and the natural environment, it is useful to return to the generic model of business activity that was introduced in the opening chapter. Here, firms were presented as transformers of inputs into outputs which were consumed by individuals to satisfy their demands, thereby creating what we subsequently referred to as **utility**. As Pearce and Turner (1990) have shown, within this on-going process of production and consumption the natural environment provides three important economic functions:

- It is a provider of resources or inputs to firms (e.g. raw materials, land, water).
- It is an assimilator of waste products emanating from production and consumption processes (e.g. litter, packaging, effluence).
- It is a source of amenity value to individuals (e.g. space for recreation, enjoyable landscapes).[1]

These three key functions can be incorporated into our original diagram as illustrated in Figure 14.1.

As far as resource provision is concerned, a useful distinction can be made between the different types of natural resources available for productive purposes. **Exhaustible (or stock) resources**, such as fossil fuels and mineral deposits, tend to be regarded as fixed in supply since they take millions of years to be created and their consumption, despite some recycling, inevitably results in a depletion of stocks. **Renewable (or flow) resources** are those which regenerate themselves naturally such as fish and forests, and which can be consumed without necessarily diminishing the total stock, although over-exploitation can lead to resource degradation. **Continuing resources** – sometimes confusingly called 'renewable' resources – are those where the supply is inexhaustible and consumption can take place without running down stocks. Examples of the latter would include wind power, wave power and solar energy.

With regard to the environment's assimilative function, it is worth noting that **residuals** such as waste and pollution are created at all stages of the

**exhaustible resources**
resources which tend to be fixed in supply and which are depleted through usage

**renewable resources**
resources which regenerate themselves naturally

**continuing resources**
resources with an inexhaustible supply

**residuals**  products left over as a result of production or consumption activity

**Figure 14.1  The firm and the natural environment**

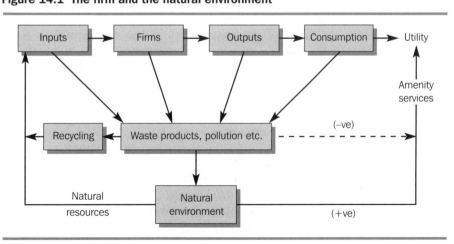

transformation process, from the acquisition of raw materials through processing and production to ultimate consumption. While some of these outputs (or economic 'bads') will either be recycled or absorbed by natural processes, a significant proportion go back into the natural environment which acts as a kind of waste sink. Given that the assimilative or carrying capacity of the environment is a finite resource (i.e. relatively scarce), unfettered economic activity can clearly damage this vital economic function, thereby reducing the ability of the natural environment to absorb future waste products. Simultaneously it may also impact negatively on the environment's third function as a source of utility, as when waste or pollutants reduce an individual's enjoyment of the countryside or the aesthetic appeal of an affected building or landscape.

As the latter example illustrates, while the three economic functions of the natural environment are listed separately, they are in practice frequently interconnected. A river, for instance, used by individuals for recreational purposes such as angling, may also supply water to a local firm for use in the production process. Both the firm and the individuals using the river may treat it as a dumping ground for rubbish, waste or effluence and this may detract from its aesthetic appeal. In the last analysis it is possible that excessive pollution of the waterway may destroy its other functions as a resource provider (to firms) as a source of amenity benefits (to individuals). In short, we need to recognise the interconnections within the natural environment as well as those between a business and the natural environment in which it operates and interacts.

## 14.3 The problem of 'free goods' and 'externalities'

While the fundamental cause of economic activity, the processes of production and consumption, as well as generate problems within the environment which can ultimately affect the ability of the economic system to carry out its various functions. Most economists would argue that without some form of intervention, the ever-rising global economic activity and the pursuit of economic growth threaten the very support systems on which we all depend (see below).

How, then, do economists explain the causes of problems such as pollution and resource depletion?

free goods goods which are not relatively scarce and therefore do not have a market price

Part of the answer lies in the notion of free goods. Whereas economic scarcity ensures that the majority of goods and services provided by the economy have positive prices and are traded in markets, some environmental resources and products are not relatively scarce and therefore do not command a price; they are effectively 'free' or 'zero priced'. Examples would include clean air, sea water and a fine view.

Elementary price theory teaches us that as price declines more tends to be demanded and that at a zero price demand is likely to outstrip supply far more significantly than if there was a positive price (see Chapter 3). In short, the fact that some environmental goods and services are not represented in the price mechanism means that their true values (i.e. as a resource to producers or a source of utility to consumers) cannot be revealed through the normal processes of buying and selling. The result is that over-use and exploitation tends to occur, as exemplified by the damage done to the ozone layer by human activity and the degradation of fish stocks.[2]

In addition, economists also point to the fact that in the process of producing (and consuming) goods and services we frequently use up some of the natural environment (e.g. when a firm dumps waste products into a river or the sea) and this can be said to represent a resource to the firm for which it effectively pays nothing. In other words, whereas the 'true' costs of production are the costs of the priced inputs (i.e. labour, materials etc.) plus a number of unpriced environmental services, the market price only tends to represent the former: what economists call the **private costs** of production. What has effectively happened is that the firm has 'externalised' some of its costs and imposed these on individuals or on society generally as in the case of polluting the environment. To the extent that such externalised costs (or in some cases 'benefits') directly affect the welfare of others who are not party to the transaction, economists call these **externalities** or **spill-over effects**.

**private costs** the costs borne by a firm or individual in carrying out an activity

**spill-over effects** the externalities of productive or consumptive behaviour

As Figure 14.2 illustrates, externalities can relate to both production and consumption and can be either positive or negative in their effect. They can also be mixed in the sense that they impact simultaneously on both producers and consumers (e.g. when individuals going on holiday in their cars help to cause traffic jams which not only frustrates them but also increases a firm's distribution costs). As far as environmental problems such as pollution are concerned, these are treated as an **external cost** or **negative externality** in that the activity of one party has resulted in a loss of welfare for another or others and this welfare loss remains uncompensated (i.e. externalised rather than internalised).[3]

**external cost** costs of consumption or production borne by people other than the consumer or producer

**negative externality** a situation in which the activity of one party has resulted in a loss of welfare for another or others

The consequences of such external costs can be illustrated using simple demand and supply analysis. Figure 14.3 shows the market for product A,

**Figure 14.2  Examples of externalities**

|   | Production externality | Consumption externality |
|---|---|---|
| + | Firm A trains its workers on computers and some take their skills to firm B. | An individual paints her/his house and thereby increases the value of neighbouring properties. |
| − | Firm X pollutes a river which increases the production costs of firm Y. | A neighbour plants fast-growing conifers blocking out the light in the next-door garden. |

Notes: 1. Production externalities exist when the production activities of one firm directly affect the production activities of another firm.
2. Consumption externalities exist when the level of consumption of a good/service has a direct effect on the welfare of another consumer.

**Figure 14.3 The impact of an external cost**

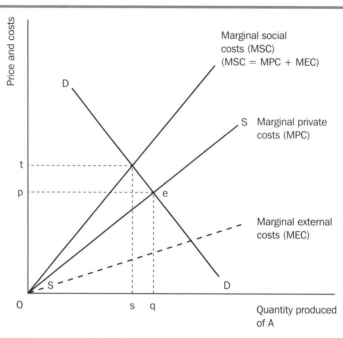

**marginal private costs**
the private costs associated
with producing additional
units of output

**marginal external costs**
the external costs
associated with producing
additional units of output

**full social costs** the
private costs of production
plus the externalities
resulting from producing a
good or service

with the demand curve DD and the supply curve SS (or **marginal private costs**
of production – MPC) intersecting at point e. If we assume that producers in
this market are imposing external costs on society in the form of say pollution
(shown as the **marginal external costs** or MEC), then the **full social costs** of
producing product A (MSC) comprise MPC plus MEC.[4] In the absence of any
externalities the market price and quantity traded would be Op and Oq
respectively and this would represent an economically efficient allocation of
resources. In this case, however, the presence of harmful spill-over effects
means that the socially optimal level of output is OS rather than Oq, representing an optimal price of Ot rather than Op.

To the economist such externalities (whether harmful or beneficial) are one
of the causes of **market failure** and, as Chapter 11 has indicated, this
inevitably raises questions about the need for government intervention in the
working of the free market. In the next two sections of this chapter we focus
on how a government can attempt to tackle such problems as pollution externalities and on some of the techniques available for assessing the
environmental impact of business decisions. The chapter concludes with a discussion of the concept of **sustainable development** and an examination of the
pressures faced by firms to become more environmentally aware and the benefits such a response can bring.

## 14.4 Governmental approaches to environmental problems: an overview

Human action alone is not responsible for causing all the environmental problems faced by the planet; natural processes are also a contributory factor. That said, it is easy to under-estimate the degree to which production and consumption decisions are at the root of many of the environmental challenges being faced today, ranging from global concerns such as ozone depletion and global warming to more localised problems such as poor air quality in cities or oil spillage in environmentally sensitive areas.

As the examples above illustrate, environmental problems resulting from human behaviour vary along a number of dimensions, including:

- *geographical scale* – local; national; regional; global
- *duration* – short-term; long-term; permanent (e.g. species loss)
- *source* – individual; firm; industry; all of us.

**green consumerism**
consumer behaviour
influenced by environmental
considerations

Accordingly, tackling these problems requires action at different spatial levels and by many different agencies, not least by individuals and firms. Proponents of **green consumerism**, for example, argue that consumers can have an impact in free markets by changing their tastes towards products which are less harmful to the environment (e.g. biodegradable detergents), thereby forcing producers to reduce the pollution content of their goods and services. Moreover, concepts such as 'think global, act local' seek to emphasise how even when decisions of this type are made locally (e.g. refusing to buy furniture made from tropical hardwoods) this can have a positive impact that can be felt at a regional and/or global level.

Persuading businesses and consumers to take steps to reduce their negative impact on the environment however, often requires intervention by government. This can range from providing information to consumers and/or forcing producers to provide more information themselves, to entering into international agreements (e.g. such as those agreed at the Earth Summits in Rio (1992) and Kyoto (1997)) or introducing directives or other forms of regulation imposed at local, national or supranational level. Broadly speaking, government intervention in practice tends to take two main forms: legal regulation and market-based approaches which use the price mechanism to change the behaviour of producers and/or consumers (i.e. by getting them to take account of the environmental consequences of the decisions they make). As the next two sections illustrate, governments often use a combination of these two approaches to achieve their environmental objectives; both have their role to play in controlling the spill-over effects of economic activity at different spatial levels.

### 14.4.1 Regulatory approaches

Virtually all industrial countries have environmental laws and policies, based at least in part on a regulatory regime imposed by government(s) at different spatial levels. Whereas local authorities tend on the whole to concentrate on environmental issues and problems of local concern (e.g. waste disposal, dog fouling), governments at national level and beyond focus on areas of broader

**directives** usually means instructions issued by a government to another party or parties and which are legally binding on those concerned

**command-and-control systems** a system where the government sets environmental standards and enforces them without the aid of market-based incentives

concern such as air quality, water quality, environmental degradation and energy consumption. The European Union, for example, has hundreds of regulations governing such areas as chemical use, pesticide use, emissions, product labelling and so on and these apply to member states which are required where necessary (e.g. through directives) to ensure compliance with the law. International agreements, in contrast, often tend to be less binding and are usually more difficult to police and/or enforce. Nevertheless they may still exert a significant degree of influence on the framework of law within which business and/or consumers operate at national and local levels.

Regulation tends to be a favoured approach to environmental problems such as those where it is difficult to measure the contribution each polluter makes to the overall problem or where system failure could give rise to a generalised effect (e.g. spillage of nuclear waste). The regulatory process usually involves government in setting overall policy objectives, deciding on standards (often in consultation with interested parties), monitoring performance and where necessary arranging for remedial action to be taken. This is often described as a 'command-and-control system'. Irrespective of whether the government appoints its own systems of inspectors to check that the regulations are being enforced or buys them in from the private sector, the process is normally relatively bureaucratic and can be costly in administrative terms. It is also criticised by the business community and its representative organisations for stifling business enterprise by placing an additional burden on employers, some of whom may be operating on very tight margins.

At an international level, regulation tends to be at its most effective when there is a general agreement amongst national governments that a particular problem needs to be tackled on a global scale and with a degree of urgency (e.g. phasing out the use of CFCs). As the incidence of acid rain and ozone depletion illustrates, state borders are no defence against some of the world's problems and their causes and effects need to be tackled that some governments tend to be more in their approach kind in order to provide their firms with singly globalised market place.

*[handwritten annotation:]* gov. Intervention

*[handwritten annotation:]* Research what the gov. has put in place to stop market failure with fisheries & road congestion / pollution

a regulatory approach to environmental turned to market-based solutions to influ ers and producers. These solutions – which nd tradeable permits – are generally seen to r control by regulation, including:

- rden on individuals, firms and government;
- l/or firms rather than the state to take into of their decisions;
- ers the responsibility for providing solutions to environmen

- providing an incentive for business to develop more environmentally sensitive approaches to economic activity (e.g. by changes in product design) and its consequences (e.g. by encouraging new approaches to pollution or resource conservation) rather than just meeting minimum standards laid down by the state.

As instruments of environmental policy, taxation and subsidies can be used to correct the problem of market failure which arises from the existence of externalities in either production or consumption.[5] Once again this can be illustrated using simple market analysis, in this case applied to a negative production externality. We saw in the previous section that the private costs of production under-estimated the full social costs where an externality of this type is present. If a government was able to impose a tax on polluting firms equivalent to the marginal external costs of their activities (the MEC curve in Figure 14.3) then the market price should rise to a point where it reflects the marginal social costs of production. This is illustrated in Figure 14.3.

It is worth noting that while an approach of this kind imposes a tax on polluting firms, part of the burden of the tax is likely to be passed on to the consumers who will see the increased costs of production through the price mechanism. Thus in Figure 14.4 at the new market price which now includes the tax, total consumer expenditure is Orgs compared to Opeq (before the tax), a tax burden on consumers of prgh. For the supplier who now receives Ot once the tax has been paid, total revenue falls from Opeq to Otfs, a loss of tpef of which tphf is the tax paid by producers (see note 4 below). As will be evident, the relative

**Figure 14.4 Pollution control through taxation: sharing the cost**

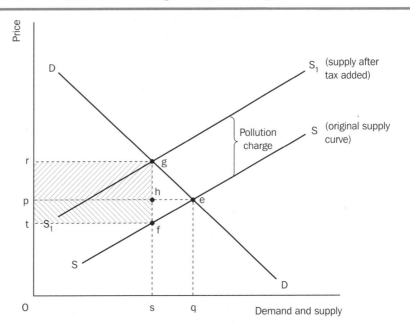

Notes: 1. Op is the original price paid (before the charge)
2. Or is the price paid including the charge (equivalent to 'gf')
3. Ot is the price received by producers after the charge
4. The areas 'ghe' and 'hef' represent the loss in consumer and producer surplus respectively that is not captured by the government when imposing this tax.

contributions of producers and consumers depends on the slope of the demand and supply curves (i.e. the price elasticities of supply and demand – see Chapters 3 and 5). In markets which are competitive on the supply side, for instance, consumers should be asked to shoulder less of the burden of a pollution tax. You might like to experiment to see (a) what happens to the tax burden if the demand curve in Figure 14.4. becomes more price inelastic and (b) how a subsidy paid to producers – in the event of a positive externality – might work and how it is affected by changes in price elasticity of demand and supply.[6]

Environmental taxes or subsidies – such as energy taxes, land fill taxes, subsidies for environmental improvements – can be applied to the good or service which is having an adverse or beneficial impact on the environment or to the inputs used to produce that good or service. In the case of a polluter, the imposition of a tax rather than a regulatory standard allows the polluting firm to choose how to adjust to the designated environmental quality standard. Thus, while polluters with significant abatement costs are likely to pay the charge, firms with low costs of abatement will tend to install anti-pollution equipment. Either way market considerations help to shape the firm's decision.

A central feature of many of the schemes currently in operation or being proposed (see mini case: Towards a green Budget) is the notion that the **polluter should pay**, a principle first adopted by the OECD over twenty five years ago and one which appears to have a widespread measure of public support. In practice putting this principle into effect is frequently problematical, since it requires government to decide the appropriate level of tax (or subsidy) to correct the externality; in effect to estimate where to draw the marginal social cost (or marginal social benefit) curve illustrated above, by no means a straightforward proposition.

**polluter pays principle**
the notion that the polluter should pay for any external costs not reflected in market prices

---

| Mini case | **Towards a green Budget?** |

Each year the government announces its monetary plans for the coming year and its fiscal projections for the next few years; this is known as the Budget. Budgets have traditionally been about raising money to pay for public expenditure by taxing economic 'goods' such as output (e.g. value-added tax) and labour (e.g. income tax). A growing number of environmentalists believe that government should shift the emphasis in the annual Budget towards taxing environmental 'bads' such as energy usage, transport, pollution and waste.

Ways in which a government could move towards a 'greener Budget' have been illustrated by the environmental pressure group, Friends of the Earth, which commissioned Cambridge Econometrics to draw up its proposals. Table 14.1 indicates some of its ideas for a more environmentally friendly approach to the public finances.

In the view of many environmental campaigners, progress towards a green Budget has been relatively slow. In the March 1998 Budget, UK Chancellor of the Exchequer, Gordon Brown, announced an extra £500 million investment in public transport (including £50 million for a rural transport fund) and a cut of £50 in the car tax for smaller, cleaner cars in the next financial year. Tony Juniper of Friends of the Earth claimed that the government had not delivered on its promise to put the environment at the heart of government policy and called upon the Treasury to impose some 'serious levies' on gas-guzzling vehicles.

**Table 14.1 Proposals for a greener budget by Friends of the Earth**

| Transport | Energy | Pollution and Waste |
|---|---|---|
| 1. Increase the tax rate on high fuel consumption cars.<br>2. Tax private, non-residential parking (e.g. at work) to discourage car usage.<br>3. Vary vehicle excise duty to encourage people to drive more economical models of car.<br>4. Cut back the road programme and use the savings to improve public transport. | 1. Remove tax breaks for the oil and gas industry.<br>2. Encourage energy efficiency and conservation through a nationwide programme of home insulation.<br>3. Cut VAT on domestic energy-saving materials. | 1. Extend the landfill tax to cover incineration and increase the rate of tax on waste disposal.<br>2. Tax new building materials such as sand and gravel to discourage usage and encourage recycling of old materials. |

Source: http://www.foe.org.uk/

**hedonic pricing** a method for estimating the extent to which a person is willing to pay for, say, living close to an environmental amenity or the disutility of living in a less favourable location

**contingency valuation** valuing a social benefit or cost by asking individuals what they would be willing to pay (to receive a benefit) or willing to accept (to bear a cost) if a market existed for the benefit/cost in question

**tradeable pollution permits** a system for regulating environmental pollution by issuing pollution permits to organisations who can buy or sell the right to pollute from other permit holders

To assist in the decision-making process, economists have developed a number of techniques to estimate the value of such nebulous concepts as 'environmental quality', many of which are based on the idea of 'willingness to pay'. **Hedonic pricing**, for example, seeks to compare the price a person is willing to pay to live close to an environmental amenity or the disutility of living in a less favourable location (e.g. in a polluted city or by an airport) by comparing (say) relative house prices of equivalent properties and using the difference to infer the capitalised value of the more desirable location. **Contingency valuation** uses surveys to estimate how much the public would be prepared to pay to achieve or preserve a certain amenity or form of behaviour such as access to a woodland or use of the car in city centres (see case study). Another approach is to estimate the value an individual places on an environmental benefit by equating it with the amount he/she is willing to pay to provide a substitute (e.g. the price of a water filter could be used to infer the value an individual places on increased water quality). In all these cases, any figures arrived at are, of course, only inferred social values placed on the environment and likely to vary between individuals as well as over time and space.

Calculations of this kind tend to be most useful at an individual project level (e.g. to reduce car usage in a city centre) rather than as a basis for environmental protection generally through an economy-wide policy of fiscal intervention. An alternative solution to a pricing approach is to use **tradeable permits** which combine elements of both regulation and market forces and can be applied at both the micro and macro level (see mini case: A permit to pollute). Under this scheme, a polluter (whether a firm or country) is given a permit to emit an agreed amount of waste such as sulphur dioxide or carbon dioxide into the environment over a specified period of time. Within the overall limits of the permits issued, individual firms (or countries) can trade permits between them, thereby allowing the market to dictate the distribution of pollution within an overall regulated total. Firms (or countries) which can meet agreed standards of emission can benefit by selling permits to those who are unable or unwilling to meet those standards. In effect they are given an incentive to improve their environmental performance over time, whilst the environment gains from the attempts to control and ideally reduce the overall level of damaging emissions associated with economic activity.

## Mini case | A permit to pollute

In seeking to reduce pollution, governments have a number of options available, ranging from regulation through taxation to market-based solutions such as tradeable permits. Under the 1990 Clean Air Act, for example, the US government laid down targets for cutting sulphur dioxide ($SO_2$) emissions – as part of its attempts to reduce acid rain – and allocated permits to the largest polluters, predominantly the energy utilities. These permits are allocated each year, with allowable emissions being reduced in line with the government's overall target of reduction. Companies which beat their target can sell spare permits to those businesses which have been unable (or unwilling) to keep pollution within permitted levels. Administering the auction and trading of permits is done by the Chicago Board of Trade, the leading US futures and options exchange.

Similar schemes to reduce carbon dioxide ($CO_2$) emissions – the main greenhouse gas blamed for global warming – have been proposed following the Kyoto Summit (1997) which allocated target levels of $CO_2$ reduction based on 1990 levels. One proposal – backed by the International Petroleum Exchange (IPE), Europe's leading energy market – essentially involves the establishment of permits which would allow countries to buy or sell the right to emit carbon dioxide; in short, a system of 'carbon trading'. Within the European Union, for instance, individual member states would be allocated targets of $CO_2$ reduction in line with Kyoto agreements and these would be translated into permits which would be given to large industrial companies. These permits could then be traded between companies and between countries.

The hope is that by creating a market in permits, a country should be able to achieve its target reductions, while its individual companies would be driven to choose between investing in cleaner processes and/or pollution controls or buying additional permits. As permits become more expensive, there would be a greater incentive for businesses to clean up their act.

Critics of pollution permits claim that such a market-based approach does little to persuade 'dirty' companies and countries to reduce levels of pollution and could lead to synthetic rather than real gains. For example, it is alleged that the US wants to buy up unused quota from Russia and the Ukraine where $CO_2$ emissions have fallen in recent years following the economic collapse of the former Soviet Union. These would then be used against future emissions. Instead of a system of permits, many environmentalists would like to see increased government regulation and the introduction of taxes on emissions. Given political considerations and, in particular, the strength of the business lobby in the major industrial economies, it seems unlikely that the latter proposals will find too much support amongst legislators at least in the foreseeable future.

## 14.5    Assessing environmental impact: techniques and approaches

Decision-makers in both government and business have a number of techniques and approaches at their disposal when seeking to assess the environmental impact of particular projects, plans, programmes and/or policies. A brief review of some of the important tools of analysis and evaluation can be found below. Students wanting a more detailed account should consult the texts cited in the Further reading section at the end of this chapter.

### 14.5.1 Cost-benefit analysis (CBA)

Decision-making, whether by individuals or firms, usually involves making a judgement about the gains and losses or advantages and disadvantages from pursuing a particular course of action. In some cases this process may be largely implicit and intuitive, like when a consumer switches from one brand of a product to another. At other times a deliberate attempt may be made to quantify the private costs and benefits of a particular decision, like the use of investment appraisal techniques which can assist corporate decision-makers to evaluate the likely outcome of committing resources to a specific project.

**investment appraisal** the analysis of prospective costs and benefits of new investment projects with a view to evaluating the desirability of committing resources to them

Whereas **investment appraisal** focuses on the financial costs and revenues associated with a project decision, **cost-benefit analysis** is concerned with the broader question of gains and losses in economic welfare; in effect it attempts to identify and evaluate the social costs and benefits associated with a project such as a new motorway or a bypass or building an additional runway at an airport (see also Chapter 13 on CBA). Since not all costs and benefits have an identifiable monetary value (e.g. increased/reduced pleasure), the analyst frequently has to impute a value, often using some of the techniques described above and will usually be required to convert the future costs and benefits of a project to their present value by applying a **discount rate**. The underlying premise to the use of CBA is that an investment project should only be undertaken if there is a net gain (i.e. the total discounted benefits exceed the total discounted costs); in practice political and/or financial considerations may override such a calculation, resulting in some projects going ahead despite an anticipated welfare loss and others being cancelled irrespective of the net benefit thought likely to accrue.

As a technique to aid decision-making, CBA is not without its problems. Difficulties facing the analyst include:

- choosing an appropriate discount rate (i.e. the danger of under- or over-estimating future costs/benefits);
- evaluating those costs and benefits which have no clear monetary value (e.g. the amount of 'pleasure');
- defining the notion of 'risk' and deciding how to measure it (e.g. damage to the environment);
- deciding whether to take account of the impact of a decision on future generations (i.e. the question of intergenerational equity);

- calculating value when something cannot be replaced (e.g. a view or an area of Special Scientific Interest).

While some of these problems are technical, others clearly have a political, social and ethical dimension and this ensures that CBA can never be more than a means of helping decision-makers to decide. CBA, in short, does not give the decision; it provides some of the information to assist those in authority to make a choice.

### 14.5.2 Environmental impact assessment (EIA)

**environment impact assessment** a technique for identifying the environmental impact of a proposed decision such as a new development

**Environmental impact assessment** (also called **environmental assessment**) is a relatively new technique which has gained prominence since it became compulsory for certain projects in the EU under a Commission directive which came into effect in 1988. As its name suggests, the purpose of EIA is to ensure that the relevant authorities (e.g. local planning authorities) are made aware of the environmental as well as the social and economic consequences of a proposed development prior to deciding whether to give approval and (where appropriate) grant planning consent. EIA is thus both an anticipatory and participatory environmental management tool which, like CBA, provides decision-makers with information which they can use to help them make a decision about controversial issues such as the route of a new bypass or the site of an out-of-town shopping centre.

Where an EIA is required by law, or requested by a government agency, responsibility for producing it invariably lies with the developers who are normally required to submit their assessment and identify the measures they propose to take to minimise any adverse effects either before or alongside any planning application. Whereas CBA tends to turn everything into monetary values, an EIA utilises measurements which are relevant to the activity or action being considered (e.g. loss of habitat or species), provides baseline information to establish the current position and evaluates how the situation is likely to change if a proposed development is allowed to go ahead. While this methodology is useful in helping decision-makers to evaluate the potential environmental consequences of sanctioning a specific project, it may under-estimate the likely cumulative effect of an individual decision such as building a motorway or expanding an existing airport. This is a problem not lost on environmental campaigners and pressure groups active is the field of transport policy.

### 14.5.3 Environmental auditing

**environmental management system** a system within an organisation for helping it to comply with environmental regulations, obtain economic and technical benefits and ensure that environmental objectives and policies are adopted and followed

Organisations seeking to monitor their environmental performance and to make improvements over time may choose to adopt a systemic approach to environmental management, normally encapsulated in the idea of an **environmental management system (EMS)**. A key component of such a system is the periodic environmental audit which may be used by organisations as part of a regular cycle of performance monitoring and evaluation in order to aid corporate decision-making.

**environmental auditing**
an examination of an
organisation's
environmental performance
against its stated objectives
and policies

Like financial auditing, **environmental auditing** is basically a process of checking what has occurred within the organisation to see if this is consistent with existing procedures, protocols, requirements and/or objectives. In the environmental context, this process would tend to include an examination of the organisation's environmental performance against its stated objectives, policies and the requirements of its environmental management system and within the context of the current legislative framework: in effect a verification that internal policies and legal requirements are being met and that its EMS is working. Armed with this information, the expectation is that management will be in a better position to make more informed decisions relating to improved environmental performance and action, thereby helping to improve the organisation's public image and helping to protect it from adverse publicity and/or possible fines and litigation.

### 14.5.4 Life cycle assessment (LCA)

Traditional environmental auditing focuses primarily on the efficacy or otherwise of systems; in contrast LCA concerns itself with the product, thus ensuring a more direct measurement of environmental impact and permitting useful comparisons to be made between the environmental consequences of producing similar products (e.g. glass containers and plastic containers).

**life cycle assessment** an
approach designed to
provide information on all
facets of a product's
environmental performance.
Also known as 'cradle to
grave' assessment

Put briefly, **life cycle assessment** involves an analysis of every stage of producing a product and its environmental impact, from the initial acquisition of raw materials through to the eventual disposal of the components and/or the recovery or decomposition of some of the elements. This is sometimes described as a cradle-to-grave approach, hence the notion of a product's life cycle (see Chapter 9).

A key advantage of the life cycle approach is that it focuses attention on the on-going impact a product may have on the natural environment, ranging from energy use through pollution to waste disposal and this information can be used by decision-makers to try to minimise environmental impact. One area where this analytical technique can be particularly useful is in the design

**eco-labelling** the labelling
of products to assist
consumers to identify
goods which are
environmentally friendly

(or redesign) of products and in their marketing. The EU **eco-labelling scheme**, for example, is based on the application of LCA and seeks to encourage the design, promotion, marketing and use of products which have a reduced environmental impact during their life cycle.

### 14.5.5 Green accounting

**environmental accounting**
an attempt to incorporate
environmental
considerations into an
organisation's accounting
and financial systems

**Environmental** or **green accounting** is a relatively new dimension to business practice and essentially involves various attempts to incorporate environmental considerations into the core functions of a firm's accounting and financial systems. One way in which this could be approached would be by introducing environmental criteria and considerations into the budgetary process so that account is taken of environmental problems (or benefits) resulting from a transaction between or within organisations. Another would be to identify the actual environmental costs a business is incurring, thus enabling it to identify possible savings or to consider changes in product or process design to minimise costs of this kind. According to the Chartered Association of Certified Accountants (CACA), environmental costs to business can range from those directly involved with a particular project or process to less tangible aspects such as company image and costs arising from contingent liabilities such as fines, future clean-up costs or the cost of meeting certain regulations.

The notion of 'accounting' for environmental impact (whether cost or benefit) can also be applied at a macro level through the national income accounts. Under conventional measurements of growth such as gross domestic product (GDP) and gross national product (GNP), little attention is paid to the impact of growth on the natural environment. Under a green approach, environmental considerations could be incorporated into the analysis by seeking to measure the physical impact of growth and development (e.g. resource depletion) and its monetary effect (e.g. an estimate of the monetary value of environmental degradation) and by subtracting these from the initial calculation of net domestic product. An increasing number of critics believe that an approach of this kind – despite all the difficulties and complexities – is a prerequisite if we are to move towards the goal of more sustainable forms of development (see below).

## 14.6    Linking economy and environment: the notion of sustainable development

Historically, economic development and growth through business activity have been portrayed as beneficial to the well-being of a society and as an important influence on the quality of life for its citizens. Accordingly, organisational practices and processes designed to increase production and consumption have generally been welcomed and encouraged, even though their detrimental effects on the natural environment have been recognised for some time.

While economic growth still remains an important objective of governments (see Chapter 12), concern about its environmental (and social) consequences has increasingly become part of the political agenda at both national and international level. Faced with problems such as ozone depletion, global warming, environmental degradation and ecosystem destruction, most national governments – albeit somewhat reluctantly – have come to accept the need for international agreement and action if we are to maintain the capacity of the planet to support human and animal life in the future. The new 'buzz word' in political circles is 'sustainability', normally used as an abbreviated form of the concept of **sustainable development**; for many this provides the main hope of reconciling the desire for future economic growth with the need to protect the natural environment on which that growth depends.

**sustainable development** economic growth which does not deplete resources which are irreplaceable, does not destroy ecological systems and which helps to reduce social inequalities

As defined in the Brundtland Report (1987), 'sustainable development' is development which meets the needs of the present without compromising the ability of future generations to meet their own needs: in effect, making sure that people who come after us can enjoy at least the same options and opportunities as we currently enjoy.[7] Implicit in this notion is the need to pay due attention to the consequences of human actions and to accept that there are absolute environmental limits on certain forms of behaviour, such as the production and consumption of greenhouse gases or the pollution of water courses through human agency and/or accident.

While much of the attention in the sustainable development debate has understandably been focused on national and international political initiatives and, in particular, on the discussions and agreements entered into at the Earth Summits (e.g. the Biodiversity Convention; the Climate Change Convention; Agenda 21), sustainability is as much about individual and organisational responsibilities as it is about government intervention at a strategic level. **'Top-down' approaches** – to return to the jargon – can only be part of the process of seeking more sustainable forms of development; much also depends on the actions of firms and individuals in the market place and on their willingness to accept responsibility for their own behaviour and its consequences. This is an issue to which we now turn.

**top-down approaches** the tendency for power and influence to lie with formal decision-makers

## 14.7 'Drivers' for change

Pressure on business organisations to contribute to more sustainable forms of development has come from a number of sources, the major ones being legislation and regulation, consumer and commercial influence and supply chain pressures.

### 14.7.1 Legislation and regulation

Reference to state intervention via legislation and regulation has been made in previous sections. It is worth reiterating, however, that in the context of the sustainable development debate pressure for change has grown gradually over time and has occurred at a variety of spatial levels. For example:

- *globally*: Agenda 21 commits signatory nations to programmes of environmental action – particularly at local level (Local Agenda 21) – which have sustainable development as their central objective;
- *supranationally*: the European Union's Fifth Action Programme (1992) aims to promote sustainability across all areas of the EU's competency;
- *nationally*: the UK government's Strategy for Sustainable Development (1994) seeks to operationalise the agreement entered into at the Rio Summit;
- *locally*: local authorities, as part of the Local Agenda 21 (LA21) process, are seeking to develop local sustainable development action plans in consultation with the business and voluntary sectors and with local citizens.

All these initiatives and other associated forms of environmental legislation and regulation have important implications for the business community and can play an important role in pushing firms towards improving their overall environmental performance. The evidence suggests that legislative requirements and standards are likely to be progressively heightened in coming years, particularly through action at the supranational level.

### 14.7.2 Consumer and commercial pressures

Pressures in the market place from consumers and other stakeholder groups have also been an important driver of change in shaping business attitudes and responses. Among some of the more noteworthy developments have been:

- an increase in consumer preferences for 'green' products;
- the growth of influential environmental pressure groups (e.g. Friends of the Earth; Greenpeace);
- increased demands made by corporate insurers – particularly where operations are hazardous or dirty;
- growing pressures on business from financial institutions, investors and shareholders to be more environmentally responsible;
- the increased incidence of contract specification (e.g. environmental clauses in contracts between firms and their clients)
- media pressures, especially the threat of bad publicity (e.g. the case of the *Sea Empress*);
- pressure on businesses from employees who are demanding higher environmental standards.

It is not a coincidence that many large organisations now have environmental policies or environmental commitments as part of their mission statements and increasingly refer to their environmental performance in their annual reports. As a growing number of companies have recognised, taking a more positive environmental approach to their activities and operations not only helps to appease important stakeholder groups, but can also provide significant commercial benefits and advantages (see below).

### 14.7.3 Supply chain pressures

**supply chain** a series of linked stages in a supply network along which a particular set of goods or services flow

As businesses have become more pressurised by the kinds of 'up-line' forces mentioned above, some in turn have exerted pressure down the **supply chain** by demanding improved environmental practices from their suppliers. The UK do-it-yourself chain B&Q, for instance, has not only audited its own products but also those of its suppliers and has de-listed businesses which cannot meet its environmental requirements (e.g. by continuing to source peat products from Sites of Special Scientific Interest). Like other types of pressure, supply chain influences look likely to grow in importance over time, particularly with developments such as LA21 and the establishment of regulatory bodies like the new Environment Agency in the UK.

## 14.8 Potential benefits of a 'greener' approach

Changes in business attitudes and practice can be linked to the pressures for change described above. Getting a firm to alter its behaviour is made much easier, however, if there are identifiable commercial advantages in doing so that cause it to go beyond mere legislative compliance. Figure 14.5 illustrates some of the potential benefits to organisations which adopt a more environmentally friendly and sensitive attitude. It should be clear to the reader that some of the commercial advantages also constitute important 'drivers' for change.

### 14.8.1 Cost advantages

Business strategists and organisations have already generated a considerable amount of pro-environmental jargon: PPP (pollution prevention pays), WOW (wipe out waste) and WRAP (waste reduction always pays) are some of the

**Figure 14.5 'Drivers' and benefits of change**

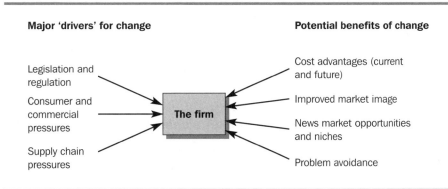

better-known acronyms. The clear message is that reducing pollution and waste is good for the organisation and for its bottom line: a means through which it can make cost savings and/or achieve efficiency gains.

Benefits of this type can arise in a variety of ways and are likely to be generated in areas such as materials and energy usage, transport, packaging and waste management. Examples include:

- reductions in the amount of waste associated with the production process
- better use of raw materials
- reduced energy consumption
- reduced need for other inputs such as pollution control equipment
- increased opportunities for recycling
- reduced waste disposal costs
- reduced insurance premiums.

In the mid-1980s, for instance, 3M claimed savings of around £200 million, mainly due to energy and material cost reductions under its PPP policy and the organisation – along with many other large companies – continues to support a policy of improved environmental performance as part of its corporate mission. Given the move towards charging polluters and waste producers for their environmental impact (e.g. by the use of landfill taxes), it makes commercial sense for an organisation to undertake an audit of its activities and to introduce some form of environmental management system to identify areas in which potential savings can be made.

### 14.8.2 Improved market image

The image a business portrays to the rest of society has become increasingly important and for many organisations can represent a source of competitive advantage (or disadvantage). Given modern communications and rapid information flows, positive or negative images can quickly spread across many markets with either beneficial or disastrous effects for the organisation concerned.

A company such as the Body Shop provides a good example of a business which has benefited commercially from having good environmental credentials and a strong positive image in the minds of consumers who are concerned with questions of 'fair trade' or the testing of products on live animals. Available evidence suggests that businesses with a more responsible environmental attitude and a capacity for communicating this to customers (e.g. through initiatives such as the Eco-label or BS 7750/ISO 14000) are likely to improve their market share and develop greater customer loyalty. Their actions may also help to improve employee morale and to boost their ability to attract skilled individuals who are keen to work for an organisation with a good environmental track record.

### 14.8.3 New market niches/new market opportunities

Concern for the environment and for the impact that business can have upon it has provided some organisations with an opportunity to identify new market possibilities or to exploit gaps in existing provision. As consumers have increasingly begun to indicate a willingness to seek out goods or services that are less harmful to the environment or are socially more acceptable, so producers have responded with new or enhanced offerings. Examples include organic fruit and vegetables, free-range eggs and meat products, biodegradable detergents, recycled paper and ethical investments. The fact that consumers are often prepared to pay extra for such products makes them an attractive proposition to would-be suppliers, particularly if margins can be increased to cover any extra costs of production or distribution.

### 14.8.4 Problem avoidance

Attempts to improve environmental performance may also be motivated by a desire to reduce or avoid future problems and/or increased costs of production, emanating from such sources as a stricter regulatory regime, supply chain developments or enhanced insurance premiums for businesses with a poor environmental record. Incurring costs now ahead of possible changes in a firm's operating environment may provide an organisation with an important source of advantage over its competitors in the market place.

## 14.9 Corporate responsibility and business objectives

Despite the potential benefits of adopting a 'greener' approach, a key question for many businesses – particularly small and medium-sized enterprises (SMEs) – still remains. Why behave in a way which is more environmentally 'sustainable' when this is likely to incur the organisation in additional costs (at least in the short term) and hence reduced profits? Put another way, what is the incentive for a firm to adopt an environmentally responsible orientation with regard to its policies, strategies and operations?

In seeking to answer this question, neo-classical economists would tend to start from the proposition that as the primary responsibility of a business is to the providers of capital, then all the resources of the organisation should be devoted to making profits and that any deviation from this by managers is contrary to the firm's objectives – a position supported by Milton Friedman who has claimed that the social responsibility of a business is to increase its profits and questions the competence of managers to make non-commercial decisions.[8] Under this approach a firm's management would only be justified in sanctioning more sustainable forms of behaviour if they added more to the organisation's revenue than to its costs.

Alternative views of the business enterprise generally go beyond this pre-occupation with short-term profitability and returns on investment (see e.g. Chapter 6). **Stakeholder theory**, for example, suggests that there are a number of groups to which a business is answerable when pursuing its aims and objectives (e.g. owners, customers, employees, etc.) and that the requirements of these different interests need to be taken into account when the organisation makes its decisions and establishes its strategy. While returns to the providers of capital remain an important consideration, the stakeholder view recognises that other factors also come into play and may at times be more important than the needs of a firm's owners. These factors could include considerations such as supply chain pressures and/or the attitudes of customers towards the firm's activities and behaviour.

More modern views of the firm – including stakeholder analysis – normally portray business organisations as unique and purposeful collectivities of individuals operating in a complex and changing environment where they are subject to broader societal influences as well as more immediate commercial pressures. Thus, while managers in some firms may pursue profit maximisation as their primary good and may never go beyond a grudging minimum level of compliance with the prevailing regime of environment regulation, others will have multiple objectives which may include demonstrating concern for their impact on the environment and on society generally, even if at times it results in reduced profits and increased short-term costs.

**social responsibility** a situation in which an organisation takes account of its impact on society including the effect of its activities on the environment

Organisations in the latter category might be described as being **socially responsible**. This is the notion that recognises that business objectives reach beyond short-term financial profit and include concern for the community and for the natural environment in which the firm exists and operates. In the environmental context, responsible organisations are those which set environmental standards above the minimum prescribed by law and seek to incorporate environmental concerns into their mainstream activities and operations. They are, in effect, seeking to conform to the current values and norms of society.

**social obligation** a situation where an organisation uses legal and economic criteria to control corporate behaviour

**social responsiveness** a situation where an organisation actively seeks social change by demonstrating and promoting socially responsible attitudes and behaviour

Sethi (1975) contrasts the notion of social responsibility with **social obligation** and **social responsiveness**.[9] Social obligation is a situation where the organisation uses legal and economic criteria to control corporate behaviour; the strategy of the business, therefore, is essentially reactive and dependent upon change instigated by the market or through legislation. In contrast, social responsiveness describes a situation where the organisation pursues a proactive strategy and actively seeks social change by demonstrating and promoting socially responsible attitudes and behaviour.

One benefit of Sethi's typology is that it draws attention to the fact that organisational responses tend to range across a continuum and are conditioned by social forces as well as by functional imperatives. This may help to explain why some organisations will voluntarily decide to act in a more environmentally responsible way while others simply meet their legal obligations. Corporate social responsibility and business responses, in other words, are rooted in the ethical standpoint of the organisation and more particularly its managers, and we need to look beyond simple economic prescriptions of management behaviour if we are to understand the motivations of organisational decision-makers. As the previous section illustrates, greater corporate social responsibility and commercial advantage are by no means contradictory objectives.

## 14.10 Conclusions: squaring the circle?

Economic activity cannot take place without the consumption of environmental resources and the discharge of wastes into the natural environment. Despite the tendency of conventional economic analysis to ignore this simple truth, it is self-evident that environmental problems at all spatial levels stem predominantly from the processes of production, consumption and distribution. In short, for society the problem is not just *what* we do but *how* we do it, indicating that any solution requires an examination of existing economic structures and processes not just types and quantities of economic output.

For many the concept of 'sustainable development' appears to offer a possible way forward which is consistent with the traditional economic view of wealth creation. Economists argue that maintaining income over time requires that the capital stock is not run down. Given that the natural environment performs the function of a capital stock for society – by providing resources and services such as the assimilation of wastes – then current economic activity can be said to be depleting this stock. While this may be socially beneficial in the short term by generating wealth, in the longer term the failure to replace or replenish this stock (like selling the family silver) reduces the capacity of the environment to meet our future needs. Sustainability, in effect, implies the need to live within our environmental means and not to pass on the costs of current activities to future generations.[10]

From a business point of view any talk of sustainable development is frequently associated with limiting growth and with increasing environmental regulation and costs: in short, a 'threat' to existing conditions and practices and one to be resisted if at all possible.[11] Not all businesses, however, take such a defensive view; an increasing number of firms are recognising that adopting a 'greener' approach can provide the organisation with both advantages and opportunities. Apart from the potential benefits referred to above (such as cost savings and new market opportunities), pursuing a more environmentally friendly strategy can encourage a business to look at areas such as product design, resource management and innovation and to identify opportunities for efficiency savings and/or market development (e.g. following the oil crisis in the early 1970s many organisations developed ways of reducing energy consumption and increasing energy efficiency). Given the likelihood that government will require higher rather than lower environmental standards in the future, businesses which tend to be more proactive in setting and maintaining new standards of behaviour are likely to be at a distinct advantage in the market place compared to their reactive counterparts.

Current evidence suggests that other stakeholder pressures, too, will continue to push organisations towards more socially responsible forms of behaviour and will require business managers to question the assumptions and values which have traditionally underpinned their perceptions of the role of business and its responsibilities. One of the important challenges facing businesses in the opening decade of the twenty-first century is how to produce products which can improve the firm's competitive position and at the same time reduce its negative impact on the environment. Any business which can square this virtuous circle is likely to find that demonstrating greater social and environmental responsibility provides it with a discernable source of corporate competitive advantage (see Chapter 15).

**Case study**  ## Tackling an environmental 'problem'

Rising income levels bring many benefits for individuals, firms and governments together with problems associated with production and consumption activities. The discussion in this chapter identifies some of the problems and some of the possible approaches which can be taken to solve or ameliorate them. In this case study we look in more detail at one such concern: the growing use of cars in city centres with its attendant problems of increased congestion, pollution and danger to pedestrians and cyclists. What insights can an economist offer to decision-makers responsible for tackling this problem? How can car usage be significantly reduced at a time when we all value increased mobility and convenience?

While the answers to this question will inevitably have political and social as well as economic dimensions, viewed from the economist's point of view three broad approaches tend to recommend themselves: (1) reduce car usage through state action (government intervention); (2) offer alternative modes of travel which are attractive to car users (substitute products); (3) control car usage through the price mechanism (manipulating demand). These three approaches can, of course, be used simultaneously or in different combinations and are not always mutually exclusive. Each is discussed below.

### State intervention

Under this approach a government could use legislation or regulation to limit the number of cars entering a city centre at any one time. This could range from a complete ban on cars in city centres at particular times or on specified days, to schemes designed to limit access to particular groups of drivers (e.g. the emergency services, older people, the disabled, etc.). In some European cities, for example, regulation has taken the form of allowing drivers into the city on certain days according to whether their number plate has an odd or an even number (e.g. Athens). While schemes of this nature clearly would reduce the number of cars allowed to enter a city centre, they tend to be expensive to police and can encourage people to run two cars (i.e. with one odd and one even number plate).

### Substitute products

In this case the approach is to get motorists to switch from their cars to alternative modes of transport. This could involve the use of the price mechanism (see below) and/or schemes to make public transport seem more attractive. With regard to the latter a number of approaches have been used:

■ *Park and ride schemes* involve motorists parking their cars in (usually) secure locations outside the city and using regular and subsidised public transport to travel into the centre (e.g. Cambridge). These schemes tend to be aimed at shoppers who may be further encouraged to use the facility by making city centre car parking difficult (e.g. reduced on-street parking) and/or more expensive (e.g. parking meters; increased car park charges). Pedestrianisation schemes can further limit the supply of parking spaces (e.g. York).

- *Bus lane priority schemes* are designed to make bus travel quicker and hence more attractive to car drivers facing congestion in neighbouring lanes.
- *Light transit systems* are modern, regular and relatively quick modes of transport, usually from outlying areas into city centres. Examples include Sheffield, Manchester and Singapore.

### Manipulating demand

This involves influencing consumer behaviour (i.e. car drivers) through the price mechanism. Among the schemes being tested and/or contemplated are:

- *Road pricing* – essentially charging people to drive into the city centre. Under experiments in cities such as Leicester and Stuttgart technology has been used to levy a toll on a chosen sample of commuters opting to use their cars to enter the city rather than travelling in by bus along priority lanes. By increasing tolls to reflect (say) air quality (e.g. more pollution, higher prices) or increased congestion, the hope is that some car drivers will be priced out of the market (i.e. they will leave their cars at home or at a park and ride site).
- *Taxing car parking spaces* – aimed at companies who provide car spaces for their employees whether in the city centre or in other locations. By taxing company car parking the hope is that individuals will be discouraged from travelling to work by car or at least may consider 'car pooling' (i.e. sharing cars).

One interesting proposal being canvassed in the late 1990s was a scheme to ban all but low and nil emission vehicles from European Union city centre streets within ten years. Under this proposal (named Alter-Europe) EU cities with populations over 100,000 were invited to participate in a joint purchasing arrangement designed to buy electric and fuel cell vehicles in bulk. By placing joint orders for thousands of vehicles the expectation was that prices of clean technology vehicles would be significantly reduced, making them more of a realistic proposition as modes of urban transport. Among the cities initially expressing interest in the scheme in 1998/9 were Athens, Barcelona, Florence, Lisbon, Oxford and Stockholm.

### Notes and references

1. Pearce, D. and Kerry Turner, R. (1990), *Economics of Natural Resources and the Environment*, Harvester Wheatsheaf, Brighton, Chapter 2.
2. See e.g. the problem of establishing property rights discussed in Pearce and Turner (1990), pp. 16–19.
3. External economies and diseconomies of scale are particular cases of production externalities.

4. Externalities can occur on the demand side as well as the supply side. Figure 14.3 assumes no demand-side externalities.

5. Taxes aimed at polluters are sometimes known as 'Pigovian' taxes after the economist Arthur Pigou who proposed them in 1920.

6. A subsidy moves the supply curve to the right of its original position.

7. World Commission on Environment and Development (The Brundtland Report) (1987), *Our Common Future*, Oxford University Press, Oxford.

8. *New York Times Magazine*, 13 September 1970, pp. 7–13.

9. Sethi, S. P. (1975), 'Dimensions of corporate performance: an analytical framework', *Californian Management Review*, Spring, pp. 58–64.

10. See e.g. Jacobs, M. (1996), *The Politics of the Real World: Meeting the New Century*, Earthscan Publications, London, p. 17.

11. Sustainable development and growth are often (incorrectly) taken to mean the same as limiting growth. This is a result of confusing two types of growth.

## Review and discussion questions

1 What are the alternatives open to a government when seeking to reduce pollution caused by car usage?

2 Should UK water companies be given the right to insist that domestic customers install water meters to conserve water stocks?

3 Discuss the ways in which a business may benefit from adopting a more environmentally friendly approach.

4 Identify ways in which a business can become more environmentally 'sustainable'.

## Assignments

1 Many large organisations claim to have an environmental policy which is often referred to in the annual report. Choosing three companies with such a policy, compare and contrast their approach to greater environmental responsibility. Produce your findings in report format.

2 Imagine you work for the local Chamber of Commerce which is keen to encourage small businesses to improve their environmental performance. Produce a leaflet for distribution to Chamber members which:
(a) – identifies areas where a small business could reduce its adverse effects on the natural environment;
(b) – indicates the potential benefits to firms which monitor and seek to reduce their environmental impact.

## Further reading

Bansal, P. and Howard, E. (eds) (1997), *Business and the Natural Environment*, Butterworth Heinemann, London.

Cairncross, F. (1995), *Green Inc: A Guide to Business and the Environment*, Earthscan Publications, London.

Griffiths, A. and Wall, S. (1999), *Applied Economics: An Introductory Course*, 8th edition, Longman, Harlow, esp. Chapter 10.

Kerry Turner, R., Pearce, D. and Bateman, I. (1994), *Environmental Economics: An Elementary Introduction*, Harvester Wheatsheaf, Brighton.

Pearce, D. *et al.* (1989), *Blueprint for a Green Economy*, Earthscan Publications, London.

Roberts, P. (1995), *Environmentally Sustainable Business: A Local and Regional Perspective*, Paul Chapman Publishing, London.

Welford, R. and Gouldson, A. (1993), *Environmental Management and Business Strategy*, Pitman, London.

Welford, R. and Starkey, R. (eds) (1996), *Business and the Environment*, Earthscan Publications, London.

# Analysis for business decision-making

# CHAPTER 15

# Linking business economics and business decision-making

Ian Worthington

## 15.1 Introduction

We began this book by portraying business activity as the process of transforming inputs into outputs for consumption purposes, with the firm at the centre of this transformation process and profit as the central driving force of economic organisation for most, if not all, business enterprises. As students of business will readily appreciate, successful firms in competitive markets tend to be those who can anticipate and meet the needs of consumers at prices the customer is both willing and able to pay. To be profitable the unit cost to the firm of producing, distributing and selling a product to customers must be below the price at which it is sold in the market place.

When described in this way, it is not difficult to see the contribution of subjects such as marketing, finance, human resource management or production to our understanding and analysis of entrepreneurial activity, particularly at an operational level. Marketing, for example, is generally held to be about the processes involved in meeting consumer needs and wants in ways which are profitable to the organisation. But what of economics? Can the study of what might seem highly abstract ideas, concepts and models be useful to organisational decision-makers seeking to gain some form of competitive advantage over their rivals? Can it help to guide decisions about what products a firm should produce, what markets it should operate in, how it should respond to the activities of its competitors or to changes in its broader environment? We hope we have demonstrated that our answer to these questions is a clear 'yes'.

To support this contention, this chapter builds on the discussions in Chapters 7 and 8 and examines some of the links which exist between the study of business economics and the notion of strategic decision-making within business organisations. Corporate Strategy, Strategic Management, Strategic Analysis or some similarly named module or subject is invariably a key area of study for students on the latter stages of business-related courses. It is appropriate, therefore, to undertake a brief review of some of the economics-based tools of analysis which can be used by firms to inform and direct the process of devising and implementing strategies aimed at acquiring and **sustaining competitive advantage**. First, however, we need to examine the notion of decision-making with business organisations and in particular the ideas of 'strategy' and 'strategic management'.

**sustainable competitive advantage** a position in which the firm is able to defend itself more effectively and thereby maintain a competitive advantage over the longer term

## 15.2 Concepts of strategy and strategy development

**strategy** a purposive course of action designed to achieve certain predetermined objectives

Like many concepts in the world of business, the term **strategy** has military origins. Dictionary definitions usually describe strategy as a plan or policy designed to achieve predetermined objectives or the processes of planning and directing a campaign (or war) to meet certain ends. Strategy, in effect, is about achieving an advantage over one's rivals, gaining the upper hand and deploying resources to establish a favourable position. Ultimately, it is about winning.

In the literature of corporate strategy/strategic management the term carries similar connotations, albeit within a variety of conceptual frameworks. Andrews (1971) talks of strategy as being a rational decision-making process by which the organisation's resources are matched with opportunities arising from the competitive environment.[1] Johnson and Scholes offer a similar definition, describing strategy as 'the direction and scope of an organisation over the long term which achieves advantage for the organisation through its configuration of resources within a changing environment, to meet the needs of markets and to fulfil stakeholder expectations'.[2] These, and similar definitions, are usually associated with the '**design**' or '**fit**' **school** of strategy development in that they portray competitive advantage as depending upon matching the organisation's internal capabilities with the changing external environment (see Figure 15.1). In contrast proponents of the **resource-based view of the firm** (see Chapter 2) have shifted the emphasis away from the firm's environment and towards its resources and internal capabilities as the primary source of competitive advantage[3] (see Figure 15.2).

**design school of strategy** broadly the view that competitive advantage depends upon achieving a match between the firm's internal and external environments

**resource-based view of the firm** the notion that the primary source of a firm's competitive advantage is its resources and internal capabilities

**corporate strategy** decisions that are concerned with the organisation as a whole, in particular where it is going and the scope of its activities

Within larger businesses the notion of strategy has relevance at three levels. At the corporate level, a firm's **corporate strategy** is concerned with decisions that are to do with the organisation as a whole and in particular where it is going and the scope of its activities (e.g. which industries and markets it competes in; whether to enter into alliances with other organisations; how to allocate resources between the different parts of the business). At the business level, its **business** (or **competitive**) **strategy** is about *how* it competes within a particular market or industry (e.g. which products it produces and in which markets), while at an operational level the **functional** or **operational strategies** relate to the major functional areas of the organisation such as marketing, production and finance.

**business strategy** strategy concerned with how a business competes within a particular market or industry

**functional strategies** strategies at the operational or functional level

**Figure 15.1  Strategy as a link between environments**

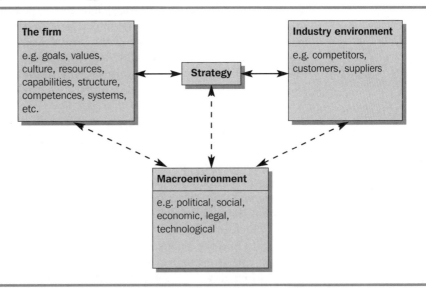

**Figure 15.2  A resource-based approach to strategy development**

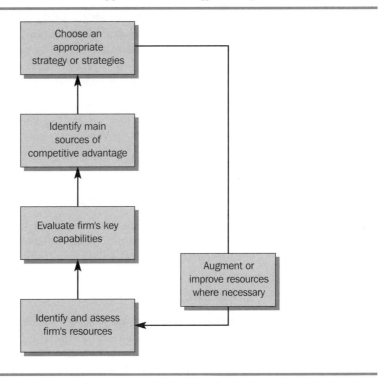

In formulating and implementing its overall strategy, a business will need to consider what policies and programmes are required to achieve its goals or objectives. Policies are perhaps best thought of as guidelines or rules which identify the limits within which actions should occur, whereas programmes normally refer to the step-by-step sequence of actions that have to be undertaken if a firm is to achieve its objectives (i.e. they indicate *how* the firm's objectives can be achieved within the limits set by the policy). Goals, policies, programmes and strategy should ideally be consistent, with strategy providing the overall direction for the enterprise: the framework within which its goals, policies and actions are integrated into a cohesive whole.

## 15.3   The three elements of strategic management

**strategic management**
management of the organisation as a whole through strategic analysis, choice and implementation

**Strategic management** is about the management of the organisation overall and as a process is usually conceived of as comprising three main elements: strategic analysis, strategic choice and strategic implementation.[4] It is tempting to see these three activities as a linear process, with analysis leading to choice, which in turn leads to implementation. As strategic managers in both the private and the public sector will verify, in practice the reality is far more complex, with questions of implementation often being an important determinant of which strategy is chosen or ultimately emerges.

### 15.3.1 Strategic analysis

**strategic analysis**
analysis designed to provide the organisation with information about its internal and external environments

As the name suggests, **strategic analysis** is concerned with providing information for decision-makers which helps them to understand and predict the current and future situation of the organisation, in particular in relation to its internal and external environment and in the context of stakeholder expectations. Some of the key questions strategic analysis seeks to answer are:

- How is the organisation's external environment likely to change in the foreseeable future and how might this affect its activities?
- What are the current strengths and weaknesses of the organisation and how can these best be exploited (or overcome) in pursuit of the organisation's objectives?
- What do **stakeholders** currently require of the organisation and is this likely to change in the coming years?

The answers to questions such as these can provide strategic decision-makers with valuable contextual information when seeking to choose between the alternative strategies the organisation might pursue.

### 15.3.2 Strategic choice

**strategic choice** the process of choosing between alternative strategies on the basis of strategic analysis

**Strategic choice** is about choosing between alternative courses of action available to the organisation in light of the circumstances revealed by a strategic analysis. As such it comprises three main activities: the generation of options, the evaluation of the different options and the eventual selection of a strategy (or strategies) from the list of those being considered (Figure 15.3).

As far as the choice of options is concerned, the logic is fairly clear: there are different means to the same ends. The task for decision-makers therefore is to decide, firstly, what the most appropriate alternatives are: what strategies to

**Figure 15.3  Making a strategic choice**

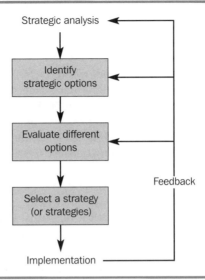

consider and what to discard. Porter, for example, has argued that the success or failure of a business depends on 'competitive advantage', which is based on the ability of the firm to deliver a product at a lower cost than its competitors or to offer unique benefits to the consumer that justify a premium price.[5] To achieve such a competitive advantage, he suggests three alternative generic strategies which a firm might consider: '**cost leadership**', '**differentiation**' and '**focus**'. Cost leadership and differentiation strategies involve the organisation in seeking a competitive advantage either through low cost or uniqueness in a broad range of industry segments (i.e. a broad competitive scope). A focus strategy, in contrast, is based on a narrow competitive scope, with the firm targeting a segment or group of segments either through cost or differentiation.

Having generated a range of alternative strategies, the next task for decision-makers is which strategy/strategies to pursue. One approach to the evaluation process could be to decide which of the options being considered offers the best 'strategic fit' between the firm's internal and external environments and against the background of its stakeholder expectations. It is in this context that the use of analytical techniques and approaches such as PEST, SWOT, scenario planning and the Delphi method can prove useful in this phase of the strategic management process (see below).

### 15.3.3 Strategic implementation

Once the firm has chosen its strategy the emphasis shifts to putting it into effect. Key aspects of the **strategy implementation** process include questions of resource allocation and of organisational structure and design. In an ideal world both the way in which resources are allocated and utilised and the structure a firm adopts should be determined by the strategy it is intending to follow; in practice this is not always the case. As practitioners are only too well aware, structure often helps to shape strategy as well as being shaped by it.

**cost leadership strategy**
a strategy in which the firm seeks a competitive advantage on the basis of low cost

**differentiation strategy**
a strategy in which the firm seeks competitive advantage through uniqueness

**focus strategy**  a strategy based on a narrow competitive scope

**strategic implementation**
the process of carrying out strategic decisions

## 15.4   Economics and business decisions

Given that firms rarely, if ever, operate in a stable external environment free from either actual or potential competition, there is an onus on business decision-makers to continually monitor and assess the performance of their organisations and, where necessary, to consider alternative strategies, policies or methods of implementation to improve the firm's competitive position. As the previous discussion of the strategic management process illustrates, when faced with making choices between alternative courses of action, managers need facts and figures about the current state of the organisation and its environment and how the situation is likely to change in the foreseeable future.

Economists can play an important role in the decision-making process by providing managers with data, information and analysis which help them to understand and predict some of the key forces affecting the firm and the market(s) in which it operates. Demand and supply theory, for instance, offers valuable insights into the factors influencing consumer behaviour and the costs of production and illustrate how changes in market conditions may have to be reflected in increases or decreases in market price. The concept of price elasticity of demand underlines the degree to which firms in less competitive markets tend to have far more discretion over price and output decisions, thereby suggesting a strategy of product differentiation (e.g. through branding and advertising) as an obvious option.

The influence of the economist and economic ways of thinking is not restricted, however, to standard texts on economic analysis but is clearly evident in the literature on strategic management and decision-making. Sections 15.4.1 to 15.4.5 below contain examples of how economic ideas, concepts and approaches underlie and inform some of the important tools for management decision-making that have been developed in recent years. They illustrate how some of the concerns of the economist are similar to those of the entrepreneur charged with the task of directing the organisation.

### 15.4.1   Analysing the firm's macroenvironment: PEST analysis

**environmental analysis**
analysis of a firm's external environment

The acronym PEST (or STEP) refers to the Political, Economic, Social and Technological environment in which firms exist and operate. As a form of **environmental analysis** or **scanning**, PEST analysis is basically a method for gathering information and data about the organisation's current external context and about possible future changes which may have important consequences for its operations (e.g. global recession; political instability in a major market). Such predictions, if accurate, not only reduce the danger that the firm will be taken by surprise by changes in its macroenvironment, but may also help to provide it with a competitive advantage within its industry, especially if its major rivals are less proactive in this sphere.

Within a PEST analysis, economic forecasting is a key component and one which relies heavily on the interpretive skills and expertise of the analyst, whether employed directly by the organisation or hired as an external consultant. Using information and data from a range of sources including government statistics (see below, Section 15.5), the forecaster basically attempts to provide an image of how the firm's economic environment is likely to change over time. At the macro level, this would typically include predictions about future levels of growth, inflation and interest rates, as well as employment-related data such as skills shortages and/or evidence of wage pressures building up in the economy.

To assist in an analysis of a firm's economic environment and its potential consequences, organisational analysts can make use of a wide variety of techniques, ranging from those involving quantitative measurements and predictions to the more qualitative or judgemental approaches associated with opinion canvassing. These might include:

- *trend extrapolation* – essentially a technique for predicting the future based on an analysis of the past, the assumption being that in the short run at least, most factors remain fairly constant and critical changes in the key variables are unlikely to occur (see Chapter 16);
- *scenario writing* – a tool for ordering decision-makers' perceptions about possible future environments in which business decisions might have to be played out; an attempt to paint a picture of the future so that managers can consider how to respond should change occur (see mini case: Shell and scenario planning).
- *expert opinion* – the Delphi method – the use of panels of experts either within the firm or from outside from which the organisation is able to distil a view of likely future developments and their root causes.

Students requiring a fuller discussion of these and other techniques are encouraged to consult Chapter 16 of our companion text.[6]

## Mini case    Shell and scenario planning

In seeking to anticipate changes in the business environment, organisations have a range of analytical techniques that they can utilise. One such technique is scenario forecasting. This is generally associated with larger organisations and tends to be used as an aid to long-range planning and strategy development.

The multinational oil giant Royal Dutch Shell is one of the world's leading commercial users of scenario forecasting. Traditionally, the company's planners used to forecast future trends in the oil market by extrapolating from current demand. In the early 1970s, however, the decision was taken to develop a range of possible future scenarios which managers could use as a starting point for decision planning under different conditions. This approach to forecasting proved particularly beneficial in the mid-1980s when a rapid fall in oil prices sent shock waves through the world oil market. Shell planners had envisaged such a possibility and its managers had planned responses in the event of such a scenario happening. As a result, effects on the company appear to have been minimal, whereas some of its competitors were less fortunate.

Shell's use of scenarios as an aid to planning continued into the 1990s and it helped the company to overcome the difficulties caused by the disruption to oil supplies during the Gulf War. Shell's current approach to forecasting appears much more streamlined than in the 1970s and it now

▶

uses relatively simple techniques to create its scenarios. Under the Shell approach, planners normally reduce the number of anticipated futures to two likely scenarios and these are used as a basis for strategic planning and decision-making. It is important to remember that scenario forecasting is only a means to an end rather than an end in itself, but it can be a useful technique in the search for robust corporate strategies. Organisations can use scenarios to examine and address the long-term threats and opportunities they face. As Shell's experience has demonstrated, an awareness of possible alternative future situations can help organisations not only to respond to changing market conditions but also to capitalise on them.

In practice the choice of analytical techniques and approaches used by firms will tend to be conditioned by a variety of factors, including resource constraints, the type of information required, the time factor and the perceived importance of the forecast to the process of organisational decision-making. At one extreme (e.g. a small business) a firm may rely predominantly on the experience and judgement of its manager(s) and the process will tend to be informal and largely intuitive. At the other extreme (e.g. a **multinational company**) there may be a sophisticated, complex and formalised system of economic information-gathering and analysis, involving the use of a range of techniques and the commitment of substantial resources to support the decision-making process. In the last analysis, of course, there is no guarantee that the latter approach will be any better than the former, given that predicting the future is far from a precise science. That said, its seems reasonable to assume that for a business, thinking about possible future economic events and contingencies – however rudimentary a process this involves – is better than not thinking at all.

### 15.4.2 Analysing the firm's microenvironment: Porter's five-forces model

Like PEST analysis, the **five-forces model** is a well-known framework for analysing the firm's business environment, in this case the focus being at the micro rather than the macro level. Rooted in the Structure–Conduct–Performance paradigm (see Chapter 7) the model was developed by industrial economist and Harvard professor Michael Porter as a means of understanding the basic structural forces affecting the organisation in a competitive environment.

The essence of Porter's argument is worth restating: namely, that an organisation's operating environment is predominantly conditioned by the intensity of competition in the industry or industries within which it is competing and that this is a critical influence not only on the competitive rules of the game, but also on the strategies potentially available to the firm. This competition, as previously indicated, is determined by five basic competitive forces – three horizontal (competition from existing suppliers, competition from substitute products, the threat of competition from new entrants) and two vertical (the bargaining power of buyers and suppliers). It is the collective strength of these forces, according to Porter, which determines the ultimate profit potential in the industry, as indicated by the rate of return on invested capital relative to capital cost (see Figure 15.4).

Porter's analysis goes on to identify the key variables which determine the strength of each of the five competitive forces. These comprise a range of concepts which will be readily familiar to students of business and economics (e.g. price sensitivity, exit barriers, fixed costs, economies of scale, supplier concentration, propensity to substitute, etc.). Under the heading 'threat of entry', for example, Porter identifies **barriers to entry** as a key factor which will affect the number of firms able to enter the industry and compete with existing organisations. According to Porter, the principal barriers faced by potential new entrants include:

- economies of scale
- capital requirements
- product differentiation
- cost advantages independent of scale
- expected retaliation by existing suppliers
- access to distribution channels
- legal and regulatory barriers.

Since Porter's model is used here for illustrative purposes, there is no need to examine the five forces in detail nor to engage in a lengthy description of

**Figure 15.4  The competitive forces in the firm's microeconomic environment**

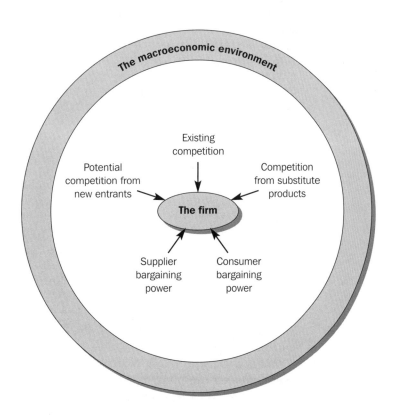

the variables affecting the different competitive elements, some of which have already been considered elsewhere (see esp. Chapter 7). The essential point to note is that, as with the Structure–Conduct–Performance paradigm, Porter identifies industry structure as a critical influence on business performance and he seeks to demonstrate the strategic implications of the five competitive forces affecting the firms within an industry. For Porter, the industry environment is the key arena in which firms compete and hence should be the primary focus of analysis and for business response.

Given its relative simplicity and value as a conceptual tool Porter's model is not without its merits and it has become a standard reference in most books on strategic management and decision-making. Critics, however, have argued that the five-forces approach to industry analysis fails to take into account the dynamic nature of competition and industry structure, in particular the degree to which, within the competitive process, industry structure can be continually changed by both the deliberate decisions of firms and the competitive interaction between organisations.

### 15.4.3 Identifying sources of competitive advantage: the value chain

Porter's five-forces model is essentially an analytical framework for understanding the competitive forces within an industry and can be used to inform the process of choosing one of the three generic strategies referred to above. Porter was equally interested in how an organisation could create and sustain a competitive advantage over its rivals and in the processes of strategy implementation – themes he took up in his book entitled *Competitive Advantage*.[7]

The economic logic of Porter's argument is plain to see. Competition is at the heart of business success or failure; successful firms are those who can create **sustainable competitive advantage** based either on the ability to deliver a product at a lower cost than their rivals or to create an offering with unique benefits to the buyer that can justify charging a premium price. The problem for the firm, in short, is to identify, understand and exploit those aspects of its activities which help it to achieve a comparative cost advantage or to differentiate itself from its rivals.

**value chain** the notion of the firm as a set of activities which help to create value for the organisation and its customers

Porter's **value chain** analysis has been widely adopted as a tool for diagnosing and enhancing sources of competitive advantage within organisations. By separating the firm into the discrete but interrelated activities involved in producing a product, Porter argues that it becomes possible to identify sources of and/or opportunities for competitive advantage which emanate from creating value for buyers (N.B. the link with notions of **marginal utility**). It is these activities from which 'value' (expressed in terms of a firm's revenue) ultimately flows.

A simplified and adapted diagrammatic representation of the generic value chain is shown in Figure 15.5 (page 468). In his analysis Porter divides the organisation's primary activities into five categories: inbound logistics, operations, outbound logistics, marketing/sales and service. These are the activities concerned with the creation, sale and transfer of the product to the buyer and after-sales support.

- *Inbound logistics* refers to those activities that are concerned with receiving, storing and distributing inputs to the product or service, such as materials handling, transport, stock control, etc.

**Mini case**    ## The search for greater price competitiveness

In markets which are highly competitive there are always winners and losers. Firms which initially establish a strong market presence can, however, find this position being eroded over time if they fail to innovate and to respond to changing customer demands and expectations. Marks and Spencer, one of the UK's best-known retailers, found itself in this situation at the end of the 1990s. As sales and profits slumped, the company found its share price under pressure and rumours of a possible takeover became rife. In response the company announced changes at boardroom level and began to put together the elements of a new strategy designed to change the company's old-fashioned image in an attempt to win back customers and to revive flagging sales and profitability. Part of this strategy involved being competitive on price as well as on quality and appeal.

To help to improve its price competitiveness Marks and Spencer announced its decision (in October 1999) to rationalise the group's supply base by reducing its main suppliers from four to three in order to achieve greater economies of scale. The unfortunate company involved, William Baird's, had been supplying Marks and Spencer with clothing for over 30 years and employed around 7,500 people in Britain and Sri Lanka supplying Marks and Spencer alone. In 1998/9 Baird's sold goods to its chief customer worth around £170 million, representing around 40 per cent of its turnover.

In a further effort to reduce its costs, Marks and Spencer announced that it would be sourcing an increased amount of its merchandise from abroad, from countries such as Morocco, Portugal and Sri Lanka where labour costs were cheaper. In an industry which has been traditionally low-skilled and labour-intensive, British textile firms have found it increasingly difficult to compete with low-wage economies. The problem has been compounded in recent years by the strength of sterling which has made exports more expensive and imports cheaper. Marks and Spencer's decision to source more goods abroad is in effect part of a general trend among firms seeking to compete more effectively in an environment of increasing globalisation.

In the last analysis, cutting shelf prices by reducing supply costs can only be part of a strategy to win back customers. As Marks and Spencer itself recognises, attention has also to be paid to the demand side which is affected by factors such as quality, product range, image, customer service and branding. Among its decisions to improve its performance in these areas Marks and Spencer has announced changes in the look of its stores, 'badging' of new lines by top designers, trendy new carrier bags and the demise of the St Michael brand (which is to remain only as a seal of quality). It remains to be seen whether this combination of demand and supply-side responses will convince the customers and the markets that Marks and Spencer can recapture its formerly dominant position in British retailing. Early indications do not look promising.

**Figure 15.5 The firm's generic value chain**

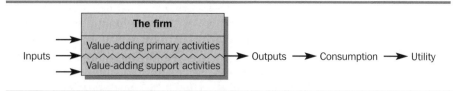

- *Operations involves* transforming the inputs into the final product form and hence would include production, packaging, assembly, testing and so on.
- *Outbound logistics* then collect, store and distribute the product to customers – activities which normally include materials handling, warehousing, transport and order processing.
- *Marketing and sales* refers to the means by which buyers are made aware of the availability of the product and are able to purchase it, e.g. promotion, advertising, selling, channel management and pricing.
- *Service* comprises those activities which help to enhance and/or maintain the value of a product, such as installation, repair, training and the provision of spares.

Each of the categories of primary activities is linked to what Porter describes as support activities. Again these are divided into a number of generic categories.

- *Procurement* refers to the process of acquiring inputs which are used in the firm's value chain (not to the resources themselves). Accordingly, it is an activity that normally occurs throughout the organisation, not just in the purchasing department.
- *Technology development* consists of a range of activities that are basically concerned with trying to improve the firm's product and processes. Examples include basic research, product design, process development and improvement.
- *Human resource management* comprises the activities involved in recruiting, hiring, training, developing and compensating people within the organisation. Like the other support activities, human resource management activities occur in different parts of the organisation; they are of primary importance to the firm and its well-being and in some industries (e.g. service industries) hold the key to competitive advantage.
- *Firm infrastructure* refers to those support activities – again spread across the organisation – that contribute to the entire value chain. The key infrastructural elements include planning, management, finance, quality control and legal activities.

As Porter recognises, to be effective a value chain analysis cannot simply be an investigation into each of the firm's activities; it also has to identify the linkages which exist both *within* and *between* value chains and to assess how these can contribute to the organisation's competitive advantage. Within the organisation, for example, the firm's marketing activities will be affected by the quality of its after-sales service and the latter may be an important source of differentiation which is not easily replicated by rival organisations. Outside the business, a considerable degree of value creation may emanate from the firm's supply and distribution arrangements, exemplified by the degree to which car manufacturers are dependent on a supply of quality components from other organisations and on the quality of service provided by their distributors. These links between an organisation's value chain and the value chains of suppliers, distributors and ultimately buyers are what Porter describes as the firm's broader value system. Like internal linkages, these vertical relationships provide the organisation with a source of competitive advantage which other firms find difficult to emulate.

In exploring how value chain analysis can assist decision-makers to identify and exploit opportunities for creating competitive advantage, Porter draws on ideas and concepts readily familiar to the business economist. On the cost side, he argues that costs can be identified in terms of the different activities within the value chain and that the behaviour of these costs depends on a number of structural factors he calls 'cost drivers'. These might include economies/diseconomies of scale, experience curve benefits, timing, the location of an activity, and institutional factors such as government pricing. To gain a competitive advantage, the firm needs either to control these cost drivers (e.g. by exploiting scale economies) or to reconfigure the value chain to its advantage (e.g. finding better ways to produce, distribute or market its product).

Differentiation is equally seen to flow from the activities within the value chain, with any value activity being a potential source of uniqueness for the organisation. As with costs, Porter argues that the firm needs to consider the factors which are driving this uniqueness, such as policy choices, locational influences, choice of suppliers or brand image. It is then in a position to enhance this differentiation in one of two ways: by improving on the source(s) of its uniqueness or reconfiguring the value chain to offer greater opportunities for achieving a uniqueness which is not easily copied by rivals (e.g. one based on a multitude of highly compatible linkages across the value chain).

### 15.4.4 The make or buy decision: transaction cost economics

Within his discussion of the configuration and economics of the value chain, Porter refers to the influence of an organisation's competitive scope. Among the questions a business has to face are:

- In which industry or industries should we compete?
- What should be our geographical spread?
- To what extent should our activities be performed in house or by outside organisations?

The answers to concerns such as these determines whether the firm adopts a narrow or broad scope and whether it operates as a largely self-sufficient entity or in coalition with other organisations (e.g. through a **joint venture** or **licensing arrangement**). As indicated previously, important questions such as the make or buy decision are central to the field of transactions cost economics (see Chapter 2).

There is no need to repeat the analysis contained in Chapter 2 (students are advised to pause at this point and to quickly revise their understanding of **transactions costs**). The essential point to note is that from a decision-making point of view firms sometimes have to decide whether the costs and benefits of

**joint venture** an undertaking involving two or more parties who co-operate for commercial purposes

**licensing** where one party permits another party access to its ideas, products, patents, trademarks, etc. in exchange for a fee or royalty

a market relationship (e.g. buying raw materials for production) outweigh those of a non-market kind (e.g. producing the materials oneself). Where the transaction costs of a market relationship are high, some firms may decide to 'internalise' these by acquiring the firm(s) supplying its raw materials or components or involved in distributing its finished goods. A strategy of **vertical integration**, in other words, may be driven at least in part by a decision by the firm to seek the net benefits of internalisation.

Transactions cost analysis can also help to provide insight into a number of other areas of corporate decision-making. For example:

- *Multinational activity* may be a preferred option for firms seeking to exploit an international market when the transaction costs of having wholly owned foreign subsidiaries is lower than the alternatives such as subcontracting, licensing or joint ventures.
- *Contract renegotiation* between firms can be linked to asset specificity and the possibilities this creates for opportunistic behaviour where one firm becomes heavily committed to a transaction because of its sunk assets.
- *Long-term contracts* may appear a better solution for firms faced with the problem of asset specificity and the possibility that a supplier, producer or distributor will try to renegotiate more favourable terms (N.B. vertical integration is an alternative course of action to prevent opportunistic behaviour arising from asset specificity).
- *'Outsourcing' decisions* may reflect a relative improvement in transaction costs compared to in-house provision as competition becomes more intense and the business environment becomes more turbulent.
- *Partnership arrangements* between firms might provide sufficient benefits (e.g. increased quality, lower costs, innovation) and flexibility within a transaction framework to obviate the need for formal integration.

In all the above cases, a central question facing the firm is whether the transaction costs of buying from (or supplying to) another organisation outweigh the administrative costs of managing the internal relationship. While this may not be the deciding factor in a firm's decision to make or buy, it is likely to be an important consideration at some stage during the decision-making process.

### 15.4.5 Analysing strategic interaction: game theory

A firm operating in a competitive market faces a degree of uncertainty regarding the actions/reactions of its rivals to any changes in its strategy. If firm X lowers its price, for instance, will its competitors follow suit? If it alters its non-price strategy, will its rivals respond by changing theirs? Questions such as these can be vitally important to the organisation and its competitive advantage, as illustrated by the periodic **price wars** in the newspaper and oil industries and the fierce competition between the major UK supermarket chains.

As demonstrated in Chapter 7, game theory provides a theoretical basis for analysing strategic interaction, particularly within **oligopoly markets**. The essence of the approach is to model the likely actions/reactions (i.e. 'strategies') of the participants (or 'players') in the game and to examine the consequences ('pay-offs') of the different responses each firm might make in a competitive situation. In the context of a game, the decisions made by the different players are said to be 'strategic', given that they not only affect the other players but also affect the choices they make.

As far as the analyst is concerned, game theory can be a useful tool for predicting the likely behaviour of firms under certain market structures. It can help managers to devise a strategy to achieve a particular desired outcome, with the strategy being the broad pattern or plan which guides the organisation's decisions in areas such as price, output, promotion, cost, etc. The 'pay-off' for the organisation of pursuing a particular course of action depends not only on the strategies being pursued by the different players, but also on the constraints that each faces (e.g. customer responses, available technology, legal restrictions, etc.). A given strategy is said to be a player's 'dominant strategy' if it offers the participant the highest pay-off regardless of what the other players do.

## 15.5 Information for business decision-making

Researching in the field of business economics and business environment can be a daunting task, given the extensive amount of information and statistical data available. To help in this direction the final section of this chapter outlines some of the key national and international information sources, which are readily accessible to both students and businesses. While the list is by no means exhaustive, it gives a good indication of the wide range of assistance available to researchers and of the different formats in which information is published by government and non-government sources for different purposes. It is worth noting that in recent years much of this information has become available in an electronic as well as a published format and can be accessed using computerised databases such as CD-ROMs. The development of the internet is also of key significance to students of business and to organisations.

### 15.5.1 Statistical sources

Statistical information is an important component of business research and students need to be aware of what is available, particularly as some data turn up in the most unexpected places. Three key guides in locating statistical information are:

1 *Guide to Official Statistics.* Published by the Office for National Statistics (ONS) and an important starting point in any search for statistical sources of information. The guide covers all official UK government statistics and some important non-official sources and provides broad descriptions of these and access through an alphabetical subject index.

2 *Sources of Unofficial UK Statistics.* Compiled by Warwick University Library and providing details of a large number of unofficial statistical publications from a wide variety of organisations (e.g. pressure groups, trade unions, professional associations).

3 *World Directory of Non-Official Statistical Sources.* Published by Euromonitor and a key guide to non-official sources in selected countries outside Western Europe, the latter being covered by the *European Directory of Non-Official Statistical Sources.* The directory concentrates particularly on sources dealing with consumer goods, consumer trends, key

industries and national economic and business trends. It has a subject and a geographical index.

Some of the main statistical sources, arranged in alphabetical order, are discussed below:

4 *Annual Abstract of Statistics.* Published by the ONS, this is an authoritative source of official statistics arranged under various headings, which include population, production, energy, transport, trade and public services. Figures usually cover a ten-year period and are presented in tabulated form. There is a detailed alphabetical index at the end.

5 *Basic Statistics of the European Union.* A pocket guide of comparative statistics on the EU, together with the United States, Canada, Japan and a number of other countries. Published by Eurostat, the annual guide covers areas such as population, finance, trade, environment and the economy and the data sometimes span several years.

6 *Business Briefing.* Produced by the British Chambers of Commerce and containing a variety of comment, information and statistical data useful to business. Good source of contemporary information.

7 *Consumer Europe.* Produced by Euromonitor and available on CD-ROM, this is a pan-European source of marketing statistics with the emphasis on consumer goods and consumer trends. The information, which is updated at yearly or two-yearly intervals, examines the main product groups and includes predictions on future levels of consumption. A *Consumer Eastern Europe* has recently been added to the series.

8 *Datastream.* A finance and economics on-line database, produced by Primark International. Accounts for public companies around the world, together with share prices and stock market indices. The economics databases cover a vast range of current and historical international economic series, including money supply, inflation and interest rates for 150 countries. Data are taken from many statistical sources, including OECD and the UK government, central banks and unofficial statistical sources.

9 *Economic Survey of Europe.* Published annually by the United Nations (UN). The survey includes data in various forms on individual countries and on geographical groupings in Europe and identifies trends in areas such as agriculture, industry, investment and trade. Tables and charts include written commentary.

10 *Economic Trends.* A monthly publication by the ONS and a key guide to the current economic indicators (e.g. prices, unemployment, trade, interest rates, exchange rates). The figures span several years, as well as the latest month or quarter, and tables and charts are provided. A quarterly supplement covering the balance of payments and the national accounts was added in March 1993.

11 *Economist Intelligence Unit Country Reports.* Reviews the business environment for countries, and is divided into six major regions of the world. Quarterly reports summarise major events, issues and trends and provide key statistics. These are available on paper, CD-ROM or the internet.

12 *Employment in Europe.* Contains an excellent overview of employment issues in Europe. Published annually by the European Commission, with a different focus in each issue.

13 *Europa World Year Book*. Published by Europa, London. An annual book which has an A–Z listing of all countries. Each entry contains a political and historical overview of a country, key statistics, contact details and basic facts about leading organisations, political parties, the media, diplomatic representation, etc.

14 *Europe in Figures*. An overview of Europe, with lots of graphs and tables. A simple introduction, but published irregularly.

15 *European Economy*. Published by the European Commission and concerned with the economic situation and other developments. The journal includes data on economic trends and business indicators and provides a statistical appendix on long-term macroeconomic indicators within Europe. There are two issues and three reports per year.

16 *European Marketing Data and Statistics*. An annual publication by Euromonitor providing statistical information on the countries of Western and Eastern Europe. The data cover a wide range of market aspects – including demographic trends, economic indicators, trade, consumer expenditure, retailing – and often show trends over a 21-year period. The information is provided primarily in a spreadsheet format and there is an alphabetical index.

17 *Family Expenditure Survey*. A comprehensive breakdown of data on households, including income, expenditure and other aspects of finance. The survey has very detailed tables and charts – mostly for the latest year – and some regional analysis is provided. Published by the Stationery Office (TSO).

18 *Financial Statistics*. A monthly publication by the ONS on a wide range of financial aspects including the accounts of the public and non-public sectors of the economy. Figures cover the latest month or quarter together with those of previous years. Data are available on floppy disk from ONS. See also www.statistics.gov.uk/statbase/mainmenu.asp.

19 *General Household Survey*. A continuous sample survey based on the financial year of the general population produced by the ONS. The survey spans a wide range of household-related aspects – including housing, health, education and employment – and is widely used as a source of background information for central government decisions on resource allocation. Since 1994 it has been renamed *Living in Britain: Results of the General Household Survey*.

20 *International Marketing Data and Statistics (IMDAS)*. An international compendium of statistical information on the Americas, Asia, Africa and Oceania published annually by Euromonitor. Information on demographics, economic trends, finance, trade, consumer expenditure and many other areas usually covers a 21-year trend period, and an alphabetical index is provided. Available on CD-ROM – *World Marketing Data and Statistics*. See also www.euromonitor. com/Imdas.html.

21 *Labour Market Trends*. Formerly the *Employment Gazette*, this is a monthly publication by the ONS that contains labour market data and a number of feature articles.

22 *Labour Market Quarterly Report*. Published by the Department for Education and Employment (DfEE), and containing information and data on labour market trends and other issues such as training.

23 *Marketing Pocket Book*. Published by NTC Publications. An essential source of statistics and information. Published annually. Sister publications include *European Marketing Pocket Book* and *Retail Pocket Book*.

24 *Monthly Digest of Statistics*. The key source of current information on national income, output and expenditure, population, employment, trade, prices and a range of other areas. Previous as well as current data are provided. Published by ONS.

25 *New Earnings Survey*. An annual publication in parts by ONS. It contains detailed statistical information on earnings by industry, occupation, region, country and age group. Available on-line via NOMIS from October 1997.

26 *National Income and Expenditure*. Now known as the *United Kingdom National Accounts* (or 'Blue Book'). Published annually by ONS, it contains data on domestic and national output, income and expenditure, and includes a sector-by-sector analysis. Figures often cover ten years or more and an alphabetical index is provided. Available on CD-ROM and on-line.

27 *Oasis*. A database containing information about sites on the world wide web that contain secondary statistical data. Most sources are free. Has links to government and other sites. Access via www.plym.ac.uk/oasis/index.html.

28 *OECD Economic Outlook*. A periodic assessment of economic trends, policies and prospects in OECD and non-member countries. Published twice a year, the *Outlook* includes articles as well as figures, tables, charts and short-term projections, and looks at developments on a country-by-country basis. Available for subscribers on the internet (www.oecd.org/eco/out/eo.htm).

29 *OECD Economic Surveys*. An annual publication by the OECD providing individual country reports of the world's advanced industrial economies. Very useful. Available on CD-ROM.

30 *Overseas Trade Statistics with Countries outside the European Community*. Published quarterly by TSO and containing statistical information on trade with non-EU countries. Available on the internet via www.tso-online.co.uk.

31 *Panorama of EU Industry*. Produced by the Office for Official Publications of the European Communities. Provides an overview of industries in Europe, with statistics, analysis and company information. Published irregularly.

32 *Quest Economics*. A collection of macroeconomic and country risk data from a variety of sources. Available as an on-line, internet or CD-ROM database.

33 *Regional Trends*. An annual ONS publication providing a wide range of information on social, demographic and economic aspects of the United Kingdom's standard planning regions, together with some data on the sub-regions and on the EU. The guide includes a subject index. Available on the internet via www.ons.gov.uk.

34 *Social Trends*. Another annual ONS publication, in this case looking at different aspects of British society, including population, education, environment, housing, leisure and transport. It provides a more detailed analysis of data produced for the *Annual Abstract of Statistics* and includes a large number of charts and diagrams. Information often spans a 15–20-year period and an alphabetical subject index is included. Available on the internet via www.ons.gov.uk.

35 *United Kingdom Balance of Payments*. Known as the Pink Book. It is a comprehensive guide to the United Kingdom's external trade performance and contains a wide range of statistics covering a ten-year period. Available on the internet (see *Social Trends*).

36 *United Nations Statistical Yearbook*. Written in both English and French, the yearbook is a detailed international comparative analysis of UN

member countries. Data cover a wide variety of topics, including international finance, transport and communications, population, trade and wages, and a World Statistical Summary is provided at the beginning.

37 *World Economic Outlook*. Published twice a year by the IMF in various languages. It is an analysis of global economic developments in the short and medium terms. It gives an overview of the world economy and looks at current global issues.

### 15.5.2 Information sources

Information on the different aspects of the business environment can be found in a variety of sources, including books, newspapers and periodicals. These often provide a wealth of contemporary data and commentary which can be located relatively easily in most cases, using indexes and other reference works designed to assist the researcher. While an increasing amount of information is available on the internet, the fastest and most reliable way of finding what you want tends to be to use newspapers and magazines, which are often available electronically (and which are loved by librarians!). In the last few years more and more abstracting databases have moved over to the web, and now also offer the full text of articles, thereby reducing the amount of time it takes to research a topic. *BHI* (see below) can be used to trace information, but there are other alternatives (e.g. *Expanded Academic ASAP* and *Academic Search Elite*). It is even possible to customise your business databases to cover the most popular titles in a particular library. But remember, the situation tends to change on a regular basis, so you need to keep up to date. Some key sources in this area are discussed below:

1 *Anbar (Anbar Management Intelligence)*. Published by MCB University Press Ltd in six issues per year. Comprising seven separate abstracting services covering fields such as accounting and finance, marketing and distribution and personnel and training and published in association with the appropriate professional body. All seven services are subsequently published as the *Complete Anbar*. Available on CD-ROM and on the internet via www.anbar.co.uk/management/home.htm (subscription required).

2 *British Humanities Index (BHI)*. A comprehensive guide to over 300 current periodicals, BHI is published quarterly and contains a number of areas relevant to students of business. Sources are arranged in alphabetical sequence and there is an author and subject index. Available on CD-ROM (*BHI Plus*).

3 *British National Bibliography (BNB)*. A record of all books published in the United Kingdom and deposited in the British Library. The subject catalogue lists books in subject order in keeping with the Dewey Classification Scheme and hence is a good source of reference on business and management. Available on CD-ROM. See also www.opac97.bl.uk, which is a very useful reference source.

4 *Business and Industry*. Covers trade and business news titles worldwide and is available as an on-line, web-based or CD-ROM database.

5 *Business Source Elite*. Covers over 1,000 full-text titles and abstracts many others in all areas of business, economics and management.

6 *Catalogue of British Official Publications Not Published by the Stationery Office*. A bi-monthly publication from TSO, annually cumulated, showing a list of publications from a range of public bodies (e.g. quangos) but which are not published by TSO. Arranged in order of department or organisation, with a combined author/subject index. Available on CD-ROM.

7 *Clover Newspaper Index*. Now known as *Newspaper Index*, a fortnightly publication covering all the main quality dailies as well as the Sunday papers. The list of articles is arranged in alphabetical order by subject and provides a readily accessible means of tracing topics of current interest. See www.cloverweb.co.uk.

8 *Emerald*. An internet version of all the journals published by MCB University Press; includes some key titles like the *European Journal of Marketing*.

9 *European Business ASAP*. A CD-ROM or web database (where the home site is called Infotrac Searchbank) which has full-text articles from the 100 most popular journals in academic business libraries in Europe.

10 *Extel*. A detailed company information service for British and overseas companies provided by Extel Financial Limited. The service is provided on CD-ROM and covers companies of various types, including quoted and unquoted business.

11 *FT McCarthy*. Available as a CD-ROM, on-line or web database, McCarthy covers business and management articles from over 50 newspapers and trade publications in the UK, Europe and further afield. Its business focus make it an excellent starting point for any research, since it usually contains relevant key stories.

12 *General BusinessFile International*. Available as a CD-ROM or web database (under the name Infotrac Searchbank General Businessfile), this database includes the European business ASAP database as well as more international titles, stockbroker research and company profiles.

13 *Guardian Index*. A monthly publication which provides a detailed index to articles appearing in the *Guardian* newspaper.

14 *HMSO Annual Catalogue* now known as the *Stationery Office Annual Catalogue*. A list of all TSO publications during a particular year. The catalogue is arranged in departmental order and has a subject index at the end. Available on the internet (www.tso-online.co.uk) and on CD-ROM (*UK Official Publications*).

15 *IMID/MICWeb*. Based on the holdings of the Institute of Management's book and journal article databases which form part of the largest collection of resources on management in Europe, focusing in all aspects of management theory and practice. *MICWeb* is updated monthly, as is the *IMID* CD-ROM. Business students can join the Institute of Management and have access to the library services.

16 *Monthly Index to the Financial Times*. An index to all the articles listed by subject and by author that have appeared in the FT during the period concerned. The *Monthly Index* cumulates as the *Official Index to the Financial Times* and both are an invaluable reference source on business matters. See www.psmedia.com.

17 *PROMT*. Another database available on-line, on the web or on CD-ROM. Covers trade and business news sources worldwide.

18 *ProQuest Direct* (also known as *ABI/Inform*). One of the best business databases because of its range and the quality of its abstracting and information retrieval. Many businesses now have access to the full text of many articles as well as summaries.

19 *Publications of the European Community*. An annual catalogue of all the publications, including periodicals, issued by EU institutions during the year. Available on the internet via www.eur-op.eu.int.

20 *Research Index*. A regularly published index to articles appearing in the commercial and industrial press and in periodicals. The index provides references to industries and subject areas and to companies by name.

21 *Scimp*. The selective co-operative index to management periodicals (hence 'scimp'), published ten times a year and a useful source of information on European publications on management issues.

22 *The Times Index*. A monthly index, dedicated to *The Times* and its associated publications (note, this does not include the FT). The index is arranged alphabetically by subject heading and by author and provides a list of the dates and the pages of the relevant publication. Available on CD-ROM for *The Times* and the *Sunday Times*.

23 *Whitaker's Books in Print*. A list of all the titles currently available in the United Kingdom. Published annually and available on microfiche and CD-ROM.

### 15.5.3 Other useful sources

1 *Bank of England Quarterly Bulletin*. An assessment of economic developments in the United Kingdom and the rest of the world. It includes articles and speeches, together with general commentary on the economy.

2 *Bank Reviews*. Quarterly publications by some of the leading clearing banks and often available free on request. These include *Barclays Economic Review* and *Lloyds Economic Bulletin*.

3 *Business Studies Update*. Published annually by Hidcote Press and a very useful source of discussion on contemporary business issues.

4 *CBI Industrial Trends Survey*. A quarterly guide to the state of UK manufacturing industry based on questionnaire responses by businesses. It provides a useful insight into business prospects and an indicator to future changes.

5 *Company Annual Reports*. Available on request from all public companies and some private ones. Many are available on-line through company websites.

6 *Consumer Goods Europe*. Replaces *Marketing in Europe*. It is a monthly publication by Corporate Intelligence on Retailing and contains detailed studies of the markets for consumer products in leading European countries.

7 *Economics Update*. Another annual publication by Hidcote Press and designed to provide a review and discussion of contemporary issues relevant to students of economics and business.

8 Ernst and Young's International Business Series. Entitled *Doing business in ...*, it contains a wide range of information on business conditions in different countries and is a very useful reference source. The information is updated fairly regularly. PriceWaterhouse Cooper has a rival publication that is also very informative.

9  *European Business Review*. A pan-European journal published by MCB University Press. It includes articles, editorial comment, news reports and a discussion of recent publications. The journal also incorporates the *New European* which looks at the more cultural, political and environmental developments within Europe. Has CD-ROM and on-line facilities.

10  *European Journal of Marketing*. Another publication by MCB University Press, relevant particularly to students of international marketing. It includes abstracts in French, German and Spanish and offers an on-line service.

11  *European Policy Analyst Quarterly*. Formerly *European Trends*. Published by the Economist Intelligence Unit, it is a quarterly review of key issues and business developments in a European context.

12  *Hambro Company Guide*. A quarterly publication providing financial data drawn predominantly from the reports and accounts of UK companies. Each issue also includes feature articles.

13  *Income Data Services*. A regular series of studies and reports on pay and other labour-market issues (e.g. teamworking, childcare, redundancy), containing valuable up-to-date information and some statistical analysis. Available on the internet via www.incomesdata.co.uk.

14  *Journal of Marketing*. A quarterly publication by the American Marketing Association and comprising articles together with recent book reviews in the field of marketing. See www.ama.org.

15  *Kelly's Business Directory*. A substantial volume giving details of the addresses and main products of UK businesses. Available via www.kellys.co.uk and on CD-ROM.

16  *Key British Enterprises*. A multivolume compendium from Dun and Bradstreet giving details of Britain's top 50,000 companies. Companies are listed alphabetically and are also indexed by trade, product and geographical location. Available on the internet via www.dunandbrad.co.uk; also on CD-ROM.

17  *Kompass UK*. A multivolume directory produced in association with the CBI and providing details on UK companies, including names, addresses, products, number of employees, and so forth. Directories for other countries are also available. See www.reedbusiness.com and CD-ROM *Kompass CD Plus*.

18  *Lloyds Bank Economic Bulletin*. A bi-monthly publication covering a topic of current interest in an easily accessible form. Internet site currently being changed.

19  *Management Decision*. Published ten times a year by MCB University Press. Looks at management strategy and issues. Available on CD-ROM and on-line.

20  *Marketing*. A weekly source of facts and articles on various aspects of marketing, presented in a journalistic style. Available on the internet via www.marketing.haynet.com.

21  *Marketing Intelligence*. Also known as *Mintel Marketing Intelligence* and an invaluable source of information and statistics on a wide range of products. Reports cover market factors, trends, market share, the supply structure and consumer characteristics, and frequently include forecasts of future prospects. Available on-line via www.mintel.co.uk.

22  *Sell's Product and Services Directory*. A useful directory in a number of sections listing products and services, company details and trade names. Produced in two volumes and available on CD-ROM.

23 *The Economist*. A standard reference source, published weekly and examining economic and political events throughout the world. It is an invaluable publication for business students and regularly contains features on specific business-related topics. It has a useful update on basic economic indicators. Available on the internet via www.economist.co.uk/ or www.economist.com/.

24 *The Times 1000*. Essentially a league table of UK top companies, with information on profitability, capital employed and other matters. Additional information is also provided on the monetary sector and on leading companies in other countries. Published annually and available on CD-ROM.

25 *Who Owns Whom*. An annual publication which identifies parent companies and their subsidiaries. It is a very useful source of information for examining the pattern of corporate ownership in the United Kingdom. Companion volumes are also available covering other parts of the world.

### 15.5.4 A final comment

When researching a business topic you are particularly recommended to use library catalogue sites, especially the British Library's OPAC97 and COPAC, which is the combined catalogue of major British academic libraries. You might also want to check references on the internet bookshop sites such as Heffers (www.heffers.co.uk), the internet bookshop (www.bookshop.co.uk) or the Book Place (www.thebookplace.co.uk), as well as Amazon.co.uk (which most people know about).

## 15.6 Conclusions

Economic concepts, ideas and models help us to understand and analyse business decisions and to shed light on some of the key forces shaping strategy at the operational, business and corporate level. As writers such as Porter have readily demonstrated, economists have made a major contribution to our understanding of the nature of markets and competition and have provided useful tools of analysis for examining the environment in which business organisations exist and operate.

For students of business and practitioners alike, access to data and other types of information is a critical part of examining and analysing this environment and an important aid to decision-making, whether at an individual or organisational level. Given the wide range of sources available and developments in the technology for accessing this information and data, there is every opportunity for interested parties to enhance their understanding of the business world and (hopefully) to make rational choices when confronted with alternative courses of action.

| Case study | **Multinational inward investment in Eastern Europe: a PEST analysis** |
|---|---|

Firms seek to gain an advantage over their competitors in a variety of ways. For some organisations, investing in production and/or service facilities in other countries is seen as a means of gaining such an advantage, whether from a cost (e.g. reduced transaction costs; lower labour costs) and/or a market point of view (e.g. exploiting new markets; extending the life cycle of existing products). Given that most industries tend to be 'footloose', one question facing organisational decision-makers who opt for this solution is where to invest: what are the relative costs and benefits in choosing Country A or B or C and so on? One way of beginning to answer this question is to undertake a PEST analysis in order to provide useful information about the broad macroenvironmental context against which the final decision has to be taken.

To illustrate how this might occur this case study looks at a hypothetical example of a consumer durables company considering direct foreign investment in Eastern Europe following the collapse of communism. Given the expectation that the transition to market-based economies would potentially provide huge new markets in countries such as Bulgaria, Poland and Russia, the company has to choose between alternative locations when building its new factory. The following PEST analysis highlights some of the key questions likely to be considered by those charged with the ultimate decision. For convenience these are presented in tabular form (Table 15.1).

**Table 15.1: A PEST approach**

| POLITICAL | ECONOMIC |
|---|---|
| ■ How stable is the government now and in the future?<br>■ Is the political regime favourable to foreign investment?<br>■ Is the government tax regime favourable to overseas-owned multinationals? | ■ Is there a favourable economic framework (e.g. institutions)?<br>■ Is the economy likely to remain stable (e.g. inflation rates) over the longer term?<br>■ What are the growth prospects for the economy?<br>■ Is there a favourable business infrastructure. |
| SOCIAL | TECHNOLOGICAL |
| ■ What are the likely public reactions to foreign companies?<br>■ Are living standards likely to provide increased market opportunities?<br>■ What skills exist within the labour force? | ■ What is the current state of technological advance?<br>■ Is technology transfer feasible (e.g. skills)?<br>■ Will the infrastructure (existing/planned) support or hinder the investment process? |

As Table 15.1 illustrates, a PEST analysis yields a valuable insight into some of the potential risks and uncertainties of a locational decision and it is not unknown for potential investors to commission a 'comparative risk analysis' in which countries are scored against a range of variables according to the perceived degree of risk (e.g. political stability, credit worthiness, market opportunities, etc.). Were this to be undertaken in this particular case it seems likely that a country such as Hungary would appear a more favourable location for investment than, say, Albania or the Ukraine. While this might not prevent a multinational organisation from becoming involved in the latter two countries, it is possible that a risk assessment of the broad macroenvironmental factors might influence both the level and nature of the investment undertaken (e.g. a joint venture might be seen as preferable to a direct commitment of funds).

## Notes and references

1. Andrews, K. R. (1971), *The Concept of Corporate Strategy*, Irwin, Burr Ridge, Ill.

2. Johnson, G. and Scholes, K. (1999), *Exploring Corporate Strategy*, 5th edition, Prentice Hall, Harlow, p.10.

3. See e.g. Grant, R. M. (1991), 'The resource-based theory of competitive advantage: implications for strategy formulation', *Californian Management Review*, 33(3), spring, pp. 114–135; Barney, J. (1991), 'Firms' resources and sustained competitive advantage', *Journal of Management*, 17, pp. 99–120.

4. See e.g. Johnson and Scholes (1999), Part 1.

5. Porter, M. E. (1985), *Competitive Advantage: Creating and Sustaining Superior Performance*, Free Press, New York, Chapter 1.

6. Worthington, I. and Britton, C. (2000), *The Business Environment*, 3rd edition, Financial Times Prentice Hall, Harlow.

7. Porter (1985), Chapter 2.

## Review and discussion questions

1 The terms 'strategy' and 'tactics' are both used commonly in a business context. What is the difference?

2 Imagine you are employed as a consultant by a multinational high technology company considering investing in the UK. Undertake a PEST analysis along the lines shown in the case study. Is the UK a risky place to invest?

3 The market for beer in the UK is dominated by a few very large companies. Discuss what the major barriers to entry are likely to be in this industry. How would you explain the significant growth in the number of micro-breweries in recent years, given the existence of entry barriers?

4 It has become fashionable in recent years for larger companies to reduce the number of firms who supply them. Can you explain the logic behind this decision using Porter's notion of the 'value chain'?

## Assignments

**1** As a business consultant you have been hired by a small company in the UK textile industry to identify a range of possible strategic responses to the intense competition from low-wage overseas producers. Produce a short report discussing what options the company is likely to have in light of the competitive environment it faces (hint: you might find Porter's generic strategies a useful tool for considering alternative options).

**2** Choose *one* recent 'strategic' decision by a business organisation and research this decision using contemporary sources of information (especially the quality press and the internet). Explain the background to the decision, what strategic choice the business made and why, and how this decision is to be implemented. Wherever possible, relate your observations to the ideas and models discussed in this chapter.

## Further reading

Cook, M. and Farquharson, C. (1998), *Business Economics: Strategy and Applications*, Pitman Publishing, London. esp. Part 4

Ferguson, P. R., Rothschild, R. and Ferguson, G. J. (1993), *Business Economics*, Macmillan, Basingstoke, Chapter 12.

Hornby, W., Gammie, R. and Wall, S. (1997), *Business Economics*, Longman, Harlow, Chapter 10.

Johnson, G. and Scholes, K. (1999), *Exploring Corporate Strategy: Text and Cases*, 5th edition, Prentice Hall, Harlow.

Porter, M. E. (1980), *Competitive Strategy*, Free Press, New York.

Porter, M. E. (1985), *Competitive Advantage: Creating and Sustaining Superior Performance*, Free Press, New York.

Rothschild, R. (1995), 'Ten simple lessons in strategy from the games people play', *Management Decision*, 33(9), pp. 24–29.

# CHAPTER 16

# Estimating and forecasting techniques

Chris Britton

**Objectives**

1 To consider the importance of empirical estimation of relationships and forecasting to business.

2 To give students an understanding of the steps involved in the statistical analysis of data.

3 To look at two alternative methods of data collection – surveys and market experiments.

4 To enable students to understand the process of forecasting in the future.

5 To take a critical look at the methods of empirical research through an appreciation of the problems involved in such research.

## 16.1 Introduction

Many of the theoretical concepts discussed in this book have great relevance to business – both in the development of long-term strategy and the day-to-day running of the organisation. For example, knowledge of the demand characteristics of the product in the market place helps the organisation decide upon its corporate identity and image and also on more operational issues such as pricing or packaging of the product. A knowledge of cost conditions helps the firm make short-term decisions about production levels and longer-term decisions about investment in new plant and machinery. For short- and long-term planning in all functional areas it is imperative that organisations can forecast into the future.

For the theoretical concepts to be useful to the organisation they need to be operationalised and estimated. This chapter looks at the empirical techniques that are used to estimate and to test these theoretical relationships. Broadly speaking these techniques fall under two headings: statistical estimation; and survey and market experiments. The problems involved in each of these are considered along with the application of these techniques to three specific areas of business economics which are of interest to the firm:

- demand estimation
- estimation of elasticities
- forecasting into the future.

There are other relationships which are of relevance, and although they are not considered here, the techniques used and the problems encountered would be very similar. At the end of the chapter there is an appendix which covers some basic mathematical concepts which aid an understanding of estimation and forecasting.

## 16.2 Statistical techniques of empirical research

In using statistical techniques to test a theoretical viewpoint, estimate a relationship or set up a forecasting model, there are five generally accepted steps that need to be followed.

### 16.2.1 Identification of the variables

Step 1 involves the identification of all the important variables involved in the relationship being considered. The estimation of a demand function will be used as an example. Both economic theory and common sense help in the identification of factors which will influence the level of demand for a particular product. These factors will vary from product to product. The weather, for example, is likely to be much more influential in determining the level of demand for ice creams than it is in the demand for computers.

In Chapter 3 a number of variables were identified as important in determining the level of demand for an individual brand of lager and these factors are repeated below:

- the price of that brand (P)
- the price of other brands, including other non-lager substitutes ($P_S$)
- the disposable income of lager drinkers (Y)
- the price of complimentary goods, for example the admission price to student night clubs ($P_C$)
- the volume and quantity of advertising on this and competing brands (A)
- the tastes of the consumer (T)
- the perceived quality of the product (Q).

Having determined the important factors, the next step is to collect data on these variables.

### 16.2.2 Collection of the data

Data are any numerically or otherwise measured values and can be thought of as lying on a continuum which runs from purely **qualitative** to **quantitative** – see Figure 16.1.

**nominal data** qualitative data

Purely **qualitative data** or **nominal data** cannot be given quantitative values. The data is sorted into categories according to some distinguishing characteristic and each characteristic is given a name – hence the term 'nomi-

**Figure 16.1  Data types**

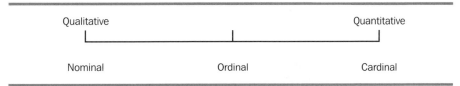

nal'. Examples of nominal data are ethnic origin or classification of students by their degree. **Ordinal data** is slightly more quantitative in nature – the data cannot be numerically measured but it can be ranked in some way. An example would be cardigan size – small, medium, large, extra large, and so on. Purely quantitative data is called **cardinal data** and has attributes that can be directly measured in numerical terms. Examples of cardinal data are income and prices which are measured in monetary terms or height and weight which are measured in appropriate units.

Statistical analysis mainly uses quantitative data but it is possible to incorporate qualitative data into the analysis. Some variables are theoretical concepts which are difficult to operationalise or to measure. In these cases **proxy variables** are often used to represent these variables – for example IQ is often used as a proxy for intelligence. Most of the variables identified above as influencing the demand for lager can be measured in quantitative terms. The exceptions are tastes and quality – these need to be operationalised in some way in order to include them in a statistical analysis.

A further distinction is made between primary and secondary data. **Primary data** are new data which have been collected for a specific purpose, usually through the use of a survey (see Section 16.3). **Secondary data** are data which already exist and have been collected by someone else, probably for a different purpose. A major source of secondary data in most countries is the government (see Chapter 15) which collects and publishes large quantities of data on a whole range of issues.[1] Secondary data have the advantage of being readily available and are relatively cheap to collect but, because they were collected by someone else for some other purpose, they might not be exactly what is required. They are also likely to have been processed in some way already. Primary data collection on the other hand can be specifically geared to the current use but can be very expensive to collect.

The final distinction is made between time series and cross-sectional data. **Time series data** are data which are collected over a period of time for the same sampling unit. **Cross-sectional data** are data which have been collected at one point in time for different sampling units. The crime rate in a particular police force area over a 20-year period is an example of time series data; while the crime rates reported by each police force area in 1998 would be cross-sectional data.

The data used for statistical calculations will typically be a combination of the types discussed above. Some will be internal to the firm and some will be external, some collected from published sources and some collected by survey. The next step is to specify the nature of the relationship to be estimated.

**ordinal data**  data which are not strictly quantitative but can be ranked

**cardinal data**  quantitative data

**proxy variables**  those chosen to represent other variables which may be difficult to measure

**primary data**  new data which have been collected for the specific purpose in hand

**secondary data**  data which are already in existence

**time series data**  data on a variable which have been collected over a period of time

**cross-sectional data**  data collected for different individuals or groups at one moment in time

### 16.2.3 **Specification of the model**

The relationship between two variables can take a variety of forms – it can be a **straight line relationship** (such as in the case of fixed costs of production where costs are constant across different levels of production), it can be **non-linear** (as in the case of average and marginal cost) or it could be part of a **simultaneous equation relationship** (as in the case of demand and supply). When specifying the model we need to choose the functional form of the equation which will best fit the data (see Appendix). For the sake of simplicity it is often assumed that the relationship is a linear one. For the demand for lager it would be:

$$\text{Demand} = a + bP + cP_S + dY + eP_C + fA + gT + hQ + u$$

In the equation a **disturbance term (u)** has been added to represent any random disturbances to the demand for lager which are not due to the specified variables. These will be unexplained and non-systematic and therefore cannot be incorporated into the equation by the inclusion of another variable.

The choice of functional form is an important one – if the wrong functional form is used there are implications for the reliability of the estimated regression line (see Section 16.2.6).

**straight line relationship** where there is a one-to-one relationship between the variables

**non-linear relationship** a relationship between variables which is not a one-to-one relationship

**simultaneous equation relationship** a model where the values of the variables are determined simultaneously, such as price and quantity in a free market

**disturbance term** a term added to a regression equation to take account of any random shocks to the relationship

### 16.2.4 **Estimating the model**

Using the techniques of **multiple regression** (Appendix 16.5) the demand function for lager can be estimated and values for the coefficients found. This can be done manually or using a computer. Both the *size* and the *sign* of the estimated coefficients are important – they show the effects on the demand for lager of changes in the independent variables. For example, if the value of b was –3 then an increase of one unit in price would lead to a fall in demand of 3 units. Although economic theory says little about the size of the coefficients, it does give an indication of the expected signs of the coefficients (see Table 16.1).

There are three desirable properties that the estimators of the regression coefficients should possess and these are best illustrated using the analogy of target practice, see Figure 16.2:[2]

**multiple regression** the estimation of a relationship in which there is more than one independent variable

1 **Unbiasedness.** An estimated coefficient is unbiased if its expected value is equal to the true value of the regression coefficient. In Figure 16.2, A and B represent **unbiased estimators** since they are both concentrated on the centre of the target. C, however, is a biased estimator.
2 **Efficiency.** An **efficient estimator** has the smallest variability among unbiased estimators of the coefficient. A is the most efficient estimator of the three shown in Figure 16.2, since it has the least variability
3 **Consistency.** A **consistent estimator** is one where, as the sample size taken increases, the bias and the variability reduce to zero.

Once the relationship has been estimated it needs to be tested according to a variety of criteria and if necessary modified.

**unbiased estimator** where the expected value of the estimate is equal to the true value being estimated

**efficient estimator** one which has the minimum variance amongst all unbiased estimators

**consistent estimator** where both the bias and the variance of the estimator reduce to zero as the sample size increases

**Table 16.1  Expected signs of coefficients in the demand function**

| Coefficient | Expected sign | Why? |
|---|---|---|
| **a – intercept** | Positive | |
| **b – own price** | Negative | A downward-sloping demand curve – as own price rises, demand falls |
| **c – price of substitutes** | Positive | As the price of substitutes rises, the demand for lager rises |
| **d – disposable income** | Positive | If lager is a normal good |
| **e – price of complementary goods** | Negative | As the price of complementary goods rises, the demand for lager falls |
| **f – volume of advertising** | Unclear | Advertising on lager in general or on this brand should have a positive effect, advertising on other brands a negative effect |
| **g – tastes** | Positive | If tastes change in favour of lager |
| | Negative | If tastes change away from lager |
| **h – perceived quality** | Positive | As perceived quality rises, so too will demand |

**Figure 16.2  The desirable properties of estimators**

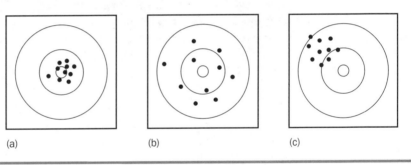

(a)                          (b)                          (c)

*Source:* Bowers, D. (1991) *Statistics for Economics and Business*, Macmillan, Basingstoke.

## 16.2.5 Testing the model

The estimated model can be evaluated according to:

- *how well it complies with the theory and previous empirical studies:* in the case of the demand for lager, how well the estimates of the regression coefficients match up with the theoretical expectations shown in Table 16.1 and any previous empirical studies of this area.
- *its statistical validity:* there are a number of statistical tests which should be carried out on an estimated regression which would give an indication of how good the model is (see Appendix 16.7). These tests can be used to give an indication of the presence of one or more of the statistical problems identified in Section 16.2.6.
- *how well it predicts:* this can be tested by using the regression line to predict a value for Y which has been collected but not included in the sample for estimation to see how close the estimation is to the observed value.

| Mini case | **The consumption function** |

Often governments wish to estimate and predict the level of consumption expenditure in the economy – it is a good indicator of general economic conditions and a major consideration in deliberations over the rate of interest. Economic theory tells us that the consumption spending of households depends upon their income levels (among other things) and the consumption function is often specified as:

$$C = a + bY$$

where
    C is consumption spending
    Y is income
    a is the intercept term
    b is the slope of the line or the marginal propensity to consume.

Data have been collected from the 2000 edition of the *Annual Abstract of Statistics* on total consumption expenditure and GDP in the UK over a 13-year period and a regression line estimated using Excel. The data are shown below, along with selections from the regression printout.

**Table 16.2 Consumption spending and GDP, UK, £ billion, current prices**

|      | GDP   | Consumption |
|------|-------|-------------|
| 1986 | 384.8 | 241.6 |
| 1987 | 423.4 | 265.3 |
| 1988 | 471.4 | 299.5 |
| 1989 | 516.0 | 327.4 |
| 1990 | 554.5 | 336.5 |
| 1991 | 583.0 | 357.8 |
| 1992 | 606.6 | 377.1 |
| 1993 | 637.8 | 399.1 |
| 1994 | 676.0 | 419.3 |
| 1995 | 712.6 | 438.5 |
| 1996 | 754.6 | 467.8 |
| 1997 | 803.9 | 498.3 |
| 1998 | 843.7 | 525.5 |

The estimated regression line is:

$$C = 6.36 + 0.61Y$$

The data have been plotted onto a scatter diagram (Figure 16.3) and the regression line added.

How well does this model perform against the tests?

■ Economic theory predicts that the marginal propensity to consume should lie between 0 and 1; therefore a value of 0.61 for b corresponds

**Summary output**

|  | Regression statistics |
| --- | --- |
| r Squared | 0.9979 |
| Adjusted r Square | 0.9977 |
| Standard error | 4.1630 |
| Observations | 13 |

|  | Coefficients | Standard error | t Stat |
| --- | --- | --- | --- |
| Intercept | 6.36 | 5.27 | 1.21 |
| X variable 1 | 0.61 | 0.01 | 72.84 |

**Figure 16.3 The consumption function**

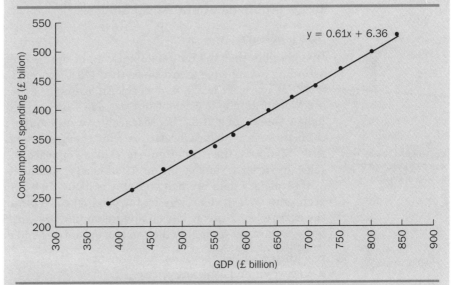

Source: Table 15.2, *Annual Abstract of Statistics*, 2000, National Statistics © Crown copyright

with theoretical expectations. It is also in line with previous empirical estimations of the consumption function. The estimated value of a as £6.36 billion also corresponds with theory. The intercept term represents the level of consumption spending when income is equal to zero and this is usually assumed to be positive. Although the income of households is zero the assumption is that they will be financing their spending out of past saving or borrowing.

■ The t statistic implies that the intercept term is not significantly different from 0 while the value of b is highly significant. The value of r squared is 0.9979 which implies that 99.79 per cent of the variation in consumption is explained by the variation in income.

■ Once data become available for these two variables for 1999, the value of income can be put into the equation and the value of consumption predicted and checked against its observed value. Given the closeness of the fit between the regression line and the data it is expected that the predictive power of this model will be high.

According to most of the tests, this model performs well. One factor which has so far been ignored is that both sets of data are measured in current values and will therefore both be affected by inflation. Thus they will both be rising (or falling) together with inflation rates. This would partly explain the strength of the relationship. The next step would be to deflate the figures to take into account the effects of inflation and repeat the exercise.

At this stage it is possible that the original model might need to be reformulated and the whole process started again.

### 16.2.6 Problems of statistical analysis

#### Data problems

It is possible that the data available might not be exactly what are required according to economic theory since theoretical concepts are often abstract ones which do not exist in the real world. An example of this is 'opportunity cost' – a powerful economic concept but not one which would be found in any published source of data. The researcher would have to operationalise and estimate such variables for each specific example, and this might be a difficult task. Similarly, theories often use 'real' as opposed to nominal values of the relevant variables and so the data will need adjustment.

**real values** values which have been adjusted to take account of inflation

If secondary data are being used it is likely that the data will already have been processed in some way by the original collector and it is important that the exact form of this is known and taken into account. The government is the largest source of secondary data in most countries and data are produced:

- with and without seasonal adjustment
- in current and constant prices
- in index numbers with varying bases.

It is important to know what the theoretical variables are and the data which are available and how well these correspond with each other. In the collection of time series data, especially over a long period of time, it is often the case that a data series is incomplete or that the definition of the variable has changed over the period.

The problems involved in the collection of primary data are discussed in Section 16.4.

#### Mis-specification of the model

Crucial in the estimation process is the specification of the exact form of the relationship. There are three common mistakes that can be made, all of which have undesirable ramifications for the reliability of the estimated regression equation and its predictive power.

### The use of the wrong functional form

**t tests** statistical tests of significance

Fitting a linear equation to a relationship which is non-linear will lead to misleading results in **t tests** of the significance of the estimated coefficients (see Appendix 16.6) and produce a regression equation which is useless for prediction. In the case of simple regression where there is one dependent variable and only one independent variable, a way of testing for non-linearity would be to plot the data on to a **scatter diagram**.

**scatter diagrams** two-dimensional graphs on which the data points of two variables have been plotted

The data in Figure 16.4 shows a non-linear relationship between the two variables and this therefore implies that using ordinary least squares OLS is not the best method of estimating the relationship. There are a number of possibilities: the data could be broken up into groups and ordinary least squares (OLS) used for each group, as Figure 16.4 shows; or the nature of the non-linearity can be identified and the model transformed as shown in Appendix 16.5. With the increased availability and sophistication of spreadsheets and dedicated statistical packages on the computer, it has become much easier to try out different functional forms.

### Omitted variables

The first step in the process of estimation is to identify all of the variables involved in the relationship. If important variables are omitted the estimates of the regression coefficients will be wrong. Both this and the use of the wrong functional form will give rise to autocorrelation as a statistical problem (see next section).

### The inclusion of irrelevant variables

The effects of this will be similar to the above and will increase the possibility of multicollinearity (see next section).

**Figure 16.4  The identification of non-linearities in the data**

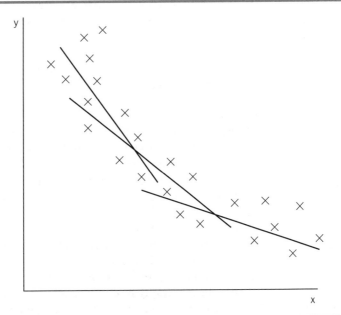

### Statistical problems

When using statistical techniques to estimate relationships, there are a number of specific problems which are very common. Although a detailed discussion of these problems is beyond the scope of this text, it is important that the reader is aware of these problems as they will affect the reliability of the estimation. They can be tested for and corrections made to the model which limit the damage they cause.

**autocorrelation** an econometric problem which stems from the existence of a relationship between the disturbance terms

■ **Autocorrelation**. If the relationship being estimated has been correctly specified and all of the relevant variables included, the values of the disturbance term (u) in the regression equation will be totally random with no systematic pattern. Autocorrelation refers to the situation in which a systematic pattern is observed and is usually due either to the misspecification of the relationship or omitted variables. The presence of autocorrelation would lead to invalid t tests on the regression coefficients.

**multicollinearity** an econometric problem which arises when there is a relationship between the independent variables

■ **Multicollinearity**. This occurs in multiple regression (see Appendix 16.5) when there is a correlation between the X variables. Such correlation is common in economic relationships and can occur in both cross-sectional and time series data. In the demand function for lager, since variables like the price of lager, other prices and income are measured in monetary terms, they will all be rising in times of inflation – therefore they will be correlated with one another. A basic assumption of regression analysis is that these variables are independent of one another. If they are not it is difficult for the computer to separate out the effects of one variable from another. The estimated regression coefficients will be unbiased but any tests performed on them will be unreliable. In the case of perfect correlation between the X variables the computer will be unable to estimate a regression line.

### Simultaneous equations and the identification problem

Using OLS to estimate a single relationship which is actually part of a simultaneous equation model produces estimates of the regression coefficients which are biased and inconsistent. The main reason for this is the 'identification problem'. To illustrate the identification problem the demand and supply model will be used. Both the quantity demanded and the quantity supplied depend on price – both equations are of the form Q = f(P). When data are collected on price and quantity, what is actually being collected are data on *equilibrium* price and quantity, i.e. the combination of both demand and supply. How can the effects of demand and supply be separated out?

**identification problem** the problem of estimating relationships when they change simultaneously

If it is known that the supply curve for a product is moving while the demand curve is stationary (see Figure 16.5), then the data on price and quantity collected must represent points on the demand curve and estimation can proceed. The same is true for the supply curve if the supply curve is stationary and the demand curve is moving.

Problems arise, however, if either the researcher has no a priori knowledge about the behaviour of demand and supply or if both curves are moving at the same time. Figure 16.6 shows that data collected on price and quantity if both curves are moving do not represent points on an individual demand curve or an individual supply curve. In fact the situation illustrated in Figure 16.6 (where supply has changed more than demand) is highly misleading, since the

**Figure 16.5  The identification of a demand curve**

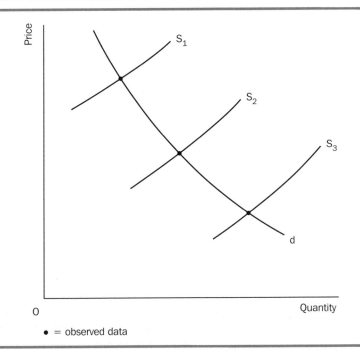

● = observed data

**Figure 16.6  The identification problem**

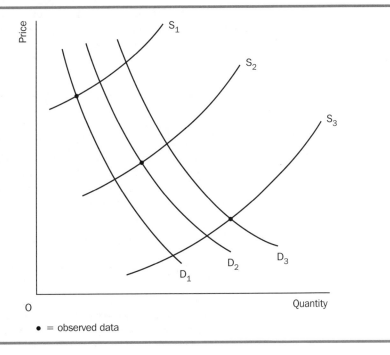

● = observed data

observed data show a downward-sloping relationship and the automatic assumption would be that these are points on a demand curve.

This is the identification problem – the demand curve cannot be identified from the supply curve. One solution to this problem stems from the likelihood that movements in demand and supply curves would be caused by different factors – for example, supply increases because of changes in technology, demand because of increases in income. The demand function is $Q = f(P, Y)$, supply is $Q = f(P, Tech)$. Thus the demand and supply functions are now different and therefore identified.[3]

## 16.3   Survey and market experiments

So far this chapter has concentrated on the statistical analysis of secondary data but as already indicated there are limitations to the use of such data. There are situations when an organisation might wish to estimate a relationship which is specific only to itself and its product. In this case it is unlikely that the appropriate secondary data will be available. The organisation will therefore have to collect its own data. If the firm wishes to estimate the elasticity of demand for its product, or how its customers perceive the quality of the product or what the likely response will be to changes in the packaging of the product, it will have to carry out or commission market research in these areas. There are two ways of collecting such data – surveys and market experiments.

### 16.3.1 Surveys

**survey** the collection of data from a sample by means of a questionnaire

Whether the organisation carries out a **survey** itself or commissions someone else to carry it out, the steps involved are the same (see Figure 16.7).

There is a large literature on the subject of surveys and survey design[4] and although a detailed discussion is beyond the scope of this book a brief consideration will be given to each of these steps. Problem definition is very

**Figure 16.7 The steps involved in carrying out a survey**

| | | |
|---|---|---|
| **Step 1** | Define the problem | Objectives of research<br>Information needed |
| **Step 2** | Planning research | Sampling frame<br>Sample size<br>Sample method<br>Method of data collection |
| **Step 3** | Design of the research instrument | Questionnaire<br>Interview structure |
| **Step 4** | Fieldwork | Pilot survey<br>Full survey |
| **Step 5** | Analysis and interpretation of results | |

**Figure 16.8  A five-point Likert scale**

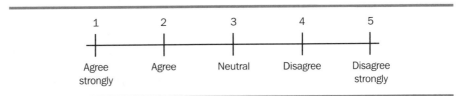

| 1 | 2 | 3 | 4 | 5 |
|---|---|---|---|---|
| Agree strongly | Agree | Neutral | Disagree | Disagree strongly |

**Likert scale** a scale used to quantify responses to a question on a scale ranging from one extreme to another

**sampling units** the units to be sampled as part of the survey

**sampling frame** the means of identifying the sampling units, for example the electoral register

**random sampling** a sampling technique where there is no human judgement involved in selecting the sample

**non-random sampling** a sampling technique which involves some human judgement in the selection of the sample

**quota sampling** where quotas are set for groups with certain characteristics (gender, for example) to ensure that the sample is representative

**judgement sampling** where human judgement is used in the selection of a sample

**stratified sample** a means of obtaining a representative sample: the population is divided into groups (or strata) and samples are taken from them

**unstructured interview** an interview in which a structured format is not followed

**structured interview** an interview in which each individual surveyed is asked the questions exactly as they appear on the questionnaire

important – incorrect specification of the research questions may result in the wrong questions being asked to the wrong people and therefore not very useful results. As in the case of statistical analysis of secondary data, this first step involves the identification of the important variables to be researched but surveys tend to be more exploratory and there is scope for the identification of additional factors which were not initially considered important. Surveys will typically collect different types of data: some data (e.g. income or number of children in a family) will be purely quantitative while some data, (e.g. gender or ethnic origin) will be qualitative data which can be coded for statistical analysis. For qualitative data on beliefs and opinions it is common to use scales like the **Likert scale** (see Figure 16.8).

Planning the research involves identifying the **sampling units** in a **sampling frame**, calculation of the required sample size and deciding upon the methodology to be used. Basically there are two methods of sampling: **random sampling** where every member of the population has a known probability of being selected and there is no human judgement involved in the selection of the sample; and **non-random sampling** where some human judgement is involved in the selection of the sample: for example, **quota sampling** and **judgement sampling**. Random samples are better statistically since the rules of probability can be used to analyse and test the results, but they are often difficult and expensive to undertake. If the main aim of the research is to obtain a representative sample there are certain methods that can be used to ensure that this is the case, e.g. **stratified sampling** where the population is divided up into groups beforehand according to some characteristic (like ethnic origin or gender) and a random sample taken from each group.

The next decision is the method of collection of data. There are a number of possibilities ranging from **unstructured** to **structured interviews** with groups or individuals to telephone surveys and postal surveys. Each of these methods has its own relative advantages and disadvantages, which are discussed briefly in Section 16.3.3. The process continues with the design of the questionnaire (if one is to be used) and the survey itself. Once the survey has been carried out, the data need to be processed. For quantitative data this will usually happen through a combination of descriptive statistics and further statistical analysis such as regression.

For the estimation of demand or demand elasticities the consumer would be asked 'what if?' questions like the buy–response test – 'if you saw this product in the shops how much would you pay for it?' The trouble with hypothetical questions of this sort is that although the respondent may answer honestly, their intentions might not be translated into action in the market place. Market experiments are an attempt to overcome this problem.

### 16.3.2 **Market experiments**

**Market experiments** are an attempt to exact information on the market under 'normal market conditions'. If an organisation is considering launching a new product it could try an experimental launch in a particular test area and project those results to a national launch. Once the decision has been made to launch a product a pilot launch in an area can be used to test specific aspects like price and packaging and the results used to modify the **marketing mix** prior to launch into other areas. Market experiments can also be used for existing products. Consumers can be given some play money and allowed to buy in an artificial shop. A group of consumers can be divided into two and each group be exposed to different stimuli (different prices or advertising messages) and the behaviour of the two groups compared. The great advantage of market experiments is that consumers are not being asked hypothetical questions and greater control can be exerted over the situation than in surveys.

### 16.3.3 **Problems of surveys and market experiments**

Collection of primary data either through survey or market experiment ensures that data can be tailored exactly to the organisation's needs; both techniques, however, carry high costs. To ensure that a sample is representative it needs to have been selected randomly and be large enough to ensure that no systematic bias has been introduced. The larger the sample, the higher the cost.

Postal surveys are the cheapest to carry out, but typically have very low response rates and if the non-respondents have different characteristics from the respondents a bias will have been introduced. Although postal questionnaires avoid the possibility of interviewer bias, it means that there is no-one present to explain or clarify particular questions and so the quality of the results might be affected. Face-to-face interviews are much more expensive to carry out but can produce a wealth of information. Interviewers need to be very well trained not to influence responses to the questions.

Whichever method is chosen, surveys are essentially posing hypothetical questions to the consumer which might produce responses which are not translated into action at the end of the day. Although this problem is partially removed with the use of market experiments, they are still artificial and if consumers are aware that they are taking part in an experiment their behaviour might be affected. The main problem in the use of market experiments is the same as for laboratory experiments – the control of experimental conditions. If the researcher is testing the effect of a price change on the demand for a particular product, all other influencing factors need to be controlled for, including, for example, the price of substitute products. It is possible that this is beyond the control of the researcher.

## 16.4 Forecasting

In addition to the estimation of relationships, firms need to be able to forecast into the future as a basis for their operational and strategic planning. An estimate of future demand will enable the firm to plan output levels, set

**forecasting**  the estimation
of variables in the future

**trend**  the underlying
movement in data over a
period of time

**seasonal fluctuations**  the
regular fluctuations that
occur in data within one
time period

**cyclical fluctuations**
fluctuations which occur in
data caused by movements
in the trade cycle

recruitment targets, plan its investment in plant and machinery, etc. **Forecasting** is carried out on time series data and is usually based on the premise that patterns identified in the past will continue into the future. Obviously the further into the future we are forecasting the more problematic this premise becomes.

Time series data fluctuate for a number of reasons: there is likely to be an underlying **trend** in the data; there will possibly also be **seasonal fluctuations** – regular fluctuations within one time period; most economic data also exhibit longer-term **cyclical fluctuations** related to the trade cycle; and other random factors. As random factors, by definition, cannot be estimated they are usually ignored in forecasting. Figure 16.9 shows these fluctuations.

The first step in the forecasting process is the identification of the underlying trend in the data. This can be done in a number of ways (moving averages and regression, for example) which are all commonly available on spreadsheet packages or statistical packages. In this section the trend is estimated using regression analysis, since this has already been covered in this chapter, but exactly the same arguments would apply to any method of trend estimation. Time is the independent variable. Once the trend has been identified it can be projected forwards. The next step is for any seasonal and/or cyclical variations to be estimated and the forecast adjusted accordingly.

Figure 16.10 shows two sets of data over time: (a) are the data on consumption spending for the UK shown in Table 16.2 and (b) shows quarterly data on the number of new car registrations in the UK between 1993 and 1999. In both graphs a linear trendline has been added and projected forward two time periods using regression analysis.

**Figure 16.9  The elements of time series data**

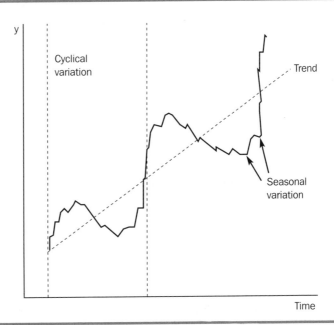

**Figure 16.10 Time series data: (a) consumption spending in the UK, 1986–1998, £ billion (b) number of new car registrations in the UK, q1 1993 to q2 1999**

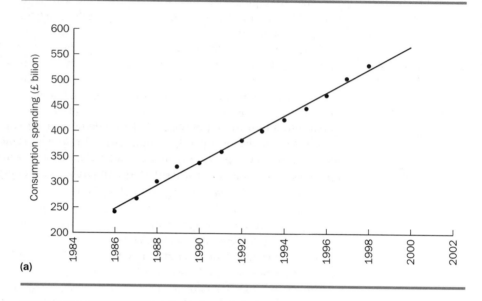

**(a)**

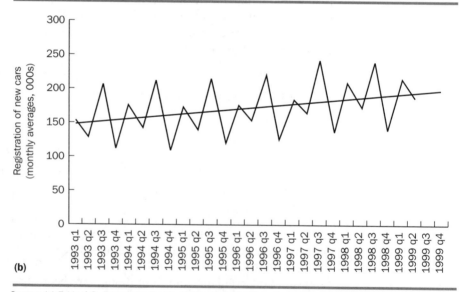

**(b)**

*Source:* (a) Table 4.8, *Economics Trends 1999*; (b) Table 15.2, *Annual Abstract of Statistics 2000*, National Statistics © Crown copyright.

Both sets of data exhibit upward trends but the pattern around those trends is very different in each case. The data on consumption lie close to the trendline – they exhibit very little cyclical variation and seasonal variation cannot be ascertained because there is no breakdown of the annual figures. The data on the registration of new cars exhibit a very strong seasonal pattern, with high levels of registrations in quarter 3 and very low levels in quarter 4. In both cases the estimated trendline can be used to make forecasts into the future.

Figure 16.10a shows that the level of consumption is forecast to be £560 billion in the year 2000, and if past patterns continue this is likely to be very close to the actual level. In the case of new car registrations, however, the situation is very different. Figure 16.10b shows that the forecast for the fourth quarter of 1999 is approximately 200,000 but if past patterns continue this is likely to be too high. The seasonal pattern shows that in each fourth quarter there is a fall in the level of registrations; therefore the true level of registrations is likely to be below the forecasted level. In the same way as the trend had to be estimated, so too the seasonal and cyclical factors have to be built into the model in order that useful forecasts can be made.[5]

Although forecasting is important for business, it must be remembered that it is based on the premise that past patterns will be repeated in the future, and although this may be true for some data series it will not be true for all and **shocks** to the system will affect the reliability of the forecasts.

## 16.5    Conclusion

This chapter has looked at the ways in which some of the theoretical concepts in business economics can be operationalised and estimated so that they are useful to business. Particular attention was paid to the estimation of demand and demand elasticities – both essential knowledge for any firm. Although a complete understanding of this area requires an extensive knowledge of mathematics, this chapter has tried to keep the treatment fairly non-mathematical. It is hoped that the reader will gain a general understanding of the concepts and principles involved, their application and their problems. There is sufficient mathematics in the appendix to this chapter to give a good understanding of the methods of statistical analysis. For readers who would like to take the analysis further there are references to further reading.

The first step in the process of estimation or forecasting is the identification of the important variables. It is here that economic theory is most useful. The next step is the collection of data and the collection of both primary and secondary data was considered along with the relative advantages and disadvantages of each. The steps involved in carrying out a statistical analysis of data were covered in some detail, as were the steps involved in carrying out a survey. Market experiments as a way of obtaining information on market characteristics were also briefly examined. In the final section of the chapter the important area of forecasting was considered.

This chapter has taken a *critical* look at each technique and procedure – the attendant problems and limitations have been stressed throughout. Most businesses require a knowledge and an understanding of the market conditions they face and the ability to forecast into the future. The importance of these for decision-making and planning in the short run and the long run cannot be under-estimated but neither should the problems and limitations of empirical analysis.

| Case study | # The estimation of elasticities of demand |

It is possible to estimate the elasticity of demand (and supply) from an estimated demand (or supply) function. This case study will only consider the estimation of elasticities of demand, but the same line of analysis can be applied to the elasticity of supply. The importance of a knowledge of elasticity of demand for the firm has already been established in Chapter 3. Eq. (5) in Chapter 3 shows own price elasticity of demand as being equal to:

$$K \times \frac{P}{Q}$$

where K is a constant which is a measure of the slope of the demand function at a single point – or, in other words, the value of the slope coefficient calculated in the regression line. At any point on the demand curve the values of P and Q will be known; therefore the value of elasticity can be calculated. A simple numerical example will be used to demonstrate the calculation of the three different elasticities of demand highlighted in Chapter 3: own price elasticity; cross-price elasticity; and income elasticity.

A set of data has been collected by a firm on the level of demand for its product ($Q_x$), the price of the product ($P_x$), the price of two other products ($P_y$ and $P_z$) and the level of income of consumers (Y). The function was assumed to be linear of the form:

$$Q_x = a + bP_x + cP_y + dP_z + eY$$

The data were entered into a computer and the demand function was estimated as follows:

$$Q_x = 10 - 2P_x - 1.5P_y + 0.3P_z + 0.25Y$$

Where:

$$P_x = 10$$
$$P_y = 20$$
$$P_z = 30$$
and $$Y = 500$$

Substituting these values into the demand function gives a level of output of 74 units, so $Q_x = 74$.

### 1 Own price elasticity of demand

$$= K \times \frac{P}{Q} \text{ or } b \times \frac{P_x}{Q_x}$$

$$= -2 \times \frac{10}{74} = -0.27$$

The demand for this good is inelastic as the value of elasticity is between 0 and –1. As mentioned in Chapter 3 it is conventional to ignore the minus sign.

## 2 Cross-price elasticity of demand

There are two other goods included in this demand function (i.e., y and z), each of which will have an associated elasticity. The formula is similar to the one given above but as cross-price elasticity measures the responsiveness of quantity demanded of good x as other prices change, the Ps in each formula have been modified:

Cross-price elasticity with respect to good y:

$$= K \times \frac{P}{Q} \text{ or } c \times \frac{P_y}{Q_x}$$

$$= -1.5 \times \frac{20}{74} = -0.4$$

Cross-price elasticity with respect to good z:

$$= K \times \frac{P}{Q} \text{ or } d \times \frac{P_z}{Q_x}$$

$$= 0.3 \times \frac{30}{74} = 0.12$$

From these calculations it can be seen that good y is a complementary good as the value of elasticity is negative. Therefore as the price of good y goes up the quantity demanded of good x falls. Good z gives a positive value for cross-price elasticity and is therefore a substitute for good x.

## 3 Income elasticity of demand

Here again the formula for calculation is a similar one but price is replaced by income since income elasticity measures the responsiveness of quantity demanded to changes in income.

$$= K \times \frac{P}{Q} \text{ or } e \times \frac{Y}{Q_x}$$

$$= 0.25 \times \frac{500}{74} = 1.69$$

This good is therefore a normal good, as the value of income elasticity is positive.

## Notes and references

1. The *Guide to Official Statistics*, published by the Office for National Statistics gives a full listing of government data.
2. Reproduced from Bowers, D. (1991), *Statistics for Economics and Business*, Macmillan, Basingstoke.
3. Griffiths, A. and Wall, S. (1996), *Intermediate Microeconomics: Theory and Applications*, Longman, Harlow.

4. Carter, M. and Williamson, D. (1996), *Quantitative Modelling for Management and Business*, Pitman, London.

5. For a full coverage of the estimation of seasonal and cyclical factors see Owen, F. and Jones, R. (1994), *Statistics*, Pitman, London.

## Review and discussion questions

1 Why might a business wish to estimate the level of demand for its product in three years time?

2 Why is it important for a firm to be aware of the value of elasticity of demand for its product?

3 Specify the target populations and the appropriate sampling frames for the following two examples:

(a) A company wishes to ascertain customer satisfaction with video recorders purchased from the company.

(b) A local authority is considering opening a nursery in a particular area but wants to know the level of demand before proceeding.

## Assignments

1 You work in the HR department of a large service sector organisation and you have been asked to carry out a survey of wages within the organisation. How would you go about designing and carrying out this research?

2 You have been asked to assess the relationship between crime and unemployment. Collect data on the crime rate from *Criminal Statistics* (ONS) and data on unemployment rates, either over a period of time or for different police force areas. Estimate a regression line for this data. What other variables should be included?

## Further reading

Carter, M. and Williamson, D. (1996), *Quantitative Modelling for Management and Business*, Pitman, London.

Crouch, S. and Housden, M. (1996), *Marketing Research for Managers*, Butterworth-Heinemann, London.

Griffiths, A. and Wall, S. (1996), *Intermediate Microeconomics: Theory and Applications*, Longman, Harlow.

## Appendix 16.1    Plotting graphs

Graphs are drawn up according to a strict mathematical convention which is (mainly) adhered to in business economics. The horizontal or X axis is the independent variable and the vertical or Y axis is the dependent variable. We are saying that the Y variable depends on the X variable.

Therefore if we were plotting the consumption spending of households against the income of households, consumption would be on the Y axis since it depends on income which would appear on the X axis. Similarly, salary of employees would be the Y variable which depends upon length of service (the X variable) where the organisation has incremental salary scales. The choice of which are the Y and which are the X variables is an important one and is largely a matter of common sense. There are, however, examples where it is unclear. In the case of the relationship between advertising and sales, for example, it seems likely that the level of sales would depend upon the level of advertising. But it is also true that the higher the level of sales the greater will be the income of the firm out of which advertising is funded. There is therefore reverse causality and the decision is not clear cut – the choice of X and Y variables depends upon what relationship you are trying to demonstrate.

There is one example in business economics where the normal mathematical convention is not followed – and that is in the case of demand and supply curves. We tend to think of the quantity demanded or supplied as being dependent upon the price of the product, but the axes are drawn the other way around. Price is shown on the Y axis and quantity on the X axis. The reason for this is that Alfred Marshall, who first drew demand and supply curves, had

**Figure 16.11  Plotting a graph**

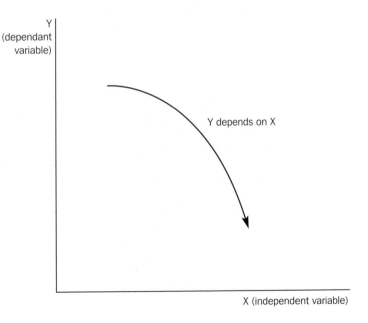

**Figure 16.12  A three-dimensional graph**

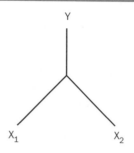

the causality running in the opposite direction, from quantity to price. Although this is not the way we now think about demand and supply, the convention continues. This is the only exception to the mathematical convention.

The graph plotted in Figure 16.11 is two-dimensional because there are two variables, X and Y. Some functions have more than one independent variable. How are these graphed? Take the simplest case of three variables – one dependent (Y) and two independent ($X_1$ and $X_2$). We are saying that Y is a function of $X_1$ and $X_2$. This means that there are three axes and the graph will be three-dimensional (see Figure 16.12). When there are more than two independent variables, the graph becomes impossible to plot since there will be an axis for each variable.

Appendix 16.2 ## The linear function

The equation of the straight line is:

$$Y = a + bX$$

where
Y  =  the dependent variable
X  =  the independent variable
a  =  the intercept term
b  =  the slope coefficient.

Two straight line functions are shown in Figure 16.13.

The value of a tells us where the line crosses the Y axis: in Figure 16.13 for both (a) and (b) this is 10. The value of a can take any value, positive or negative – if it is equal to 0 the line will pass through the origin. The value of b (or the slope of the line) in Figure 16.13a is equal to 2 and in 16.13b it is equal to –0.5. This tells us the relationship between changes in X and changes in Y. For (a) it tells us that a 1 unit increase in X will cause the value of Y to increase by 2 units; for (b) it tells us that a 1 unit increase in X causes a decrease in Y of 0.5 of a unit. Figure 16.13a illustrates a positive relationship and 16.13b illustrates a negative relationship between X and Y.

**Figure 16.13 The straight line function: (a) Y = 10 + 2X; (b) Y = 10 – 0.5X**

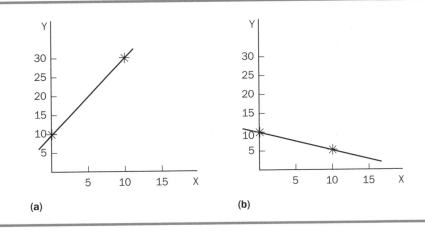

(a)                                    (b)

Appendix 16.3  ## Non-linear functions

In business economics we tend to assume straight-line relationships wherever possible because these are much easier to estimate and to use. However, there are many relationships in business economics which are not linear – cost curves, for example, are usually assumed to be U-shaped. There are many different forms of non-linear functions and it is beyond the scope of this book to consider them all, but here are a few important ones:

The quadratic function: $Y = aX^2 + bX + c$

This function has an $X^2$ as the highest power, therefore this function has one 'bump' and would be typical of an average cost curve or a marginal cost curve. In this function the constant term c still represents the intercept on the Y axis, the coefficient on X (b) still indicates the slope of the function and the coefficient on $X^2$ (a) indicates whether this is a 'hill' or a 'valley'. If the value of a is positive it is a valley, if a is negative it is a hill.

The cubic function: $Y = aX^3 + bX^2 + cX + d$

This function has $X^3$ as the highest power and therefore has two 'bumps' – this would be typical of a total revenue curve.

The exponential function: $Q = aP^b$

This function is a hyperbola and is the equation of the demand curve which has constant elasticity along its whole length. The special case of constant unitary elasticity shown in Figure 3.7c is where the value of b is equal to –1.

## Appendix 16.4    Simple linear regression

**line of best fit** the straight
line which best represents
the data that is available

A straight line which **best fits** a set of data can be estimated in a number of ways. The simplest method involves drawing a line freehand which seems to fit the data best. The problem with this method is that if ten people were asked to draw the line of best fit on to a scatter diagram it is likely that they would end up with ten different lines. This is not a very scientific method and has clear implications for forecasting the future – with ten different lines of best fit there will be ten different forecasts of the future! A more scientific method which produces *the* line of best fit is to fit a regression line using the method of ordinary least squares (OLS).

OLS fits a straight line $(Y = a + bX)$ to the data by minimising the vertical differences between the data points in the scatter diagram and the line – the e's in Figure 16.14. As some of these will be positive (above the line) and some will be negative (below the line) the sum of these distances will be zero and so OLS fits the line which minimises the sum of these differences **squared**. This line can either be calculated manually using formulae for a and b or can be done using a computer. Most spreadsheet packages and all statistical packages will calculate a regression line. Figure 16.15 shows a set of data, a scatter diagram of this data and the fitted OLS line using Excel.

**Figure 16.14  The method of ordinary least squares**

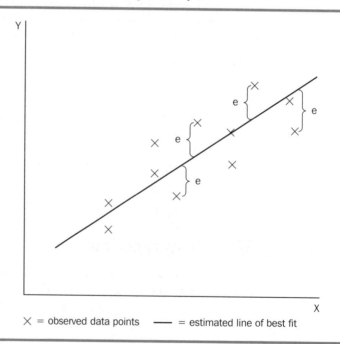

X = observed data points    —— = estimated line of best fit

**Figure 16.15  A regression line**

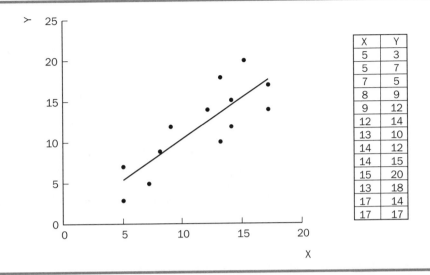

| X | Y |
|----|----|
| 5 | 3 |
| 5 | 7 |
| 7 | 5 |
| 8 | 9 |
| 9 | 12 |
| 12 | 14 |
| 13 | 10 |
| 14 | 12 |
| 14 | 15 |
| 15 | 20 |
| 13 | 18 |
| 17 | 14 |
| 17 | 17 |

---

## Appendix 16.5  Multiple regression

It is clear from discussions elsewhere in this book that relationships are more complex than a simple regression line with only one independent variable. The quantity demanded of a product $(Q_x)$, for example, depends not only upon the price of the product $(P_x)$ but also income levels (Y), tastes (T), the prices of other goods $(P_y)$. These can all be incorporated into the analysis (provided we have data on them) by estimating a multiple regression line:

$$Q_x = a + bP_x + cP_y + dY + eT$$

The technique is similar to the above but complicated by the fact that there is more than one independent variable. This makes it impossible to draw, since there would be more than three axes, and impossible to calculate manually – it would have to be done using a computer.

## Appendix 16.6  Non-linear functions

It is possible to extend the analysis to estimate non-linear relationships. As indicated above, there are two types of non-linear functions:

1 *Functions which are linear in the coefficients but non-linear in variables:*

$$Y = aX^3 + bX^2 + cX + d$$

Such a function can be estimated using the method of OLS by 'creating' new variables – for example $Z = X^3$ and $V = X^2$. These can be calculated as new columns in the spreadsheet and included in the estimation of multiple regression:

$$Y = aZ + bV + cX + d.$$

2 *Functions which are linear in variables but non-linear in the coefficients:*

$$Q = aP^b$$

This type of function can be estimated using OLS by taking logs of the function:

$$\log Q = \log a + b \log P$$

This transforms the function into one which is log linear and estimation of multiple regression can take place, but care must be taken in the interpretation of the estimated coefficients.

These techniques are beyond the scope of this book but most spreadsheet packages on computers will calculate these very easily for you.

---

## Appendix 16.7    Testing regression lines

Only two tests of the regression line are considered here but there are many more tests than this – for autcorrelation and multicollinearity, for example. These would be covered in an advanced statistics book. The two tests covered are the most important ones:

1 *t tests on the regression coefficients.* Each estimated coefficient in the regression equation should be tested for statistical significance – i.e. whether the value of the coefficient is equal to 0 or not. This is tested by using a t test. If a t test concludes that the intercept term is equal to 0, then the intercept term does not exist and the regression line passes through the origin. The intercept term is therefore not **statistically significant** in that regression equation. If a t test concludes that b the coefficient on X is equal to 0 this implies that the variable X is not significant in the regression equation – in explaining Y. t statistics for each coefficient can be calculated manually or will be given on the computer regression printout. See Table 16.2 for an example of output from Excel. The rule of thumb for the t test is that if the t statistic is less than −2 or greater than +2 the coefficient is statistically significant and does have a place in the regression equation.

2. *The coefficient of determination (r squared).* This measures the overall explanatory power of the regression equation. For example an r squared of 0.978 means that 97.8 per cent of the variation in the dependent variable is 'explained' by the regression equation. Again Table 16.2 gives the printout from Excel.

Computer packages give very detailed printouts which contain a number of statistics which would be used to test the statistical validity of the regression analysis.

# Index

Page numbers in **bold** refer to marginal definitions.